BASIC ECONOMICS

A Common Sense Guide to the Economy

THOMAS SOWELL

Fifth Edition

BASIC BOOKS
A Member of the Perseus Books Group
New York

A few lines of reasoning can change the way we see the world.

Steven E. Landsburg

Books published by Basic Books are available at special discounts for bulk purchases in the United States by corporations, institutions, and other organizations. For more information, please contact the Special Markets Department at the Perseus Books Group, 2300 Chestnut Street, Suite 200, Philadelphia, PA 19103, or call (800) 810-4145, ext. 5000, or e-mail special.markets@perseusbooks.com.

Library of Congress Control Number: 2014945836

ISBN: 978-0-465-06073-3 (hardcover)
ISBN: 978-0-465-05684-2 (e-book)

LSC-C

10 9

CONTENTS

PREFACE

The most obvious difference between this book and other introductory economics books is that *Basic Economics* has no graphs or equations. It is also written in plain English, rather than in economic jargon, so that it can be readily understood by people with no previous knowledge of economics. This includes both the general public and beginning students in economics.

A less obvious, but important, feature of *Basic Economics* is that it uses real-life examples from countries around the world to make economic principles vivid and memorable, in a way that graphs and equations might not. Through its various editions, the fundamental idea behind *Basic Economics* has remained the same: Learning economics should be as uncomplicated as it is eye-opening.

Readers' continuing interest in these new editions at home, and a growing number of translations into foreign languages overseas,* suggest that there is a widespread desire for this kind of introduction to economics, when it is presented in a readable way.

Just as people do, this book has put on weight with the passing years, as new chapters have been added and existing chapters updated and expanded to stay abreast of changing developments in economies around the world.

Readers who have been puzzled by the large disparities in economic development, and standards of living, among the nations of the world will find a new chapter— Chapter 23, the longest chapter in the book— devoted to exploring geographic, demographic, cultural and other reasons why such striking disparities have existed for so long. It also examines factors which are said to have been major causes of international economic disparities and finds that the facts do not always support such claims.

Most of us are necessarily ignorant of many complex fields, from botany to brain surgery. As a result, we simply do not attempt to operate in, or

---

* Previous editions have been translated into Spanish, Chinese, Hebrew, Japanese, Swedish, Korean, and Polish.

comment on, those fields. However, every voter and every politician that they vote for affects economic policies. We cannot opt out of economic issues and decisions. Our only options are to be informed, uninformed, or misinformed, when making our choices on issues and candidates. *Basic Economics* is intended to make it easier to be informed. The fundamental principles of economics are not hard to understand, but they are easy to forget, especially amid the heady rhetoric of politics and the media.

In keeping with the nature of *Basic Economics* as an introduction to economics, not only have jargon, graphs and equations been left out, so have the usual endnotes. However, those who wish to check up on some of the surprising facts they will learn here can find the sources listed on my website (www.tsowell.com) or on a website established by the publisher (sowellbasiceconomics.com). For instructors who are using *Basic Economics* as a textbook in their courses, or for parents who are homeschooling their children, more than a hundred questions are available in the back of the book, with pages listed after each question, showing where the answer to that question can be found in the text.

THOMAS SOWELL
Hoover Institution
Stanford University

ACKNOWLEDGMENTS

L ike other books of mine, this one owes much to my two extraordinary research assistants, Na Liu and Elizabeth Costa. In addition to their tracking down all sorts of information for me, Ms. Costa did the copyediting and fact-checking of the manuscript, which Ms. Liu then converted into galleys and helped to index, after which the resulting Quark file was sent to the publisher, who could have the book printed directly from her computer file. The chapter on the history of economics was read by distinguished emeritus Professor William R. Allen of UCLA, a former colleague whose insightful comments and suggestions were very much appreciated, even when I did not make full use of all of them. Needless to say, any errors or shortcomings that remain after all these people's efforts can only be my responsibility.

And of course none of this would be possible without the support of the Hoover Institution and the research facilities of Stanford University.

Chapter 1

WHAT IS ECONOMICS?

> *Whether one is a conservative or a radical, a protectionist or a free trader, a cosmopolitan or a nationalist, a churchman or a heathen, it is useful to know the causes and consequences of economic phenomena.*
>
> *George J. Stigler*

Economic events often make headlines in the newspapers or "breaking news" on television. Yet it is not always clear from these news stories what caused these particular events, much less what future consequences can be expected.

The underlying principles involved in most economic events are usually not very complicated in themselves, but the political rhetoric and economic jargon in which they are discussed can make these events seem murky. Yet the basic economic principles that would clarify what is happening may remain unknown to most of the public and little understood by many in the media.

These basic principles of economics apply around the world and have applied over thousands of years of recorded history. They apply in many very different kinds of economies— capitalist, socialist, feudal, or whatever— and among a wide variety of peoples, cultures, and governments. Policies which led to rising price levels under Alexander the Great have led to rising price levels in America, thousands of years later. Rent control laws have led to a very similar set of consequences in Cairo, Hong Kong, Stockholm, Melbourne, and New York. So have similar agricultural policies in India and in the European Union countries.

1

We can begin the process of understanding economics by first being clear as to what economics means. To know what economics is, we must first know what an economy is. Perhaps most of us think of an economy as a system for the production and distribution of the goods and services we use in everyday life. That is true as far as it goes, but it does not go far enough. The Garden of Eden was a system for the production and distribution of goods and services, but it was not an economy, because everything was available in unlimited abundance. Without scarcity, there is no need to economize— and therefore no economics. A distinguished British economist named Lionel Robbins gave a classic definition of economics:

> *Economics is the study of the use of scarce resources which have alternative uses.*

SCARCITY

What does "scarce" mean? It means that what everybody wants adds up to more than there is. This may seem like a simple thing, but its implications are often grossly misunderstood, even by highly educated people. For example, a feature article in the *New York Times* laid out the economic woes and worries of middle-class Americans— one of the most affluent groups of human beings ever to inhabit this planet. Although this story included a picture of a middle-class American family in their own swimming pool, the main headline read: "The American Middle, Just Getting By." Other headings in the article included:

> Wishes Deferred and Plans Unmet
> Goals That Remain Just Out of Sight
> Dogged Saving and Some Luxuries

In short, middle-class Americans' desires exceed what they can comfortably afford, even though what they already have would be considered unbelievable prosperity by people in many other countries around the world— or even by earlier generations of Americans. Yet both they and the reporter regarded them as "just getting by" and a Harvard sociologist was quoted as saying "how budget-constrained these people really are." But it is not something as man-made as a budget which constrains them: Reality constrains them. There has never been enough to satisfy everyone completely. That is the real constraint. That is what scarcity means.

The *New York Times* reported that one of these middle-class families "got in over their heads in credit card spending" but then "got their finances in order."

> "But if we make a wrong move," Geraldine Frazier said, "the pressure we had from the bills will come back, and that is painful."

To all these people— from academia and journalism, as well as the middle-class people themselves— it apparently seemed strange somehow that there should be such a thing as scarcity and that this should imply a need for both productive efforts on their part and personal responsibility in spending the resulting income. Yet nothing has been more pervasive in the history of the human race than scarcity and all the requirements for economizing that go with scarcity.

Regardless of our policies, practices, or institutions— whether they are wise or unwise, noble or ignoble— there is simply not enough to go around to satisfy all our desires to the fullest. "Unmet needs" are inherent in these circumstances, whether we have a capitalist, socialist, feudal, or other kind of economy. These various kinds of economies are just different institutional ways of making trade-offs that are inescapable in any economy.

PRODUCTIVITY

Economics is not just about dealing with the existing output of goods and services as consumers. It is also, and more fundamentally, about *producing* that output from scarce resources in the first place— turning inputs into output.

requires judgmt; value subjective

In other words, economics studies the consequences of decisions that are made about the use of land, labor, capital and other resources that go into producing the volume of output which determines a country's standard of living. Those decisions and their consequences can be more important than the resources themselves, for there are poor countries with rich natural resources and countries like Japan and Switzerland with relatively few natural resources but high standards of living. The values of natural resources per capita in Uruguay and Venezuela are several times what they are in Japan and Switzerland, but real income per capita in Japan and Switzerland is more than double that of Uruguay and several times that of Venezuela.

Not only scarcity but also "alternative uses" are at the heart of economics. If each resource had only one use, economics would be much simpler. But water can be used to produce ice or steam by itself or innumerable mixtures and compounds in combination with other things. Similarly, from petroleum comes not only gasoline and heating oil, but also plastics, asphalt and Vaseline. Iron ore can be used to produce steel products ranging from paper clips to automobiles to the frameworks of skyscrapers.

How much of each resource should be allocated to each of its many uses? Every economy has to answer that question, and each one does, in one way or another, efficiently or inefficiently. Doing so efficiently is what economics is about. Different kinds of economies are essentially different ways of making decisions about the allocation of scarce resources— and those decisions have repercussions on the life of the whole society.

During the days of the Soviet Union, for example, that country's industries used more electricity than American industries used, even though Soviet industries produced a smaller amount of output than American industries produced. Such inefficiencies in turning inputs into outputs translated into a lower standard of living, in a country richly endowed with natural resources— perhaps more richly endowed than any other country in the world. Russia is, for example, one of the few industrial nations that produces more oil than it consumes. But an abundance of resources does not automatically create an abundance of goods.

Efficiency in production— the rate at which inputs are turned into output— is not just some technicality that economists talk about. It affects the standard of living of whole societies. When visualizing this process, it helps to think about the real things— the iron ore, petroleum, wood and other inputs that go into the production process and the furniture, food and automobiles that come out the other end— rather than think of economic decisions as being simply decisions about money. Although the word "economics" suggests money to some people, for a society as a whole money is just an artificial device to get real things done. Otherwise, the government could make us all rich by simply printing more money. It is not money but the volume of goods and services which determines whether a country is poverty stricken or prosperous.

THE ROLE OF ECONOMICS

Among the misconceptions of economics is that it is something that tells you how to make money or run a business or predict the ups and downs of the stock market. But economics is not personal finance or business administration, and predicting the ups and downs of the stock market has yet to be reduced to a dependable formula.

When economists analyze prices, wages, profits, or the international balance of trade, for example, it is from the standpoint of how decisions in various parts of the economy affect the allocation of scarce resources in a way that raises or lowers the material standard of living of the people as a whole.

Economics is not simply a topic on which to express opinions or vent emotions. It is a systematic study of cause and effect, showing what happens when you do specific things in specific ways. In economic analysis, the methods used by a Marxist economist like Oskar Lange did not differ in any fundamental way from the methods used by a conservative economist like Milton Friedman. It is these basic economic principles that this book is about.

One of the ways of understanding the consequences of economic decisions is to look at them in terms of the *incentives* they create, rather than simply the *goals* they pursue. This means that consequences matter more than intentions— and not just the immediate consequences, but also the longer run repercussions.

Nothing is easier than to have good intentions but, without an understanding of how an economy works, good intentions can lead to counterproductive, or even disastrous, consequences for a whole nation. Many, if not most, economic disasters have been a result of policies intended to be beneficial— and these disasters could often have been avoided if those who originated and supported such policies had understood economics.

While there are controversies in economics, as there are in science, this does not mean that the basic principles of economics are just a matter of opinion, any more than the basic principles of chemistry or physics are just a matter of opinion. Einstein's analysis of physics, for example, was not just Einstein's opinion, as the world discovered at Hiroshima and Nagasaki. Economic reactions may not be as spectacular or as tragic, as of a given day, but the worldwide depression of the 1930s plunged millions of people into poverty, even in the richest countries, producing malnutrition in countries with surplus food, probably causing more deaths around the world than those at Hiroshima and Nagasaki.

Conversely, when India and China— historically, two of the poorest nations on earth— began in the late twentieth century to make fundamental changes in their economic policies, their economies began growing dramatically. It has been estimated that 20 million people in India rose out of destitution in a decade. In China, the number of people living on a dollar a day or less fell from 374 million— one third of the country's population in 1990— to 128 million by 2004, now just 10 percent of a growing population. In other words, nearly a quarter of a billion Chinese were now better off as a result of a change in economic policy.

Things like this are what make the study of economics important— and not just a matter of opinions or emotions. Economics is a tool of cause and effect analysis, a body of tested knowledge— and principles derived from that knowledge.

Money doesn't even have to be involved to make a decision be economic. When a military medical team arrives on a battlefield where soldiers have a variety of wounds, they are confronted with the classic economic problem of allocating scarce resources which have alternative uses. Almost never are there enough doctors, nurses, or paramedics to go around, nor enough medications. Some of the wounded are near death and have little chance of being saved, while others have a fighting chance if they get immediate care, and still others are only slightly wounded and will probably recover whether they get immediate attention or not.

If the medical team does not allocate its time and medications efficiently, some wounded soldiers will die needlessly, while time is being spent attending to others not as urgently in need of care or still others whose wounds are so devastating that they will probably die in spite of anything that can be done for them. It is an economic problem, though not a dime changes hands.

Most of us hate even to think of having to make such choices. Indeed, as we have already seen, some middle-class Americans are distressed at having to make much milder choices and trade-offs. But life does not ask us what we want. It presents us with options. Economics is one of the ways of trying to make the most of those options.

PART I: PRICES AND MARKETS

Chapter 2

THE ROLE OF PRICES

The wonder of markets is that they reconcile the choices of myriad individuals.

William Easterly

Since we know that the key task facing any economy is the allocation of scarce resources which have alternative uses, the next question is: How does an economy do that?

Different kinds of economies obviously do it differently. In a feudal economy, the lord of the manor simply told the people under him what to do and where he wanted resources put: Grow less barley and more wheat, put fertilizer here, more hay there, drain the swamps. It was much the same story in twentieth century Communist societies, such as the Soviet Union, which organized a far more complex modern economy in much the same way, with the government issuing orders for a hydroelectric dam to be built on the Volga River, for so many tons of steel to be produced in Siberia, so much wheat to be grown in the Ukraine. By contrast, in a market economy coordinated by prices, there is no one at the top to issue orders to control or coordinate activities throughout the economy.

How an incredibly complex, high-tech economy can operate without any central direction is baffling to many. The last President of the Soviet Union, Mikhail Gorbachev, is said to have asked British Prime Minister Margaret Thatcher: "How do you see to it that people get food?" The answer was that she didn't. Prices did that. Moreover, the British people were better fed than people in the Soviet Union, even though the British have not produced

11

enough food to feed themselves in more than a century. Prices bring them food from other countries.

Without the role of prices, imagine what a monumental bureaucracy it would take to see to it that the city of London alone is supplied with the tons of food, of every variety, which it consumes every day. Yet such an army of bureaucrats can be dispensed with— and the people that would be needed in such a bureaucracy can do productive work elsewhere in the economy— because the simple mechanism of prices does the same job faster, cheaper and better.

This is also true in China, where the Communists still run the government but, by the early twenty-first century, were allowing free markets to operate in much of that country's economy. Although China has one-fifth of the total population of the world, it has only 10 percent of the world's arable land, so feeding its people could continue to be the critical problem that it once was, back in the days when recurring famines took millions of lives each in China. Today prices attract food to China from other countries:

> China's food supplement is coming from abroad— from South America, the U.S. and Australia. This means prosperity for agricultural traders and processors like Archer Daniels Midland. They're moving into China in all of the ways you'd expect in a $100 billion national market for processed food that's growing more than 10% annually. It means a windfall for farmers in the American Midwest, who are enjoying soybean prices that have risen about two-thirds from what they were a year ago. It means a better diet for the Chinese, who have raised their caloric intake by a third in the past quarter-century.

Given the attractive power of prices, the American fried-chicken company KFC was by the early twenty-first century making more sales in China than in the United States. China's per capita consumption of dairy products nearly doubled in just five years. A study estimated that one-fourth of the adults in China were overweight— not a good thing in itself, but a heartening development in a country once afflicted with recurring famines.

ECONOMIC DECISION-MAKING

The fact that no given individual or set of individuals controls or coordinates all the innumerable economic activities in a market economy does not mean that these things just happen randomly or chaotically. Each consumer, producer, retailer, landlord, or worker makes individual transactions with other individuals on whatever terms they can mutually agree on. Prices convey those terms, not just to the particular individuals immediately involved but throughout the whole economic system— and indeed, throughout the world. If someone else somewhere else has a better product or a lower price for the same product or service, that fact gets conveyed and acted upon through prices, without any elected official or planning commission having to issue orders to consumers or producers— indeed, faster than any planners could assemble the information on which to base their orders.

If someone in Fiji figures out how to manufacture better shoes at lower costs, it will not be long before you are likely to see those shoes on sale at attractive prices in the United States or in India, or anywhere in between. After the Second World War ended, Americans could begin buying cameras from Japan, whether or not officials in Washington were even aware at that time that the Japanese made cameras. Given that any modern economy has millions of products, it is too much to expect the leaders of any country to even know what all those products are, much less know how much of each resource should be allocated to the production of each of those millions of products. Prices play a crucial role in determining how much of each resource gets used where and how the resulting products get transferred to millions of people. Yet this role is seldom understood by the public and it is often disregarded entirely by politicians. Prime Minister Margaret Thatcher in her memoirs said that Mikhail Gorbachev "had little understanding of economics," even though he was at that time the leader of the largest nation on earth. Unfortunately, he was not unique in that regard. The same could be said of many other national leaders around the world, in countries large and small, democratic or undemocratic.

In countries where prices coordinate economic activities automatically, that lack of knowledge of economics does not matter nearly as much as in countries where political leaders try to direct and coordinate economic activities.

Many people see prices as simply obstacles to their getting the things they want. Those who would like to live in a beach-front home, for example, may abandon such plans when they discover how extremely expensive beach-front property can be. But high prices are not the reason we cannot all live in beach-front houses. On the contrary, the inherent reality is that there are not nearly enough beach-front homes to go around, and prices simply convey that underlying reality. When many people bid for a relatively few homes, those homes become very expensive because of supply and demand. But it is not the prices that cause the scarcity. There would be the same scarcity under feudalism or socialism or in a tribal society.

If the government today were to come up with a "plan" for "universal access" to beach-front homes and put "caps" on the prices that could be charged for such property, that would not change the underlying reality of the extremely high ratio of people to beach-front land. With a given population and a given amount of beach-front property, rationing without prices would have to take place by bureaucratic fiat, political favoritism or random chance— but the rationing would still have to take place. Even if the government were to decree that beach-front homes were a "basic right" of all members of society, that would still not change the underlying scarcity in the slightest.

Prices are like messengers conveying news— sometimes bad news, in the case of beach-front property desired by far more people than can possibly live at the beach, but often also good news. For example, computers have been getting both cheaper and better at a very rapid rate, as a result of technological advances. Yet the vast majority of beneficiaries of those high-tech advances have not the foggiest idea of just what specifically those technological changes are. But prices convey to them the end results— which are all that matter for their own decision-making and their own enhanced productivity and general well-being from using computers.

Similarly, if vast new rich iron ore deposits were suddenly discovered somewhere, perhaps no more than one percent of the population would be likely to be aware of it, but everyone would discover that things made of steel were becoming cheaper. People thinking of buying desks, for example, would discover that steel desks had become more of a bargain compared to wooden desks and some would undoubtedly change their minds as to which kind of desk to purchase because of that. The same would be true when comparing various other products made of steel to competing products made of aluminum, copper, plastic, wood, or other materials. In short, price changes would enable a whole society— indeed, consumers around the world— to adjust automatically to a greater abundance of known iron ore deposits, even if 99 percent of those consumers were wholly unaware of the new discovery.

Prices are not just ways of transferring money. Their primary role is to provide financial incentives to affect behavior in the use of resources and their resulting products. Prices not only guide consumers, they guide producers as well. When all is said and done, producers cannot possibly know what millions of different consumers want. All that automobile manufacturers, for example, know is that when they produce cars with a certain combination of features they can sell those cars for a price that covers their production costs and leaves them a profit, but when they manufacture cars with a different combination of features, these don't sell as well. In order to get rid of the unsold cars, the sellers must cut the prices to whatever level is necessary to get them off the dealers' lots, even if that means taking a loss. The alternative would be to take a bigger loss by not selling them at all.

Although a free market economic system is sometimes called a profit system, it is in reality a profit-and-loss system— and the losses are equally important for the efficiency of the economy, because losses tell producers what to *stop* doing— what to stop producing, where to stop putting resources, what to stop investing in. Losses *force* the producers to stop producing what consumers don't want. Without really knowing why consumers like one set of features rather than another, producers automatically produce more of what earns a profit and less of what is losing money. That amounts to producing what the consumers want and stopping the production of what they don't want. Although the producers are only looking out for themselves and their companies' bottom line, nevertheless from the standpoint of the economy as a whole the society is using its scarce resources more efficiently because decisions are guided by prices.

Prices formed a worldwide web of communication long before there was an Internet. Prices connect you with anyone, anywhere in the world where markets are allowed to operate freely, so that places with the lowest prices for particular goods can sell those goods around the world. As a result, you can end up wearing shirts made in Malaysia, shoes produced in Italy, and slacks made in Canada, while driving a car manufactured in Japan, rolling on tires produced in France.

Price-coordinated markets enable people to signal to other people how much they want and how much they are willing to offer for it, while other people signal what they are willing to supply in exchange for what compensation. Prices responding to supply and demand cause natural resources to move from places where they are abundant, like Australia, to places where they are almost non-existent, like Japan. The Japanese are willing to pay higher prices than Australians pay for those resources. These higher prices will cover shipping costs and still leave a larger profit than selling the same resources within Australia, where their abundance makes their prices lower. A discovery of large bauxite deposits in India would reduce the cost of aluminum baseball bats in America. A disastrous failure of the wheat crop in Argentina would raise the incomes of farmers in Ukraine, who would now find more demand for their wheat in the world market, and therefore higher prices.

When more of some item is supplied than demanded, competition among sellers trying to get rid of the excess will force the price down, discouraging future production, with the resources used for that item being set free for use in producing something else that is in greater demand. Conversely, when the demand for a particular item exceeds the existing supply, rising prices due to competition among consumers encourage more production, drawing resources away from other parts of the economy to accomplish that.

The significance of free market prices in the allocation of resources can be seen more clearly by looking at situations where prices are *not* allowed to perform this function. During the era of the government-directed economy of the Soviet Union, for example, prices were not set by supply and demand but by central planners who sent resources to their various uses by direct commands, supplemented by prices that the planners raised or lowered as they saw fit. Two Soviet economists, Nikolai Shmelev and Vladimir Popov, described a situation in which their government raised the price it would pay for moleskins, leading hunters to get and sell more of them:

> State purchases increased, and now all the distribution centers are filled with these pelts. Industry is unable to use them all, and they often rot in warehouses before they can be processed. The Ministry of Light Industry has already requested Goskomtsen twice to lower purchasing prices, but the "question has not been decided" yet. And this is not surprising. Its members are too busy to decide. They have no time: besides setting prices on these pelts, they have to keep track of another 24 *million* prices.

However overwhelming it might be for a government agency to try to keep track of 24 million prices, a country with more than a hundred million people can far more easily keep track of those prices individually, because no given individual or enterprise has to keep track of more than the relatively few prices that are relevant to their own decision-making. The over-all coordination of these innumerable isolated decisions takes place through the effect of supply and demand on prices and the effect of prices on the behavior of consumers and producers. Money talks— and people listen. Their reactions are usually faster than central planners could get their reports together.

While telling people what to do might seem to be a more rational or orderly way of coordinating an economy, it has turned out repeatedly to be far less effective in practice. The situation as regards pelts was common for many other goods during the days of the Soviet Union's centrally planned economy, where a chronic problem was a piling up of unsold goods in warehouses at the very time when there were painful shortages of other things that could have been produced with the same resources. In a market economy, the prices of surplus goods would fall automatically by supply and demand, while the prices of goods in short supply would rise automatically for the same reason— the net result being a shifting of resources from the former to the latter, again automatically, as producers seek to gain profits and avoid losses.

The problem was not that particular planners made particular mistakes in the Soviet Union or in other planned economies. Whatever the mistakes made by central planners, there are mistakes made in all kinds of economic systems— capitalist, socialist, or whatever. The more fundamental problem with central planning has been that the task taken on has repeatedly proven to be too much for human beings, in whatever country that task has been taken on. As Soviet economists Shmelev and Popov put it:

> No matter how much we wish to organize everything rationally, without waste, no matter how passionately we wish to lay all the bricks of the economic structure tightly, with no chinks in the mortar, it is not yet within our power.

PRICES AND COSTS

Prices in a market economy are not simply numbers plucked out of the air or arbitrarily set by sellers. While you may put whatever price you wish on the goods or services you provide, those prices will become economic realities only if others are willing to pay them— and that depends not on whatever prices you have chosen but on how much consumers want what you offer and on what prices other producers charge for the same goods and services.

Even if you produce something that would be worth $100 to a customer and offer it for sale at $80, that customer will still not buy it from you if another producer offers the same thing for $70. Obvious as all this may seem, its implications are not at all obvious to some people— those who blame high prices on "greed," for example, for that implies that a seller can set prices at will and make sales at those arbitrary prices. For example, a front-page newspaper story in *The Arizona Republic* began:

> Greed drove metropolitan Phoenix's home prices and sales to new records in 2005. Fear is driving the market this year.

This implies that lower prices meant less greed, rather than *changed circumstances* that reduce the sellers' ability to charge the same prices as before and still make sales. The changed circumstances in this case included the fact that homes for sale in Phoenix remained on the market longer before being sold than during the year before, and the fact that home builders were "struggling to sell even deeply discounted new homes." There was not the slightest indication that sellers were any less interested in getting as much money as they could for the houses they sold— that is, that they were any less "greedy."

Competition in the market is what limits how much anyone can charge and still make sales, so what is at issue is not anyone's disposition, whether greedy or not, but what the circumstances of the market cause to happen. A seller's feelings— whether "greedy" or not— tell us nothing about what the buyer will be willing to pay.

Resource Allocation by Prices

We now need to look more closely at the process by which prices allocate scarce resources that have alternative uses. The situation where the consumers want product *A* and don't want product *B* is the simplest example of how prices lead to efficiency in the use of scarce resources. But prices are equally important in more common and more complex situations, where consumers want both *A* and *B*, as well as many other things, some of which require the same ingredients in their production. For example, consumers not only want cheese, they also want ice cream and yogurt, as well as other products made from milk. How do prices help the economy to determine how much milk should go to each of these products?

In paying for cheese, ice cream, and yogurt, consumers are in effect also bidding indirectly for the milk from which these products are produced. In other words, money that comes in from the sales of these products is what enables the producers to again buy milk to use to continue making their respective products. When the demand for cheese goes up, cheese-makers use their additional revenue to bid away some of the milk that before went into making ice cream or yogurt, in order to increase the output of their own product to meet the rising demand. When the cheese-makers demand more milk, this increased demand forces up the price of milk— to everyone, including the producers of ice cream and yogurt. As the producers of these other products raise the prices of ice cream and yogurt to cover the higher cost of the milk that goes into them, consumers are likely to buy less of these other dairy products at these higher prices.

How will each producer know just how much milk to buy? Obviously they will buy only as much milk as will repay its higher costs from the higher prices of these dairy products. If consumers who buy ice cream are not as discouraged by rising prices as consumers of yogurt are, then very little of the additional milk that goes into making more cheese will come from a reduced production of ice cream and more will come from a reduced production of yogurt.

 What this all means as a general principle is that *the price which one producer is willing to pay for any given ingredient becomes the price that other producers are forced to pay for that same ingredient.* This applies whether we are talking about the milk that goes into making cheese, ice cream, and yogurt or we are talking about the wood that goes into making baseball bats, furniture, and paper. If the amount of paper demanded doubles, this means that the demand for wood pulp to make paper goes up. As the price of wood rises in response to this increased demand, that in turn means that the prices of baseball bats and furniture will have to go up, in order to cover the higher costs of the wood from which they are made.

The repercussions go further. As the price of milk rises, dairies have incentives to produce more milk, which can mean buying more cows, which in turn can mean that more cows will be allowed to grow to maturity, instead of being slaughtered for meat as calves. Nor do the repercussions stop there. As fewer cows are slaughtered, there is less cowhide available, and the prices of baseball gloves can rise because of supply and demand. Such repercussions spread throughout the economy, much as waves spread across a pond when a stone drops into the water.

No one is at the top coordinating all of this, mainly because no one would be capable of following all these repercussions in all directions. Such a task has proven to be too much for central planners in country after country.

Incremental Substitution

Since scarce resources have alternative uses, the value placed on one of these uses by one individual or company sets the cost that has to be paid by others who want to bid some of these resources away for their own use. From the standpoint of the economy as a whole, this means that *resources tend to flow to their most valued uses* when there is price competition in the marketplace. This does not mean that one use categorically precludes all other uses. On the contrary, adjustments are incremental. Only that amount of milk which is as valuable to ice cream consumers or consumers of yogurt as it is to cheese purchasers will be used to make ice cream or yogurt. Only that amount of wood which is as valuable to the makers of baseball bats or furniture as it is to the producers of paper will be used to make bats and furniture.

Now look at the demand from the consumers' standpoint: Whether considering consumers of cheese, ice cream, or yogurt, some will be anxious to have a certain amount, less anxious to have additional amounts, and finally— beyond some point— indifferent to having any more, or even unwilling to consume any more after becoming satiated. The same principle applies when more wood pulp is used to make paper and the producers and consumers of furniture and baseball bats have to make their incremental adjustments accordingly. In short, prices coordinate the use of resources, so that only that amount is used for one thing which is equal in value to what it is worth to others in other uses. That way, a price-coordinated economy does not flood people with cheese to the point where they are sick of it, while others are crying out in vain for more ice cream or yogurt.

Absurd as such a situation would be, it has happened many times in economies where prices are *not* used to allocate scarce resources. Pelts were not the only unsalable goods that were piling up in Soviet warehouses while people were waiting in long lines trying to get other things that were in short supply.* The efficient allocation of scarce resources which have alternative uses is not just some abstract notion of economists. It determines how well or how badly millions of people live.

Again, as in the example of beach-front property, prices convey an underlying reality. *From the standpoint of society as a whole, the "cost" of anything is the value that it has in alternative uses.* That cost is reflected in the market when the price that one individual is willing to pay becomes a cost

---

* A visitor to the Soviet Union in 1987 reported "long lines of people still stood patiently for hours to buy things: on one street corner people were waiting to buy tomatoes from a cardboard box, one to a customer, and outside a shop next to our hotel there was a line for three days, about which we learned that on the day of our arrival that shop had received a new shipment of men's undershirts." Midge Decter, *An Old Wife's Tale*, p. 169.

that others are forced to pay, in order to get a share of the same scarce resource or the products made from it. But, no matter whether a particular society has a capitalist price system or a socialist economy or a feudal or other system, the real cost of anything is still its value in alternative uses. The real cost of building a bridge is whatever else could have been built with that same labor and material. This is also true at the level of a given individual, even when no money is involved. The cost of watching a television sitcom or soap opera is the value of the other things that could have been done with that same time.

Economic Systems

Different economic systems deal with this underlying reality in different ways and with different degrees of efficiency, but the underlying reality exists independently of whatever particular kind of economic system happens to exist in a given society. Once we recognize that, we can then compare how economic systems which use prices to force people to share scarce resources among themselves differ in efficiency from economic systems which determine such things by having kings, politicians, or bureaucrats issue orders saying who can get how much of what.

During a brief era of greater openness in the last years of the Soviet Union, when people became more free to speak their minds, the two Soviet economists already mentioned wrote a book giving a very candid account of how their economy worked, and this book was later translated into English.* As Shmelev and Popov put it, production enterprises in the Soviet Union "always ask for more than they need" from the government in the way of raw materials, equipment, and other resources used in production. "They take everything they can get, regardless of how much they actually need, and they don't worry about economizing on materials," according to these economists. "After all, nobody 'at the top' knows exactly what the real requirements are," so "squandering" made sense— from the standpoint of the manager of a Soviet enterprise.

Among the resources that were squandered were workers. These economists estimated that "from 5 to 15 percent of the workers in the

---

* *The Turning Point: Revitalizing the Soviet Economy* (New York: Doubleday, 1989).

majority of enterprises are surplus and are kept 'just in case.'" The consequence was that far more resources were used to produce a given amount of output in the Soviet economy as compared to a price-coordinated economic system, such as that in Japan, Germany and other market economies. Citing official statistics, Shmelev and Popov lamented:

> To make one ton of copper we use about 1,000 kilowatt hours of electrical energy, as against 300 in West Germany. To produce one ton of cement we use twice the amount of energy that Japan does.

The Soviet Union did not lack for resources, but was in fact one of the most richly endowed nations on earth— if not *the* most richly endowed in natural resources. Nor was it lacking in highly educated and well-trained people. What it lacked was an economic system that made efficient use of its resources.

Because Soviet enterprises were not under the same financial constraints as capitalist enterprises, they acquired more machines than they needed, "which then gather dust in warehouses or rust out of doors," as the Soviet economists put it. In short, Soviet enterprises were not forced to economize— that is, to treat their resources as both scarce and valuable in alternative uses, for the alternative users were not bidding for those resources, as they would in a market economy. While such waste cost individual Soviet enterprises little or nothing, they cost the Soviet people dearly, in the form of a lower standard of living than their resources and technology were capable of producing.

Such a waste of inputs as these economists described could not of course continue in the kind of economy where these inputs would have to be purchased in competition with alternative users, and where the enterprise itself could survive only by keeping its costs lower than its sales receipts. In such a price-coordinated capitalist system, the amount of inputs ordered would be based on the enterprise's most accurate estimate of what was really required, not on how much its managers could persuade higher government officials to let them have.

These higher officials could not possibly be experts on all the wide range of industries and products under their control, so those with the power in the central planning agencies were to some extent dependent on those with the knowledge of their own particular industries and enterprises. This separation of power and knowledge was at the heart of the problem.

Central planners could be skeptical of what the enterprise managers told them but skepticism is not knowledge. If resources were denied, production could suffer— and heads could roll in the central planning agencies. The net result was the excessive use of resources described by the Soviet economists. The contrast between the Soviet economy and the economies of Japan and Germany is just one of many that can be made between economic systems which use prices to allocate resources and those which have relied on political or bureaucratic control. In other regions of the world as well, and in other political systems, there have been similar contrasts between places that used prices to ration goods and allocate resources versus places that have relied on hereditary rulers, elected officials or appointed planning commissions.

When many African colonies achieved national independence in the 1960s, a famous bet was made between the president of Ghana and the president of the neighboring Ivory Coast as to which country would be more prosperous in the years ahead. At that time, Ghana was not only more prosperous than the Ivory Coast, it had more natural resources, so the bet might have seemed reckless on the part of the president of the Ivory Coast. However, he knew that Ghana was committed to a government-run economy and the Ivory Coast to a freer market. By 1982, the Ivory Coast had so surpassed Ghana economically that the poorest 20 percent of its people had a higher real income per capita than most of the people in Ghana.

This could not be attributed to any superiority of the country or its people. In fact, in later years, when the government of the Ivory Coast eventually succumbed to the temptation to control more of their country's economy, while Ghana finally learned from its mistakes and began to loosen government controls on the market, these two countries' roles reversed— and now Ghana's economy began to grow, while that of the Ivory Coast declined.

Similar comparisons could be made between Burma and Thailand, the former having had the higher standard of living before instituting socialism, and the latter a much higher standard of living afterwards. Other countries— India, Germany, China, New Zealand, South Korea, Sri Lanka— have experienced sharp upturns in their economies when they freed those economies from many government controls and relied more on prices to allocate resources. As of 1960, India and South Korea were at comparable economic levels but, by the late 1980s, South Korea's per capita income was ten times that in India.

India remained committed to a government-controlled economy for many years after achieving independence in 1947. However, in the 1990s, India "jettisoned four decades of economic isolation and planning, and freed the country's entrepreneurs for the first time since independence," in the words of the distinguished London magazine *The Economist*. There followed a new growth rate of 6 percent a year, making it "one of the world's fastest-growing big economies." From 1950 to 1990, India's average growth rate had been 2 percent. The cumulative effect of growing three times as fast as before was that millions of Indians rose out of poverty.

In China, the transition to a market economy began earlier, in the 1980s. Government controls were at first relaxed on an experimental basis in particular economic sectors and in particular geographic regions earlier than in others. This led to stunning economic contrasts within the same country, as well as rapid economic growth overall.

Back in 1978, less than 10 percent of China's agricultural output was sold in open markets, instead of being turned over to the government for distribution. But, by 1990, 80 percent was sold directly in the market. The net result was more food and a greater variety of food available to city dwellers in China, and a rise in farmers' income by more than 50 percent within a few years. In contrast to China's severe economic problems when there was heavy-handed government control under Mao, who died in 1976, the subsequent freeing up of prices in the marketplace led to an astonishing economic growth rate of 9 percent per year between 1978 and 1995.

While history can tell us that such things happened, economics helps explain *why* they happened—what there is about prices that allows them to accomplish what political control of an economy can seldom match. There is more to economics than prices, but understanding how prices function is the foundation for understanding much of the rest of economics. A rationally planned economy sounds more plausible than an economy coordinated only by prices linking millions of separate decisions by individuals and organizations. Yet Soviet economists who saw the actual consequences of a centrally planned economy reached very different conclusions— namely, "there are far too many economic relationships, and it is impossible to take them all into account and coordinate them sensibly."

Knowledge is one of the most scarce of all resources, and a pricing system economizes on its use by forcing those with the most knowledge of their own particular situation to make bids for goods and resources based on that knowledge, rather than on their ability to influence other people in planning commissions, legislatures, or royal palaces. However much articulation may be valued by intellectuals, it is not nearly as efficient a way of conveying accurate information as confronting people with a need to "put your money where your mouth is." That forces them to summon up their most accurate information, rather than their most plausible words.

Human beings are going to make mistakes in any kind of economic system. The key question is: What kinds of incentives and constraints will force them to correct their own mistakes? In a price-coordinated economy, any producer who uses ingredients which are more valuable elsewhere in the economy is likely to discover that the costs of those ingredients cannot be repaid from what the consumers are willing to pay for the product. After all, the producer has had to bid those resources away from alternative users, paying more than the resources are worth to some of those alternative users. If it turns out that these resources are not more valuable in the uses to which this producer puts them, then he is going to lose money. There will be no choice but to discontinue making that product with those ingredients.

For those producers who are too blind or too stubborn to change, continuing losses will force their businesses into bankruptcy, so that the waste of the resources available to the society will be stopped that way. That is why losses are just as important as profits, from the standpoint of the economy, even though losses are not nearly as popular with businesses.

In a price-coordinated economy, employees and creditors insist on being paid, regardless of whether the managers and owners have made mistakes. This means that capitalist businesses can make only so many mistakes for so long before they have to either stop or get stopped— whether by an inability to get the labor and supplies they need or by bankruptcy. In a feudal economy or a socialist economy, leaders can continue to make the same mistakes indefinitely. The consequences are paid by others in the form of a standard of living lower than it would be if there were greater efficiency in the use of scarce resources.

In the absence of compelling price signals and the threat of financial losses to the producers that they convey, inefficiency and waste in the Soviet Union could continue until such time as each particular instance of waste reached proportions big enough and blatant enough to attract the attention of central planners in Moscow, who were preoccupied with thousands of other decisions.

Ironically, the problems caused by trying to run an economy by direct orders or by arbitrarily-imposed prices created by government fiat were foreseen in the nineteenth century by Karl Marx and Friedrich Engels, whose ideas the Soviet Union claimed to be following.

Engels pointed out that price fluctuations have "forcibly brought home to the individual commodity producers what things and what quantity of them society requires or does not require." Without such a mechanism, he demanded to know "what guarantee we have that necessary quantity and not more of each product will be produced, that we shall not go hungry in regard to corn and meat while we are choked in beet sugar and drowned in potato spirit, that we shall not lack trousers to cover our nakedness while trouser buttons flood us in millions." Marx and Engels apparently understood economics much better than their latter-day followers. Or perhaps Marx and Engels were more concerned with economic efficiency than with maintaining political control from the top.

There were also Soviet economists who understood the role of price fluctuations in coordinating any economy. Near the end of the Soviet Union, two of these economists, Shmelev and Popov, whom we have already quoted, said: "Everything is interconnected in the world of prices, so that the smallest change in one element is passed along the chain to millions of others." These Soviet economists were especially aware of the role of prices from having seen what happened when prices were not allowed to perform that role. But economists were not in charge of the Soviet economy. Political leaders were. Under Stalin, a number of economists were shot for saying things he did not want to hear.

SUPPLY AND DEMAND

There is perhaps no more basic or more obvious principle of economics than the fact that people tend to buy more at a lower price and less at a higher price. By the same token, people who produce goods or supply services tend to supply more at a higher price and less at a lower price. Yet the implications of these two simple principles, singly or in combination, cover a remarkable range of economic activities and issues— and contradict an equally remarkable range of misconceptions and fallacies.

Demand versus "Need"

When people try to quantify a country's "need" for this or that product or service, they are ignoring the fact that there is no fixed or objective "need." Seldom, if ever, is there a fixed quantity demanded. For example, communal living in an Israeli kibbutz was based on its members' collectively producing and supplying each other with goods and services, without resort to money or prices. However, supplying electricity and food without charging prices led to a situation where people often did not bother to turn off electric lights during the day and members would bring friends from outside the kibbutz to join them for meals. But, after the kibbutz began to charge prices for electricity and food, there was a sharp drop in the consumption of both. In short, there was no fixed quantity of "need" or demand for food or electricity, despite how indispensable both might be.

Likewise, there is no fixed supply. Statistics on the amount of petroleum, iron ore, or other natural resources seem to indicate that this is just a simple matter of how much physical stuff there is in the ground. In reality, the costs of discovery, extraction and processing of natural resources vary greatly from one place to another. There is some oil that can be extracted and processed from some places for $20 a barrel and other oil elsewhere that cannot repay all its production costs at $40 a barrel, but which can at $60 a barrel. With goods in general, *the quantity supplied varies directly with the price*, just as the quantity demanded varies inversely with the price.

When the price of oil falls below a certain point, low-yield oil wells are shut down because the cost of extracting and processing the oil from those particular wells would exceed the price that the oil would sell for in the market. If the price later rises— or if the cost of extraction or processing is lowered by some new technology— then such oil wells will be put back into operation again. Certain sands containing oil in Venezuela and in Canada had such low yields that they were not even counted in the world's oil reserves until oil prices hit new highs in the early twenty-first century. That changed things, as the *Wall Street Journal* reported:

> These deposits were once dismissed as "unconventional" oil that couldn't be recovered economically. But now, thanks to rising global oil prices and improved technology, most oil-industry experts count oil sands as recoverable reserves. That recalculation has vaulted Venezuela and Canada to first and third in global reserves rankings. . .

The Economist magazine likewise reported:

> Canada's oil sands, or tar sands, as the goo is known, are outsized in every way. They contain 174 billion barrels of oil that can be recovered profitably, and another 141 billion that might be worth exploiting if the oil price rises or the costs of extraction decrease— enough to give Canada bigger oil reserves than Saudi Arabia.

In short, there is no fixed supply of oil— or of most other things. In some ultimate sense, the earth has a finite amount of each resource but, even when that amount may be enough to last for centuries or millennia, at any given time the amount that is economically feasible to extract and process varies directly with the price for which it can be sold. Many false predictions over the past century or more that we were "running out" of various natural resources in a few years were based on confusing the economically available current supply at current prices with the ultimate physical supply in the earth, which is often vastly greater.

Natural resources are not the only things that will be supplied in greater quantities when their prices rise. That is true of many commodities and even workers. When people project that there will be a shortage of engineers or teachers or food in the years ahead, they usually either ignore prices or implicitly assume that there will be a shortage at today's prices. But shortages are precisely what cause prices to rise. At higher prices, it may be no harder to fill vacancies for engineers or teachers than today and no harder to find food, as rising prices cause more crops to be grown and more livestock to be raised. In short, a larger quantity is usually supplied at higher prices than at lower prices, whether what is being sold is oil or apples, lobsters or labor.

"Real" Value

The producer whose product turns out to have the combination of features that are closest to what the consumers really want may be no wiser than his competitors. Yet he can grow rich while his competitors who guessed wrong go bankrupt. But the larger result is that society as a whole gets more benefits from its limited resources by having them directed toward where those resources produce the kind of output that millions of people want, instead of producing things that they don't want.

Simple as all this may seem, it contradicts many widely held ideas. For example, not only are high prices often blamed on "greed," people often speak of something being sold for more than its "real" value, or of workers being paid less than they are "really" worth— or of corporate executives, athletes, and entertainers being paid more than they are "really" worth. The fact that prices fluctuate over time, and occasionally have a sharp rise or a steep drop, misleads some people into concluding that prices are deviating from their "real" values. But their usual level under usual conditions is no more real or valid than their much higher or much lower levels under different conditions.

When a large employer goes bankrupt in a small community, or simply moves away to another region or country, many of the business' former employees may decide to move away themselves from a place that now has fewer jobs— and when their numerous homes go on sale in the same small area at the same time, the prices of those houses are likely to be driven down by competition. But this does not mean that people are selling their homes for less than their "real" value. The value of living in that particular community has simply declined with the decline of job opportunities, and housing prices reflect this underlying fact.

The most fundamental reason why there is no such thing as an objective or "real" value is that there would be no rational basis for economic transactions if there were. When you pay a dollar for a newspaper, obviously the only reason you do so is that the newspaper is more valuable to you than the dollar is. At the same time, the only reason people are willing to sell the newspaper is that a dollar is more valuable to them than the newspaper is. If there were any such thing as a "real" or objective value of a newspaper— or anything else— neither the buyer nor the seller would benefit from making a transaction at a price equal to that objective value, since what would be acquired would be of no greater value than what was given up. In that case, why bother to make the transaction in the first place?

On the other hand, if either the buyer or the seller was getting more than the objective value from the transaction, then the other person must be getting less— in which case, why would the other party continue making such transactions while being continually cheated? Continuing transactions between buyer and seller make sense only if value is subjective, each getting what is worth more subjectively. Economic transactions are not a zero-sum process, where one person loses whatever the other person gains.

Competition

Competition is the crucial factor in explaining why prices usually cannot be maintained at arbitrarily set levels. Competition is the key to the operation of a price-coordinated economy. It not only forces prices toward equality, it likewise causes capital, labor, and other resources to flow toward where their rates of return are highest— that is, where the unsatisfied demand is greatest— until the returns are evened out through competition, much like water seeking its own level. However, the fact that water seeks its own level does not mean that the ocean has a glassy smooth surface. Waves and tides are among the ways in which water seeks its own level, without being frozen indefinitely at a given level. Similarly, in an economy, the fact that prices and rates of return on investments tend to equalize means only that their fluctuations, relative to one another, are what move resources from places where their earnings are lower to where their earnings are higher— that is, from where the quantity supplied is greatest, relative to the quantity demanded, to where there is the most unsatisfied demand. It does *not* mean that prices remain the same over time or that some ideal pattern of allocation of resources remains the same indefinitely.

Prices and Supplies

Prices not only ration existing supplies, they also act as powerful incentives to cause supplies to rise or fall in response to changing demand. When a crop failure in a given region creates a sudden increase in demand for imports of food into that region, food suppliers elsewhere rush to be the first to get there, in order to capitalize on the high prices that will prevail until more supplies arrive and drive food prices back down again through competition. What this means, from the standpoint of the hungry people in that region, is that food is being rushed to them at maximum speed by "greedy" suppliers, probably much faster than if the same food were being transported to them by salaried government employees sent on a humanitarian mission.

Those spurred on by a desire to earn top dollar for the food they sell may well drive throughout the night or take short cuts over rough terrain, while those operating "in the public interest" are more likely to proceed at a less hectic pace and by safer or more comfortable routes. In short, people tend to do more for their own benefit than for the benefit of others. Freely fluctuating prices can make that turn out to be beneficial to others. In the case of food supplies, earlier arrival can be the difference between temporary hunger and death by starvation or by diseases to which people are more susceptible when they are undernourished. Where there are local famines in Third World countries, it is not at all uncommon for food supplied by international agencies to the national government to sit spoiling on the docks while people are dying of hunger inland.* However unattractive greed may be, it is likely to move food much faster, saving more lives.

In other situations, the consumers may not want more, but less. Prices also convey this. When automobiles began to displace horses and buggies in the early twentieth century, the demand for saddles, horseshoes, carriages and other such paraphernalia declined. As the manufacturers of such products faced losses instead of profits, many began to abandon their businesses or were forced to shut down by bankruptcy. In a sense, it is unfair when some people

---

* The same thing can happen when the food arrives by land. See "Death by Bureaucracy," in the December 8, 2001 issue of *The Economist* (page 40), for examples of Afghan refugees dying of starvation while waiting for paperwork to be completed by aid workers.

are unable to earn as much as others with similar levels of skills and diligence, because of innovations which were as unforeseen by most of the producers who benefitted as by most of the producers who were made worse off. Yet this unfairness to particular individuals and businesses is what makes the economy as a whole operate more efficiently for the benefit of vastly larger numbers of others. Would creating more fairness among producers, at the cost of reduced efficiency and a resulting lower standard of living, be fair to consumers?

The gains and losses are not isolated or independent events. The crucial role of prices is in tying together a vast network of economic activities among people too widely scattered to all know each other. However much we may think of ourselves as independent individuals, we are all dependent on other people for our very lives, as well as being dependent on innumerable strangers who produce the amenities of life. Few of us could grow the food we need to live, much less build a place to live in, or produce such things as computers or automobiles. Other people have to be induced to create all these things for us, and economic incentives are crucial for that purpose. As Will Rogers once said, "We couldn't live a day without depending on everybody." Prices make that dependence viable by linking their interests with ours.

"UNMET NEEDS"

One of the most common— and certainly one of the most profound— misconceptions of economics involves "unmet needs." Politicians, journalists, and academicians are almost continuously pointing out unmet needs in our society that should be supplied by some government program or other. Most of these are things that most of us wish our society had more of.

What is wrong with that? Let us go back to square one. If economics is the study of the use of scarce resources which have alternative uses, then it follows that there will always be unmet needs. Some particular desires can be singled out and met 100 percent, but that only means that other desires will be even more unfulfilled than they are now. Anyone who has driven in most big cities will undoubtedly feel that there is an unmet need for more parking spaces. But, while it is both economically and technologically possible to build cities in such a way as to have a parking space available for anyone who wants one, anywhere in the city, at any hour of the day or night, does it follow that we should do it?

The cost of building vast new underground parking garages, or of tearing down existing buildings to create parking garages above ground, or of designing new cities with fewer buildings and more parking lots, would all be astronomically costly. What other things are we prepared to give up, in order to have this automotive Utopia? Fewer hospitals? Less police protection? Fewer fire departments? Are we prepared to put up with even more unmet needs in these areas? Maybe some would give up public libraries in order to have more places to park. But, whatever choices are made and however it is done, there will still be more unmet needs elsewhere, as a result of meeting an unmet need for more parking spaces.

We may differ among ourselves as to what is worth sacrificing in order to have more of something else. The point here is more fundamental. Merely demonstrating an unmet need is not sufficient to say that it should be met— not when resources are scarce and have alternative uses.

In the case of parking spaces, what might appear to be cheaper, when measured only by government expenditures, would be to restrict or forbid the use of private automobiles in cities, adjusting the number of cars to the number of existing parking spaces, instead of vice versa. Moreover, passing and enforcing such a law would cost a tiny fraction of the cost of greatly expanding the number of parking spaces. But this saving in government expenditures would have to be weighed against the vast private expenditures currently devoted to the purchase, maintenance, and parking of automobiles in cities. Obviously these expenditures would not have been undertaken in the first place if those who pay these prices did not find the benefits to be worth it to them. To go back to square one again, *costs are foregone opportunities*, not government expenditures. Forcing thousands of people to forego opportunities for which they have willingly paid vast amounts of money is a cost that may far outweigh the money saved by not having to build more parking spaces or do the other things necessary to accommodate cars in cities. None of this says that we should have either more parking spaces or fewer parking spaces in cities. What it says is that the way this issue— and many others— is presented makes no sense in a world of scarce resources which have alternative uses. That is a world of trade-offs, not solutions—and whatever trade-off is decided upon will still leave unmet needs.

So long as we respond gullibly to political rhetoric about unmet needs, we will arbitrarily choose to shift resources to whatever the featured unmet need of the day happens to be and away from other things. Then, when another politician— or perhaps even the same politician at a later time— discovers that robbing Peter to pay Paul has left Peter worse off, and now wants to help Peter meet his unmet needs, we will start shifting resources in another direction. In short, we will be like a dog chasing his tail in a circle and getting no closer, no matter how fast he runs.

This is not to say that we have the ideal trade-offs already and should leave them alone. Rather, it says that whatever trade-offs we make or change should be seen from the outset as trade-offs— not meeting unmet needs.

The very word "needs" arbitrarily puts some desires on a higher plane than others, as categorically more important. But, however urgent it may be to have *some* food and some water, for example, in order to sustain life itself, nevertheless— beyond some point— both become not only unnecessary but even counterproductive and dangerous. Widespread obesity among Americans shows that food has already reached that point and anyone who has suffered the ravages of flood (even if it is only a flooded basement) knows that water can reach that point as well. In short, even the most urgently required things remain necessary only within a given range. We cannot live half an hour without oxygen, but even oxygen beyond some concentration level can promote the growth of cancer and has been known to make newborn babies blind for life. There is a reason why hospitals do not use oxygen tanks willy-nilly.

In short, nothing is a "need" categorically, regardless of how urgent it may be to have particular amounts at particular times and places. Unfortunately, most laws and government policies apply categorically, if only because of the dangers in leaving every government official to become a petty despot in interpreting what these laws and policies mean and when they should apply. In this context, calling something a "need" categorically is playing with fire. Many complaints that some basically good government policy has been applied stupidly may fail to address the underlying problem of categorical laws in an incremental world. There may not have been any intelligent way to apply categorically a policy designed to meet desires whose benefits vary incrementally and ultimately cease to be benefits.

By its very nature as a study of the use of scarce resources which have alternative uses, economics is about incremental trade-offs— not about "needs" or "solutions." That may be why economists have never been as popular as politicians who promise to solve our problems and meet our needs.

Chapter 3

PRICE CONTROLS

> The record of price controls goes as far back as human
> history. They were imposed by the Pharaohs of ancient
> Egypt. They were decreed by Hammurabi, king of
> Babylon, in the eighteenth century B.C. They were tried
> in ancient Athens.

Henry Hazlitt

Nothing makes us understand the many roles of electricity in our lives like a power failure. Similarly, nothing shows more vividly the role and importance of price fluctuations in a market economy than the *absence* of such price fluctuations when the market is controlled. What happens when prices are not allowed to fluctuate freely according to supply and demand, but instead their fluctuations are fixed within limits set by law under various kinds of price controls?

Q

Typically, price controls are imposed in order to keep prices from rising to the levels that they would reach in response to supply and demand. The political rationales for such laws have varied from place to place and from time to time, but there is seldom a lack of rationales whenever it becomes politically expedient to hold down some people's prices in the interest of other people whose political support seems more important.

To understand the effects of price control, it is first necessary to understand how prices rise and fall in a free market. There is nothing esoteric about it, but it is important to be very clear about what happens. Prices rise because the amount demanded exceeds the amount supplied *at existing prices*. Prices fall because the amount supplied exceeds the amount demanded *at existing prices*.

key

The first case is called a "shortage" and the second is called a "surplus"— but both depend on *existing prices*. Simple as this might seem, it is often misunderstood, sometimes with disastrous consequences.

PRICE "CEILINGS" AND SHORTAGES

When there is a "shortage" of a product, there is not necessarily any less of it, either absolutely or relative to the number of consumers. During and immediately after the Second World War, for example, there was a very serious housing shortage in the United States, even though the country's population and its housing supply had both increased by about 10 percent from their prewar levels— and there was no shortage when the war began. In other words, even though the ratio between housing and people had not changed, nevertheless many Americans looking for an apartment during this period had to spend weeks or months in an often futile search for a place to live, or else resorted to bribes to get landlords to move them to the top of waiting lists. Meanwhile, they doubled up with relatives, slept in garages or used other makeshift living arrangements, such as buying military surplus Quonset huts or old trolley cars to live in.

Although there was no less housing space per person than before the war, the shortage was very real and very painful *at existing prices*, which were kept artificially lower than they would have been, because of rent control laws that had been passed during the war. At these artificially low prices, more people had a demand for more housing space than before rent control laws were enacted. This is a practical consequence of the simple economic principle already noted in Chapter 2, that the quantity demanded varies according to how high or how low the price is.

When some people used more housing than usual, other people found less housing available. The same thing happens under other forms of price control: Some people use the price-controlled goods or services more generously than usual because of the artificially lower price and, as a result, other people find that less than usual remains available for them. There are other consequences to price controls in general, and rent control provides examples of these as well.

Demand under Rent Control

Some people who would normally not be renting their own apartments, such as young adults still living with their parents or some single or widowed elderly people living with relatives, were enabled by the artificially low prices created by rent control to move out and into their own apartments. These artificially low prices also caused others to seek larger apartments than they would ordinarily be living in or to live alone when they would otherwise have to share an apartment with a roommate, in order to be able to afford the rent.

Some people who do not even live in the same city as their rent-controlled apartment nevertheless keep it as a place to stay when they are visiting the city— Hollywood movie stars who keep rent-controlled apartments in New York or a couple living in Hawaii who kept a rent-controlled residence in San Francisco, for example. More tenants seeking both more apartments and larger apartments create a shortage, even when there is not any greater physical scarcity of housing relative to the total population.

When rent control ended after World War II, the housing shortage quickly disappeared. After rents rose in a free market, some childless couples living in four-bedroom apartments could decide that they would live in two-bedroom apartments and save the difference in rent. Some late teenagers could decide that they would continue living with their parents a little longer, until their pay rose enough for them to be able to afford their own apartment, now that rent was no longer artificially cheap. The net result was that families looking for a place to stay found more places available, now that rent-control laws were no longer keeping such places occupied by people with less urgent requirements. In other words, the housing shortage immediately eased, even before there was time for new housing to be built, in response to market conditions that now made it possible to recover the cost of building more housing and earn a profit.

Just as price fluctuations allocate scarce resources which have alternative uses, price controls which limit those fluctuations reduce the incentives for individuals to limit their own use of scarce resources desired by others. Rent control, for example, tends to lead to many apartments being occupied by just one person. A study in San Francisco showed that 49 percent of that city's rent-controlled apartments had only a single occupant, while a severe housing shortage in the city had thousands of people living considerable distances away and making long commutes to their jobs in San Francisco. Meanwhile, a Census report showed likewise that 46 percent of all households in Manhattan, where nearly half of all apartments are under some form of rent control, are occupied by only one person— compared to 27 percent nationwide.

In the normal course of events, people's demand for housing space changes over a lifetime. Their demand for space usually increases when they get married and have children. But, years later, after the children have grown up and moved away, the parents' demand for space may decline, and it often declines yet again after a spouse dies and the widow or widower moves into smaller quarters or goes to live with relatives or in an institution for the elderly. In this way, a society's total stock of housing is shared and circulated among people according to their changing individual demands at different stages of their lives.

This sharing takes place, not because the individuals themselves have a sense of cooperation, but because of the prices— rents in this case— which confront them. In a free market, these prices are based on the value that other tenants put on housing. Young couples with a growing family are often willing to bid more for housing, even if that means buying fewer consumer goods and services, in order to have enough money to pay for additional housing space. A couple who begin to have children may cut back on how often they go out to restaurants or to movies, or they may wait longer to buy new clothes or a new car, in order that each child may have his or her own bedroom. But, once the children are grown and gone, such sacrifices may no longer make sense, when additional other amenities can now be enjoyed by reducing the amount of housing space being rented.

Given the crucial role of prices in this process, suppression of that process by rent control laws leaves few incentives for tenants to change their behavior as their circumstances change. Elderly people, for example, have less incentive to vacate apartments that they would normally vacate when their children are gone, or after a spouse dies, if that would result in a significant reduction in rent, leaving them more money with which to improve their living standards in other respects. Moreover, the chronic housing shortages which accompany rent control greatly increase the time and effort required to search for a new and smaller apartment, while reducing the financial reward for finding one. In short, rent control reduces the rate of housing turnover.

New York City has had rent control longer and more stringently than any other major American city. One consequence has been that the annual rate of turnover of apartments in New York is less than half the national average, and the proportion of tenants who have lived in the same apartment for 20 years or more is more than double the national average. As the *New York Times* summarized the situation:

> New York used to be like other cities, a place where tenants moved frequently and landlords competed to rent empty apartments to newcomers, but today the motto may as well be: No Immigrants Need Apply. While immigrants are crowded into bunks in illegal boarding houses in the slums, upper-middle-class locals pay low rents to live in good neighborhoods, often in large apartments they no longer need after their children move out.

Supply under Rent Control

Rent control has effects on supply as well as on demand. Nine years after the end of World War II, not a single new apartment building had been built in Melbourne, Australia, because of rent control laws there which made such buildings unprofitable. In Egypt, rent control was imposed in 1960. An Egyptian woman who lived through that era and wrote about it in 2006 reported:

> The end result was that people stopped investing in apartment buildings, and a huge shortage in rentals and housing forced many Egyptians to live in horrible conditions with several families sharing one small apartment. The effects of the harsh rent control is still felt today in Egypt. Mistakes like that can last for generations.

Declines in building construction have likewise followed in the wake of rent control laws elsewhere. After rent control was instituted in Santa Monica, California in 1979, building permits declined to less than one-tenth of what they were just five years earlier. A housing study in San Francisco found that three quarters of its rent-controlled housing was more than half a century old and 44 percent of it was more than 70 years old.

Although the construction of office buildings, factories, warehouses, and other commercial and industrial buildings requires much of the same kind of labor and materials used to construct apartment buildings, it is not uncommon for many new office buildings to be constructed in cities where very few new apartment buildings are built. Rent control laws often do not apply to industrial or commercial buildings. Thus, even in cities with severe housing shortages, there may be much vacant space in commercial and industrial buildings. Despite a severe housing shortage in New York, San Francisco, and other cities with rent control, a nationwide survey in 2003 found the vacancy rates in buildings used by business and industry to be nearly 12 percent, the highest in more than two decades.

This is just one more piece of evidence that housing shortages are a price phenomenon. High vacancy rates in commercial buildings show that there are obviously ample resources available to construct buildings, but rent control keeps those resources from being used to construct apartments, and thereby diverts these resources into constructing office buildings, industrial plants, and other commercial properties.

Not only is the supply of new apartment construction less after rent control laws are imposed, even the supply of existing housing tends to decline, as landlords provide less maintenance and repair under rent control, since the housing shortage makes it unnecessary for them to maintain the appearance of their premises in order to attract tenants. Thus housing tends to deteriorate faster under rent control and to have fewer replacements when it wears out. Studies of rent control in the United States, England, and France have found rent-controlled housing to be deteriorated far more often than non-rent-controlled housing.

Typically, the rental housing stock is relatively fixed in the short run, so that a shortage occurs first because more people want more housing at the artificially low price. Later, there may be a real increase in scarcity as well, as rental units deteriorate more rapidly with reduced maintenance, while not enough new units are being built to replace them as they wear out, because new privately built housing can be unprofitable under rent control. Under rent control in England and Wales, for example, privately-built rental housing fell from being 61 percent of all housing in 1947 to being just 14 percent by 1977.

A study of rent control in various countries concluded: "New investment in private unsubsidized rented housing is essentially nonexistent in all the European countries surveyed, except for luxury housing."

In short, a policy intended to make housing affordable for the poor has had the net effect of shifting resources toward the building of housing that is affordable only by the affluent or the rich, since luxury housing is often exempt from rent control, just as office buildings and other commercial properties are. Among other things, this illustrates the crucial importance of making a distinction between intentions and consequences. Economic policies need to be analyzed in terms of the incentives they create, rather than the hopes that inspired them.

The incentives towards a reduced supply of housing under rent control are especially pronounced when people who have been renting out rooms or apartments in their own homes, or bungalows in their back yards, decide that it is no longer worth the bother, when rents are kept artificially low under rent control laws. In addition, there are often conversions of apartments to condominiums. During 8 years of rent control in Washington during the 1970s, that city's available rental housing stock declined absolutely, from just over 199,000 units on the market to just under 176,000 units. After rent control was introduced in Berkeley, California, the number of private rental housing units available to students at the university there declined by 31 percent in five years.

None of this should be surprising, given the incentives created by rent control laws. In terms of incentives, it is likewise easy to understand what happened in England when rent control was extended in 1975 to cover furnished rental units. According to *The Times* of London:

> Advertisements for furnished rented accommodation in the London *Evening Standard* plummeted dramatically in the first week after the Act came into force and are now running at about 75 per cent below last year's levels.

Since furnished rooms are often in people's homes, these represent housing units that are easily withdrawn from the market when the rents no longer compensate for the inconveniences of having renters living with you. The same principle applies where there are small apartment buildings like duplexes, where the owner is also one of the tenants. Within three years after rent control was imposed in Toronto in 1976, 23 percent of all rental units in owner-occupied dwellings were withdrawn from the housing market.

Even when rent control applies to apartment buildings where the landlord does not live, eventually the point may be reached where the whole building becomes sufficiently unprofitable that it is simply abandoned. In New York City, for example, many buildings have been abandoned after their owners found it impossible to collect enough rent to cover the costs of services that they are required by law to provide, such as heat and hot water. Such owners have simply disappeared, in order to escape the legal consequences of their abandonment, and such buildings often end up vacant and boarded up, though still physically sound enough to house people, if they continued to be maintained and repaired.

The number of abandoned buildings taken over by the New York City government over the years runs into the thousands. It has been estimated that there are at least four times as many abandoned housing units in New York City as there are homeless people living on the streets there. Homelessness is not due to a physical scarcity of housing, but to a price-related shortage, which is painfully real nonetheless. As of 2013, there were more than 47,000 homeless people in New York City, 20,000 of them children.

Such inefficiency in the allocation of resources means that people are sleeping outdoors on the pavement on cold winter nights— some dying of exposure— while the means of housing them already exist, but are not being used because of laws designed to make housing "affordable." Once again, this demonstrates that the efficient or inefficient allocation of scarce resources is not just some abstract notion of economists, but has very real consequences, which can even include matters of life and death. It also illustrates that the goal of a law— "affordable housing," in this case— tells us nothing about its actual consequences.

The Politics of Rent Control

Politically, rent control is often a big success, however many serious economic and social problems it creates. Politicians know that there are always more tenants than landlords and more people who do not understand economics than people who do. That makes rent control laws something likely to lead to a net increase in votes for politicians who pass rent control laws.

Often it is politically effective to represent rent control as a way to keep greedy rich landlords from "gouging" the poor with "unconscionable" rents. In reality, rates of return on investments in housing are seldom higher than on alternative investments, and landlords are often people of very modest means. This is especially so for owners of small, low-end apartment buildings that are in constant need of repair, the kinds of places where tenants are likely to be low-income people. Many of the landlords with buildings like this are handymen who use their own skills and labor as carpenters or plumbers to repair and maintain the premises, while trying to pay off the mortgage with the rents they collect. In short, the kind of housing likely to be rented by the poor often has owners who are by no means rich.*

Where rent control laws apply on a blanket basis to all housing in existence as of the time the law goes into effect, even luxurious housing becomes low-rent housing. Then, after the passage of time makes clear that no new housing is likely to be built unless it is exempted from rent control, such exemptions or relaxations of rent control for new housing mean that even new apartments that are very modest in size and quality may rent for far more than older, more spacious and more luxurious apartments that are still under rent control. This non-comparability of rents has been common in European cities under rent control, as well as in New York and other American cities. Similar incentives produce similar results in many different settings. A news story in the *Wall Street Journal* pointed up this non-comparability of rents under New York City's rent control laws:

> Les Katz, a 27-year-old acting student and doorman, rents a small studio apartment on Manhattan's Upper West Side for $1,200— with two roommates. Two sleep in separate beds in a loft built atop the kitchen, the third on a mattress in the main room.

---

* My wife was once an attorney for a non-profit organization that often represented tenants in disputes with landlords. After observing how often the landlords were people of obviously modest economic and educational levels, she began to rethink the assumptions that led her into supporting rent control and its accompanying housing regulations.

> Across town on Park Avenue, Paul Haberman, a private investor, and his wife live in a spacious, two-bedroom apartment with a solarium and two terraces. The apartment in an elegant building on the prestigious avenue is worth at least $5,000 a month, real-estate professionals say. The couple pay around $350, according to rent records.

This example of cheap rent for the affluent or the wealthy under rent control was by no means unique. Ironically, a statistical study indicated that the biggest difference between prices under New York's rent control law and free-market prices is in luxury apartments. In other words, the affluent and the wealthy get more economic benefit from rent control than do the poor who are invoked to justify such laws. Meanwhile, city welfare agencies have paid much higher rents than those just mentioned when they housed poverty-stricken families in cramped and roach-infested apartments in run-down hotels. In 2013, the *New York Times* reported that the city's Department of Homeless Services was "spending over $3,000 a month for each threadbare room without a bathroom or kitchen" in a single room occupancy hotel— half of that money going to the landlord for rent and the other half for "security and social services for homeless tenants."

The image that rent control protects poor tenants from rich landlords may be politically effective, but often it bears little resemblance to the reality. The people who actually benefit from rent control can be at any income level and so can those who lose out. It depends on who happens to be on the inside looking out, and who happens to be on the outside looking in, when such laws are passed.

San Francisco's rent control laws are not as old as those in New York City but they are similarly severe— and have produced very similar results. A study published in 2001 showed that more than one-fourth of the occupants of rent-controlled apartments in San Francisco had household incomes of more than $100,000 a year. It should also be noted that this was the first empirical study of rent control commissioned by the city of San Francisco. Since rent control began there in 1979, this means that for more than two decades these laws were enforced and extended, with no serious attempt being made to measure their actual economic and social consequences, as distinguished from their political popularity.

Ironically, cities with strong rent control laws, such as New York and San Francisco, tend to end up with *higher* average rents than cities without rent control. Where such laws apply only to rents below some specified level, presumably to protect the poor, builders then have incentives to build only apartments luxurious enough to be priced above the rent-control level. Not surprisingly, this leads to higher average rents, and homelessness tends to be greater in cities with rent control— New York and San Francisco again being classic examples.

One of the reasons for the political success of rent control laws is that many people accept words as indicators of reality. They believe that rent control laws actually control rents. So long as they believe that, such laws are politically viable, as are other laws that proclaim some apparently desirable goals, whether those goals end up being served or not.

Scarcity versus Shortage

One of the crucial distinctions to keep in mind is the distinction between an increased scarcity— where fewer goods are available relative to the population— and a "shortage" as a *price* phenomenon. Just as there can be a growing shortage without an increased scarcity, so there can be a growing scarcity without a shortage.

As already noted, there was a severe housing shortage in the United States during and immediately after the Second World War, even though the ratio of housing to people was the same as it had been before the war, when there was no housing shortage. It is also possible to have the opposite situation, where the actual amount of housing suddenly declines in a given area without any price control— and without any shortage. This happened in the wake of the great San Francisco earthquake and fire of 1906. More than half the city's housing supply was destroyed in just three days during that catastrophe. Yet there was no housing shortage. When the *San Francisco Chronicle* resumed publication a month after the earthquake, its first issue contained 64 advertisements of apartments or homes for rent, compared to only 5 ads from people seeking apartments to live in.

Of the 200,000 people suddenly made homeless by the earthquake and fire, temporary shelters housed 30,000 and an estimated 75,000 left the city.

Still, that left nearly 100,000 people to be absorbed into the local housing market. Yet the newspapers of that time mention no housing shortage. Rising prices not only allocate existing housing, they provide incentives for rebuilding and for renters to use less space in the meantime, as well as incentives for those with space in their homes to take in roomers while rents are high. In short, just as there can be a shortage without any greater physical scarcity, so there can be a greater physical scarcity without any shortage. People made homeless by the huge 1906 San Francisco earthquake found housing more readily than people made homeless by New York's rent control laws that took thousands of buildings off the market.

Hoarding

In addition to shortages and quality deterioration under price controls, there is often hoarding— that is, individuals keeping a larger inventory of the price-controlled goods than they would ordinarily under free market conditions, because of the uncertainty of being able to find it in the future. Thus, during the gasoline shortages of the 1970s, motorists were less likely to let their gas tanks get down as low as usual before going to a filling station to buy more gas.

Some motorists with their tanks half full would drive into any filling station that happened to have gas, and fill up the other half, as a precaution. With millions of motorists driving around with their gas tanks more full than usual, vast amounts of gasoline disappeared into individual inventories, leaving less available for sale from the general inventory at filling stations. Thus a relatively small shortage of gasoline nationally could turn into a very serious problem for those motorists who happened to run out of gas and had to look for a filling station that was open and had gas to sell. The sudden severity of the gasoline shortage— given how little difference there was in the total amount of gasoline produced— baffled many people and produced various conspiracy theories.

One of these conspiracy theories was that oil companies had their tankers from the Middle East circling around in the ocean, waiting for a price increase before coming ashore with their cargoes. Although none of these conspiracy theories stood up under scrutiny, there was a kernel of sense behind them, as there usually is behind most fallacies. A severe shortage of gasoline with very little difference in the total amount of gasoline produced meant that there had to be a large amount of gasoline being diverted somewhere. Few of those who created or believed conspiracy theories suspected that the excess was being stored in their own gas tanks, rather than in oil tankers circling in the ocean. This increased the severity of the gasoline shortage because maintaining millions of larger individual inventories of gasoline in cars and trucks was less efficient than maintaining general inventories in filling stations' storage tanks.

The feasibility of hoarding varies with different goods, so the effect of price controls also varies. For example, price controls on strawberries might lead to less of a shortage than price controls on gasoline, since strawberries are too perishable to be hoarded for long. Price controls on haircuts or other services may also create less of a shortage because services cannot be hoarded. That is, you would not get two haircuts on the same day if you found a barber with time available, in order to go twice as long before the next haircut, even though barbers might be less available when the price of haircuts was kept down by price controls.

Nevertheless, some unlikely things do get hoarded under price controls. For example, under rent control, people may keep an apartment that they seldom use, as some Hollywood stars have kept rent-controlled apartments in Manhattan where they would stay when visiting New York. Mayor Ed Koch kept his rent-controlled apartment during the entire 12 years when he lived in Gracie Mansion, the official residence of New York's mayor. In 2008, it was revealed that New York Congressman Charles Rangel had four rent-controlled apartments, one of which he used as an office.

Hoarding is a special case of the more general economic principle that more is demanded at a lower price and of the corollary that price controls allow lower priority uses to preempt higher priority uses, increasing the severity of the shortages, whether of apartments or of gasoline.

Sometimes the reduction in supply under price controls takes forms that are less obvious. Under World War II price controls, *Consumer Reports* magazine found that 19 out of 20 candy bars that it tested in 1943 were smaller in size than they had been four years earlier. Some producers of canned foods let the quality deteriorate, but then sold these lower quality foods under a different label, in order to preserve the reputation of their regular brand.

Black Markets

While price controls make it illegal for buyer and seller to make some transactions on terms that they would both prefer to the shortages that price controls entail, bolder and less scrupulous buyers and sellers make mutually advantageous transactions outside the law. Price controls almost invariably produce black markets, where prices are not only higher than the legally permitted prices, but also higher than they would be in a free market, since the legal risks must also be compensated. While small-scale black markets may function in secrecy, large-scale black markets usually require bribes to officials to look the other way. In Russia, for example, a local embargo on the shipment of price-controlled food beyond regional boundaries was dubbed the "150-ruble decree," since this was the cost of bribing police to let the shipments pass through checkpoints.

Even during the early Soviet period, when operating a black market in food was punishable by death, black markets still existed. As two Soviet economists of a later era put it: "Even at the height of War Communism, speculators and food smugglers at the risk of their lives brought as much grain into the cities as all the state purchases made under *prodrazverstka*."

Statistics on black market activity are by nature elusive, since no one wants to let the whole world know that they are violating the law. However, sometimes there are indirect indications. Under American wartime price controls during and immediately after the Second World War, employment in meat-packing plants declined as meat was diverted from legitimate packing houses into black markets. This often translated into empty meat counters in butcher shops and grocery stores.*

As in other cases, however, this was not due simply to an actual physical scarcity of meat but to its diversion into illegal channels. Within one month

---

* In many cases, goods in short supply were kept in the back of the store for sale to those people who were willing to offer more than the legal price. Black markets were not always separate operations, but were also a sideline of some otherwise legitimate businesses.

after price controls were ended, employment in meat-packing plants rose from 93,000 to 163,000 and then rose again to 180,000 over the next two months. This nearly doubling of employment in meat-packing plants in just three months indicated that meat was clearly no longer being diverted from the packing houses after price controls were ended.

In the Soviet Union, where price controls were more pervasive and longer lasting, two Soviet economists wrote of a "gray market" where people paid "additional money for goods and services." Although these illegal transactions "are not taken into account by official statistics," the Soviet economists estimated that 83 percent of the population used these forbidden economic channels. These illegal markets covered a wide range of transactions, including "almost half of the repair of apartments," 40 percent of automobile repairs and more video sales than in the legal markets: "The black market trades almost 10,000 video titles, while the state market offers fewer than 1,000."

Quality Deterioration

One of the reasons for the political success of price controls is that part of their costs are concealed. Even the visible shortages do not tell the whole story. Quality deterioration, such as already noted in the case of housing, has been common with many other products and services whose prices have been kept artificially low by government fiat.

One of the fundamental problems of price control is defining just what it is whose price is being controlled. Even something as simple as an apple is not easy to define because apples differ in size, freshness, and appearance, quite aside from the different varieties of apples. Produce stores and supermarkets spend time (and hence money) sorting out different kinds and qualities of apples, throwing away those that fall below a certain quality that their respective customers expect. Under price control, however, the amount of apples demanded at an artificially low price exceeds the amount supplied, so there is no need to spend so much time and money sorting out apples, as they will all be sold anyway. Some apples that would ordinarily be thrown away under free market conditions may, under price control, be kept for sale to those people who arrive after all the good apples have been sold.

As with apartments under rent control, there is less incentive to maintain high quality when everything will sell anyway during a shortage.

Some of the most painful examples of quality deterioration have occurred in countries where there are price controls on medical care. At artificially low prices, more people go to doctors' offices with minor ailments like sniffles or skin rashes that they might otherwise ignore, or else might treat with over-the-counter medications, perhaps with a pharmacist's advice. But all this changes when price controls reduce the cost of visits to the doctor's office, and especially when these visits are paid for by the government and are therefore free to the patient.

In short, more people make more claims on doctors' time under price control, leaving less time for other people with more serious, or even urgent, medical problems. Thus, under Britain's government-controlled medical system, a twelve-year-old girl was given a breast implant while 10,000 people waited 15 months or more for surgery. A woman with cancer had her operation postponed so many times that the malignancy eventually became inoperable. The priorities which prices automatically cause individuals to consider are among the first casualties of price controls.

A study conducted by the international agency Organisation for Economic Co-operation and Development found that, among five English-speaking countries surveyed, only in the United States was the percentage of patients waiting for elective surgery for more than four months in single digits. All the other English-speaking countries— Australia, Canada, New Zealand, and the United Kingdom— had more than 20 percent of their patients waiting more than four months, with 38 percent of those in the United Kingdom waiting at least that long. In this group, the United States was the only country without government-set prices for medical treatment. Incidentally, the term "elective surgery" was not confined to cosmetic surgery or other medically unnecessary procedures, but in this study included cataract surgery, hip replacement and coronary bypass surgery.

Delayed medical treatment is one aspect of quality deterioration when prices are set below the levels that would prevail under supply and demand. The quality of the treatment received is also affected when doctors spend less time per patient. In countries around the world, the amount of time that physicians spend per patient visit has been shorter under government-controlled medical care prices, compared to the time spent by physicians where prices are not controlled.

Black markets are another common feature of price controls that apply to medical care as to other things. In China and Japan, black markets have taken the form of bribes to doctors to get expedited treatment. In short, whether the product or service has been housing, apples, or medical care, quality deterioration under price control has been common in the most disparate settings.

PRICE "FLOORS" AND SURPLUSES

Just as a price set below the level that would prevail by supply and demand in a free market tends to cause more to be demanded and less to be supplied, creating a shortage at the imposed price, so a price set *above* the free market level tends to cause more to be supplied than demanded, creating a surplus.

Among the tragedies of the Great Depression of the 1930s was the fact that many American farmers simply could not make enough money from the sale of their crops to pay their bills. The prices of farm products fell much more drastically than the prices of the things that farmers bought. Farm income fell from just over $6 billion in 1929 to $2 billion in 1932.

As many farmers lost their farms because they could no longer pay the mortgages, and as other farm families suffered privations as they struggled to hang on to their farms and their traditional way of life, the federal government sought to restore what was called "parity" between agriculture and other sectors of the economy by intervening to keep farm prices from falling so sharply.

This intervention took various forms. One approach was to reduce by law the amount of various crops that could be grown and sold, so as to prevent the supply from driving the price below the level that government officials had decided upon. Thus, supplies of peanuts and cotton were restricted by law. Supplies of citrus fruit, nuts and various other farm products were regulated by local cartels of farmers, backed up by the authority of the Secretary of

Agriculture to issue "marketing orders" and prosecute those who violated these orders by producing and selling more than they were authorized to produce and sell. Such arrangements continued for decades after the poverty of the Great Depression was replaced by the prosperity of the economic boom following World War II, and many of these restrictions continue to this day.

These indirect methods of keeping prices artificially high were only part of the story. The key factor in keeping farm prices artificially higher than they would have been under free market supply and demand was the government's willingness to buy up the surpluses created by its control of prices. This they did for such farm products as corn, rice, tobacco, and wheat, among others— and many of these programs continue on to the present as well. Regardless of what group was initially supposed to be helped by these programs, the very existence of such programs benefitted others as well, and these new beneficiaries made it politically difficult to end such programs, even long after the initial conditions had changed and the initial beneficiaries were now a small part of the constituency politically organized and determined to keep these programs going.*

Price control in the form of a "floor" under prices, preventing these prices from falling further, produced surpluses as dramatic as the shortages produced by price control in the form of a "ceiling" preventing prices from rising higher. In some years, the federal government bought more than one-fourth of all the wheat grown in the United States and took it off the market, in order to maintain prices at a pre-determined level.

During the Great Depression of the 1930s, agricultural price support programs led to vast amounts of food being deliberately destroyed, at a time when malnutrition was a serious problem in the United States and hunger marches were taking place in cities across the country. For example, the federal government bought 6 million hogs in 1933 alone and destroyed them. Huge amounts of farm produce were plowed under, in order to keep it off the market and maintain prices at the officially fixed level, while vast amounts of milk were poured down the sewers for the same reason. Meanwhile, many American children were suffering from diseases caused by malnutrition.

---

* This is not an uncommon pattern in the evolution of other kinds of government programs.

Still, there was a food surplus. A surplus, like a shortage, is a *price* phenomenon. A surplus does not mean that there is some excess relative to the people. There was not "too much" food relative to the population during the Great Depression. The people simply did not have enough money to buy everything that was produced at the artificially high prices set by the government. A very similar situation existed in poverty-stricken India at the beginning of the twenty-first century, where there was a surplus of wheat and rice under government price supports. The *Far Eastern Economic Review* reported:

> India's public stock of food grains is at an all-time high, and next spring, it will grow still further to a whopping 80 million tonnes, or four times the amount necessary in case of a national emergency. Yet while that wheat and rice sits idle— in some cases for years, to the point of rotting— millions of Indians don't have enough to eat.

A report from India in the *New York Times* told a very similar story under the headline, "Poor in India Starve as Surplus Wheat Rots":

> Surplus from this year's wheat harvest, bought by the government from farmers, sits moldering in muddy fields here in Punjab State. Some of the previous year's wheat surplus sits untouched, too, and the year's before that, and the year's before that.
> To the south, in the neighboring state of Rajasthan, villagers ate boiled leaves or discs of bread made from grass seeds in late summer and autumn because they could not afford to buy wheat. One by one, children and adults— as many as 47 in all— wilted away from hunger-related causes, often clutching pained stomachs.

A surplus or "glut" of food in India, where malnutrition is still a serious problem, might seem like a contradiction in terms. But food surpluses under "floor" prices are just as real as the housing shortages under "ceiling" prices. In the United States, the vast amount of storage space required to keep surplus crops off the market once led to such desperate expedients as storing these farm products in unused warships, when all the storage facilities on land had been filled to capacity. Otherwise, American wheat would have had to be left outside to rot, as in India.

A series of bumper crops in the United States could lead to the federal government's having more wheat in storage than was grown by American farmers all year. In India, it was reported in 2002 that the Indian government was spending more on storage of its surplus produce than on rural development, irrigation and flood control combined. It was a classic example of a *misallocation* of scare resources which have alternative uses, especially in a poor country.

So long as the market price of the agricultural product covered by price controls stays above the level at which the government is legally obligated to buy it, the product is sold in the market at a price determined by supply and demand. But, when there is either a sufficient increase in the amount supplied or a sufficient reduction in the amount demanded, the resulting lower price can fall to a level at which the government buys what the market is unwilling to buy. For example, when powdered milk was selling in the United States for about $2.20 a pound in 2007, it was sold in the market but, when the price fell to 80 cents a pound in 2008, the U.S. Department of Agriculture found itself legally obligated to buy about 112 million pounds of powdered milk at a total cost exceeding $90 million.

None of this is peculiar to the United States or to India. The countries of the European Union spent $39 billion in direct subsidies in 2002 and their consumers spent twice as much as that in the inflated food prices created by these agricultural programs. Meanwhile, the surplus food has been sold below cost on the world market, driving down the prices that Third World farmers could get for their produce. In all these countries, not only the government but also the consumers are paying for agricultural price-support programs— the government directly in payments to farmers and storage companies, and the consumers in inflated food prices. As of 2001, American consumers were paying $1.9 billion a year in artificially higher prices, just for products containing sugar, while the government was paying $1.4 million per *month* just to store the surplus sugar. Meanwhile, the *New York Times* reported that sugar producers were "big donors to both Republicans and Democrats" and that the costly sugar price support program had "bipartisan support."

Sugar producers are even more heavily subsidized in the European Union countries than in the United States, and the price of sugar in these countries is among the highest in the world. In 2009, the *New York Times* reported that sugar subsidies in the European Union were "so lavish it even prompted cold-weather Finland to start producing more sugar," even though sugar can be produced from cane grown in the tropics for much lower costs than from sugar beets grown in Europe.

In 2002, the U.S. Congress passed a farm subsidy bill that was estimated to cost the average American family more than $4,000 over the following decade in taxes and inflated food prices. Nor was this a new development. During the mid-1980s, when the price of sugar on the world market was four cents a pound, the wholesale price within the United States was 20 cents a pound. The government was subsidizing the production of something that Americans could have gotten cheaper by not producing it at all, and buying it from countries in the tropics. This has been true of sugar for decades. Moreover, sugar is not unique in this respect, nor is the United States. In the nations of the European Union, the prices of lamb, butter, and sugar are all more than twice as high as their world market prices. As a writer for the *Wall Street Journal* put it, every cow in the European Union gets more subsidies per day than most sub-Saharan Africans have to live on.

Although the original rationale for the American price-support programs was to save family farms, in practice more of the money went to big agricultural corporations, some of which received millions of dollars each, while the average farm received only a few hundred dollars. Most of the money from the 2002 bipartisan farm bill will likewise go to the wealthiest 10 percent of farmers— including David Rockefeller, Ted Turner, and a dozen companies on the *Fortune* 500 list. In Mexico as well, 85 percent of agricultural subsidies go to the largest 15 percent of farmers.

What is crucial from the standpoint of understanding the role of prices in the economy is that persistent surpluses are as much a result of keeping prices artificially high as persistent shortages are of keeping prices artificially low. Nor were the losses simply the sums of money extracted from the taxpayers or the consumers for the benefit of agricultural corporations and farmers. These are internal transfers within a nation, which do not directly reduce the total wealth of the country. The real losses to the country as a whole come from the misallocation of scarce resources which have alternative uses.

Scarce resources such as land, labor, fertilizer, and machinery are needlessly used to produce more food than the consumers are willing to consume at the artificially high prices decreed by the government. All the vast resources used to produce sugar in the United States are wasted when sugar can be imported from countries in the tropics, where it is produced much more cheaply in a natural environment more conducive to its growth. Poor people, who spend an especially high percentage of their income on food, are forced to pay far more than necessary to get the amount of food they receive, leaving them with less money for other things. Those on food stamps are able to buy less food with those stamps when food prices are artificially inflated.

From a purely economic standpoint, it is working at cross purposes to subsidize farmers by forcing food prices up and then subsidize some consumers by bringing down their particular costs of food with subsidies— as is done in both India and the United States. However, from a political standpoint, it makes perfect sense to gain the support of two different sets of voters, especially since most of them do not understand the full economic implications of the policies.

Even when agricultural subsidies and price controls originated during hard times as a humanitarian measure, they have persisted long past those times because they developed an organized constituency which threatened to create political trouble if these subsidies and controls were removed or even reduced. Farmers have blocked the streets of Paris with their farm machinery when the French government showed signs of scaling back its agricultural programs or allowing more foreign farm produce to be imported. In Canada, farmers protesting low wheat prices blocked highways and formed a motorcade of tractors to the capital city of Ottawa.

While only about one-tenth of farm income in the United States comes from government subsidies, about half of farm income in South Korea comes from such subsidies, as does 60 percent in Norway.

THE POLITICS OF PRICE CONTROLS

Simple as basic economic principles may be, their ramifications can be quite complex, as we have seen with the various effects of rent control laws and agricultural price support laws. However, even this basic level of economics is seldom understood by the public, which often demands political "solutions" that turn out to make matters worse. Nor is this a new phenomenon of modern times in democratic countries.

When a Spanish blockade in the sixteenth century tried to starve Spain's rebellious subjects in Antwerp into surrender, the resulting high prices of food within Antwerp caused others to smuggle food into the city, even through the blockade, enabling the inhabitants to continue to hold out. However, the authorities within Antwerp decided to solve the problem of high food prices by laws fixing the maximum price to be allowed to be charged for given food items and providing severe penalties for anyone violating those laws.

There followed the classic consequences of price control— a larger consumption of the artificially lower-priced goods and a reduction in the supply of such goods, since suppliers were less willing to run the risk of sending food through the Spanish blockade without the additional incentive of higher prices. Therefore, the net effect of price control was that "the city lived in high spirits until all at once provisions gave out" and Antwerp had no choice but to surrender to the Spaniards.

Halfway around the world, in eighteenth-century India, a local famine in Bengal brought a government crackdown on food dealers and speculators, imposing price controls on rice. Here the resulting shortages led to widespread deaths by starvation. However, when another famine struck India in the nineteenth century, now under the colonial rule of British officials and during the heyday of free market economics, opposite policies were followed, with opposite results:

> In the earlier famine one could hardly engage in the grain trade without becoming amenable to the law. In 1866 respectable men in vast numbers went into the trade; for the Government, by publishing weekly returns of the rates in every district, rendered the traffic both easy and safe. Everyone knew where to buy grain cheapest and where to sell it dearest and food was accordingly bought from the districts which could best spare it and carried to those which most urgently needed it.

As elementary as all this may seem, in terms of economic principles, it was made possible politically only because the British colonial government was not accountable to local public opinion. In an era of democratic politics, the same actions would require either a public familiar with basic economics or political leaders willing to risk their careers to do what needed to be done. It is hard to know which is less likely.

Politically, price controls are always a tempting "quick fix" for inflation, and certainly easier than getting the government to cut back on its own spending that is often behind the inflation. It may be considered especially important to keep the prices of food from rising. Accordingly, Argentina put price controls on wheat in the early twenty-first century. Predictably, Argentine farmers reduced the amount of land that they planted with wheat, from 15 million acres in 2000 to 9 million acres in 2012. Since there is a large international market for wheat, where the price is higher than the price permitted domestically in Argentina, the government also found it necessary to block wheat exports that would have made the domestic wheat shortage worse.

The greater the difference between free market prices and the prices decreed by price control laws, the more severe the consequences of price control. In 2007, Zimbabwe's government responded to runaway inflation by ordering sellers to cut prices in half or more. Just a month later, the *New York Times* reported, "Zimbabwe's economy is at a halt." It detailed some specifics:

> Bread, sugar and cornmeal, staples of every Zimbabwean's diet, have vanished, seized by mobs who denuded stores like locusts in wheat fields. Meat is virtually nonexistent, even for members of the middle class who have money to buy it on the black market. Gasoline is nearly unobtainable. Hospital patients are dying for lack of basic medical supplies. Power blackouts and water cutoffs are endemic.

As with price controls in other times and places, price controls were viewed favorably by the public when they were first imposed in Zimbabwe. "Ordinary citizens initially greeted the price cuts with a euphoric— and short-lived— shopping spree," according to the *New York Times*. Both the initial reactions and the later consequences were much as they had been in Antwerp, centuries earlier.

When a local area is devastated by a hurricane or some other natural disaster, many people consider it unconscionable if businesses in that area suddenly raise the prices of such things as bottled water, flashlights or gasoline— or if local hotels double or triple the prices of their rooms when there are many local people suddenly made homeless who are seeking temporary shelter. Often price controls are regarded as a necessary quick fix in this situation.

The political response has often been to pass laws against "price gouging" to stop such unpopular practices. Yet the role of prices in allocating scarce resources is even more urgently needed when local resources have suddenly become more scarce than usual, relative to the increased demand from people suddenly deprived of the resources normally available to them, as a result of the destruction created by storms or wildfires or some other natural disaster.

Where homes have been destroyed, for example, the demand for local hotel rooms may rise suddenly, while the supply of hotel rooms at best remains the same, assuming that none of these hotels has been damaged or destroyed. When the local population wants more hotel rooms than there are available locally, these rooms will have to be rationed, one way or another, whether by prices or in some other way.

If the prices of hotel rooms remain what they have been in normal times, those who happen to arrive at the hotels first will take all the rooms, and those who arrive later will either have to sleep outdoors, or in damaged homes that may offer little protection from the weather, or else leave the local area and thus leave their homes vulnerable to looters. But, if hotel prices rise sharply, people will have incentives to ration themselves. A couple with children, who might rent one hotel room for themselves and another for their children, when the prices are kept down to their normal level, will have incentives to rent just one room for the whole family when the rents are abnormally high— that is, when there is "price gouging."

Similar principles apply when there are local shortages of other things suddenly in higher demand in the local area. If electric power has been knocked out locally, the demand for flashlights may greatly exceed the supply. If the prices of flashlights remain the same as before, those who arrive first at stores selling flashlights may quickly exhaust the local supply, so that those who arrive later are unable to find any more flashlights available. However, if the prices of flashlights skyrocket, a family that might otherwise buy multiple flashlights for its members is more likely to make do with just one of the unusually expensive flashlights— which means that there will be more flashlights left for others.

If there is an increased demand for gasoline, whether for electric generators or to drive automobiles to other areas to shop for things in short supply locally, or to move out of the stricken local area entirely, this can create a shortage of gasoline until new supplies can arrive at filling stations or until electric power is fully restored, so that the pumps at more filling stations can operate. If the price of gasoline remains what it has been in normal times, those who get to the filling stations first may fill up their gas tanks and exhaust the local supply, leaving those who arrive later with no gasoline to buy. But, if the price of gasoline skyrockets, motorists who arrive earlier may buy just enough of the unusually expensive gasoline to get them out of the area of local destruction, so that they can then fill up their gas tanks much less expensively in places less affected by the natural disaster. That leaves more gasoline available locally for others.

When local prices spike, that affects supply as well, both before and after the natural disaster. The arrival of a hurricane is usually foreseen by meteorologists, and their predictions of approaching hurricanes are usually widely reported. Supplies of all sorts of things that are usually needed after a hurricane strikes— flashlights, bottled water, gasoline and lumber, for example— are more likely to be rushed to the area where the hurricane is likely to strike, before the hurricane actually gets there, if suppliers anticipate higher prices. This means that shortages can be mitigated in advance. But if only the usual prices in normal times can be expected, there is less incentive to incur the extra costs of rushing things to an area where disaster is expected to strike.

Similar incentives exist after a hurricane or other disaster has struck. To replenish supplies in a devastated area can cost more, due to damaged roads and highways, debris and congested traffic from people fleeing the area. Skyrocketing local prices can overcome the reluctance to take on these local obstacles that entail additional costs. Moreover, each supplier has incentives to try to be the first to arrive on the scene, since that is when prices will be highest, before additional suppliers arrive and their competition drives prices back down. Time is also of great importance to people in a disaster area, who need a continuous supply of food and other necessities.

Prices are not the only way to ration scarce resources, either in normal times or in times of sudden increases in scarcity. But the question is whether alternative systems of rationing are usually better or worse. History shows repeatedly the effect of price controls on food in creating hunger or even starvation. It might be possible for sellers to ration how much they will sell to one buyer. But this puts the seller in the unenviable role of offending some of his customers by refusing to let them buy as much as they want— and he may lose some of those customers after things return to normal. Few sellers may be willing to risk that.

The net result of having neither price rationing nor non-price rationing may well be the situation described in the wake of the super storm "Sandy" in 2012, as reported in the *Wall Street Journal*:

> At one New Jersey supermarket, shoppers barely paused for a public loudspeaker announcement urging them to buy only the provisions needed for a couple of days of suburban paralysis. None seemed to be deterred as they loaded their carts to the gunwales with enough canned tuna to last six weeks. A can of Bumblebee will keep for years: Shoppers take no risk in buying out a store's entire supply at the normal price.

Appeals to people to limit their purchases during an emergency, like other forms of non-price rationing, are seldom as effective as raising prices.

Chapter 4

AN OVERVIEW OF PRICES

*We need education in the obvious more
than investigation of the obscure.*

Justice Oliver Wendell Holmes

Many of the basic principles of economics may seem obvious but the implications to be drawn from them are not— and it is the implications that matter. Someone once pointed out that Newton was not the first man who saw an apple fall. His fame was based on his being the first to understand its implications.

Economists have understood for centuries that when prices are higher, people tend to buy less than when prices are lower. But, even today, many people do not yet understand the many implications of that simple fact. For example, one consequence of not thinking through the implications of this simple fact is that government-provided medical care has repeatedly cost far more than initially estimated, in various countries around the world. These estimates have usually been based on current usage of doctors, hospitals, and pharmaceutical drugs. But the introduction of free or subsidized medical care leads to vastly greater usage, simply because its price is lower, and this entails vastly greater costs than initially estimated.

Understanding any subject requires that it first be defined, so that you are clear in your own mind as to what you are talking about— and what you are not talking about. Just as a poetic discussion of the weather is not meteorology, so an issuance of moral pronouncements or political creeds about the economy is not economics. Economics is an analysis of *cause-and-effect* relationships in an economy. Its purpose is to discern the consequences of various ways of allocating scarce resources which have alternative uses. It has nothing to say about social philosophy or moral values, any more than it has anything to say about humor or anger.

These other things are not necessarily any less important. They are simply not what economics is about. No one expects mathematics to explain love, and no one should expect economics to be something other than what it is or to do something other than what it can. But both mathematics and economics can be very important where they apply. Careful and complex mathematical calculations can be the difference between having an astronaut who is returning to earth from orbit end up crashing in the Himalayas or landing safely in Florida. We have also seen similar social disasters from misunderstanding the basic principles of economics.

CAUSE AND EFFECT

Analyzing economic actions in cause-and-effect terms means examining the logic of the incentives being created, rather than simply thinking about the desirability of the goals being sought. It also means examining the empirical evidence of what actually happens under such incentives.

The kind of causation at work in an economy is often *systemic interactions*, rather than the kind of simple one-way causation involved when one billiard ball hits another billiard ball and knocks it into a pocket. Systemic causation involves more complex reciprocal interactions, such as adding lye to hydrochloric acid and ending up with salty water,* because both chemicals are transformed by their effects on one another, going from being two deadly substances to becoming one harmless one.

In an economy as well, the plans of buyers and sellers are transformed as they discover each other's reactions to supply and demand conditions, and the resulting price changes that force them to reassess their plans. Just as those who start out planning to buy a villa at the beach may end up settling for a

---

* Do *not* try this at home. Professional chemists can handle these dangerous chemicals, with appropriate safeguards, in a laboratory but either can be fatal in other hands.

bungalow farther inland, after they discover the high prices of villas at the beach, suppliers likewise sometimes end up selling their goods for less than they paid to buy them or produce them, when the demand is inadequate to get any higher price from the consuming public, and the alternative is to get nothing at all for an item that is unsalable at the price originally planned.

Systemic Causation

Because systemic causation involves reciprocal interactions, rather than one-way causation, that reduces the role of individual intentions. As Friedrich Engels put it, "what each individual wills is obstructed by everyone else, and what emerges is something that no one willed." Economics is concerned with what *emerges*, not what anyone intended. If the stock market closes at 14,367 on a given day, that is the end result of a process of complex interactions among innumerable buyers and sellers of stocks, none of whom may have intended for the market to close at 14,367, even though it was their own actions in pursuit of other intentions which caused it to do so.

While causation can sometimes be explained by intentional actions and sometimes by systemic interactions, too often the results of systemic interactions are falsely explained by individual intentions. Just as primitive peoples tended to attribute such things as the swaying of trees in the wind to some intentional action by an invisible spirit, rather than to such systemic causes as variations in atmospheric pressure, so there is a tendency toward intentional explanations of systemic events in the economy, when people are unaware of basic economic principles. For example, while rising prices are likely to reflect changes in supply and demand, people ignorant of economics may attribute price rises to "greed."

People shocked by the high prices charged in stores in low-income neighborhoods have often been quick to blame greed or exploitation on the part of the people who run such businesses. Similar conclusions about intentions have often been reached when people noticed the much higher interest rates charged by pawnbrokers and small finance companies that operate in low-income neighborhoods, as compared to the interest rates charged by banks in middle-class communities. Companies that charge for cashing checks also usually operate in low-income neighborhoods, while people in middle-class neighborhoods usually get their checks cashed free of charge at their local banks. Yet profit rates are generally no higher in inner city businesses than elsewhere, and the fact that many businesses are leaving such neighborhoods— and others, such as supermarket chains, are staying away— reinforces that conclusion.

The painful fact that poor people end up paying more than affluent people for many goods and services has a very plain— and systemic— explanation: It often costs more to deliver goods and services in low-income neighborhoods. Higher insurance costs and higher costs for various security precautions, due to higher rates of crime and vandalism, are just some of the systemic reasons that get ignored by those seeking an explanation in terms of personal intentions. In addition, the cost of doing business tends to be higher per dollar of business in low-income neighborhoods. Lending $100 each to fifty low-income borrowers at pawn shops or local finance companies takes more time and costs more money to process the transactions than lending $5,000 at a bank to one middle-class customer, even though the same total sum of money is involved in both cases.*

About 10 percent of American families do not have a checking account, and undoubtedly this percentage is higher among low-income families, so that many of them resort to local check-cashing agencies to cash their paychecks, Social Security checks or other checks. An armored car delivering money in small denominations to a neighborhood finance company or a small check-cashing agency in a ghetto costs just as much as an armored car delivering a hundred times as much value of money, in larger denominations of bills, to a bank in a suburban shopping mall. With the cost of doing business being higher per dollar of business in the low-income

---

* In many cases, the middle-class borrower who already has a checking account at the bank from which he wishes to borrow also has an automatic line of credit available with that checking account. When the need for a $5,000 loan arises, there may be no need even to file an application. The borrower simply writes $5,000 more in checks than there is money in the account, and the automatic line of credit covers it, with minimum time and trouble to both the borrower and the bank, since the potential borrower's credit rating was already established when the account was first opened and the size of the line of credit was established on the basis of that credit rating. Cashing a check in such situations involves little risk or cost to the bank, as distinguished from the risks and costs incurred by a check-cashing company whose customers typically have no bank accounts.

community, it is hardly surprising that these higher costs get passed on in higher prices and higher interest rates.

Higher prices for people who can least afford them are a tragic end-result, but the causes are systemic. This is not merely a philosophic or semantic distinction. There are major practical consequences to the way causation is understood. Treating the causes of higher prices and higher interest rates in low-income neighborhoods as being personal greed or exploitation, and trying to remedy it by imposing price controls and interest rate ceilings only ensures that even less will be supplied to people living in low-income neighborhoods thereafter. Just as rent control reduces the supply of housing, so price controls and interest rate controls can reduce the number of stores, pawn shops, local finance companies, and check-cashing agencies willing to operate in neighborhoods with higher costs, when those costs cannot be recovered by legally permissible prices and interest rates.

The alternative, for many residents of low-income neighborhoods, may be to go outside the legal money-lending organizations and borrow from loan sharks, who charge even higher rates of interest and have their own methods of collecting, such as physical violence.

When stores and financial institutions close down in low-income neighborhoods, more people in such neighborhoods are then forced to travel to other neighborhoods to shop for groceries or other goods, paying money for bus fare or taxi fare, in addition to the costs of their purchases. Such business closings have already occurred for a variety of reasons, including riots and higher rates of shoplifting and vandalism, with the net result that many people in low-income neighborhoods already have to go elsewhere for shopping or banking.

"First, do no harm" is a principle that has endured for centuries. Understanding the distinction between systemic causation and intentional causation is one way to do less harm with economic policies. It is especially important to do no harm to people who are already in painful economic circumstances. It is also worth noting that most people are not criminals, even in high-crime neighborhoods. The fraction of dishonest people in such neighborhoods are the real source of many of the higher costs behind the higher prices charged by businesses operating in those neighborhoods. But it is both intellectually and emotionally easier to blame high prices on those who collect them, rather than on those who cause them. It is also more politically popular to blame outsiders, especially if those outsiders are of a different ethnic background.

Systemic causes, such as those often found in economics, provide no such emotional release for the public, or moral melodrama for the media and politicians, as such intentional causes as "greed," "exploitation," "gouging," "discrimination," and the like. Intentional explanations of cause and effect may also be more natural, in the sense that less sophisticated individuals and less sophisticated societies tend to turn first to such explanations. In some cases, it has taken centuries for intentional explanations embodied in superstitions about nature to give way to systemic explanations based on science. It is not yet clear whether it will take that long for the basic principles of economics to replace many people's natural tendency to try to explain systemic results by intentional causes.

Complexity and Causation

Although the basic principles of economics are not really complicated, the very ease with which they can be learned also makes them easy to dismiss as "simplistic" by those who do not want to accept analyses which contradict some of their cherished beliefs. Evasions of the obvious are often far more complicated than the plain facts. Nor is it automatically true that complex effects must have complex causes. The ramifications of something very simple can become enormously complex. For example, the simple fact that the earth is tilted on its axis causes innumerable very complex reactions in plants, animals, and people, as well as in such non-living things as ocean currents, weather changes and changes in the length of night and day.

If the earth stood straight up on its axis,* night and day would be the same length all year round and in all parts of the world. Climate would still differ between the equator and the poles but, at any given place, the climate would be the same in winter as in summer. The fact that the earth is tilted

---

* Purists can say that there is no up or down in space, but that simply requires rephrasing the same facts by saying that the axis on which the earth rotates is not perpendicular to the plane of the planet's orbit around the sun.

on its axis means that sunlight is striking the same country at different angles at different points during the planet's annual orbit around the sun, leading to changing warmth and changing lengths of night and day.

In turn, such changes trigger complex biological reactions in plant growth, animal hibernations and migrations, as well as psychological changes in human beings and many seasonal changes in their economies. Changing weather patterns affect ocean currents and the frequency of hurricanes, among many other natural phenomena. Yet all of these complications are due to the one simple fact that the earth is tilted on its axis, instead of being straight up.

In short, complex effects may be a result of either simple causes or complex causes. The specific facts can tell us which. *A priori* pronouncements about what is "simplistic" cannot. An explanation is *too* simple if its conclusions fail to match the facts or its reasoning violates logic. But calling an explanation "simplistic" is too often a substitute for examining either its evidence or its logic.

Few things are more simple than the fact that people tend to buy more at lower prices and buy less at higher prices. But, when putting that together with the fact that producers tend to supply more at higher prices and less at lower prices, that is enough to predict many sorts of complex reactions to price controls, whether in the housing market or in the market for food, electricity, or medical care. Moreover, these reactions have been found on all inhabited continents and over thousands of years of recorded history. Simple causes and complex effects have been common among wide varieties of peoples and cultures.

Individual Rationality versus Systemic Rationality

The tendency to personalize causation leads not only to charges that "greed" causes high prices in market economies, but also to charges that "stupidity" among bureaucrats is responsible for many things that go wrong in government economic activities. In reality, many of the things that go wrong in these activities are due to perfectly rational actions, *given the incentives* faced by government officials who run such activities, and given the inherent constraints on the amount of knowledge available to any given decision-maker or set of decision-makers.

Where a policy or institution has been established by top political leaders, officials subject to their authority may well hesitate to contradict their beliefs, much less point out the counterproductive consequences that later follow from these policies and institutions. Messengers carrying bad news could be risking their careers or— under Stalin or Mao— their lives.

Officials carrying out particular policies may be quite rational, however negative the impact of these policies may prove to be for society at large. During the Stalin era in the Soviet Union, for example, there was at one time a severe shortage of mining equipment, but the manager of a factory producing such machines kept them in storage after they were built, rather than sending them out to the mines, where they were sorely needed. The reason was that the official orders called for these machines to be painted with red, oil-resistant paint and the manufacturer had on hand only green, oil-resistant paint and red varnish that was not oil-resistant. Nor could he readily get the prescribed paint, since there was no free market.

Disobeying official orders in any respect was a serious offense under Stalin and "I don't want to get eight years," the manager said.

When he explained the situation to a higher official and asked for permission to use the green, oil-resistant paint, the official's response was: "Well, I don't want to get eight years either." However, the higher official cabled to his ministry for their permission to give his permission. After a long delay, the ministry eventually granted his request and the mining machinery was finally shipped to the mines. None of these people was behaving stupidly. They were responding quite rationally to the incentives and constraints of the system in which they worked. Under any economic or political system, people can make their choices only among the alternatives actually available— and different economic systems present different alternatives.

Even in a democratic government, where the personal dangers would be far less, a highly intelligent person with a record of outstanding success in the private sector is often unable to repeat that success when appointed to a high position in government. Again, the point is that the incentives and constraints are different in different institutions. As Nobel Prizewinning economist George J. Stigler put it:

> A large number of successful businessmen have gone on to high administrative posts in the national government, and many— I think most— have been less than distinguished successes in that new environment. They are surrounded and overpowered by informed and entrenched subordinates, they must deal with legislators who can be relentless in their demands, and almost everything in their agency that should be changed is untouchable.

INCENTIVES VERSUS GOALS

Incentives matter because most people will usually do more for their own benefit than for the benefit of others. Incentives link the two concerns together. A waitress brings food to your table, not because of your hunger, but because her salary and tips depend on it. In the absence of such incentives, service in restaurants in the Soviet Union was notoriously bad. Unsold goods piling up in warehouses were not the only consequences of a lack of the incentives that come with a free market price system. Prices not only help determine which particular things are produced, they are also one of the ways of rationing the inherent scarcity of all goods and services, as well as rationing the scarce resources that go into producing those goods and services. However, prices do not create that scarcity, which will require some form of rationing under any other economic system.

Simple as all this may seem, it goes counter to many policies and programs designed to make various goods and services "affordable" or to keep them from becoming "prohibitively expensive." But being prohibitive is precisely how prices limit how much each person uses. If everything were made affordable by government decree, there would still not be any more to go around than when things were prohibitively expensive. There would simply have to be some alternative method of rationing the inherent scarcity. Whether that method was through the government's issuing ration coupons, the emergence of black markets, or just fighting over things when they go on sale, the rationing would still have to be done, since artificially making things affordable does not create any more total output. On the contrary, price "ceilings" tend to cause less output to be produced.

Many apparently humanitarian policies have backfired throughout history because of a failure to understand the role of prices. Attempts to keep food prices down by imposing price controls have led to hunger and even starvation, whether in seventeenth-century Italy, eighteenth-century India, France after the French Revolution, Russia after the Bolshevik revolution, or in a number of African countries after they obtained independence during the 1960s. Some of these African countries, like some of the countries in Eastern Europe, once had such an abundance of food that they were food exporters before the era of price control and government planning turned them into countries unable to feed themselves.

Failure to supply goods, as a result of government restrictions, must be sharply distinguished from an inability to produce them. Food can be in short supply in a country with extraordinarily fertile soil, as in post-Communist Russia that had not yet achieved a free-market economy:

> Undulating gently through pastoral hills 150 miles south of Moscow, the Plava River Valley is a farmer's dream come true. This is the gateway to what Russians call "Chernozym"— "Black Earth country"— which boasts some of the most fertile soil in Europe, within three hours' drive of a giant, hungry metropolis. . . Black Earth country has the natural wealth to feed an entire nation. But it can barely feed itself.

It is hard even to imagine, in a free market economy, a hungry city, dependent on imports of foreign food, when there is extraordinarily fertile farmland not far away. Yet the people on that very fertile farmland were as poor as the city dwellers were hungry. The workers harvesting that land earned the equivalent of about $10 a week, with even this small amount being paid in kind— sacks of potatoes or cucumbers— because of a lack of money. As the mayor of a town in this region said:

> We ought to be rich. We have wonderful soil. We have the scientific know-how. We have qualified people. But what does it add up to?

If nothing else, it adds up to a reason for understanding economics as a means of achieving an efficient allocation of scarce resources which have alternative uses. All that was lacking in Russia was a market to connect the hungry city with the products of the fertile land and a government that would allow such a market to function freely. But, in some places, local Russian officials forbad the movement of food across local boundary lines, in order to assure low food prices within their own jurisdictions, and therefore local political support for themselves. Again, it is necessary to emphasize that this was not a stupid policy, from the standpoint of officials trying to gain local popularity with consumers by maintaining low food prices. This protected their political careers, however disastrous such policies were for the country as a whole.

While systemic causation in a free market is in one sense impersonal, in the sense that its outcomes are not specifically predetermined by any given person, "the market" is ultimately a way by which many people's individual personal desires are reconciled with those of other people. Too often a false contrast is made between the impersonal marketplace and the supposedly compassionate policies of various government programs. But both systems face the same scarcity of resources and both systems make choices within the constraints of that scarcity. The difference is that one system involves each individual making choices for himself or herself, while the other system involves a small number of people making choices for millions of others.

The mechanisms of the market are impersonal but the choices made by individuals are as personal as choices made anywhere else. It may be fashionable for journalists to refer to "the whim of the marketplace," as if that were something different from the desires of people, just as it was once fashionable to advocate "production for use, rather than profit"— as if profits could be made by producing things that people cannot use or do not want to use. The real contrast is between choices made by individuals for themselves and choices made for them by others who presume to define what these individuals "really" need.

SCARCITY AND COMPETITION

Scarcity means that everyone's desires cannot be satisfied completely, regardless of which particular economic system or government policy we choose— and regardless of whether an individual or a society is poor or prosperous, wise or foolish, noble or ignoble. Competition among people for scarce resources is inherent. It is not a question whether we like or dislike competition. Scarcity means that we do not have the option to *choose* whether or not to have an economy in which people compete. That is the only kind of economy that is possible— and our only choice is among the particular methods that can be used for that competition.

Economic Institutions

Most people may be unaware that they are competing when making purchases, and simply see themselves as deciding how much of various things to buy at whatever prices they find. But scarcity ensures that they are competing with others, even if they are conscious only of weighing their own purchasing decisions against the amount of money they have available.

One of the incidental benefits of competing and sharing through prices is that different people are not as likely to think of themselves as rivals, nor to develop the kinds of hostility that rivalry can breed. For example, much the same labor and construction material needed to build a Protestant church could be used to build a Catholic church. But, if a Protestant congregation is raising money to build a church for themselves, they are likely to be preoccupied with how much money they can raise and how much is needed for the kind of church they want. Construction prices may cause them to scale back some of their more elaborate plans, in order to fit within the limits of what they can afford. But they are unlikely to blame Catholics, even though the competition of Catholics for the same construction materials makes their prices higher than otherwise.

If, instead, the government were in the business of building churches and giving them to different religious groups, Protestants and Catholics would be explicit rivals for this largess and neither would have any financial incentive to cut back on their building plans to accommodate the other.

Instead, each would have an incentive to make the case, as strongly as possible, for the full extent of their desires, to mobilize their followers politically to insist on getting what they want, and to resent any suggestion that they scale back their plans. The inherent scarcity of materials and labor would still limit what could be built, but that limit would now be imposed politically and would be seen by each as due to the rivalry of the other.

The Constitution of the United States of course prevents the American government from building churches for religious groups, no doubt in order to prevent just such political rivalries and the bitterness, and sometimes bloodshed, to which such rivalries have led in other countries and in other times.

The same economic principle, however, applies to groups that are not based on religion but on ethnicity, geographic regions, or age brackets. All are inherently competing for the same resources, simply because these resources are scarce. However, competing indirectly by having to keep your demands within the limits of your own pocketbook is very different from seeing your desires for government benefits thwarted directly by the rival claims of some other group. The self-rationing created by prices not only tends to mean less social and political friction but also more economic efficiency, since each individual knows his or her own preferences better than any third party can, and can therefore make incremental trade-offs that are more personally satisfying within the limits of the available resources.

Rationing through pricing also limits the amount of each individual's claims on the output of others to what that individual's own productivity has created for others, and thereby earned as income. What price controls, subsidies, or other substitutes for price allocation do is reduce the incentives for self-rationing. That is why people with minor ailments go to doctors when medical care is either free or heavily subsidized by the government, and why farmers receiving government-subsidized water from irrigation projects grow crops requiring huge amounts of water, which they would never grow if they had to pay the full costs of that water themselves.

Society as a whole always has to pay the full costs, regardless of what prices are or are not charged to individuals. When price controls make goods artificially cheaper, that allows greater self-indulgence by some, which means that less is left for others. Thus many apartments occupied by just one person under rent control means that others have trouble finding a place to stay, even when they are perfectly willing and able to pay the current rent. Moreover, since rationing must take place with or without prices, this means that some form of non-price rationing becomes a substitute.

Simply waiting until what you want becomes available has been a common form of non-price rationing. This can mean waiting in long lines at stores, as was common in the Soviet economy, or being put on a waiting list for surgery, as patients often are in countries where government-provided medical care is either free or heavily subsidized.

Luck and corruption are other substitutes for price rationing. Whoever happens to be in a store when a new shipment of some product in short supply arrives can get the first opportunity to buy it, while people who happen to learn about it much later can find the coveted product all gone by the time they get there. In other cases, personal or political favoritism or bribery takes the place of luck in gaining preferential access, or formal rationing systems may replace favoritism with some one-size-fits-all policy administered by government agencies. However it is done, the rationing that is done by prices in market economies cannot be gotten rid of by getting rid of prices or by the government's lowering the level of prices.

Incremental Substitution

As important as it is to understand the role of substitutions, it is also important to keep in mind that the efficient allocation of resources requires that these substitutions be *incremental*, not total. For example, one may believe that health is more important than entertainment but, however reasonable that may sound as a general principle, no one really believes that having a twenty-year's supply of Band-Aids in the closet is more important than having to give up all music in order to pay for it. A price-coordinated economy facilitates incremental substitution, but political decision-making tends toward categorical *priorities*— that is, declaring one thing absolutely more important than another and creating laws and policies accordingly.

When some political figure says that we need to "set national priorities" about one thing or another, what that amounts to is making *A* categorically more important than *B*. This is the opposite of incremental substitution, in which the value of each depends on how much of each we already have at the moment, and therefore on the changing amount of *A* that we are willing to give up in order to get more *B*.

This variation in the relative values of things can be so great as to convert something that is beneficial into something that is detrimental, or vice versa. For example, human beings cannot live without salt, fat and cholesterol, but most Americans get so much of all three that their lifespan is reduced. Conversely, despite the many problems caused by alcohol, from fatal automobile accidents to deaths from cirrhosis of the liver, studies show that very modest amounts of alcohol have health benefits that can be life-saving.* Alcohol is not categorically good or bad.

Whenever there are two things which each have some value, one cannot be categorically more valuable than another. A diamond may be worth much more than a penny, but enough pennies will be worth more than any diamond. That is why incremental trade-offs tend to produce better results than categorical priorities.

There are chronic complaints about government red tape in countries around the world, but the creation of red tape is understandable in view of the incentives facing those who create government forms, rules, and requirements for innumerable activities that require official approval. Nothing is easier than thinking of additional requirements that might be useful in some way or other, at some time or other, and nothing is harder than remembering to ask the crucial incremental question: *At what cost?*

People who are spending their own money are confronted with those costs at every turn, but people who are spending the taxpayers' money— or who are simply imposing uncounted costs on businesses, homeowners, and others— have no real incentives to even find out how much the additional costs are,

---

* Men who drank either nothing alcoholic or just one drink per week had a reduction in cardiovascular disease when they increased their alcohol intake by from one to six drinks per week. However, among men who already averaged seven or more alcoholic drinks per week, an increase in their drinking led to more cardiovascular disease, according to the *Archives of Internal Medicine* (September 25, 2000 issue). The medical publication *The Lancet* reported that "light-to-moderate alcohol consumption is associated with a reduced risk of dementia in individuals aged 55 years or older" in its January 26, 2002 issue.

much less to hold off on adding requirements when the incremental costs threaten to become larger than the incremental benefits to those on whom these costs are imposed by the government. Red tape grows as a result.

Any attempt to get rid of some of this red tape is likely to be countered by government officials, who can point out what useful purpose these requirements may serve in some circumstances. But they are unlikely even to pose the question whether the incremental benefit exceeds the incremental costs. There are no incentives for them to look at things that way. Nor are the media likely to. A *New York Times* article, for example, argued that there were few, if any, "useless" regulations— as if that was the relevant criterion. But neither individuals nor businesses are willing or able to pay for everything that is not useless, when they are spending their own money.

No doubt there are reasons, or at least rationales, for the many government regulations imposed on businesses in Italy, for example, but the real question is whether their costs exceed their benefits:

> Imagine you're an ambitious Italian entrepreneur, trying to make a go of a new business. You know you will have to pay at least two-thirds of your employees' social security costs. You also know you're going to run into problems once you hire your 16th employee, since that will trigger provisions making it either impossible or very expensive to dismiss a staffer.
> But there's so much more. Once you hire employee 11, you must submit an annual self-assessment to the national authorities outlining every possible health and safety hazard to which your employees might be subject. These include stress that is work-related or caused by age, gender and racial differences. You must also note all precautionary and individual measures to prevent risks, procedures to carry them out, the names of employees in charge of safety, as well as the physician whose presence is required for the assessment.
> . . . By the time your firm hires its 51st worker, 7% of the payroll must be handicapped in some way. . . Once you hire your 101st employee, you must submit a report every two years on the gender dynamics within the company. This must include a tabulation of the men and women employed in each production unit, their functions and level within the company, details of compensation and benefits, and dates and reasons for recruitments, promotions and transfers, as well as the estimated revenue impact.

As of the time that this description of Italian labor laws appeared in the *Wall Street Journal*, the unemployment rate in Italy was 10 percent and the Italian economy was contracting, rather than growing.

Subsidies and Taxes

Ideally, prices allow alternative users to compete for scarce resources in the marketplace. However, this competition is distorted to the extent that special taxes are put on some products or resources but not on others, or when some products or resources are subsidized by the government but others are not.

Prices charged to the consumers of such specially taxed or specially subsidized goods and services do not convey the real costs of producing them and therefore do not lead to the same trade-offs as if they did. Yet there is always a political temptation to subsidize "good" things and tax "bad" things. However, when neither good things nor bad things are good or bad categorically, this prevents our finding out just how good or how bad any of these things is by letting people choose freely, uninfluenced by politically changed prices. People who want special taxes or subsidies for particular things seem not to understand that what they are really asking for is for the prices to *misstate* the relative scarcities of things and the relative values that the users of these things put on them.

One of the factors in California's recurring water crises, for example, is that California farmers' use of water is subsidized heavily. Farmers in California's Imperial Valley pay $15 for the same amount of water that costs $400 in Los Angeles. The net result is that agriculture, which accounts for less than 2 percent of the state's output, consumes 43 percent of its water. California farmers grow crops requiring great amounts of water, such as rice and cotton, in a very dry climate, where such crops would never be grown if farmers had to pay the real costs of the water they use. Inspiring as it may be to some observers that California's arid lands have been enabled to produce vast amounts of fruits and vegetables with the aid of subsidized water, those same fruits and vegetables could be produced more cheaply elsewhere with water supplied free of charge from the clouds.

The way to tell whether the California produce is worth what it costs to grow is to allow all those costs to be paid by California farmers who compete with farmers in other states that have higher rainfall levels. There is no need for government officials to decide arbitrarily— and categorically— whether it is a good thing or a bad thing for particular crops to be grown in California with water artificially supplied below cost from federal irrigation projects. Such questions can be decided incrementally, by those directly confronting the alternatives, through price competition in a free market.

California is, unfortunately, not unique in this respect. In fact, this is not a peculiarly American problem. Halfway around the world, the government of India provides "almost free electricity and water" to farmers, according to *The Economist* magazine, encouraging farmers to plant too much "water-guzzling rice," with the result that water tables in the Punjab "are dropping fast." Making anything artificially cheap usually means that it will be wasted, whatever that thing might be and wherever it might be located.

From the standpoint of the allocation of resources, government should either not tax resources, goods, and services or else tax them all equally, so as to minimize the distortions of choices made by consumers and producers. For similar reasons, particular resources, goods, and services should not be subsidized, even if particular people are subsidized out of humanitarian concern over their being the victims of natural disasters, birth defects, or other misfortunes beyond their control. Giving poor people money would accomplish the same humanitarian purpose without the same distortion in the allocation of resources created by subsidizing or taxing different products differently.

However much economic efficiency would be promoted by letting resource prices be unchanged by taxes or subsidies, from a political standpoint politicians win votes by doing special favors for special interests or putting special taxes on whomever or whatever might be unpopular at the moment. The free market may work best when there is a level playing field, but politicians win more votes by tilting the playing field to favor particular groups. Often this process is rationalized politically in terms of a need to help the less fortunate but, once the power and the practice are established, they provide the means of subsidizing all sorts of groups who are not the least bit unfortunate. For example, the *Wall Street Journal* reported:

A chunk of the federal taxes and fees paid by airline passengers are awarded to small airports used mainly by private pilots and globe-trotting corporate executives.

The Meaning of "Costs"

Sometimes the rationale for removing particular things from the process of weighing costs against benefits is expressed in some such question as: "How can you put a price on art?"— or education, health, music, etc. The fundamental fallacy underlying this question is the belief that prices are simply "put" on things. So long as art, education, health, music, and thousands of other things all require time, effort, and raw material, the costs of these inputs are inherent. These costs do not go away because a law prevents them from being conveyed through prices in the marketplace. Ultimately, to society as a whole, costs are the other things that could have been produced with the same resources. Money flows and price movements are symptoms of that fact— and suppressing those symptoms will not change the underlying fact.

One reason for the popularity of price controls is a confusion between prices and costs. For example, politicians who say that they will "bring down the cost of medical care" almost invariably mean that they will bring down the *prices* paid for medical care. The actual costs of medical care— the years of training for doctors, the resources used in building and equipping hospitals, the hundreds of millions of dollars for years of research to develop a single new medication— are unlikely to decline in the slightest. Nor are these things even likely to be addressed by politicians. What politicians mean by bringing down the cost of medical care is reducing the price of medicines and reducing the fees charged by doctors or hospitals.

Once the distinction between prices and costs is recognized, then it is not very surprising that price controls have the negative consequences that they do, because price ceilings mean a refusal to pay the full costs. Those who supply housing, food, medications or innumerable other goods and services are unlikely to keep on supplying them in the same quantities and qualities when they cannot recover the costs that such quantities and qualities require. This may not become apparent immediately, which is why price controls are often popular, but the consequences are lasting and often become worse over time.

Housing does not disappear immediately when there is rent control but it deteriorates over time without being replaced by sufficient new housing as it wears out. Existing medicines do not necessarily vanish under price controls but new medicines to deal with cancer, AIDS, Alzheimer's and numerous other afflictions are unlikely to continue to be developed at the same pace when the money to pay for the costs and risks of creating new medications is just not there any more. But all this takes time to unfold, and memories may be too short for most people to connect the bad consequences they experience to the popular policies they supported some years back.

Despite how obvious all this might seem, there are never-ending streams of political schemes designed to escape the realities being conveyed by prices— whether through direct price controls or by making this or that "affordable" with subsidies or by having the government itself supply various goods and services free, as a "right." There may be more ill-conceived economic policies based on treating prices as just nuisances to get around than on any other single fallacy. What all these schemes have in common is that they exempt some things from the process of weighing costs and benefits against one another*— a process essential to maximizing the benefits from scarce resources which have alternative uses.

The most valuable economic role of prices is in conveying information about an underlying reality— while at the same time providing incentives to respond to that reality. Prices, in a sense, can summarize the end results of a complex reality in a simple number. For example, a photographer who wants to buy a telephoto lens may confront a choice between two lenses that produce images of equal quality and with the same magnification, but one of which admits twice as much light as the other. This second lens can take

---

* A *New York Times* writer, for example, said "we need high-quality, universal, subsidized day care." (Alissa Quart, "Crushed by the Cost of Child Care," *New York Times*, August 18, 2013, Sunday Review Section, p. 4). In other words, some people should make the decision to have children and simultaneously pursue a career, leaving the costs to be paid by taxpayers who had nothing to do with these decisions, and with no one basing these decisions on weighing the costs against the benefits— except, perhaps, third-party observers with no personal stake in the outcome and with no adverse consequences for being wrong.

pictures in dimmer light, but there are optical problems created by a wider lens opening that admits more light.

While the photographer may be wholly unaware of these optical problems, their solution can require a more complex lens made of more expensive glass. What the photographer is made aware of is that the lens with the wider opening has a higher price. The only decision to be made by the photographer is whether the higher price is worth it for the particular kinds of pictures he takes. A landscape photographer who takes pictures outdoors on sunny days may find the higher-priced lens not worth the extra money, while a photographer who takes pictures indoors in museums that do not permit flashes to be used may have no choice but to pay more for the lens with the wider opening.

Because knowledge is one of the scarcest of all resources, prices play an important role in economizing on the amount of knowledge required for decision-making by any given individual or organization. The photographer needs no knowledge of the science of optics in order to make an efficient trade-off when choosing among lenses, while the lens designer who knows optics need have no knowledge of the rules of museums or the market for photographs taken in museums and in other places with limited amounts of light.

In a different economic system which does not rely on prices, but relies instead on a given official or a planning commission to make decisions about the use of scarce resources, a vast amount of knowledge of the various complex factors behind even a relatively simple decision like producing and using a camera lens would be required, in order to make an efficient use of scarce resources which have alternative uses. After all, glass is used not only in camera lenses but also in microscopes, telescopes, windows, mirrors and innumerable other things. To know how much glass should be allocated to the production of each of these many products would require more expertise in more complex subjects than any individual, or any manageable sized group, can be expected to master.

Although the twentieth century began with many individuals and groups looking forward to a time when price-coordinated economies would be replaced by centrally planned economies, the rise and fall of centrally planned economies took place over several decades. By the end of the twentieth century, even most socialist and communist governments around the world had returned to the use of prices to coordinate their economies. However attractive central planning may have seemed before it was tried, concrete experience led even its advocates to rely more and more on price-coordinated markets. An international study of free markets in 2012 found the world's freest market to be in Hong Kong— in a country with a communist government.

PART II:

INDUSTRY AND COMMERCE

Chapter 5

THE RISE AND FALL
OF BUSINESSES

Failure is part of the natural cycle of business. Companies
are born, companies die, capitalism moves forward.

Fortune *magazine*

Ordinarily, we tend to think of businesses as simply money-making enterprises, but that can be very misleading, in at least two ways. First of all, about one-third of all new businesses fail to survive for two years, and more than half fail to survive for four years, so obviously many businesses are losing money. Nor is it only new businesses that lose money. Businesses that have lasted for generations— sometimes more than a century— have eventually been forced by red ink on the bottom line to close down. More important, from the standpoint of economics, is not what money the business owner hopes to make or whether that hope is fulfilled, but how all this affects the use of scarce resources which have alternative uses— and therefore how it affects the economic well-being of millions of other people in the society at large.

ADJUSTING TO CHANGES

The businesses we hear about, in the media and elsewhere, are usually those which have succeeded, and especially those which have succeeded on a grand scale— Microsoft, Toyota, Sony, Lloyd's of London, Credit Suisse. In an earlier era, Americans would have heard about the A & P grocery chain, once the largest retail chain in any field, anywhere in the world. Its 15,000 stores in 1929 were more than that of any other retailer in America. The fact that A & P has now shrunk to a minute fraction of its former size, and is virtually unknown, suggests that industry and commerce are not static things, but dynamic processes, in which particular products, individual companies and whole industries rise and fall, as a result of relentless competition under ever changing conditions.

In just one year— between 2010 and 2011— 26 businesses dropped off the list of the *Fortune* 500 largest companies, including Radio Shack and Levi Strauss. Such processes of change have been going on for centuries and include changes in whole financial centers. From the 1780s to the 1830s, the financial center of the United States was Chestnut Street in Philadelphia but, for more than a century and a half since then, New York's Wall Street replaced Chestnut Street as the leading financial center in America, and later replaced the City of London as the financial center of the world.

At the heart of all of this is the role of profits— and of *losses*. Each is equally important from the standpoint of forcing companies and industries to use scarce resources efficiently. Industry and commerce are not just a matter of routine management, with profits rolling in more or less automatically. Masses of ever-changing details, within an ever-changing surrounding economic and social environment, mean that the threat of losses hangs over even the biggest and most successful businesses. There is a reason why business executives usually work far longer hours than their employees, and why only 35 percent of new companies survive for ten years. Only from the outside does it look easy.

Just as companies rise and fall over time, so do profit rates— even more quickly. When the *Wall Street Journal* reported the profits of Sun Microsystems at the beginning of 2007, it noted that the company's profit was "its first since mid-2005." When compact discs began rapidly replacing vinyl records back in the late 1980s, Japanese manufacturers of CD players "thrived" according to the *Far Eastern Economic Review*. But "within a few years, CD-players only offered manufacturers razor-thin margins."

This has been a common experience with many products in many industries. The companies which first introduce a product that consumers like may make large profits, but those very profits attract more investments into existing companies and encourage new companies to form, both of which add to output, driving down prices and profit margins through competition, as prices decline in response to supply and demand. Sometimes prices fall so low that profits turn to losses, forcing some firms into bankruptcy until the industry's supply and demand balance at levels that are financially sustainable.

Longer run changes in the relative rankings of firms in an industry can be dramatic. For example, United States Steel was founded in 1901 as the largest steel producer in the world. It made the steel for the Panama Canal, the Empire State Building, and more than 150 million automobiles. Yet, by 2011, U.S. Steel had fallen to 13th place in the industry, losing $53 million that year and $124 million the following year. Boeing, producer of the famous B-17 "flying fortress" bombers in World War II and since then the largest producer of commercial airliners such as the 747, was in 1998 selling more than twice as many such aircraft as its nearest rival, the French firm Airbus. But, in 2003, Airbus passed Boeing as the number one producer of commercial aircraft in the world and had a far larger number of back orders for planes to be delivered in the future. Yet Airbus too faltered and, in 2006, its top managers were fired for falling behind schedule in the development of new aircraft, while Boeing regained the lead in sales of planes.

In short, although corporations may be thought of as big, impersonal and inscrutable institutions, they are ultimately run by human beings who all differ from one another and who all have shortcomings and make mistakes, as happens with economic enterprises in every kind of economic system and in countries around the world. Companies superbly adapted to a given set of conditions can be left behind when those conditions change suddenly and their competitors are quicker to respond. Sometimes the changes are technological, as in the computer industry, and sometimes these changes are social or economic.

Social Changes

The A & P grocery chain was for decades a company superbly adapted to social and economic conditions in the United States. It was by far the leading grocery chain in the country, renowned for its high quality and low prices. During the 1920s the A & P chain was making a phenomenal rate of profit on its investment— never less than 20 percent per year, about double the national average— and it continued to prosper on through the decades of the 1930s, 1940s and 1950s. But all this began to change drastically in the 1970s, when A & P lost more than $50 million in one 52-week period. A few years later, it lost $157 million over the same span of time. Its decline had begun and, in the years that followed, many thousands of A & P stores were forced to close, as the chain shrank to become a mere shadow of its former self.

A & P's fate, both when it prospered and when it lost out to rival grocery chains, illustrates the dynamic nature of a price-coordinated economy and the role of profits and losses. When A & P was prospering up through the 1950s, it did so by charging *lower* prices than competing grocery stores. It could do this because its exceptional efficiency kept its costs lower than those of most other grocery stores and chains, and the resulting lower prices attracted vast numbers of customers. Later, when A & P began to lose customers to other grocery chains, this was because these other chains now had lower costs than A & P, and could therefore sell for lower prices. Changing conditions in the surrounding society brought this about— together with differences in the speed with which different companies spotted these changes, realized their implications and adjusted accordingly.

What were these changes? In the years following the end of World War II, suburbanization and the American public's rising prosperity gave huge supermarkets in shopping malls with vast parking lots decisive advantages over neighborhood stores— such as those of A & P— located along the streets in the central cities. As the ownership of automobiles, refrigerators and freezers became far more widespread, this completely changed the economics of the grocery industry.

The automobile, which made suburbanization possible, also made possible greater economies of scale for both customers and supermarkets. Shoppers could now buy far more groceries at one time than they could have carried home in their arms from an urban neighborhood store before the war. That was the crucial role of the automobile. Moreover, the far more widespread ownership of refrigerators and freezers now made it possible to stock up on perishable items like meat and dairy products. This led to fewer trips to grocery stores, with larger purchases each time.

What this meant to the supermarket itself was a larger volume of sales at a given location, which could now draw customers in automobiles from miles around, whereas a neighborhood store in the central city was unlikely to draw customers on foot from ten blocks away. High volume meant savings in delivery costs from the producers to the supermarket, as compared to the cost of delivering the same total amount of groceries in smaller individual lots to many scattered and smaller neighborhood stores, whose total sales would add up to what one supermarket sold. This also meant savings in the cost of selling within the supermarket, because it did not take as long to check out one customer buying $100 worth of groceries at a supermarket as it did to check out ten customers buying $10 worth of groceries each at a neighborhood store. Because of these and other differences in the costs of doing business, supermarkets could be very profitable while charging prices lower than those in neighborhood stores that were struggling to survive.

All this not only lowered the costs of delivering groceries to the consumer, it changed the relative economic advantages and disadvantages of different locations for stores. Some supermarket chains, such as Safeway, responded to these radically new conditions faster and better than A & P did. The A & P stores lingered in the central cities longer and also did not follow the shifts of population to California and other sunbelt regions.

A & P was also reluctant to sign long leases or pay high prices for new locations where the customers and their money were now moving. As a result, after years of being the lowest-price major grocery chain, A & P suddenly found itself being undersold by rivals with even lower costs of doing business.

Lower costs reflected in lower prices is what made A & P the world's leading retail chain in the first half of the twentieth century. Similarly, lower costs reflected in lower prices is what enabled other supermarket chains to take A & P's customers away in the second half of the twentieth century. While A & P succeeded in one era and failed in another, what is far more important is that the economy as a whole succeeded in *both* eras in getting its groceries at the lowest prices possible at the time— from whichever company happened to have the lowest prices. Such displacements of industry leaders continued in the early twenty-first century, when general merchandiser Wal-Mart moved to the top of the grocery industry, with nearly double the number of stores selling groceries as Safeway had.

Many other corporations that once dominated their fields have likewise fallen behind in the face of changes or have even gone bankrupt. Pan American Airways, which pioneered in commercial flights across the Atlantic and the Pacific in the first half of the twentieth century, went out of business in the late twentieth century, as a result of increased competition among airlines in the wake of the deregulation of the airline industry.

Famous newspapers like the *New York Herald-Tribune*, with a pedigree going back more than a century, stopped publishing in a new environment, after television became a major source of news and newspaper unions made publishing more costly. Between 1949 and 1990, the total number of copies of all the newspapers sold daily in New York City fell from more than 6 million copies to less than 3 million. New York was not unique. Nationwide, daily newspaper circulation per capita dropped 44 percent between 1947 and 1998. The *Herald-Tribune* was one of many local newspapers across the country to go out of business with the rise of television. The *New York Daily Mirror*, with a circulation of more than a million readers in 1949, went out of business in 1963.

By 2004, the only American newspapers with daily circulations of a million or more were newspapers sold nationwide— *USA Today*, the *Wall Street Journal* and the *New York Times*. Back in 1949, New York City alone had two local newspapers that each sold more than a million copies daily— the *Daily Mirror* at 1,020,879 and the *Daily News* at 2,254,644. The decline was still continuing in the twenty-first century, as newspaper circulation nationwide fell nearly an additional 4 million between 2000 and 2006.

Other great industrial and commercial firms that have declined or become extinct are likewise a monument to the unrelenting pressures of competition. So is the rising prosperity of the consuming public. The fate of particular companies or industries is not what is most important. Consumers are the principal beneficiaries of lower prices made possible by the more efficient allocation of scarce resources which have alternative uses. The key roles in all of this are played not only by prices and profits, but also by losses. These losses force businesses to change with changing conditions or find themselves losing out to competitors who spot the new trends sooner or who understand their implications better and respond faster.

Knowledge is one of the scarcest of all resources in any economy, and the insight distilled from knowledge is even more scarce. An economy based on prices, profits, and losses gives decisive advantages to those with greater knowledge and insight.

Put differently, knowledge and insight can guide the allocation of resources, even if most people, including the country's political leaders, do not share that knowledge or do not have the insight to understand what is happening. Clearly this is not true in the kind of economic system where political leaders control economic decisions, for then the necessarily limited knowledge and insights of those leaders become decisive barriers to the progress of the whole economy. Even when leaders have more knowledge and insight than the average member of the society, they are unlikely to have nearly as much knowledge and insight as exists scattered among the millions of people subject to their governance.

Knowledge and insight need not be technological or scientific for it to be economically valuable and decisive for the material well-being of the society as a whole. Something as mundane as retailing changed radically during the course of the twentieth century, revolutionizing both department stores and grocery stores— and raising the standard of living of millions of people by lowering the costs of delivering goods to them.

Individual businesses are forced to make drastic changes internally over time, in order to survive. For example, names like Sears and Wards came to mean department store chains to most Americans by the late twentieth century. However, neither of these enterprises began as department store chains. Montgomery Ward— the original name of Wards department stores— began as a mail order house in the nineteenth century. Under the conditions of that time, before there were automobiles or trucks, and with most Americans living in small rural communities, the high costs of delivering consumer goods to small and widely-scattered local stores was reflected in the prices that were charged. These prices, in turn, meant that ordinary people could seldom afford many of the things that we today regard as basic.

Montgomery Ward cut delivery costs by operating as a mail order house, selling directly to consumers all over the country from its huge warehouse in Chicago. Using the existing railway freight shipping services, and later the post office, allowed Montgomery Ward to deliver its products to customers at lower costs that were reflected in lower prices than those charged by local stores in rural areas. Under these conditions, Montgomery Ward became the world's largest retailer in the late nineteenth century.

During that same era, a young railroad agent named Richard Sears began selling watches on the side, and ended up creating a rival mail order house that grew over the years to eventually become several times the size of Montgomery Ward. Moreover, the Sears retail empire outlasted the demise of its rival in 2001, when the latter closed its doors for the last time under its more recent name, Wards department stores. One indication of the size of these two retail giants in their heyday as mail order houses was that each had railroad tracks running through its Chicago warehouse. That was one of the ways they cut delivery costs, allowing them to charge lower prices than those charged by local retail stores in what was still a predominantly rural country in the early twentieth century. In 1903, the *Chicago Daily Tribune* reported that mail order houses were driving rural stores out of business.

More important than the fates of these two businesses was the fact that millions of people were able to afford a higher standard of living than if they had to be supplied with goods through costlier channels. Meanwhile, there were changes over the years in American society, with more and more people beginning to live in urban communities. This was not a secret, but not everyone noticed such gradual changes and even fewer had the insight to understand their implications for retail selling. It was 1920 before the census showed that, for the first time in the country's history, there were more Americans living in urban areas than in rural areas.

One man who liked to pore over such statistics was Robert Wood, an executive at Montgomery Ward. Now, he realized, selling merchandise through a chain of urban department stores would be more efficient and more profitable than selling exclusively by mail order. Not only were his insights not shared by the head of Montgomery Ward, Wood was fired for trying to change company policy.

Meanwhile, a man named James Cash Penney had the same insight and was already setting up his own chain of department stores. From very modest beginnings, the J.C. Penney chain grew to almost 300 stores by 1920 and more than a thousand by the end of the decade. Their greater efficiency in delivering goods to urban consumers was a boon to those consumers— and Penney's competition became a big economic problem for the mail order giants Sears and Montgomery Ward, both of which began losing money as department stores began taking customers away from mail order houses. The fired Robert Wood went to work for Sears and was more successful there in convincing their top management to begin building department stores of their own. After they did, Montgomery Ward had no choice but to do the same belatedly, though it was never able to catch up to Sears again.

Rather than get lost in the details of the histories of particular businesses, we need to look at this from the standpoint of the economy as a whole and the standard of living of the people as a whole. One of the biggest advantages of an economy coordinated by prices and operating under the incentives created by profit and loss is that it can tap scarce knowledge and insights, even when most of the people— or even their intellectual and political elites— do not have such knowledge or insights.

The competitive advantages of those who are right can overwhelm the numerical, or even financial, advantages of those who are wrong. James Cash Penney did not start with a lot of money. He was in fact raised in poverty and began his retail career as just a one-third partner in a store in a little town in Wyoming, at a time when Sears and Montgomery Ward were unchallenged giants of nationwide retailing. Yet his insights into the changing conditions of retailing eventually forced these giants into doing things his way, on pain of extinction.

In a later era, a clerk in a J.C. Penney store named Sam Walton would learn retailing from the ground up, and then put his knowledge and insights to work in his own store, which would eventually expand to become the Wal-Mart chain, with sales larger than those of Sears and J.C. Penney combined.

One of the great handicaps of economies run by political authorities, whether under medieval mercantilism or modern communism, is that insights which arise among the masses have no such powerful leverage as to force those in authority to change the way they do things. Under any form of economic or political system, those at the top tend to become complacent, if not arrogant. Convincing them of anything is not easy, especially when it is some new way of doing things that is very different from what they are used to. The big advantage of a free market is that you don't have to convince anybody of anything. You simply compete with them in the marketplace and let that be the test of what works best.

Imagine a system in which James Cash Penney had to verbally convince the heads of Sears and Montgomery Ward to expand beyond mail order retailing and build a nationwide chain of stores. Their response might well have been: "Who is this guy Penney— a part-owner of some little store in a hick town nobody ever heard of— to tell us how to run the largest retail companies in the world?"

In a market economy, Penney did not have to convince anybody of anything. All he had to do was deliver the merchandise to the consumers at lower prices. His success, and the millions of dollars in losses suffered by Sears and Montgomery Ward as a result, left these corporate giants no choice but to imitate this upstart, in order to become profitable again. Although J.C. Penney grew up in worse poverty than most people who are on welfare today, his ideas and insights prevailed against some of the richest men of his time, who eventually realized that they would not remain rich much longer if Penney and others kept taking away their customers, leaving their companies with millions of dollars in losses each year.

Economic Changes

Economic changes include not only changes in the economy but also changes within the managements of firms, especially in their responses to external economic changes. Many things that we take for granted today, as features of a modern economy, were resisted when first proposed and had to fight uphill to establish themselves by the power of the marketplace. Even something as widely used today as bank credit cards were initially resisted. When BankAmericard and Master Charge (later MasterCard) first appeared in the 1960s, leading New York department stores such as Macy's and Bloomingdale's said that they had no intention of accepting bank credit cards as payments for purchases in their stores, even though there were already millions of people with such cards in the New York metropolitan area.

Only after the success of these credit cards in smaller stores did the big department stores finally relent and begin accepting credit cards. In 2003, for the first time, more purchases were made by credit cards or debit cards than by cash. That same year, *Fortune* magazine reported that a number of companies made more money from their own credit card business, with its interest charges, than from selling goods and services. Sears made more than half its profits from its credit cards and Circuit City made all of its profits from its credit cards, while losing $17 million on its sales of electronic merchandise.

Neither individuals nor companies are successful forever. Death alone guarantees turnover in management. Given the importance of the human factor and the variability among people— or even with the same person at different stages of life— it can hardly be surprising that dramatic changes over time in the relative positions of businesses have been the norm.

Some individual executives are very successful during one era in the country's evolution, or during one period in their own lives, and very ineffective at a later time. Sewell Avery, for example, was for many years during the twentieth century a highly successful and widely praised leader of U.S. Gypsum and later of Montgomery Ward. Yet his last years were marked by public criticism and controversy over the way he ran Montgomery Ward, and by a bitter fight for control of the company that he was regarded as mismanaging. When Avery resigned as chief executive officer, the value of Montgomery Ward's stock rose immediately. Under his leadership, Montgomery Ward had put aside so many millions of dollars, as a cushion against an economic downturn, that *Fortune* magazine called it "a bank with a store front." Meanwhile, rivals like Sears were using their money to expand into new markets.

What is important is not the success or failure of particular individuals or companies, but the success of particular knowledge and insights in prevailing despite the blindness or resistance of particular business owners and managers. Given the scarcity of mental resources, an economy in which knowledge and insights have such decisive advantages in the competition of the marketplace is an economy which itself has great advantages in creating a higher standard of living for the population at large. A society in which only members of a hereditary aristocracy, a military junta, or a ruling political party can make major decisions is a society which has thrown away much of the knowledge, insights, and talents of most of its own people. A society in which such decisions can only be made by males has thrown away half of its knowledge, talents, and insights.

Contrast societies with such restricted sources of decision-making ability with a society in which a farm boy who walked eight miles to Detroit to look for a job could end up creating the Ford Motor Company and changing the face of America with mass-produced automobiles— or a society in which a couple of young bicycle mechanics could invent the airplane and change the whole world. Neither a lack of pedigree, nor a lack of academic degrees, nor even a lack of money could stop ideas that worked, for investment money is always looking for a winner to back and cash in on. A society which can tap all kinds of talents from all segments of its population has obvious advantages over societies in which only the talents of a preselected few are allowed to determine its destiny.

No economic system can depend on the continuing wisdom of its current leaders. A price-coordinated economy with competition in the marketplace does not have to, because those leaders can be forced to change course— or be replaced— whether because of red ink, irate stockholders, outside investors ready to move in and take over, or because of bankruptcy. Given such economic pressures, it is hardly surprising that economies under the thumbs of kings or commissars have seldom matched the track record of economies based on competition and prices.

Technological Changes

For decades during the twentieth century, television sets were built around a cathode ray tube, in which an image was projected from the small back end of the tube to the larger front screen, where the picture was viewed. But a new century saw this technology replaced by new technologies that produced a thinner and flatter screen, with sharper images. By 2006, only 21 percent of the television sets sold in the United States had picture tube technology, while 49 percent of all television sets sold had liquid crystal display (LCD) screens and another 10 percent had plasma screens.

For more than a century, Eastman Kodak company was the largest photographic company in the world. In 1976, Kodak sold 90 percent of all the film sold in the United States and 85 percent of all the cameras. But new technology created new competitors. At the end of the twentieth century and the beginning of the twenty-first century, digital cameras began to be produced not only by such traditional manufacturers of cameras for film as Nikon, Canon, and Minolta, but also by producers of other computerized products such as Sony and Samsung. Moreover, "smart phones" could now take pictures, providing easy substitutes for the kinds of small, simple and inexpensive cameras that Kodak manufactured.

Film sales began falling for the first time after 2000, and digital camera sales surpassed the sales of film cameras for the first time three years later. This sudden change left Kodak scrambling to convert from film photography to digital photography, while companies specializing in digital photography took away Kodak's customers. The ultimate irony in all this was that the digital camera was invented by Kodak. But apparently other companies saw its potential earlier and developed the technology better.

By the third quarter of 2011, Eastman Kodak reported a $222 million loss, its ninth quarterly loss in three years. Both the price of its stock and the number of its employees fell to less than one-tenth of what they had once been. In January 2012, Eastman Kodak filed for bankruptcy. Meanwhile, its biggest competitor in the business, the Japanese firm Fuji, which produced both film and cameras, diversified into other fields, including cosmetics and flat-screen television.

Similar technological revolutions have occurred in other industries and in other times. Clocks and watches for centuries depended on springs and gears to keep time and move the hour and minute hands. The Swiss became renowned for the high quality of the internal watch mechanisms they produced, and the leading American watch company in the mid-twentieth century— Bulova— used mechanisms made in Switzerland for its best-selling watches. However, the appearance of quartz time-keeping technology in the early 1970s, which was more accurate and had lower costs, led to a dramatic fall in the sales of Bulova watches, and vanishing profits for the company that made them. As the *Wall Street Journal* reported:

> For 1975, the firm reported a $21 million loss on $55 million in sales. That year, the company was reported to have 8% of domestic U.S. watch sales, one-tenth of what it claimed at its zenith in the early 1960s.

Changes in Business Leadership

Perhaps the most overlooked fact about industry and commerce is that they are run by people who differ greatly from one another in insight, foresight, leadership, organizational ability, and dedication— just as people do in every other walk of life. Therefore the companies they lead likewise differ in the efficiency with which they perform their work. Moreover, these differences change over time.

The automobile industry is just one example. According to *Forbes* business magazine in 2003, "other automakers can't come close to Toyota on how much it costs to build cars" and this shows up on the bottom line. "Toyota earned $1,800 for every vehicle sold, GM made $300 and Ford lost $240," *Forbes* reported. Toyota "makes a net profit far bigger than the combined total for Detroit's Big three," according to *The Economist* magazine in 2005. But, by 2010 Detroit's big three automakers were earning more profits per vehicle than the average of Toyota and Honda. By 2012, the Ford Motor Company's annual profit was $5.7 billion, while General Motors earned $4.9 billion and Toyota earned $3.45 billion.

Toyota's lead in the quality of its cars was likewise not permanent. *BusinessWeek* in 2003 reported that, although Toyota spent fewer hours manufacturing each automobile, its cars had fewer defects than those of any of the American big three automakers. High rankings for quality by *Consumer Reports* magazine during the 1970s and 1980s have been credited with helping Toyota's automobiles gain widespread acceptance in the American market and, though Honda and Subaru overtook Toyota in the *Consumer Reports* rankings in 2007, Toyota continued to outrank any American automobile manufacturer in quality at that time. Over the years, however, competition from Japanese automakers brought marked improvements in American-made cars, "closing the quality gap with Asian auto makers," according to the *Wall Street Journal*. However, in 2012, *Consumer Reports* reported that "a perfect storm of reliability problems" dropped the Ford Motor Company out of the top ten, while Toyota "swept the top spots."

Although Toyota surpassed General Motors as the world's largest automobile manufacturer, in 2010 it had to stop production and recall more than 8 million cars because of problems with their acceleration. Neither quality leadership, nor any other kind of leadership, is permanent in a market economy.

What matters far more than the fate of any given business is how much its efficiency can benefit consumers. As *BusinessWeek* said of the Wal-Mart retail chain:

> At Wal-Mart, "everyday low prices" is more than a slogan; it is the fundamental tenet of a cult masquerading as a company. . . New England Consulting estimates that Wal-Mart saved its U.S. customers $20 billion last year alone.

Business leadership is a factor, not only in the relative success of various enterprises but more fundamentally in the advance of the economy as a whole through the spread of the impact of new and better business methods to competing companies and other industries. While the motives for these improvements are the bottom lines of the companies involved, the bottom line for the economy as a whole is the standard of living of the people who buy the products and services that these companies produce.

Although we measure the amount of petroleum in barrels, which is how it was once shipped in the nineteenth century, today it is actually shipped in railroad tank cars or tanker trucks on land or in gigantic oil tankers at sea. The most famous fortune in American history, that of John D. Rockefeller, was made by revolutionizing the way oil was refined and distributed, drastically lowering the cost of delivering its various finished products to the consumer. When Rockefeller entered the oil business in the 1860s, there were no automobiles, so the principal use of petroleum was to produce kerosene for lamps, since there were no electric lights then either. When petroleum was refined to produce kerosene, the gasoline that was a by-product was so little valued that some oil companies simply poured it into a river to get rid of it.

In an industry where many investors and businesses went bankrupt, Rockefeller made the world's largest fortune by revolutionizing the industry. Shipping his oil in railroad tank cars, rather than in barrels like his competitors, was just one of the cost-saving innovations that made Rockefeller's Standard Oil Company the biggest and most profitable enterprise in the petroleum industry. He also hired scientists to create numerous new products from petroleum, ranging from paints to paraffin to anesthetics to vaseline— and they used gasoline for fuel in the production process, instead of letting it go to waste. Kerosene was still the principal product of petroleum but, because Standard Oil did not have to recover all its production costs from the sale of kerosene, it was able to sell the kerosene more cheaply. The net result, from a business standpoint, was that Standard Oil ended up selling about 90 percent of the kerosene in the country.

From the standpoint of the consumers, the results were even more striking. Kerosene was literally the difference between light and darkness for most people at night. As the price of kerosene fell from 58 cents a gallon in 1865 to 26 cents a gallon in 1870, and then to 8 cents a gallon during the 1870s, far more people were able to have light after sundown. As a distinguished historian put it:

> Before 1870, only the rich could afford whale oil and candles. The rest had to go to bed early to save money. By the 1870s, with the drop in the price of kerosene, middle and working class people all over the nation could afford the one cent an hour that it cost to light their homes at night. Working and reading became after-dark activities new to most Americans in the 1870s.

The later rise of the automobile created a vast new market for gasoline, just as Standard Oil's more efficient production of petroleum products facilitated the growth of the automobile industry.

It is not always one individual who is the key to the success of a given business, as Rockefeller was to the success of Standard Oil. What is really key is the role of knowledge and insights in the economy, whether they are concentrated in one individual or more widely dispersed. Some business leaders are very good at some aspects of management and very weak in other aspects. The success of the business then depends on which aspects happen to be crucial at a particular time. Sometimes two executives with very different skills and weaknesses combine to produce a very successful management team, whereas either one of them might have failed completely if operating alone.

Ray Kroc, founder of the McDonald's chain, was a genius at operating details and may well have known more about hamburgers, milk shakes, and French fries than any other human being— and there is a lot to know— but he was out of his depth in complex financial operations. These matters were handled by Harry Sonneborn, who was a financial genius whose improvisations rescued the company from the brink of bankruptcy more than once during its rocky early years. But Sonneborn didn't even eat hamburgers, much less have any interest in how they were made or marketed. However, as a team, Kroc and Sonneborn made McDonald's one of the leading corporations in the world.

When an industry or a sector of the economy is undergoing rapid change through new ways of doing business, sometimes the leaders of the past find it hardest to break the mold of their previous experience. For example, when the fast food revolution burst forth in the 1950s, existing leaders in restaurant franchises such as Howard Johnson were very unsuccessful in trying to compete with upstarts like McDonald's in the fast food segment of the market. Even when Howard Johnson set up imitations of the new fast food restaurants under the name "Howard Johnson Jr.," these imitations were unable to compete successfully, because they carried over into the fast food business approaches and practices that were successful in conventional restaurants, but which slowed down operations too much to be successful in the new fast food sector, where rapid turnover with inexpensive food was the key to profits.

Selecting managers can be as chancy as any other aspect of a business. Only by trial and error did the new McDonald's franchise chain discover back in the 1950s what kinds of people were most successful at running their restaurants. The first few franchisees were people with business experience, who nevertheless did very poorly. The first two really successful McDonald's franchisees— who were *very* successful— were a working class married couple who drained their life's savings in order to go into business for themselves. They were so financially strained at the beginning that they even had trouble coming up with the $100 needed to put into the cash register on their opening day, so as to be able to make change. But they ended up millionaires.

Other working class people who put everything they owned on the line to open a McDonald's restaurant also succeeded on a grand scale, even when they had no experience in running a restaurant or managing a business. When McDonald's set up its own company-owned restaurants, these restaurants did not succeed nearly as well as restaurants owned by people whose life's savings were at stake. But there was no way to know that in advance.

The importance of the personal factor in the performance of corporate management was suggested in another way by a study of chief executive officers in Denmark. A death in the family of a Danish CEO led, on average, to a 9 percent decline in the profitability of the corporation. If it was the death of a spouse, the decline was 15 percent and, if it was a child who died, 21 percent. According to the *Wall Street Journal*, "The drop was sharper when the child was under 18, and greater still if it was the death of an only child." Although corporations are often spoken of as impersonal institutions operating in an impersonal market, both the market and the corporations reflect the personal priorities and performances of people.

Market economies must rely not only on price competition between various producers to allow the most successful to continue and expand, they must also find some way to weed out those business owners or managers who do not get the most from the nation's resources. Losses accomplish that. Bankruptcy shuts down the entire enterprise that is consistently failing to come up to the standards of its competitors or is producing a product that has been superseded by some other product.

Before reaching that point, however, losses can force a firm to make internal reassessments of its policies and personnel. These include the chief executive, who can be replaced by irate stockholders who are not receiving the dividends they expected.

A poorly managed company is more valuable to outside investors than to its existing owners, when these outside investors are convinced that they can improve its performance. Outside investors can therefore offer existing stockholders more for their stock than it is currently worth, and still make a profit, if that stock's value later rises to the level expected when existing management is replaced by more efficient managers. For example, if the stock is selling in the market for $50 a share under inefficient management, outside investors can start buying it up at $60 a share until they own a controlling interest in the corporation.

After using that control to fire existing managers and replace them with a more efficient management team, the value of the stock may then rise to $100 a share. While this profit is what motivates the investors, from the standpoint of the economy as a whole what matters is that such a rise in stock prices usually means that either the business is now serving more customers, or offering them better quality or lower prices, or is operating at lower cost— or some combination of these things.

Like so many other things, running a business looks easy from the outside. On the eve of the Bolshevik revolution the leader of the Communist movement, V.I. Lenin, declared that "accounting and control" were the key factors in running an enterprise, and that capitalism had already "reduced" the administration of businesses to "extraordinarily simple operations" that "any literate person can perform"— that is, "supervising and recording, knowledge of the four rules of arithmetic, and issuing appropriate receipts." Such "exceedingly simple operations of registration, filing and checking" could, according to Lenin, "easily be performed" by people receiving ordinary workmen's wages.

After just a few years in power as ruler of the Soviet Union, however, Lenin confronted a very different— and very bitter— reality. He himself wrote of a "fuel crisis" which "threatens to disrupt all Soviet work," of economic "ruin, starvation and devastation" in the country and even admitted that peasant uprisings had become "a common occurrence" under Communist rule. In short, the economic functions which had seemed so easy and simple before having to perform them now seemed almost overwhelmingly difficult.

Belatedly, Lenin saw a need for people "who are versed in the art of administration" and admitted that "there is nowhere we can turn to for such people except the old class"— that is, the capitalist businessmen. In his address to the 1920 Communist Party Congress, Lenin warned his comrades: "Opinions on corporate management are all too frequently imbued with a spirit of sheer ignorance, an antiexpert spirit." The apparent simplicities of just three years earlier now required experts. Thus began Lenin's New Economic Policy, which allowed more market activity, and under which the economy began to revive.

Nearly a hundred years later, with the Russian economy growing at less than two percent annually, the same lesson was learned anew by another Russian leader. A front-page story in the *New York Times* in 2013 reported how, "with the Russian economy languishing, President Vladimir V. Putin has devised a plan for turning things around: offer amnesty to some of the imprisoned business people."

Chapter 6

THE ROLE OF PROFITS— AND LOSSES

Rockefeller got rich selling oil. . . He found cheaper ways to get oil from the ground to the gas pump.

John Stossel

To those who run businesses, profits are obviously desirable and losses deplorable. But economics is not business administration. From the standpoint of the economy as a whole, and from the standpoint of the central concern of economics— the allocation of scarce resources which have alternative uses— profits and losses play equally important roles in maintaining and advancing the standards of living of the population as a whole.

Part of the efficiency of a price-coordinated economy comes from the fact that goods can simply "follow the money," without the producers really knowing just why people are buying one thing here and something else there and yet another thing during a different season. However, it is necessary for those who run businesses to keep track not only of the money coming in from the customers, it is equally necessary to keep track of how much money is going out to those who supply raw materials, labor, electricity, and other inputs. Keeping careful track of these numerous flows of money in and out can make the difference between profit and loss. Therefore electricity, machines or cement cannot be used in the same careless way that caused far more of such inputs to be used per unit of output in the Soviet economy than in the German or Japanese economy. From the standpoint of the economy as a whole, and the well-being of the consuming public, the threat of losses is just as important as the prospect of profits.

When one business enterprise in a market economy finds ways to lower its costs, competing enterprises have no choice but to scramble to try to do the same. After the general merchandising chain Wal-Mart began selling groceries in 1988, it moved up over the years to become the nation's largest grocery seller by the early twenty-first century. Its lower costs benefitted not only its own customers, but those of other grocers as well. As the *Wall Street Journal* reported:

> When two Wal-Mart Supercenters and a rival regional grocery opened near a Kroger Co. supermarket in Houston last year, the Kroger's sales dropped 10%. Store manager Ben Bustos moved quickly to slash some prices and cut labor costs, for example, by buying ready-made cakes instead of baking them in-house, and ordering precut salad-bar items from suppliers. His employees used to stack displays by hand: Now, fruit and vegetables arrive stacked and gleaming for display.
>
> Such moves have helped Mr. Bustos cut worker-hours by 30% to 40% from when the store opened four years ago, and lower the prices of staples such as cereal, bread, milk, eggs and disposable diapers. Earlier this year, sales at the Kroger finally edged up over the year before.

In short, the economy operated more efficiently, to the benefit of the consumers, not only because of Wal-Mart's ability to cut its own costs and thereby lower prices, but also because this forced Kroger to find ways to do the same. This is a microcosm of what happens throughout a free market economy. "When Wal-Mart begins selling groceries in a community," a study showed, "the average price of groceries in that community falls by 6 to 12 percent." Similar competition by low-cost sellers in other industries tends to produce similar results in those industries. It is no accident that people in such economies tend to have higher standards of living.

PROFITS

Profits may be the most misconceived subject in economics. Socialists have long regarded profits as simply "overcharge," as Fabian socialist George Bernard Shaw called it, or a "surplus value" as Karl Marx called it. "Never talk to me about profit," India's first prime minister, Jawaharlal Nehru, warned his country's leading industrialist, "It is a dirty word." Philosopher John Dewey demanded that "production for profit be subordinated to production for use."

From all these men's perspectives, profits were simply unnecessary charges added on to the inherent costs of producing goods and services, driving up the cost to consumers. One of the great appeals of socialism, especially back when it was simply an idealistic theory without any concrete examples in the real world, was that it sought to eliminate these supposedly unnecessary charges, making things generally more affordable, especially for people with lower incomes. Only after socialism went from being a theory to being an actual economic system in various countries around the world did the fact become painfully apparent that people in socialist countries had a harder time trying to afford things that most people in capitalist countries could afford with ease and took for granted.

With profits eliminated, prices should have been lower in socialist countries, according to theory, and the standard of living of the masses correspondingly higher. Why then was it not that way in practice?

Profits as Incentives

Let us go back to square one. The hope for profits and the threat of losses is what forces a business owner in a capitalist economy to produce at the lowest cost and sell what the customers are most willing to pay for. In the absence of these pressures, those who manage enterprises under socialism have far less incentive to be as efficient as possible under given conditions, much less to keep up with changing conditions and respond to them quickly, as capitalist enterprises must do if they expect to survive.

It was a Soviet premier, Leonid Brezhnev, who said that his country's enterprise managers shied away from innovation "as the devil shies away from incense." But, given the incentives of government-owned and government-controlled enterprises, why should those managers have stuck their necks out by trying new methods or new products, when they stood to gain little or nothing if innovation succeeded and might have lost their jobs (or worse) if it failed? Under Stalin, failure was often equated with sabotage, and was punished accordingly.

Even under the milder conditions of democratic socialism, as in India for decades after its independence, innovation was by no means necessary for protected enterprises, such as automobile manufacturing. Until the freeing up of markets that began in India in 1991, the country's most popular car was the Hindustan Ambassador— an unabashed copy of the British Morris Oxford. Moreover, even in the 1990s, *The Economist* referred to the Ambassador as "a barely upgraded version of a 1950s Morris Oxford." A London newspaper, *The Independent*, reported: "Ambassadors have for years been notorious in India for their poor finish, heavy handling and proneness to alarming accidents." Nevertheless, there was a waiting list for the Ambassador— with waits lasting for months and sometimes years— since foreign cars were not allowed to be imported to compete with it.

Under free market capitalism, the incentives work in the opposite direction. Even the most profitable business can lose its market if it doesn't keep innovating, in order to avoid being overtaken by its competitors. For example, IBM pioneered in creating computers, including one 1944 model occupying 3,000 cubic feet. But, in the 1970s, Intel created a computer chip smaller than a fingernail that could do the same things as that computer. Yet Intel itself was then constantly forced to improve its chips at an exponential rate, as rivals like Advanced Micro Devices (AMD), Cyrix, and others began catching up with them technologically. More than once, Intel poured such huge sums of money into the development of improved chips as to risk the financial survival of the company itself. But the alternative was to allow itself to be overtaken by rivals, which would have been an even bigger risk to Intel's survival.

Although Intel continued as the leading seller of computer chips in the world, continuing competition from Advanced Micro Devices spurred both companies to feverish innovation, as *The Economist* reported in 2007:

> For a while it seemed that AMD had pulled ahead of Intel in chip design. It devised a clever way to enable chips to handle data in both 32-bit and 64-bit chunks, which Intel reluctantly adopted in 2004. And in 2005 AMD launched a new processor that split the number-crunching between two "cores", the brains of a chip, thus boosting performance and reducing energy-consumption. But Intel came back strongly with its own dual-core designs. . . Next year it will launch new chips with eight cores on a single slice of silicon, at least a year ahead of AMD.

Although this technological rivalry was very beneficial to computer users, it has had large and often painful economic consequences for both Intel and AMD. The latter had losses of more than a billion dollars in 2002 and its stock lost four-fifths of its value. But, four years later, the price of Intel stock fell by 20 percent in just three months, and Intel announced that it would lay off 1,000 managers, as its profits fell by 57 percent while the profits of AMD rose by 53 percent. All this feverish competition took place in an industry where Intel sells more than 80 percent of all the computer chips in the world.

In short, even among corporate giants, competition in innovation can become desperate in a free market, as the see-saw battle for market share in microchips indicates. The dean of the Yale School of Management described the computer chip industry as "an industry in constant turmoil" and the Chief Executive Officer of Intel wrote a book titled *Only the Paranoid Survive.*

The fate of AMD and Intel is not the issue. The issue is how the consumers benefit from both technological advances and lower prices as a result of these companies' fierce competition to gain profits and avoid losses. Nor is this industry unique. In 2011, 45 of the *Fortune* 500 companies reported losses, totaling in the aggregate more than $50 billion. Such losses play a vital role in the economy, forcing corporate giants to change what they are doing, under penalty of extinction, since no one can sustain losses of that magnitude indefinitely.

Inertia may be a common tendency among human beings around the world— whether in business, government or other walks of life— but businesses operating in a competitive market are forced by red ink on the bottom line to realize that they cannot keep drifting along like the Hindustan Motor Corporation, protected from competition by the Indian government.

Even in India, the freeing of markets toward the end of the twentieth century created competition in cars, forcing Hindustan Motors to invest in improvements, producing new Ambassadors that were now "much more reliable than their predecessors," according to *The Independent* newspaper, and now even had "perceptible acceleration" according to *The Economist* magazine. Nevertheless, the Hindustan Ambassador lost its long-standing position of the number one car in sales in India to a Japanese car manufactured in India, the Maruti. In 1997, 80 percent of the cars sold in India were Marutis. Moreover, in the now more competitive automobile market in India, "Marutis too are improving, in anticipation of the next invaders," according to *The Economist*. As General Motors, Volkswagen and Toyota began investing in new factories in India, the market share of Maruti dropped to 38 percent by 2012.

There was a similar pattern in India's wrist watch industry. In 1985, the worldwide production of electronic watches was more than double the production of mechanical watches. But, in India the HMT watch company produced the vast majority of the country's watches, and more than 90 percent of its watches were still mechanical. By 1989, more than four-fifths of the watches produced in the world were electronic but, in India, more than 90 percent of the watches produced by HMT were still the obsolete mechanical watches. However, after government restrictions on the economy were greatly reduced, electronic watches quickly became a majority of all watches produced in India by 1993–1994, and other watch companies displaced HMT, whose market share fell to 14 percent.

While capitalism has a visible cost— profit— that does not exist under socialism, socialism has an invisible cost— inefficiency— that gets weeded out by losses and bankruptcy under capitalism. The fact that most goods are more widely affordable in a capitalist economy implies that profit is less costly than inefficiency. Put differently, profit is a price paid for efficiency. Clearly the greater efficiency must outweigh the profit or else socialism would in fact have had the more affordable prices and greater prosperity that its theorists expected, but which failed to materialize in the real world.

If in fact the cost of profits exceeded the value of the efficiency they promote, then non-profit organizations or government agencies could get the same work done cheaper or better than profit-making enterprises, and could therefore displace them in the competition of the marketplace. Yet that seldom, if ever, happens, while the opposite happens increasingly— that is, private profit-making companies taking over various functions formerly performed by government agencies or by non-profit organizations such as colleges and universities.[*]

---

[*] Further discussion of this phenomenon can be found in Chapter 24 in a section titled "Non-Profit Organizations."

While capitalists have been conceived of as people who make profits, what a business owner really gets is legal ownership of whatever residual is left over after the costs of production have been paid out of the money received from customers. That residual can turn out to be positive, negative, or zero. Workers must be paid and creditors must be paid— or else they can take legal action to seize the company's assets. Even before that happens, they can simply stop supplying their inputs when the company stops paying them. The only person whose payment is contingent on how well the business is doing is the owner of that business. This is what puts unrelenting pressure on the owner to monitor everything that is happening in the business and everything that is happening in the market for the business' products or services.

In contrast to the layers of authorities monitoring the actions of those under them in a government-run enterprise, the business owner is essentially an *unmonitored monitor* as far as the economic efficiency of the business is concerned. Self-interest takes the place of external monitors, and forces far closer attention to details and far more expenditure of time and energy at work than any set of rules or authorities is likely to be able to do. That simple fact gives capitalism an enormous advantage. More important, it gives the people living in price-coordinated market economies visibly higher standards of living.

It is not just ignorant people, but also highly educated and highly intellectual people like George Bernard Shaw, Karl Marx, Jawaharlal Nehru and John Dewey who have misconceived profits as arbitrary charges added on to the inherent costs of producing goods and services. To many people, even today, high profits are often attributed to high prices charged by those motivated by "greed." In reality, most of the great fortunes in American history have resulted from someone's figuring out how to reduce costs, so as to be able to charge *lower* prices and therefore gain a mass market for the product. Henry Ford did this with automobiles, Rockefeller with oil, Carnegie with steel, and Sears, Penney, Walton and other department store chain founders with a variety of products.

A supermarket chain in a capitalist economy can be very successful charging prices that allow about a penny of clear profit on each dollar of sales. Because several cash registers are usually bringing in money simultaneously all day long in a big supermarket, those pennies can add up to a very substantial annual rate of return on the supermarket chain's investment, while adding very little to what the customer pays. If the entire contents of a store get sold out in about two weeks, then that penny on a dollar becomes more like a quarter on the dollar over the course of a year, when that same dollar comes back to be re-used 25 more times. Under socialism, that penny on each dollar would be eliminated, but so too would be all the economic pressures on the management to keep costs down. Instead of prices falling to 99 cents, they might well rise above a dollar, after the enterprise managers lose the incentives and pressures to keep production costs down.

Profit Rates

When most people are asked how high they think the average rate of profit is, they usually suggest some number much higher than the actual rate of profit. Over the entire period from 1960 through 2005, the average rate of return on corporate assets in the United States ranged from a high of 12.4 percent to a low of 4.1 percent, before taxes. After taxes, the rate of profit ranged from a high of 7.8 percent to a low of 2.2 percent. However, it is not just the numerical rate of profit that most people misconceive. Many misconceive its whole role in a price-coordinated economy, which is to serve as incentives— and it plays that role wherever its fluctuations take it. Moreover, some people have no idea that there are vast differences between profits on sales and profits on investments.

If a store buys widgets for $10 each and sells them for $15 each, some might say that it makes $5 in profits on each widget that it sells. But, of course, the store has to pay the people who work there, the company that supplies electricity to the store, as well as other suppliers of other goods and services needed to keep the business running. What is left over after all these people have been paid is the net profit, usually a lot less than the gross profit. But that is still not the same as profit on investment. It is simply net profits on sales, which still ignores the cost of the investments which built the store in the first place.

It is the profit on the whole investment that matters to the investor. When someone invests $10,000, what that person wants to know is what annual rate of return it will bring, whether it is invested in stores, real estate, or stocks and bonds. Profits on particular sales are not what matter most. It is the profit on the total capital that has been invested in the business that matters. That profit matters not just to those who receive it, but to the economy as a whole, because differences in profit rates in different sectors of the economy are what cause investments to flow into and out of these various sectors, until profit rates are equalized, like water seeking its own level. Changing rates of profit allocate resources in a market economy— when these are rates of profit on investment.

Profits on sales are a different story. Things may be sold at prices that are much higher than what the seller paid for them and yet, if those items sit on a shelf in the store for months before being sold, the profit on investment may be less than with other items that have less of a mark-up in price but which sell out within a week. A store that sells pianos undoubtedly makes a higher percentage profit on each sale than a supermarket makes selling bread. But a piano sits in the store for a much longer time waiting to be sold than a loaf of bread does. Bread would go stale and moldy waiting for as long as a piano to be sold. When a supermarket chain buys $10,000 worth of bread, it gets its money back much faster than when a piano dealer buys $10,000 worth of pianos. Therefore the piano dealer must charge a higher percentage mark-up on the sale of each piano than a supermarket charges on each loaf of bread, if the piano dealer is to make the same annual percentage rate of return on a $10,000 investment.

Competition among those seeking money from investors makes profit rates tend to equalize, even when that requires different mark-ups to compensate for different turnover rates among different products. Piano stores can continue to exist only when their higher mark-ups in prices compensate for slower turnover in sales. Otherwise investors would put their money elsewhere and piano stores would start disappearing.

When the supermarket gets its money back in a shorter period of time, it can turn right around and re-invest it, buying more bread or other grocery items. In the course of a year, the same money turns over many times in a supermarket, earning a profit each time, so that a penny of profit on the dollar can produce a total profit rate for the year on the initial investment equal to what a piano dealer makes charging a much higher percentage mark-up on an investment that turns over much more slowly.

Even firms in the same business may have different turnover rates. For example, Wal-Mart's inventory turns over more times per year than the inventory at Target stores. In the United States in 2008, an automobile spent an average of three months on a dealer's lot before being sold, compared to two months the previous year. However, in 2008 Volkswagens sold in about two months in the U.S. while Chryslers took more than four months. Although supermarkets tend to have especially low rates of profit on sales, because of their high rates of turnover, other businesses' profit rates on sales are also usually lower than what many people imagine. Companies that made the *Fortune* magazine list of the 500 largest companies in America averaged "a return on revenues [sales] of a penny on the dollar" in 2002, compared to "6 cents in 2000, the peak profit year."

Profits on sales and profits on investment are not merely different concepts. They can move in opposite directions. One of the keys to the rise to dominance of the A & P grocery chain in the 1920s was a conscious decision by the company management to cut profit margins on sales, in order to increase the profit rate on investment. With the new and lower prices made possible by selling with lower profits per item, A & P was able to attract greatly increased numbers of customers, making far more total profit because of the increased volume of sales. Making a profit of only a few cents on the dollar on sales, but with the inventory turning over nearly 30 times a year, A & P's profit rate on investment soared. This low price and high volume strategy set a pattern that spread to other grocery chains and to other kinds of enterprises as well. Consumers benefitted from lower prices while A & P benefitted from higher profits on their investment— further evidence that economic transactions are not a zero-sum process.

In a later era, huge supermarkets were able to shave the profit margin on sales still thinner, because of even higher volumes of sales, enabling them to displace A & P from industry leadership by charging still lower prices.

Conversely, a study of prices in low-income neighborhoods found that there were larger than usual mark-ups in prices charged their customers but, at the same time, there were lower than usual rates of profit on investment.

Higher profits on sales helped compensate for the higher costs of doing business in low-income neighborhoods but apparently not completely, as indicated by the avoidance of such neighborhoods by many businesses, including supermarket chains.

A limiting factor in how high stores in low-income neighborhoods can raise their prices to compensate for higher costs is the fact that many low-income residents already shop in stores in higher-income neighborhoods, where the prices are lower, even though this may entail paying bus fare or taxi fare. The higher the prices rise in low-income neighborhoods, the more people are likely to shop elsewhere. Thus stores in such neighborhoods are limited in the extent to which they can offset higher costs and slower turnover with higher prices, often leaving them in a precarious financial position, even while they are being denounced for "exploiting" their customers with high prices.

It should also be noted that, where there are higher costs of doing business in low-income neighborhoods when there are higher rates of crime and vandalism, such additional costs can easily overwhelm the profit margin and make many businesses unsustainable in such neighborhoods. If a store clears a penny of profit on an item that costs a quarter, then if just one out of every 25 of these items gets stolen by shoplifters, that can make it unprofitable to sell in that neighborhood. The majority of people in the neighborhood may be honest consumers who pay for what they get at the store, but it takes only a fraction as many who are shoplifters (or robbers or vandals) to make it uneconomic for stores to locate there.

COSTS OF PRODUCTION

Among the crucial factors in prices and profits are the costs of producing whatever goods or services are being sold. Not everyone is equally efficient in production and not everyone's circumstances offer equal opportunities to achieve lower costs. Unfortunately, costs are misconceived almost as much as profits.

Economies of Scale

First of all, there is no such thing as "the" cost of producing a given product or service. Henry Ford proved long ago that the cost of producing an automobile was very different when you produced 100 cars a year than when you produced 100,000. He became the leading automobile manufacturer in the early twentieth century by pioneering mass production methods in his factories, revolutionizing not only his own company but businesses throughout the economy, which followed the mass production principles that he introduced. The time required to produce a Ford Model T chassis shrank from 12 man-hours to an hour and a half. With a mass market for automobiles, it paid to invest in expensive but labor-saving mass production machinery, whose cost per car would turn out to be modest when spread out over a huge number of automobiles. But, if there were only half as many cars sold as expected, then the cost of that machinery per car would be twice as much.

Large fixed costs are among the reasons for lower costs of production per unit of output as the amount of output increases. Lower costs per unit of output as the number of units increases is what economists call "economies of scale."

It has been estimated that the minimum amount of automobile production required to achieve the fullest economies of scale today runs into the hundreds of thousands of cars per year. Back at the beginning of the twentieth century, the largest automobile manufacturer in the United States produced just six cars a day. At that level of output, the cost of production was so high that only the truly rich could afford to buy a car. But Henry Ford's mass production methods brought the cost of producing cars down within the price range of ordinary Americans. Moreover, he continued to improve the efficiency of his factories. The price of a Model T Ford was cut in half between 1910 and 1916.

Similar principles apply in other industries. It does not cost as much to deliver a hundred cartons of milk to one supermarket as it does to deliver ten cartons of milk to each of ten different neighborhood stores scattered around town. Economies in beer production include advertising. Although Anheuser-Busch spends millions of dollars a year advertising Budweiser and its other beers, its huge volume of sales means that its advertising cost per barrel of beer is less than that of its competitors Coors and Miller. Such savings add up, permitting larger enterprises to have either lower prices or larger profits, or both. Small retail stores have long had difficulty surviving in competition with large chain stores charging lower prices, whether A & P in the first half of the twentieth century, Sears in the second half, or Wal-Mart in the twenty-first century. The higher costs per unit in the smaller stores will not permit them to charge prices as low as the big chain stores' prices.

Advertising has sometimes been depicted as simply another cost added on to the cost of producing goods and services. However, in so far as advertising causes more of the advertised product to be sold, economies of scale can reduce production costs, so that the same product may cost less when it is advertised, rather than more. Advertising itself of course has costs, both in the financial sense and in the sense of using resources. But it is an empirical question, rather than a foregone conclusion, whether the costs of advertising are greater or less than the reductions of production costs made possible by the economies of scale which it promotes. This can obviously vary from one firm or industry to another.

Diseconomies of Scale

Economies of scale are only half the story. If economies of scale were the whole story, the question would then have to be asked: Why not produce cars in even more gigantic enterprises? If General Motors, Ford, and Chrysler all merged together, would they not be able to produce cars even more cheaply and thereby make more sales and profit than when they produce separately?

Probably not. There comes a point, in every business, beyond which the cost of producing a unit of output no longer declines as the amount of production increases. In fact, costs per unit actually rise after an enterprise becomes so huge that it is difficult to monitor and coordinate, when the right hand may not always know what the left hand is doing.* Back in the 1960s, when the American Telephone & Telegraph Company was the largest corporation in the world, its own chief executive officer put it this way: "A.T.

---

* A book of mine was reviewed in the *New York Times* on two consecutive days by two different people— one favorably and the other unfavorably— apparently because the weekly edition and the Sunday edition were under two different departments.

& T. is so big that, if you gave it a kick in the behind today, it would be two years before the head said 'ouch.'"

In a survey of banks around the world in 2006, *The Economist* magazine reported their tendency to keep growing larger and the implications of this for lower levels of efficiency:

> Management will find it harder and harder to aggregate and summarise everything that is going on in the bank, opening the way to the duplication of expense, the neglect of concealed risks and the failure of internal controls.

In other words, the risks inherent in banking may be well under control, as far as the top management is aware, but somewhere in their sprawling financial empire there may be transactions being made that expose the bank to risks that the top management is unaware of. Unknown to the top management at an international bank's New York headquarters, some bank official at a branch in Singapore may be making transactions that create not only financial risks but risks of criminal prosecution. This is not a problem peculiar to banks or to the United States. As a professor at the London Business School put it, some organizations have "reached a scale and complexity that made risk-management errors almost inevitable, while others had become so bureaucratic and top-heavy that they had lost the capacity to respond to changing market demands." Smaller rivals may be able to respond faster because their decision-makers do not have to go through so many layers of bureaucracy to get approval for their actions.

During General Motors' long tenure as the largest manufacturer of motor vehicles in the world, its cost of production per car was estimated to be hundreds of dollars more than the costs of Ford, Chrysler, or leading Japanese manufacturers. Problems associated with size can affect quality as well as price. Among hospitals, for example, surveys suggest that smaller and more specialized hospitals are usually safer for patients than large hospitals treating a wide range of maladies.

Economies of scale and diseconomies of scale can exist simultaneously in the same business at various levels of output. That is, there may be some things that a given company could do better if it were larger and other things that it could do better if it were smaller. As an entrepreneur in India put it, "What small companies give up in terms of financial clout, technological resources, and staying power, they gain in flexibility, lack of bureaucracy, and speed of decision making." People in charge of a company's operations in Calcutta may decide what needs to be done to improve business in that city but, if they then have to also convince the top management at the company's headquarters in New Delhi, their decisions cannot be put into operation as quickly, or perhaps as fully, and sometimes the people in New Delhi may not understand the situation in Calcutta well enough to approve a decision that makes sense to people who live there.

With increasing size, eventually the diseconomies begin to outweigh the economies, so it does not pay a firm to expand beyond that point. That is why industries usually consist of a number of firms, instead of one giant, super-efficient monopoly.

In the Soviet Union, where there was a fascination with economies of scale and a disregard of diseconomies of scale, both its industrial and agricultural enterprises were the largest in the world. The average Soviet farm, for example, was ten times the size of the average American farm and employed more than ten times as many workers. But Soviet farms were notoriously inefficient. Among the reasons for this inefficiency cited by Soviet economists was "deficient coordination." One example may illustrate a general problem:

> In the vast common fields, fleets of tractors fanned out to begin the plowing. Plan fulfillment was calculated on the basis of hectares worked, and so it was to the drivers' advantage to cover as much territory as quickly as possible. The drivers started by cutting deep furrows around the edge of the fields. As they moved deeper into the fields, however, they began to lift the blade of the plow and race the tractor, and the furrows became progressively shallower. The first furrows were nine to ten inches deep. A little farther from the road, they were five to six inches deep, and in the center of the field, where the tractor drivers were certain that no one would check on them, the furrows were as little as two inches deep. Usually, no one discovered that the furrows were so shallow in the middle of the field until it became obvious that something was wrong from the stunted nature of the crop.

Once again, counterproductive behavior from the standpoint of the economy was not irrational behavior from the standpoint of the person engaging in it. Clearly, the tractor drivers understood that their work could be more easily monitored at the edge of a field than in the center, and they adjusted the kind and quality of work they did accordingly, so as to maximize their own pay, based on how much land they plowed. By not plowing as deeply into the ground where they could not be easily monitored by farm officials, tractor drivers were able to go faster and cover more ground in a given amount of time, even if they covered it less effectively.

No such behavior would be likely by a farmer plowing his own land in a market economy, because his actions would be controlled by the incentive of profit, rather than by external monitors.

The point at which the disadvantages of size begin to outweigh the advantages differs from one industry to another. That is why restaurants are smaller than steel mills. A well-run restaurant usually requires the presence of an owner with sufficient incentives to continuously monitor the many things necessary for successful operation, in a field where failures are all too common. Not only must the food be prepared to suit the tastes of the restaurant's clientele, the waiters and waitresses must do their jobs in a way that encourages people to come back for another pleasant experience, and the furnishings of the restaurant must also be such as to meet the desires of the particular clientele that it serves.

These are not problems that can be solved once and for all. Food suppliers must be continuously monitored to see that they are still sending the kind and quality of produce, fish, meats, and other ingredients needed to satisfy the customers. Cooks and chefs must also be monitored to see that they are continuing to meet existing standards— as well as adding to their repertoires, as new foods and drinks become popular and old ones are ordered less often by the customers. The normal turnover of employees also requires the owner to be able to select, train, and monitor new people on an on-going basis. Moreover, changes outside the restaurant— in the kind of neighborhood around it, for example— can make or break its business. All these factors, and more, must be kept in mind, weighed by the owner and continuously adjusted to, if the business is to survive, much less be profitable.

Such a spectrum of details, requiring direct personal knowledge and control by someone on the scene and with incentives going beyond a fixed salary, limits the size of restaurants, as compared to the size of steel mills, automobile factories, or mining companies. Even where there are nationwide restaurant chains, often these are run by individual owners operating with franchises from some national organization that supplies such things as advertising and general guidance and standards, leaving the numerous on-site monitoring tasks to local owners. Howard Johnson pioneered in restaurant franchising in the 1930s, supplying half the capital, with the local manager supplying the other half. This gave the local franchisee a vested interest in the restaurant's profitability, rather than simply a fixed salary for his time.

Costs and Capacity

Costs vary not only with the volume of output, and to varying degrees from one industry to another, they also vary according to the extent to which existing capacity is being used.

In many industries and enterprises, capacity must be built to handle the peak volume— which means that there is excess capacity at other times. The cost of accommodating more users of the product or service during the times when there is excess capacity is much less than the cost of handling those who are served at peak times. A cruise ship, for example, must receive enough money from its passengers to cover not only such current costs as paying the crew, buying food and using fuel, it must also be able to pay such overhead costs as the purchase price of the ship and the expenses at the headquarters of the cruise line.

To handle twice as many passengers on a given cruise at the peak season may require buying another ship, as well as hiring another crew and buying twice as much food and fuel. However, if the number of passengers in the off season is only one-third of what it is at the peak, then a doubling of the number of off-season passengers need not require buying another ship. Existing ships can simply sail with fewer empty cabins. Therefore, it pays the cruise line to try to attract economy-minded passengers by offering much reduced fares during the off season. Groups of retired people, for example, can usually schedule their cruises at any time of the year, not being tied down to the vacation schedules of jobs and usually not having young children whose school schedules would limit their flexibility. It is common for seniors to get large discounts in off-season travel, both on land and at sea. Businesses in general can afford to do this because their costs are lower in the off season— and each particular business is forced to do it because its competitors will take customers away otherwise.

Excess capacity can also result from over-optimistic building. Because of what the *Wall Street Journal* called "an ill-timed building frenzy in luxury ships," luxury cruise lines added more than 4,000 new berths in a little over a year during the early twenty-first century. When they found that there was no such demand as to fill all the additional cabins at their existing prices, the net result was that Crystal Cruises, for example, offered their usual $2,995 cruise through the Panama Canal for $1,695 and Seabourn Cruise Line cut the price of its Caribbean cruise from $4,495 to $1,999. They would hardly have done this unless the pressures of competition left them no choice— and unless their incremental costs, when they had excess capacity, were lower than their reduced prices.

Unutilized capacity can cause price anomalies in many sectors of the economy. In Cancun, Mexico, the cheapest room available at the modest Best Western hotel there was $180 a night in mid-2001, while the more luxurious Ritz-Carlton nearby was renting rooms for $169 a night. The Best Western happened to be filled up and the Ritz-Carlton happened to have vacancies. Nor was this peculiar to Mexico. A four-star hotel in Manhattan was renting rooms for less than a two-star hotel nearby, and the posh Phoenician in Phoenix was renting rooms for less than the Holiday Inn in the same city.

Why were normally very expensive hotels renting rooms for less than hotels that were usually much lower in price? Again, the key was the utilization of capacity. Tourists going to popular resorts on limited budgets had made reservations at the low-cost hotels well in advance, in order to be sure of finding something affordable. This meant that fluctuations in the number of tourists would be absorbed by the higher-priced hotels. A general decline in tourism in 2001 thus led to vacancies at the luxury hotels, which then had no choice but to cut prices in order to attract more people to fill their rooms. Thus the luxurious Boca Raton Resort & Spa in Florida gave guests their third night free and tourists were able to get last-minute bargains on luxurious beachfront villas at Hilton Head, South Carolina, where reservations usually had to be made six months in advance.

Conversely, a rise in tourism would also have more effect on luxury hotels, which could raise their prices even more than usual. After three consecutive years of declining profits, hotels in 2004 began "yanking the discounts," as the *Wall Street Journal* put it, when increased travel brought more guests. The luxury hotels' reactions took the form of both price increases— $545 a night for the smallest and cheapest room at the Four Seasons Hotel in New York— and elimination of various free extras:

> It's already tougher this year for families to find the offers of free breakfasts and other perks that business hotels have been freely distributing for the past three years in an effort to fill empty beds.

Because prices can vary so widely for the same room in the same hotel, according to whether or not there is excess capacity, auxiliary businesses have been created to direct travelers where they can get the best deals on a given day— Priceline and Travelocity being examples of such businesses that have sprung up to match bargain-hunters with hotels that have unexpected vacancies.

Since all these responses to excess capacity are due to incentives created by the prospect of profits and the threat of losses in a market economy, the same principles do *not* apply where the government provides a good or service and charges for it. There are few incentives for government officials to match prices with costs— and sometimes they charge more to those who create the least cost.

When a bridge, for example, is built or its capacity is expanded, the costs created are essentially the cost of building the capacity to handle rush-hour traffic. The cars that drive across the bridge between the morning and evening rush hours cost almost nothing because the bridge has idle capacity during those hours. Yet, when tolls are charged, often there are books of tickets or electronic passes available at lower prices per trip than the prices charged to those who drive across the bridge only occasionally during off-peak hours.

Although it is the regular rush-hour users who create the huge costs of building or expanding a bridge's capacity, they pay less because it is they who are more numerous voters and whose greater stake in toll policies makes them more likely to react politically to toll charges. What may seem like economic folly can be political prudence on the part of politically appointed officials operating the bridges and trying to protect their own jobs. The net economic result is that there is more bridge traffic during rush hours than if different tolls reflected costs at different times of day. Higher rush hour tolls would provide incentives for some drivers to cross the bridge either earlier or later than the rush hours. In turn, that would mean that the amount of capacity required to handle rush hour traffic would be less, reducing costs in both money terms and in terms of the use of scarce resources which have alternative uses.

"Passing On" Costs and Savings

It is often said that businesses pass on whatever additional costs are placed on them, whether these costs are placed on them by higher taxes, rising fuel costs, raises for their employees under a new union contract, or a variety of other sources of higher costs. By the same token, whenever costs come down for some reason, whether because of a tax cut or a technological improvement, for example, the question is often raised as to whether these lower costs will be passed on in lower prices to the consumers.

The idea that sellers can charge whatever price they want is seldom expressed explicitly, but the implication that they can often lurks in the background of such questions as what they will pass on to their customers. But the passing on of either higher costs or savings in costs is not an automatic process and, in both cases, it depends on the kind of competition faced by each business and how many of the competing companies have the same cost increases or decreases.

If you are running a gold mining company in South Africa and the government there increases the tax on gold by $10 an ounce, you cannot pass that on in higher prices to buyers of gold in the world market because gold producers in other countries do not have to pay that extra $10. To buyers around the world, gold is gold, wherever it is produced. There is no way that these buyers are going to pay $10 an ounce more for your gold than for somebody else's gold. Under these circumstances, a $10 tax on your gold means that your profits on gold sales in the world market will simply decline by $10 an ounce.

The same principle applies when there are rising costs of transportation. If you ship your product to market by railroad and the railroads raise their freight charges, you can pass that on to the buyers only to the extent that your competitors also ship their product by rail. But, if your competitors are shipping by truck or by barge, while your location will not allow you to do the same, then raising your prices to cover the additional rail charges will simply allow your competitors, with lower costs, to take away some of your customers by charging lower prices. On the other hand, if all your competitors ship by rail and for similar distances, then all of you can pass on the higher railroad freight charges to all your customers. But if you ship your output an average of 100 miles and your competitors ship their output an average of only 10 miles, then you can only raise your prices to cover the additional cost of rail charges for 10 miles and take a reduction in profit by the cost of the other 90 miles.

Similar principles apply when it comes to passing on savings to customers. If you alone introduce a new technology that cuts your production costs in half, then you can keep all the additional profits resulting from these cost savings by continuing to charge what your higher-cost competitors are charging. Alternatively— and this is what has often happened— you can cut your prices and take customers away from your competitors, which can lead to even larger total profits, despite lowering your profits per unit sold. Many of the great American fortunes— by Rockefeller, Carnegie, and others— came from finding lower cost ways of producing and delivering the product to the customer, and then charging lower prices than their higher-cost competitors could meet, thus luring away their customers.

Over a period of time, competitors usually begin to use similar technological or organizational advances to cut costs and reduce prices, but fortunes can be made by pioneering innovators in the meantime. That provides incentives for enterprises in profit-seeking market economies to be on the lookout for new ways of doing things, in contrast to enterprises in either government-run economies like those in the days of the Soviet Union or in economies where laws protect private businesses from domestic or international competition, as in India before they began to open their economy to competition in the world market.

SPECIALIZATION AND DISTRIBUTION

A business firm is limited, not only in its over-all size, but also in the range of functions that it can perform efficiently. General Motors makes millions of automobiles, but not a single tire. Instead, it buys its tires from Goodyear, Michelin and other tire manufacturers, who can produce this part of the car more efficiently than General Motors can. Nor do automobile manufacturers own their own automobile dealerships across the country. Typically, automobile producers sell cars to local people who in turn sell to the public. There is no way that General Motors can keep track of all the local conditions across the length and breadth of the United States, which determine how much it will cost to buy or lease land on which to locate an automobile dealership, or which locations are best in a given community, much less evaluate the condition of local customers' used cars that are being traded in on new ones.

No one can sit in an automobile company's headquarters and decide how much trade-in value to allow on a particular Chevrolet in Seattle with some dents and scratches, or a particular used Honda in mint condition in Miami. And if the kind of salesmanship that works in Los Angeles does not work in Boston, those on the scene are likely to know that better than any automobile executive in Michigan can. In short, the automobile manufacturer specializes in manufacturing automobiles, leaving other functions to people who develop different knowledge and different skills needed to specialize in those particular functions.

Middlemen

The perennial desire to "eliminate the middleman" is perennially thwarted by economic reality. The range of human knowledge and expertise is limited for any given person or for any manageably-sized collection of administrators. Only a certain number of links in the great chain of production and distribution can be mastered and operated efficiently by the same set of people. Beyond some point, there are other people with different skills and experience who can perform the next step in the sequence more cheaply or more effectively— and, therefore, at that point it pays a firm to sell its output to some other businesses that can carry on the next part of the operation more efficiently. That is because, as we have noted in earlier chapters, *goods tend to flow to their most valued uses* in a free market, and goods are more valuable to those who can handle them more efficiently at a given stage. Furniture manufacturers usually do not own or operate furniture stores, and most authors do not do their own publishing, much less own their own bookstores.

Prices play a crucial role in all of this, as in other aspects of a market economy. Any economy must not only allocate scarce resources which have alternative uses, it must determine how long the resulting products remain in whose hands before being passed along to others who can handle the next stage more efficiently. Profit-seeking businesses are guided by their own bottom line, but this bottom line is itself determined by what others can do and at what cost.

When a product becomes more valuable in the hands of somebody else, that somebody else will bid more for the product than it is worth to its current owner. The owner then sells, not for the sake of the economy, but for the owner's own sake. However, the end result is a more efficient economy, where goods move to those who value them most. Despite superficially appealing phrases about "eliminating the middleman," middlemen continue to exist because they can do their phase of the operation more efficiently than others can. It should hardly be surprising that people who specialize in one phase can do that particular phase more efficiently than others.

Third World countries have tended to have more middlemen than more industrialized nations have, a fact much lamented by observers who have not considered the economics of the situation. Farm produce tends to pass through more hands between the African farmer who grows peanuts, for example, to the company that processes it into peanut butter than would be the case in the United States. A similar pattern was found with consumer goods moving in the opposite direction. Boxes of matches may pass through more hands between the manufacturer of matches and the African consumer who ultimately buys them. A British economist in mid-twentieth century West Africa described and explained such situations there:

West African agricultural exports are produced by tens of thousands of Africans operating on a very small scale and often widely dispersed. They almost entirely lack suitable storage facilities, and they have no, or only very small, cash reserves. . . The large number and the long line of intermediaries in the purchase of export produce essentially derive from the economies to be obtained from bulking very large numbers of small parcels. . . In produce marketing the first link in the chain may be the purchase, hundreds of miles from Kano, of a few pounds of groundnuts, which after several stages of bulking arrive there as part of a wagon or lorry load of several tons.

Instead of ten farmers in a given area all taking time off from their farming to carry their individually small amounts of produce to a distant town for sale, one middleman can collect the produce of the many farmers and drive it all to a produce buyer at one time, allowing these farmers to apply their scarce resources— time and labor— to the alternative uses of those resources for growing more produce. Society as a whole thus saves on the amount of resources required to move produce from the farm to the next buyer, as well as saving on the number of individual negotiations required at the final points of sale. This saving of time is especially important during the harvest season, when some of the crop may become over-ripe before it is picked or spoil afterwards if it is not picked promptly and then gotten into a storage or processing facility quickly.

In a wealthier country, each farm would have more produce, and motorized transport on modern highways would reduce the time required to get it to the next point of sale, so that the time lost per ton of crop would be less and fewer middlemen would be required to move it. Moreover, modern farmers in prosperous countries would be more likely to have their own storage facilities, harvesting machinery, and other aids. What is and is not efficient— either from the standpoint of the individual farmer or of society as a whole— depends on the circumstances. Since these circumstances can differ radically between rich and poor countries, very different methods may be efficient in each country and no given method need be right for both.

For similar reasons, there are often more intermediaries between the industrial manufacturer and the ultimate consumer in poor countries. However, the profits earned by each of these intermediaries is not just so much waste, as often assumed by third-party observers, especially observers from a different society. Here the limiting factor is the poverty of the consumer, which restricts how much can be bought at one time. Again, West Africa in the mid-twentieth century provided especially clear examples:

> Imported merchandise arrives in very large consignments and needs to be distributed over large areas to the final consumer who, in West Africa, has to buy in extremely small quantities because of his poverty. . . The organization of retail selling in Ibadan (and elsewhere) exemplifies the services rendered by petty traders both to suppliers and to consumers. Here there is no convenient central market, and it is usual to see petty traders sitting with their wares at the entrances to the stores of the European merchant firms. The petty traders sell largely the same commodities as the stores, but in much smaller quantities.

This might seem to be the ideal situation in which to "eliminate the middleman," since the petty traders were camped right outside stores selling the same merchandise, and the consumers could simply walk right on past them to buy the same goods inside at lower prices per unit. But these traders would sell in such tiny quantities as ten matches or half a cigarette, while it would be wasteful for people in the stores behind them to spend their time breaking down their packaged goods that much, in view of the better paying alternative uses of their labor and capital.

The alternatives available to the African petty traders were seldom as remunerative, so it made sense for these traders to do what it would not make sense for the European merchant to do. Moreover, it made sense for the very poor African consumer to buy from the local traders, even if the latter's additional profit raised the price of the commodity, because the consumer often could not afford to buy the commodity in the quantities sold by the European merchants.

Obvious as all this may seem, it has been misunderstood by renowned writers and— worse yet— by both colonial and post-colonial governments hostile to middlemen and prone to creating laws and policies expressing that hostility.

Socialist Economies

As in other cases, one of the best ways of understanding the role of prices, profits, and losses is to see what happens in their absence. Socialist economies not only lack the kinds of incentives which force individual enterprises toward efficiency and innovation, they also lack the kinds of financial incentives that lead each given producer in a capitalist economy to limit its work to those stages of production and distribution at which it has lower costs than alternative enterprises. Capitalist enterprises buy components from others who have lower costs in producing those particular components, and sell their own output to whatever middlemen can most efficiently carry out its distribution. But a socialist economy may forego these advantages of specialization— and for perfectly rational reasons, given the very different circumstances in which they operate.

In the Soviet Union, for example, many enterprises produced their own components, even though specialized producers of such components existed and could manufacture them at lower costs. Two Soviet economists estimated that the costs of components needed for a machine-building enterprise in the U.S.S.R. were two to three times as great as the costs of producing those same components in specialized enterprises. But why would cost matter to the individual enterprise making these decisions in a system where profits and losses were not decisive? What was decisive was fulfilling the monthly production quotas set by government authorities, and that could be assured most readily by an enterprise making its own components, since it could not depend on timely deliveries from other enterprises that lacked the profit-and-loss incentives of a supplier in a market economy.

This was not peculiar to machine-building enterprises. According to the same Soviet economists, "the idea of self-sufficiency in supply penetrates all the tiers of the economic administrative pyramid, from top to bottom." Just over half the bricks in the U.S.S.R. were produced by enterprises that were *not* set up for that purpose, but which made their own bricks in order to build whatever needed building to house their main economic activity. That was because these Soviet enterprises could not rely on deliveries from the Ministry of the Industry of Construction Materials, which had no financial incentives to be reliable in delivering bricks on time or of the quality required.

For similar reasons, far more Soviet enterprises were producing machine tools than were specifically set up to do so. Meanwhile, specialized plants set up for that purpose worked below their capacity— which is to say, at higher production costs per unit than if their overhead had been spread out over more units of output— because so many other enterprises were producing these machine tools for themselves. Capitalist producers of bricks or machine tools have no choice but to produce what is wanted by the customer, and to be reliable in delivering it, if they intend to keep those customers in competition with other producers of bricks or machine tools. That, however, is not the case when there is one nationwide monopoly of a particular product under government control, as was the situation in the Soviet Union.

In China's economy as well, when it was government-planned for decades after the Communists took over in 1949, many enterprises supplied their own transportation for the goods they produced, unlike most companies in the United States that pay trucking firms or rail or air freight carriers to transport their products. As the *Far Eastern Economic Review* put it: "Through decades of state-planned development, nearly all big Chinese firms transported their own goods, however inefficiently." Although theoretically firms specializing in transportation might operate more efficiently, the absence of financial incentives for a government monopoly enterprise to satisfy their customers made specialized transport enterprises too unreliable, both as to times of delivery and as to the care— or lack of care— when handling goods in transit. A company manufacturing television sets in China might not be as efficient in transporting those sets as a specialized transport enterprise would be, but at least they were less likely to damage their own TV sets by handling them roughly in transit.

One of the other side effects of unreliable deliveries has been that Chinese firms have had to keep more goods in inventory, foregoing the advantages of "just in time" delivery practices in Japan, which reduce the Japanese firms' costs of maintaining inventories. Dell Computers in the United States likewise operates with very small inventories, relative to their sales, but this is possible only because there are shipping firms like Federal Express or UPS that Dell can rely on to get components to them and computers to their customers quickly and safely.

The net result of habits and patterns of behavior left over from the days of a government-run economy is that China spends about twice as high a share of its national income on transportation as the United States does, even though the U.S. has a larger territory, including two states separated by more than a thousand miles from the other 48 states.

Contrasts in the size— and therefore costs— of inventories can be extreme from one country to another. Japan carries the smallest inventories, while the Soviet Union carried the largest, with the United States in between. As two Soviet economists pointed out:

> Spare parts are literally used right "off the truck": in Japan producers commonly deliver supplies to their ordering companies three to four times a day. At Toyota the volume of warehoused inventories is calculated for only an hour of work, while at Ford the inventories are for up to three weeks.

In the Soviet Union, these economists said, "we have in inventories almost as much as we create in a year." In other words, most of the people who work in Soviet industry "could take a year's paid vacation" and the economy could live on its inventories. This is not an advantage but a handicap because inventories cost money— and don't earn any. From the standpoint of the economy as a whole, the production of inventory uses up resources without adding anything to the standard of living of the public. As the Soviet economists put it, "our economy is always burdened by the heavy weight of inventories, much heavier than those that weigh on a capitalist economy during the most destructive recessions."

Yet the decisions to maintain huge inventories were not irrational decisions, given the circumstances of the Soviet economy and the incentives and constraints inherent in those circumstances. Soviet enterprises had no real choice but to maintain these costly inventories. The less reliable the suppliers, the more inventory it pays to keep, so as not to run out of vital components.* Nevertheless, inventories add to the costs of production, which add to the price, which in turn reduces the public's purchasing power and therefore its standard of living.

---

* Far from being excessive under the circumstances, inventories in the Soviet Union often proved to be inadequate, as manufacturing enterprises still ran out of components. According to Soviet economists, "a third of all cars come off the assembly line with parts missing." Shmelev and Popov, *The Turning Point*, p. 136.

Geography can also increase the amount of inventory required. As a result of severe geographical handicaps that limit transportation in parts of sub-Saharan Africa,* large inventories of both agricultural produce and industrial output have had to be maintained there because regions heavily dependent on rivers and streams for transportation can be cut off if those rivers and streams fall too low to be navigable because the rainy season is either delayed or ends prematurely. In short, geographic handicaps to land transportation and drastic differences in rainfall at different times of the year add huge inventory costs in sub-Saharan Africa, contributing to that region's painfully low standard of living. In Africa, as elsewhere, maintaining large inventories means using up scarce resources without a corresponding addition to the consumers' standard of living.

The reason General Motors can produce automobiles, without producing any tires to go on them, is because it can rely on Goodyear, Michelin, and whoever else supplies their tires to have those tires waiting to go on the cars as they move down off the production lines. If those suppliers failed to deliver, it would of course be a disaster for General Motors. But it would be even more catastrophic for the tire companies themselves. To leave General Motors high and dry, with no tires to go on its Cadillacs or Chevrolets, would be financially suicidal for a tire company, since it would lose a customer for millions of tires each year, quite aside from the billions of dollars in damages from lawsuits over breach of contract. Under these circumstances, it is hardly surprising that General Motors does not have to produce all its own components, as many Soviet enterprises did.

Absurd as it might seem to imagine Cadillacs rolling off the assembly lines and finding no tires to go on them, back in the days of the Soviet Union one of that country's own high officials complained that "hundreds of thousands of motor vehicles stand idle without tires." The fact that complex coordination takes place so seemingly automatically in one economic system that people hardly even think about it does not mean that coordination will be similarly automatic in another economic system

---

* See my *Conquests and Cultures,* pages 101–108.

operating on different principles.* Ironically, it is precisely where there is no one controlling the whole economy that it is automatically coordinated by price movements, while in deliberately planned economies a similar level of coordination has repeatedly turned out to be virtually impossible to achieve.

Reliability is an inherent accompaniment of the physical product when keeping customers is a matter of economic life and death under capitalism, whether at the manufacturing level or the retail level. Back in the early 1930s, when refrigerators were just beginning to become widely used in the United States, there were many technological and production problems with the first mass-produced refrigerators sold by Sears. The company had no choice but to honor its money-back guarantee by taking back 30,000 refrigerators, at a time when Sears could ill afford to do so, in the depths of the Great Depression, when businesses were as short of money as their customers were. This situation put enormous financial pressure on Sears to either stop selling refrigerators (which is what some of its executives and many of its store managers wanted) or else greatly improve their reliability. What they eventually did was improve the reliability of their refrigerators, thereby becoming one of the leading sellers of refrigerators in the country.

---

* This is not to say that there are *never* component suppliers who fail to deliver in a market economy. Planes costing hundreds of millions of dollars can sit idle after being built, waiting for a cooking galley, a toilet or some other component to arrive from another company before it can be sold. As one Boeing official put it, "You have a huge asset that's not moving, waiting on a galley." An Airbus executive said, "The issue can even escalate to the point that I have to go and ask, 'What the hell's going on?'" Such a question from a company that is buying millions of dollars' worth of a component supplier's output is more than an exercise in rhetoric. In short, human beings have the same shortcomings in all economic systems but the difference is in the pressures that can be brought to bear to force corrections. Daniel Michaels and J. Lynn Lunsford, "Lack of Seats, Galleys Delays Boeing, Airbus," *Wall Street Journal*, August 8, 2008, pp. B1, B4.

Chapter 7

THE ECONOMICS OF
BIG BUSINESS

*Competition always has been and always will be
troublesome to those who have to meet it.*

Frédéric Bastiat

B ig businesses can be big in different ways. They can be big absolutely,
like Wal-Mart— with billions of dollars in sales annually, making it the
biggest business in the nation— without selling more than a modest
percentage of the total merchandise in its industry as a whole. Other
businesses can be big in the sense of making a high percentage of all the
sales in their industries, as Microsoft does with sales of operating systems for
personal computers around the world. There are major economic differences
between bigness in these two senses. An absolute monopoly in one industry
may be smaller in size than a much larger company in another industry
where there are numerous competitors.

The incentives and constraints in a competitive market are quite different
from those in a market where one company enjoys a monopoly, and such
differences lead to different behavior with different consequences for the
economy as a whole. Markets controlled by monopolies, oligopolies or
cartels require a separate analysis. But, before turning to such analysis, let us
consider big businesses in general, whether big absolutely or big relative to
the market for their industry's products. One of the general characteristics
of big businesses has already been noted in Chapter 6— economies of scale

and diseconomies of scale, which together determine the actual scale of production of companies that are likely to survive and prosper in a given industry. Another of the general characteristics of big businesses is that they typically take the form of a corporation, rather than being owned by a given individual, family, or partnership. The reasons for this particular kind of organization and its consequences require examination.

CORPORATIONS

Corporations are not all businesses. The first corporation in America was the Harvard Corporation, formed in the seventeenth century to govern America's first college. Corporations are different from enterprises owned by individuals, families or partners. In these other kinds of enterprises, the owners are personally responsible for all the financial obligations of the organization. If such organizations do not happen to have enough money on hand to pay their bills or to pay any damages resulting from lawsuits, a court can order the seizure of the bank accounts or other personal property of those who own the enterprise. A corporation, however, has a separate legal identity, so that the individual owners of the corporation are not personally liable for its financial obligations. The corporation's legal liability is limited to its own corporate assets— hence the abbreviation "Ltd." (for limited liability) after the names of British corporations, serving the same purpose as "Inc." (incorporated) after the names of American corporations.

This limited liability is more than a convenient privilege for corporate stockholders. It has major implications for the economy as a whole. Huge companies, doing billions of dollars' worth of business annually, can seldom be created or maintained by money from a few rich investors. There are not nearly enough rich people for that to happen, and even those who are rich would seldom risk their entire fortune in one enterprise. Instead, gigantic corporations are usually owned by thousands, or even millions, of stockholders. These include not only people who directly own shares of corporate stocks, but also many other people who may never think of themselves as stockholders, but whose money paid into pension funds has been used by those funds to purchase corporate stock. Directly or indirectly, about half of the American population are investors in corporate stocks.

Like many other things, the significance of limited legal liability can be understood most easily by seeing what happens in its absence. Back during the First World War, Herbert Hoover organized a philanthropic enterprise to buy and distribute food to vast numbers of people who were suffering hunger and starvation across the continent of Europe, as a result of blockades and disruptions growing out of the military conflict. A banker whom he had recruited to help him in this enterprise asked Hoover if this was a limited liability organization. When Hoover said that it was not, the banker resigned immediately because, otherwise, his life's savings could be wiped out if the organization did not receive enough donations from the public to pay for all the millions of dollars' worth of food that it would buy to feed all the hungry people across Europe.

The importance of limited liability to those particular individuals creating or investing in corporations is obvious. But the limited liability of stockholders is of even greater importance to the larger society, including people who do not own any corporate stock nor have any other affiliation with a corporation. What limited liability does for the economy and for the society as a whole is to permit many gigantic economic activities to be undertaken that would be too large to be financed by a given individual, and too risky to invest in by large numbers of individuals, if each investor became liable for the debts of an enterprise that is too large for all its stockholders to monitor its performance closely.

The economies of scale, and the lower prices which large corporations can achieve as a result, and the correspondingly higher standards of living resulting from these economies of scale, enable vast numbers of consumers to be able to afford many goods and services that could otherwise be beyond their financial means. In short, the significance of the corporation in the economy at large extends far beyond those people who own, manage, or work for corporations.

What of creditors, who can collect the debts that corporations owe them only to the extent of the corporation's own assets, and who cannot recover any losses beyond that from those who own the corporation? The "Ltd." or

"Inc." after a corporation's name warns creditors in advance, so that they can limit their lending accordingly and charge interest rates adjusted to the risk.

Corporate Governance

Unlike other kinds of businesses, where those who own the enterprise also manage it, a major corporation has far too many stockholders for them to be able to direct its operations. Executives are put in charge of corporate management, hired and if need be fired by a board of directors who hold the ultimate authority in a corporation. This arrangement applies beyond business enterprises. Colleges and universities are usually also managed by administrators who are hired and fired by a board of trustees, who hold the ultimate legal authority but who do not manage day-to-day operations in the classrooms or in academic administration.

Like limited liability, the separation of ownership and management is a key characteristic of corporations. It is also a key target of critics of corporations. Many have argued that a "separation of ownership and control" permits corporate managements to run these enterprises in their own interests, at the expense of the interests of the stockholders. Certainly the massive and highly publicized corporate scandals of the early twenty-first century confirm the potential for fraud and abuse. However, since fraud and abuse have also occurred in non-corporate enterprises, including both democratic and totalitarian governments, as well as in the United Nations and in non-profit charities, it is not clear whether the limited liability corporation is any more prone to such things than other kinds of organizations, or any less subject to the detection and punishment of those who commit crimes.

Complaints about the separation of ownership and control often overlook the fact that owners of a corporation's stock do not necessarily *want* the time-consuming responsibilities that go with control. Many people want the rewards of investing without the headaches of managing. This is especially obvious in the case of large stockholders, whose investments would be sufficient for them to start their own businesses, if they wanted management responsibilities. The corporate form enables those who simply want to invest their money, without taking on the burdens of running a business, to have institutions which permit them to do that, leaving the task of monitoring the honesty of existing management to regulatory and law enforcement institutions, and the monitoring of management efficiency to the competition of the marketplace.

Outside investment specialists are always on the lookout for companies whose management efficiency they expect to be able to improve by buying enough stock to take over these corporations and run them differently. This threat has been sufficiently felt by many managements to get them to lobby state governments to pass laws impeding this process. But these outside investors have both the incentives and the expertise available to evaluate a corporation's efficiency better than most of the rank-and-file stockholders can.

Complaints that corporations are "undemocratic" miss the point that stockholders may not want them to be democratic and neither may consumers, despite the efforts of people who call themselves "consumer advocates" to promote laws that would force corporations to cede management controls to either stockholders or to outsiders who proclaim themselves representatives of the public interest. The very reason for the existence of any business enterprise is that those who run such enterprises know how to perform the functions necessary to the organization's survival and well-being better than outsiders with no financial stake— and with no expertise being required for calling themselves "consumer advocates" or "public interest" organizations. Significantly, attempts by various activists to create greater stockholder input into such things as the compensation of chief executive officers have been opposed by mutual funds holding corporate stock. These mutual funds do not want their huge investments in corporations jeopardized by people whose track record, skills and agendas are unlikely to serve the purposes of corporations.

The economic fate of a corporation, like that of other business enterprises, is ultimately controlled by innumerable individual consumers. But most consumers may be no more interested in taking on management responsibility than stockholders are. Nor is it enough that those consumers who don't want to be bothered don't have to be. The very existence of enhanced powers for non-management individuals to have a say in the running of a corporation would force other consumers and stockholders to either take time to represent their own views and interests in this process or risk having people with other agendas over-ride their interests and interfere with the management of the enterprise, without these outsiders having to pay any price for being wrong.

Different countries have different laws regarding the legal rights of corporate stockholders— and very different results. According to a professor of law who has specialized in the study of business organizations, writing in the *Wall Street Journal*:

> American corporate law severely limits shareholders' rights. So does Japanese, German and French corporate law. In contrast, the United Kingdom seems a paradise for shareholders. In the U.K., shareholders can call a meeting to remove the board of directors at any time. They can pass resolutions telling boards to take certain actions, they are entitled to vote on dividends and CEO pay, and they can force a board to accept a hostile takeover bid the board would prefer to reject.

How does the economic performance of British corporations compare with that of corporations in other countries? According to the British magazine *The Economist*, 13 of the world's 30 largest corporations are American, 6 are Japanese, and 3 each are German and French. Only one is British and another is half owned by Britons. Even a small country like the Netherlands has a larger share of the world's largest corporations. Whatever the psychic benefits of stockholder participation in corporate decisions in Britain, its track record of business benefits is unimpressive.

Questions about the role of corporations, as such, are very different from questions about what particular corporations do in particular circumstances. The people who manage corporations run the gamut, from the wisest to the most foolish and from the most honest to the most dishonest, as do people in other institutions and activities— including people who choose to call themselves "consumer advocates" or members of "public interest" organizations or advocates of "shareholder democracy."

Executive Compensation

The average compensation package of chief executive officers of corporations large enough to be listed in the Standard & Poor's Index was $10 million a year in 2010. While that is much more than most people make, it is also much less than is made by any number of professional athletes and entertainers, not to mention financiers.

Some critics have claimed that corporate executives, and especially chief executive officers (CEOs), have been overly generously rewarded by boards of directors carelessly spending the stockholders' money. However, this belief can be tested by comparing the pay of CEOs of public corporations, owned by many stockholders, with the pay of CEOs of corporations owned by a small number of large financial institutions. In the latter case, financiers with their own money at stake set the salaries of CEOs— and it is precisely these kinds of corporations which set the highest salaries for CEOs. Since it is their own money, financiers have no incentive to over-pay, but neither do they have any reason to be penny-wise and pound-foolish when hiring someone to manage a corporation in which they have billions of dollars at stake. Nor do they need to fear the adverse reactions of numerous stockholders who may be susceptible to complaints in the media that corporate executives are paid too much.

What has provoked special outcries are the severance packages in the millions of dollars for executives who are let go because of their own failures. However, no one finds it strange that some divorces cost much more than the original wedding cost or that one spouse or the other can end up being rewarded for being impossible to live with. In the corporate world, it is especially important to end a relationship quickly, even at a cost of millions of dollars for a "golden parachute," because keeping a failing CEO on can cost a company billions through the bad decisions that the CEO can continue to make. Delays over the firing of a CEO, whether these are delays within the company or within the courts, can easily cost far more than the golden parachute.

MONOPOLIES AND CARTELS

Although much of the discussion in previous chapters has been about the way free competitive markets function, competitive free markets are not the only kinds of markets, nor are government-imposed price controls or central planning the only interferences with the operations of such markets.

Monopolies, oligopolies, and cartels also produce economic results very different from those of a free market.

A monopoly means literally one seller. However, a small number of sellers— an "oligopoly," as economists call it— may cooperate with one another, either explicitly or tacitly, in setting prices and so produce results similar to those of a monopoly. Where there is a formal organization in an industry to set prices and output— a cartel— its results can also be somewhat like those of a monopoly, even though there may be numerous sellers in the cartel. Although these various kinds of non-competitive industries differ among themselves, their generally detrimental effects have led to laws and government policies designed to prevent or counter these negative effects. Sometimes this government intervention takes the form of direct regulation of the prices and policies of non-competing firms in industries where there is little or no competition. In other cases, government prohibits particular practices without attempting to micro-manage the companies involved. The first and most fundamental question, however, is: How are monopolistic firms detrimental to the economy?

Sometimes one company produces the total output of a given good or service in a region or a country. For many years, each local telephone company in the United States was a monopoly in its region of the country and that remains true in some other countries. For about half a century before World War II, the Aluminum Company of America (Alcoa) produced all the virgin ingot aluminum in the United States. Such situations are unusual, but they are important enough to deserve some serious attention.

Most big businesses are not monopolies and not all monopolies are big business. In the days before the automobile and the railroad, a general store in an isolated rural community could easily be the only store for miles around, and was as much of a monopoly as any corporation on the *Fortune* 500 list, even though the general store was usually an enterprise of very modest size. Conversely, today even multi-billion-dollar nationwide grocery chains like Safeway or Kroger have too many competitors to be able to set prices on the goods they sell the way a monopolist would set prices on those goods.

Monopoly Prices vs. Competitive Prices

Just as we can understand the function of prices better after we have seen what happens when prices are not allowed to function freely, so we can understand the role of competition in the economy better after we contrast what happens in competitive markets with what happens in markets that are not competitive.

Take something as simple as apple juice. How do consumers know that the price they are being charged for apple juice is not far above the cost of producing it and distributing it, including a return on investment sufficient to keep those investments being made? After all, most people do not grow apples, much less process them into juice and then bottle the juice, transport and store it, so they have no idea how much any or all of this costs. Competition in the marketplace makes it unnecessary to know. Those few people who do know such things, and who are in the business of making investments, have every incentive to invest wherever there are higher rates of return and to reduce their investments where the rates of return are lower or negative. If the price of apple juice is higher than necessary to compensate for the costs incurred in producing it, then higher rates of profit will be made— and will attract ever more investment into this industry until the competition of additional producers drives prices down to a level that just compensates the costs with the same average rate of return on similar investments available elsewhere in the economy.

Only then will the in-flow of investments from other sectors of the economy stop, with the incentives for these in-flows now being gone. If, however, there were a monopoly in producing apple juice, the situation would be very different. Chances are that monopoly prices would remain at levels higher than necessary to compensate for the costs and efforts that go into producing apple juice, including paying a rate of return on capital sufficient to attract the capital required. The monopolist would earn a rate of return higher than necessary to attract the capital required. But with no competing company to produce competing output to drive down prices, the monopolist could continue to make profits above and beyond what is necessary to attract investment.

Many people object to the fact that a monopolist can charge higher prices than a competitive business could. But the ability to transfer money from other members of the society to itself is not the sole harm done by a monopoly. From the standpoint of the economy as a whole, these internal transfers do not change the total wealth of the society, even though such transfers redistribute wealth in a manner that may be considered objectionable. What adversely affects the total wealth in the economy as a whole is the effect of a monopoly on the allocation of scarce resources which have alternative uses.

When a monopoly charges a higher price than it could charge if it had competition, consumers tend to buy less of the product than they would at a lower competitive price. In short, a monopolist produces less output than a competitive industry would produce with the same available resources, technology and cost conditions. The monopolist stops short at a point where consumers are still willing to pay enough to cover the cost of production (including a normal rate of profit) of more output.

In terms of the allocation of resources which have alternative uses, the net result is that some resources which could have been used to produce more apple juice instead go into producing other things elsewhere in the economy, even if those other things are not as valuable as the apple juice that could and would have been produced in a free competitive market. In short, the economy's resources are used inefficiently when there is monopoly, because these resources would be transferred from more valued uses to less valued uses.

Fortunately, monopolies are very hard to maintain without laws to protect the monopolistic firms from competition. The ceaseless search of investors for the highest rates of return virtually ensures that such investments will flood into whatever segment of the economy is earning higher profits, until the rate of profit in that segment is driven down by the increased competition caused by that flood of investment. It is like water seeking its own level. But, just as dams can prevent water from finding its own level, so government intervention can prevent a monopoly's profit rate from being reduced by competition.

In centuries past, government permission was required to open businesses in many parts of the economy, especially in Europe and Asia, and monopoly rights were granted to various business owners, who either paid the government directly for these rights or bribed officials who had the power to grant such rights, or both. However, by the end of the eighteenth century, the development of economics had reached the point where increasingly large numbers of people understood how this was detrimental to society as a whole and counter-pressures developed toward freeing the economy from monopolies and government control. Monopolies have therefore become much rarer, at least at the national level, though restrictions on competition remain common in many cities where restrictive licensing laws limit how many taxis are allowed to operate, causing fares to be artificially higher than necessary and cabs less available than they would be in a free market.

Again, the loss is not simply that of the individual consumers. The economy as a whole loses when people who are perfectly willing to drive taxis at fares that consumers are willing to pay are nevertheless prevented from doing so by artificial restrictions on the number of taxi licenses issued, and thus either do some other work of lesser value or remain unemployed. If the alternative work were of greater value, and were compensated accordingly, then such people would never have been potential taxi drivers in the first place.

From the standpoint of the economy as a whole, monopolistic pricing means that consumers of a monopolist's product are foregoing the use of scarce resources which would have a higher value to them than in alternative uses. That is the inefficiency which causes the economy as a whole to have less wealth under monopoly than it would have under free competition. It is sometimes said that a monopolist "restricts output," but this is not the intent, nor is the monopolist the one who restricts output. The monopolist would love to have the consumers buy more at its inflated price, but the consumers stop short of the amount that they would buy at a lower price under free competition. It is the monopolist's higher price which causes the consumers to restrict their own purchases and therefore causes the monopolist to restrict production to what can be sold. But the monopolist may be advertising heavily to try to persuade consumers to buy more.

Similar principles apply to a cartel— that is, a group of businesses which agree among themselves to charge higher prices or otherwise avoid competing with one another. In theory, a cartel could operate collectively the same as a monopoly. In practice, however, individual members of cartels tend to cheat on one another secretly— lowering the cartel price to some customers, in order to take business away from other members of the cartel.

When this practice becomes widespread, the cartel becomes irrelevant, whether or not it formally ceases to exist.

When railroads were formed in the nineteenth century, they often had competing lines between major cities, such as Chicago and New York. These were called "trunk lines," as distinguished from "branch lines" leading from the trunk lines to smaller communities that might be served by only one railroad each. This led to monopoly prices on the branch lines and prices so competitive on the trunk lines that the cost of shipping freight a long distance on a trunk line was often cheaper than shipping it a shorter distance on a branch line. More important, from the railroads' point of view, the trunk line prices were so low as to jeopardize profits. In order to deal with this problem, the railroads got together to form a cartel:

> These cartels kept breaking down. . . The cost of sending a train from here to there is largely independent of how much freight it carries. Therefore, above a break-even point, each additional ton of freight yields nearly pure profit. Sooner or later, the temptation to offer secret rebates to shippers in order to capture this profitable-at-any-price traffic would become irresistible. Once the secret rebates started, price wars soon followed and the cartel would collapse.

For very similar reasons, the steamboat companies had attempted to form a cartel before the railroads did— and for similar reasons those cartels collapsed, as many other cartels have since then. A successful cartel requires not only an agreement among the companies involved but also some method by which they can check up on each other, to make sure all the cartel members are living up to the agreement, and also some way to prevent competition from other companies outside the cartel. All these things are easier said than done. One of the most successful cartels, that in the American steel industry, was based on a pricing system that made it easy for the companies to check up on one another,* but that system was eventually outlawed by the courts under the anti-trust laws.

---

* This was a system where all steel prices in the United States were based on the fixed price of steel plus the cost of shipping it by rail from Pittsburgh— regardless of whether the steel was actually produced in Pittsburgh, Birmingham or anywhere else, and regardless of whether it was shipped by rail, barge or by other means. Otherwise, it would be easy for individual steel producers to hide price reductions

Governmental and Market Responses

Because some kinds of huge business organizations were once known as "trusts," legislation designed to outlaw monopolies and cartels became known as "anti-trust laws." However, such laws are not the only way of fighting monopolies and cartels. Private businesses that are not part of the cartel have incentives to fight them in the marketplace. Moreover, private businesses can take action much faster than the years required for the government to bring a major anti-trust case to a successful conclusion.

Back in the heyday of American trusts, Montgomery Ward was one of their biggest opponents. Whether the trust involved agricultural machinery, bicycles, sugar, nails or twine, Montgomery Ward would seek out manufacturers that were not part of the trust and buy from them below the cartel price, reselling to the general public below the retail price of the goods produced by members of the cartel. Since Montgomery Ward was the number one retailer in the country at that time, it was also big enough to set up its own factories and make the product itself, if need be. The later rise of other huge retailers like Sears and the A & P grocery chain likewise confronted the big producers with corporate giants able to either produce their own competing products to sell in their own stores or able to buy enough from some small enterprise outside the cartel, enabling that enterprise to grow into a big competitor.

Sears did both. It produced stoves, shoes, guns, and wallpaper, among other things, in addition to subcontracting the production of other products. A & P imported and roasted its own coffee, canned its own salmon, and baked half a billion loaves of bread a year for sale in its stores. While giant firms like Sears, Montgomery Ward and A & P were unique in being able

---

in the large and variable freight charges for shipping a heavy product like steel from different places by different modes of transportation, making it far more difficult to tell who was undercutting the price agreed to by the cartel. But, under the cartel's pricing system, it was easy to tell what the total delivered cost of steel— price plus rail shipment cost from Pittsburgh— should be at any point in the country, regardless of where it was produced or how it was shipped. From the standpoint of the economy, however, this system led to a misallocation of resources, since someone located near Birmingham would just as soon buy steel produced in Pittsburgh as in Birmingham, since they had to pay the same price plus the same rail freight cost from Pittsburgh, either way. This meant that far more steel was transported greater distances than would have been the case in a free, competitive market.

to compete against a number of cartels simultaneously, smaller companies could also take away sales from cartels in their respective industries. Their incentive was the same as that of the cartel— profit. Where a monopoly or cartel maintains prices that produce higher than normal profits, other businesses are attracted to the industry. This additional competition then tends to force prices and profits down. In order for a monopoly or cartel to continue to succeed in maintaining profits above the competitive level, it must find ways to prevent others from entering the industry.

One way to keep out potential competitors is to have the government make it illegal for others to operate in particular industries. Kings granted or sold monopoly rights for centuries, and modern governments have restricted the issuance of licenses for various industries and occupations, ranging from airlines to trucking to the braiding of hair. Political rationales are never lacking for these restrictions, but their net economic effect is to protect existing enterprises from additional potential competitors and therefore to maintain prices at artificially high levels.

For much of the late twentieth century, the government of India not only decided which companies it would license to produce which products, it imposed limits on how much each company could produce. Thus an Indian manufacturer of scooters was hauled before a government commission because he had produced more scooters than he was allowed to and a producer of medicine for colds was fearful that the public had bought "too much" of his product during a flu epidemic in India. Lawyers for the cold medicine manufacturer spent months preparing a legal defense for having produced and sold more than they were allowed to, in case they were called before the same commission. All this costly legal work had to be paid for by someone and that someone was ultimately the consumer.

In the absence of government prohibition against entry into particular industries, various clever schemes can be used privately to try to erect barriers to keep out competitors and protect monopoly profits. But other businesses have incentives to be just as clever at circumventing these barriers. Accordingly, the effectiveness of barriers to entry has varied from industry to industry and from one era to another in the same industry. The computer industry was once difficult to enter, back in the days when a computer was a huge machine taking up thousands of cubic feet of space, and the cost of manufacturing such machines was likewise huge. But the development of microchips meant that smaller computers could do the same work and chips were now inexpensive enough to produce that they could be manufactured by smaller companies. These include companies located around the world, so that even a nationwide monopoly does not preclude competition in an industry. Although the United States pioneered in the creation of computers, the actual manufacturing of computers spread quickly to East Asia, which supplied much of the American market with computers, even when those computers carried American brand names.

Chapter 8

REGULATION AND
ANTI-TRUST LAWS

*Competition is not easily suppressed even when there are
only a few independent firms. . . competition is a tough
weed, not a delicate flower.*

George J. Stigler

In the late nineteenth century, the American government began to
respond to monopolies and cartels by both directly regulating the prices
which monopolies and cartels were allowed to charge and by taking punitive
legal action against these monopolies and cartels under the Sherman Anti-
Trust Act of 1890 and other later anti-trust legislation. Complaints about
the high prices charged by railroads in places where they had a monopoly
led to the creation of the Interstate Commerce Commission in 1887, the
first of many federal regulatory commissions created to control the prices
charged by monopolists.

During the era when local telephone companies were monopolies in their
respective regions and their parent company— the American Telephone and
Telegraph Company— had a monopoly of long-distance service, the Federal
Communications Commission controlled the prices charged by A.T.&T.,
while state regulatory agencies controlled the price of local phone service.
Another approach has been to pass laws against the creation or maintenance
of a monopoly or against various practices, such as price discrimination,
growing out of non-competitive markets. These anti-trust laws were
intended to allow businesses to operate without the kinds of detailed

government supervision which exist under regulatory commissions, but with a sort of general surveillance, like that of traffic police, with intervention occurring only when there are specific violations of laws.

REGULATORY COMMISSIONS

Although the functions of a regulatory commission are fairly straightforward in theory, in practice its task is far more complex and, in some respects, impossible. Moreover, the political climate in which regulatory commissions operate often leads to policies and results directly the opposite of what was expected by those who created such commissions.

Ideally, a regulatory commission would set prices where they would have been if there were a competitive marketplace. In practice, there is no way to know what those prices would be. Only the actual functioning of a market itself could reveal such prices, with the less efficient firms being eliminated by bankruptcy and only the most efficient surviving, and their lower prices now being the market prices. No outside observers can know what the most efficient ways of operating a given firm or industry are. Indeed, many managements within an industry discover the hard way that what they thought was the most efficient way to do things was not efficient enough to meet the competition, and have ended up losing customers as a result. The most that a regulatory agency can do is accept what appear to be reasonable production costs and allow the monopoly to make what seems to be a reasonable profit over and above such costs.

Determining the cost of production is by no means always easy. As noted in Chapter 6, there may be no such thing as "the" cost of production. The cost of generating electricity, for example, can vary enormously, depending on when and where it is generated. When you wake up in the middle of the night and turn on a light, that electricity costs practically nothing to supply, because the electricity-generating system must be kept operating around the clock, so it has much unused capacity in the middle of the night, when most people are asleep. But, when you turn on your air conditioner on a hot summer afternoon, when millions of other homes and offices already have their air conditioners on, that may help strain the system to its limit and necessitate turning on costly standby generators, in order to avoid blackouts.

It has been estimated that the cost of supplying the electricity required to run a dishwasher, for example, at a time of peak electricity usage, can be 100 times greater than the cost of running that same dishwasher at a time when there is a low demand for electricity. Turning on your dishwasher in the middle of the night, like turning on a light in the middle of the night, costs the electricity-generating system practically nothing, since the electricity has to be generated around the clock in any case.

There are many reasons why additional electricity, beyond the usual capacity of the system, may be many times more costly per kilowatt hour than the usual costs when the system is functioning within its usual capacity. The main system that supplies vast numbers of consumers can make use of economies of scale to produce electricity at its lowest cost, while standby generators typically produce less electricity and therefore cannot take full advantage of economies of scale, but must produce at higher costs per kilowatt hour. Sometimes technological progress gives the main system lower costs, while obsolete equipment is kept as standby equipment, rather than being junked, and the costs of producing additional electricity with this obsolete equipment is of course higher. Where additional electricity has to be purchased from outside sources when the local generating capacity is at its limit, the additional cost of transmitting that electricity from greater distances raises the cost of the additional electricity to much higher levels than the cost of electricity generated closer to the consumers.

More variations in "the" cost of producing electricity come from fluctuations in the costs of the various fuels— oil, gas, coal, nuclear— used to run the generators. Since all these fuels are used for other things besides generating electricity, the fluctuating demand for these fuels from other industries, or for use in homes or automobiles, makes their prices unpredictable. Hydroelectric dams likewise vary in how much electricity they can produce when rainfall varies, increasing or reducing the amount of water that flows through the generators. When the fixed costs of the dam are spread over differing amounts of electricity, the cost per kilowatt hour varies accordingly.

How is a regulatory commission to set the rates to be charged consumers of electricity, given that the cost of generating electricity can vary so widely and unpredictably? If state regulatory commissions set electricity rates based on "average" costs of generating electricity, then when there is a higher demand or a shorter supply within the state, out-of-state suppliers may be unwilling to sell electricity at prices lower than their own costs of generating the additional electricity from standby units. This was part of the reason for the much-publicized blackouts in California in 2001. "Average" costs are irrelevant when the costs of generation are far above average at a particular time or far below average at other times.

Because the public is unlikely to be familiar with all the economic complications involved, they are likely to be outraged at having to pay electricity rates far higher than they are used to. In turn, this means that politicians are tempted to step in and impose price controls based on the old rates. And, as already noted in other contexts, price controls create shortages— in this case, shortages of electricity that result in blackouts. A larger quantity demanded and a smaller quantity supplied has been a very familiar response to price controls, going back in history long before electricity came into use. However, politicians' success does not depend on their learning the lessons of history or of economics. It depends far more on their going along with what is widely believed by the public and the media, which may include conspiracy theories or belief that higher prices are due to "greed" or "gouging."

Halfway around the world, attempts to raise electricity rates in India were met by street demonstrations, as they were in California. In the Indian state of Karnataka, controlled politically by India's Congress Party at the time, efforts to change electricity rates were opposed in the streets by one of the opposition parties. However, in the neighboring state of Andhra Pradesh, where the Congress Party was in the opposition, it led similar street demonstrations against electricity rate increases. In short, what was involved in these demonstrations was neither ideology nor party but an opportunistic playing to the gallery of public misconceptions.

The economic complexities involved when regulatory agencies set prices are compounded by political complexities. Regulatory agencies are often set up after some political crusaders have successfully launched investigations or

publicity campaigns that convince the authorities to establish a permanent
commission to oversee and control a monopoly or some group of firms few
enough in number to be a threat to behave in collusion as if they were one
monopoly. However, after a commission has been set up and its powers
established, crusaders and the media tend to lose interest over the years and
turn their attention to other things. Meanwhile, the firms being regulated
continue to take a keen interest in the activities of the commission and to
lobby the government for favorable regulations and favorable appointments
of individuals to these commissions.

The net result of these asymmetrical outside interests on these agencies is
that commissions set up to keep a given firm or industry within bounds, for
the benefit of the consumers, often metamorphose into agencies seeking to
protect the existing regulated firms from threats arising from new firms with
new technology or new organizational methods. Thus, in the United States,
the Interstate Commerce Commission— initially created to keep railroads
from charging monopoly prices to the public— responded to the rise of the
trucking industry, whose competition in carrying freight threatened the
economic viability of the railroads, by extending the commission's control to
include trucking.

The original rationale for regulating railroads was that these railroads
were often monopolies in particular areas of the country, where there was
only one rail line. But now that trucking undermined that monopoly, by
being able to go wherever there were roads, the response of the I.C.C. was
not to say that the need for regulating transportation was now less urgent or
perhaps even unnecessary. Instead, it sought— and received from
Congress— broader authority under the Motor Carrier Act of 1935, in
order to restrict the activities of truckers. This allowed railroads to survive
under the new economic conditions, despite truck competition that was
more efficient for various kinds of freight hauling and could therefore often
charge lower prices than the railroads charged. Trucks were now permitted
to operate across state lines only if they had a certificate from the Interstate
Commerce Commission declaring that the trucks' activities served "public
convenience and necessity" as defined by the I.C.C. This kept truckers from

driving railroads into bankruptcy by taking away as many of their customers as they could have in an unregulated market.

In short, freight was no longer being hauled in whatever way required the use of the least resources, as it would be under open competition, but only by whatever way met the arbitrary requirements of the Interstate Commerce Commission. The I.C.C. might, for example, authorize a particular trucking company to haul freight from New York to Washington, but not from Philadelphia to Baltimore, even though these cities are on the way. If the certificate did not authorize freight to be carried back from Washington to New York, then the trucks would have to return empty, while other trucks carried freight from D.C. to New York.

From the standpoint of the economy as a whole, enormously greater costs were incurred than were necessary to get the work done. But what this arrangement accomplished politically was to allow far more companies— both truckers and railroads— to survive and make a profit than if there were an unrestricted competitive market, where the transportation companies would have no choice but to use the most efficient ways of hauling freight, even if lower costs and lower prices led to the bankruptcy of some railroads whose costs were too high to survive in competition with trucks. The use of more resources than necessary entailed the survival of more companies than were necessary.

While open and unfettered competition would have been economically beneficial to the society as a whole, such competition would have been politically threatening to the regulatory commission. Firms facing economic extinction because of competition would be sure to resort to political agitation and intrigue against the survival in office of the commissioners and against the survival of the commission and its powers. Labor unions also had a vested interest in keeping the status quo safe from the competition of technologies and methods that might require fewer workers to get the job done.

After the I.C.C.'s powers to control the trucking industry were eventually reduced by Congress in 1980, freight charges declined substantially and customers reported a rise in the quality of the service. This was made possible by greater efficiency in the industry, as there were now fewer trucks driving around empty and more truckers hired workers whose pay was determined by supply and demand, rather than by union contracts. Because truck deliveries were now more dependable in a competitive industry, businesses using their services were able to carry smaller inventories, saving in the aggregate tens of billions of dollars.

The inefficiencies created by regulation were indicated not only by such savings after federal deregulation, but also by the difference between the costs of interstate shipments and the costs of *intrastate* shipments, where strict state regulation continued after federal regulation was cut back. For example, shipping blue jeans within the state of Texas from El Paso to Dallas cost about 40 percent more than shipping the same jeans internationally from Taiwan to Dallas.

Gross inefficiencies under regulation were not peculiar to the Interstate Commerce Commission. The same was true of the Civil Aeronautics Board, which kept out potentially competitive airlines and kept the prices of air fares in the United States high enough to ensure the survival of existing airlines, rather than force them to face the competition of other airlines that could carry passengers cheaper or with better service. Once the CAB was abolished, airline fares came down, some airlines went bankrupt, but new airlines arose and in the end there were far more passengers being carried than at any time under the constraints of regulation. Savings to airline passengers ran into the billions of dollars.

These were not just zero-sum changes, with airlines losing what passengers gained. The country as a whole benefitted from deregulation, for the industry became more efficient. Just as there were fewer trucks driving around empty after trucking deregulation, so airplanes began to fly with a higher percentage of their seats filled with passengers after airline deregulation, and passengers usually had more choices of carriers on a given route than before. Much the same thing happened after European airlines were deregulated in 1997, as competition from new discount airlines like Ryanair forced British Airways, Air France and Lufthansa to lower their fares.

In these and other industries, the original rationale for regulation was to keep prices from rising excessively but, over the years, this turned into regulatory restrictions against letting prices *fall* to a level that would threaten the survival of existing firms. Political crusades are based on plausible rationales but, even when those rationales are sincerely believed and honestly applied, their actual consequences may be completely different from their initial goals. People make mistakes in all fields of human endeavor but, when major mistakes are made in a competitive economy, those who were mistaken can be forced from the marketplace by the losses that follow. In politics, however, those regulatory agencies often continue to survive, after the initial rationale for their existence is gone, by doing things that were never contemplated when their bureaucracies and their powers were created

ANTI-TRUST LAWS

With anti-trust laws, as with regulatory commissions, a sharp distinction must be made between their original rationales and what they actually do. The basic rationale for anti-trust laws is to prevent monopoly and other non-competitive conditions which allow prices to rise above where they would be in a free and competitive marketplace. In practice, most of the famous anti-trust cases in the United States have involved some business that charged *lower* prices than its competitors. Often it has been complaints from these competitors which caused the government to act.

Competition versus Competitors

The basis of many government prosecutions under the anti-trust laws is that some company's actions threaten competition. However, the most important thing about competition is that it is a *condition* in the marketplace. This condition cannot be measured by the number of competitors existing in a given industry at a given time, though politicians, lawyers and assorted others have confused the existence of competition with the number of surviving competitors. But competition as a condition is precisely what eliminates many competitors.

Obviously, if it eliminates all competitors, then the surviving firm would be a monopoly, at least until new competitors arise, and could in the interim charge far higher prices than in a competitive market. But that is extremely rare. However, the specter of monopoly is often used to justify government policies of intervention where there is no serious danger of a monopoly. For example, back when the A & P grocery chain was the largest retail chain in the world, more than four-fifths of all the groceries in the United States were sold by *other* grocery stores. Yet the Justice Department brought an anti-trust action against A & P, using the company's low prices, and the methods by which it achieved those low prices, as evidence of "unfair" competition against rival grocers and rival grocery chains.

Throughout the history of anti-trust prosecutions, there has been an unresolved confusion between what is detrimental to competition and what is detrimental to competitors. In the midst of this confusion, the question of what is beneficial to the consumer has often been lost sight of.

What has often also been lost sight of is the question of the efficiency of the economy as a whole, which is another way of looking at the benefits to the consuming public. For example, fewer scarce resources are used when products are bought and sold in carload lots, as large chain stores are often able to do, than when the shipments are sold and delivered in much smaller individual quantities to numerous smaller stores. Both delivery costs and selling costs are less per unit of product when the product is bought and sold in large enough amounts to fill a railroad boxcar. The same principle applies when a huge truck delivers a vast amount of merchandise to a Wal-Mart Supercenter, as compared to delivering the same total amount of merchandise to numerous smaller stores scattered over a wider area.

Production costs are also lower when the producer receives a large enough order to be able to schedule production far ahead, instead of finding it necessary to pay overtime to fill many small and unexpected orders that happen to arrive at the same time.

Unpredictable orders also increase the likelihood of slow periods when there is not enough work to keep all the workers employed. Workers who have to be laid off at such times may find other jobs, and not all of them may return when the first employer has more orders to fill, thus making it necessary for that employer to hire new workers, which entails training costs and lower productivity until the new workers gain enough experience to reach peak efficiency. Moreover, employers unable to offer steady employment may find recruiting workers to be more difficult, unless they offer higher pay to offset the uncertainties of the job.

In all these ways, production costs are higher when there are unpredictable orders than when a large purchaser, such as a major department store chain, can contract for a large amount of the supplier's output over a considerable span of time, enabling cost savings to be made in production, part of which go to the chain in lower prices as well as to the producer as lower production costs that leave more profit. Yet this process has long been represented as big chain stores using their "power" to "force" suppliers to sell to them for less. For example, a report in the *San Francisco Chronicle* said:

> For decades, big-box retailers such as Target and Wal-Mart Stores have used their extraordinary size to squeeze lower prices from suppliers, which have a vested interest in keeping them happy.

But what is represented as a "squeeze" on suppliers for the sole benefit of a retail chain with "power" is in fact a reduction in the use of scarce resources, benefitting the economy by freeing some of those resources for use elsewhere. Moreover, despite the use of the word "power," chain stores have no ability to reduce the options otherwise available to the producers. A producer of towels or toothpaste has innumerable alternative buyers and was under no compulsion to sell to A & P in the past or to Target or Wal-Mart today. Only if the economies of scale make it profitable to supply a large buyer with towels or toothpaste (or other products) will the supplier find it advantageous to cut the price below what would otherwise be charged. All economic transactions involve mutual accommodation and each transactor has to make the deal a net benefit to the other transactor, in order to have a deal at all.

Despite economies of scale, the government has repeatedly taken anti-trust action against various companies that gave quantity discounts that the authorities did not like or understand. There was, for example, a well-known anti-trust action against the Morton Salt Company in the 1940s for giving discounts to buyers who bought carload lots of their product. Businesses that bought less than a carload lot of salt were charged $1.60 a case, those who bought carload lots were charged $1.50 a case, and those who bought 50,000 cases or more in a year's time were charged $1.35. Because there were relatively few companies that could afford to buy so much salt and many more that could not, "the competitive opportunities of certain merchants were injured," according to the Supreme Court, which upheld the Federal Trade Commission's actions against Morton Salt.

The government likewise took action against the Standard Oil Company in the 1950s for allowing discounts to those dealers who bought oil by the tank car. The Borden Company was similarly brought into court in the 1960s for having charged less for milk to big chain stores than to smaller grocers. In all these cases, the key point was that such price differences were considered "discriminatory" and "unfair" to those competing firms unable to make such large purchases.

While the sellers were allowed to defend themselves in court by referring to cost differences in selling to different classes of buyers, the apparently simple concept of "cost" is by no means simple when argued over by rival lawyers, accountants and economists. Where neither side could prove anything conclusively about the costs— which was common— the accused lost the case. In a fundamental departure from the centuries-old traditions of Anglo-American law, the government need only make a superficial or *prima facie* case, based on gross numbers, to shift the burden of proof to the accused. This same principle and procedure were to reappear, years later, in employment discrimination cases under the civil rights laws. As with anti-trust cases, these employment discrimination cases likewise produced many consent decrees and large out-of-court settlements by companies well aware of the virtual impossibility of proving their innocence, regardless of what the facts might be.

The emphasis on protecting competitors, in the name of protecting competition, takes many forms and has appeared in other countries besides the United States. A European anti-trust case against Microsoft was based on the idea that Microsoft had a duty to accommodate competitors who might want to attach their software products to the Microsoft operating system. Moreover, the rationale of the European decision was defended in a *New York Times* editorial:

> Microsoft's resounding defeat in a European antitrust case establishes welcome principles that should be adopted in the United States as guideposts for the future development of the information economy.

The court agreed with European regulators that Microsoft had abused its operating system monopoly by incorporating its Media Player, which plays music and films, into Windows. That shut out rivals, like RealPlayer. The decision sets a sound precedent that companies may not leverage their dominance in one market (the operating system) to extend it into new ones (the player).

The court also agreed that Microsoft should provide rival software companies the information they need to make their products work with Microsoft's server software.

The *New York Times* editorial seemed surprised that others saw the principle involved in this anti-trust decision as "a mortal blow against capitalism itself." But when free competition in the marketplace is replaced by third-party intervention to force companies to facilitate their competitors' efforts, it is hard to see that as fostering competition, as distinguished from protecting competitors.

The confusion between the two things is long standing. Back when Kodachrome was the leading color film in the world, it was also what was aptly called "the most complicated film there is to process." Since Eastman Kodak had a huge stake in maintaining the reputation of Kodachrome, it sought to protect that reputation by processing all Kodachrome itself, so it sold the processing and the film together, rather than risk having other processors turn out substandard results that could be seen by consumers as deficiencies of the film. Yet an anti-trust lawsuit forced Kodak to sell the processing and the film separately, in order not to foreclose that market to other film processors. The fact that all other Kodak films were sold without processing included might suggest that Kodak was not out to foreclose the processing market but to protect the quality and reputation of one particular film that was especially difficult to process. Yet the focus on protecting competitors prevailed in the courts.

"Control" of the Market

The rarity of genuine monopolies in the American economy has led to much legalistic creativity, in order to define various companies as monopolistic or as potential or "incipient" monopolies. How far this could go was illustrated when the Supreme Court in 1962 broke up a merger between two shoe companies that would have given the new combined company less than 7 percent of the shoe sales in the United States. The court likewise in 1966 broke up a merger of two local supermarket chains which, put together, sold less than 8 percent of the groceries in the Los Angeles area. Similarly arbitrary categorizations of businesses as "monopolies" were imposed in India under the Monopolies and Restrictive Trade Practices Act of 1969, where any enterprises with assets in excess of a given amount (about $27 million) were declared to be monopolies and restricted from expanding their business.

A standard practice in American courts and in the literature on anti-trust laws is to describe the percentage of sales made by a given company as the share of the market which it "controls." By this standard, such now defunct companies as Pan American Airways "controlled" a substantial share of their respective markets, when in fact the passage of time showed that they controlled nothing, or else they would never have allowed themselves to be forced out of business. The severe shrinkage in size of such former giants as .A & P likewise suggests that the rhetoric of "control" bears little relationship to reality. But such rhetoric remains effective in courts of law and in the court of public opinion.

Even in the rare case where a genuine monopoly exists on its own— that is, has not been created or sustained by government policy— the consequences in practice have tended to be much less dire than in theory. During the decades when the Aluminum Company of America (Alcoa) was the only producer of virgin ingot aluminum in the United States, its annual profit rate on its investment was about 10 percent after taxes. Moreover, the price of aluminum went down over the years to a fraction of what it had been before Alcoa was formed. Yet Alcoa was prosecuted under the anti-trust laws and convicted.

Why were aluminum prices going down under a monopoly, when in theory they should have been going up? Despite its "control" of the market for aluminum, Alcoa was well aware that it could not jack up prices at will, without risking the substitution of other materials— steel, tin, wood, plastics— for aluminum by many users. Technological progress lowered the costs of producing all these materials and economic competition forced the competing firms to lower their prices accordingly.

This raises a question which applies far beyond the aluminum industry. Percentages of the market "controlled" by this or that company ignore the role of substitutes that may be officially classified as products of other industries, but which can nevertheless be used as substitutes by many buyers, if the price of the monopolized product rises significantly. Whether in a monopolized or a competitive market, a technologically very different product may serve as a substitute, as television did when it replaced many newspapers as sources of information and entertainment or when "smart phones" that could take pictures provided devastating competition for the simple, inexpensive cameras that had long been profitable for Eastman Kodak. Phones and cameras would be classified as being in separate industries when calculating what percentage of the market was "controlled" by Kodak, but the economic reality said otherwise.

In Spain, when high-speed trains began operating between Madrid and Seville, the division of passenger traffic between rail and air travel went from 33 percent rail and 67 percent air to 82 percent rail and 18 percent air. Clearly many people treated air and rail traffic as substitute ways of traveling between these two cities. No matter how high a percentage of the air traffic between Madrid and Seville might be carried ("controlled") by one airline, and no matter how high a percentage of the rail traffic might be carried by one railroad, each would still face the competition of all air lines and all rail lines operating between these cities.

Similarly, in earlier years, ocean liners carried a million passengers across the Atlantic in 1954 while planes carried 600,000. But, eleven years later, the ocean liners were carrying just 650,000 passengers while planes now carried four million. The fact that these were technologically very different things did not mean that they could not serve as economic substitutes. In twenty-first century Latin America, airlines have even competed successfully with buses. According to the *Wall Street Journal*:

> The new low-cost carriers in Brazil, Mexico and Colombia are largely avoiding competition with incumbent full-service airlines. Instead, they are stimulating new traffic by adding cheap, no-frills flights to secondary cities that, for many residents, had long required day-long bus rides.
>
> Largely as a result, the number of airline passengers in these countries has surged. The newfound mobility has opened up the flow of commerce

and drastically cut travel times in areas with poor roads, virtually no rail service and stretches of harsh terrain.

One low-cost airline offers flights into Mexico City for "about half the price of the 14-hour overnight bus ride." In Brazil and Colombia it is much the same story. In both these countries, new low-cost airlines have reduced bus travel somewhat and greatly increased air travel, as the total number of people traveling has grown. Planes and buses are obviously very different technologically, but they can serve the same purpose and compete against each other in the marketplace— a crucial fact overlooked by those who compile data on how large a share of the market some company "controls."

Those bringing anti-trust lawsuits generally seek to define the relevant market narrowly, so as to produce high percentages of the market "controlled" by the enterprise being prosecuted. In the famous anti-trust case against Microsoft at the turn of the century, for example, the market was defined as that for computer operating systems for stand-alone personal computers using microchips of the kind manufactured by Intel. This left out not only the operating systems running Apple computers but also other operating systems such as those produced by Sun Microsystems for multiple computers or the Linux system for stand-alone computers.

In its narrowly defined market, Microsoft clearly had a "dominant" share. The anti-trust lawsuit, however, did not accuse Microsoft of jacking up prices unconscionably, in the classic manner of monopoly theory. Rather, Microsoft had added an Internet browser to its Windows operating system free of charge, undermining rival browser producer Netscape.

The existence of all the various sources of potential competition from outside the narrowly defined market may well have had something to do with the fact that Microsoft did not raise prices, as it could have gotten away with in the short run— but at the cost of jeopardizing its long-run sales and profits, since other operating systems could have been substituted for Microsoft's system, if the prices of these other operating systems were right. In 2003, the city government of Munich in fact switched from using Microsoft Windows in its 14,000 computers to using Linux— one of the systems excluded from the definition of the market that Microsoft "controlled," but which was nevertheless obviously a substitute.

In 2013, the Department of Justice filed an anti-trust lawsuit to prevent the brewers of Budweiser and other beers from buying full ownership of the brewer of Corona beer. Ownership of all the different brands of beer involved would have given the brewers of Budweiser "control" of 46 percent of all beer sales in the United States, as "control" is defined in anti-trust rhetoric. In reality, the merger would still leave a majority of the beer sold in the country in the hands of other brewers, of which more than 400 new brewers were added the previous year, raising the total number of brewers to an all-time high of 2,751. More fundamentally, defining the relevant market as the beer market ignored the fact that beer was just one alcoholic beverage— and "beer has been losing market share on this wider playing field for a decade or more" to other alcoholic drinks, according to the *Wall Street Journal*.

The spread of international free trade means that even a genuine monopoly of a particular product in a particular country may mean little if that same product can be imported from other countries. If there is only one producer of widgets in Brazil, that producer is not a monopoly in any economically meaningful sense if there are a dozen widget manufacturers in neighboring Argentina and hundreds of widget makers in countries around the world. Only if the Brazilian government prevents widgets from being imported does the lone manufacturer in the country become a monopoly in a sense that would allow higher prices to be charged than would be charged in a competitive market.

If it seems silly to arbitrarily define a market and "control" of that market by a given firm's current sales of domestically produced products, it was not too silly to form the basis of a landmark U.S. Supreme Court decision in 1962, which defined the market for shoes in terms of "domestic production of nonrubber shoes." By eliminating sneakers, deck shoes, and imported shoes of all kinds, this definition increased the defined market share of the firms being charged with violating the anti-trust laws— who in this case were convicted.

Thus far, whether discussing widgets, shoes, or computer operating systems, we have been considering markets defined by a given product performing a given function. But often the same function can be performed by technologically different products. Corn and petroleum may not seem to be similar products belonging in the same industry but producers of plastics can use the oil from either one to manufacture goods made of plastic.

When petroleum prices soared in 2004, Cargill Dow's sales of a resin made from corn oil rose 60 percent over the previous year, as plastics manufacturers switched from the more expensive petroleum oil. Whether or not two things are substitutes economically does not depend on whether they look alike or are conventionally defined as being in the same industry. No one considers corn as being in the petroleum industry or considers either of these products when calculating what percentage of the market is "controlled" by a given producer of the other product. But that simply highlights the inadequacy of "control" statistics.

Even products that have no functional similarity may nevertheless be substitutes in economic terms. If golf courses were to double their fees, many casual golfers might play the game less often or give it up entirely, and in either case seek recreation by taking more trips or cruises or by pursuing a hobby like photography or skiing, using money that might otherwise have been used for playing golf. The fact that these other activities are functionally very different from golf does not matter. In economic terms, when higher prices for A cause people to buy more of B, then A and B are substitutes, whether or not they look alike or operate alike. But laws and government policies seldom look at things this way, especially when defining how much of a given market a given firm "controls."

Domestically, as well as internationally, as the area that can be served by given producers expands, the degree of statistical dominance or "control" by local producers in any given area means less and less. For example, as the number of newspapers published in given American communities declined substantially after the middle of the twentieth century, with the rise of television, much concern was expressed over the growing share of local markets "controlled" by the surviving papers. In many communities, only one local newspaper survived, making it a monopoly as defined by the share of the market it "controlled." Yet the fact that newspapers published elsewhere became available over wider and wider areas made such statistical "control" less and less meaningful economically.

For example, someone living in the small community of Palo Alto, California, 30 miles south of San Francisco, need not buy a Palo Alto newspaper to find out what movies are playing in town, since that information is readily available from the *San Francisco Chronicle*, which is widely sold in Palo Alto, with home delivery being easy to arrange. Still less does a Palo Alto resident have to rely on a local paper for national or international news.

Technological advances have enabled the *New York Times* and the *Wall Street Journal* to be printed in California as readily as in New York, and at the same time, so that these became national newspapers, available in communities large and small across America. *USA Today* achieved the largest circulation in the country with no local origin at all, being printed in numerous communities across the country.

The net result of such widespread availability of newspapers beyond the location of their headquarters has been that many local "monopoly" newspapers had difficulties even surviving financially, in competition with larger regional and national newspapers, much less making any extra profits associated with monopoly. Yet anti-trust policies based on market share statistics among locally headquartered newspapers continued to impose restrictions on mergers of local papers, lest such mergers leave the surviving newspapers with too much "control" of their local market. But the market as defined by the location of a newspaper's headquarters had become largely irrelevant economically.

An extreme example of how misleading market share statistics can be was the case of a local movie chain that showed 100 percent of all the first-run movies in Las Vegas. It was prosecuted as a monopoly but, by the time the case reached the 9th Circuit Court of Appeals, another movie chain was showing more first-run movies in Las Vegas than the "monopolist" that was being prosecuted. Fortunately, sanity prevailed in this instance. Judge Alex Kozinski of the 9th Circuit Court of Appeals pointed out that the key to monopoly is not market share— even when it is 100 percent— but the ability to keep others out. A company which cannot keep competitors out is not a monopoly, no matter what percentage of the market it may have at a given moment. That is why the *Palo Alto Daily News* is not a monopoly in any economically meaningful sense, even though it is the only local daily newspaper published in town.

Focusing on market shares at a given moment has also led to a pattern in which the U. S. government has often prosecuted leading firms in an industry just when they were about to lose that leadership. In a world where it is common for particular companies to rise and fall over time, anti-trust lawyers can take years to build a case against a company that is at its peak— and about to head over the hill. A major anti-trust case can take a decade or more to be brought to a final conclusion. Markets often react much more quickly than that against monopolies and cartels, as early twentieth century trusts found when giant retailers like Sears, Montgomery Ward and A & P outflanked them long before the government could make a legal case against them.

"Predatory" Pricing

One of the remarkable theories which has become part of the tradition of anti-trust law is "predatory pricing." According to this theory, a big company that is out to eliminate its smaller competitors and take over their share of the market will lower its prices to a level that dooms the competitor to unsustainable losses, forcing it out of business when the smaller company's resources run out. Then, having acquired a monopolistic position, the larger company will raise its prices— not just to the previous level, but to new and higher levels in keeping with its new monopolistic position. Thus, it recoups its losses and enjoys above-normal profits thereafter, at the expense of the consumers, according to the theory of predatory pricing.

One of the most remarkable things about this theory is that those who advocate it seldom even attempt to provide any concrete examples of when this ever actually happened. Perhaps even more remarkable, they have not had to do so, even in courts of law, in anti-trust cases. Nobel Prizewinning economist Gary Becker has said: "I do not know of any documented predatory-pricing case."

Yet both the A & P grocery chain in the 1940s and the Microsoft Corporation in the 1990s were accused of pursuing such a practice in anti-trust cases, but without a single example of this process having gone to completion. Instead, their current low prices (in the case of A & P) and the inclusion of a free Internet browser in Windows software (in the case of Microsoft) have been interpreted as directed toward that end— though not with having actually achieved it.

Since it is impossible to prove a negative, the accused company cannot disprove that it was pursuing such a goal, and the issue simply becomes a question of whether those who hear the charge choose to believe it.

Predatory pricing is more than just a theory without evidence. It is something that makes little or no economic sense. A company that sustains losses by selling below cost to drive out a competitor is following a very risky strategy. The only thing it can be sure of is losing money initially. Whether it will ever recover enough extra profits to make the gamble pay off in the long run is problematical. Whether it can do so and escape the anti-trust laws as well is even more problematical— and anti-trust laws can lead to millions of dollars in fines and/or the dismemberment of the company. But, even if the would-be predator manages somehow to overcome these formidable problems, it is by no means clear that eliminating all existing competitors will mean eliminating competition.

Even when a rival firm has been forced into bankruptcy, its physical equipment and the skills of the people who once made it viable do not vanish into thin air. A new entrepreneur can come along and acquire both, perhaps at low distress sale prices for both the physical equipment and the unemployed workers, enabling the new competitor to have lower costs than the old— and hence to be a more dangerous competitor, able to afford to charge lower prices or to provide higher quality at the same price.

As an illustration of what can happen, back in 1933 the *Washington Post* went bankrupt, though not because of predatory pricing. In any event, this bankruptcy did not cause the printing presses, the building, or the reporters to disappear. All were acquired by publisher Eugene Meyer, at a price that was less than one-fifth of what he had bid unsuccessfully for the same newspaper just four years earlier. In the decades that followed, under new ownership and management, the *Washington Post* grew to become the largest newspaper in the nation's capital. By the early twenty-first century, the *Washington Post* had one of the five largest circulations in the country.

Had some competitor driven the paper into bankruptcy by predatory pricing back in 1933, that predatory competitor would have accomplished nothing except to enable the *Post* to rise again, with Eugene Meyer now having lower production costs than the previous owner— and therefore being a more formidable competitor.

Bankruptcy can eliminate particular owners and managers, but it does not eliminate competition in the form of new people, who can either take over an existing bankrupt enterprise or start their own new business from scratch in the same industry. Destroying a particular competitor— or even all existing competitors— does not mean destroying competition, which can take the form of new firms being formed. In short "predatory pricing" can be an expensive venture, with little prospect of recouping the losses by subsequent monopoly profits. It can hardly be surprising that predatory pricing remains a theory without concrete examples. What is surprising is how seriously that unsubstantiated theory is taken in anti-trust cases.

Benefits and Costs of Anti-Trust Laws

Perhaps the most clearly positive benefit of American anti-trust laws has been a blanket prohibition against collusion to fix prices. This is an automatic violation, subject to heavy penalties, regardless of any justification that might be attempted. Whether this outweighs the various negative effects of other anti-trust laws on competition in the marketplace is another question.

The more stringent anti-monopoly laws in India produced many clearly counterproductive results before these laws were eventually repealed in 1991. Some of India's leading industrialists were prevented from expanding their highly successful enterprises, lest they exceed an arbitrary financial limit used to define a "monopoly"— regardless of how many competitors that "monopolist" might have. As a result, Indian entrepreneurs often applied their efforts and capital outside of India, providing goods, employment, and taxes in other countries where they were not so restricted. One such Indian entrepreneur, for example, produced fiber in Thailand from pulp bought in Canada and sent this fiber to his factory in Indonesia for converting to yarn. He then exported the yarn to Belgium, where it would be made into carpets.

It is impossible to know how many other Indian businesses invested outside of India because of the restrictions against "monopoly." What is known is that the repeal of the Monopolies and Restrictive Trade Practices Act in 1991 was followed by an expansion of large-scale enterprises in India, both by Indian entrepreneurs and by foreign entrepreneurs who now found India a better place to establish or expand businesses. What also increased dramatically was the country's economic growth rate, reducing the number of people in poverty and increasing the Indian government's ability to help them, because tax revenues rose with the rising economic activity in the country.

Although India's Monopolies and Restrictive Trade Practices Act was intended to rein in big business, its actual effect was to cushion businesses from the pressures of competition, domestic and international— and the effect of that was to reduce incentives toward efficiency. Looking back on that era, India's leading industrialist, Ratan Tata of Tata Industries, said of his own huge conglomerate:

> The group operated in a protected environment. The less-sensitive companies didn't worry about their competition, didn't worry about their costs and had not looked at newer technology. Many of them didn't even look at market shares.

In short, cushioned capitalism produced results similar to those under socialism. When India's economy was later opened up to competition, at home and abroad, it was a shock. Some of the directors of Tata Steel "held their heads in their hands" when they learned that the company now faced an annual loss of $26 million because freight rates had gone up. In the past, they could simply have raised the price of steel accordingly but now, with other steel producers free to compete, local freight charges could not simply be passed on in higher prices to the consumers, without risking bigger losses through a loss of customers to global competitors. Tata Steel had no choice but to either go out of business or change the way they did business. According to *Forbes* magazine:

> Tata Steel has spent $2.3 billion closing decrepit factories and modernizing mines, collieries and steelworks as well as building a new blast furnace. . .From 1993 to 2004 productivity skyrocketed from 78

tons of steel per worker per year to 264 tons, thanks to plant upgrades and fewer defects.

By 2007, the *Wall Street Journal* was reporting that Tata Steel's claim to be the world's lowest-cost producer of steel had been confirmed by analysts. But none of these adjustments would have been necessary if this and other companies in India had continued to be sheltered from competition under the guise of preventing "monopoly." India's steel industry, like its automobile industry and its watch industry, among others, were revolutionized by competition.

Chapter 9

MARKET AND NON-MARKET ECONOMIES

In general, "the market" is smarter than the smartest of its individual participants.

Robert L. Bartley

Although business enterprises based on profit have become one of the most common economic institutions in modern industrialized nations, an understanding of how businesses operate internally and how they fit into the larger economy and society is not nearly as common. The prevalence of business enterprises in many economies around the world has been so taken for granted that few people ask the question why this particular way of providing the necessities and amenities of life has come to prevail over alternative ways of carrying out economic functions.

Among the many economically productive endeavors at various times and places throughout history, capitalist businesses are just one. Human beings lived for thousands of years without businesses. Tribes hunted and fished together. During the centuries of feudalism, neither serfs nor nobles were businessmen. Even in more recent centuries, millions of families in America lived on self-sufficient farms, growing their own food, building their own houses, and making their own clothes. Even in more recent times, there have been cooperative groups, such as the Israeli kibbutz, where people have voluntarily supplied one another with goods and services, without money changing hands. In the days of the Soviet Union, a whole modern, industrial economy had government-owned and government-operated enterprises doing the same kinds of things that businesses do in a capitalist economy, without in fact being businesses in either their incentives or constraints.

Even in countries where profit-seeking businesses have become the norm, there are many private non-profit enterprises such as colleges, foundations, hospitals, symphony orchestras and museums, providing various goods and services, in addition to government-run enterprises such as post offices and public libraries. Although some of these enterprises supply goods and services different from those supplied by profit-seeking businesses, others supply similar or overlapping goods and services.

Universities publish books and stage sports events that bring in millions of dollars in gate receipts. *National Geographic* magazine is published by a non-profit organization, as are other magazines published by the Smithsonian Institution and a number of independent, non-profit research institutions ("think tanks") such as the Brookings Institution, the American Enterprise Institute and the Hoover Institution. Some functions of a Department of Motor Vehicles, such as renewing automobile licenses, are also handled by the American Automobile Association, a non-profit organization, which also arranges airline and cruise ship travel, like commercial travel agencies.

In short, the activities engaged in by profit-seeking and non-profit organizations overlap. So do the activities of some governmental agencies, whether local, national or international. Moreover, many activities can shift from one of these kinds of organizations to another with the passage of time.

Municipal transit, for example, was once provided by private profit-seeking businesses in the United States before many city governments took over trolleys, buses, and subways. Activities have also shifted the other way in more recent times, when such governmental functions as garbage collection and prison management have in some places shifted to private, profit-seeking businesses, and such functions of non-profit colleges and universities as running campus bookstores have been turned over to companies like Follet or Barnes & Noble. Traditional non-profit academic institutions have also been supplemented by the creation of profit-seeking universities such as the University of Phoenix, which not only has more students than any of the private non-profit academic institutions but more students than even some whole state university systems.

The simultaneous presence of a variety of organizations doing similar or overlapping things provides opportunities for insights into how different ways of organizing economic activities affect the differing incentives and constraints facing decision-makers in these organizations, and how that in turn affects the efficiency of their activities and the way these enterprises affect the larger economy and society.

Misconceptions of business are almost inevitable in a society where most people have neither studied nor run businesses. In a society where most people are employees and consumers, it is easy to think of businesses as "them"— as impersonal organizations, whose internal operations are largely unknown and whose sums of money may sometimes be so huge as to be unfathomable.

BUSINESSES VERSUS
NON-MARKET PRODUCERS

Since non-market ways of producing goods and services preceded markets and businesses by centuries, if not millennia, the obvious question is: Why have businesses displaced these non-market producers to such a large extent in so many countries around the world?

The fact that businesses have largely displaced many other ways of organizing the production of goods and services suggests that the cost advantages, reflected in prices, are considerable. This is not just a conclusion of free market economists. In *The Communist Manifesto*, Marx and Engels said of capitalist business, "The cheap prices of its commodities are the heavy artillery with which it batters down all Chinese walls." That by no means spared business from criticism, then or later.

Since there are few, if any, people who want to return to feudalism or to the days of self-sufficient family farms, government enterprises are the primary alternative to capitalist businesses today. These government enterprises may be either isolated phenomena or part of a comprehensive set of organizations based on government ownership of the means of production, namely socialism. There have been many theories about the merits or demerits of market versus non-market ways of producing goods and services. But the actual track record of market and non-market producers is the real issue.

In principle, either market or non-market economic activity can be carried on by competing enterprises or by monopolistic enterprises. In practice, however, competing enterprises have been largely confined to market economies, while governments have usually created one agency with an exclusive mandate to do one specific thing.

Monopoly is the enemy of efficiency, whether under capitalism or socialism. The difference between the two systems is that monopoly is the norm under socialism. Even in a mixed economy, with some economic activities being carried out by government and others being carried out by private industry, the government's activities are typically monopolies, while those in the private marketplace are typically activities carried out by rival enterprises.

Thus, when a hurricane, flood, or other natural disaster strikes some part of the United States, emergency aid usually comes both from the Federal Emergency Management Agency (FEMA) and from numerous private insurance companies, whose customers' homes and property have been damaged or destroyed. FEMA has been notoriously slower and less efficient than the private insurance companies. One insurance company cannot afford to be slower in getting money into the hands of its policy-holders than a rival insurance company is in getting money to the people who hold its policies. Not only would existing customers in the disaster area be likely to switch insurance companies if one dragged its feet in getting money to them, while their neighbors received substantial advances from a different insurance company to tide them over, word of any such difference would spread like wildfire across the country, causing millions of people elsewhere to switch billions of dollars' worth of insurance business from the less efficient company to the more efficient one.

A government agency, however, faces no such pressure. No matter how much FEMA may be criticized or ridiculed for its failures to get aid to disaster victims in a timely fashion, there is no rival government agency that these people can turn to for the same service. Moreover, the people who run these agencies are paid according to fixed salary schedules, not by how quickly or how well they serve people hit by disaster. In rare cases where a government monopoly is forced to compete with private enterprises doing the same thing, the results are often like that of the government postal service in India:

> When Mumbai Region Postmaster General A.P. Srivastava joined the postal system 27 years ago, mailmen routinely hired extra laborers to help carry bulging gunnysacks of letters they took all day to deliver.
>
> Today, private-sector couriers such as FedEx Corp. and United Parcel Service Inc. have grabbed more than half the delivery business nationwide. That means this city's thousands of postmen finish their rounds before lunch. Mr. Srivastava, who can't fire excess staffers, spends much of his time cooking up new schemes to keep his workers busy. He's ruled out selling onions at Mumbai post offices: too perishable. Instead, he's considering marketing hair oil and shampoo.

India Post, which carried 16 billion pieces of mail in 1999, carried less than 8 billion pieces by 2005, after FedEx and UPS moved in. The fact that competition means losers as well as winners may be obvious but that does not mean that its implications are widely understood and accepted. A *New York Times* reporter in 2010 found it a "paradox" that a highly efficient German manufacturer of museum display cases is "making life difficult" for manufacturers of similar products in other countries. Other German manufacturers of other products have likewise been very successful but "some of their success comes at the expense of countries like Greece, Spain and Portugal." His all too familiar conclusion: "The problem that policy makers are wrestling with is how to correct the economic imbalances that German competitiveness creates."

In the United States, for decades a succession of low-price retailers have been demonized for driving higher-cost competitors out of business. The Robinson-Patman Act of 1936 was sometimes called "the anti-Sears, Roebuck Act" and Congressman Patman also denounced those who ran the A & P grocery chain. In the twenty-first century, Wal-Mart has inherited the role of villain because it too makes it harder for higher-cost competitors to survive. Where, as in India, the higher-cost competitor is a government agency, the rigidities of its rules— such as not being able to fire unneeded workers— make adjustments even harder than they would be for a private enterprise trying to survive in the face of new competition.

From the standpoint of society as a whole, it is not superior quality or efficiency which are a problem, but inertia and inefficiency. Inertia is common to people under both capitalism and socialism, but the market exacts a price for inertia. In the early twentieth century, both Sears and Montgomery Ward were reluctant to begin operating out of stores, after decades of great success selling exclusively from their mail order catalogs. It was only when the 1920s brought competition from chain stores that cut into their profits and caused red ink to start appearing on the bottom line that they had no choice but to become chain stores themselves. In 1920, Montgomery Ward lost nearly $10 million and Sears was $44 million in debt— all this in dollars many times more valuable than today. Under socialism, Sears and Montgomery Ward could have remained mail order retailers indefinitely, and there would have been little incentive for the government to pay to set up rival chain stores to complicate everyone's life.

Socialist and capitalist economies differ not only in the quantity of output they produce but also in the quality. Everything from cars and cameras to restaurant service and airline service were of notoriously low quality in the Soviet Union. Nor was this a happenstance. The incentives are radically different when the producer has to satisfy the consumer, in order to survive financially, than when the test of survivability is carrying out production quotas set by the government's central planners. The consumer in a market economy is going to look not only at quantity but quality. But a central planning commission is too overwhelmed with the millions of products they oversee to be able to monitor much more than gross output.

That this low quality is a result of incentives, rather than being due to traits peculiar to Russians, is shown by the quality deterioration that has taken place in the United States or in Western Europe when free market prices have been replaced by rent control or by other forms of price controls and government allocation. Both excellent service and terrible service can occur in the same country, when there are different incentives, as a salesman in India found:

Every time I ate in a roadside cafe or dhaba, my rice plate would arrive in three minutes flat. If I wanted an extra roti, it would arrive in thirty seconds. In a saree shop, the shopkeeper showed me a hundred sarees even if I did not buy a single one. After I left, he would go through the laborious and thankless job of folding back each saree, one at a time, and placing it back on the shelf. In contrast, when I went to buy a railway ticket, pay my telephone bill, or withdraw money from my nationalized bank, I was mistreated or regarded as a nuisance, and made to wait in a long queue. The bazaar offered outstanding service because the shopkeeper knew that his existence depended on his customer. If he was courteous and offered quality products at a competitive price, his customer rewarded him. If not, his customers deserted him for the shop next door. There was no competition in the railways, telephones, or banks, and their employees could never place the customer in the center.

London's *The Economist* magazine likewise pointed out that in India one can "watch the tellers in a state-owned bank chat amongst themselves while the line of customers stretches on to the street." Comparisons of government-run institutions with privately-run institutions often overlook the fact that ownership and control are not the only differences between them. Government-run institutions are almost always monopolies, while privately-run institutions usually have competitors. Competing government institutions performing the same function are referred to negatively as "needless duplication." Whether the frustrated customers waiting in line at a government-run bank would consider an alternative bank to be needless duplication is another question. Privatization helped provide an answer to that question in India, as the *Wall Street Journal* reported:

> The banking sector is still dominated by the giant State Bank of India but the country's growing middle class is taking most of its business to the high-tech private banks, such as HDFC Bank Ltd. and ICICI Bank Ltd. leaving the state banks with the least-profitable businesses and worst borrowers.

While some privately owned businesses in various countries can and do give poor service, or cut corners on quality in a free market, they do so at the risk of their own survival. When the processed food industry first began in nineteenth century America, it was common for producers to adulterate food items with less expensive fillers. Horseradish, for example, was often sold in colored bottles, to conceal the adulteration. But when Henry J.

Heinz began selling unadulterated horseradish in clear bottles, this gave him a decisive advantage over his competitors, who fell by the wayside while the Heinz company went on to become one of the enduring giants of American industry, still in business in the twenty-first century and highly successful. When the H.J. Heinz company was sold in 2013, the price was $23 billion.

Similarly with the British food processing company Crosse & Blackwell, which sold quality foods not only in Britain but in the United States as well. It too remained one of the giants of the industry throughout the twentieth century and into the twenty first. Perfection is not found in either market or non-market economies, nor in any other human endeavors, but market economies exact a price from enterprises that disappoint their customers and reward those that fulfill their obligations to the consuming public. The great financial success stories in American industry have often involved companies almost fanatical about maintaining the reputation of their products, even when these products have been quite mundane and inexpensive.

McDonald's built its reputation on a standardized hamburger and maintained quality by having its own inspectors make unannounced visits to its meat suppliers, even in the middle of the night, to see what was being put into the meat it was buying. Colonel Sanders was notorious for showing up unexpectedly at Kentucky Fried Chicken restaurants. If he didn't like the way the chickens were being cooked, he would dump them all into a garbage can, put on an apron, and proceed to cook some chickens himself, to demonstrate how he wanted it done. His protégé Dave Thomas later followed similar practices when he created his own chain of Wendy's hamburger restaurants. Although Colonel Sanders and Dave Thomas could not be everywhere in a nationwide chain, no local franchise owner could take a chance on seeing his profits being thrown into a garbage can by the head honcho of the chain.

In the credit card era, protecting card users' identity from theft or misuse has become part of the quality of a credit card service. Accordingly, companies like Visa and MasterCard "have levied fines, sent warning letters and held seminars to pressure restaurants into being more careful about protecting the information" about card-users, according to the *Wall Street Journal*, which added: "All companies that accept plastic must follow a complex set of security rules put in place by Visa, MasterCard, American Express Co. and Morgan Stanley's Discover unit."

Behind all of this is the basic fact that a business is selling not only a physical product, but also the reputation which surrounds that product. Motorists traveling in an unfamiliar part of the country are more likely to turn into a hamburger restaurant that has a McDonald's or Wendy's sign on it than one which does not. That reputation translates into dollars and cents— or, in this case, billions of dollars. People with that kind of money at stake are unlikely to be very tolerant of anyone who would compromise their reputation. Ray Kroc, the founder of the McDonald's chain, would explode in anger if he found a McDonald's parking lot littered. His franchisees were expected to keep not only their own premises free of litter, but also to see that there was no McDonald's litter on the streets within a radius of two blocks of their restaurants.

When speaking of quality in this context, what matters is the kind of quality that is relevant to the particular clientele being served. Hamburgers and fried chicken may not be regarded by others as either gourmet food or health food, nor can a nationwide chain mass-producing such meals reach quality levels achievable by more distinctive, fancier, and pricier restaurants. What the chain can do is assure quality within the limits expected by their particular customers. Those quality standards, however, often exceed those imposed or used by the government. As *USA Today* reported:

> The U.S. Department of Agriculture says the meat it buys for the National School Lunch Program "meets or exceeds standards in commercial products."
>
> That isn't always the case. McDonald's, Burger King and Costco, for instance, are far more rigorous in checking for bacteria and dangerous pathogens. They test the ground beef they buy five to 10 times more often than the USDA tests beef made for schools during a typical production day.
>
> And the limits Jack in the Box and other big retailers set for certain bacteria in their burgers are up to 10 times more stringent than what the USDA sets for school beef.
>
> For chicken, the USDA has supplied schools with thousands of tons of meat from old birds that might otherwise go to compost or pet food. Called "spent hens" because they're past their egg-laying prime, the chickens don't pass muster with Colonel Sanders— KFC won't buy them— and they don't

pass the soup test, either. The Campbell Soup Company says it stopped using them a decade ago based on "quality considerations."

While a market economy is essentially an impersonal mechanism for allocating resources, some of the most successful businesses have prospered by their attention to the personal element. One of the reasons for the success of the Woolworth retail chain in years past was founder F.W. Woolworth's insistence on the importance of courtesy to the customers. This came from his own painful memories of store clerks treating him like dirt when he was a poverty-stricken farm boy who went into stores to buy or look.

Ray Kroc's zealous insistence on maintaining McDonald's reputation for cleanliness paid off at a crucial juncture in the early years, when he desperately needed a loan to stay in business, for the financier who toured McDonald's restaurants said later: "If the parking lots had been dirty, if the help had grease stains on their aprons, and if the food wasn't good, McDonald's never would have gotten the loan." Similarly, Kroc's good relations with his suppliers— people who sold paper cups, milk, napkins, etc., to McDonald's— had saved him before when these suppliers agreed to lend him money to bail him out of an earlier financial crisis.

What is called "capitalism" might more accurately be called consumerism. It is the consumers who call the tune, and those capitalists who want to remain capitalists have to learn to dance to it. The twentieth century began with high hopes for replacing the competition of the marketplace by a more efficient and more humane economy, planned and controlled by government in the interests of the people. However, by the end of that century, all such efforts were so thoroughly discredited by their actual results, in countries around the world, that even most communist nations abandoned central planning, while socialist governments in democratic countries began selling off government-run enterprises, whose chronic losses had been a heavy burden to the taxpayers.

Privatization was embraced as a principle by such conservative governments as those of Prime Minister Margaret Thatcher in Britain and President Ronald Reagan in the United States. But the most decisive evidence for the efficiency of the marketplace was that even socialist and communist governments, led by people who were philosophically opposed to capitalism, turned back towards the free market after seeing what happens when industry and commerce operate without the guidance of prices, profits and losses.

WINNERS AND LOSERS

Many people who appreciate the prosperity created by market economies may nevertheless lament the fact that particular individuals, groups, industries, or regions of the country do not share fully in the general economic advances, and some may even be worse off than before. Political leaders or candidates are especially likely to deplore the inequity of it all and to propose various government "solutions" to "correct" the situation.

Whatever the merits or demerits of various political proposals, what must be kept in mind when evaluating them is that the good fortunes and misfortunes of different sectors of the economy may be closely related as cause and effect— and that preventing bad effects can prevent good effects. It was not coincidental that Smith Corona began losing millions of dollars a year on its typewriters when Dell began making millions on its computers. Computers were replacing typewriters. Nor was it coincidental that sales of film began declining with the rise of digital cameras. The fact that scarce resources have alternative uses implies that some enterprises must lose their ability to use those resources, in order that others can gain the ability to use them.

Smith Corona had to be *prevented* from using scarce resources, including both materials and labor, to make typewriters, when those resources could be used to produce computers that the public wanted more. Some of the resources used for manufacturing cameras that used film had to be redirected toward producing digital cameras. Nor was this a matter of anyone's fault. No matter how fine the typewriters made by Smith Corona were or how skilled and conscientious its employees, typewriters were no longer what the public wanted after they had the option to achieve the same end result— and more— with computers. Some excellent cameras that used film were discontinued when new digital cameras were created.

During all eras, scarcity implies that resources must be taken from some in order to go to others, if new products and new methods of production are to raise living standards.

It is hard to know how industry in general could have gotten the millions of workers that they added during the twentieth century, whose output contributed to dramatically rising standards of living for the public at large, without the much-lamented decline in the number of farms and farm workers that took place during that same century. Few individuals or businesses are going to want to give up what they have been used to doing, especially if they have been successful at it, for the greater good of society as a whole. But, in one way or another— under any economic or political system— they are going to have to be forced to relinquish resources and change what they themselves are doing, if rising standards of living are to be achieved and sustained.

The financial pressures of the free market are just one of the ways in which this can be done. Kings or commissars could instead simply order individuals and enterprises to change from doing *A* to doing *B*. No doubt other ways of shifting resources from one producer to another are possible, with varying degrees of effectiveness and efficiency. What is crucial, however, is that it must be done. Put differently, the fact that some people, regions, or industries are being "left behind" or are not getting their "fair share" of the general prosperity is not necessarily a problem with a political solution, as abundant as such proposed solutions may be, especially during election years.

However more pleasant and uncomplicated life might be if all sectors of the economy grew simultaneously at the same lockstep pace, that has never been the reality in any changing economy. When and where new technologies and new methods of organizing or financing production will appear cannot be predicted. To know what the new discoveries were going to be would be to make the discoveries before the discoveries were made. It is a contradiction in terms.

The political temptation is to have the government come to the aid of particular industries, regions or segments of the population that are being adversely affected by economic changes. But this can only be done by taking resources from those parts of the economy that are advancing and redirecting those resources to those whose products or methods are less productive— in other words, by impeding or thwarting the economy's allocation of scarce resources to their most valued uses, on which the standard of living of the whole society depends. Moreover, since economic changes are never-ending, this same policy of preventing resources from going to the uses most valued by millions of people must be on-going as well, if the government succumbs to the political temptation to intervene on behalf of particular industries, regions or segments of the population, sacrificing the standard of living of the population as a whole.

What can be done instead is to recognize that economic changes have been going on for centuries and that there is no sign that this will stop— or that the adjustments necessitated by such changes will stop. This applies to government, to industries and to the people at large. Neither enterprises nor individuals can spend all their current income, as if there are no unforeseeable contingencies to prepare for. Yet many observers continue to lament that even people who are financially prepared are forced to make adjustments, as a *New York Times* economic reporter lamented in a book about job losses with the grim title, *The Disposable American*. Among others, it described an executive whose job at a major corporation was eliminated in a reorganization of the company, and who consequently had to sell "two of the three horses" she owned and also sell "$16,500 worth of Procter stock, cutting into savings to support herself while she hunted for work."

Although this executive had more than a million dollars in savings and owned a seventeen-acre estate, it was presented as some tragic failure of society that she had to make adjustments to the ever-changing economy which had produced such prosperity in the first place.

PART III: WORK AND PAY

Chapter 10

PRODUCTIVITY AND PAY

Government data, if misunderstood or improperly used, can lead to many false conclusions.

Steven R. Cunningham

In discussing the allocation of resources, we have so far been concerned largely with inanimate resources. But people are a key part of the inputs which produce output. Most people do not volunteer their labor free of charge, so they must be either paid to work or forced to work, since the work has to be done in any case, if we are to live at all, much less enjoy the various amenities that go into our modern standard of living. In many societies of the past, people were forced to work, whether as serfs or slaves. In a free society, people are paid to work. But pay is not just income to individuals. It is also a set of incentives facing everyone working or potentially working, and a set of constraints on employers, so that they do not use the scarce resource of labor as was done in the days of the Soviet Union, keeping extra workers on hand "just in case," when those workers could be doing something productive somewhere else.

In short, the payment of wages and salaries has an economic role that goes beyond the provision of income to individuals. From the standpoint of the economy as a whole, payment for work is a way of allocating scarce resources which have alternative uses. Labor is a scarce resource because there is always more work to do than there are people with the time to do it all, so the time of those people must be allocated among competing uses of their time and talents. If the pay of truck drivers doubles, some taxi drivers may decide that they would rather drive a truck. Let the income of engineers double and some students who were thinking of majoring in math or physics may decide to major in engineering instead. Let pay for all jobs double and some people who are retired may decide to go back to work, at least part-time, while others who were thinking of retiring may decide to postpone that for a while.

How much people are paid depends on many things. Stories about the astronomical pay of professional athletes, movie stars, or chief executives of big corporations often cause journalists and others to question how much this or that person is "really" worth.

Fortunately, since we know from Chapter 2 that there is no such thing as "real" worth, we can save all the time and energy that others put into such unanswerable questions. Instead, we can ask a more down-to-earth question: What determines how much people get paid for their work? To this question there is a very down-to-earth answer: Supply and Demand. However, that is just the beginning. Why does supply and demand cause one individual to earn more than another?

Workers would obviously like to get the highest pay possible and employers would like to pay the least possible. Only where there is overlap between what is offered and what is acceptable can anyone be hired. But why does that overlap take place at a pay rate that is several times as high for an engineer as for a messenger?

Messengers would of course like to be paid what engineers are paid, but there is too large a supply of people capable of being messengers to force employers to raise their pay scales to that level. Because it takes a long time to train an engineer, and not everyone is capable of mastering such training, there is no such abundance of engineers relative to the demand. That is the supply side of the story. But what determines the demand for labor? What determines the limit of what an employer is willing to pay?

It is not merely the fact that engineers are scarce that makes them valuable. It is what engineers can add to a company's earnings that makes employers willing to bid for their services— and sets a limit to how high the bids can go. An engineer who added $100,000 to a company's earnings and asked for a $200,000 salary would obviously not be hired. On the other hand, if the engineer added a quarter of a million dollars to a company's earnings, that engineer would be worth hiring at $200,000— provided that there were no other engineers who would do the same job for a lower salary.

PRODUCTIVITY

While the term "productivity" may be used to describe an employee's contribution to a company's earnings, this word is often also defined inconsistently in other ways. Sometimes the implication is left that each worker has a certain productivity that is inherent in that particular worker, rather than being dependent on surrounding circumstances as well.

A worker using the latest modern equipment can obviously produce more output per hour than the very same worker employed in another firm whose equipment is not quite as up-to-date or whose management does not have production organized as efficiently. For example, Japanese-owned cotton mills in China during the 1930s paid higher wages than Chinese-owned cotton mills there, but the Japanese-run mills had lower labor costs per unit of output because they had higher output per worker. This was not due to different equipment— they both used the same machinery— but to more efficient management brought over from Japan.

Similarly, in the early twenty-first century, an international consulting firm found that American-owned manufacturing enterprises in Britain had far higher productivity than British-owned manufacturing enterprises. According to the British magazine *The Economist*, "British industrial companies have underperformed their American counterparts startlingly badly," so that when it comes to "economy in the use of time and materials," fewer than 40 percent of British manufacturers "have paid any attention to this." Moreover, "Britain's top engineering graduates prefer to work for foreign-owned companies." In short, lower productivity in British-owned companies reflected differences in management practices, even when productivity was measured in terms of output per unit of labor.

In general, the productivity of any input in the production process depends on the quantity and quality of other inputs, as well as its own. Thus workers in South Africa have higher productivity than workers in Brazil, Poland, Malaysia, or China because, as *The Economist* magazine pointed out, South African firms "rely more on capital than labour." In other words, South African workers are not necessarily working any harder or any more skillfully than workers in these other countries. They just have more or better equipment to work with.

The same principle applies outside what we normally think of as economic activities, and it applies to what we normally think of as a purely individual feat, such as a baseball player hitting a home run. A slugger gets more chances to hit home runs if he is batting ahead of another slugger. But, if the batter hitting after him is not much of a home run threat, pitchers are more likely to walk the slugger, whether by pitching to him extra carefully or by deliberately walking him in a tight situation, so that he may get significantly fewer opportunities to hit home runs over the course of a season.

During Ted Williams' career, for example, he had one of the highest percentages of home runs— in proportion to his times at bat— in the history of baseball. Yet he had only one season in which he hit as many as 40 homers, because he was walked as often as 162 times a season, averaging more than one walk per game during the era of the 154-game season.

By contrast, Hank Aaron had eight seasons in which he hit 40 or more home runs, even though his home-run percentage was not quite as high as that of Ted Williams. Although Aaron hit 755 home runs during his career, he was never walked as often as 100 times in any of his 23 seasons in the major leagues. Batting behind Aaron during much of his career was Eddie Mathews, whose home-run percentage was nearly identical with that of Aaron, so that there was not much point in walking Aaron to pitch to Mathews with one more man on base. In short, Hank Aaron's productivity as a home-run hitter was greater because he batted with Eddie Mathews in the on-deck circle.

More generally, in almost any occupation, your productivity depends not only on your own work but also on cooperating factors, such as the quality of the equipment, management and other workers around you. Movie stars like to have good supporting actors, good make-up artists and good directors, all of whom enhance the star's performance. Scholars depend heavily on their research assistants, and generals rely on their staffs, as well as their troops, to win battles.

Whatever the source of a given individual's productivity, that productivity determines the upper limit of how far an employer will go in bidding for that person's services. Just as any worker's value can be enhanced by complementary factors— whether fellow workers, machinery, or more efficient management—(so the worker's value can also be reduced by other factors over which the individual worker has no control.)

Even workers whose output per hour is the same can be of very different value if the transportation costs in one place are higher than in another, so that the employer's net revenue from sales is lower where these higher transportation costs must be deducted from the revenue received. Where the same product is produced by businesses with different transportation costs and sold in a competitive market, those firms with higher transportation costs cannot pass all those costs along to their customers because competing firms whose costs are not as high would be able to charge a lower price and take their customers away. Businesses in Third World countries without modern highways, or efficient trains and airlines, may have to absorb higher transportation costs. Even when they sell the same product for the same price as businesses in more advanced economies, the net revenue from that product will be less, and therefore the value of the labor that went into producing that product will also be worth correspondingly less.

In countries with high levels of corruption, the bribes necessary to get bureaucrats to permit the business to operate likewise have to be deducted from sales revenues and likewise reduce the value of the product and of the workers who produce it, even if these workers have the same output per hour as workers in more modern and less corrupt economies. In reality, Third World workers more typically have lower output per hour, and the higher costs of transportation and corruption which must be deducted from sales revenues can leave such workers earning a fraction of what workers earn for doing similar work in other countries.

In short, productivity is not just a result solely of what the individual worker does but is a result of numerous other factors as well. To say that the demand for labor is based on the value of the worker's productivity is not to say that pay is based on merit. Merit and productivity are two very different things, just as morality and causation are two different things.

PAY DIFFERENCES

Thus far the discussion has been about things affecting the demand for labor. What about supply? Employers seldom bid as much as they would if they had to, because there are other individuals willing and able to supply the same services for less.

Wages and salaries serve the same economic function as other prices— that is, they guide the utilization of scarce resources which have alternative uses, so that each resource gets used where it is most valued. Yet because these scarce resources are human beings, we tend to look on wages and salaries differently from the way we look on prices paid for other inputs into the production process. Often we ask questions that are emotionally powerful, even if they are logically meaningless and wholly undefined. For example: Are the wages "fair"? Are the workers "exploited"? Is this "a living wage"?

No one likes to see fellow human beings living in poverty and squalor, and many are prepared to do something about it, as shown by the vast billions of dollars that are donated to a wide range of charities every year, on top of the additional billions spent by governments in an attempt to better the condition of poor people. These socially important activities occur alongside an economy coordinated by prices, but the two things serve different purposes. Attempts to make prices, including the prices of people's labor and talents, be something other than signals to guide resources to their most valued uses make those prices less effective for their basic purpose, on which the prosperity of the whole society depends. Ultimately, it is economic prosperity which makes it possible for billions of dollars to be devoted to helping the less fortunate.

Income "Distribution"

Nothing is more straightforward and easy to understand than the fact that some people earn more than others, for a variety of reasons. Some people are simply older than others, for example, and their additional years have given them opportunities to acquire more experience, skills, formal education and on-the-job-training— all of which allow them to do a given job more efficiently or to take on more complicated jobs that would be overwhelming for a beginner or for someone with only limited experience or training. It is hardly surprising that this leads to higher incomes. With the passing years, older individuals may also become more knowledgeable about job opportunities, while increasing numbers of other people become more aware of them and their individual abilities, leading to offers of new jobs or promotions where they are currently working. It is not uncommon for most of the people in the top 5 percent of income-earners to be 45 years old and up.

These and other common sense reasons for income differences among individuals are often lost sight of in abstract discussions of the ambiguous term "income distribution." Although people in the top income brackets and the bottom income brackets— "the rich" and "the poor," as they are often called— may be discussed as if they were different classes of people, often they are in fact people at different stages of their lives. Three-quarters of those American workers who were in the bottom 20 percent in income in 1975 were also in the top 40 percent at some point over the next 16 years.

This is not surprising. After 16 years, people usually have had 16 years more work experience, perhaps including on-the-job training or formal education. Those in business or the professions have had 16 years in which to build up a clientele. It would be surprising if they were not able to earn more money as a result.

None of this is unique to the United States. A study of eleven European countries found similar patterns. One-half of the people in Greece and two-thirds of the people in Holland who were below the poverty line in a given year had risen above that line within two years. A study in Britain found similar patterns when following thousands of individuals over a five-year period. At the end of five years, nearly two-thirds of the individuals who were initially in the bottom 10 percent in income had risen out of that bracket. Studies in New Zealand likewise showed significant rises of individuals out of the bottom 20 percent of income earners in just one year and of course larger numbers rising out of this bracket over a period of several years.

When some people are born, live, and die in poverty, while others are born, live, and die in luxury, that is a very different situation from one in which young people have not yet reached the income level of older people, such as their parents. But the kind of statistics often cited in the media, and even in academia, typically do not distinguish these very different situations.

Moreover, those who publicize such statistics usually proceed as if they are talking about income differences between classes rather than differences between age brackets. But, while it is possible for people to stay in the same income bracket for life, though they seldom do, it is not equally possible for them to stay in the same age bracket for life.

Because of the movement of people from one income bracket to another over the years, the degree of income inequality over a lifetime is not the same as the degree of income inequality in a given year. A study in New Zealand found that the degree of income inequality over a working lifetime there was less than the degree of inequality in *any* given year during those lifetimes.

Much discussion of "the rich" and "the poor"— or of the top and bottom 10 or 20 percent— fail to say just what kinds of incomes qualify to be in those categories. As of 2011, a household income of $101,583 was enough to put those who earned it in the top 20 percent of Americans. But a couple earning a little over $50,000 a year each are hardly "the rich." Even to make the top 5 percent required a household income of just over $186,000— that is, about $93,000 apiece for a working couple. That is a nice income, but rising to that level after working for decades at lower levels is hardly a sign of being rich.

Describing people in certain income brackets as "rich" is false for a more fundamental reason: Income and wealth are different things. No matter how much income passes through your hands in a given year, your wealth depends on how much you have retained and accumulated over the years. If you receive a million dollars in a year and spend a million and a half, you are not getting rich. But many frugal people on modest incomes have been found, after their deaths, to have left surprisingly large amounts of wealth to their heirs.

Even among the truly rich, there is turnover. When *Forbes* magazine ran its first list of the 400 richest Americans in 1982, that list included 14 Rockefellers, 28 du Ponts and 11 Hunts. Twenty years later, the list included 3 Rockefellers, one Hunt and no du Ponts. Just over one-fifth of the people on the 1982 *Forbes* list of the wealthiest Americans inherited their wealth. By 2006, however, only two percent of the people on the list had inherited their wealth.

Although there is much talk about "income distribution," most income is of course *not* distributed at all, in the sense in which newspapers or Social

Security checks are distributed from some central place. Most income is distributed only in the figurative statistical sense in which there is a distribution of heights in a population— some people being 5 foot 4 inches tall, others 6 foot 2 inches, etc.— but none of these heights was sent out from some central location. Yet it is all too common to read journalists and others discussing how "society" *distributes* its income, rather than saying in plain English that some people make more money than others.

silly

There is no collective decision by "society" as to how much each individual's work is worth. In a market economy, those who get the direct benefit of an individual's goods or services decide how much they are prepared to pay for what they receive. People who would prefer collective decision-making on such things can argue their case for that particular method of decision-making. But it is misleading to suggest that today "society" *distributes* its income with one set of results and should simply change to distributing its income with different results in the future.

More is involved than a misleading metaphor. Often the very units in which income differences are discussed are as misleading as the metaphor. Family income or household income statistics can be especially misleading as compared to individual income statistics. An individual always means the same thing— one person— but the sizes of families and households differ substantially from one time period to another, from one racial or ethnic group to another, and from one income bracket to another.

For example, a detailed analysis of U.S. Census data showed that there were 40 million people in the bottom 20 percent of households in 2002 but 69 million people in the top 20 percent of households. Although the unwary might assume that these quintiles represent dividing the country into "five equal layers," as two well-known economists have misstated it in a popular book, there is nothing equal about those layers. They represent grossly different numbers of people.

Not only do the numbers of people differ considerably between low-income households and high-income households, the proportions of people who work also differ by very substantial amounts between these households. In the year 2010, the top 20 percent of households contained 20.6 million heads of households who worked, compared to 7.5 million heads of households who worked in the bottom 20 percent of households. These striking disparities do not even take into account whether they are working full-time or part-time. When it comes to working full-time the year-round, even the top *5 percent* of households contained more heads of households who worked full-time for 50 or more weeks than did the bottom 20 percent. That is, there were more heads of households *in absolute numbers*— 4.3 million versus 2.2 million— working full-time and year-round in the top 5 percent of households compared to the bottom 20 percent.

At one time, back in the 1890s, people in the top 10 percent in income worked fewer hours than people in the bottom 10 percent, but that situation has long since reversed. We are no longer talking about the idle rich versus the toiling poor. Today we are usually talking about those who work regularly and those who, in most cases, do not work regularly or at all. Under these conditions, the more that pay for work increases the more income inequality increases. Among the top 6 percent of income earners in a survey published in the *Harvard Business Review*, 62 percent worked more than 50 hours a week and 35 percent worked more than 60 hours a week.

The sizes of families and households have differed not only from one income bracket to another at a given time, but also have differed over time. These differences are not incidental. They radically change the implications of trends in "income distribution" statistics. For example, real income per American household rose only 6 percent over the entire period from 1969 to 1996, but real per capita income rose 51 percent over that same period. The discrepancy is due to the fact that the average size of families and households was declining during those years, so that smaller households— including some with only one person— were now earning about the same as larger households had earned a generation earlier. Looking at a still longer period, from 1967 to 2007, real median household income rose by 30 percent over that span, but real per capita income rose by 100 percent over that same span. Declining numbers of persons per household were the key to these differences.

Rising prosperity contributed to the decline in household size. As early as 1966, the U.S. Bureau of the Census reported that the number of households was increasing faster than the number of people and concluded: "The main reason for the more rapid rate of household formation is the increased tendency, particularly among unrelated individuals, to maintain their own homes or apartments rather than live with relatives or move into existing households as roomers, lodgers, and so forth." Yet these consequences of rising prosperity generate household income statistics that are widely used to suggest that there has been no real economic progress.

A *Washington Post* writer, for example, declared "the incomes of most American households have remained stubbornly flat over the past three decades." It might be more accurate to say that some writers have remained stubbornly blind to economic facts. When two working people in one household today earn the same total amount of money that three working people were earning in one household in the past, that is a 50 percent increase in income per person— even when household income remains the same.

Despite some confused or misleading discussions of "the rich" and "the poor," based on people's transient positions in the income stream, genuinely rich and genuinely poor people do exist— people who are going to be living in luxury or in poverty all their lives— but they are much rarer than gross income statistics would suggest. Just as most American "poor" do not stay poor, so most rich Americans were not born rich. Four-fifths of American millionaires earned their fortunes within their own lifetimes, having inherited nothing. Moreover, the genuinely rich are rare, like the genuinely poor.

Even if we take a million dollars in net worth as our criterion for being rich, only about 3.5 percent of American households are at that level. This is in fact a fairly modest level, given that net worth counts everything from household goods and clothing to the total amount of money in an individual's pension fund. If we count as genuinely poor that 5 percent of the population which remains in the bottom 20 percent over a period of years, then the genuinely rich and the genuinely poor— put together— add up to less than 10 percent of the American population. Nevertheless, some political rhetoric might suggest that most people are either "haves" or "have nots."

Trends over Time

If our concern is with the economic well-being of flesh-and-blood human beings, as distinguished from statistical comparisons between income brackets, then we need to look at real income per capita, because people do not live on percentage shares. They live on real income. Among those Americans who were in the bottom 20 percent in 1975, 98 percent had higher real incomes in 1991— and two-thirds had higher real incomes in 1991 than the average American had back in 1975, when they were in the bottom 20 percent.

Even when narrowly focusing on income brackets, the fact that the share of the bottom 20 percent of households declined from 4 percent of all income in 1985 to 3.5 percent in 2001 did not prevent the real income of the households in this bracket from rising by thousands of dollars in absolute terms, quite aside from the movement of actual people out of the bottom 20 percent between the two years.

Radically different trends are found when looking at statistics based on comparisons of top and bottom income brackets over time, rather than following individual income-earners over the same span of time. For example, it is a widely publicized fact that census data show the percentage of the national income going to those in the bottom 20 percent bracket has been declining over the years, while the percentage going to those in the top 20 percent has been rising— and the amount going to those in the top one percent has been rising especially sharply. This has led to the familiar refrain that "the rich are getting richer and the poor are getting poorer"— a notion that provides the media with the kind of dramatic and alarming news stories that sell newspapers and attract television audiences, as well as being ideologically satisfying to some and politically useful to others. The real question, however, is: Is it true?

A diametrically opposite picture is found when comparing what happens to *specific individuals* over time. Unfortunately, most statistics, including those from the U.S. Bureau of the Census, do *not* follow particular individuals over time, even though the illusion that they do may be fostered by data on income categories over time. Among the few studies which have actually followed individual Americans over time, one from the University of Michigan and another from the Internal Revenue Service, show patterns similar to each other but radically different from the often-cited patterns in data from the Census Bureau and other sources. The University of Michigan study followed the same individuals from 1975 through 1991 and the

Internal Revenue Service study followed individuals through their income tax returns from 1996 through 2005.

The University of Michigan study found that, among working Americans who were in the bottom 20 percent in income in 1975, approximately 95 percent had risen out of that bracket by 1991— including 29 percent who had reached the *top* quintile by 1991, compared to only 5 percent who still remained in the bottom quintile. The largest absolute amount of increase in income between 1975 and 1991 was among those people who were initially in the bottom quintile in 1975 and the least absolute increase in income was among those who were initially in the top quintile in 1975.

In other words, the incomes of people who were initially at the bottom rose *more* than the incomes of people who were initially at the top. This is the direct opposite of the picture presented by Census data, based on following income brackets over time, instead of following the people who are moving in and out of those brackets.

Similar patterns appeared in statistics from the Internal Revenue Service, which also followed given individuals. The IRS found that between 1996 and 2005 the income of individuals who had been in the bottom 20 percent of income tax filers in 1996 had increased by 91 percent by 2005, and the income of those individuals who were in the top one percent in 1996 had *fallen* by 26 percent. It may seem almost impossible that the data from the Bureau of the Census and the data from the IRS and the University of Michigan can all be correct, but they are. Studies of income brackets over time and studies of individual people over time are measuring fundamentally different things that are often confused with one another.

A study of individual incomes over time in Canada turned up patterns very similar to those in the United States. During the period from 1990 to 2009, Canadians who were initially in the bottom 20 percent had both the highest absolute increase in income and the highest percentage increase in income. Only 13 percent of the Canadians who were initially in the bottom quintile in 1990 were still there in 2009, while 21 percent of them had risen all the way to the top quintile.

Whatever the relationship between one income bracket and another, that is not necessarily the relationship between *people*, because people are moving from one bracket to another as time goes on. Therefore the fate of brackets and the fate of people can be very different— and, in many cases, completely opposite. When income-earning Americans in the bottom income bracket have their incomes nearly double in a decade, they end up *no longer* in the bottom bracket. There is nothing mysterious about this, since most people begin their careers in entry-level jobs and their growing experience over the years leads to higher incomes. Nor is it surprising that people whose incomes are at the peak of the income pyramid seem often also to be at or near their own peak incomes and do not continue to rise as dramatically as those who started at the bottom.

Some Americans reach the top one percent in income— approximately $369,500 and up in 2010— in a given year because of some particular boost to their income during that particular year. Someone who sells a house may have an income that year which is some multiple of the income received in any year before or since. Similarly for someone who receives a large inheritance in a given year, or cashes in stock options that have been accumulating over the years. Such spikes in income account for a substantial proportion of those whose incomes in a given year reach the top levels. More than half the people in the top one percent in income in 1996 were no longer at that level in 2005. Among those in the top one-hundredth of one percent in income in 1996, three-quarters were no longer at that level in 2005.

Many people who never have a spike in income that would put them in the top one percent may nevertheless end up in the top 20 percent after many years of moving up in the course of a career. They are not "rich" in any meaningful sense, even though they may be called that in political, media or even academic rhetoric. As already noted, the amount of income required to reach the top 20 percent is hardly enough to live the lifestyle of the rich and famous. Nor will being in the top one percent, for that half of the people in that bracket who do not remain there.

Just as there are spikes in income from time to time, so there are troughs in income in particular years. Thus many people who are genuinely affluent, or even rich, can have business losses or off years in their professions or investments, so that their income in a given year may be very low or even negative, without their being poor in any meaningful sense. This may help explain such anomalies as hundreds of thousands of people with incomes below $20,000 a year who are living in homes costing $300,000 and up.

The fundamental confusion that makes income bracket data and individual income data seem mutually contradictory is the implicit assumption that people in particular income brackets at a given time are an enduring "class" at that level. If that were true, then trends over time in comparisons between income brackets would be the same as trends over time between individuals. Because that is *not* the case, however, the two sets of statistics lead not only to different conclusions but even to opposite conclusions that seem to contradict each other.

The higher up the income scale people are, the more volatile are their incomes. "During the past three recessions, the top 1% of earners (those making $380,000 or more in 2008) experienced the largest income shocks in percentage terms of any income group in the U.S." the *Wall Street Journal* reported. When the incomes of people making $50,000 or less fell by 2 percent between 2007 and 2009, the incomes of people making a million dollars or more fell by nearly 50 percent.

Conversely, when the economy grows, the incomes of the top one percent "grow up to three times faster than the rest of the country's." This is not really surprising, since incomes at the highest levels are less likely to be due to salaries and more likely to be due to income from investments or sales, both of which can vary greatly when the economy goes up or down. Similar patterns apply to wealth as to income. "During the 1990 and 2001 recessions, the richest 5% of Americans (measured by net worth) experienced the largest decline in their wealth," the *Wall Street Journal* reported.

Differences in Skills

Among the many reasons for differences in productivity and pay is that some people have more skills than others. No one is surprised that engineers earn more than messengers or that experienced shipping clerks tend to earn higher pay than inexperienced shipping clerks— and experienced pilots tend to earn more than either. Although workers may be thought of as people who simply supply labor, what most people supply is not just their ability to engage in physical exertions, but also their ability to apply mental proficiency to their tasks. The time when "a strong back and a weak mind" were sufficient for many jobs is long past in most modern economies. Obvious as this may seem, its implications are not equally obvious nor always widely understood.

In those times and places where physical strength and stamina have been the principal work requirements, productivity and pay have tended to reach their peak in the youthful prime of life, with middle-aged laborers receiving less pay or less frequent employment, or both. A premium on physical strength likewise favored male workers over female workers.

In some desperately poor countries living close to the edge of subsistence, such as China in times past, the sex differential in performing physical labor was such that it was not uncommon for the poorest people to kill female infants. While a mother was necessary for the family, an additional woman's productivity in arduous farm labor on small plots of land with only primitive tools might not produce enough food to keep her alive— and her drain on the food produced by others would thus threaten the survival of the whole family, at a time when malnutrition and death by starvation were ever-present dangers. One of the many benefits of economic development has been making such desperate and brutal choices unnecessary.

The rising importance of skills and experience relative to physical strength has changed the relative productivities of youth compared to age, and of women compared to men. This has been especially so in more recent times, as the power of machines has replaced human strength in industrial societies and as skills have become crucial in high-tech economies. Even within a relatively short span of time, the age at which most people receive their peak earnings has shifted upward. In 1951, most Americans reached their peak earnings between 35 and 44 years of age, and people in that age bracket earned 60 percent more than workers in their early twenties. By 1973, however, people in the 35 to 44-year-old bracket earned more than double the income of the younger workers. Twenty years later, the peak earnings bracket had moved up to people aged 45 to 54 years, and people in that bracket earned more than three times what workers in their early twenties earned.

Meanwhile, the dwindling importance of physical strength also reduced or eliminated the premium for male workers in an ever-widening range of occupations. This did not require all employers to have enlightened self-interest. Those who persisted in paying more for male workers who were not correspondingly more productive were at a competitive disadvantage compared to rival firms that got their work done at lower costs by eliminating the male premium, equalizing the pay of women and men to match their productivities. The most unenlightened or prejudiced employers had higher labor costs, which risked the elimination of their businesses by the ruthlessness of market competition. Thus the pay of women began to equal that of men of similar qualifications even before there were laws mandating equal pay.

While the growing importance of skills tended to reduce economic inequalities between the sexes, it tended to increase the inequality between those with skills and those without skills. Moreover, rising earnings in general, growing out of a more productive economy with more skilled people, tended to increase the inequality between those who worked regularly and those who did not. As already noted, there are striking differences between the numbers and proportions of people who work and those who don't work, as between the top income brackets and the bottom income brackets. A simultaneous rise in rewards for work and a growing welfare state that allows more people to live without working virtually guarantees increasing inequality in earnings and incomes, when many of the welfare state benefits are received in kind rather than in money, such as subsidized housing or subsidized medical care, since these benefits are not counted in income statistics.

One of the seemingly most obvious reasons for different individuals (or nations) to live at very different economic levels is that they *produce* at very different economic levels. As economies grow more technologically and economically more complex, and the work less physically demanding, those individuals with higher skills are more in demand and more highly rewarded. The growing disparities between upper level income brackets and lower level income brackets are hardly surprising under these conditions.

Job Discrimination

While pay differences often reflect differences in skills, experience, or willingness to do hard or dangerous work, these differences may also reflect discrimination against particular segments of society, such as ethnic minorities, women, lower castes, or other groups. However, in order to determine whether there is discrimination or how severe it is, we first need to define what we mean.

Sometimes discrimination is defined as judging individuals from different groups by different standards when hiring, paying or promoting. In its severest form, this can mean refusal to hire at all. "No Irish Need Apply" was a stock phrase in advertisements for many desirable jobs in nineteenth-century and early twentieth-century America. Before World War II, many hospitals in the United States would not hire black doctors or Jewish doctors, and some prestigious law firms would not hire anyone who was not a white Protestant male from the upper classes. In other cases, people might be hired from a number of groups, but individuals from different groups were channeled into different kinds of jobs.

None of this has been peculiar to the United States or to the modern era. On the contrary, members of different groups have been treated differently in laws and practices all around the world and for thousands of years of recorded history. It is the idea of treating all individuals the same, regardless of what group they come from, that is relatively recent as history is measured, and by no means universally observed around the world today.

Overlapping with discrimination, and often confused with it, are employment differences based on substantial differences in skills, experience, work habits and behavior patterns from one group to another. Mohawk Indians, for example, were long sought after to work on the construction of skyscrapers in the United States, for they walked around high up on the steel frameworks with no apparent fear or distraction from their work. In times past, Chinese laborers on rubber plantations in colonial Malaya were found to collect twice as much sap from rubber trees in a given amount of time as Malay workers did.

While preferences for some groups and reluctance or unwillingness to hire others have often been described as due to "bias," "prejudice," or "stereotypes," third-party observers cannot so easily dismiss the first-hand knowledge of those who are backing their beliefs by risking their own money. Even in the absence of different beliefs about different groups, application of the same employment criteria to different groups can result in very different proportions of these groups being hired, fired, or promoted. Distinguishing discrimination from differences in qualifications and performances is not easy in practice, though the distinction is fundamental in principle. Seldom do statistical data contain sufficiently detailed information on skills, experience, performance, or absenteeism, much less work habits and attitudes, to make possible comparisons between truly comparable individuals from different groups.

Women, for example, have long had lower incomes than men, but most women give birth to children at some point in their lives and many stay out of the labor force until their children reach an age where they can be put into some form of day care while their mothers return to work. These interruptions of their careers cost women workplace experience and seniority, which in turn inhibit the rise of their incomes over the years, relative to that of men who have been working continuously in the meantime. However, as far back as 1971, American single women who worked continuously from high school into their thirties earned slightly *more* than single men of the same description, even though women as a group earned substantially less than men as a group.

This suggests that employers were willing to pay women of the same experience the same as men, if only because they are forced to by competition in the labor market, and that women with the same experience may even outperform men and therefore earn more. But differences in domestic responsibilities prevent the sexes from having identical workplace experience or identical incomes based on that experience. None of this should be surprising. If, for example, women were paid only 75 percent of what men *of the same level of experience and performance* were paid, then any employer could hire four women instead of three men for the same money and gain a decisive advantage in production costs over competing firms.

Put differently, any employer who discriminated against women in this situation would be incurring unnecessarily higher costs, risking profits, sales, and survival in a competitive industry. It is worth noting again the distinction made in Chapter 4 between *intentional* and *systemic* causation. Even if not a single employer consciously or intentionally thought about the economic implications of discriminating against women, the systemic effects of competition would tend to weed out over time those employers who paid a sex differential not corresponding to a difference in productivity. This process would be hastened to the extent that women set up their own businesses, as many increasingly do, and do not discriminate against other women.

Substantial pay differentials between women and men are not the same across the board, but vary between those women who become mothers and those who do not. In one study, women without children earned 95 percent of what men earned, while women with children earned just 75 percent of what men earned. Moreover, even those women without children need not be in the same occupations as men. The very possibility of having children makes different occupations have different attractions to women, even before they become mothers. Occupations like librarians or teachers, which one can resume after a few years off to take care of small children, are more attractive to women who anticipate becoming mothers. But occupations such as computer engineers, where just a few years off from work can leave you far behind in this rapidly changing field, tend to be less attractive to many women. In short, women and men make different occupational choices and prepare for many of these occupations by specializing in a very different mix of subjects while being educated.

The question as to whether or how much discrimination women encounter in the labor market is a question about whether there are substantial differences in pay between women and men in the same fields with the same qualifications. The question as to whether there is or is not income parity between the sexes is very different, since differences in occupational choices, educational choices, and continuous employment all affect incomes. Men also tend to work in more hazardous occupations, which usually pay more than similar occupations that are safer. As one study noted, "although 54 percent of the workplace is male, men account for 92 percent of all job-related deaths."

Similar problems in trying to compare truly comparable individuals make it difficult to determine the presence and magnitude of discrimination between groups that differ by race or ethnicity. It is not uncommon, both in the United States and in other countries, for one racial or ethnic group to differ in age from another by a decade or more— and we have already seen how age makes a big difference in income. While gross statistics show large income differences among American racial and ethnic groups, finer breakdowns usually show much smaller differences. For example, black, white, and Hispanic males of the same age (29) and IQ (100) have all had average annual incomes within a thousand dollars of one another. In New Zealand, while there are substantial income differences between the Maori population and the white population, these differences likewise shrink drastically when comparing Maoris with other New Zealanders of the same age and with the same skills and literacy levels.

Much discussion of discrimination proceeds as if employers are free to make whatever arbitrary decisions they wish as to hiring or pay. This ignores the fact that employers do not operate in isolation but in markets. Businesses compete against each other for employees as well as competing for customers. Mistaken decisions incur costs in both product markets and labor markets and, as we have seen in earlier chapters, the costs of being wrong can have serious consequences. Moreover, these costs vary with conditions in the market.

While it is obvious that discrimination imposes a cost on those being discriminated against, in the form of lost opportunities for higher incomes, it is also true that discrimination can impose costs on those who do the discriminating, where they too lose opportunities for higher incomes. For example, when a landlord refuses to rent an apartment to people from the "wrong" group, that can mean leaving the apartment vacant longer. Clearly, that represents a loss of rent— if this is a free market. However, if there is rent control, with a surplus of applicants for vacant apartments, then such discrimination costs the landlord nothing, since there will be no delay in finding a new tenant, under these conditions.

Similar principles apply in job markets. An employer who refuses to hire qualified individuals from the "wrong" groups risks leaving his jobs unfilled longer in a free market. This means that he must either leave some work undone and some orders from customers unfilled— or else pay overtime to existing employees to get the job done. Either way, this costs the employer more money. However, in a market where wages are set artificially above the level that would exist through supply and demand, the resulting surplus of job applicants can mean that discrimination costs the employer nothing, since there would be no delay in filling the job under these conditions.

Whether these artificially higher wages are set by a labor union or by a minimum wage law does not change the principle. Empirical evidence strongly indicates that racial discrimination tends to be greater when the costs are lower and lower when the costs are greater.

Even in white-ruled South Africa during the era of apartheid, where racial discrimination against blacks was required by law, white employers in competitive industries often hired more blacks and in higher occupations than they were permitted to do by the government— and were often fined when caught doing so. This was because it was in the employers' economic self-interest to hire blacks. Similarly, whites who wanted homes built in Johannesburg typically hired illegal black construction crews, often with a token white nominally in charge to meet the requirements of the apartheid laws, rather than pay the higher price of hiring a white construction crew as the government wanted them to do. White South African landlords likewise often rented to blacks in areas where only whites were legally allowed to live.

The cost of discrimination to the discriminators is crucial for understanding such behavior. Employers who are spending other people's money— government agencies or non-profit organizations, for example— are much less affected by the cost of discrimination. In countries around the world, discrimination by government has been greater than discrimination by businesses operating in private, competitive markets. Understanding the basic economics of discrimination makes it easier to understand why blacks were starring on Broadway in the 1920s, at a time when they were not permitted to enlist in the U.S. Navy and were kept out of many civilian government jobs as well. Broadway producers were not about to lose big money that they could make by hiring black entertainers who could attract big audiences, but the costs of government discrimination were paid by the taxpayers, whether they realized it or not.

Just as minimum wage laws reduce the cost of discrimination to the employer, *maximum* wage laws increase the employer's cost of discrimination. Among the few examples of maximum wage laws in recent centuries were the wage and price controls imposed in the United States during World War II. Because wages were not allowed to rise to the level that they would reach under supply and demand, there was a shortage of workers, just as there is a shortage of housing under rent control. Many employers who had not hired blacks or women before, or who had not hired them for desirable jobs before the war, now began to do so. The "Rosie the Riveter" image that came out of World War II was in part a result of wage and price controls.

CAPITAL, LABOR AND EFFICIENCY

While everything requires some labor for its production, practically nothing can be produced by labor alone. Farmers need land, taxi drivers need cars, artists need something to draw on and something to draw with. Even a stand-up comedian needs an inventory of jokes, which is his capital, just as hydroelectric dams are the capital of companies that generate electricity.

Capital complements labor in the production process, but it also competes with labor for employment. In other words, many goods and services can be produced either with much labor and little capital or much capital and little labor. When transit workers' unions force bus drivers' pay rates much above what they would be in a competitive labor market, transit companies tend to add more capital, in order to save on the use of the more expensive labor. Buses grow longer, sometimes becoming essentially two buses with a flexible connection between them, so that one driver is using twice as much capital as before and is capable of moving twice as many passengers.

Some might think that this is more "efficient," but efficiency is not so easily defined. If we arbitrarily define efficiency as output per unit of labor, as some do, then it is merely circular reasoning to say that having one bus driver moving more passengers is more efficient. It may in fact cost more money per passenger to move them, as a result of the additional capital needed for the expanded buses and the more expensive labor of the drivers.

If bus drivers were not unionized and were paid no more than was necessary to attract qualified people, then undoubtedly their wage rates would be lower and it would then be profitable for the transit companies to hire more of them and use shorter buses. Not only would the total cost of moving passengers be less, passengers would have less time to wait at bus stops because of the shorter and more numerous buses. This is not a small concern to people waiting on street corners on cold winter days or in high-crime neighborhoods at night.

"Efficiency" cannot be meaningfully defined without regard to human desires and preferences. Even the efficiency of an automobile engine is not simply a matter of physics. All the energy generated by the engine will be used in some way— either in moving the car forward, overcoming internal friction among the engine's moving parts, or shaking the automobile body in various ways. It is only when we define our goal— moving the car forward— that we can regard the percentage of the engine's power that is used for that task as indicating its efficiency, and the other power dissipated in various other ways as being "wasted."

Europeans long regarded American agriculture as "inefficient" because output per acre was much lower in the United States than in much of Europe. On the other hand, output per agricultural worker was much higher in the United States than in Europe. The reason was that land was far more plentiful in the U.S. and labor was more scarce. An American farmer would spread himself thinner over far more land and would have correspondingly less time to devote to each acre. In Europe, where land was more scarce, and therefore more expensive because of supply and demand, the European farmer concentrated on the more intensive cultivation of what land he could get, spending more time clearing away weeds and rocks, or otherwise devoting more attention to ensuring the maximum output per acre.

Similarly, Third World countries often get more use out of given capital equipment than do wealthier and more industrialized countries. Such tools as hammers and screwdrivers may be plentiful enough for each worker in an American factory or shop to have his own, but that is much less likely to be the case in a much poorer country, where such tools are more likely to be shared, or shared more widely, than among Americans making the same products. Looked at from another angle, each hammer in a poor country is likely to drive more nails per year, since it is shared among more people and has less idle time. That does not make the poorer country more "efficient." It is just that the relative scarcities of capital and labor are different.

Capital tends to be scarcer and hence more expensive in poorer countries, while labor is more abundant and hence cheaper than in richer countries. Poor countries tend to economize on the more expensive factor, just as richer countries economize on a different factor that is more expensive and scarce there, namely labor. In the richer countries, it is capital that is more plentiful and cheaper, while labor is more scarce and more expensive.

When a freight train comes into a railroad stop, workers are needed to unload it. When a freight train arrives in the middle of the night, it can either be unloaded then and there, so that the train can proceed on its way intact, or some boxcars can be detached and left on a siding until the workers come to work the next morning to unload them.

In a country where such capital as railroad boxcars are very scarce and labor is more plentiful, it makes sense to have workers available around the clock, so that they can immediately unload boxcars, and this very scarce resource does not remain idle. But, in a country that is rich in capital, it may often be more economical to detach individual boxcars from a train, letting the train continue on its way. Thus the detached boxcars can sit idle on a siding, waiting to be unloaded the next morning, rather than have expensive workers sitting around idle during the night, waiting for the next train to arrive.

This is not just a question about these particular workers' paychecks or this particular railroad company's monetary expenses. From the standpoint of the economy as a whole, the more fundamental question is: What are the alternative uses of these workers' time and the alternative uses of the railroad boxcars? In other words, it is not just a question of money. The money only reflects underlying realities that would be the same in a socialist, feudal or other non-market economy. Whether it makes sense to leave the boxcars idle waiting for the workers to arrive or to leave the workers idle waiting for trains to arrive depends on the relative scarcities of labor and capital and their relative productivity in alternative uses.

During the era of the Soviet Union and its Cold War competition with the United States, the Soviets used to boast of the fact that an average Soviet boxcar moved more freight per year than an average American boxcar. But, far from indicating that their economy was more efficient, this showed that Soviet railroads lacked the abundant capital of the American railroad industry, and that Soviet labor had less valuable alternative uses of its time than did American labor. Similarly, a study of West African economies in the mid-twentieth century noted that trucks there "are in service twenty-four hours a day for seven days a week and are generally tightly packed with passengers and freight."

For similar reasons, automobiles tend to have longer lives in poor countries than in richer countries. Not only does it pay many poorer countries to keep their own automobiles in use longer, it pays them to buy used cars from richer countries. In just one year, 90,000 used cars from Japan were sold to the United Arab Emirates. Dubai, one of those emirates, has become a center for the sale of these used vehicles to other Middle Eastern and African countries. The *Wall Street Journal* reported: "Many African cities are already teeming with Toyotas, even though very few new cars have been sold there." In Cameroon, the taxis "are beaten-up old Toyotas, carrying four in the back and three in the front." Even cars needing repairs are sold internationally:

> Japan's exporters also ship out thousands of cars that have been dented or damaged. Mechanics in Dubai can repair vehicles for a fraction of the price in Japan, where high labor costs make it one of the world's most expensive places to fix a car.

By and large, it pays richer countries to junk their cars, refrigerators, and other capital equipment in a shorter time than it would pay people in poorer countries to do so. Nor is this a matter of being able to afford "waste." It would be a waste to keep repairing this equipment, when the same efforts elsewhere in the Japanese economy— or the American economy or German economy— would produce more than enough wealth to provide replacements. But it would not make sense for poorer countries, whose alternative uses of time are not as productive, to junk their equipment at the same times when richer countries junk theirs. The fact that labor is cheaper in Dubai than in Japan is not a happenstance. Labor is more productive in richer countries. That is one of the reasons why these countries are more prosperous in the first place. The sale of used equipment from rich countries to poor countries can be an efficient way of handling the situation for both kinds of countries.

In a modern industrial economy, many goods are mass produced, thereby lowering their production costs, and hence prices, because of economies of scale. But repairs on those products are still typically done individually by hand, without the benefit of economies of scale, and therefore relatively expensively. In such a mass production economy, repeated repairs can in many cases quickly reach the point where it would be cheaper to get a new, mass-produced replacement. The number of television repair shops in the United States has therefore not kept pace with the growing number of television sets, as mass production has reduced television prices to the point where many malfunctioning sets can be more cheaply replaced than repaired.

A book by two Russian economists, back in the days of the Soviet Union, pointed out that in the Union of Soviet Socialist Republics "equipment is endlessly repaired and patched up," so that the "average service life of capital stock in the U.S.S.R. is forty-seven years, as against seventeen in the United States." They were not bragging. They were complaining.

Chapter 11

MINIMUM WAGE LAWS

*Supply-and-demand says that above-market prices create
unsaleable surpluses, but that has not stopped most of
Europe from regulating labor markets into decades of
depression-level unemployment.*

Bryan Caplan

Just as we can better understand the economic role of prices in general
when we see what happens when prices are not allowed to function, so we
can better understand the economic role of workers' pay by seeing what
happens when that pay is not allowed to vary with the supply and demand
for labor. Historically, political authorities set maximum wage levels
centuries before they set minimum wage levels. Today, however, only the
latter are widespread.

Minimum wage laws make it illegal to pay less than the government-
specified price for labor. By the simplest and most basic economics, a price
artificially raised tends to cause more to be supplied and less to be demanded
than when prices are left to be determined by supply and demand in a free
market. The result is a surplus, whether the price that is set artificially high
is that of farm produce or labor.

Making it illegal to pay less than a given amount does not make a worker's
productivity worth that amount— and, if it is not, that worker is unlikely to
be employed. Yet minimum wage laws are almost always discussed politically
in terms of the benefits they confer on workers receiving those wages.
Unfortunately, the real minimum wage is always zero, regardless of the laws,
and that is the wage that many workers receive in the wake of the creation or

escalation of a government-mandated minimum wage, because they either lose their jobs or fail to find jobs when they enter the labor force. The logic is plain and an examination of the empirical evidence from various countries around the world tends to back up that logic, as we shall see.

UNEMPLOYMENT

Because the government does not hire surplus labor the way it buys surplus agricultural output, a labor surplus takes the form of unemployment, which tends to be higher under minimum wage laws than in a free market.

Unemployed workers are not surplus in the sense of being useless or in the sense that there is no work around that needs doing. Most of these workers are perfectly capable of producing goods and services, even if not to the same extent as more skilled or more experienced workers. The unemployed are made idle by wage rates artificially set above the level of their productivity. Those who are idled in their youth are of course delayed in acquiring the job skills and experience which could make them more productive— and therefore higher earners— later on. That is, they not only lose the low pay that they could have earned in an entry-level job, they lose the higher pay that they could have moved on to and begun earning after gaining experience in entry-level jobs. Younger workers are disproportionately represented among people with low rates of pay in countries around the world. Only about three percent of American workers over the age of 24 earn the minimum wage, for example.

Although most modern industrial societies have minimum wage laws, not all do. Switzerland has been a rare exception— and has had very low unemployment rates. In 2003, *The Economist* magazine reported: "Switzerland's unemployment neared a five-year high of 3.9% in February." Swiss labor unions have been trying to get a minimum wage law passed, arguing that this would prevent "exploitation" of workers. However, the Swiss cabinet still rejected the proposed minimum wage law in January 2013. Its unemployment rate at that time was 3.1 percent.

Singapore likewise has no minimum wage law and its unemployment rate has likewise been 2.1 percent. Back in 1991, when Hong Kong was still a

British colony, it too had no minimum wage law, and its unemployment rate was under 2 percent. In the United States, during the Coolidge administration— the last administration before there was any federal minimum wage law— the annual unemployment rate got as low as 1.8 percent.

The explicit minimum wage rate understates the labor costs imposed by European governments, which also mandate various employer contributions to pension plans and health benefits, among other things. Higher costs in the form of mandated benefits have the same economic effect as higher costs in the form of minimum wage laws. Europe's unemployment rates shot up when such government-mandated benefits, to be paid for by employers, grew sharply during the 1980s and 1990s.

In Germany, such benefits accounted for half of the average labor cost per hour. By comparison, such benefits accounted for less than one-fourth the average labor costs per hour in Japan and the United States. Average hourly compensation of manufacturing employees in the European Union countries in general is higher than in the United States or Japan. So is unemployment.

Comparisons of Canada with the United States show similar patterns. Over a five-year period, Canadian provinces had minimum wage rates that were a higher percentage of output per capita than in American states, and unemployment rates were correspondingly higher in Canada, as was the average duration of unemployment, while the Canadian rate of job creation lagged behind that in the United States. Over this five-year period, three Canadian provinces had unemployment rates in excess of 10 percent, with a high of 16.9 percent in Newfoundland, but none of the 50 American states averaged unemployment rates in double digits over that same five-year period.

A belated recognition of the connection between minimum wage laws and unemployment by government officials has caused some countries to allow their real minimum wage levels to be eroded by inflation, avoiding the political risks of trying to repeal these laws explicitly, when so many voters think of these laws as being beneficial to workers. Such laws are in fact beneficial to those workers who continue to be employed— those who are on the inside looking out, but at the expense of the unemployed who are on the outside looking in.

Labor unions also benefit from minimum wage laws, and are among the strongest proponents of such laws, even though their own members typically make much more than the minimum wage rate. There is a reason for this. Just as most goods and services can be produced with either much labor and little capital or vice versa, so can most things be produced using varying proportions of low-skilled labor and high-skilled labor, depending on their respective costs, relative to one another. Thus experienced unionized workers are competing for employment against younger, inexperienced, and less skilled workers, whose pay is likely to be at or near the minimum wage. The higher the minimum wage goes, the more the unskilled and inexperienced workers are likely to be displaced by more experienced and higher skilled unionized workers.

Just as businesses seek to have government impose tariffs on imported goods that compete with their own products, so labor unions use minimum wage laws as tariffs to force up the price of non-union labor that competes with their members for jobs.

Among 3.6 million Americans earning no more than the minimum wage in 2012, just over half were from 16 to 24 years of age— and 64 percent of them worked part-time. Yet political campaigns to increase the minimum wage often talk in terms of providing "a living wage" sufficient to support a family of four— such families as most minimum wage workers do not have, and would be ill-advised to have before they reach the point where they can feed and clothe their children. The average family income of a minimum wage worker is more than $44,000 a year— far more than can be earned by someone working at minimum wages. But 42 percent of minimum-wage workers live with parents or some other relative. In other words, they are not supporting a family but often a family is supporting them. Only 15 percent of minimum-wage workers are supporting themselves and a dependent, the kind of person envisioned by those who advocate a "living wage."

Nevertheless, a number of American cities have passed "living wage" laws, which are essentially local minimum wage laws specifying a higher wage rate than the national minimum wage law. Their effects have been similar to the effects of national minimum wage laws in the United States and other countries— that is, the poorest people have been the ones who have most often lost jobs.

The huge financial, political, emotional, and ideological investment of various groups in issues revolving around minimum wage laws means that dispassionate analysis is not always the norm. Moreover, the statistical complexities of separating out the effects of minimum wage rates on employment from all the other ever-changing variables which also affect employment mean that honest differences of opinion are possible when examining empirical data. However, when all is said and done, most empirical studies indicate that minimum wage laws reduce employment in general, and especially the employment of younger, less skilled, and minority workers.

A majority of professional economists surveyed in Britain, Germany, Canada, Switzerland, and the United States agreed that minimum wage laws increase unemployment among low-skilled workers. Economists in France and Austria did not. However, the majority among Canadian economists was 85 percent and among American economists was 90 percent. Dozens of studies of the effects of minimum wages in the United States and dozens more studies of the effects of minimum wages in various countries in Europe, Latin America, the Caribbean, Indonesia, Canada, Australia, and New Zealand were reviewed in 2006 by two economists at the National Bureau of Economic Research. They concluded that, despite the various approaches and methods used in these studies, this literature as a whole was one "largely solidifying the conventional view that minimum wages reduce employment among low-skilled workers."

Those officially responsible for administering minimum wage laws, such as the U. S. Department of Labor and various local agencies, prefer to claim that these laws do not create unemployment. So do labor unions, which have a vested interest in such laws as protection for their own members' jobs. In South Africa, for example, *The Economist* reported:

> The main union body, the Congress of South African Trade Unions (Cosatu) says joblessness has nothing to do with labour laws. The problem, it says, is that businesses are not trying hard enough to create jobs.

In Britain, the Low Pay Commission, which sets the minimum wage, has likewise resisted the idea that the wages it set were responsible for an unemployment rate of 17.3 percent among workers under the age of 25, at a time when the overall unemployment rate was 7.6 percent.

Even though most studies show that unemployment tends to increase as minimum wages are imposed or increased, those few studies that seem to indicate otherwise have been hailed in some quarters as having "refuted" this "myth." However, one common problem with some research on the employment effects of minimum wage laws is that surveys of employers before and after a minimum wage increase can survey only those particular businesses which survived in both periods. Given the high rates of business failures in many industries, the results for the surviving businesses may be completely different from the results for the industry as a whole.* Using such research methods, you could survey people who have played Russian roulette and "prove" from their experiences that it is a harmless activity, since those for whom it was not harmless are unlikely to be around to be surveyed. Thus you would have "refuted" the "myth" that Russian roulette is dangerous.

It would be comforting to believe that the government can simply decree higher pay for low-wage workers, without having to worry about unfortunate repercussions, but the preponderance of evidence indicates that labor is not exempt from the basic economic principle that artificially high prices cause surpluses. In the case of surplus human beings, that can be a special tragedy when they are already from low-income, unskilled, or minority backgrounds and urgently need to get on the job ladder, if they are to move up the ladder by acquiring experience and skills.

Unemployment varies not only in its quantity as of a given time, it varies also in how long workers remain unemployed. Like the unemployment rate,

---

* Imagine that an industry consists of ten firms, each hiring 1,000 workers before a minimum wage increase, for an industry total of 10,000 employees. If three of these firms go out of business between the first and the second surveys, and only one new firm enters the industry, then only the seven firms that were in existence both "before" and "after" can be surveyed and their results reported. With fewer firms, employment per firm may increase, even if employment in the industry as a whole decreases. If, for example, the seven surviving firms and the new firm each hire 1,100 employees, this means that the industry as a whole will have 8,800 employees— fewer than before the minimum wage increase— and yet a study of the seven surviving firms would show a 10 percent *increase* in employment in the firms surveyed, rather than the 12 percent *decrease* for the industry as a whole. Since minimum wages can cause unemployment by (1) reducing employment among all the firms, (2) by pushing marginal firms into bankruptcy, or (3) discouraging the entry of replacement firms, reports based on surveying only survivors can create as false a conclusion as interviewing people who have played Russian roulette.

the *duration* of unemployment varies considerably from country to country. Countries which drive up labor costs with either high minimum wages or generous employee benefits imposed on employers by law, or both, tend to have longer-lasting unemployment, as well as higher rates of unemployment. In Germany, for example, there is no national minimum wage law but government-imposed mandates on employers, job security laws, and strong labor unions artificially raise labor costs anyway. As of the year 2000, 51.5 percent of the unemployed in Germany were unemployed for a year or more, while just 6 percent of the unemployed in the United States were unemployed that long. However, as the U.S. Congress extended the period during which unemployment compensation would be paid, the share of Americans who remained unemployed for a year or longer rose to 31.3 percent in 2011, compared to 48 percent in Germany.

Informal Minimum Wages

Sometimes a minimum wage is imposed not by law, but by custom, informal government pressures, labor unions or— especially in the case of Third World countries— by international public opinion or boycotts pressuring multinational companies to pay Third World workers wages comparable to the wages usually found in more industrially developed countries. Although organized public pressures for higher pay for Third World workers in Southeast Asia and Latin America have made news in the United States in recent years, such pressures are not new nor confined to Americans. Similar pressures were put on companies operating in colonial West Africa in the middle of the twentieth century.

Informal minimum wages imposed in these ways have had effects very similar to those of explicit minimum wage laws. An economist studying colonial West Africa in the mid-twentieth century found signs telling job applicants that there were "no vacancies" almost everywhere. Nor was this peculiar to West Africa. The same economist— P.T. Bauer of the London School of Economics— noted that it was "a striking feature of many under-developed countries that money wages are maintained at high levels" while "large numbers are seeking but unable to find work." These were of course not high levels of wages compared to what was earned by workers in more industrialized economies, but high wages relative to Third World workers' productivity and high relative to their alternative earning opportunities, such as in agriculture, domestic service, or self-employment as street vendors and the like— that is, in sectors of the economy not subject to external pressures to maintain an artificially inflated wage rate.

The magnitude of the unemployment created by artificially high wages that multinational companies felt pressured to pay in West Africa was indicated by Professor Bauer's first-hand investigations:

> I asked the manager of the tobacco factory of the Nigerian Tobacco Company (a subsidiary of the British-American Tobacco Company) in Ibadan whether he could expand his labour force without raising wages if he wished to do so. He replied that his only problem would be to control the mob of applicants. Very much the same opinion was expressed by the Kano district agent of the firm of John Holt and Company in respect of their tannery. In December 1949 a firm of produce buyers in Kano dismissed two clerks and within two days received between fifty and sixty applications for the posts without having publicized the vacancies. The same firm proposed to erect a groundnut crushing plant. By June 1950 machinery had not yet been installed; but without having advertised a vacancy it had already received about seven hundred letters asking for employment. . . I learnt that the European-owned brewery and the recently established manufacturers of stationery constantly receive shoals of applications for employment.

Nothing had changed fundamentally more than half a century later, when twenty-first century job seekers in South Africa were lined up far in excess of the number of jobs available, as reported in the *New York Times*:

> When Tiger Wheels opened a wheel plant six years ago in this faded industrial town, the crush of job seekers was so enormous that the chief executive, Eddie Keizan, ordered a corrugated iron roof to shield them from the midday heat.
> "There were hundreds and hundreds of people outside our gate, just sitting there, in the sun, for days and days," Mr. Keizan recalled in an interview. "We had no more jobs, but they refused to believe us."

Why then did wage rates not come down in response to supply and demand, leading to more employment at a lower wage level, as basic economic principles might lead us to expect? According to the same report:

In other developing countries, legions of unskilled workers have kept
down labor costs. But South Africa's leaders, vowing not to let their
nation become the West's sweatshop, heeded the demands of politically
powerful labor unions for new protections and benefits.

Such "protections and benefits" included minimum wages set at levels
higher than the productivity of many South African workers. The net result
was that when Tiger Wheels, which had made aluminum wheels solely in
South Africa for two decades, expanded its production, it expanded by hiring
more workers in Poland, where it earned a profit, rather than in South Africa,
where it could only break even or sustain a loss. The misfortunes of eager but
frustrated African job applicants throughout the South African economy were
only part of the story. The output that they could have produced, if employed,
would have made a particularly important contribution to the economic well-
being of the consuming public in a very poor region, lacking many things that
others take for granted in more prosperous societies.

It is not at all clear that workers as a whole are benefitted by artificially
high wage rates in the Third World. Employed workers— those on the
inside looking out— obviously benefit, while those on the outside looking
in lose. For the population as a whole, including consumers, it would be hard
to make a case that there is a net benefit, since there are fewer consumer
goods when people who are willing to work cannot find jobs producing
those consumer goods. The only category of clear beneficiaries are people
living in richer countries, who can enjoy the feeling that they are helping
people in poorer countries, or Third World leaders too proud to let their
workers be hired at wage rates commensurate with their productivity.

While South African workers' productivity is twice that of workers in
Indonesia, they are paid five times as much— when they can find jobs at all.
In short, these productive South African workers are not "surplus" or
"unemployable" in any sense other than being priced out of the market by
politicians.

As already noted in Chapter 10, South African firms use much capital per
worker. This is more efficient for the firms, but only because South African
labor laws make labor artificially more expensive, both with minimum wage
laws and with laws that make laying off workers costly. "Labour costs are more

than three-and-a-half times higher than in the most productive areas of China and a good 75% higher than in Malaysia or Poland," according to *The Economist*. With such artificially high costs of South African labor, it pays employers to use more capital, but this is not greater efficiency for the economy as a whole, which is worse off for having so many people unemployed, which is to say, with so many resources idled instead of being allocated.

South Africa is not unique. A National Bureau of Economic Research study, comparing the employment of low-skilled workers in Europe and the United States found that, since the 1970s, such workers have been disproportionately displaced by machinery in European countries where there are higher minimum wages and more benefits mandated to be paid for by employers. The study pointed out that it was since the 1970s that European labor markets moved toward more control by governments and labor unions, while in the United States the influence of government and labor unions on labor markets became less.

The net result has been that, despite more technological change in the United States, the substitution of capital for labor in low-skilled occupations has been greater in Europe. Sometimes the work of low-skilled labor is not displaced by capital but simply dispensed with, as the study noted:

> It is close to impossible to find a parking attendant in Paris, Frankfurt or Milan, while in New York City they are common. When you arrive even in an average Hotel in an American city you are received by a platoon of bag carriers, door openers etc. In a similar hotel in Europe you often have to carry your bags on your own. These are not simply trivial traveler's pointers, but indicate a deeper and widespread phenomenon: low skilled jobs have been substituted away for machines in Europe, or eliminated, much more than in the US, while technological progress at the "top" i.e. at the high-tech sector, is faster in the US than in Europe.

Just as a price set by government below the free market level tends to cause quality deterioration in the product that is being sold, because a shortage means that buyers will be forced to accept things of lower quality than they would have otherwise, so a price set above the free market level tends to cause a rise in average quality, as the surplus allows the buyers to cherry-pick and purchase only the better quality items. What that means in the labor market is that job qualification requirements are likely to rise and that some workers who would ordinarily be hired in a free market may become "unemployable" when there are minimum wage laws. Unemployability, like shortages and surpluses, is not independent of price.

In a free market, low-productivity workers are just as employable at a low wage rate as high-productivity workers are at a high wage rate. During the long era from the late nineteenth century to the mid-twentieth century, when black Americans received lower quantities and lower qualities of education than whites in the South where most lived, the labor force participation rates of black workers were nevertheless slightly higher than those of white workers. For most of that era, there were no minimum wage laws to price them out of jobs and, even after a nationwide minimum wage law was passed in 1938, the wartime inflation of the 1940s raised wages in the free market above the legally prescribed minimum wage level, making the law largely irrelevant by the late 1940s. The law was amended in 1950, beginning a series of minimum wage escalations.

If low-wage employers make workers worse off than they would be otherwise, then it is hard to imagine why workers would work for them. "Because they have no alternative" may be one answer. But that answer implies that low-wage employers provide a better option than these particular workers have otherwise— and so are *not* making them worse off. Thus the argument against low-wage employers making workers worse off is internally self-contradictory. What would make low-wage workers worse off would be foreclosing one of their already limited options. This is especially harmful when considering that low-wage workers are often young, entry-level workers for whom work experience can be more valuable in the long run than the immediate pay itself.

DIFFERENTIAL IMPACT

Because people differ in many ways, those who are unemployed are not likely to be a random sample of the labor force. In country after country around the world, those whose employment prospects are reduced most by minimum wage laws are those who are younger, less experienced or less skilled. This pattern has been found in New Zealand, France, Canada, the Netherlands, and the United States, for example. It should not be surprising that those whose productivity falls furthest short of the minimum wage level would be the ones most likely to be unable to find a job.

In Australia, the *lowest* unemployment rate for workers under the age of 25, during the entire period from 1978 to 2002, never fell below 10 percent, while the *highest* unemployment rate for the population in general barely reached 10 percent once during that same period. Australia has an unusually high minimum wage, relatively speaking, since its minimum wage level is nearly 60 percent of that country's median wage rate, while the minimum wage in the United States has been less than 40 percent of the American median wage rate.

In early twenty-first century France, the national unemployment rate was 10 percent but, among workers under the age of twenty five, the unemployment rate was more than 20 percent. In Belgium, the unemployment rate for workers under the age of twenty five was 22 percent and in Italy 27 percent. During the global downturn in 2009, the unemployment rate for workers under the age of 25 was 21 percent in the European Union countries as a whole, with more than 25 percent in Italy and Ireland, and more than 40 percent in Spain.

As American laws and policies moved more in the direction of those in other modern industrial nations in the early twenty-first century, the unemployment rate among Americans who were from 25 to 34 years old went from being lower than unemployment rates in the same age bracket in Canada, Britain, Germany, France and Japan in 2000 to being *higher* than in these same countries in 2011.

Some countries in Europe set lower minimum wage rates for teenagers than for adults, and New Zealand simply exempted teenagers from the coverage of its minimum wage law until 1994. This was tacit recognition of the fact that those workers less in demand were likely to be hardest hit by unemployment created by minimum wage laws.

Another group disproportionately affected by minimum wage laws are members of unpopular racial or ethnic minority groups. Indeed, minimum wage laws were once advocated explicitly because of the likelihood that such laws would reduce or eliminate the competition of particular minorities, whether they were Japanese in Canada during the 1920s or blacks in the United States and South Africa during the same era. Such expressions of overt racial discrimination were both legal and socially accepted in all three countries at that time.

The history of black workers in the United States illustrates the point. As already noted, from the late nineteenth-century on through the middle of the twentieth century, the labor force participation rate of black Americans was slightly higher than that of white Americans. In other words, blacks were just as employable at the wages they received as whites were at their very different wages. The minimum wage law changed that. Before federal minimum wage laws were instituted in the 1930s, the black unemployment rate was slightly *lower* than the white unemployment rate in 1930. But then followed the Davis-Bacon Act of 1931, the National Industrial Recovery Act of 1933 and the Fair Labor Standards Act of 1938— all of which imposed government-mandated minimum wages, either on a particular sector or more broadly.

The National Labor Relations Act of 1935, which promoted unionization, also tended to price black workers out of jobs, in addition to union rules that kept blacks from jobs by barring them from union membership. The National Industrial Recovery Act raised wage rates in the Southern textile industry by 70 percent in just five months, and its impact nationwide was estimated to have cost blacks half a million jobs. While this Act was later declared unconstitutional by the Supreme Court, the Fair Labor Standards Act of 1938, establishing a national minimum wage, was upheld by the High Court. As already noted, the inflation of the 1940s largely nullified the effect of the Fair Labor Standards Act, until it was amended in 1950 to raise minimum wages to a level that would have some actual effect on current wages.

The unemployment rates of young black males during the late 1940s— the years prior to the repeated escalations of the minimum wage that began in 1950— contrast sharply with their unemployment rates in later years. As of 1948, for example, the unemployment rate for blacks aged 16–17 years was 9.4 percent, while that of whites the same ages was 10.2 percent. For blacks 18–19 years of age, the unemployment rate that year was 10.5 percent, while that of whites the same ages was 9.4 percent. In short, teenage unemployment rates were a fraction of what they were to become in later years, and black and white teenage unemployment rates were very similar.

Even though the following year— 1949— was a recession year, rising black teenage male unemployment rates that year still did not reach 20 percent. The black teenage unemployment rate during the recession of 1949 was lower than it was to be at any time during even the boom years of the 1960s and later decades. Black 16 and 17 year-olds had an unemployment rate of 15.8 percent in the 1949 recession year, but that was less than half of what it would be in every year from 1971 through 1997, and less than one-third of what it would be in 2009. Repeated increases in the minimum wage marked these later years of much higher unemployment rates among black teenagers.

The wide gap between the unemployment rates of black and white teenage males likewise dates from the escalation of the minimum wage and the spread of its coverage in the 1950s. The usual explanations of higher unemployment among black teenagers— less education, lack of skills, racism— cannot explain their rising unemployment, since all these handicaps were worse during the earlier period when black teenage unemployment was much lower.

Chapter 12

SPECIAL PROBLEMS IN LABOR MARKETS

The promotion of economic equality and the alleviation of poverty are distinct and often conflicting.

Peter Bauer

Although the basic economic principles underlying the allocation of labor are not fundamentally different from the principles underlying the allocation of inanimate resources, it is not equally easy to look at labor and its pay rates in the same way one looks at the prices of iron ore or bushels of wheat. Moreover, we are concerned about the conditions where people work in a way that we are not concerned about the conditions where machinery is used or where raw materials are processed, except in so far as these conditions affect people.

Other issues that arise with labor that do not arise with inanimate factors of production include job security, collective bargaining, occupational licensing and questions about whether labor is "exploited" in any of the various meanings of that word.

The statistics that measure what is happening in labor markets also present special problems that are not present when considering statistics about inanimate factors of production. The unemployment rate is one example.

UNEMPLOYMENT STATISTICS

The unemployment rate is a very important statistic, as an indicator of the health of the economy and society. But, for that very reason, it is necessary to know the limitations of such statistics.

Because human beings have volition and make choices, unlike inanimate factors of production, many people choose not to be in the labor force at a given time and place. They may be students, retired people or housewives who work in their own homes, taking care of their families, but are not on any employer's payroll. Children below some legally specified age are not even allowed to be gainfully employed at all. Those people who are officially counted as unemployed are people who are in the labor force, seeking employment but not finding it. Patients in hospitals, people serving in the military forces and inmates of prisons are also among those people who are not counted as part of the labor force.

While unemployment statistics can be very valuable, they can also be misleading if their definitions are not kept in mind. The unemployment rate is based on what percentage of the people who are in the labor force are not working. However, people's choices as to whether or not to be in the labor force at any given time means that unemployment rates are not wholly objective data, but vary with choices made differently under different conditions, and varying from country to country.

Although the unemployment rate is supposed to indicate what proportion of the people in the labor force do and do not have jobs, sometimes the unemployment rate goes down while the number of people without jobs is going up. The reason is that a prolonged recession or depression may lead some people to stop looking for a job, after many long and futile searches. Since such people are no longer counted as being in the labor force, their exodus will reduce the unemployment rate, even if the proportion of people without jobs has not been reduced at all.

In the wake of the downturn of the American economy in the early twenty-first century, the unemployment rate rose to just over 10 percent. Then the unemployment rate began to decline— as more and more people stopped looking for jobs, and thus dropped out of the labor force. The labor force participation rate declined to levels not seen in decades. Although some saw the declining unemployment rate as an indication of the success of government policies, much of that decline represented people who had simply given up looking for jobs, and subsisted on resources provided by various government programs. For example, more than 3.7 million workers went on Social Security disability payments from the middle of 2009 to early 2013, "the fastest enrollment pace ever," according to *Investor's Business Daily*.

Rather than relying solely on the unemployment rate, an alternative way of measuring unemployment is to compare what percentage of the adult population outside of institutions (colleges, the military, hospitals, prisons, etc.) are working. This avoids the problem of people who have given up looking for work not being counted as unemployed, even if they would be glad to have a job if they thought there was any reasonable chance of finding one. In the first half of 2010, for example, while the unemployment rate remained steady at 9.5 percent, the proportion of the non-institutional adult population with jobs continued a decline that was the largest in more than half a century. The fact that more people were giving up looking for jobs kept the official unemployment rate from rising to reflect the increased difficulty of finding a job.

Things become more complicated when comparing different countries. For example, *The Economist* magazine found that more than 80 percent of the male population between the ages of 15 and 64 were employed in Iceland but fewer than 70 percent were in France. Any number of things could account for such differences. Not only are there variations from country to country in the number of people going to college but there are also variations in the ease or difficulty with which people qualify for government benefits that make it unnecessary for them to work, or to look for work, or to accept jobs that do not meet their hopes or expectations.

High as the unemployment rate has been in France for years, French unemployment statistics tend to *understate* how many adults are not working. That is because the French welfare state makes it easier for senior citizens to withdraw from the labor force altogether— and unemployment rates are based on the size of the labor force. Thus, while more than 70 percent of people who are from 55 to 64 years of age are working in Switzerland, only 37 percent of the people in that same age bracket are working in France.

The point here is that, while people who choose not to look for work are not employed, they are also not automatically classified as unemployed. Therefore statistics on employment rates and unemployment rates do not necessarily move in opposite directions. Both rates can rise at the same time or fall at the same time, depending on how easy or how difficult it is for people to live without working. Unemployment compensation is one obvious way for people to live for some period of time without working. How long that time is and how generous the benefits are vary from country to country. According to *The Economist*, unemployment compensation in the United States "pays lower benefits for less time and to a smaller share of the unemployed" than in other industrialized countries. It is also true that unemployed Americans spend more time per day looking for work— more than four times as much time as unemployed workers in Germany, Britain or Sweden.

"Even five years after losing his job, a sacked Norwegian worker can expect to take home almost three-quarters of what he did while employed," *The Economist* reported. Some other Western European countries are almost as generous for the first year after losing a job: Spain, France, Sweden and Germany pay more than 60 percent of what the unemployed worker earned while working, but only in Belgium does this level of generosity continue for five years. In the United States, unemployment benefits usually expire after one year, though Congress has, at some times, extended these benefits longer.

There are various kinds of unemployment, and unemployment statistics alone cannot tell you what kind of unemployment currently exists. There is, for example, what economists call "frictional unemployment." People who graduate from high school or college do not always have jobs waiting for them or find jobs the first day they start looking. Meanwhile, job vacancies remain unfilled while there are unemployed people looking for work, because it takes time for the right employers and the right workers to find one another. If you think of the economy as a big, complex machine, then there is always going to be some loss of efficiency by social versions of internal friction. That is why the unemployment rate is never literally zero, even in boom years when employers are having a hard time trying to find enough people to fill their job vacancies.

Such transient unemployment must be distinguished from long-term unemployment. Countries differ in how long unemployment lasts. A study by the Organisation for Economic Co-operation and Development showed that, among the unemployed, those who were unemployed for a year or more constituted 9 percent of all unemployed in the United States, 23 percent in Britain, 48 percent in Germany and 59 percent in Italy. In short, even the difference between American and European rates of unemployment as a whole understates the difference in a worker's likelihood of finding a job. Ironically, it is in countries with strong job security laws, like Germany, where it is harder to find a new job. Fewer job opportunities in such countries often take the form of fewer hours worked per year, as well as higher unemployment rates and longer periods of unemployment.

One form of unemployment that has long stirred political emotions and led to economic fallacies is technological unemployment. Virtually every advance in technological efficiency puts somebody out of work. This is nothing new:

> By 1830 Barthélemy Thimonnier, a French tailor who had long been obsessed with the idea, had patented and perfected an effective sewing machine. When eighty of his machines were making uniforms for the French army, Paris tailors, alarmed at the threat to their jobs, smashed the machines and drove Thimonnier out of the city.

Such reactions were not peculiar to France. In early nineteenth century Britain, people called Luddites smashed machinery when they realized that the industrial revolution threatened their jobs. Opposition to technological efficiency— as well as other kinds of efficiency, ranging from new organizational methods to international trade— has often focused on the effects of efficiency on jobs. These are almost invariably the short run effects on particular workers, in disregard of the effects on consumers or on workers in other fields.

The rise of the automobile industry, for example, no doubt caused huge losses of employment among those raising and caring for horses, as well as among the makers of saddles, horseshoes, whips, horse-drawn carriages and other paraphernalia associated with this mode of transportation. But these were not *net* losses of jobs, as the automobile industry required vast numbers of workers, as did industries producing gasoline, batteries, and car repair services, as well as other sectors of the economy catering to motorists, such as motels, fast food restaurants, and suburban shopping malls.

WORKING CONDITIONS

Both governments and labor unions have regulated working conditions, such as the maximum hours of work per week, safety rules, and various amenities to make the job less stressful or more pleasant.

The economic effects of regulating working conditions are very similar to the effects of regulating wages, because better working conditions, like higher wage rates, tend to make a given job both more attractive to the workers and more costly to the employers. Moreover, employers take these costs into account thereafter, when deciding how many workers they can afford to hire when there are higher costs per worker, as well as how high they can afford to bid for workers, since money spent creating better working conditions is the same as money spent for higher wage rates per hour.

Other things being equal, better working conditions mean lower pay than otherwise, so that workers are in effect buying improved conditions on the job. Employers may not cut pay whenever working conditions are improved but, when rising worker productivity leads to rising pay scales through competition among employers for workers, those pay scales are unlikely to rise as much as they would have if the costs of better working conditions did not have to be taken into account. That is, employers' bids are limited not only by the productivity of the workers but also by all the other costs besides the rate of pay. In some countries, these non-wage costs of labor are much higher than in others— about twice as high in Germany, for example, as in the United States, making German labor more expensive than American labor that is paid the same wage rate.

While it is always politically tempting for governments to mandate benefits for workers, to be paid for by employers— since that wins more votes from workers than it loses among employers, and costs the government nothing— the economic repercussions seldom receive much attention from either the politicians who create such mandates or from the voting public. But one of the reasons why the unemployed may not begin to be hired as output increases, such as when an economy is rising out of a recession, is that working the existing workers overtime may be cheaper for the employer than hiring new workers.

That is because an increase in working hours from existing employees does not require paying for additional mandated benefits, as hiring new workers would. Despite higher pay required for overtime hours, it may in many cases still be cheaper to work the existing employees longer, instead of hiring new workers.

In November 2009, under the headline "Overtime Creeps Back Before Jobs," the *Wall Street Journal* reported: "In October, the manufacturing sector shed 61,000 people, while those still employed were working more hours: Overtime increased." The reason: "Overtime enables companies to increase productivity to meet rising customer orders without adding fixed costs such as health-care benefits for new hires." It also enables companies to meet temporary increases in demand for their products without taking on the expenses of training people who will have to be let go when the temporary increase in consumer demand passes. The cost of training a new worker includes reducing the output of an already trained worker who is assigned to train the new worker, both of them being paid while neither of them is producing as much output as other workers who are already trained.

Although it is easier to visualize the consequences of more costly working conditions in a capitalist economy, where these can be conceived in dollars and cents terms, similar conditions applied in the days of the socialist economy in the Soviet Union. For example, a study of the Soviet economy noted that "juveniles (under 18) are entitled to longer holidays, shorter hours, study leave; consequently managers prefer to avoid employing juveniles." There is no free lunch in a socialist economy any more than in a capitalist economy.

Because working conditions were often much worse in the past— fewer safety precautions, longer hours, more unpleasant and unhealthy surroundings— some advocates of externally regulated working conditions, whether regulated by government or unions, argue as if working conditions would never have improved otherwise. But wage rates were also much lower in the past, and yet they have risen in both unionized and non-unionized occupations, and in occupations covered and those not covered by minimum wage laws. Growth in per capita output permits both higher pay and better working conditions, while competition for workers forces individual employers to make improvements in both, just as they are forced to improve the products they sell to the consuming public for the same reason.

Safety Laws

While safety is one aspect of working conditions, it is a special aspect because, in some cases, leaving its costs and benefits to be weighed by employers and employees leaves out the safety of the general public that may be affected by the actions of employers and employees. Obvious examples include pilots, truck drivers, and train crews, because their fatigue can endanger many others besides themselves when a plane crashes, a big rig goes out of control on a crowded highway, or a train derails, killing not only passengers on board but also spreading fire or toxic fumes to people living near where the derailment occurs. Laws have accordingly been passed, limiting how many consecutive hours individuals may work in these occupations, even if longer hours might be acceptable to both employers and employees in these occupations.

Child Labor Laws

In most countries, laws to protect children in the workplace began before there were laws governing working conditions for adults. Such laws reflected public concerns because of the special vulnerability of children, due to their inexperience, weaker bodies, and general helplessness against the power of adults. At one time, children were used for hard and dangerous work in coal mines, as well as working around factory machinery that could maim or kill a child who was not alert to the dangers. However, laws passed under one set of conditions often remain on the books long after the circumstances that gave rise to those laws have changed. As a twenty-first century observer noted:

> Child labor laws passed to protect children from dangerous factories now keep strapping teenagers out of air-conditioned offices.

Such results are not mere examples of irrationality. Like other laws, child labor laws were not only passed in response to a given constituency— humanitarian individuals and groups, in this case— but also developed new constituencies among those who found such laws useful to their own interests. Labor unions, for example, have long sought to keep children and adolescents out of the work force, where they would compete for jobs with the unions' own members. Educators in general and teachers' unions in particular likewise have a vested interest in keeping young people in school longer, where their attendance increases the demand for teachers and can be used politically to argue for larger expenditures on the school system.

While keeping strapping teenagers from working in air-conditioned offices might seem irrational in terms of the original reasons for child labor laws advanced by the original humanitarian constituency, it is quite rational from the standpoint of the interests of these new constituencies. Whether it is rational from the standpoint of society as a whole to have so many young people denied legal ways to earn money, while illegal ways abound, is another question.

Hours of Work

One of the working conditions that can be quantified is the length of the work week. Most modern industrial countries specify the maximum number of hours per week that can be worked, either absolutely or before the employer is forced by law to pay higher rates for overtime work beyond those specified hours. This imposed work week varies from country to country. France, for example, specified 35 hours as the standard work week, with employers being mandated to continue to pay the same amount for this shorter work week as they had paid in weekly wages before. In addition, French law requires employees to be given 25 days of paid vacation per year, plus paid holidays— neither of which is required under American laws.

Given these facts, it is hardly surprising that the average number of hours worked annually in France is less than 1,500, compared to more than 1,800 in the United States and Japan. Obviously the extra 300 or more hours a year worked by American workers has an effect on annual output and therefore on the standard of living. Nor are all these differences financial. According to *BusinessWeek* magazine:

> Doctors work 20% less, on average. Staff shortages in hospitals and nursing homes due to the 35-hour week was a key reason August's heat wave killed 14,000 in France.

The French tradition of long summer vacations would have made the under-staffing problem worse during an August heat wave.

Sometimes, in various countries, especially during periods of high unemployment, a government-mandated shorter work week is advocated on grounds that this would share the work among more workers, reducing the unemployment rate. In other words, instead of hiring 35 workers to work 40 hours each, an employer might hire 40 workers to work 35 hours each. Plausible as this might seem, the problem is that shorter work weeks, whether imposed by government or by labor unions, often involve maintaining the same weekly pay as before, as it did in France. What this amounts to is a higher wage rate per hour, which tends to reduce the number of workers hired, instead of increasing employment as planned.

Western European nations in general tend to have more generous time-off policies mandated by law. According to the *Wall Street Journal*, the average European worker "took off 11.3 days in 2005, compared with 4.5 days for the average American."

Spain is especially generous in this regard. The *Wall Street Journal* in 2012 reported that in Spain the law requires that workers receive 14 paid holidays off annually, plus 22 days of paid vacation, 15 days off to get married and 2 to 4 days off when anyone in an employee's family has a wedding, birth, hospitalization or death. Employees who themselves are off from work due to illness can continue to get most or all of their wages paid, if they have a note from a doctor, for the duration of their illness, up to 18 months. Should the employer choose to fire an ill worker, the severance pay required to compensate that worker can be up to what that worker would have earned in two years.

Such mandated generosity is not without its costs, not simply to the employer but to the economy in general and workers in particular. Spain has had chronically high levels of unemployment— 25 percent in 2012, but ranging up to 52 percent for younger workers. Moreover, 49 percent of the unemployed in Spain in the second quarter of 2013 had been unemployed for a year or more, compared to 27 percent in the United States.

The labor market is affected not only by mandated employer benefits to workers, but also by government-provided benefits that make it unnecessary for many people to work. In Denmark, for example, a 36-year-old single mother of two "was getting about $2,700 a month, and she had been on welfare since she was 16," according to the *New York Times*, which also noted that "in many regions of the country people without jobs now outnumber those with them."

Third World Countries

Some of the worst working conditions exist in some of the poorest countries— that is, countries where the workers could least afford to accept lower pay as the price of better surroundings or circumstances on the job. Multinational companies with factories in the Third World often come under severe criticism in Europe or America for having working conditions in those factories that would not be tolerated in their own countries. What this means is that more prosperous workers in Europe or America in effect buy better working conditions, just as they are likely to buy better housing and better clothing than people in the Third World can afford. If employers in the Third World are forced by law or public pressures to provide better working conditions, the additional expense reduces the number of workers hired, just as wage rates higher than would be required by supply and demand left many Africans frustrated in their attempts to get jobs with multinational companies.

However much the jobs provided by multinational companies to Third World workers might be disdained for their low pay or poor working conditions by critics in Europe or the United States, the real question for workers in poor countries is how these jobs compare with their local alternatives. A *New York Times* writer in Cambodia, for example, noted: "Here in Cambodia factory jobs are in such demand that workers usually have to bribe a factory insider with a month's salary just to get hired." Clearly these are jobs highly sought after. Nor is Cambodia unique. Multinational companies typically pay about double the local wage rate in Third World countries.

It is much the same story with working conditions. Third World workers compare conditions in multinational companies with their own local alternatives. The same *New York Times* writer reporting from Cambodia described one of these alternatives— working as a scavenger picking through garbage dumps where the "stench clogs the nostrils" and where burning produces "acrid smoke that blinds the eyes," while "scavengers are chased by swarms of flies and biting insects." Speaking of one of these scavengers, the *Times* writer said:

> Nhep Chanda averages 75 cents a day for her efforts. For her, the idea of being exploited in a garment factory— working only six days a week, inside instead of in the broiling sun, for up to $2 a day— is a dream.

Would it not be even better if this young woman could be paid what workers in Europe or America are paid, and work under the same kinds of conditions found on their jobs? Of course it would. The real question is: How can her productivity be raised to the same level as that of workers in Europe or the United States— and what is likely to happen if productivity issues are waved aside and better working conditions are simply imposed by law or public pressures? There is little reason to doubt that the results would be similar to what happens when minimum wage rates are prescribed in disregard of productivity.

This does not mean that workers in poorer countries are doomed forever to low wages and bad working conditions. On the contrary, to the extent that more and more multinational companies locate in poor countries, working conditions as well as productivity and pay are affected when increasing numbers of multinationals compete for labor that is increasingly experienced in modern production methods— that is, workers with increasing amounts of valuable human capital, for which employers must compete in the labor market. In 2013, *The Economist* magazine reported, "Wages in China and India have been going up by 10–20% a year for the past decade." A decade earlier, "wages in emerging markets were a tenth of their level in the rich world." But between 2001 and 2011, the difference between what computer programmers in India were paid and what computer programmers in the United States were paid constantly narrowed.

The competition of multinational corporations for workers has affected wages not only among their employees, but also among employees of indigenous businesses that have had to compete for the same workers. In 2006, *BusinessWeek* magazine reported that a Chinese manufacturer of air-conditioner compressors "has seen turnover for some jobs hit 20% annually," with the general manager observing that "it's all he can do to keep his 800 employees from jumping ship to Samsung, Siemens, Nokia, and other multinationals" operating in his area. In Guangdong province, factories "have been struggling to find staff for five years, driving up wages at double-digit rates," the *Far Eastern Economic Review* reported in 2008.

These upward competitive pressures on wages have continued. According to the *New York Times* in 2012, "Labor shortages are already so acute in many Chinese industrial zones that factories struggle to find enough people to operate their assembly lines" and "often pay fees to agents who try to recruit workers arriving on long-haul buses and trains from distant provinces." That same year the *Wall Street Journal* reported that average urban wages in China rose by 13 percent in one year.

Competitive pressures have affected working conditions as well as wages:

> That means managers can no longer simply provide eight-to-a-room dorms and expect laborers to toil 12 hours a day, seven days a week. . . In addition to boosting salaries, Yongjin has upgraded its dormitories and improved the food in the company cafeteria. Despite those efforts, its five factories remain about 10% shy of the 6,000 employees they need.

In 2012 the *New York Times* reported that workers assembling iPads in a factory in China, who had previously been sitting on "a short, green plastic stool" that left their backs unsupported and sore, were suddenly supplied with decorated wooden chairs with "a high, sturdy back." Nor were such changes isolated, given the competitive labor markets, where even companies in different industries were competing for many of the same workers. According to the *New York Times*:

"When the largest company raises wages and cuts hours, it forces every other factory to do the same thing whether they want to or not," said Tony Prophet, a senior vice president at Hewlett-Packard. "A firestorm has started, and these companies are in the glare now. They have to improve to compete. It's a huge change from just 18 months ago."

The difference between having such improvements in working conditions emerge as a result of market competition and having them imposed by government is that markets bring about such improvements as a result of more options for the workers— due to more employer competition for workers, who are increasingly more experienced and therefore more valuable employees— while government impositions tend to reduce existing options, by raising the cost of hiring labor in disregard of whether those costs exceed the labor's productivity.

A free market is not a zero-sum system, where the gains of one party have to come at the expense of losses to another party. Because this is a process that creates a larger total output as workers acquire more human capital, these workers, their employers and the consumers can all benefit at the same time. However, politicians in various Asian countries have sought to simply impose higher pay rates through minimum wage laws, which can impede this process and create other problems that are all too familiar from the track record of minimum wage laws in other countries.

Informal pressures for better working conditions by international non-governmental organizations likewise tend to disregard costs and their repercussions when setting their standards. Tragic events, such as the 2013 collapse of a factory in Bangladesh that killed more than a thousand workers, create international public opinion pressures on multinational corporations to either pay for safer working conditions or to leave countries whose governments do not enforce safety standards. But such pressures are also used to push for higher minimum wage laws and more labor unions, usually without regard to the costs and employment repercussions of such things.

Third-party observers face none of the inherent constraints and trade-offs that are inescapable for both employers and employees, and therefore these third parties have nothing to force them to even think in such terms.

COLLECTIVE BARGAINING

In previous chapters we have been considering labor markets in which both workers and employers are numerous and compete individually and independently, whether with or without government regulation of pay and working conditions. However, these are not the only kinds of markets for labor. Some workers are members of labor unions which negotiate pay and working conditions with employers, whether employers are acting individually or in concert as members of an employers' association.

Employer Organizations

In earlier centuries, it was the employers who were more likely to be organized and setting pay and working conditions as a group. In medieval guilds, the master craftsmen collectively made the rules determining the conditions under which apprentices and journeymen would be hired and how much customers would be charged for the products. Today, major league baseball owners collectively make the rules as to what is the maximum of the total salaries that any given team can pay to its players without incurring financial penalties from the leagues.

Clearly, pay and working conditions tend to be different when determined collectively than in a labor market where employers compete against one another individually for workers and workers compete against one another individually for jobs. It would obviously not be worth the trouble of organizing employers if they were not able to gain by keeping the salaries they pay lower than they would be in a free market. Much has been said about the fairness or unfairness of the actions of medieval guilds, modern labor unions or other forms of collective bargaining. Here we are studying their economic consequences— and especially their effects on the allocation of scarce resources which have alternative uses.

Almost by definition, all these organizations exist to keep the price of labor from being what it would be otherwise in free and open competition in the market. Just as the tendency of market competition is to base rates of pay on the productivity of the worker, thereby bidding labor away from where it is less productive to where it is more productive, so organized efforts to make wages artificially low or artificially high defeat this process and thereby make the allocation of resources less efficient for the economy as a whole.

For example, if an employers' association keeps wages in the widget industry below the level that workers of similar skills receive elsewhere, fewer workers are likely to apply for jobs producing widgets than if the pay rate were higher. If widget manufacturers are paying $10 an hour for labor that would get $15 an hour if employers had to compete with each other for workers in a free market, then some workers will go to other industries that pay $12 an hour. From the standpoint of the economy as a whole, this means that people capable of producing $15 an hour's worth of output are instead producing only $12 an hour's worth of output somewhere else. This is a clear loss to the consumers— that is, to society as a whole, since everyone is a consumer.

The fact that it is a more immediate and more visible loss to the workers in the widget industry does not make that the most important fact from an economic standpoint. Losses and gains between employers and employees are social or moral issues, but they do not change the key *economic* issue, which is how the allocation of resources affects the total wealth available to society as a whole. What makes the total wealth produced by the economy less than it would be in a free market is that wages set below the market level cause workers to work where they are not as productive, but where they are paid more because of a competitive labor market in the less productive occupation.

The same principle applies where wages are set above the market level. If a labor union is successful in raising the wage rate for the same workers in the widget industry to $20 an hour, then employers will employ fewer workers at this higher rate than they would at the $15 an hour rate that would have prevailed in free market competition. In fact, the only workers that will be worth hiring are workers whose productivity is at least $20 an hour. This higher productivity can be reached in a number of ways, whether by retaining only the most skilled and experienced employees, by adding more capital to enable the labor to turn out more products per hour, or by other means— none of them free.

Those workers displaced from the widget industry must go to their second-best alternative. As before, those worth $15 an hour producing widgets may end up working in another industry at $12 an hour. Again, this is not simply a loss to those particular workers who cannot find employment at the higher wage rate, but a loss to the economy as a whole, because scarce resources are not being allocated where their productivity is highest.

Where unions set wages above the level that would prevail under supply and demand in a free market, widget manufacturers are not only paying more money for labor, they are also paying for additional capital or other complementary resources to raise the productivity of labor above the $20 an hour level. Higher labor productivity may seem on the surface to be greater "efficiency," but producing fewer widgets at higher cost per widget does not benefit the economy, even though less labor is being used. Other industries receiving more labor than they normally would, because of the workers displaced from the widget industry, can expand their output. But that expanding output is not the most productive use of the additional labor. It is only the artificially-imposed union wage rate which causes the shift from a more productive use to a less productive use.

Either artificially low wage rates caused by an employer association or artificially high wage rates caused by a labor union reduces employment in the widget industry. One side or the other must now go to their second-best option— which is also second-best from the standpoint of the economy as a whole, because scarce resources have not been allocated to their most valued uses. The parties engaged in collective bargaining are of course preoccupied with their own interests, but those judging the process as a whole need to focus on how such a process affects the economic interests of the entire society, rather than the internal division of economic benefits among contending members of the society.

Even in situations where it might seem that employers could do pretty much whatever they wanted to do, history often shows that they could not— because of the effects of competition in the labor market. Few workers have been more vulnerable than newly freed blacks in the United States after the Civil War. They were extremely poor, most completely uneducated, unorganized, and unfamiliar with the operation of a market economy. Yet organized attempts by white employers and landowners in the South to hold down their wages and limit their decision-making as sharecroppers all eroded away in the market, amid bitter mutual recriminations among white employers and landowners.

When the pay scale set by the organized white employers was below the actual productivity of black workers, that made it profitable for any given employer to offer more than the others were paying, in order to lure more workers away, so long as his higher offer was still not above the level of the black workers' productivity. With agricultural labor especially, the pressure on each employer mounted as the planting season approached, because the landowner knew that the size of the crop for the whole year depended on how many workers could be hired to do the spring planting. That inescapable reality often over-rode any sense of loyalty to fellow landowners. The percentage rate of increase of black wages was higher than the percentage rate of increase in the wages of white workers in the decades after the Civil War, even though the latter had higher pay in absolute terms.

One of the problems of cartels in general is that, no matter what conditions they set collectively to maximize the benefits to the cartel as a whole, it is to the advantage of individual cartel members to violate those conditions, if they can get away with it, often leading to the disintegration of the cartel. That was the situation of white employer cartels in the postbellum South. It was much the same story out in California in the late nineteenth and early twentieth centuries, when white landowners there organized to try to hold down the pay of Japanese immigrant farmers and farm laborers. These cartels too collapsed amid bitter mutual recriminations among whites, as competition among landowners led to widespread violations of the agreements which they had made in collusion with one another.

The ability of employer organizations to achieve their goals depends on their being able to impose discipline on their own members, and on keeping competing employers from arising outside their organizations. Medieval guilds had the force of law behind their rules. Where there has been no force of law to maintain internal discipline within the employer organization, or to keep competing employers from arising outside the organization, employer cartels have been much less successful.

In special cases, such as the employer organization in major league baseball, this is a monopoly legally exempted from anti-trust laws. Therefore internal rules can be imposed on each team, since none of these teams can hope to withdraw from major league baseball and have the same financial support from baseball fans, or the same media attention, when they are no longer playing other major league teams. Nor would it be likely, or even feasible, for new leagues to arise to compete with major league baseball, with any hope of getting the same fan support or media attention. Therefore, major league baseball can operate as an employer organization, exercising some of the powers once used by medieval guilds, before they lost the crucial support of law and faded away.

Labor Unions

Although employer organizations have sought to keep employees' pay from rising to the level it would reach by supply and demand in a free competitive market, while labor unions seek to raise wage rates above where they would be in a free competitive market, these very different intentions can lead to similar consequences in terms of the allocation of scarce resources which have alternative uses.

Legendary American labor leader John L. Lewis, head of the United Mine Workers from 1920 to 1960, was enormously successful in winning higher pay for his union's members. However, an economist also called him "the world's greatest oil salesman," because the resulting higher price of coal and the disruptions in its production due to numerous strikes caused many users of coal to switch to using oil instead. This of course reduced employment in the coal industry.

By the 1960s, declining employment in the coal industry left many mining communities economically stricken and some became virtual ghost towns. Media stories of their plight seldom connected their current woes with the former glory days of John L. Lewis. In fairness to Lewis, he made a conscious decision that it was better to have fewer miners doing dangerous work underground and more heavy machinery down there, since machinery could not be killed by cave-ins, explosions and the other hazards of mining.

To the public at large, however, these and other trade-offs were largely unknown. Many simply cheered at what Lewis had done to improve the wages of miners and, years later, were compassionate toward the decline of mining communities— but made little or no connection between the two things. Yet what was involved was one of the simplest and most basic principles of economics, that less is demanded at a higher price than at a lower price. That principle applies whether considering the price of coal, of the labor of mine workers, or anything else.

Very similar trends emerged in the automobile industry, where the danger factor was not what it was in mining. Here the United Automobile Workers' union was also very successful in getting higher pay, more job security and more favorable work rules for its members. In the long run, however, all these additional costs raised the price of automobiles and made American cars less competitive with Japanese and other cars, not only in the United States but in markets around the world.

As of 1950, the United States produced three-quarters of all the cars in the world and Japan produced less than one percent of what Americans produced. Twenty years later, Japan was producing almost two-thirds as many automobiles as the United States and, ten years after that, more automobiles. By 1990, one-third of the cars sold within the United States were Japanese. In a number of years since then, more Honda Accords or Toyota Camrys were sold in the United States than any car made by any American car company. All this of course had its effect on employment. By 1990, the number of jobs in the American automobile industry was 200,000 less than it had been in 1979.

Political pressures on Japan to "voluntarily" limit its export of cars to the U.S. led to the creation of Japanese automobile manufacturing plants in the United States, hiring American workers, to replace the lost exports. By the early 1990s, these transplanted Japanese factories were producing as many cars as were being exported to the United States from Japan— and, by 2007, 63 percent of Japanese cars sold in the United States were manufactured within the United States. Many of these transplanted Japanese car companies had work forces that were non-union— and which rejected unionization when votes were taken among the employees in secret ballot elections conducted by the government. The net result, by the early twenty-first century, was that Detroit automakers were laying off workers by the thousands, while Toyota was hiring American workers by the thousands.

The decline of unionized workers in the automobile industry was part of a more general trend among industrial workers in the United States. The United Steelworkers of America was another large and highly successful union in getting high pay and other benefits for its members. But here too the number of jobs in the industry declined by more than 200,000 in a decade, while the steel companies invested $35 billion in machinery that replaced these workers, and while the towns where steel production was concentrated were economically devastated.

The once common belief that unions were a blessing and a necessity for workers was now increasingly mixed with skepticism and apprehension about the unions' role in the economic declines and reduced employment in many industries. Faced with the prospect of seeing some employers going out of business or having to drastically reduce employment, some unions were forced into "give-backs"— that is, relinquishing various wages and benefits they had obtained for their members in previous years. Painful as this was, many unions concluded that it was the only way to save members' jobs. A front page news story in the *New York Times* summarized the situation in the early twenty-first century:

> In reaching a settlement with General Motors on Thursday and in recent agreements with several other industrial behemoths— Ford, DaimlerChrysler, Goodyear and Verizon— unions have shown a new willingness to rein in their demands. Keeping their employers competitive, they have concluded, is essential to keeping unionized jobs from being lost to nonunion, often lower-wage companies elsewhere in this country or overseas.

Unions and their members had, over the years, learned the hard way what is usually taught early on in introductory economics courses— that people buy less at higher prices than at lower prices. It is not a complicated principle, but it often gets lost sight of in the swirl of events and the headiness of rhetoric.

The proportion of the American labor force that is unionized has declined over the years, as skepticism about unions' economic effects spread among workers who have increasingly voted against being represented by unions. Unionized workers were 32 percent of all workers in the middle of the twentieth century, but only 14 percent by the end of the century. Moreover, there was a major change in the composition of unionized workers.

In the first half of the twentieth century, the great unions in the U.S. economy were in mining, automobiles, steel, and trucking. But, by the end of that century, the largest and most rapidly growing unions were those of government employees. By 2007, only 8 percent of private sector employees were unionized. The largest union in the country by far was the union of teachers— the National Education Association.

The economic pressures of the marketplace, which had created such problems for unionized workers in private industry and commerce, did not apply to government workers. Government employees could continue to get pay raises, larger benefits, and job security without worrying that they were likely to suffer the fate of miners, automobile workers, and other unionized industrial workers. Those who hired government workers were not spending their own money but the taxpayers' money, and so had little reason to resist union demands. Moreover, they seldom faced such competitive forces in the market as would force them to lose business to imports or to substitute products. Most government agencies have a monopoly of their particular function.* Only the Internal Revenue Service collects taxes for the federal government and only the Department of Motor Vehicles issues states' driver licenses.

In private industry, many companies have remained non-union by a policy of paying their workers at least as much as unionized workers received. Such a policy implies that the cost to an employer of having a union exceeds the wages and benefits paid to workers. The hidden costs of union rules on seniority and many other details of operations are for some companies worth being rid of for the sake of greater efficiency, even if that means paying their employees more than they would have to pay to unionized workers. The unionized big three American automobile makers, for example, have required from 26 hours to 31 hours of labor per car, while the largely non-unionized Japanese automakers required from 17 to 22 hours.

Western European labor unions have been especially powerful, and the many benefits that they have gotten for their members have had their repercussions on the employment of workers and the growth rates of whole

---

* This is not always true: Some state and local governments have paid private businesses to carry out some functions traditionally done by government employees, such as garbage collection and running prisons. The federal government has also outsourced some of its functions to private companies, both in the United States and overseas. The extent to which these things can be done is, however, limited by political reactions.

economies. Western European countries have for years lagged behind the United States both in economic growth and in the creation of jobs. A belated recognition of such facts led some European unions and European governments to relax some of their demands and restrictions on employers in the wake of an economic slump. In 2006, the *Wall Street Journal* reported:

> Europe's economic slump has given companies new muscle in their negotiations with workers. Governments in Europe have been slow to overhaul worker-friendly labor laws for fear of incurring voters' wrath. That slowed job growth as companies transferred operations overseas where labor costs were lower. High unemployment in Europe depressed consumer spending, helping limit economic growth in the past five years to a meager 1.4% average in the 12 countries that use the euro.

In the wake of a relaxation of labor union and government restrictions in the labor market, the growth rate in these countries rose from 1.4 percent to 2.2 percent and the unemployment rate fell from 9.3 percent to 8.3 percent. Neither of these statistics was as good as those in the United States at the time, but they were an improvement over what existed under previous policies and practices in the European Union countries.

EXPLOITATION

Usually those who decry "exploitation" make no serious attempt to define it, so the word is often used simply to condemn either prices that are higher than the observer would like to see or wages lower than the observer would like to see. There would be no basis for objecting to this word if it were understood by all that it is simply a statement about someone's internal emotional reactions, rather than being presented as a statement about some fact in the external world. We have seen in Chapter 4 how higher prices charged by stores in low-income neighborhoods have been called "exploitation" when in fact there are many economic factors which account for these higher prices, often charged by local stores that are struggling to survive, rather than stores making unusually high profits. Similarly, we have seen in Chapter 10 some of the factors behind low pay for Third World workers whom many regard as being "exploited" because they are not paid what workers in more prosperous countries are paid.

The general idea behind "exploitation" theories is that some people are somehow able to receive more than enough money to compensate for their contributions to the production and distribution of output, by either charging more than is necessary to consumers or paying less than is necessary to employees. In some circumstances, this is in fact possible. But we need to examine those circumstances— and to see when such circumstances exist or do not exist in the real world.

As we have seen in earlier chapters, earning a rate of return on investment that is greater than what is required to compensate people for their risks and contributions to output is virtually guaranteed to attract other people who wish to share in this bounty by either investing in existing firms or setting up their own new firms. This in turn virtually guarantees that the above-average rate of return will be driven back down by the increased competition caused by expanded investment and production whether by existing firms or by new firms. Only where there is some way to prevent this new competition can the above-average earnings on investment persist.

Governments are among the most common and most effective barriers to the entry of new competition. During the Second World War, the British colonial government in West Africa imposed a wide range of wartime controls over production and trade, as also happened within Britain itself. This was the result, as reported by an economist on the scene in West Africa:

> During the period of trade controls profits were much larger than were necessary to secure the services of the traders. Over this period of great prosperity the effective bar to the entry of new firms reserved the very large profits for those already in the trade.

This was not peculiar to Africa or to the British colonial government there. The Civil Aeronautics Board and the Interstate Commerce Commission in the United States have been among the many government agencies, at both the national and local levels, which have restricted the number of firms or individuals allowed to enter various occupations and industries. In fact, governments around the world have at various times and places restricted how many people, and which people, would be allowed to engage in particular occupations or to establish firms in particular industries. This was even more common in past centuries, when kings often conferred monopoly rights on particular individuals or enterprises to engage in the production of salt or wine or many other commodities, sometimes as a matter of generosity to royal favorites and often because the right to a monopoly was purchased for cash.

The purpose or the net effect of barriers to entry has been a persistence of a level of earnings higher than that which would exist under free market competition and higher than necessary to attract the resources required. This could legitimately be considered "exploitation" of the consumers, since it is a payment over and beyond what is necessary to cause people to supply the product or service in question. However, higher earnings than would exist under free market competition do not always or necessarily mean that these earnings are higher than earnings in competitive industries. Sometimes inefficient firms are able to survive under government protection when such firms would not survive in the competition of a free market. Therefore even modest rates of return received by such inefficient firms still represent consumers being forced to pay more money than necessary in a free market, where more efficient firms would produce a larger share of the industry's output, while driving the less efficient firms out of business by offering lower prices.

While such situations could legitimately be called exploitation— defined as prices higher than necessary to supply the goods or services in question— these are not usually the kinds of situations which provoke that label. It would also be legitimate to describe as exploitation a situation where people are paid less for their work than they would receive in a free market or less than the amount necessary to attract a continuing supply of people with their levels of skills, experience, and talents. However, such situations are far more likely to involve people with high skills and high incomes than people with low skills and low incomes.

Where exploitation is defined as the difference between the wealth that an individual creates and the amount that individual is paid, then Babe Ruth may well have been the most exploited individual of all time. Not only was

Yankee Stadium "the house that Ruth built," the whole Yankee dynasty was built on the exploits of Babe Ruth. Before he joined the team, the New York Yankees had never won a pennant, much less a World Series, and they had no ballpark of their own, playing their games in the New York Giants' ballpark when the Giants were on the road. Ruth's exploits drew huge crowds, and the huge gate receipts provided the financial foundation on which the Yankees built teams that dominated baseball for decades.

Ruth's top salary of $80,000 a year— even at 1932 prices— did not begin to cover the financial difference that he made to the team. But the exclusive, career-long contracts of that era meant that the Yankees did not have to bid for Babe Ruth's services against the other teams who would have paid handsomely to have him in their lineups. Here, as elsewhere, the prevention of competition is essential to exploitation. It is also worth noting that, while the Yankees could exploit Babe Ruth, they could not exploit the unskilled workers who swept the floors in Yankee Stadium, because these workers could have gotten jobs sweeping floors in innumerable offices, factories or homes, so there was no way for them to be paid less than comparable workers received elsewhere.

In some situations, people in a given occupation may be paid less currently than the rate of pay necessary to continue to attract a sufficient supply of qualified people to that occupation. Doctors, for example, have already invested huge sums of money in getting an education in expensive medical schools, in addition to an investment in the form of foregone earnings during several years of college and medical school, followed by low pay as interns before finally becoming fully qualified to conduct their own independent medical practice. Under a government-run medical system the government can at any given time set medical salary scales, or pay scales for particular medical treatments, which are not sufficient to continue to attract as many people of the same qualifications into the medical profession in the future.

In the meantime, however, existing doctors have little choice but to accept what the government authorizes, if the government either pays all medical bills or hires all doctors. Seldom will there be alternative professions which existing doctors can enter to earn better pay, because becoming a lawyer or an engineer would require yet another costly investment in education and training. Therefore most doctors seldom have realistic alternatives available and are unlikely to become truck drivers or carpenters, just because they would not have gone into the medical profession if they had known in advance what the actual level of compensation would turn out to be.

Low-paid workers can also be exploited in circumstances where they are unable to move, or where the cost of moving would be high, whether because of transportation costs or because they live in government-subsidized housing that they would lose if they moved somewhere else, where they would have to pay market prices for a home or an apartment, at least while being on waiting lists for government-subsidized housing at their new location. In centuries past, slaves could of course be exploited because they were held by force. Indentured servants or contract laborers, especially those working overseas, likewise had high costs of moving, and so could be exploited in the short run. However, many very low-paid contract workers chose to sign up for another period of work at jobs whose pay and working conditions they already knew about from personal experience, clearly indicating that— however low their pay and however bad their working conditions— these were sufficient to attract them into this occupation. Here the explanation was less likely to be exploitation than a lack of better alternatives or the skills to qualify for better alternatives.

Where there is only one employer for a particular kind of labor, then of course that employer can set pay scales which are lower than what is required to attract new people into that occupation. But this is more likely to happen to highly specialized and skilled people, such as astronauts, rather than to unskilled workers, since unskilled workers are employed by a wide variety of businesses, government agencies, and even private individuals. In the era before modern transportation was widespread, local labor markets might be isolated and a given employer might be the only employer available for many local people in particular occupations. But the spread of low-cost transportation has made such situations much rarer than in the past.

Once we see that barriers to entry or exit— the latter absolute in the case of slaves or expensive in the case of exit for doctors or for people living in local subsidized housing, for example— are key, then the term exploitation often legitimately applies to people very different from those to whom this term is usually applied. It would also apply to businesses which have invested large amounts of fixed and hard to remove capital at a particular location. A company that builds a hydroelectric dam, for example, cannot move that dam elsewhere if the local government doubles or triples its tax rates or requires the company to pay much higher wage rates to its workers than similar workers receive elsewhere in a free market. In the long run, however, fewer businesses tend to invest in places where the political climate produces such results— the exit of many businesses from California being a striking example— but those who have already invested in such places have little recourse but to accept a lower rate of return there.

Whether the term "exploitation" applies or does not apply to a particular situation is not simply a matter of semantics. Different *consequences* follow when policies are based on a belief that is false instead of beliefs that are true. Imposing price controls to prevent consumers from being "exploited" or minimum wage laws to prevent workers from being "exploited" can make matters worse for consumers or workers if in fact neither is being exploited, as already shown in Chapters 3 and 11. Where a given employer, or a small set of employers operating in collusion, constitute a local cartel in hiring certain kinds of workers, then that cartel can pay lower salaries, and in these circumstances a government-imposed increase in salary may— within limits— not result in workers losing their jobs, as would tend to happen with an imposed minimum wage in what would otherwise be a competitive market. But such situations are very rare and such employer cartels are hard to maintain, as indicated by the collapsing employer cartels in the postbellum South and in nineteenth-century California.

The tendency to regard low-paid workers as exploited is understandable as a desire to seek a remedy in moral or political crusades to right a wrong. But, as noted economist Henry Hazlitt said, years ago:

> The real problem of poverty is not a problem of "distribution" but of production. The poor are poor not because something is being withheld from them but because, for whatever reason, they are not producing enough.

This does not make poverty any less of a problem but it makes a solution more difficult, less certain and more time-consuming, as well as requiring the cooperation of those in poverty, in addition to others who may wish to help them, but who cannot solve the problem without such cooperation. The poor themselves may not be to blame because their poverty may be due to many factors beyond their control— including the past, which is beyond anyone's control today. Some of those circumstances will be dealt with in Chapter 23.

Job Security

Virtually every modern industrial nation has faced issues of job security, whether they have faced these issues realistically or unrealistically, successfully or unsuccessfully. In some countries— France, Germany, India, and South Africa, for example— job security laws make it difficult and costly for a private employer to fire anyone. Labor unions try to have job security policies in many industries and in many countries around the world. Teachers' unions in the United States are so successful at this that it can easily cost a school district tens of thousands of dollars— or more than a hundred thousand in some places— to fire just one teacher, even if that teacher is grossly incompetent.

The obvious purpose of job security laws is to reduce unemployment but that is very different from saying that this is the actual effect of such laws. Countries with strong job security laws typically do not have lower unemployment rates, but instead have higher unemployment rates, than countries without widespread job protection laws. In France, which has some of Europe's strongest job security laws, double-digit unemployment rates are not uncommon. But in the United States, Americans become alarmed when the unemployment rate approaches such a level. In South Africa, the government itself has admitted that its rigid job protection laws have had "unintended consequences," among them an unemployment rate that has remained around 25 percent for years, peaking at 31 percent in 2002. As the British magazine *The Economist* put it: "Firing is such a costly headache that many prefer not to hire in the first place." This consequence is by no means unique to South Africa.

The very thing that makes a modern industrial society so efficient and so effective in raising living standards— the constant quest for newer and better ways of getting work done and more goods produced— makes it impossible to keep on having the same workers doing the same jobs in the same way. For example, back at the beginning of the twentieth century, the United States had about 10 million farmers and farm laborers to feed a population of 76 million people. By the end of the twentieth century, there were fewer than one-fifth this many farmers and farm laborers, feeding a population more than three times as large. Yet, far from having less food, Americans' biggest problems now included obesity and trying to find export markets for their surplus agricultural produce. All this was made possible because farming became a radically different enterprise, using machinery, chemicals and methods unheard of when the century began— and requiring the labor of far fewer people.

There were no job security laws to keep workers in agriculture, where they were now superfluous, so they went by the millions into industry, where they added greatly to the national output. Farming is of course not the only sector of the economy to be revolutionized during the twentieth century. Whole new industries sprang up, such as aviation and computers, and even old industries like retailing have seen radical changes in which companies and which business methods have survived. More than 17 million workers in the United States lost their jobs between 1990 and 1995. But there were never 17 million Americans unemployed at any given time during that period, nor anything close to that. In fact, the unemployment rate in the United States fell to its lowest point in years during the 1990s. Americans were moving from one job to another, rather than relying on job security in one place. The average American has nine jobs between the ages of 18 and 34.

In Europe, where job security laws and practices are much stronger than in the United States, jobs have in fact been harder to come by. During the decade of the 1990s, the United States created jobs at triple the rate of industrial nations in Europe. In the private sector, Europe actually lost jobs, and only its increased government employment led to any net gain at all. This should not be surprising. Job security laws make it more expensive to hire workers— and, like anything else that is made more expensive, labor is less in demand at a higher price than at a lower price. Job security policies save the jobs of existing workers, but at the cost of reducing the flexibility and efficiency of the economy as a whole, thereby inhibiting production of the wealth needed for the creation of new jobs for other workers.

Because job security laws make it risky for private enterprises to hire new workers, during periods of rising demand for their products existing employees may be worked overtime instead, or capital may be substituted for labor, such as using huge buses instead of hiring more drivers for more regular-sized buses. However it is done, increased substitution of capital for labor leaves other workers unemployed. For the working population as a whole, there may be no net increase in job security but instead a concentration of the insecurity on those who happen to be on the outside looking in, especially younger workers entering the labor force or women seeking to re-enter the labor force after taking time out to raise children.

The connection between job security laws and unemployment has been understood by some officials but apparently not by much of the public, including the educated public. When France tried to deal with its high youth unemployment rate of 23 percent by easing its stringent job security laws for people on their first job, students at the Sorbonne and other French universities rioted in Paris and other cities across the country in 2006.

OCCUPATIONAL LICENSING

Job security laws and minimum wage laws are just some of the ways in which government intervention in labor markets makes those markets differ from what they would be under free competition. Among the other ways that government intervention changes labor markets are laws requiring a government-issued license to engage in some occupations. One cannot be a physician or an attorney without a license, for the obvious reason that people without the requisite training and skill would be perpetrating a dangerous fraud if they sought to practice in these professions. However, once the government has a rationale for exercising a particular power, that power can be extended to other circumstances far removed from that rationale. That has long been the history of occupational licensing.

Although economists often proceed by first explaining how a free competitive market operates and then move on to show how various infringements on that kind of market affect economic outcomes, what happened in history is that controlled markets preceded free markets by centuries. Requirements for government permission to engage in various occupations were common centuries ago. The rise of free markets was aided by the rise and spread of classical economics in the nineteenth century. Although both product markets and labor markets became freer in the nineteenth century, the forces that sought protection from competition were never completely eradicated. Gradually, over the years, more occupations began to require licenses— a process accelerated in bad economic times, such as the Great Depression of the 1930s, or after government intervention in the economy began to become more accepted again.

Although the rationale for requiring licenses in particular occupations has usually been to protect the public from various risks created by unqualified or unscrupulous practitioners, the demand for such protection has seldom come from the public. Almost invariably the demand for requiring a license has come from existing practitioners in the particular occupation. That the real goal is to protect themselves from competition is suggested by the fact that it is common for occupational licensing legislation to exempt existing practitioners, who are automatically licensed, as if it can be assumed that the public requires no protection from incompetent or dishonest practitioners already in the occupation.

Occupational licensing can take many forms. In some cases, the license is automatically issued to all the applicants who can demonstrate competence in the particular occupation, with perhaps an additional requirement of a clean record as a law-abiding citizen. In other cases, there is a numerical limit placed on the number of licenses to be issued, regardless of how many qualified applicants there are. A common example of the latter is a license to drive a taxi. New York City, for example, has been limiting the number of taxi licenses since 1937, when it began issuing special medallions authorizing each taxi to operate. The resulting artificial scarcity of taxis has had many repercussions, the most obvious of which has been a rising cost of taxi medallions, which first sold for $10 in 1937, rising to $80,000 in the 1980s and selling for more than a million dollars in 2011.

PART IV: TIME AND RISK

Chapter 13

INVESTMENT

*A tourist in New York's Greenwich Village decided to
have his portrait sketched by a sidewalk artist. He received
a very fine sketch, for which he was charged $100.
   "That's expensive," he said to the artist, "but I'll pay it,
because it is a great sketch. But, really, it took you only five
minutes."
   "Twenty years and five minutes," the artist replied.*

Artistic ability is only one of many things which are accumulated over time for use later on. Some people may think of investment as simply a transaction with money. But, more broadly and more fundamentally, it is the sacrificing of real things today in order to have more real things in the future.

In the case of the Greenwich Village artist, it was time that was invested for two decades, in order to develop the skills that allow a striking sketch to be made in five minutes. For society as a whole, investment is more likely to take the form of foregoing the production of some consumer goods today so that the labor and capital that would have been used to produce those consumer goods will be used instead to produce machinery and factories that will cause future production to be greater than it would be otherwise. The accompanying financial transactions may be what the attention of individual investors are focused on but here, as elsewhere, for society as a whole money is just an artificial device to facilitate real things that constitute real wealth.

Because the future cannot be known in advance, investments necessarily involve risks, as well as the tangible things that are invested. These risks must be compensated if investments are to continue. The cost of keeping people alive while waiting for their artistic talent to develop, their oil explorations to finally find places where oil wells can be drilled, or their academic credits to

269

eventually add up to enough to earn their degrees, are all investments that must be repaid if such investments are to continue to be made.

The repaying of investments is not a matter of morality, but of economics. If the return on the investment is not enough to make it worthwhile, fewer people will make that particular investment in the future, and future consumers will therefore be denied the use of the goods and services that would otherwise have been produced.

No one is under any obligation to make *all* investments pay off, but how many need to pay off, and to what extent, is determined by how many consumers value the benefits of other people's investments, and to what extent.

Where the consumers do not value what is being produced, the investment should *not* pay off. When people insist on specializing in a field for which there is little demand, their investment has been a waste of scarce resources that could have produced something else that others wanted. The low pay and sparse employment opportunities in that field are a compelling signal to them— and to others coming after them— to stop making such investments.

The principles of investment are involved in activities that do not pass through the marketplace, and are not normally thought of as economic. Putting things away after you use them is an investment of time in the present to reduce the time required to find them in the future. Explaining yourself to others can be a time-consuming, and even unpleasant, activity but it is engaged in as an investment to prevent greater unhappiness in the future from avoidable misunderstandings.

KINDS OF INVESTMENTS

Investments take many forms, whether the investment is in human beings, steel mills, or transmission lines for electricity. Risk is an inseparable part of these investments and others. Among the ways of dealing with risk are speculation, insurance and the issuance of stocks and bonds.

Human Capital

While human capital can take many forms, there is a tendency of some to equate it with formal education. However, not only may many other valuable forms of human capital be overlooked this way, the value of formal schooling may be exaggerated and its counterproductive consequences in some cases not understood.

The industrial revolution was not created by highly educated people but by people with practical industrial experience. The airplane was invented by a couple of bicycle mechanics who had never gone to college. Electricity and many inventions run by electricity became central parts of the modern world because of a man with only three months of formal schooling, Thomas Edison. Yet all these people had enormously valuable knowledge and insights— human capital— acquired from experience rather than in classrooms.

Education has of course also made major contributions to economic development and rising standards of living. But this is not to say that all kinds of education have. From an economic standpoint, some education has great value, some has no value and some can even have a negative value. While it is easy to understand the great value of specific skills in medical science or engineering, for example, or the more general foundation for a number of professions provided by mathematics, other subjects such as literature make no pretense of producing marketable skills but are available for whatever they may contribute in other ways.

In a country where education or higher levels of education are new or rare, those who have obtained diplomas or degrees may feel that many kinds of work are now beneath them. In such societies, even engineers may prefer sitting at a desk to standing in the mud in hip boots at a construction site. Depending on what they have studied, the newly educated may have higher levels of expectations than they have higher levels of ability to create the wealth from which their expectations can be met.

In the Third World especially, those who are the first members of their families to reach higher education typically do not study difficult and demanding subjects like science, medicine, or engineering, but instead tend toward easier and fuzzier subjects which provide them with little in the way of marketable skills— which is to say, skills that can create prosperity for themselves or their country.

Large numbers of young people with schooling, but without economically meaningful skills, have produced much unemployment in Third World nations. Since the marketplace has little to offer such people that would be commensurate with their expectations, governments have created swollen bureaucracies to hire them, in order to neutralize their potential for political disaffection, civil unrest or insurrection. In turn, these bureaucracies and the voluminous and time-consuming red tape they generate can become obstacles to others who *do* have the skills and entrepreneurship needed to contribute to the country's economic advancement.

In India, for example, two of its leading entrepreneurial families, the Tatas and the Birlas, have been repeatedly frustrated in their efforts to obtain the necessary government permission to expand their enterprises:

> The Tatas made 119 proposals between 1960 and 1989 to start new businesses or expand old ones, and all of them ended in the wastebaskets of the bureaucrats. Aditya Birla, the young and dynamic inheritor of the Birla empire, who had trained at MIT, was so disillusioned with Indian policy that he decided to expand Birla enterprises outside India, and eventually set up dynamic companies in Thailand, Malaysia, Indonesia, and the Philippines, away from the hostile atmosphere of his home.

The vast array of government rules in India, micro-managing businesses, "ensured that every businessman would break some law or the other every month," according to an Indian executive. Large businesses in India set up their own bureaucracies in Delhi, parallel to those of the government, in order to try to keep track of the progress of their applications for the innumerable government permissions required to do things that businesses do on their own in free market economies, and to pay bribes as necessary to secure these permissions.

The consequences of suffocating bureaucratic controls in India have been shown not only by such experiences while they were in full force but also by the country's dramatic economic improvements after many of these controls were relaxed or eliminated. The Indian economy's growth rate increased dramatically after reforms in 1991 freed many of its entrepreneurs from some of the worst controls, and foreign investment in India rose from $150 million to $3 billion— in other words, by twenty times.

Hostility to entrepreneurial minorities like the Chinese in Southeast Asia or the Lebanese in West Africa has been especially fierce among the newly educated indigenous people, who see their own diplomas and degrees bringing them much less economic reward than the earnings of minority business owners who may have less formal schooling than themselves.

In short, more schooling is not automatically more human capital. It can in some cases reduce a country's ability to use the human capital that it already possesses. Moreover, to the extent that some social groups specialize in different kinds of education, or have different levels of performance as students, or attend educational institutions of differing quality, the same number of years of schooling does not mean the same education in any economically meaningful sense. Such qualitative differences have in fact been common in countries around the world, whether comparing the Chinese and the Malays in Malaysia, Sephardic and Ashkenazic Jews in Israel, Tamils and Sinhalese in Sri Lanka or comparing various ethnic groups with one another in the United States.

Financial Investments

When millions of people invest money, what they are doing more fundamentally is foregoing the use of current goods and services, which they have the money to buy, in hopes that they will receive back more money in the future— which is to say, that they may be able to receive a larger quantity of goods and services in the future. From the standpoint of the economy as a whole, investments mean that many resources that would otherwise have gone into producing current consumer goods like clothing, furniture, or pizzas will instead go into producing factories, ships or hydroelectric dams that will provide future goods and services. Money totals give us some idea of the magnitude of investments but the investments themselves are ultimately additions to the real capital of the country, whether physical capital or human capital.

Investments may be made directly by individuals who buy corporate stock, for example, supplying corporations with money now in exchange for a share of the additional future value that these corporations are expected to add by using the money productively.

Much investment, however, is by institutions such as banks, insurance companies, and pension funds. Financial institutions around the world owned a total of $60 trillion in investments in 2009, of which American institutions owned 45 percent.

The staggering sums of money owned by various investment institutions are often a result of aggregating individually modest sums of money from millions of people, such as stockholders in giant corporations, depositors in savings banks or workers who pay modest but regular amounts into pension funds. What this means is that vastly larger numbers of people are owners of giant corporations than those who are direct individual purchasers of corporate stock, as distinguished from those whose money makes its way into corporations through some financial intermediary. By the late twentieth century, just over half the American population owned stock, either directly or through their pension funds, bank accounts or other financial intermediaries.

Financial institutions allow vast numbers of individuals who cannot possibly all know each other personally to nevertheless use one another's money by going through some intermediary institution which assumes the responsibility of assessing risks, taking precautions to reduce those risks, and making transfers through loans to individuals or institutions, or by making investments in businesses, real estate or other ventures.

Financial intermediaries not only allow the pooling of money from innumerable individuals to finance huge economic undertakings by businesses, they also allow individuals to redistribute their own individual consumption over time. Borrowers in effect draw on future income to pay for current purchases, paying interest for the convenience. Conversely, savers postpone purchases till a later time, receiving interest for the delay.

Everything depends on the changing circumstances of each individual's life, with many— if not most— people being both debtors and creditors at different stages of their lives. People who are middle-aged, for example, tend to save more than young people, not only because their incomes are higher but also because of a need to prepare financially for retirement in the years ahead and for the higher medical expenses that old age can be expected to bring. In the United States, Canada, Britain, Italy, and Japan, the highest rates of saving have been in the 55 to 59 year old bracket and the lowest in the under 30 year old bracket— the whole under 30 cohort having zero net savings in Canada and negative net savings in the United States. While those who are saving may not think of themselves as creditors, the money that they put into banks is then lent out by those banks, acting as intermediaries between those who are saving and those who are borrowing.

What makes such activities something more than matters of personal finance is that these financial transactions are for the economy as a whole another way of allocating scarce resources which have alternative uses— allocating them over time, as well as among individuals and enterprises at a given time. To build a factory, a railroad, or a hydroelectric dam requires that labor, natural resources, and other factors of production that would otherwise go into producing consumer goods in the present be diverted to creating something that may take years before it begins to produce any output that can be used in the future.

In short, from the standpoint of society as a whole, present goods and services are sacrificed for the sake of future goods and services. Only where those future goods and services are more valuable than the present goods and services that are being sacrificed will financial institutions be able to receive a rate of return on their investments that will allow them to offer a high enough rate of return to innumerable individuals to induce those individuals to sacrifice their current consumption by supplying the savings required.

With financial intermediaries as with other economic institutions, nothing shows their function more clearly than seeing what happens when they are not able to function. A society without well-functioning financial institutions has fewer opportunities to generate greater wealth over time. Poor countries may remain poor, despite having an abundance of natural resources, when they have not yet developed the complex financial institutions required to mobilize the scattered savings of innumerable individuals, so as to be able to make the large investments required to turn natural resources into usable output. Sometimes foreign investors from countries which do have such institutions are the only ones able to come in to perform this function. At other times, however, there is not the legal framework of dependable laws and secure property rights required for either domestic or foreign investors to function.

Financial institutions not only transfer resources from one set of consumers to another and transfer resources from one use to another, they also create wealth by joining the entrepreneurial talents of people who lack money to the savings of many others, in order to finance new firms and new industries. Many, if not most, great American industries and individual fortunes began with entrepreneurs who had very limited financial resources at the outset. The Hewlett-Packard Corporation, for example, began as a business in a garage rented with borrowed money, and many other famous entrepreneurs— Henry Ford, Thomas Edison, and Andrew Carnegie, for example— had similarly modest beginnings. That these individuals and the enterprises they founded later became wealthy was an incidental by-product of the fact that they created vast amounts of wealth for the country as a whole. But the ability of poorer societies to follow similar paths is thwarted when they lack the financial institutions to allocate resources to those with great entrepreneurial ability but little or no money.

Such institutions took centuries to develop in the West. Nineteenth-century London was the greatest financial capital in the world, but there were earlier centuries when the British were so little versed in the complexities of finance that they were dependent on foreigners to run their financial institutions— notably Lombards and Jews. That is why there is a Lombard Street in London's financial district today and another street there named Old Jewry. Not only some Third World countries, but also some countries in the former Communist bloc of nations in Eastern Europe, have yet to develop the kinds of sophisticated financial institutions which promote economic development. They may now have capitalism, but they have not yet developed the financial institutions that would mobilize capital on a scale found in Western European countries and their overseas offshoots, such as the United States.

It is not that the wealth is not there in less developed economies. The problem is that their wealth cannot be collected from innumerable small sources, concentrated, and then allocated in large amounts to particular entrepreneurs, without financial institutions equal to the complex task of evaluating risks, markets, and rates of return.

In recent years, American banks and banks from Western Europe have gone into Eastern Europe to fill the vacuum. As of 2005, 70 percent of the assets in Poland's banking system were controlled by foreign banks, as were more than 80 percent of the banking assets in Bulgaria. Still, these countries lagged behind other Western nations in the use of such things as credit cards or even bank accounts. Only one-third of Poles had a bank account and only two percent of purchases in Poland were made with credit cards.

The complexity of financial institutions means that relatively few people are likely to understand them— which makes them vulnerable politically to critics who can depict their activities as sinister. Where those who have the expertise to operate such institutions are either foreigners or domestic minorities, they are especially vulnerable. Money-lenders have seldom been popular and terms like "Shylock" or even "speculator" are not terms of endearment. Many unthinking people in many countries and many periods of history have regarded financial activities as not "really" contributing anything to the economy, and have regarded the people who engage in such financial activities as mere parasites.

This was especially so at a time when most people engaged in hard physical labor in agriculture or industry, and were both suspicious and resentful of people who simply sat around handling pieces of paper, while producing nothing that could be seen or felt. Centuries-old hostilities have arisen— and have been acted upon— against minority groups who played such roles, whether they were Jews in Europe, overseas Chinese minorities in Southeast Asia, or Chettiars in their native India or in Burma, East Africa, or Fiji. Often such groups have been expelled or harassed into leaving the country— sometimes by mob violence— because of popular beliefs that they were parasitic.

Those with such misconceptions have then often been surprised to discover economic activity and the standard of living declining in the wake of their departure. An understanding of basic economics could have prevented many human tragedies, as well as many economic inefficiencies.

RETURNS ON INVESTMENT

Delayed rewards for costs incurred earlier are a return on investment, whether these rewards take the form of dividends paid on corporate stock or increases in incomes resulting from having gone to college or medical school. One of the largest investments in many people's lives consists of the time and energy expended over a period of years in raising their children. At one time, the return on that investment included having the children take care of the parents in old age, but today the return on this investment often consists only of the parents' satisfaction in seeing their children's well-being and progress. From the standpoint of society as a whole, each generation that makes this investment in its offspring is repaying the investment that was made by the previous generation in raising those who are parents today.

"Unearned Income"

Although making investments and receiving the delayed return on those investments takes many forms and has been going on all over the world throughout the history of the human race, misunderstandings of this process have also been long standing and widespread. Sometimes these delayed benefits are called "unearned" income, simply because they do not represent rewards for contributions made during the current time period. Investments that build a factory may not be repaid until years later, after workers and managers have been hired and products manufactured and sold.

During the particular year when dividends finally begin to be paid, investors may not have contributed anything, but this does not mean that the reward they receive is "unearned," simply because it was not earned by an investment made during that particular year.

What can be seen physically is always more vivid than what cannot be seen. Those who watch a factory in operation can see the workers creating a product before their eyes. They cannot see the investment which made that factory possible in the first place. Risks are invisible, even when they are present risks, and the past risks surrounding the initial creation of the business are readily forgotten by observers who see only a successful enterprise after the fact.

Also easily overlooked are the many management decisions that had to be made in determining where to locate, what kind of equipment to acquire, and what policies to follow in dealing with suppliers, consumers, and employees— any one of which decisions could spell the difference between success and failure. And of course what also cannot be seen are all the similar businesses that went out of business because they did not do all the things done by the surviving business we see before our eyes, or did not do them equally well.

It is easy to regard the visible factors as the sole or most important factors, even when other businesses with those same visible factors went bankrupt, while an expertly managed enterprise in the same industry flourished and grew. Nor are such misunderstandings inconsequential, either economically or politically. Many laws and government economic policies have been based on these misunderstandings. Elaborate ideologies and mass movements have also been based on the notion that only the workers "really" create wealth, while others merely skim off profits, without having contributed anything to producing the wealth in which they unjustly share.

Such misconceptions have had fateful consequences for money-lenders around the world. For many centuries, money-lenders have been widely condemned in many cultures for receiving back more money than they lent— that is, for getting an "unearned" income for waiting for payment and for taking risks. Often the social stigma attached to money-lending has been so great that only minorities who lived outside the existing social system anyway have been willing to take on such stigmatized activities. Thus, for centuries, Jews predominated in such occupations in Europe, as the Chinese did in Southeast Asia, the Chettiars and Marwaris in India, and other minority groups in other parts of the world.

Misconceptions about money-lending often take the form of laws attempting to help borrowers by giving them more leeway in repaying loans. But anything that makes it difficult to collect a debt when it is due makes it less likely that loans will be made in the first place, or will be made at the lower interest rates that would prevail in the absence of such debtor-protection policies by governments.

In some societies, people are not expected to charge interest on loans to relatives or fellow members of the local community, nor to be insistent on prompt payment according to the letter of the loan agreement. These kinds of preconditions discourage loans from being made in the first place, and sometimes they discourage individuals from letting it be known that they have enough money to be able to lend. In societies where such social pressures are particularly strong, incentives for acquiring wealth are reduced. This is not only a loss to the individual who might otherwise have made wealth by going all out, it is a loss to the whole society when people who are capable of producing things that many others are willing to pay for may not choose to go all out in doing so.

Investment and Allocation

Interest, as the price paid for investment funds, plays the same allocational role as other prices in bringing supply and demand into balance. When interest rates are low, it is more profitable to borrow money to invest in building houses or modernizing a factory or launching other economic ventures. On the other hand, low interest rates reduce the incentives to save. Higher interest rates lead more people to save more money but lead fewer investors to borrow that money when borrowing is more expensive. As with supply and demand for products in general, imbalances between supply and demand for money lead to rises or falls in the price— in this case, the interest rate. As *The Economist* magazine put it:

> Most of the time, mismatches between the desired levels of saving and investment are brought into line fairly easily through the interest-rate mechanism. If people's desire to save exceeds their desire to invest, interest rates will fall so that the incentive to save goes down and the willingness to invest goes up.

In an unchanging world, these mismatches between savings and investment would end, and investors would invest the same amount that savers were saving, with the result that interest rates would be stable because they would have no reason to change. But, in the real world as it is, interest rate fluctuations, like price fluctuations in general, constantly redirect resources in different directions as technology, demand and other factors change. Because interest rates are symptoms of an underlying reality, and of the constraints inherent in that reality, laws or government policies that change interest rates have repercussions far beyond the purpose for which the interest rate is changed, with reverberations throughout the economy.

For example, when the U.S. Federal Reserve System in the early twenty-first century lowered interest rates, in order to try to sustain production and employment, in the face of signs that the growth of national output and employment might be slowing down, the repercussions included an increase in the prices of houses. Lower interest rates meant lower mortgage payments and therefore enabled more people to be able to afford to buy houses. This in turn led fewer people to rent apartments, so that apartment rents fell because of a reduced demand. Artificially low interest rates also provided fewer incentives for people to save.

These were just some of many changes that spread throughout the economy, brought about by the Federal Reserve's changes in interest rates. More generally, this showed how intricately all parts of a market economy are tied together, so that changes in one part of the system are transmitted automatically to innumerable other parts of the system.

Not everything that is called interest is in fact interest, however. When loans are made, for example, what is charged as interest includes not only the rate of return necessary to compensate for the time delay in receiving the money back, but also an additional amount to compensate for the risk that the loan will not be repaid, or repaid on time, or repaid in full. What is called interest also includes the costs of processing the loan. With small loans, especially, these process costs can become a significant part of what is charged because process costs do not vary as much as the amount of the loan varies. That is, lending a thousand dollars does not require ten times as much paperwork as lending a hundred dollars.

In other words, process costs on small loans can be a larger share of what is loosely called interest. Many of the criticisms of small financial institutions that operate in low-income neighborhoods grow out of misconstruing various charges that are called interest but are not, in the strict sense in which economists use the term for payments received for time delay in receiving repayment and the risk that the repayment will not be made in full or on time, or perhaps at all.

Short-term loans to low-income people are often called "payday loans," since they are to be repaid on the borrower's next payday or when a Social Security check or welfare check arrives, which may be only a matter of weeks, or even days, away. Such loans, according to the *Wall Street Journal*, are "usually between $300 and $400." Obviously, such loans are more likely to be made to people whose incomes and assets are so low that they need a modest sum of money immediately for some exigency and simply do not have it.

The media and politicians make much of the fact that the *annual* rate of interest (as they loosely use the term "interest") on these loans is astronomical. The *New York Times*, for example referred to "an annualized interest rate of 312 percent" on some such loans. But payday loans are not made for a year, so the annual rate of interest is irrelevant, except for creating a sensation in the media or in politics. As one owner of a payday loan business pointed out, discussing annual interest rates on payday loans is like saying salmon costs more than $15,000 a ton or a hotel room rents for more than $36,000 a year, since most people never buy a ton of salmon or rent a hotel room for a year.

Whatever the costs of processing payday loans, those costs as well as the cost of risk must be recovered from the interest charged— and the shorter the period of time involved, the higher the annual interest rate must be to cover those fixed costs. For a two-week loan, payday lenders typically charge $15 in interest for every $100 lent. When laws restrict the annual interest rate to 36 percent, this means that the interest charged for a two-week loan would be less than $1.50— an amount unlikely to cover even the cost of processing the loan, much less the risk involved. When Oregon passed a law capping the annual interest rate at 36 percent, three-quarters of the hundreds of payday lenders in the state closed down. Similar laws in other states have also shut down many payday lenders.

So-called "consumer advocates" may celebrate such laws but the low-income borrower who cannot get the $100 urgently needed may have to pay more than $15 in late fees on a credit card bill or pay in other consequences— such as having a car repossessed or having the electricity cut off— that the borrower obviously considered more detrimental than paying $15, or the transaction would not have been made in the first place.

The lower the interest rate ceiling, the more reliable the borrowers would have to be, in order to make it pay to lend to them. At a sufficiently low interest rate ceiling, it would pay to lend only to millionaires and, at a still lower interest rate ceiling, it would pay to lend only to billionaires. Since different ethnic groups have different incomes and different average credit scores, interest rate ceilings virtually guarantee that there will be disparities in the proportions of these groups who are approved for mortgage loans, credit cards and other forms of lending.

In the United States, for example, Asian Americans have higher average credit scores than Hispanic Americans or black Americans— or white Americans, for that matter. Yet people who favor interest rate ceilings are often shocked to discover that some racial or ethnic groups are turned down for mortgage loans more often than others, and attribute this to racial discrimination by the lenders. But, since most American lenders are apt to be white, and they turn down whites at a much higher rate than they turn down Asian Americans, racial discrimination seems an unlikely explanation.

Where there are lenders who specialize in large, short-term loans to high-income people with expensive possessions to use as collateral, these "collateral lenders" (essentially pawn shops for the affluent or rich) charge interest rates that can exceed 200 percent on an annual basis. These interest rates are high for the same reasons that payday loans to low-income people are high. But, because the high-income loans are secured by collateral that can be sold if the loan is not repaid, the high interest rates are not as high as with loans to low-income people without collateral. Moreover, because a collateral lender like Pawngo makes loans averaging between $10,000 to $15,000, the fixed process costs are a much smaller percentage of the loans, and so add correspondingly less to the interest rate charged.

SPECULATION

Most market transactions involve buying things that exist, based on whatever value they have to the buyer and whatever price is charged by the seller. Some transactions, however, involve buying things that do not yet exist or whose value has yet to be determined— or both. For example, the price of stock in the Internet company Amazon.com rose for years before the company made its first dollar of profits. People were obviously speculating that the company would eventually make profits or that others would keep bidding up the price of its stock, so that the initial stockholder could sell the stock for a profit, whether or not Amazon.com itself ever made a profit. Amazon.com was founded in 1994. After years of operating at a loss, it finally made its first profit in 2001.

Exploring for oil is another costly speculation, since millions of dollars may be spent before discovering whether there is in fact any oil at all where the exploration is taking place, much less whether there is enough oil to repay the money spent.

Many other things are bought in hopes of future earnings which may or may not materialize— scripts for movies that may never be made, pictures painted by artists who may or may not become famous some day, and foreign currencies that may go up in value over time, but which could just as easily go down. Speculation as an economic activity may be engaged in by people in all walks of life but there are also professional speculators for whom this is their whole career.

One of the professional speculator's main roles is in relieving other people from having to speculate as part of their regular economic activity, such as farming for example, where both the weather during the growing season and the prices at harvest time are unpredictable. Put differently, risk is inherent in all aspects of human life. Speculation is one way of having some people specialize in bearing these risks, for a price. For such transactions to take place, the cost of the risk being transferred from whoever initially bears that risk must be greater than what is charged by whoever agrees to take on the risk. At the same time, the cost to whoever takes on that risk must be less than the price charged.

In other words, the risk must be *reduced* by this transfer, in order for the transfer to make sense to both parties. The reason for the speculator's lower cost may be more sophisticated methods of assessing risk, a larger amount of capital available to ride out short-run losses, or because the number and variety of the speculator's risks lowers his over-all risk. No speculator can expect to avoid losses on particular speculations but, so long as the gains exceed the losses over time, speculation can be a viable business.

The other party to the transaction must also benefit from the net reduction of risk. When an American wheat farmer in Idaho or Nebraska is getting ready to plant his crop, he has no way of knowing what the price of wheat will be when the crop is harvested. That depends on innumerable other wheat farmers, not only in the United States but as far away as Russia or Argentina.

If the wheat crop fails in Russia or Argentina, the world price of wheat will shoot up, because of supply and demand, causing American wheat farmers to get very high prices for their crop. But if there are bumper crops of wheat in Russia and Argentina, there may be more wheat on the world market than anybody can use, with the excess having to go into expensive storage facilities. That will cause the world price of wheat to plummet, so that the American farmer may have little to show for all his work, and may be lucky to avoid taking a loss on the year. Meanwhile, he and his family will have to live on their savings or borrow from whatever sources will lend to them.

In order to avoid having to speculate like this, the farmer may in effect pay a professional speculator to carry the risk, while the farmer sticks to farming. The speculator signs contracts to buy or sell at prices fixed in advance for goods to be delivered at some future date. This shifts the risk of the activity from the person engaging in it— such as the wheat farmer, in this case— to someone who is, in effect, betting that he can guess the future prices better than the other person and has the financial resources to ride out the inevitable wrong bets, in order to make a net profit over all because of the bets that turn out better.

Speculation is often misunderstood as being the same as gambling, when in fact it is the opposite of gambling. What gambling involves, whether in games of chance or in actions like playing Russian roulette, is creating a risk that would otherwise not exist, in order either to profit or to exhibit one's skill or lack of fear. What economic speculation involves is coping with an *inherent* risk in such a way as to minimize it and to leave it to be borne by whoever is best equipped to bear it.

When a commodity speculator offers to buy wheat that has not yet been planted, that makes it easier for a farmer to plant wheat, without having to wonder what the market price will be like later, at harvest time. A futures contract guarantees the seller a specified price in advance, regardless of what the market price may turn out to be at the time of delivery. This separates farming from economic speculation, allowing each to be done by different people, who specialize in different economic activities. The speculator uses his knowledge of the market, and of economic and statistical analysis, to try to arrive at a better guess than the farmer may be able to make, and thus is able to offer a price that the farmer will consider an attractive alternative to waiting to sell at whatever price happens to prevail in the market at harvest time.

Although speculators seldom make a profit on every transaction, they must come out ahead in the long run, in order to stay in business. Their profit depends on paying the farmer a price that is lower on average than the price which actually emerges at harvest time. The farmer also knows this, of course. In effect, the farmer is paying the speculator for carrying the risk, just as one pays an insurance company. As with other goods and services, the question may be raised as to whether the service rendered is worth the price charged. At the individual level, each farmer can decide for himself whether the deal is worth it. Each speculator must of course bid against other speculators, as each farmer must compete with other farmers, whether in making futures contracts or in selling at harvest time.

From the standpoint of the economy as a whole, competition determines what the price will be and therefore what the speculator's profit will be. If that profit exceeds what it takes to entice investors to risk their money in this volatile field, more investments will flow into this segment of the market until competition drives profits down to a level that just compensates the expenses, efforts, and risks.

Competition is visibly frantic among speculators who shout out their offers and bids in commodity exchanges. Prices fluctuate from moment to moment and a five-minute delay in making a deal can mean the difference between profits and losses. Even a modest-sized firm engaging in commodity speculation can gain or lose hundreds of thousands of dollars in a single day, and huge corporations can gain or lose millions in a few hours.

Commodity markets are not just for big businesses or even for farmers in technologically advanced countries. A *New York Times* dispatch from India reported:

At least once a day in this village of 2,500 people, Ravi Sham Choudhry turns on the computer in his front room and logs in to the Web site of the Chicago Board of Trade.

He has the dirt of a farmer under his fingernails and pecks slowly at the keys. But he knows what he wants: the prices for soybean commodity futures.

This was not an isolated case. As of 2003, there were 3,000 organizations in India putting as many as 1.8 million Indian farmers in touch with the world's commodity markets. The farmer just mentioned served as an agent for fellow farmers in surrounding villages. As one sign of how fast such Internet commodity information is spreading, Mr. Choudhry earned $300 the previous year from this activity that is incidental to his farming, but now earned that much in one month. That is a very significant sum in a poor country like India.

Agricultural commodities are not the only ones in which commodity traders speculate. One of the most dramatic examples of what can happen with commodity speculation involved the rise and fall of silver prices in 1980. Silver was selling at $6.00 an ounce in early 1979 but skyrocketed to a high of $50.05 an ounce by early 1980. However, this price began a decline that reached $21.62 on March 26th. Then, in just one day, that price was cut by more than half to $10.80. In the process, the billionaire Hunt brothers, who were speculating heavily in silver, lost more than a billion dollars *within a few weeks*. Speculation is one of the financially riskiest activities for the individual speculator, though it reduces risks for the economy as a whole.

Speculation may be engaged in by people who are not normally thought of as speculators. As far back as the 1870s, a food-processing company headed by Henry Heinz signed contracts to buy cucumbers from farmers at pre-arranged prices, regardless of what the market prices might be when the cucumbers were harvested. Then as now, those farmers who did *not* sign futures contracts with anyone were necessarily engaging in speculation about prices at harvest time, whether or not they thought of themselves as speculators. Incidentally, the deal proved to be disastrous for Heinz when there was a bumper crop of cucumbers, well beyond what he expected or could afford to buy, forcing him into bankruptcy. It took him years to recover financially and start over, eventually founding the H.J. Heinz company that continues to exist today.

Because risk is the whole reason for speculation in the first place, being wrong is a common experience, though being wrong too often means facing financial extinction. Predictions, even by very knowledgeable people, can be wrong by vast amounts. The distinguished British magazine *The Economist* predicted in March 1999 that the price of a barrel of oil was heading down, when in fact it headed up— and by December oil was selling for five times the price suggested by *The Economist*. In the United States, predictions about inflation by the Federal Reserve System have more than once turned out to be wrong, and the Congressional Budget Office has likewise predicted that a new tax law would bring in more tax revenue, when in fact tax revenues fell instead of rising, and in other cases the CBO predicted falling revenues from a new tax law, when in fact revenues rose.

Futures contracts are made for delivery of gold, oil, soybeans, foreign currencies and many other things at some price fixed in advance for delivery on a future date. Commodity speculation is only one kind of speculation. People also speculate in real estate, corporate stocks, or other things.

The full cost of risk is not only the amount of money involved, it is also the worry that hangs over the individual while waiting to see what happens. A farmer may expect to get $1,000 a ton for his crop but also knows that it could turn out to be $500 a ton or $1,500. If a speculator offers to guarantee to buy his crop at $900 a ton, that price may look good if it spares the farmer months of sleepless nights wondering how he is going to support his family if the harvest price leaves him too little to cover his costs of growing the crop.

Not only may the speculator be better equipped financially to deal with being wrong, he may be better equipped psychologically, since the kind of people who worry a lot do not usually go into commodity speculation. A commodity speculator I knew had one year when his business was operating at a loss going into December, but things changed so much in December that he still ended up with a profit for the year— to his surprise, as much as anyone else's. This is not an occupation for the faint of heart.

Economic speculation is another way of allocating scarce resources— in this case, knowledge. Neither the speculator nor the farmer knows what the prices will be when the crop is harvested. But the speculator happens to have more knowledge of markets and of economic and statistical analysis than the farmer, just as the farmer has more knowledge of how to grow the crop. My commodity speculator friend admitted that he had never actually seen a soybean and had no idea what they looked like, even though he had probably bought and sold millions of dollars' worth of soybeans over the years. He simply transferred ownership of his soybeans on paper to soybean buyers at harvest time, without ever taking physical possession of them from the farmer. He was not really in the soybean business, he was in the risk management business.

INVENTORIES

Inherent risks must be dealt with by the economy not only through economic speculation but also by maintaining inventories. Put differently, *inventory is a substitute for knowledge*. No food would ever be thrown out after a meal, if the cook knew beforehand exactly how much each person would eat and could therefore cook just that amount. Since inventory costs money, a business enterprise must try to limit how much inventory it has on hand, while at the same time not risking running out of their product and thereby missing sales.

Japanese automakers are famous for carrying so little inventory that parts for their automobiles arrive at the factory several times a day, to be put on the cars as they move down the assembly line. This reduces the costs of carrying a large inventory of parts and thereby reduces the cost of producing a car. However, an earthquake in Japan in 2007 put one of its piston-ring suppliers out of commission. As the *Wall Street Journal* reported:

> For want of a piston ring costing $1.50, nearly 70% of Japan's auto production has been temporarily paralyzed this week.

Having either too large or too small an inventory means losing money. Clearly, those businesses which come closest to the optimal size of inventory will have their profit prospects enhanced. More important, the total resources of the economy will be allocated more efficiently, not only because each enterprise has an incentive to be efficient, but also because those firms which turn out to be right more often are more likely to survive and continue making such decisions, while those who repeatedly carry far too large an inventory, or far too small, are likely to disappear from the market through bankruptcy.

Too large an inventory means excess costs of doing business, compared to the costs of their competitors, who are therefore in a position to sell at lower prices and take away customers. Too small an inventory means running out of what the customers want, not only missing out on immediate sales but also risking having those customers look elsewhere for more dependable suppliers in the future. As noted in Chapter 6, in an economy where deliveries of goods and parts were always uncertain, such as that of the Soviet Union, huge inventories were the norm.

Some of the same economic principles involving risk apply to activities far removed from the marketplace. A soldier going into battle does not take just the number of bullets he will fire or just the amount of first aid supplies he will need if wounded in a particular way, because neither he nor anyone else has the kind of foresight required to do that. The soldier carries an inventory of both ammunition and medical supplies to cover various contingencies. At the same time, he cannot go into battle loaded down with huge amounts of everything that he might possibly need in every conceivable circumstance. That would slow him down and reduce his maneuverability, making him an easier target for the enemy. In other words, beyond some point, attempts to increase his safety can make his situation more dangerous.

Inventory is related to knowledge and risk in another way. In normal times, each business tends to keep a certain ratio of inventory to its sales. However, when times are more uncertain, such as during a recession or depression, sales may be made from existing inventories without producing replacements. During the third quarter of 2003, for example, as the United States was recovering from a recession, its sales, exports, and profits were all rising, but *BusinessWeek* magazine reported that manufacturers, wholesalers, and retailers were "selling goods off their shelves" and "the ratio of inventories to sales hit a record low."

The net result was that far fewer jobs were created than in similar periods of increased business activity in the past, leading to the phrase "a jobless recovery" to describe what was happening, as businesses were not confident that this recovery would last. In short, for sellers the selling of inventory was a way of coping with economic risks. Only after inventories had hit bottom did the hiring of more people to produce more goods increase on such a large scale as to make the phrase "a jobless recovery" no longer applicable.

PRESENT VALUE

Although many goods and services are bought for immediate use, many other benefits come in a stream over time, whether as a season's ticket to baseball games or an annuity that will make monthly pension payments to you after you retire. That whole stream of benefits may be purchased at a given moment for what economists call its "present value"— that is, the price of a season's ticket or the price paid for an annuity. However, more is involved than simply determining the price to be paid, important as that is. The implications of present value affect economic decisions and their consequences, even in areas that are not normally thought of as economic, such as determining the amount of natural resources available for future generations.

Prices and Present Values

Whether a home, business, or farm is maintained, repaired or improved today determines how long it will last and how well it will operate in the future. However, the owner who has paid for repairs and maintenance does not have to wait to see the future effects on the property's value. These future benefits are immediately reflected in the property's *present value*. The "present value" of an asset is in fact nothing more than its anticipated future benefits, added up and discounted for the fact that they are delayed. Your home, business, or farm may be functioning no better than your neighbor's today, but if the prospective toll of wear and tear on your property over time is reduced by installing heavier pipes, stronger woods, or other more durable building materials, then your property's market value will *immediately* be worth more than that of your neighbor, even if there is no visible difference in the way they are functioning today.

Conversely, if the city announces that it is going to begin building a sewage treatment plant next year, on a piece of land next to your home, the value of your home will decline *immediately*, before the adjoining land has been touched. The present value of an asset reflects its future benefits or detriments, so that anything which is expected to enhance or reduce those benefits or detriments will immediately affect the price at which the asset can be sold today.

Present value links the future to the present in many ways. It makes sense for a ninety-year-old man to begin planting fruit trees that will take 20 years before they reach their maturity because his land will *immediately* be worth more as a result of those trees. He can sell the land a month later and go live in the Bahamas if he wishes, because he will be receiving additional value from the fruit that is expected to grow on those trees, years after he is no longer alive. Part of the value of his wealth today consists of the value of food that has not yet been grown— and which will be eaten by children who have not yet been born.

One of the big differences between economics and politics is that politicians are not forced to pay attention to future consequences that lie beyond the next election. An elected official whose policies keep the public happy up through election day stands a good chance of being voted another term in office, even if those policies will have ruinous consequences in later years. There is no "present value" to make political decision-makers today take future consequences into account, when those consequences will come after election day.

Although the general public may not have sufficient knowledge or training to realize the long-run implications of today's policies, financial specialists who deal in government bonds do. Thus the Standard & Poor's bond-rating service downgraded California's state bonds in the midst of that state's electricity crisis in 2001, even though there had been no defaults on those bonds, nor any lesser payments made to those who had bought California bonds, and there were billions of dollars of surplus in the state's treasury.

What Standard & Poor's understood was that the heavy financial responsibilities taken on by the California government to meet the electricity crisis meant that heavy taxes or heavy debt were waiting over the horizon. That increased the risk of future defaults or delay in payments to bondholders— thereby reducing the present value of those bonds.

Any series of future payments can be reduced to a present value that can be paid immediately in a lump sum. Winners of lotteries who are paid in installments over a period of years can sell those payments to a financial institution that will give them a fixed sum immediately. So can accident victims who have been awarded installment payments from insurance companies. Because the present value of a series of payments due over a period of decades may be considerably less than the sum total of all those payments, due to discounting for delays, the lump sums paid may be less than half of those totals, causing some people who sold, in order to relieve immediate financial problems, to later resent the deal they made. Others, however, are pleased and return to make similar deals in the future.

Conversely, some individuals may wish to convert a fixed sum of money into a stream of future payments. Elderly people who are retiring with what seems like an adequate amount to live on must be concerned with whether they will live longer than expected— "outlive their money" as the expression goes— and end up in poverty. In order to avoid this, they may use a portion of their money to purchase an annuity from an insurance company. For example, in the early twenty-first century, a seventy year old man could purchase an annuity for a price of $100,000 and thereafter receive $772 a month for life— whether that life was three more years or thirty more years. In other words, the risk would be transferred to the insurance company, for a price.

As in other cases, the risk is not only shifted but reduced, since the insurance company can more accurately predict the average lifespan of millions of people to whom it has sold annuities than any given individual can predict his own lifespan. Incidentally, a woman aged 70 would get somewhat smaller monthly payments— $725— for the same price, given that women usually live longer than men.

The key point is that the reduced risk comes from the greater predictability of large numbers. A news story some years ago told of a speculator who made a deal with an elderly woman who needed money. In exchange for her making him the heir to her house, he agreed to pay her a fixed sum every month as long as she lived. However, this one-to-one deal did not work out as planned because she lived far longer than anyone expected and the speculator died before she did. An insurance company not only has the advantage of large numbers, it has the further advantage that its existence is not limited to the human lifespan.

Natural Resources

Present value profoundly affects the discovery and use of natural resources. There may be enough oil underground to last for centuries or millennia, but its present value determines how much oil will repay what it costs anyone to discover it at any given time— and that may be no more than enough oil to last for a dozen or so years. A failure to understand this basic economic reality has, for generations, led to numerous and widely publicized false predictions that we were "running out" of petroleum, coal, or some other natural resource.

In 1960, for example, a best-selling book said that the United States had only a 13-year supply of domestic petroleum at the existing rate of usage. At that time, the known petroleum reserves of the United States were not quite 32 billion barrels. At the end of the 13 years, the known petroleum reserves of the United States were more than 36 billion barrels. Yet the original statistics and the arithmetic based on them were both accurate. Why then did the United States not run out of oil by 1973? Was it just dumb luck that more oil was discovered— or were there more fundamental economic reasons?

Just as shortages and surpluses are not simply a matter of how much physical stuff there is, either absolutely or relative to the population, so known reserves of natural resources are not simply a matter of how much physical stuff there is in the ground. For natural resources as well, prices are crucial. So are present values.

How much of any given natural resource is known to exist depends on how much it costs to know. Oil exploration, for example, is very costly. In 2011, the *New York Times* reported:

> Two miles below the ocean floor, on a ridge the size of metropolitan Houston, modern-day wildcatters have pinpointed what they believe is a major oil field. Now all they have to do is spend $100 million to find out if they're right.

The cost of producing oil includes not only the costs of geological exploration but also the costs of drilling expensive dry holes before striking oil. As these costs mount up while more and more oil is being discovered around the world, the growing abundance of known supplies of oil reduces its price through supply and demand. Eventually the point is reached where the cost per barrel of finding more oil in a given place and processing it exceeds the present value per barrel of the oil that you are likely to find there. At that point, it no longer pays to keep exploring. Depending on a number of circumstances, the total amount of oil discovered at that point may well be no more than the 13 years' supply which led to dire predictions that we were running out. But, as the existing supplies of oil are being used up, rising prices lead to more huge investments in oil exploration.

As one example of the kinds of costs that can be involved, a major oil exploration venture in the Gulf of Mexico spent $80 million on the initial exploration and leases, and another $120 million for exploratory drilling, just to see if it looked like there was enough oil to justify continuing further. Then there were $530 million spent for building drilling platforms, pipelines, and other infrastructure, and— finally— $370 million for drilling for oil where there were proven reserves. This adds up to a total of $1.1 billion.

Imagine if the interest rate had been twice as high on this much money borrowed from banks or investors, making the total cost of exploration even higher. Or imagine that the oil companies had this much money of their own and could put it in a bank to earn twice the usual interest in safety. Would they have sunk as much money as they did into the more risky investment of looking for oil? Would you? Probably not. A higher interest rate would probably have meant less oil exploration and therefore smaller amounts of known reserves of petroleum. But that would not mean that we were any closer to running out of oil than if the interest rate were lower and the known reserves were correspondingly higher.

As more and more of the known reserves of oil get used up, the present value of each barrel of the remaining oil begins to rise and, once more, exploration for additional oil becomes profitable. But, as of any given time, it never pays to discover all the oil that exists in the ground or under the sea. In fact, it does not pay to discover more than a minute fraction of that oil. What does pay is for people to write hysterical predictions that we are running out of natural resources. It pays not only in book sales and television ratings, but also in political power and in personal notoriety.

In the early twenty-first century, a book titled *Twilight in the Desert* concluded that "Sooner or later, the worldwide use of oil must peak" and that is because "oil, like the other two fossil fuels, coal and natural gas, is nonrenewable." That is certainly true in the abstract, just as it is true in the abstract that sooner or later the sun must grow cold. But that is very different from saying that this has any relevance to any problem confronting us in the next century or the next millennium. The insinuation, however, was that we faced some enduring energy crisis in our own time, and the fact that the price of crude oil had shot up to $147 a barrel, with the price of gasoline shooting up to $4 a gallon, lent credence to that insinuation. But, in 2010, the *New York Times* reported:

> Just as it seemed that the world was running on fumes, giant oil fields were discovered off the coasts of Brazil and Africa, and Canadian oil sands projects expanded so fast, they now provide North America with more oil than Saudi Arabia. In addition, the United States has increased domestic oil production for the first time in a generation.

Even the huge usages of energy resources during the entire twentieth century did not reduce the known reserves of the natural resources used to generate that energy. Given the enormous drain on energy resources created historically by such things as the spread of railroad networks, factory machinery, and the electrification of cities, it has been estimated that more energy was consumed in the first two decades of the twentieth century than in all the previously recorded history of the human race. Moreover, energy usage continued to escalate throughout the century— and yet known petroleum reserves rose. At the end of the twentieth century, the known reserves of petroleum were more than ten times as large as they were in the middle of the twentieth century. Improvements in technology made oil discovery and its extraction more efficient. In the 1970s, only about one-sixth of all wells drilled in search of oil turned out to actually produce oil. But, by the early twenty-first century, two-thirds of these exploratory wells produced oil.

The economic considerations which apply to petroleum apply to other natural resources as well. No matter how much iron ore there is in the ground, it will never pay to discover more of it when its present value per ton is less than the cost per ton of exploration and processing. Yet, despite the fact that the twentieth century saw vast expansions in the use of iron and steel, the proven reserves of iron ore increased several fold. So did the known reserves of copper, aluminum, and lead, among other natural resources. As of 1945, the known reserves of copper were 100 million metric tons. After a quarter of a century of unprecedented increases in the use of copper, the known reserves of copper were *three times* what they were at the outset and, by 1999, copper reserves had doubled again. The known reserves of natural gas in the United States rose by about one-third (from 1,532 trillion cubic feet to 2,074 trillion cubic feet), just from 2006 to 2008.

Even after a pool of petroleum has been discovered underground or under the sea and the oil is being extracted and processed, economic considerations prevent that pool of oil from being drained dry. As *The Economist* magazine put it:

> A few decades ago, the average oil recovery rate from reservoirs was 20%; thanks to remarkable advances in technology, this has risen to about 35% today.

In other words, nearly two-thirds of the oil in an underground pool is left in the pool, because it would be too costly to drain out all of it— or even most of it— with today's technology and today's oil prices. But the oil is still there and its location is already known. If and when we are genuinely "running out" of oil that is available at today's costs of extraction and processing, then the next step would be to begin extracting and processing oil that costs a little more and, later, oil that costs a little more than that. But we are clearly not at that point when most of the oil that has been discovered is still left underground or under the sea. As technology improves, a higher rate of production of oil from existing wells becomes economically feasible. In 2007 the *New York Times* reported a number of examples, such as this:

> The Kern River oil field, discovered in 1899, was revived when Chevron engineers here started injecting high-pressured steam to pump out more oil. The field, whose production had slumped to 10,000 barrels a day in the 1960s, now has a daily output of 85,000 barrels.

Such considerations are not unique to petroleum. When coal was readily available above ground, it did not pay to dig into the ground and build coal mines, since the coal extracted at higher costs underground could not compete in price with coal that could be gathered at lower cost on the surface. Only after the coal available at the lowest cost was exhausted did it pay to begin digging into the ground for more.

The difference between the economic approach and the hysterical approach to natural resource usage was demonstrated by a bet between economist Julian Simon and environmentalist Paul Ehrlich. Professor Simon offered to bet anyone that any set of five natural resources they chose would not have risen in real cost over any time period they chose. A group led by Professor Ehrlich took the bet and chose five natural resources. They also chose ten years as the time period for measuring how the real costs of these natural resources had changed. At the end of that decade, not only had the real cost of that set of five resources declined, so had the cost of every single resource which they had expected to rise in cost! Obviously, if we had been anywhere close to running out of those resources, their costs would have risen because the present value of these potentially more scarce resources would have risen.

In some ultimate sense, the total quantity of resources must of course be declining. However, a resource that would run out centuries after it becomes obsolete, or a thousand years after the sun grows cold, is not a serious practical problem. If it is going to run out within some time period that is a matter of practical relevance, then the rising present value of the resource whose exhaustion looms ahead will automatically force conservation, without either public hysteria or political exhortation.

Just as prices cause us to share scarce resources and their products with each other at a given time, present value causes us to share those resources over time with future generations— without even being aware that we are sharing. It is of course also possible to share politically, by having the government assume control of natural resources, as it can assume control of other assets, or in fact of the whole economy.

The efficiency of political control versus impersonal control by prices in the marketplace depends in part on which method conveys the underlying realities more accurately. As already noted in earlier chapters, price controls and direct allocation of resources by political institutions require far more explicit knowledge by a relatively small number of planners than is required for a market economy to be coordinated by prices to which millions of people respond according to their own first-hand knowledge of their own individual circumstances and preferences— and the relative handful of prices that each individual has to deal with.

Planners can easily make false projections, either from ignorance or from various political motives, such as seeking more power, re-election, or other goals. For example, during the 1970s, government scientists were asked to estimate the size of the American reserves of natural gas and how long it would last at the current rate of usage. Their estimate was that the United States had enough natural gas to last for more than a thousand years! While some might consider this good news, politically it was bad news at a time when the President of the United States was trying to arouse public support for more government programs to deal with the energy "crisis." This estimate was repudiated by the Carter administration and a new study begun, which reached more politically acceptable results.

Sometimes the known reserves of a natural resource seem especially small because the amount available at currently feasible costs is in fact nearing exhaustion within a few years. There may be vast amounts available at a slightly higher cost of extraction and processing, but these additional amounts will of course not be touched until the amount available at a lower cost is exhausted. For example, back when there were large coal deposits available on top of the ground, someone could sound an alarm that we were "running out" of coal that is "economically feasible" to use, coal that can be gotten without "prohibitive costs." But again, the whole purpose of prices is to be prohibitive. In this case, that prohibition prevented more costly resources from being resorted to needlessly, so long as there were less costly sources of the same resource available.

A similar situation exists today, when most of the petroleum found in an oil pool is left there because the costs of extracting more than the most easily accessible oil cannot be repaid by the current market price. During the oil crisis of 2005, when the price of gasoline in the United States shot up to double what it had been less than two years earlier, and people worried that the world was running out of petroleum, the *Wall Street Journal* reported:

> The Athabasca region in Alberta, Canada, for instance, theoretically could produce about 1.7 trillion to 2.5 trillion barrels of oil from its 54,000 square miles of oil-sands deposits— making it second to Saudi Arabia in oil reserves. The Athabasca reserves remain largely untapped because getting the oil out of the sand is expensive and complicated. It takes about two tons of sand to extract one barrel of oil. But if oil prices remain near current levels— indeed, if prices stay above $30 a barrel, as they have since late 2003— oil-sands production would be profitable. Limited investment and production has been under way in Athabasca.

If technology never improved, then all resources would become more costly over time, as the most easily obtained and most easily processed deposits were used up first and the less accessible, or less rich, or more difficult to process deposits were then resorted to. However, with improving technology, it can actually cost less to acquire future resources when their time comes, as happened with the resources that Julian Simon and Paul Ehrlich bet on. For example, the average cost of finding a barrel of oil fell from $15 in 1977 to $5 by 1998. It is hardly surprising that there were larger known oil reserves after the cost of knowing fell.

Petroleum is by no means unique in having its supply affected by prices. The same is true for the production of nickel as well, for example. When the price of nickel rose in the early twenty-first century, the *Wall Street Journal* reported:

> A few years ago, it would have been hard to find a better example of a failed mining project than Murrin Murrin, a huge, star-crossed nickel operation deep in the Western Australian desert.
>
> Now, Murrin Murrin is an investor favorite. Shares of the company that runs it. . .have more than tripled in the past year, and some analysts see room for more.
>
> The surprising turnaround highlights a central fact of the current commodity boom: With prices this high— especially for nickel— even technically difficult or chronically troubled projects look good. Nickel is most widely used to make stainless steel.

Although the reserves of natural resources in a nation are often discussed in terms of physical quantities, economic concepts of cost, prices, and present values must be considered if practical conclusions are to be reached. In addition to needless alarms about natural resources running out, there have also been, conversely, unjustifiably optimistic statements that some poor country has so many billions of dollars' worth of "natural wealth" in the form of iron ore or bauxite deposits or some other natural resource.

Such statements mean very little without considering how much it would cost to extract and process those resources— and this varies greatly from place to place. Extraction of petroleum from Canada's oil sands, for example, costs so much that until recent years the oil there was not even counted in the world's petroleum reserves. But, when the price of oil shot up past $100 a barrel, Canada became one of the world's leaders in petroleum reserves.

Chapter 14

STOCKS, BONDS AND INSURANCE

Risk-taking is the mother's milk of capitalism.

Wall Street Journal

Risks inherent in economic activities can be dealt with in a wide variety of ways. In addition to the commodity speculation and inventory management discussed in the previous chapter, other ways of dealing with risk include stocks and bonds. There are also other economic activities analogous to stocks and bonds which deal with risks in ways that are legally different, though similar economically.

Whenever a home, a business, or any other asset increases in value over time, that increase is called a "capital gain." While it is another form of income, it differs from wages and salaries in not being paid right after it is earned, but usually only after an interval of some years. A thirty-year bond, for example, can be cashed in only after thirty years. If you never sell your home, then whatever increase in value it has will be called an "unrealized capital gain." The same is true for someone who opens a grocery store that grows more valuable as its location becomes known throughout the neighborhood, and as it develops a set of customers who get into the habit of shopping at that particular store. Perhaps after the owner dies, the surviving spouse or children may decide to sell the store— and only then will the capital gain be realized.

Sometimes a capital gain comes from a purely financial transaction, where you simply pay someone a certain amount of money today in order to get back a somewhat larger amount of money later on. This happens when you put money into a savings account that pays interest, or when a pawnbroker lends money, or when you buy a $10,000 U. S. Treasury bond for somewhat less than $10,000.

However it is done, this is a trade-off of money today for money in the future. The fact that interest is paid implies that money today is worth more than the same amount of money in the future. How much more depends on many things, and varies from time to time, as well as from country to country at the same time.

In the heyday of nineteenth-century British industrialization, railroad companies could raise the huge sums of money required to build miles of tracks and buy trains, by selling bonds that paid about 5 percent per year. This was possible only because the public had great confidence in both the railroads and the stability of the money. If the rate of inflation had been 6 percent a year, those who bought the bonds would have lost real value instead of gaining it. But the value of the British pound sterling was very stable and reliable during that era.

Since those times, inflation has become more common, so the interest rate would now have to cover whatever level of inflation was expected and still leave a prospect of a real gain in terms of an increase in purchasing power. The risk of inflation varies from country to country and from one era to another, so the rate of return on investments must include an allowance for the risk of inflation, which also varies. At the beginning of the twenty-first century, Mexico's government bonds paid 2.5 percentage points higher interest than those of the United States, while those of Brazil paid five percentage points higher than those of Mexico. Brazil's interest rate then shot up another ten percentage points after the emergence of a left-wing candidate for president of the country.

In short, varying risks— of which inflation is just one— are reflected in varying risk premiums added on to the underlying pure interest rate, which is a payment for postponed repayment. The risk premium component included in what is more loosely and more generally called the interest rate can become larger than what economists might call the pure interest rate. As of April 2003, for example, short-term interest rates (in the more general sense) ranged from less than 2 percent in Hong Kong to 18 percent in Russia and 39 percent in Turkey.

Leaving inflation aside, how much would a $10,000 bond that matures a year from now be worth to you today? That is, how much would you bid today for a bond that can be cashed in for $10,000 next year? Clearly it would not be worth $10,000, because future money is not as valuable as the same amount of present money. Even if you felt certain that you would still be alive a year from now, and even if there were no inflation expected, you would still prefer to have the same amount of money right now rather than later. If nothing else, money that you have today can be put in a bank and earn a year's interest on it. For the same reason, if you had a choice between buying a bond that matures a year from now and another bond of the same face value that matures ten years from now, you would not be willing to bid as much for the one that matures a decade later.

What this says is that the same nominal amount of money has different values, depending on how long you must wait to receive it. At a sufficiently high interest rate, you might be willing to wait decades to get your money back. People buy 30-year bonds regularly, though usually at a higher rate of return than what is paid on financial securities that mature in a year. On the other hand, at a sufficiently low interest rate, you would not be willing to wait any time at all to get your money back.

Somewhere in between is an interest rate at which you would be indifferent between lending money or keeping it. At that interest rate, the present value of a given amount of future money is equal to some smaller amount of present money. For example if you are indifferent at 4 percent, then a hundred dollars today is worth $104 a year from now to you. Any business or government agency that wants to borrow $100 from you today with a promise to pay you back a year from now will have to make that repayment at least $104. If everyone else has the same preferences that you do, then the interest rate in the economy as a whole will be 4 percent.

What if everyone does not have the same preferences that you do? Suppose that others will lend only when they get back 5 percent more at the end of the year? In that case, the interest rate in the economy as a whole will be 5 percent, simply because businesses and government cannot borrow the money they want for any less and they do not have to offer any more. Faced with a national interest rate of 5 percent, you would have no reason to accept less, even though you would take 4 percent if you had to.

In this situation, let us return to the question of how much you would be willing to bid for a $10,000 bond that matures a year from now. With an interest rate of 5 percent being available in the economy as a whole, it would not pay you to bid more than $9,523.81 for a $10,000 bond that matures a year from now. By investing that same amount of money somewhere else today at 5 percent, you could get back $10,000 in a year. Therefore, there is no reason for you to bid more than $9,523.81 for the $10,000 bond.

What if the interest rate in the economy as a whole had been 12 percent, rather than 5 percent? Then it would not pay you to bid more than $8,928.57 for a $10,000 bond that matures a year from now. In short, what people will bid for bonds depends on how much they could get for the same money by putting it somewhere else. That is why bond prices go down when the interest rate goes up, and vice versa.

What this also says is that, when the interest rate is 5 percent, $9,523.81 in the year 2014 is the same as $10,000 in the year 2015. This raises questions about the taxation of capital gains. If someone buys a bond for the former price and sells it a year later for the latter price, the government will of course want to tax the $476.19 difference. But is that really the same as an increase in value, if the two sums of money are just equivalent to one another? What if there has been a one percent inflation, so that the $10,000 received back would not have been enough to compensate for waiting, if the investor had expected inflation to reduce the real value of the bond? What if there had been a 5 percent inflation, so that the amount received back was worth no more than the amount originally lent, with no reward at all for waiting for the postponed repayment? Clearly, the investor would be worse off than if he or she had never bought the bond. How then can this "capital gain" really be said to be a gain?

These are just some of the considerations that make the taxation of capital gains more complicated than the taxation of such other forms of income as wages and salaries. Some governments in some countries do not tax capital gains at all, while the rate at which such gains are taxed in the United States remains a matter of political controversy.

VARIABLE RETURNS VERSUS

FIXED RETURNS

There are many ways of confronting the fact that the real value of a given sum of money varies with when it is received and with the varying likelihood that it will be received at all. Stocks and bonds are among the many ways of dealing with differing risks. But people who are not considering buying these financial securities must nevertheless confront the same principles in other ways, when choosing a career for themselves or when considering public policy issues for the country as a whole.

Stocks versus Bonds

Bonds differ from stocks because bonds are legal commitments to pay fixed amounts of money on a fixed date. Stocks are simply shares of the business that issues them, and there is no guarantee that the business will make a profit in the first place, much less pay out dividends instead of re-investing their profits in the business itself. Bondholders have a legal right to be paid what they were promised, whether the business is making money or losing money. In that respect, they are like the business' employees, to whom fixed commitments have been made as to how much they would be paid per hour or per week or month. They are legally entitled to those amounts, regardless of whether the business is profitable or unprofitable. The owners of a business— whether that is a single individual or millions of stockholders— are not legally entitled to anything, except whatever happens to be left over after a business has paid its employees, bondholders and other creditors.

Considering the fact that most new businesses fail within a few years, what is left over can just as easily be negative as positive. In other words, people who set up businesses may not only fail to make a profit but may even lose part or all of what they originally invested. In short, stocks and bonds have different amounts of risk. Moreover, the mixture of stocks and bonds sold by different kinds of businesses may reflect the inherent risks of these businesses themselves.

Imagine that someone is raising money to go into a business where (1) the chances are 50–50 that he will go bankrupt and (2) if the business does survive financially, the value of the initial investment will increase ten-fold. Perhaps the entrepreneur is drilling for oil or speculating in foreign currencies. What if the entrepreneur wants you to contribute $5,000 to this venture? Would you be better off buying $5,000 worth of stock in this enterprise or $5,000 worth of this company's bonds?

If you buy bonds, your chances are still only 50–50 of getting all your money back. And if this enterprise prospers, you are only entitled to whatever rate of return was specified in the bond at the outset, no matter how many millions of dollars the entrepreneur makes with your money. Buying bonds in such a venture would obviously not be a worthwhile deal. Buying stocks, on the other hand, might make sense, if you can afford the risk. If the business goes bankrupt, your stock could be worthless, while a bond would have some residual value, based on whatever assets might remain to be sold, even if that only pays the bondholders and other creditors pennies on the dollar. On the other hand, if the business succeeds and its assets increase ten-fold, then the value of your stock likewise increases ten-fold.

This is the kind of investment often called "venture capital," as distinguished from buying the stocks or bonds of some long-established corporation that is unlikely to either go bankrupt or to have a spectacular rate of return on its investments. As a rule of thumb, it has been estimated that a venture capitalist needs at least a 50 percent rate of return on successful investments, in order to cover the losses on the many unsuccessful investments and still come out ahead over all. In real life, rates of return on venture capital can vary greatly from year to year. For the 12 months ending September 30, 2001, venture capital funds *lost* 32.4 percent. That is, not only did these venture capitalists as a whole not make any net profit, they lost nearly one-third of the money they had invested. But, just a couple of years earlier venture capitalists averaged a rate of return of 163 percent.

The question of whether this kind of activity is worthwhile from the standpoint of the venture capitalist can be left to the venture capitalist to worry about. From the standpoint of the economy as a whole, the question is whether this kind of financial activity represents an efficient allocation of scarce resources which have alternative uses. Although individual venture capitalists can go bankrupt, just like the companies they invest in, the venture capital industry as a whole usually does not lose money— that is, it does not waste the available resources of the economy. It is in fact remarkable that something which looks as risky as venture capital usually works out from the standpoint of the economy as a whole, even if not from the standpoint of each venture capitalist.

Now look at stocks and bonds from the standpoint of the entrepreneur who is trying to raise money for a risky undertaking. Knowing that bonds would be unattractive to investors and that a bank would likewise be reluctant to lend to him because of the high risks, the entrepreneur would almost certainly try to raise money by selling stocks instead. At the other end of the risk spectrum, consider a public utility that supplies something for which the public has a continuing demand, such as water or electricity. There is usually very little risk involved in putting money into such an enterprise, so the utility can issue and sell bonds, without having to pay the higher amounts that investors would earn on stocks.* In recent years, some pension funds seeking safe, long-run investments from which to pay their retirees have invested in the building of toll highways, from whose receipts they can expect a continuing stream of returns for years to come.

In short, risks vary among businesses and their financial arrangements vary accordingly. At one extreme, a commodity speculator can go from profits to losses and back again, not only from year to year but even from hour to hour on a given day. That is why there are television pictures of frantic shouting and waving in commodity exchanges, where prices are changing so rapidly that the difference between making a deal right now and making it five minutes from now can be vast sums of money.

A more common pattern among those businesses that succeed is one of low income or no income at the beginning, followed by higher earnings after

---

* There are exceptions to virtually every rule. People who bought bonds in California's electric utility companies, as a safe investment for their retirement years, saw most of the value of those investments vanish into thin air during that state's electricity crisis of 2001. The state forced these utilities to sell electricity to their customers for less than they were paying their suppliers. As these utilities went billions of dollars into debt, their bonds were downgraded to the level of junk bonds.

the enterprise develops a clientele and establishes a reputation. For example, a dentist first starting out in his profession after graduating from dental school and buying the costly equipment needed to get started, may have little or no net income the first year, before becoming known widely enough in the community to attract a large clientele. During that interim, the dentist's secretary may be making more money than the dentist. Later on, of course, the situation will reverse and some observers may then think it unfair that the dentist makes several times the income of the secretary.

Even when variable sums of money add up to the same total as fixed sums of money, they are unlikely to be equally attractive. Would you be equally as likely to enter two occupations with the same average income— say, $50,000 a year— over the next decade if one occupation paid $50,000 every year while the income in the other occupation might vary from $10,000 one year to $90,000 the next year and back again, in an unpredictable pattern? Chances are you would require a somewhat higher average income in the occupation with variable pay, to make it equally attractive with the occupation with a reliably fixed income. Accordingly, stocks usually yield a higher average rate of return than bonds, since stocks have a variable rate of return (including, sometimes, no return at all), while bonds have a guaranteed fixed rate of return. It is not some moral principle that makes this happen. It happens because people will not take the risk of buying stocks unless they can expect a higher average rate of return than they get from bonds.

The degree of risk varies not only with the kind of investment but also with the period of time involved. For a period of one year, bonds are likely to be much safer than stocks. But for a period of 20 or 30 years, the risk of inflation threatens the value of bonds or other assets with fixed-dollar amounts, such as bank accounts, while stock prices tend to rise with inflation like real estate, factories, or other real assets. Being shares of real assets, stocks rise in price as the assets themselves rise in price during inflation. Therefore the relative safety of stocks and bonds can be quite different in the long run than in the short run.

Someone planning for retirement decades in the future may find a suitable mixture of stocks a much safer investment than someone who will need the money in a year or two. "Like money in the bank" is a popular phrase used to indicate something that is a very safe bet, but money in the bank is not particularly safe over a period of decades, when inflation can steal much of its value. The same is true of bonds. Eventually, after reaching an age when the remaining life expectancy is no longer measured in decades, it may be prudent to begin transferring money out of stocks and into bonds, bank accounts, and other assets with greater short-run safety.

Risk and Time

The stock market as a whole is not as risky as commodity speculation or venture capital but neither is it a model of stability. Even during a boom in the economy and in stocks, the Dow Jones Industrial Average, which measures movements in the stocks of major corporations, can go down on a given day. In the entire history of the American stock market, the longest streak of consecutive business days when the Dow Jones average ended up higher was fourteen— back in 1897. In 2007, the *Wall Street Journal* reported: "Until yesterday, the Dow Jones Industrial Average was on its longest winning streak since 2003— up for eight straight sessions. Had it continued one more day, it would have been the longest streak in more than a decade." Yet the media often report the ups and downs of the stock market as if it were big news, sometimes offering guesses for a particular day's rise or fall. But stock prices around the world have been going up and down for centuries.

As an extreme example of how the relative risks of different kinds of investments can vary over time, a dollar invested in bonds in 1801 would have been worth nearly a thousand dollars by 1998, while a dollar invested in stocks that same year would have been worth more than half a million dollars. All this is in real terms, taking inflation into account. Meanwhile, a dollar invested in gold in 1801 would in 1998 be worth just 78 cents. The phrase "as good as gold" can be as misleading as the phrase "money in the bank," when talking about the long run. While there have been many short-run periods when bonds and gold held their values as stock prices plummeted, the relative safety of these different kinds of investments varies greatly with how long a time period you have in mind. Moreover, the pattern is not the same in all eras.

The real rate of return on American stocks was just 3.6 percent during the Depression decade from 1931 to 1940, while bonds paid 6.4 percent.

However, bonds had a negative rate of return in real terms during the succeeding decades of the 1940s, 1950s, 1960s and 1970s, while stocks had positive rates of return during that era. In other words, money invested in bonds during those inflationary decades would not buy as much when these bonds were cashed in as when the bonds were bought, even though larger sums of money were received in the end. With the restoration of price stability in the last two decades of the twentieth century, both stocks and bonds had positive rates of real returns. But, during the first decade of the twenty-first century, all that changed, as the *New York Times* reported:

> If you invested $100,000 on Jan. 1, 2000, in the Vanguard index fund that tracks the Standard & Poor's 500, you would have ended up with $89,072 by mid-December of 2009. Adjust that for inflation by putting it in January 2000 dollars and you're left with $69,114.

With a more diversified portfolio and a more complex investment strategy, however, the original $100,000 investment would have grown to $313,747 over the same time period, worth $260,102 in January 2000 dollars, taking inflation into account.

Risk is always specific to the time at which a decision is made. "Hindsight is twenty-twenty," but risk always involves looking forward, not backward. During the early, financially shaky years of McDonald's, the company was so desperate for cash at one point that its founder, Ray Kroc, offered to sell half interest in McDonald's for $25,000— and no one accepted his offer. If anyone had, that person would have become a billionaire over the years. But, at the time, it was neither foolish for Ray Kroc to make that offer nor for others to turn it down.

The relative safety and profitability of various kinds of investments also depends on your own knowledge. An experienced expert in financial transactions may grow rich speculating in gold, while people of more modest knowledge are losing big. However, with gold you are unlikely to be completely wiped out, since gold always has a value for jewelry and industrial uses, while any given stock can end up not worth the paper it is written on. Nor is it only novices who lose money in the stock market. In 2001 the 400 richest Americans lost a total of $283 billion.

Risk and Diversification

The various degrees and varieties of risk can be dealt with by having a variety of investments— a "portfolio," as they say— so that when one kind of investment is not doing well, other kinds may be flourishing, thereby reducing the over-all risk to your total assets. For example, as already noted, bonds may not be doing well during a period when stocks are very profitable, or vice versa. A portfolio that includes a combination of stocks and bonds may be much less risky than investing exclusively in either. Even adding an individually risky investment like gold, whose price is very volatile, to a portfolio can reduce the risk of the portfolio as a whole, since gold prices tend to move in the opposite direction from stock prices.

A portfolio consisting mostly— or even solely— of stocks can have its risks reduced by having a mixture of stocks from different companies. These may be a group of stocks selected by a professional investor who charges others for selecting and managing their money in what is called a "mutual fund." Where the selection of stocks bought by the mutual fund is simply a mixture based on whatever stocks make up the Dow Jones Industrial Average or the Standard & Poor's Index, then there is less management required and less may be charged for the service. Mutual funds manage vast sums of investors' money: More than fifty mutual funds have assets of at least $10 billion each.

Theoretically, those mutual funds where the managers actively follow the various markets and then pick and choose which stocks to buy and sell should average a higher rate of return than those mutual funds which simply buy whatever stocks happen to make up the Dow Jones average or Standard & Poor's Index. Some actively managed mutual funds do in fact do better than index mutual funds, but in many years the index funds have had higher rates of return than most of the actively managed funds, much to the embarrassment of the latter. In 2005, for example, of 1,137 actively managed mutual funds dealing in large corporate stocks, just 55.5 percent did better than the Standard & Poor's Index.

On the other hand, the index funds offer little chance of a big killing, such as a highly successful actively managed fund might. A reporter for the *Wall Street Journal* who recommended index funds for people who don't have the time or the confidence to buy their own stocks individually said: "True, you

might not laugh all the way to the bank. But you will probably smile smugly."
However, index mutual funds lost 9 percent of their value in the year 2000, so
there is no complete freedom from risk anywhere. For mutual funds as a
whole— both managed funds and index funds— a $10,000 investment in early
1998 would by early 2003 be worth less than $9,000. Out of a thousand
established mutual funds, just one made money every year of the decade ending
in 2003. What matters, however, is whether they usually make money.

While mutual funds made their first appearance in the last quarter of the
twentieth century, the economic principles of risk-spreading have long been
understood by those investing their own money. In centuries past,
shipowners often found it more prudent to own 10 percent of ten different
ships, rather than own one ship outright. The dangers of a ship sinking were
much greater in the days of wooden ships and sails than in the modern era
of metal, mechanically powered ships. Owning 10 percent shares in ten
different ships increased the danger of a loss through a sinking of at least
one of those ships, but greatly reduced how catastrophic that loss would be.

Investing in Human Capital

Investing in human capital is in some ways similar to investing in other
kinds of capital and in some ways different. People who accept jobs with no
pay, or with pay much less than they could have gotten elsewhere, are in effect
investing their working time, rather than money, in hopes of a larger future
return than they would get by accepting a job that pays a higher salary
initially. But, where someone invests in another person's human capital, the
return on this investment is not as readily recovered by the investor. Typically,
those who use other people's money to pay for their education, for example,
either receive that money as a gift— from parents, philanthropic individuals
or organizations, or from the government— or else borrow the money.

While students can, in effect, issue bonds, they seldom issue stocks. That
is, many students go into debt to pay for their education but rarely sell
percentage shares of their future earnings. In the few cases where students
have done the latter, they have often felt resentful in later years at having to
continue contributing a share of their income after their payments have
already covered all of the initial investment made in them. But dividends

from corporations that issue stock likewise continue to be paid in disregard of whether the initial purchase price of the stock has already been repaid. That is the difference between stocks and bonds.

It is misleading to look at this situation only after an investment in human capital has paid off. Stocks are issued precisely because of risks that the investment will not pay off. Given that a substantial number of college students will never graduate, and that even some of those who do may have meager incomes, the pooling of risks enables more private financing to be made available to college students in general.

Ideally, if prospective students could and did issue both stocks and bonds in themselves, it would be unnecessary for parents or taxpayers to subsidize their education, and even poverty-stricken students could go to the most expensive colleges without financial aid. However, legal problems, institutional inertia, and social attitudes have kept such arrangements from becoming widespread in colleges and universities. When Yale University in the 1970s offered loans whose future repayment amounts varied with the students' future earnings, those students who were going into law, business, and medicine usually would not borrow from the university under this program, since their high anticipated incomes would mean paying back far more than was borrowed. They preferred issuing bonds rather than stock.

In some kinds of endeavors, however, it is feasible to have human beings in effect issue both stocks and bonds in themselves. Boxing managers have often owned percentage shares of their fighters' earnings. Thus many poor youngsters have received years of instruction in boxing that they would have been unable to pay for. Nor would simply going into debt to pay for this instruction be feasible because the risks are too high for lenders to lend in exchange for a fixed repayment. Some boxers never make it to the point where their earnings from fighting would enable them to repay the costs of their instruction and management. Nor are such boxers likely to have alternative occupations from which they could repay large loans to cover the costs of their failed boxing careers. Professional boxers are more likely to have been in prison or on welfare than to have a college degree.

Given the low-income backgrounds from which most boxers have come and the high risk that they will never make any substantial amount of money, financing their early training in effect by stocks makes more sense than financing it by bonds. A fight manager can collect a dozen young men from tough neighborhoods as boxing prospects, knowing that most will never repay his investment of time and money, but calculating that a couple probably will, if he has made wise choices. Since there is no way to know in advance which ones these will be, the point is to have enough financial gains from shares in the winning fighters to offset the losses on the fighters who never make enough money to repay the investment.

For similar reasons, Hollywood agents have acquired percentage shares in the future earnings of unknown young actors and actresses who looked promising, thus making it worthwhile to invest time and money in the development and marketing of their talent. The alternative of having these would-be movie stars pay for this service by borrowing the money would be far less feasible, given the high risk that the majority who fail would never be able to repay the loans and might well disappear after it was clear that they were going nowhere in Hollywood.

At various times and places, it has been common for labor contractors to supply teams of immigrant laborers to work on farms, factories, or construction sites, in exchange for a percentage share of their earnings. In effect, the contractor owns stock in the workers, rather than bonds. Such workers have often been both very poor and unfamiliar with the language and customs of the country, so that their prospects of finding their own jobs individually have been very unpromising. In the nineteenth and early twentieth centuries, vast numbers of contract laborers from Italy went to countries in the Western Hemisphere and contract laborers from China went to countries in Southeast Asia, while contract laborers from India spread around the world to British Empire countries from Malaysia to Fiji to British Guiana.

In short, investment in human capital, as in other capital, has been made in the form of stocks as well as bonds. Although these are not the terms usually applied, that is what they amount to economically.

INSURANCE

Many things are called "insurance" but not all of those things are in fact insurance. After first dealing with the principles on which insurance has operated for centuries, we can then see the difference between insurance and various other programs which have arisen in more recent times and have been called "insurance" in political rhetoric.

Insurance in the Marketplace

Like commodity speculators, insurance companies deal with inherent and inescapable risks. Insurance both transfers and reduces those risks. In exchange for the premium paid by its policy-holder, the insurance company assumes the risk of compensating for losses caused by automobile accidents, houses catching fire, earthquakes, hurricanes, and numerous other misfortunes that befall human beings. There are nearly 36,000 insurance carriers in the United States alone.

In addition to transferring risks, an insurance company seeks to reduce them. For example, it charges lower prices to safe drivers and refuses to insure some homes until brush and other flammable materials near a house are removed. People working in hazardous occupations are charged higher premiums. In a variety of ways, insurance companies segment the population and charge different prices to people with different risks. That way it reduces its own over-all risks and, in the process, sends a signal to people working in dangerous jobs or living in dangerous neighborhoods, conveying to them the costs created by their chosen activity, behavior or location.

The most common kind of insurance— life insurance— compensates for a misfortune that cannot be prevented. Everyone must die but the risk involved is in the time of death. If everyone were known in advance to die at age 80, there would be no point in life insurance, because there would be no risk involved. Each individual's financial affairs could be arranged in advance to take that predictable time of death into account. Paying premiums to an insurance company would make no sense, because the total amount to which those premiums grew over the years would have to add up to an amount no less than the compensation to be received by one's surviving beneficiaries. A life insurance company would, in effect, become an issuer of bonds redeemable on fixed dates. Buying life insurance at age 20 would be the same as buying a 60-year bond and buying life insurance at age 30 would be the same as buying a 50-year bond.

What makes life insurance different from a bond is that neither the individual insured nor the insurance company knows when that particular individual will die. The financial risks to others that accompany the death of a family breadwinner or business partner are transferred to the insurance company, for a price. Those risks are also reduced because the average death rate among millions of policy-holders is far more predictable than the death of any given individual. As with other forms of insurance, risks are not simply transferred from one party to another, but reduced in the process. That is what makes buying and selling an insurance policy a mutually beneficial transaction. The insurance policy is worth more to the buyer than it costs the seller because the seller's risk is less than the risk that the buyer would face without insurance.

Where a given party has a large enough sample of risks, there may be no benefit from buying an insurance policy. The Hertz car rental agency, for example, owns so many automobiles that its risks are sufficiently spread that it need not pay an insurance company to assume those risks. It can use the same statistical methods used by insurance companies to determine the financial costs of its risks and incorporate that cost into what it charges people who rent their cars. There is no point transferring a risk that is not reduced in the process, because the insurer must charge as much as the risk would cost the insured— plus enough more to pay the administrative costs of doing business and still leave a profit to the insurer. Self-insurance is therefore a viable option for those with a large enough sample of risks.

Insurance companies do not simply save the premiums they receive and later pay them out when the time comes. In 2012, for example, more than half the current premiums on homeowners' insurance were paid out in current claims— 60 percent by State Farm and 53 percent by Allstate. Insurance companies can then invest what is left over after paying claims and other costs of doing business. Because of these investments, the insurance companies will have more money available than if they had let the money they receive from policy-holders gather dust in a vault. About two-thirds of life insurance companies' income comes from the premiums paid by their policy-holders and about one-fourth from earnings on their investments. Obviously, the money invested has to be put into relatively safe investments— government securities and conservative real estate loans, for example, rather than commodity speculation.

If, over a period of ten years, you pay a total of $9,000 in premiums for insurance to cover some property and then suffer $10,000 in property damages that the insurance company must pay for, it might seem that the insurance company has lost money. If, however, your $9,000 in premium payments have been invested and have grown to $12,000 by the time you require reimbursement for property damage, then the insurance company has come out $2,000 ahead. According to *The Economist* magazine, "premiums alone are rarely enough to cover claims and expenses," and in the United States "this has been true of property/casualty insurers for the past 25 years." In 2004, automobile and property insurers in the United States made a profit from the actual insurance underwriting itself for the first time since 1978.

While it might seem that an insurance company could just keep the profit from its investments for itself, in reality competition forces the price of insurance down, as it forces other prices down, to a level that will cover costs and provide a rate of return sufficient to compensate investors, without attracting additional competing investment. In an economy where investors are always on the lookout for higher profits, an inflated rate of profit in the insurance industry would tend to cause new insurance companies to be created, in order to share in this bonanza. There are already many competitors in the insurance industry, none of them dominant. Among American property and casualty insurance companies in 2010 the four largest, put together, collected just 28 percent of the premiums, while the next 46 largest insurance companies collected 52 percent.

The role of competition in forcing prices and profits into line can be seen in the decline of the price of term life insurance after an Internet website began to list all the insurance companies providing this service and their respective prices. Other changes in circumstances are also reflected in changing prices, as a result of competition. For example, when the large baby boomer generation became middle-aged, their declining automobile accident rates as they moved into the safest age brackets were reflected in the ending of the sharply rising automobile insurance rates in previous years. Crackdowns on automobile insurance frauds also helped.

With insurance, as with advertising, the costs paid do not simply add to the price of products sold by a business that is insured. With advertising, as noted in Chapter 6, the increased sales that it produces can allow a business and its customers to benefit from economies of scale that produce lower prices. In the case of insurance, the risk that it insures against would have to be covered in the price of the product sold if there were no insurance. Since the whole point of buying insurance is to reduce risk, the cost of the insurance has to be less than the cost of the uninsured risk. Therefore the cost of producing the insured product is less than the cost of producing the product without insurance, so that the price tends to be lower than it would be if the risk had to be guarded against by charging higher prices.

"Moral Hazard" and "Adverse Selection"

While insurance generally reduces risks as it transfers them, there are also risks created by the insurance itself. Someone who is insured may then engage in more risky behavior than if he or she were not insured. An insured motorist may park a car in a neighborhood where the risk of theft or vandalism would be too great to risk parking an uninsured vehicle. Jewelry that is insured may not be as carefully kept under lock and key as if it were uninsured. Such increased risk as a result of having insurance is known as "moral hazard."

Such changes in behavior, as a result of having insurance, make it more difficult to calculate the right premium to charge. If one out of every 10,000 automobiles suffers $1,000 worth of damage from vandalism annually, then it might seem as if charging each of the 10,000 motorists ten cents more to cover damage from vandalism would be sufficient. However, if *insured* motorists become sufficiently careless that one out of every 5,000 cars now suffers the same damage from vandalism, then the premium would need to be twice as large to cover the costs. In other words, statistics showing how motorists currently behave and what damages they currently incur may under-estimate what damages they will incur after they are insured. That is what makes "moral hazard" a hazard to the insurance companies and a source of higher premiums to those who buy insurance.

For similar reasons, knowing what percentage of the population comes down with a given illness can also be misleading as to how much it would cost to sell insurance to pay for treatment of that illness. If one out of every 100,000 people comes down with disease X and the average cost of treating that disease is $10,000, it might seem that adding insurance coverage for disease X to a policy would cost the insurance company only an additional ten cents per policy. But what if some people are more likely to get that disease than others— and those people know it?

What if people who work in and around water are more likely to come down with this disease than people who work in dry, air-conditioned offices? Then fishermen, lifeguards and sailors are more likely to buy this insurance coverage than are secretaries, executives, or computer programmers. People living in Hawaii would be more likely to buy insurance coverage for this disease than people living in Arizona. This is known as "adverse selection" because statistics on the incidence of disease X in the population at large may seriously under-estimate its incidence among the kinds of people who are likely to buy insurance coverage for a disease that is more likely to strike people living or working near water.

Although determining costs and probabilities for various kinds of insurance involve complex statistical calculations of risk, this can never be reduced to a pure science because of such unpredictable things as changes in behavior caused by the insurance itself as well as differences among people who choose or do not choose to be insured against a given risk.

Government Regulation

Government regulation can either increase or decrease the risks faced by insurance companies and their customers. The power of government can be used to forbid some dangerous behavior, such as storing flammable liquids in schools or driving on tires with thin treads. This limits "moral hazard"— that is, how much additional risky behavior and its consequent damage may occur among people who are insured. Forcing everyone to have a given kind of insurance coverage, such as automobile insurance for all drivers, likewise eliminates the "adverse selection" problem. But government regulation of the insurance industry does not always bring net benefits, however, because there are other kinds of government regulation which increase risks and costs.

During the Great Depression of the 1930s, for example, the federal government forced all banks to buy insurance that would reimburse depositors if their bank went bankrupt. There was no reason why banks could not have bought such insurance voluntarily before, but those banks which followed sufficiently cautious policies, and which had a sufficient diversification of their assets that setbacks in some particular sector of the economy would not ruin them, found such insurance not worth paying for.

Despite the thousands of banks that went out of business during the Great Depression, the vast majority of these were small banks with no branch offices. That is, their loans and their depositors were typically from a given geographic location, so that their risks were concentrated, rather than diversified. None of the largest and most diversified banks failed.

Forcing all banks and savings & loan associations to have deposit insurance eliminated the problem of adverse selection— but it increased the problem of moral hazard. That is, insured financial institutions could attract depositors who no longer worried about whether those institutions' policies were prudent or reckless, because deposits were insured up to a given amount, even if the bank or savings & loan association went bankrupt. In other words, those who managed these institutions no longer had to worry about depositors pulling their money out when the managements made risky investments. The net result was more risky behavior— "moral hazard"— which led to losses of more than half a trillion dollars by savings & loan associations during the 1980s.

Government regulation can also adversely affect insurance companies and their customers when insurance principles conflict with political principles. For example, arguments are often made— and laws passed accordingly— that it is "unfair" that a safe young driver is charged a higher premium because other young drivers have higher accident rates,* or that young male drivers are charged more than female drivers the same age for similar reasons,

---

* Although fatality rates from motor vehicle deaths are highest for drivers 20 to 24 years of age, the declining fatality rates end from 55 to 59 years of age, and then rise again, with drivers aged 80 to 84 having fatality rates from motor vehicle deaths being similar to drivers aged 16 to 19. (Insurance Information Institute, *2012 Insurance Fact Book*, p. 155.

or that people with similar driving records are charged different premiums according to where they live. A City Attorney in Oakland, California, called a press conference in which he asked: "Why should a young man in the Fruitvale pay 30 percent more for insurance" than someone living in another community. "How can this be fair?" he demanded.

Implicit in such political arguments is the notion that it is wrong for people to be penalized for things that are not their fault. But insurance is about risk— not fault— and risks are greater when you live where your car is more likely to be stolen, vandalized, or wrecked in a collision with local drag racers. Fraudulent insurance claims also differ from one location to another, with insurance premiums being higher in places where such fraud is more prevalent. Thus the same insurance coverage for the same car can vary from city to city and even from one part of the same city to another.

The same automobile insurance coverage that costs $5,162 in Detroit costs $3,225 in Los Angeles and $948 in Green Bay. The same insurance coverage for the same car costs more in Brooklyn than in Manhattan because Brooklyn has been one of the hotspots for insurance fraud.

These are all risks that differ from one place to another with a given driver. Forcing insurance companies to charge the same premiums to groups of people with different risks means that premiums must rise over all, with safer groups subsidizing those who are either more dangerous in themselves or who live where they are vulnerable to more dangerous other people or where insurance fraud rings operate. In the case of automobile insurance, this also means that more unsafe drivers can afford to be on the road, so that their victims pay the highest and most unnecessary price of all in injuries and deaths.

Concern for politically defined "fairness" over risk also led to a 95-to-nothing vote in the United States Senate in 2003 for a bill banning insurance companies from "discriminating" against people whose genetic tests show them to have a higher risk of certain diseases. It is certainly not these people's fault that their genes happen to be what they are, but insurance premiums are based on risk, not fault. Laws forbidding risks to be reflected in insurance premiums and coverage mean that premiums in general must rise, not only to cover higher uncertainties when knowledge of certain risks is banned, but also to cover the cost of increased litigation from policy-holders who claim discrimination, whether or not such claims turn out to be true.

Such political thinking is not peculiar to the United States. Charging different premiums by sex is banned in France, and efforts have been made to extend this ban to other countries in the European Union. In a free market, premiums paid for insurance or annuities would reflect the fact that men have more car accidents and women live longer. Therefore men would pay more for car insurance and life insurance in general, while women would pay more for an annuity providing the same annual income as an annuity for men, since that amount would usually have to be paid for more years for a woman.

Unisex insurance and annuities would cost more total money than insuring the sexes separately and charging them different amounts for given insurance or annuities. That is because, with one sex subsidizing the other, an insurance company's profit-and-loss situation would be very different if more women than expected bought annuities or more men than expected bought life insurance. Since those who buy insurance or annuities choose which companies to buy from, no given company can know in advance how many women or men will buy their insurance or annuities, even though their own profit or loss depends on which sex buys what. In other words, there would be more financial risk to selling unisex insurance policies and annuities, and this additional risk would have to be covered by charging higher prices for both products.

GOVERNMENT "INSURANCE"

Government programs that deal with risk are often analogized to insurance, or may even be officially called "insurance" without in fact being insurance. For example, the National Flood Insurance Program in the United States insures homes in places too risky for a real insurance company, and charges premiums far below what would be necessary to cover the costs, so that taxpayers cover the remainder. In addition, the Federal Emergency Management Agency (FEMA) helps victims of floods, hurricanes and other natural disasters to recover and rebuild. Far from being confined to helping people struck by unpredictable disasters, FEMA also helps affluent resort communities built in areas known in advance to face high levels of danger.

As a former mayor of one such community— Emerald Isle, North Carolina— put it: "Emerald Isle basically uses FEMA as an insurance policy." Shielded by heavily subsidized financial protection, many vulnerable coastal communities have been built along the North Carolina shore. As the *Washington Post* reported:

> In the past two decades, beach towns have undergone an unprecedented building boom, transforming sleepy fishing villages into modern resorts. Land values have doubled and tripled, with oceanfront lots selling for $1 million or more. Quaint shore cottages have been replaced by hulking rentals with 10 bedrooms, game rooms, elevators, whirlpool bathtubs and pools.

All this has been made possible by the availability of government money to replace all this vulnerable and expensive real estate, built on a shore often struck by hurricanes. After one such hurricane, FEMA bought "an estimated $15 million worth of sand" to replace sand washed away from the beach in the storm, according to the *Washington Post*.

Unlike real insurance, such programs as FEMA and the National Flood Insurance Program do not reduce the over-all risks. Often people rebuild homes and businesses in the well-known paths of hurricanes and floods, often to the applause of the media for their "courage." But the financial risks created are not paid by those who create them, as with insurance, but are instead paid by the taxpayers. What this means is that the government makes it less expensive for people to live in risky places— and more costly to society as a whole, when people distribute themselves in more risky patterns than they would do if they had to bear the costs themselves, either in higher insurance premiums or in financial losses and anxieties.

Television reporter John Stossel's experience was typical:

> In 1980, I built a beach house. A wonderful one. Four bedrooms— every room with a view of the Atlantic Ocean.
> It was an absurd place to build. It was on *the edge of the ocean*. All that stood between my house and ruin was a hundred feet of sand. My father told me, "Don't do it, it's too risky. No one should build so close to an ocean."

But I built anyway.

Why? As my eager-for-the-business architect said, "Why not? If the ocean destroys your house, the government will pay for a new one."

Four years later, the ocean surged in and ruined the first floor of Mr. Stossel's house— and the government replaced it. Then, a decade after that, the ocean came in again— and this time it wiped out the whole house. The government then paid for the entire house and its contents. John Stossel described the premiums he paid for coverage under the National Flood Insurance Program as "dirt cheap," while the same coverage from a private insurance company would undoubtedly have been "prohibitively expensive." But this is not a program for low-income people. It covers mansions in Malibu and vacation homes owned by wealthy families in Hyannis and Kennebunkport. The National Flood Insurance Program is in fact the largest property insurer in the country.

More than 25,000 properties have received flood insurance payments from the federal government on more than four different occasions each. One property in Houston was flooded 16 times, requiring more than $800,000 worth of repairs— several times the value of the property itself. It was one of more than 4,500 properties whose insurance payments exceeded the value of the property during the period from 1978 to 2006.

There is an almost irresistible political inclination to provide disaster relief to people struck by earthquakes, wildfires, tornadoes and other natural disasters, as well as providing money to rebuild. The tragic pictures on television over-ride any consideration of what the situation was when they decided to live where disaster victims did. The cost of rebuilding New Orleans after Hurricane Katrina struck has been estimated to be enough to pay every New Orleans family of four $800,000, which they could use to relocate to some safer place if they wished. But no such offer is likely to be made, either in New Orleans or in other places subject to predictable and recurrent natural disasters ranging from wildfires to hurricanes.

Even when there is no current natural disaster, just the prospect of such a disaster often evokes calls for government subsidies, as in a *New York Times* editorial:

> With premiums rising relentlessly and insurers cutting hundreds of
> thousands of homeowner policies from the Gulf of Mexico up the East
> Coast to Florida and Long Island, there is a real danger that millions
> might soon be unable to purchase insurance. That's a compelling
> argument for government help.

Such arguments proceed as if the only real issue is covering the cost of
damage, rather than reducing the risk of damage in the first place by not
locating in dangerous places. Private insurance provides incentives to
relocate by charging higher premiums for dangerous locations. But
government-imposed price controls on insurance companies have had
predictable results, as the same editorial noted— "private insurers have
jacked up premiums as much as they can and, when barred from raising
prices, dropped coverage of riskier homes."

Disaster relief from the government differs from private payments from
insurance companies in another way. Competition among insurance
companies involves not only price but service.

When floods, hurricanes or other disasters strike an area, insurance
company *A* cannot afford to be slower than insurance company *B* in getting
money to their policy-holders.

Imagine a policy-holder whose home has been destroyed by a flood or
hurricane, and who is still waiting for his insurance agent to show up, while
his neighbor's insurance agent arrives on the scene within hours to advance
a few thousand dollars immediately, so that the family can afford to go find
shelter somewhere. Not only will the customer of the tardy insurance
company be likely to change companies afterward, so will people all across
the country, if word gets out as to who provides prompt service and who
drags their feet. For the tardy insurance company, that can translate into
losing billions of dollars' worth of business nationwide. The lengths to
which some insurance companies go to avoid being later than competing
insurance companies was indicated by a *New York Times* story:

> Prepared for the worst, some insurers had cars equipped with global
> positioning systems to help navigate neighborhoods with downed street
> signs and missing landmarks, and many claims adjusters carried
> computer-produced maps identifying the precise location of every
> customer.

After the catastrophic hurricane Katrina struck New Orleans in 2005, the difference between private and governmental responses was reported in the *Wall Street Journal*:

> The private-sector planning began *before* Katrina hit. Home Depot's "war room" had transferred high-demand items— generators, flashlights, batteries and lumber— to distribution areas surrounding the strike area. Phone companies readied mobile cell towers and sent in generators and fuel. Insurers flew in special teams and set up hotlines to process claims.

The same difference in response time was observed in the recovery after Katrina:

> In August, 2005, Hurricane Katrina flattened two bridges, one for cars, one for trains, that span the two miles of water separating this city of 8,000 from the town of Pass Christian. Sixteen months later, the automobile bridge remains little more than pilings. The railroad bridge is busy with trains.
>
> The difference: The still-wrecked bridge is owned by the U.S. government. The other is owned by railroad giant CSX Corp. of Jacksonville, Fla. Within weeks of Katrina's landfall, CSX dispatched construction crews to fix the freight line; six months later, the bridge reopened. Even a partial reopening of the road bridge, part of U.S. Highway 90, is at least five months away.

The kind of market competition which forces faster responses in the private sector is of course lacking in government emergency programs, which have no competitors. They may be analogized to insurance but do not have the same incentives or results. Political incentives can even delay getting aid to victims of natural disasters. When there were thousands of deaths in the wake of a huge cyclone that struck India in 1999, it was reported in that country's press that the government was unwilling to call on international agencies for help, for fear that this would be seen as admitting the inadequacies of India's own government. The net result was that many villages remained without either aid or information, two weeks after the disaster.

Chapter 15

SPECIAL PROBLEMS OF
TIME AND RISK

*The purpose of capital markets is to direct scarce capital to
its highest uses.*

Robert L. Bartley

Perhaps the most important thing about risk is its inescapability. Particular individuals, groups, or institutions may be sheltered from risk— but only at the cost of having someone else bear that risk. For a society as a whole, there is no someone else. Obvious as this may seem, it is easy to forget, especially by those who are sheltered from risk, as many are, to varying degrees. At one time, when most people were engaged in farming, risk was as widely perceived as it was pervasive: droughts, floods, insects, and plant diseases were just some of the risks of nature, while economic risks hung over each farmer in the form of the uncertainties about the price that the crop would bring at harvest time. Risks are no less pervasive today but the perception of them, and an understanding of their inescapability, are not, because fewer people are forced to face those risks themselves.

Most people today are employees with guaranteed rates of pay, and sometimes with guaranteed tenure on their jobs, when they are career civil servants, tenured professors, or federal judges. All that this means is that the inescapable risks are now concentrated on those who have given them these guarantees. All risks have by no means been eliminated for all employees but, by and large, a society of employees does not live with risks as plainly and vividly seen as in the days when most people worked on farms, at the mercy of both nature and the market, neither of which they could control or even influence. One consequence of an employee society is that incomes derived from risky fluctuations are often seen as being at best strange, and at worst suspicious or sinister. "Speculator" is not a term of endearment and "windfall gains" are viewed suspiciously, if not as being illegitimate, as compared to the earnings of someone who receives a more or less steady and prescribed income for their work.

Many think that the government should intervene when business earnings deviate from what is, or is thought to be, a normal profit rate. The concept of a "normal" rate of profit may be useful in some contexts but it can be a source of much confusion and mischief in others. The rate of return on investment or on entrepreneurship is, by its very nature and the unpredictability of events, a variable return. A firm's profits may soar, or huge losses pile up, within a few years of each other— or sometimes even within the same year. Both profits and losses serve a key economic function, moving resources from where they are less in demand to where they are more in demand. If the government steps in to reduce profits when they are soaring or to subsidize large losses, then it defeats the whole purpose of market prices in allocating scarce resources which have alternative uses.

Economic systems that depend on individual rewards to get all the innumerable things done that have to be done— whether labor, investment, invention, research, or managerial organization— must then confront the fact that time must elapse between the performance of these vital tasks and receiving the rewards that flow from completing them successfully. Moreover, the amount of time varies enormously. Someone who shines shoes is paid immediately after the shoes are shined, but a decade or more can elapse between the time when an oil company begins exploring for petroleum deposits and the time when gasoline from those deposits finally comes out of a pump at a filling station, and earns money to begin repaying the costs incurred years earlier.

Different people are willing to wait different amounts of time. One labor contractor created a profitable business by hiring men who normally worked only intermittently for money to meet their immediate wants. Such men were unwilling to work on Monday morning for wages that they would not receive until Friday afternoon, so the labor contractor paid them all at the end of each day, waiting until Friday to be reimbursed by the employer for whom the work was being done. On the other hand, some people buy thirty-year bonds and wait for them to mature during their retirement years. Most of us are somewhere in between.

Somehow, all these different time spans between contributions and their rewards must be coordinated with innumerable individual differences in patience and risk-taking. But, for this to happen, there must be some over-all assurance that the reward will be there when it is due. That is, there must be property rights that specify who has exclusive access to particular things and to whatever financial benefits flow from those things. Moreover, the protection of these property rights of individuals is a precondition for the economic benefits to be reaped by society at large.

UNCERTAINTY

In addition to risk, there is another form of contingency known as "uncertainty." Risk is calculable: If you play Russian roulette, there is one chance in six that you will lose. But if you anger a friend, it is uncertain what that friend will do, with the possibilities including the loss of friendship or even revenge. It is not calculable.

The distinction between risk and uncertainty is important in economics, because market competition can take risk into account more readily, whether by buying insurance or setting aside a calculable sum of money to cover contingencies. But, if the market has uncertainty as to what the government's ever-changing policies are likely to be during the life of an investment that may take years to pay off, then many investors may choose not to invest until the situation becomes clarified. When investors, consumers and others simply sit on their money because of uncertainty, this lack of demand can then adversely affect the whole economy.

A 2013 article in the *Wall Street Journal*, titled "Uncertainty Is the Enemy of Recovery," pointed out that many businesses "are in good shape and have money to spend," even though the economic recovery was slow, and asked:

"So why aren't they pumping more capital back into the economy, creating jobs and fueling the country's economic engine?" Their answer: Uncertainty. A financial advisory group estimated that the cost of uncertainty to the American economy was $261 billion over a two-year period. In addition, there were an estimated 45,000 more jobs per month that would have been created, in the absence of the current uncertainty, or more than one million jobs over a two-year period.

Such situations are not peculiar to the United States or to the economic problems of the early twenty-first century. During the Great Depression of the 1930s, President Franklin D. Roosevelt said:

> The country needs and, unless I mistake its temper, the country demands bold, persistent experimentation. It is common sense to take a method and try it; if it fails, admit it frankly and try another. But above all, try something.

Whatever the merits or demerits of the particular policies tried, this approach generates uncertainty, which can make investors, consumers and others reluctant to spend money, when they cannot form reliable expectations of when or how the government will change the rules that govern the economy, or what the economic consequences of those unpredictable rule changes will be. The rate of circulation of money declined during the uncertainties of the Great Depression, and some have regarded this as one reason for the record amount of time it took for the economy to recover.

TIME AND MONEY

The old adage, "time is money" is not only true but has many serious implications. Among other things, it means that whoever has the ability to delay has the ability to impose costs on others— sometimes devastating costs.

People who are planning to build housing, for example, often borrow millions of dollars to finance the construction of homes or apartment buildings, and must pay the interest on these millions, whether or not their construction is proceeding on schedule or is being delayed by some legal challenge or by some political decision or indecision by officials who are in no hurry to decide. Huge interest payments can be added to the cost of the construction itself while claims of environmental dangers are investigated or while local planning commissioners wrangle among themselves or with the builders over whether the builder should be required to add various amenities such as gardens, ponds, or bicycle paths, including amenities for the benefit of the general public, as well as for those to whom homes will be sold or apartments rented.

Weighing the costs of these amenities against the costs of delay, the builder may well decide to build things that neither he nor his customers want enough to pay for otherwise. But pay they will, in higher home prices and higher apartment rents. The largest cost of all may be hidden— fewer homes and apartments built when extra costs are imposed by third parties through the power of delay. In general, wherever *A* pays a low cost to impose high costs on *B* through delay, then *A* can either extort money from *B* or thwart *B*'s activities that *A* does not like, or some combination of the two.

Slow-moving government bureaucracies are a common complaint around the world, not only because bureaucrats usually receive the same pay whether they move slowly or quickly, but also because in some countries corrupt bureaucrats can add substantially to their incomes by accepting bribes to speed things up. The greater the scope of the government's power and the more red tape is required, the greater the costs that can be imposed by delay and the more lucrative the bribes that can be extorted.

In less corrupt countries, bribes may be taken in the form of things extorted indirectly for political purposes, such as forcing builders to build things that third parties want— or not build at all, where either local homeowners or environmental movements prefer leaving the status quo unchanged. The direct costs of demanding an environmental impact report may be quite low, compared to the costs of the delay which preparing this report will impose on builders, in the form of mounting interest charges on millions of dollars of borrowed money that is left idle while this time-consuming process drags on.

Even if the report ends up finding no environmental dangers whatever, the report itself may nevertheless have imposed considerable economic damage, sometimes enough to force the builder to abandon plans to build in that community. As a result, other builders may choose to stay away from such jurisdictions, in view of the great uncertainties generated by regulatory agencies with large and arbitrary powers that are unpredictable in their application.

Similar principles apply when it comes to health regulations applied to imported fruits, vegetables, flowers, or other perishable things. While some health regulations have legitimate functions, just as some environmental regulations do, it is also true that either or both can be used as ways of preventing people from doing what third parties object to, by the simple process of imposing high costs through delay.

Time is money in yet another way. Merely by changing the age of retirement, governments can help stave off the day of reckoning when the pensions they have promised exceed the money available to pay those pensions. Hundreds of billions of dollars may be saved by raising the retirement age by a few years. This violation of a contract amounts to a government default on a financial obligation on which millions of people were depending. But, to those who do not stop to think that time is money, it may all be explained away politically in wholly different terms.

Where the retirement age is not simply that of government employees but involves that of people employed by private businesses as well, the government not only violates its own commitments but violates prior agreements made between private employers and employees. In the United States, the government is explicitly forbidden by the Constitution from changing the terms of private contracts, but judges have over the years "interpreted" this Constitutional provision more or less out of existence.

Where the government has changed the terms of private employment agreements, the issue has often been phrased politically as putting an end to "mandatory retirement" for older workers. In reality, there has seldom, if ever, been any requirement for mandatory retirement. What did exist was simply an age beyond which a given business was no longer committed to employing those who worked for it. These people remained free to work wherever others wished to employ them, usually while continuing to receive their pensions. Thus a professor who retired from Harvard might go teach at one of the campuses of the University of California, military officers could go to work for companies producing military equipment, engineers or economists could work for consulting firms, while people in innumerable other occupations could market their skills to whoever wanted to hire them.

There was no mandatory retirement. Yet those skilled in political rhetoric were able to depict the government's partial default on its own obligations to pay pensions at a given age as a virtuous rescue of older workers, rather than as a self-serving transfer of billions of dollars in financial liabilities from the government itself to private employers.*

Sometimes time costs money, not as a deliberate strategy, but as a by-product of delays that grow out of an impasse between contending individuals or groups who pay no price for their failure to reach agreement. For example, a 2004 dispute over how a new span of the Bay Bridge in San Francisco should be built, after it was damaged in a 1989 earthquake, created delays that ended up costing California an additional $81 million before construction was resumed in 2005. Construction of the new span was completed and the span opened to traffic in September 2013— 24 years after the earthquake.

Remembering that time is money is, among other things, a defense against political rhetoric, as well as an important economic principle in itself.

ECONOMIC ADJUSTMENTS

Time is important in another sense, in that most economic adjustments take time, which is to say, the consequences of decisions unfold over time— and markets adjust at different rates for different decisions.

---

* Elimination of the ability of private employers to cease employing people at a given age had further economic repercussions, the most obvious being that it now became harder for younger workers to move up the occupational ladder, with older employees at the top blocking their rise by staying on. From the standpoint of the economy as a whole, that was a loss of efficiency. The elimination of a "mandatory retirement" age meant that, instead of automatically phasing out employees when they reached the age at which productivity usually begins to decline, employers now faced the prospect of having to prove that decline in each individual case to the satisfaction of third parties in government, in order to avoid an "age discrimination" lawsuit. The costs and risks of this meant that many older people would be kept employed when there were younger people who could perform their duties more efficiently. As for those older individuals whose productivity did not decline at the usual age, employers had always had an option to waive retirements on an individual basis. Neither for the employer nor the employee was there in fact a mandatory retirement age.

The fact that economic consequences take time to unfold has enabled government officials in many countries to have successful political careers by creating current benefits at future costs. Government-financed pension plans are perhaps a classic example, since great numbers of voters are pleased to be covered by government-provided pension plans, while only a few economists and actuaries point out that there is not enough wealth being set aside to cover the promised benefits— but it will be decades before the economists and actuaries are proved right.

With time comes risk, given the limitations of human foresight. This *inherent* risk must be sharply distinguished from the kinds of risk that are created by such activities as gambling or playing Russian roulette. Economic activities for dealing with inescapable risks seek both to minimize these risks and shift them to those best able to carry them. Those who accept these risks typically have not only the financial resources to ride out short-run losses but also have lower risks from a given situation than the person who transferred the risk. A commodity speculator can reduce risks overall by engaging in a wider variety of risky activities than a farmer does, for example.

While a wheat farmer can be wiped out if bumper crops of wheat around the world force the price far below what was expected when the crop was planted, a similar disaster would be unlikely to strike wheat, gold, cattle, and foreign currencies simultaneously, so that a professional speculator who speculated in all these things would be in less danger than someone who speculated in any one of them, as a wheat farmer does.

Whatever statistical or other expertise the speculator has further reduces the risks below what they would be for the farmer or other producer. More fundamentally, from the standpoint of the efficient use of scarce resources, speculation reduces the costs associated with risks for the economy as a whole. One of the important consequences, in addition to more people being able to sleep well at night because of having a guaranteed market for their output, is that more people find it worthwhile to produce things under risky conditions than would have otherwise. In other words, the economy can produce more soybeans because of soybean speculators, even if the speculators themselves know nothing about growing soybeans.

It is especially important to understand the interlocking mutual interests of different economic groups— the farmer and the speculator being just one example— and, above all, the effects on the economy as a whole, because these are things often neglected or distorted in the zest of the media for emphasizing conflicts, which is what sells newspapers and gets larger audiences for television news programs. Politicians likewise benefit from portraying different groups as enemies of one another and themselves as the saviors of the group they claim to represent.

When wheat prices soar, for example, nothing is easier for a demagogue than to cry out against the injustice of a situation where speculators, sitting comfortably in their air-conditioned offices, grow rich on the sweat of farmers toiling in the fields for months under a hot sun. The years when the speculators took a financial beating at harvest time, while the farmers lived comfortably on the guaranteed wheat prices paid by speculators, are of course forgotten.

Similarly, when an impending or expected shortage drives up prices, much indignation is often expressed in politics and the media about the higher retail prices being charged for things that the sellers bought from their suppliers when prices were lower. What things cost under earlier conditions is history; what the supply and demand are today is economics.

During the early stages of the 1991 Persian Gulf War, for example, oil prices rose sharply around the world, in anticipation of a disruption of Middle East oil exports because of impending military action in the region. At this point, a speculator rented an oil tanker and filled it with oil purchased in Venezuela to be shipped to the United States. However, before the tanker arrived at an American port, the Gulf War of 1991 was over sooner than anyone expected and oil prices fell, leaving the speculator unable to sell his oil for enough to recover his costs. Here too, what he paid in the past was history and what he could get now was economics.

From the standpoint of the economy as a whole, different batches of oil purchased at different times, under different sets of expectations, are the same when they enter the market today. There is no reason why they should be priced differently, if the goal is to allocate scarce resources in the most efficient way.

Time and Politics

Politics and economics differ radically in the way they deal with time. For example, when it becomes clear that the fares being charged on municipal buses are too low to permit those buses to be replaced as they wear out, the logical economic conclusion for the long run is to raise the fares. However, a politician who opposes the fare increase as "unjustified" may gain the votes of bus riders at the next election. Moreover, since all the buses are not going to wear out immediately, or even simultaneously at some future date, the consequences of holding down the fare will not appear all at once but will be spread out over time. It may be some years before enough buses start breaking down and wearing out, without adequate replacements, for the bus riders to notice that there now seem to be longer waits between buses and buses do not arrive on schedule as often as they used to.

By the time the municipal transit system gets so bad that many people begin moving out of the city, taking the taxes they pay with them, so many years may have elapsed since the political bus fare controversy that few people remember it or see any connection between that controversy and their current problems. Meanwhile, the politician who won municipal elections by assuming the role of champion of the bus riders may now have moved on up to statewide office, or even national office, on the basis of that popularity. As a declining tax base causes deteriorating city services and neglected infrastructure, the erstwhile hero of the bus riders may even be able to boast that things were never this bad when he was a city official, and blame the current problems on the failings of his successors.

In economics, however, future consequences are anticipated in the concept of "present value." If, instead of fares being regulated by a municipal government, these fares were set by a private bus company operating in a free market, any neglect of financial provisions for replacing buses as they wear out would begin *immediately* to reduce the value of the bus company's stock. In other words, the present value of the bus company would decline as a result of the long-run consequences anticipated by professional investors concerned about the safety and profitability of their own money.

If a private bus company's management decided to keep fares too low to maintain and replace its buses as they wore out, perhaps deciding to pay themselves higher executive salaries instead of setting aside funds for the maintenance of their bus fleet, 99 percent of the public might still be unaware of this or its long-run consequences. But among the other one percent who would be far more likely to be aware would be those in charge of financial institutions that owned stock in the bus company, or were considering buying that stock or lending money to the bus company. For these investors, potential investors, or lenders examining financial records, the company's present value would be seen as reduced, long before the first bus wore out.

As in other situations, a market economy allows accurate knowledge to be effective in influencing decision-making, even if 99 percent of the population do not have that knowledge. In politics, however, the 99 percent who do not understand can create immediate political success for elected officials and for policies that will turn out in the end to be harmful to society as a whole. It would of course be unreasonable to expect the general public to become financial experts or any other kind of experts, since there are only 24 hours in the day and people have lives to lead. What may be more reasonable is to expect enough voters to see the dangers in letting many economic decisions be made through political processes.

Time can turn economies of scale from an economic advantage to a political liability. After a business has made a huge investment in a fixed installation— a gigantic automobile factory, a hydroelectric dam or a skyscraper, for example— the fact that this asset cannot be moved makes it a tempting target for high local taxation or for the unionization of employees who can shut it down with a strike and impose huge losses unless their demands are met. Where labor costs are a small fraction of the total costs of an enterprise with a huge capital investment, even a doubling of wages may be a price worth paying to keep a multi-billion-dollar operation going. This does not mean that investors will simply accept a permanently reduced rate of return in this company or industry. As in other aspects of an economy, a change in one factor has repercussions elsewhere.

While a factory or dam cannot be moved, an office staff— even the headquarters staff of a national or international corporation— can much more readily be relocated elsewhere, as New York discovered after its high taxes caused many of its big corporations to move their headquarters out of the city.

With enough time, even many industries with huge fixed installations can change their regional distribution— not by physically moving existing dams, buildings, or other structures, but by not building any new ones in the unpromising locations where the old ones are, and by placing new and more modern structures and installations in states and localities with a better track record of treating businesses as economic assets, rather than economic prey. Meanwhile, places that treated businesses as prey— Detroit being a classic example— are sympathized with as victims of bad luck when the businesses leave and take their taxes and jobs with them.

A hotel cannot move across state lines, but a hotel chain can build their new hotels somewhere else. New steel mills with the latest technology can likewise be built elsewhere, while the old obsolete steel mill is closed down or phased out. As in the case of bus fares kept too low to sustain the same level and quality of service in the long run, here too the passage of time may be so long that few people connect the political policies and practices of the past with the current deterioration of the region into "rustbelt" communities with declining employment opportunities for its young people and a declining tax base to support local services.

"Rustbelts" are not simply places where jobs are disappearing. Jobs are always disappearing, even at the height of prosperity. The difference is that old jobs are constantly being replaced by new jobs in places where businesses are allowed to flourish. But in rustbelt communities or regions that have made businesses unprofitable with high taxes, red tape and onerous requirements by either governments or labor unions that impair efficiency, there may not be nearly as many new jobs as would be required to replace the old jobs that disappear with the passage of time and the normal changes in economic circumstances.

While politicians or people in the media may focus on the old jobs that have disappeared, the real story consists of the new jobs that do not come to replace them, but go elsewhere instead of to rustbelt communities that have made themselves hostile environments for economic activity.

Time and Foresight

Even though many government officials may not look ahead beyond the next election, individual citizens who are subjected to the laws and policies that officials impose nevertheless have foresight that causes many of these laws and policies to have very different consequences from those that were intended. For example, when money was appropriated by the U.S. government to help children with learning disabilities and psychological problems, the implicit assumption was that there was a more or less given number of such children. But the availability of the money created incentives for more children to be classified into these categories. Organizations running programs for such children had incentives to diagnose problem children as having the particular problem for which government money was available. Some low-income mothers on welfare have even told their children to do badly on tests and act up in school, so as to add more money to their meager household incomes.

New laws and new government policies often have unanticipated consequences when those subject to these laws and policies react to the changed incentives. For example, getting relief from debts through bankruptcy became more difficult for Americans under a new law passed in 2005. Prior to this law, the number of bankruptcy filings in the United States averaged about 30,000 a week but, just before the new law went into effect, the number of bankruptcy filings spiked at more than 479,000 per week— and immediately afterwards fell below 4,000 a week. Clearly, some people anticipated the change in the bankruptcy law and rushed to file before the new law took effect.

Where Third World governments have contemplated confiscation of land for redistribution to poor farmers, many years can elapse between the political campaign for redistribution of land and the time when the land is actually transferred. During those years, the foresight of existing landowners is likely to lead them to neglect to maintain the property as well as they did when they expected to reap the long-term benefits of investing time and money in weeding, draining, fencing and otherwise caring for the land. By the time the land actually reaches the poor, it may be much poorer land. As one development economist put it, land reform can be "a bad joke played on those who can least afford to laugh."

The political popularity of threatening to confiscate the property of rich foreigners— whether land, factories, railroads or whatever— has led many Third World leaders to make such threats, even when they were too fearful of the economic consequences to actually carry out these threats. Such was the case in Sri Lanka in the middle of the twentieth century:

> Despite the ideological consensus that the foreign estates should be nationalized, the decision to do so was regularly postponed. But it remained a potent political threat, and not only kept the value of the shares of the tea companies on the London exchange low in relation to their dividends, but also tended to scare away foreign capital and enterprise.

Even very general threats or irresponsible statements can affect investment, as in Malaysia, during an economic crisis:

> Malaysia's prime minister, Mahathir Mohamad, tried to blame Jews and whites who "still have the desire to rule the world," but each time he denounced some foreign scapegoat, his currency and stock market fell another 5 percent. He grew quieter.

In short, people have foresight, whether they are landowners, welfare mothers, investors, taxpayers or whatever. A government which proceeds as if the planned effect of its policies is the only effect often finds itself surprised or shocked because those subject to its policies react in ways that benefit or protect themselves, often with the side effect of causing the policies to produce very different results from what was planned.

Foresight takes many forms in many different kinds of economies. During periods of inflation, when people spend money faster, they also tend to hoard consumer goods and other physical assets, accentuating the imbalance between the reduced amount of real goods available in the market and the increased amount of money available to purchase these goods. In other words, they anticipate future difficulties in finding goods that they will need or in having assets set aside for a rainy day, when money is losing its value too rapidly to fulfill that role as well. During the runaway inflation in the Soviet Union in 1991, both consumers and businesses hoarded:

Hoarding reached unprecedented proportions, as Russians stashed huge supplies of macaroni, flour, preserved vegetables, and potatoes on their balconies and filled their freezers with meat and other perishable goods.

Business enterprises likewise sought to deal in real goods, rather than money:

> By 1991, enterprises preferred to pay each other in goods rather than rubles. (Indeed, the cleverest factory managers struck domestic and international barter deals that enabled them to pay their employees, not with rubles, but with food, clothing, consumer goods, even Cuban rum.)

Both social and economic policies are often discussed in terms of the goals they proclaim, rather than the incentives they create. For many, this may be due simply to shortsightedness. For professional politicians, however, the fact that their time horizon is often bounded by the next election means that any goal that is widely accepted can gain them votes, while the long-run consequences come too late to be politically relevant at election time, and the lapse of time can make the connection between cause and effect too difficult to prove without complicated analysis that most voters cannot or will not engage in.

In the private marketplace, however, experts can be paid to engage in such analysis and exercise such foresight. Thus the bond-rating services Moody's and Standard & Poor's downgraded California's state bonds in 2001, even though there had been no default and the state budget still had a surplus in its treasury. What Moody's and Standard & Poor's realized was that the huge costs of dealing with California's electricity crisis were likely to strain the state's finances for years to come, raising the possibility of a default on state bonds or a delay in payment, which amounts to a partial default. A year after these agencies had downgraded the state's bonds, it became public knowledge that the state's large budget surplus had suddenly turned into an even larger budget deficit— and many people were shocked by the news.

PART V:

THE NATIONAL ECONOMY

Chapter 16

NATIONAL OUTPUT

*Commonsense observation as well as statistics are
necessary for assessing the success of an economy.*

Theodore Dalrymple

Just as there are basic economic principles which apply in particular
markets for particular goods and services, so there are principles which
apply to the economy as a whole. For example, just as there is a demand for
particular goods and services, so there is an aggregate demand for the total
output of the whole nation. Moreover, aggregate demand can fluctuate, just
as demand for individual products can fluctuate. In the four years following
the great stock market crash of 1929, the money supply in the United States
declined by a staggering one-third. This meant that it was now impossible
to continue to sell as many goods and hire as many people *at the old price
levels*, including the old wage levels.

If prices and wage rates had also declined immediately by one-third, then of
course the reduced money supply could still have bought as much as before, and
the same real output and employment could have continued. There would have
been the same amount of real things produced, just with smaller numbers on
their price tags, so that paychecks with smaller numbers on them could have
bought just as much as before. In reality, however, a complex national economy
can never adjust that fast or that perfectly, so there was a massive decline in
total sales, with corresponding declines in production and employment. The
nation's real output in 1933 was one-fourth lower than it was in 1929.

Stock prices plummeted to a fraction of what they had been and American
corporations as a whole operated at a loss for two years in a row.

Unemployment, which had been 3 percent in 1929, rose to 25 percent in 1933. It was the greatest economic catastrophe in the history of the United States. Moreover, the depression was not confined to the United States but was worldwide. In Germany, unemployment hit 34 percent in 1931, setting the stage for the Nazis' electoral triumph in 1932 that brought Hitler to power in 1933. Around the world, the fears, policies and institutions created during the Great Depression of the 1930s were still evident in the twenty-first century.

THE FALLACY OF COMPOSITION

While some of the same principles which apply when discussing markets for particular goods, industries, or occupations may also apply when discussing the national economy, it cannot be assumed in advance that this is always the case. When thinking about the national economy, a special challenge will be to avoid what philosophers call "the fallacy of composition"— the mistaken assumption that what applies to a part applies automatically to the whole. For example, the 1990s were dominated by news stories about massive reductions in employment in particular American firms and industries, with tens of thousands of workers being laid off by some large companies and hundreds of thousands in some industries. Yet the rate of unemployment in the U.S. economy as a whole was the lowest in years during the 1990s, while the number of jobs nationwide rose to record high levels.

What was true of the various sectors of the economy that made news in the media was the opposite of what was true of the economy as a whole.

Another example of the fallacy of composition would be adding up all individual investments to get the total investments of the country. When individuals buy government bonds, for example, that is an investment for those individuals. But, for the country as a whole, there are no more real investments— no more factories, office buildings, hydroelectric dams, etc.— than if those bonds had never been purchased. What the individuals have purchased is a right to sums of money to be collected from future taxpayers. These individuals' additional assets are the taxpayers' additional liabilities, which cancel out for the country as a whole.

The fallacy of composition is not peculiar to economics. In a sports stadium, any given individual can see the game better by standing up but, if everybody stands up, everybody will not see better. In a burning building, any given individual can get out faster by running than by walking. But, if everybody runs, the stampede is likely to create bottlenecks at doors, preventing escapes by people struggling against one another to get out, causing some of those people to lose their lives needlessly in the fire. That is why there are fire drills, so that people will get in the habit of leaving during an emergency in an orderly way, so that more lives can be saved.

What is at the heart of the fallacy of composition is that it ignores *interactions* among individuals, which can prevent what is true for one of them from being true for them all.

Among the common economic examples of the fallacy of composition are attempts to "save jobs" in some industry threatened with higher unemployment for one reason or another. Any given firm or industry can always be rescued by a sufficiently large government intervention, whether in the form of subsidies, purchases of the firm's or industry's products by government agencies, or by other such means. The interaction that is ignored by those advocating such policies is that everything the government spends is taken from somebody else. The 10,000 jobs saved in the widget industry may be at the expense of 15,000 jobs lost elsewhere in the economy by the government's taxing away the resources needed to keep those other people employed. The fallacy is not in believing that jobs can be saved in given industries or given sectors of the economy. The fallacy is in believing that these are *net* savings of jobs for the economy as a whole.

OUTPUT AND DEMAND

One of the most basic things to understand about the national economy is how much its total output adds up to. We also need to understand the important role of money in the national economy, which was so painfully demonstrated in the Great Depression of the 1930s. The government is almost always another major factor in the national economy, even though it may or may not be in particular industries. As in many other areas, the facts are relatively straightforward and not difficult to understand. What gets complicated are the misconceptions that have to be unravelled.

One of the oldest confusions about national economies is reflected in fears that the growing abundance of output threatens to reach the point where it exceeds what the economy is capable of absorbing. If this were true, then masses of unsold goods would lead to permanent cutbacks in production, leading in turn to massive and enduring unemployment. Such an idea has appeared from time to time over more than two centuries, though usually not among economists. However, a Harvard economist of the mid-twentieth century named Seymour Harris seemed to express such views when he said: "Our private economy is faced with the tough problem of selling what it can produce." A popular best-selling author of the 1950s and 1960s named Vance Packard expressed similar worries about "a threatened overabundance of the staples and amenities and frills of life" which have become "a major national problem" for the United States.

President Franklin D. Roosevelt blamed the Great Depression of the 1930s on people of whom it could be said that "the products of their hands had exceeded the purchasing power of their pocketbooks." A widely used history textbook likewise explained the origins of the Great Depression of the 1930s this way:

> What caused the Great Depression? One basic explanation was overproduction by both farm and factory. Ironically, the depression of the 1930s was one of abundance, not want. It was the "great glut" or the "plague of plenty."

Yet today's output is several times what it was during the Great Depression, and many times what it was in the eighteenth and nineteenth centuries, when others expressed similar views. Why has this not created the problem that so many have feared for so long, the problem of insufficient income to buy the ever-growing output that has been produced?

First of all, while income is usually measured in money, real income is measured by what that money can buy, how much real goods and services. The national output likewise consists of real goods and services. The total real income of everyone in the national economy and the total national output are one and the same thing. They do not simply happen to be equal at a given time or place. They are necessarily equal always because they are the same thing looked at from different angles— that is, from the standpoint of income and from the standpoint of output. The fear of a permanent barrier to economic growth, based on output exceeding real income, is as inherently groundless today as it was in past centuries when output was a small fraction of what it is today.

What has lent an appearance of plausibility to the idea that total output can exceed total real income is the fact that both output and income fluctuate over time, sometimes disastrously, as in the Great Depression of the 1930s. At any given time, for any of a number of reasons, either consumers or businesses— or both— may hesitate to spend their income. Since everyone's income depends on someone else's spending, such hesitations can reduce aggregate money income and with it aggregate money demand. When various government policies generate uncertainty and apprehensions, this can lead individuals and businesses to want to hold on to their money until they see how things are going to turn out.

When millions of people do this at the same time, that in itself can make things turn out badly because aggregate demand falls below aggregate income and aggregate output. An economy cannot continue producing at full capacity if people are no longer spending and investing at full capacity, so cutbacks in production and employment may follow until things sort themselves out. How such situations come about, how long it will take for things to sort themselves out, and what policies are best for coping with these problems are all things on which different schools of economists may disagree. However, what economists in general agree on is that this situation is very different from the situation feared by those who foresaw a national economy simply glutted by its own growing abundance because people lack the income to buy it all. What people may lack is the desire to spend or invest all their income.

Simply saving part of their income will not necessarily reduce aggregate demand because the money that is put into banks or other financial institutions is in turn lent or invested elsewhere. That money is then spent by different people for different things but it is spent nonetheless, whether to buy homes, build factories, or otherwise. For aggregate demand to decline, either consumers or investors, or both, have to hesitate to part with their money, for one reason or another. That is when current national output cannot all be sold and producers cut back their production to a level that can be sold at prices that cover production costs. When this happens throughout the economy, national output declines and unemployment increases, since fewer workers are hired to produce a smaller output.

During the Great Depression of the 1930s, some people saved their money at home in a jar or under a mattress, since thousands of bank failures had led them to distrust banks. This reduced aggregate demand, since this money that was saved was not invested.

Some indication of the magnitude and duration of the Great Depression can be found in the fact that the 1929 level of output— $104 billion, in the dollars of that year— fell to $56 billion by 1933. Taking into account changes in the value of money during this era, the 1929 level of real output was not reached again until 1936. For an economy to take seven years to get back to its previous level of output is extraordinary— one of the many extraordinary things about the Great Depression of the 1930s.

MEASURING NATIONAL OUTPUT

The distinction between income and wealth that was made when discussing individuals in Chapter 10 applies also when discussing the income and wealth of the nation as a whole. A country's total wealth includes everything it has accumulated from the past. Its income or national output, however, is what is produced during the current year. Accumulated wealth and current output are both important, in different ways, for indicating how much is available for different purposes, such as maintaining or improving the people's standard of living or for carrying out the functions of government, business, or other institutions.

National output during a year can be measured in a number of ways. The most common measure today is the Gross Domestic Product (GDP), which is the sum total of everything produced within a nation's borders. An older and related measure, the Gross National Product (GNP) is the sum total of all the goods and services produced by the country's people, wherever they or their resources may be located. These two measures of national output are sufficiently similar that people who are not economists need not bother about the differences. For the United States, the difference between GDP and GNP has been less than one percent.

The real distinction that must be made is between both these measures of national output during a given year— a *flow* of real income— versus the accumulated *stock* of wealth as of a given time.* At any given time, a country can live beyond its current production by using up part of its accumulated stock of wealth from the past. During World War II, for example, American production of automobiles stopped, so that factories which normally produced cars could instead produce tanks, planes and other military equipment. This meant that existing cars simply deteriorated with age, without being replaced. So did most refrigerators, apartment buildings and other parts of the national stock of wealth. Wartime government posters said:

> Use it up,
> Wear it out,
> Make it do,
> Or do without.

After the war was over, there was a tremendous increase in the production of cars, refrigerators, housing, and other parts of the nation's accumulated stock of wealth which had been allowed to wear down or wear out while production was being devoted to urgent wartime purposes. The durable equipment of consumers declined in real value between 1944 and 1945, the last year of the war— and then more than doubled in real value over the next five years, as the nation's stock of durable assets that had been depleted during the war was replenished. This was an unprecedented rate of growth. Businesses as well had an accelerated growth of durable equipment after the war.

---

* Those familiar with calculus will recognize the former as a derivative and the latter as an integral.

Just as national income does not refer to money or other paper assets, so national wealth does not consist of these pieces of paper either, but of the real goods and services that money can buy. Otherwise, any country could get rich immediately just by printing more money. Sometimes national output or national wealth is added up by using the money prices of the moment, but most serious long-run studies measure output and wealth in real terms, taking into account price changes over time. This is necessarily an inexact process because the prices of different things change differently over time. In the century between 1900 and 2000, for example, the real cost of electricity, eggs, bicycles, and clothing all declined in the United States, while the real cost of bread, beer, potatoes, and cigarettes all rose.

The Changing Composition of Output

Prices are not the only things that change over time. The real goods and services which make up the national output also change. The cars of 1950 were not the same as the cars of 2000. The older cars usually did not have air conditioning, seat belts, anti-lock brakes, or many other features that have been added over the years. So when we try to measure how much the production of automobiles has increased in real terms, a mere count of how many such vehicles there were in both time periods misses a huge qualitative difference in what we are arbitrarily defining as being the same thing— cars. A J.D. Power survey in 1997 found both cars and trucks to be the best they had ever tested. Similarly, a 2003 report on sports utility vehicles by *Consumer Reports* magazine began:

> All five of the sport-utilities we tested for this report performed better overall than the best SUV of five years ago.

Housing has likewise changed qualitatively over time. The average American house at the end of the twentieth century was much larger, had more bathrooms, and was far more likely to have air conditioning and other amenities than houses which existed in the United States in the middle of that century. Merely counting how many houses there were at both times does not tell us how much the production of housing had increased. Just between 1983 and 2000, the median square feet in a new single-family house in the United States increased from 1,565 to 2,076.

While these are problems which can be left for professional economists and statisticians to try to wrestle with, it is important for others to at least be aware of such problems, so as not to be misled by politicians or media pundits who throw statistics around for one purpose or another. Just because the same word is used— a "car" or a "house"— does not mean that the same thing is being discussed.

Over a period of generations, the goods and services which constitute national output change so much that statistical comparisons can become practically meaningless, because they are comparing apples and oranges. At the beginning of the twentieth century, the national output of the United States did not include any airplanes, television sets, computers or nuclear power plants. At the end of that century, American national output no longer included typewriters, slide rules (once essential for engineers, before there were pocket calculators), or a host of equipment and supplies once widely used in connection with horses that formerly provided the basic transportation of many societies around the world.

What then, does it mean to say that the Gross Domestic Product was X percent more in the year 2000 than in 1900, when it consisted largely of very different things at these different times? It may mean something to say that output this year is 5 percent higher or 3 percent lower than it was last year because it consists of much the same things in both years. But the longer the time span involved, the more such statistics approach meaninglessness.

A further complication in comparisons over time is that attempts to measure real income depend on statistical adjustments which have a built-in inflationary bias. Money income is adjusted by taking into account the cost of living, which is measured by the cost of some collection of items commonly bought by most people. The problem with that approach is that what people buy is affected by price. When videocassette recorders were first produced, they sold for $30,000 each and were sold at luxury-oriented Neiman Marcus stores. Only many years later, after their prices had fallen below $200, were videocassette recorders so widely used that they were now included in the collection of items used to determine the cost of living, as measured by the consumer price index. But all the previous years of dramatically declining prices of videocassette recorders had no effect on the statistics used to compile the consumer price index.

The same general pattern has occurred with innumerable other goods that went from being rare luxuries of the rich to common items used by most consumers, since it was only after becoming commonly purchased items that they began to be included in the collection of goods and services whose prices were used to determine the consumer price index.

Thus, while many goods that are declining in price are not counted when measuring the cost of living, common goods that are increasing in price are measured. A further inflationary bias in the consumer price index or other measures of the cost of living is that many goods which are increasing in price are also increasing in quality, so that the higher prices do not necessarily reflect inflation, as they would if the prices of the same identical goods were rising. The practical— and political— effects of these biases can be seen in such assertions as the claim that the real wages of Americans have been declining for years. Real wages are simply money wages adjusted for the cost of living, as measured by the consumer price index. But if that index is biased upward, then that means that real wage statistics are biased downward.

Various economists' estimates of the upward bias of the consumer price index average about one percentage point or more. That means that when the consumer price index shows 3 percent inflation per year, it is really more like 2 percent inflation per year. That might seem like a small difference but the consequences are not small. A difference of one percentage point per year, compounded over a period of 25 years, means that in the end the average American income per person is under-estimated by almost $9,000 a year. In other words, at the end of a quarter-century, an American family of three has a real income of more than $25,000 a year higher than the official statistics on real wages would indicate.

Alarms in the media and in politics about statistics showing declining real wages over time have often been describing a statistical artifact rather than an actual fact of life. It was during a period of "declining real wages" that the average American's consumption increased dramatically and the average American's net worth more than doubled.

A further complication in measuring changes in the standard of living is that more of the increase in compensation for work takes the form of job-related benefits, rather than direct wages. Thus, in the United States, total compensation rose during a span of years when there were "declining real wages."

International Comparisons

The same problems which apply when comparing a given country's output over time can also apply when comparing the output of two very different countries at the same time. If some Caribbean nation's output consists largely of bananas and other tropical crops, while some Scandinavian country's output consists more of industrial products and crops more typical of cold climates, how is it possible to compare totals made up of such differing items? This is not just comparing apples and oranges, it may be comparing cars and sugar.

The qualitative differences found in output produced in the same country at different times are also found in comparisons of output from one country to another at a given time. In the days of the Soviet Union, for example, its products from cameras to cars were notorious for their poor quality and often technological obsolescence, while the service that people received from people working in Soviet restaurants or in the national airline, Aeroflot, was equally notorious for poor quality. When the watches produced in India during the 1980s were overwhelmingly mechanical watches, while most of the watches in the rest of the world were electronic, international comparisons of the output of watches were equally as misleading as comparisons of Soviet output with output in Western industrial nations.

Moreover, a purely quantitative record of increased output in India, after many of its government restrictions on the economy were lifted in the late twentieth century, understates the economic improvement, by not being able to quantify the dramatic qualitative improvements in India's watches, cars, television sets and telephone service, as these industries responded to increased competition from both domestic and international enterprises. These qualitative improvements ranged from rapid technological advances to being able to buy these goods and services immediately, instead of being put on waiting lists.

Just as some statistics understate the economic differences between nations, other statistical data overstate these differences. Statistical comparisons of incomes in Western and non-Western nations are affected by the same age differences that exist among a given population within a given nation. For example, the median ages in Nigeria, Afghanistan, and Tanzania are all below twenty, while the median ages in Japan, Italy, and Germany are all over forty. Such huge age gaps mean that the real significance of some international differences in income may be seriously overstated. Just as nature provides— free of charge— the heat required to grow pineapples or bananas in tropical countries, while other countries would run up huge heating bills growing those same fruits in greenhouses, so nature provides free for the young many things that can be very costly to provide for older people.

Enormously expensive medications and treatments for dealing with the many physical problems that come with aging are all counted in statistics about a country's output, but fewer such things are necessary in a country with a younger population. Thus statistics on real income per capita overstate the difference in economic well-being between older people in Western nations and younger people in non-Western nations.

If it were feasible to remove from national statistics all the additional wheelchairs, pacemakers, nursing homes, and medications ranging from Geritol to Viagra— all of which are ways of providing for an older population things which nature provides free to the young— then international comparisons of real income would more accurately reflect actual levels of economic well-being. After all, an elderly person in a wheelchair would gladly change places with a young person who does not need a wheelchair, so the older person cannot be said to be economically better off than the younger person by the value of the wheelchair— even though that is what gross international statistical comparisons would imply.

One of the usual ways of making international comparisons is to compare the total money value of outputs in one country versus another. However, this gets us into other complications created by official exchange rates between their respective currencies, which may or may not reflect the actual purchasing power of those currencies. Governments may set their official exchange rates anywhere they wish, but that does not mean that the actual purchasing power of the money will be whatever they say it is. Purchasing power depends on what sellers are willing to sell for a given amount of money. That is why there are black markets in foreign currencies, where unofficial money changers may offer more of the local currency for a dollar than the government specifies, when the official exchange rate overstates what the local currency is worth in the market.

Country *A* may have more output per capita than Country *B* if we measure by official exchange rates, while it may be just the reverse if we measure by the purchasing power of the money. Surely we would say that Country *B* has the larger total value of output if it could purchase everything produced in country *A* and still have something left over. As in other cases, the problem is not with understanding the basic economics involved. The problem is with verbal confusion spread by politicians, the media and others trying to prove some point with statistics.

Some have claimed, for example, that Japan has had a higher per capita income than the United States, using statistics based on official exchange rates of the dollar and the yen. But, in fact, the average American's annual income could buy everything the average Japanese annual income buys and still have thousands of dollars left over. Therefore the average American has a higher standard of living than the average Japanese.

Yet statistics based on official exchange rates may show the average Japanese earning thousands of dollars more than the average American in some years, leaving the false impression that the Japanese are more prosperous than Americans. In reality, purchasing power per person in Japan is about 71 percent of that in the United States.

Another complication in comparisons of output between nations is that more of one nation's output may have been sold through the marketplace, while more of the other nation's output may have been produced by government and either given away or sold at less than its cost of production. When too many automobiles have been produced in a market economy to be sold profitably, the excess cars have to be sold for whatever price they can get, even if that is less than what it cost to produce them. When the value of national output is added up, these cars are counted according to what they sold for. But, in an economy where the government provides many free or subsidized goods, these goods are valued at what it cost the government to produce them.

These ways of counting exaggerate the value of government-provided goods and services, many of which are provided by government precisely because they would never cover their costs of production if sold in a free market economy. Given this tendency to overvalue the output of socialist economies relative to capitalist economies when adding up their respective Gross Domestic Products, it is all the more striking that statistics still generally show higher output per capita in capitalist countries.

Despite all the problems with comparisons of national output between very different countries or between time periods far removed from one another, Gross Domestic Product statistics provide a reasonable, though rough, basis for comparing similar countries at the same time— especially when population size differences are taken into account by comparing Gross Domestic Product per capita. Thus, when the data show that the Gross Domestic Product per capita in Norway in 2009 was more than double what it was in Italy that same year, we can reasonably conclude that the Norwegians had a significantly higher standard of living. But we need not pretend to precision. As John Maynard Keynes said, "It is better to be roughly right than precisely wrong."

Ideally, we would like to be able to measure people's personal sense of well-being but that is impossible. The old saying that money cannot buy happiness is no doubt true. However, opinion polls around the world indicate some rough correlation between national prosperity and personal satisfaction. Nevertheless, correlation is not causation, as statisticians often warn, and it is possible that some of the same factors which promote happiness— security and freedom, for example— also promote economic prosperity.

Which statistics about national output are most valid depends on what our purpose is. If the purpose of an international comparison is to determine which countries have the largest total output— things that can be used for military, humanitarian, or other purposes— then that is very different from determining which countries have the highest standard of living. For example, in 2009 the countries with the five highest Gross Domestic Products, measured by purchasing power, were:

1. United States
2. China
3. Japan
4. India
5. Germany

Although China had the second highest Gross Domestic Product in the world, it was by no means among the leaders in Gross Domestic Product *per capita*, since its output is divided among the largest population in the world. The Gross Domestic Product per capita in China in 2009 was in fact less than one-tenth that of Japan.

None of the countries with the five highest Gross Domestic Products were among those with the five highest GDP per capita, all of the latter being very small countries that were not necessarily comparable to the major nations that dominate the list of countries with the largest Gross Domestic Products. Some small countries like Bermuda are tax havens that attract the wealth of rich people from other countries, who may or may not become citizens while officially having a residence in the tax-haven country. But the fact that the Gross Domestic Product per capita of Bermuda is higher than that of the United States does not mean that the average permanent resident of Bermuda has a higher standard of living than the average American.

Statistical Trends

One of the problems with comparisons of national output over some span of time is the arbitrary choice of the year to use as the beginning of the time span. For example, one of the big political campaign issues of 1960 was the rate of growth of the American economy under the existing administration. Presidential candidate John F. Kennedy promised to "get America moving again" economically if he were elected, implying that the national economic growth rate had stagnated under the party of his opponent. The validity of this charge depended entirely on which year you chose as the year from which to begin counting. The long-term average annual rate of growth of the Gross National Product of the United States had been about 3 percent per year. As of 1960, this growth rate was as low as 1.9 percent (since 1945) or as high as 4.4 percent (since 1958).

Whatever the influence of the existing administration on any of this, whether it looked like it was doing a wonderful job or a terrible job depended entirely on the base year arbitrarily selected.

Many "trends" reported in the media or proclaimed in politics likewise depend entirely on which year has been chosen as the beginning of the trend. Crime in the United States has been going up if you measure from 1960 to the present, but down if you measure from 1990 to the present. The degree of income inequality was about the same in 1939 and 1999 but, in the latter year, you could have said that income inequality had increased from the 1980s onward because there were fluctuations in between the years in which it was about the same. At the end of 2003, an investment in a Standard & Poor's 500 mutual fund would have earned nearly a 10.5 percent annual rate of return (since 1963) or nearly a zero percent rate of return (since 1998). It all depended on the base year chosen.

Trends outside economics can be tricky to interpret as well. It has been claimed that automobile fatality rates have declined since the federal government began imposing various safety regulations. This is true— but it is also true that automobile fatality rates were declining for decades before the federal government imposed any safety regulations. Is the continuation of a trend that existed long before a given policy was begun proof of the effectiveness of that policy?

In some countries, especially in the Third World, so much economic activity takes place "off the books" that official data on national output miss much— if not most— of the goods and services produced in the economy. In all countries, work done domestically and not paid for in wages and salary— cooking food, raising children, cleaning the home— goes uncounted. This inaccuracy does not directly affect trends over time if the same percentage of economic activity goes uncounted in one era as in another. In reality, however, domestic economic activities have undergone major changes over time in many countries, and vary greatly from one society to another at a given time.

For example, as more women have entered the work force, many of the domestic chores formerly performed by wives and mothers without generating any income statistics are now performed for money by child care centers, home cleaning services and restaurants or pizza-delivery companies. Because money now formally changes hands in the marketplace, rather than informally between husband and wife in the home, today's statistics count as output things that did not get counted before. This means that national output trends reflect not only real increases in the goods and services being produced, but also an increased counting of things that were not counted before, even though they existed before.

The longer the time period being considered, the more the shifting of economic activities from the home to the marketplace makes the statistics not comparable. In centuries past, it was common for a family's food to be grown in its own garden or on its own farm, and this food was often preserved in jars by the family rather than being bought from stores where it was preserved in cans. In 1791, Alexander Hamilton's *Report on Manufactures* stated that four fifths of the clothing worn by the American people was homemade. In pioneering times in America, or in some Third World countries today, the home itself might have been constructed by the family, perhaps with the help of friends and neighbors.

As these and other economic activities moved from the family to the marketplace, the money paid for them made them part of official statistics. This makes it harder to know how much of the statistical trends in output over time represent real increases in totals and how much of these trends represent differences in how much has been recorded or has gone unrecorded.

Just as national output statistics can overstate increases over time, they can also understate these increases. In very poor Third World countries, increasing prosperity can look statistically like stagnation. One of the ravages of extreme poverty is a high infant mortality rate, as well as health risks to others from inadequate food, shelter, medical services and sewage disposal. As Third World countries rise economically, one of the first consequences of higher income per capita is that more infants, small children, and frail old people are able to survive, now that they can afford better nutrition and medical care.

This is particularly likely at the lower end of the income scale. But, with more poor people now surviving, both absolutely and relative to the more prosperous classes, a higher percentage of the country's population now consists of these poor people. Statistically, the averaging in of more poor people can understate the country's average rise in real income, or can even make the average income decline statistically, even if every individual in the country has higher incomes than in the past.*

---

* Imagine a Third World country with 100 million people, one-fourth of whom average $1,000 a year in per capita income, another fourth average $2,000, another fourth $4,000 and the top fourth $5,000. Now imagine that (1) *everyone's* income rises by 20 percent and (2) the two poorest classes double in size as a result of reduced mortality rates among those most vulnerable to malnutrition and inadequate medical care, while the two top classes remain the same size. If you work out the arithmetic, you will see that per capita income for the country as a whole remains the same, even though every individual's income has risen by one-fifth. Obviously, if the income had risen by less than one-fifth, per capita income would have *fallen*, even though each individual's income rose.

Chapter 17

MONEY AND THE

BANKING SYSTEM

A system established largely to prevent bank panics produced the most severe banking panic in American history.

Milton Friedman

Money is of interest to most people but why should banking be of interest to anyone who is not a banker? Both money and banking play crucial roles in promoting the production of goods and services, on which everyone's standard of living depends, and they are crucial factors in the ability of the economy as a whole to maintain full employment of its people and resources. While money is not wealth— otherwise the government could make us all twice as rich by simply printing twice as much money— a well-designed and well-maintained monetary system facilitates the production and distribution of wealth.

The banking system plays a vital role in that process because of the vast amounts of real resources— raw materials, machines, labor— which are transferred by the use of money, and whose allocation is affected by the huge sums of money— trillions of dollars— that pass through the banking system. American banks had $14 trillion in assets in 2012, for example. One way to visualize such a vast sum is that a trillion seconds ago, no one on this planet could read or write. Neither the Roman Empire nor the ancient Chinese dynasties had yet been formed and our ancestors lived in caves.

363

THE ROLE OF MONEY

Many economies in the distant past functioned without money. People simply bartered their products and labor with one another. But these have usually been small, uncomplicated economies, with relatively few things to trade, because most people provided themselves with food, shelter and clothing, while trading with others for a limited range of implements, amenities or luxuries.

Barter is awkward. If you produce chairs and want some apples, you certainly are not likely to trade one chair for one apple, and you may not want enough apples to add up to the value of a chair. But if chairs and apples can both be exchanged for some third thing that can be subdivided into very small units, then more trades can take place using that intermediary means of exchange, benefitting both chair-makers and apple-growers, as well as everyone else. All that people have to do is to agree on what will be used as an intermediary means of exchange and that means of exchange becomes money.

Some societies have used sea shells as money, others have used gold or silver, and still others have used special pieces of paper printed by their governments. In colonial America, where hard currency was in short supply, warehouse receipts for tobacco circulated as money. In the early colonial era in British West Africa, bottles and cases of gin were sometimes used as money, often passing from hand to hand for years without being consumed. In a prisoner-of-war camp during the Second World War, cigarettes from Red Cross packages were used as money among the prisoners, producing economic phenomena long associated with money, such as interest rates and Gresham's Law.* During the early, desperate and economically chaotic days of the Soviet Union, "goods such as flour, grain, and salt gradually assumed the role of money," according to two Soviet economists who studied that era, and "salt or baked bread could be used to buy virtually anything a person might need."

In the Pacific islands of Yap, a part of Micronesia, doughnut-shaped rocks function as money, even though the largest of these rocks are 12 feet

---

* Gresham's Law is that bad money drives good money out of circulation. In the P.O.W. camp, the least popular brands of cigarettes circulated as money, while the most popular brands were smoked.

in diameter and obviously cannot circulate physically. What circulates is the *ownership* of these rocks, so that this primitive system of money functions in this respect like the most modern systems today, in which ownership of money can change instantaneously by electronic transfers without any physical movement of currency or coins.

. What made all these different things money was that people would accept them in payment for the goods and services which actually constituted real wealth. Money is equivalent to wealth for an individual only because other individuals will supply the real goods and services desired in exchange for that money. But, from the standpoint of the national economy as a whole, money is not wealth. It is just an artifact used to transfer wealth or to give people incentives to produce wealth.

While money facilitates the production of real wealth— greases the wheels, as it were— this is not to say that its role is inconsequential. Wheels work much better when they are greased. When a monetary system breaks down for one reason or another, and people are forced to resort to barter, the clumsiness of that method quickly becomes apparent to all. In 2002, for example, the monetary system in Argentina broke down, leading to a decline in economic activity and a resort to barter clubs called *trueque*:

> This week, the bartering club pooled its resources to "buy" 220 pounds of bread from a local baker in exchange for half a ton of firewood the club had acquired in previous trades— the baker used the wood to fire his oven. . . .The affluent neighborhood of Palermo hosts a swanky *trueque* at which antique china might be traded for cuts of prime Argentine beef.

Although money itself is not wealth, an absence of a well-functioning monetary system can cause losses of real wealth, when transactions are reduced to the crude level of barter. Argentina is not the only country to revert to barter or other expedients when the monetary system broke down. During the Great Depression of the 1930s, when the money supply contracted drastically, there were in the United States an estimated "150 barter and/or scrip systems in operation in thirty states."

Usually everyone seems to want money, but there have been particular times in particular countries when no one wanted money, because they considered it worthless. In reality, it was the fact that no one would accept money that made it worthless. When you can't buy anything with money, it becomes just useless pieces of paper or useless little metal disks. In France during the 1790s, a desperate government passed a law prescribing the death penalty for anyone who refused to sell in exchange for money. What all this suggests is that the mere fact that the government prints money does not mean that it will automatically be accepted by people and actually function as money. We therefore need to understand how money functions, if only to avoid reaching the point where it malfunctions. Two of its most important malfunctions are inflation and deflation.

Inflation

Inflation is a general rise in prices. The national price level rises for the same reason that prices of particular goods and services rise— namely, that there is more demanded than supplied at a given price. When people have more money, they tend to spend more. Without a corresponding increase in the volume of output, the prices of existing goods and services simply rise because the quantity demanded exceeds the quantity supplied at current prices and either people bid against each other during the shortage or sellers realize the increased demand for their products at existing prices and raise their prices accordingly.

Whatever the money consists of— sea shells, gold, or whatever— more of it in the national economy means higher prices, unless there is a correspondingly larger supply of goods and services. This relationship between the total amount of money and the general price level has been seen for centuries. When Alexander the Great began spending the captured treasures of the Persians, prices rose in Greece. Similarly, when the Spaniards removed vast amounts of gold from their colonies in the Western Hemisphere, price levels rose not only in Spain, but across Europe, because the Spaniards used much of their wealth to buy imports from other European countries. Sending their gold to those countries to pay for these purchases added to the total money supply across the continent.

None of this is hard to understand. Complications and confusion come in when we start thinking about such mystical and fallacious things as the "intrinsic value" of money or believe that gold somehow "backs up" our money or in some mysterious way gives it value.

For much of history, gold has been used as money by many countries. Sometimes the gold was used directly in coins or (for large purchases) in nuggets, gold bars or other forms. Even more convenient for carrying around were pieces of paper money printed by the government that were redeemable in gold whenever you wanted it redeemed. It was not only more convenient to carry around paper money, it was also safer than carrying large sums of money as metal that jingled in your pockets or was conspicuous in bags, attracting the attention of criminals.

The big problem with money created by the government is that those who run the government always face the temptation to create more money and spend it. Whether among ancient kings or modern politicians, this has happened again and again over the centuries, leading to inflation and the many economic and social problems that follow from inflation. For this reason, many countries have preferred using gold, silver, or some other material that is inherently limited in supply, as money. It is a way of depriving governments of the power to expand the money supply to inflationary levels.

Gold has long been considered ideal for this purpose, since the supply of gold in the world usually cannot be increased rapidly. When paper money is convertible into gold whenever the individual chooses to do so, then the money is said to be "backed up" by gold. This expression is misleading only if we imagine that the value of the gold is somehow transferred to the paper money, when in fact the real point is that the gold simply limits the amount of paper money that can be issued.

The American dollar was once redeemable in gold on demand, but that was ended back in 1933. Since then, the United States has simply had paper money, limited in supply only by what officials thought they could or could not get away with politically. Many economists have pointed out what a dangerous power this gives to government officials. John Maynard Keynes, for example, wrote: "By a continuing process of inflation, governments can confiscate, secretly and unobserved, an important part of the wealth of their citizens."

As an example of the cumulative effects of inflation, in 2013 *Investor's Business Daily* pointed out that in 1960, "you could buy six times more stuff for a dollar than you can buy today." Among other things, this means that people who saved money in 1960 had more than four-fifths of its value silently stolen from them.

Sobering as such inflation may be in the United States, it pales alongside levels of inflation reached in some other countries. "Double-digit inflation" during a given year in the United States creates political alarms, but various countries in Latin America and Eastern Europe have had periods when the annual rate of inflation was in four digits.

Since money is whatever we accept as money in payment for real goods and services, there are a variety of other things that function in a way very similar to the official money issued by the government. Credit cards, debit cards, and checks are obvious examples. Mere promises may also function as money, serving to acquire real goods and services, when the person who makes the promises is highly trusted. IOUs from reliable merchants were once passed from hand to hand as money. As noted in Chapter 5, more purchases were made in 2003 by credit cards or debit cards than by cash.

What this means is that aggregate demand is created not only by the money issued by the government but also by credits originating in a variety of other sources. What this also means is that a liquidation of credits, for whatever reason, reduces aggregate demand, just as if the official money supply had contracted.

Some banks used to issue their own currency, which had no legal standing, but which was nevertheless widely accepted in payment when the particular bank was regarded as sufficiently reliable and willing to redeem their currency in gold. Back in the 1780s, currency issued by the Bank of North America was more widely accepted than the official government currency of that time.

Sometimes money issued by some other country is preferred to money issued by one's own. Beginning in the late tenth century, Chinese money was preferred to Japanese money in Japan. In twentieth century Bolivia, most of the savings accounts were in dollars in 1985, during a period of runaway inflation of the Bolivian peso. In 2007, the *New York Times* reported: "South Africa's rand has replaced Zimbabwe's essentially worthless dollar as the currency of choice." During the later stages of the American Civil War,

Southerners tended to use the currency issued in Washington, rather than the currency of their own Confederate government.

Gold continues to be preferred to many national currencies, even though gold earns no interest, while money in the bank does. The fluctuating price of gold reflects not only the changing demands for it for making jewelry— the source of about 80 percent of the demand for gold— or in some industrial uses but also, and more fundamentally, these fluctuations reflect the degree of worry about the possibility of inflation that could erode the purchasing power of official currencies. That is why a major political or military crisis can send the price of gold shooting up, as people dump their holdings of the currencies that might be affected and begin bidding against each other to buy gold, as a more reliable way to hold their existing wealth, even if it does not earn any interest or dividends.

Since the price of gold depends on people's expectations as regards the value of money, that price can rise or fall sharply, and reverse promptly, in response to changing economic and political conditions. The sharpest rate of increase in the price of gold in one year was 135 percent in 1979— and the sharpest fall in the price of gold was 32 percent just two years later.

Existing or expected inflation usually leads to rising prices of gold, as people seek to shelter their wealth from the government's silent confiscations by inflation. But long periods of prosperity with price stability are likely to see the price of gold fall, as people move their wealth out of gold and into other financial assets that earn interest or dividends and can therefore increase their wealth. When the economic crises of the late 1970s and early 1980s passed, and were followed by a long period of steady growth and low inflation, the price of gold fell over the years from about $800 an ounce to about $250 an ounce by 1999. Still later, after record-breaking federal deficits in the United States and similar problems in a number of European countries in the early years of the twenty-first century, the price of gold soared well over $1,000 an ounce.

The great unspoken fear behind the demand for gold is the fear of inflation. Nor is this fear irrational, given how often governments of all types— from monarchies to democracies to dictatorships— have resorted to inflation, as a means of getting more wealth without having to directly confront the public with higher taxes.

Raising tax rates has always created political dangers to those who hold political power. Political careers can be destroyed when the voting public turns against those who raised their tax rates. Sometimes public reaction to higher taxes can range all the way up to armed revolts, such as those that led to the American war of independence from Britain. In addition to adverse political reactions to higher taxes, there can be adverse economic reactions. As tax rates reach ever higher levels, particular economic activities may be abandoned by those who do not find the net rate of return on these activities, after taxes, to be enough to justify their efforts. Thus many people abandoned agriculture and moved to the cities during the declining era of the Roman Empire, adding to the number of people needing to be taken care of by the government, at the very time when the food supply was declining because of those who had stopped farming.

In order to avoid the political dangers that raising tax rates can create, governments around the world have for thousands of years resorted to inflation instead. As John Maynard Keynes observed:

> There is no record of a prolonged war or a great social upheaval which has not been accompanied by a change in the legal tender, but an almost unbroken chronicle in every country which has a history, back to the earliest dawn of economic record, of a progressive deterioration in the real value of the successive legal tenders which have represented money.

If fighting a major war requires half the country's annual output, then rather than raise tax rates to 50 percent of everyone's earnings in order to pay for it, the government may choose instead to create more money for itself and spend that money buying war materiel. With half the country's resources being used to produce military equipment and supplies, civilian goods will become more scarce just as money becomes more plentiful. This changed ratio of money to civilian goods will lead to inflation, as more money is bid for fewer goods, and prices rise as a result.

Not all inflation is caused by war, though inflation has often accompanied military conflicts. Even in peacetime, governments have found many things to spend money on, including luxurious living by kings or dictators and numerous showy projects that have been common under both democratic and undemocratic governments. To pay for such things, using the government's power to create more money has often been considered easier and politically safer than raising tax rates. Put differently, inflation is in effect a hidden tax. The money that people have saved is robbed of part of its purchasing power, which is quietly transferred to the government that issues new money.

Inflation is not only a hidden tax, it is also a broad-based tax. A government may announce that it will not raise taxes, or will raise taxes only on "the rich"— however that is defined— but, by creating inflation, it in effect transfers some of the wealth of everyone who has money, which is to say, it siphons off wealth across the whole range of incomes and wealth, from the richest to the poorest. To the extent that the rich have their wealth invested in stocks, real estate or other tangible assets that rise in value along with inflation, they escape some of this de facto taxation, which people in lower income brackets may not be able to escape.

In the modern era of paper money, increasing the money supply is a relatively simple matter of turning on the printing presses. However, long before there were printing presses, governments were able to create more money by the simple process of reducing the amount of gold or silver in coins of a given denomination. Thus a French franc or a British pound might begin by containing a certain amount of precious metal, but coins later issued by the French or British government would contain less and less of those metals, enabling these governments to issue more money from a given supply of gold or silver. Since the new coins had the same legal value as the old, the purchasing power of them all declined as coins became more abundant.

More sophisticated methods of increasing the quantity of money have been used in countries with government-controlled central banks, but the net result is still the same: An increase in the amount of money, without a corresponding increase in the supply of real goods, means that prices rise— which is to say, inflation. Conversely, when output increased during Britain's industrial revolution in the nineteenth century, the country's prices declined because its money supply did not increase correspondingly.

Doubling the money supply while the amount of goods remains the same may more than double the price level, as the speed with which the money circulates increases when people lose confidence in its retaining its value. During the drastic decline in the value of the Russian ruble in 1998, a

Moscow correspondent reported: "Many are hurrying to spend their shrinking rubles as fast as possible while the currency still has some value."

Something very similar happened in Russia during the First World War and in the years immediately after the revolutions of 1917. By 1921, the amount of currency issued by the Russian government was hundreds of times greater than the currency in circulation on the eve of the war in 1913— and the price level rose to *thousands* of times higher than in 1913. When the money circulates faster, the effect on prices is the same as if there were more money in circulation. When both things happen on a large scale simultaneously, the result is runaway inflation. During the last, crisis-ridden year of the Soviet Union in 1991, the value of the ruble fell so low that Russians used it for wallpaper and toilet paper, both of which were in short supply.

Perhaps the most famous inflation of the twentieth century occurred in Germany during the 1920s, when 40 marks were worth one dollar in July 1920, but it took more than 4 trillion marks to be worth one dollar by November 1923. People discovered that their life's savings were not enough to buy a pack of cigarettes. The German government had, in effect, stolen virtually everything they owned by the simple process of keeping more than 1,700 printing presses running day and night, printing money. Some have blamed the economic chaos and bitter disillusionment of this era for setting the stage for the rise of Adolf Hitler and the Nazis. During this runaway inflation, Hitler coined the telling phrase, "starving billionaires," for there were Germans with a billion marks that would not buy enough food to feed themselves.

The rate of inflation is often measured by changes in the consumer price index. Like other indexes, the consumer price index is only an approximation because the prices of different things change differently. For example, when consumer prices in the United States rose over the previous 12 months by 3.4 percent in March 2006, these changes ranged from a rise of 17.3 percent for energy to 4.1 percent for medical care and an actual decline of 1.2 percent in the prices of apparel.

While the effects of deflation are more obvious than the effects of inflation— since less money means fewer purchases, and therefore lower production of new goods, with correspondingly less demand for labor— the effects of inflation can likewise bring an economy to a halt. Runaway inflation means that producers find it risky to produce, when the price at which they can sell their output may not represent as much purchasing power as the money they spent producing that output. When inflation in Latin America peaked at about 600 percent per year in 1990, real output in Latin America fell absolutely that same year. But, after several subsequent years of no inflation, real output hit a robust growth rate of 6 percent per year.

Deflation

While inflation has been a problem that is centuries old, at particular times and places deflation has also created problems, some of them devastating.

From 1873 through 1896, price levels declined by 22 percent in Britain, and 32 percent in the United States. These and other industrial nations were on the gold standard and output was growing faster than the world's gold supply. While the prices of current output and inputs were declining, debts specified in money terms remained the same— in effect, making mortgages and other debts more of a burden in real purchasing power terms than when these debts were incurred. This problem for debtors became a problem for creditors as well, when the debtors could no longer pay and simply defaulted.

Farmers were especially hard hit by declining price levels because agricultural produce declined especially sharply in price, while the things that farmers bought did not decline as much, and mortgages and other farm debts required the same amounts of money as before.

An even more disastrous deflation occurred in twentieth-century America. As noted at the beginning of Chapter 16, the money supply in the United States declined by one-third from 1929 to 1933, making it impossible for Americans to buy as many goods and services as before *at the old prices*. Prices did come down— the Sears catalog for 1931 had many prices that were lower than they had been a decade earlier— but some prices could not change because there were legal contracts involved.

Mortgages on homes, farms, stores, and office buildings all specified monthly mortgage payments in specific money amounts. These terms might have been quite reasonable and easy to meet when the total amount of money in the economy was substantially larger, but now it was the same as if these payments had been arbitrarily raised— as in fact they were raised in real purchasing power terms. Many homeowners, farmers and businesses simply could not pay after the national money supply contracted— and therefore they lost the places that housed them. People with leases faced very similar problems, as it became increasingly difficult to come up with the money to pay the rent. The vast amounts of goods and services purchased on credit by businesses and individuals alike produced debts that were now harder to pay off than when the credit was extended in an economy with a larger money supply.

Those whose wages and salaries were specified in contracts— ranging from unionized workers to professional baseball players— were now legally entitled to more real purchasing power than when these contracts were originally signed. So were government employees, whose salary scales were fixed by law. But, while deflation benefitted members of these particular groups *if they kept their jobs*, the difficulty of paying them meant that many would lose their jobs.

Similarly, banks that owned the mortgages which many people were struggling to pay were benefitted by receiving mortgage payments worth more purchasing power than before— *if they received the payments at all*. But so many people were unable to pay their debts that many banks began to fail. More than 9,000 banks suspended operations over a four year period from 1930 through 1933. Other creditors likewise lost money when debtors simply could not pay them.

Just as inflation tends to be made worse by the fact that people spend a depreciating currency faster than usual, in order to buy something with it before it loses still more value, so a deflation tends to be made worse by the fact that people hold on to money longer, especially during a depression, with widespread unemployment making everyone's job or business insecure. Not only was there less money in circulation during the downturn in the economy from 1929 to 1932, what money there was circulated more slowly, which further reduced demand for goods and services. That in turn reduced demand for the labor to produce them, creating mass unemployment.

Theoretically, the government could have increased the money supply to bring the price level back up to where it had been before. The Federal Reserve System had been set up, nearly 20 years earlier during the Woodrow Wilson administration, to deal with changes in the nation's money supply.

President Wilson explained that the Federal Reserve "provides a currency which expands as it is needed and contracts when it is not needed" and that "the power to direct this system of credits is put into the hands of a public board of disinterested officers of the Government itself" to avoid control by bankers or other special interests.

However reasonable that sounds, what a government can do theoretically is not necessarily the same as what it is likely to do politically, or what its leaders understand intellectually. Moreover, the fact that government officials have no personal *financial* interest in the decisions they make does not mean that they are "disinterested" as regards the *political* interests involved in their decisions.

Even if Federal Reserve officials were unaffected by either financial or political interests, that does not mean that their decisions are necessarily competent— and, unlike people whose decisions are subject to correction by the market, government decision-makers face no such automatic correction. Looking back on the Great Depression of the 1930s, both conservative and liberal economists have seen the Federal Reserve System's monetary policies during that period as confused and counterproductive. Milton Friedman called the people who ran the Federal Reserve System in those years "inept" and John Kenneth Galbraith called them a group with "startling incompetence." For example, the Federal Reserve raised the interest rate in 1931, as the downturn in the economy was nearing the bottom, with businesses failing and banks collapsing by the thousands all across the country, along with massive unemployment.

Today, anyone with just a basic knowledge of economics would be expected to understand that you do not get out of a depression by raising the interest rate, since higher interest rates reduce the amount of credit, and therefore further reduce aggregate demand at a time when more demand is required to restore the economy.

Nor were the presidents who were in office during the Great Depression any more economically sophisticated than the Federal Reserve officials. Both Republican President Herbert Hoover and his Democratic successor, Franklin D. Roosevelt, thought that wage rates should not be reduced, so this way of adjusting to deflation was discouraged by the federal government— for both humanitarian and political reasons. The theory was that maintaining wage rates in money terms meant maintaining purchasing power, so as to prevent further declines in sales, output and employment.

Unfortunately, this policy works only so long as people keep their jobs— and higher wage rates under given conditions, especially deflation, mean lower employment. Therefore higher real wage rates per hour did not translate into higher aggregate earnings for labor, and so provided no basis for the higher aggregate demand that both presidents expected. Joseph A. Schumpeter, a leading economist of that era, saw resistance to downward adjustments in money wages as making the Great Depression worse. Writing in 1931, he said:

> The depression has not been brought about by the rate of wages, but having been brought about by other factors, is much intensified by this factor.

It was apparently not necessary to be an economist, however, to understand what both Presidents Hoover and Roosevelt did not understand. Columnist Walter Lippmann, writing in 1934, said, "in a depression men cannot sell their goods or their service at pre-depression prices. If they insist on pre-depression prices for goods, they do not sell them. If they insist on pre-depression wages, they become unemployed." The millions of unemployed— many in desperate economic circumstances— were not the ones demanding pre-depression wages. It was politicians who were trying to keep wages at pre-depression levels.

Both the Hoover administration and the subsequent Roosevelt administration applied the same reasoning— or lack of reasoning— to agriculture that they had applied to labor: The prices of farm products were to be kept up by the government, in order to maintain the purchasing power of farmers. President Hoover decided that the federal government should "give indirect support to prices which had seriously declined" in agriculture. President Roosevelt later institutionalized this policy in agricultural price support programs which led to mass destructions of food at a time of widespread hunger. In short, misconceptions of economics were both common and bipartisan.

Nor were misconceptions of economics confined to the United States. Writing in 1931, John Maynard Keynes said of the British government's monetary policies that the arguments being made for those policies "could not survive ten minutes' rational discussion."

Monetary policy is just one of many areas in which it is not enough that the government *could* do things to make a situation better. What matters is what government is in fact *likely* to do, which can in many cases make the situation worse.

It is not only during national and international catastrophes, such as the Great Depression of the 1930s, that deflation can become a serious problem. During the heyday of the gold standard in the nineteenth and early twentieth centuries, whenever the production of goods and services grew faster than the gold supply, prices tended to decline, just as prices tend to rise when the money supply grows faster than the supply of the things that money buys.

The average price level in the United States, for example, was lower at the end of the nineteenth century than at the beginning. As in other cases of deflation— that is, an increase in the purchasing power of money— this made mortgages, leases, contracts, and other legal obligations payable in money grow in real value. In short, debtors in effect owed more— in real purchasing power— than they had agreed to pay when they borrowed money.

In addition to problems created by legal obligations fixed in money terms, there are other problems created by deflation that result from different people's incomes being affected differently by price changes. Deflation— like inflation— affects different prices differently. In the United States, as already noted, the prices of what farmers sold tended to fall faster than the prices of what they bought:

> The price of wheat, which had hovered around a dollar a bushel for decades, closed out 1892 under ninety cents, 1893 around seventy-five cents, 1894 barely sixty cents. In the dead of the winter of 1895–1896, the price went below fifty cents a bushel.

Meanwhile, farmers' mortgage payments remained where they had always been in money terms— and therefore were growing in real terms during deflation. Moreover, payments on these mortgages now had to be paid out of farm incomes that were half or less of what they had been when these mortgages were taken out. This was the background for William

Jennings Bryan's campaign for the presidency in 1896, based on a demand to end the gold standard, and was climaxed by his dramatic speech saying "you shall not crucify mankind upon a cross of gold."

At a time when more people lived in the country than in the cities and towns, he was narrowly defeated by William McKinley. What really eased the political pressures to end the gold standard was the discovery of new gold deposits in South Africa, Australia, and Alaska. These discoveries led to rising prices for the first time in twenty years, including the prices of farm produce, which rose especially rapidly.

With the deflationary effects of the gold standard now past, not only was the political polarization over the issue eased in the United States, more countries around the world went onto the gold standard at the end of the nineteenth century and the beginning of the twentieth century. However, the gold standard does not prevent either inflation or deflation, though it restricts the ability of politicians to manipulate the money supply, and thereby keeps both inflation and deflation within narrower limits. Just as the growth of output faster than the growth of the gold supply has caused a general fall in the average price level, so discoveries of large gold deposits— as in nineteenth century California, South Africa, and the Yukon— caused prices to rise to inflationary levels.

THE BANKING SYSTEM

Why are there banks in the first place?

One reason is that there are economies of scale in guarding money. If restaurants or hardware stores kept all the money they received from their customers in a back room somewhere, criminals would hold up far more restaurants, hardware stores, and other businesses and homes than they do. By transferring their money to a bank, individuals and enterprises are able to have their money guarded by others at lower costs than guarding it themselves.

Banks can invest in vaults and guards, or pay to have armored cars come around regularly to pick up money from businesses and take it to some other heavily guarded place for storage. In the United States, Federal Reserve

Banks store money from private banks and money and gold owned by the U.S. government. The security systems there are so effective that, although private banks get robbed from time to time, no Federal Reserve Bank has ever been robbed. Nearly half of all the gold owned by the German government was at one time stored in the Federal Reserve Bank of New York. In short, economies of scale enable banks to guard wealth at lower costs per unit of wealth than either private businesses or homes, and enable the Federal Reserve Banks to guard wealth at lower costs per unit of wealth than private banks.

THE ROLE OF BANKS

Banks are not just storage places for money. They play a more active role than that in the economy. As noted in earlier chapters, businesses' incomes are unpredictable and can go from profits to losses and back again repeatedly. Meanwhile, businesses' legal obligations— to pay their employees every payday and pay their electricity bills regularly, as well as paying those who supply them with all the other things needed to keep the business running— must be paid steadily, whether or not the bottom line has red ink or black ink at the moment. This means that someone must supply businesses with money when they don't have enough of their own to meet their obligations at the time when payment is due. Banks are a major source of this money, which must of course be repaid from later profits.

Businesses typically do not apply for a separate loan each time their current incomes will not cover their current obligations. It saves time and money for both the businesses and the banks if the bank grants them a line of credit for a given sum of money and the business uses up to that amount as circumstances require, repaying it when profits come in, thus replenishing the fund behind the line of credit.

Theoretically, each individual business could save its own money from the good times to tide it over the bad times, as businesses do to some extent. But here, again, there are economies of scale in having commercial banks maintain a large central fund from which individual businesses can draw money as needed to maintain a steady cash flow to pay their employees and others. Commercial banks of course charge interest for this service but, because economies of scale and risk-pooling make the commercial banks' costs lower than that of their customers, both the banks and their customers are better off financially because of this shifting of risks to where the costs of those risks are lower.

Banks not only have their own economies of scale, they are one of a number of financial institutions which enable individual businesses to achieve economies of scale— and thereby raise the general public's standard of living through lower production costs that translate into lower prices. In a complex modern economy, businesses achieve lower production costs by operating on a huge scale requiring far more labor, machinery, electricity and other resources than even rich individuals are able to afford. Most giant corporations are not owned by a few rich people but draw on money from vast numbers of people whose individually modest sums of money are aggregated and then transferred in vast amounts to the business by financial intermediaries like banks, insurance companies, mutual funds and pension funds.

Many individuals also transfer their own money more directly to businesses by buying stocks and bonds. But that means doing their own risk assessments, while others transfer their money through financial intermediaries who have the expertise and experience to evaluate investment risks and earnings prospects in a way that most individuals do not.

What is evaluated by individual owners of money that is transferred through financial institutions is the riskiness and earnings prospects of the financial institutions themselves. Individuals decide whether to put their money into an insured savings account, into a pension plan, or into a mutual fund or with commodity speculators, while these financial intermediaries in turn evaluate the riskiness and earnings prospects of those to whom they transfer this money.

Banks also finance consumer purchases by paying for credit card purchases by people who later reimburse the credit card companies and the banks behind them, by paying monthly installments that include interest. The banking system is thus a major part of an elaborate system of financial intermediaries which enables millions of people to spend money that belongs to millions of strangers, not only for investments in businesses but also for consumer purchases. For example, the leading credit card company, Visa, forms a network in which 14,800 banks and other financial institutions provide the money for purchases made by more than 100 million credit card users who buy goods from 20 million merchants around the world.

The importance of financial intermediaries to the economy as a whole can be seen by looking at places where there are not enough sufficiently knowledgeable, experienced, and trustworthy intermediaries to enable strangers to turn vast sums of money over to other strangers. Such countries are often poor, even when they are rich in natural resources. Financial intermediaries can facilitate turning these natural resources into goods and services, homes and businesses— in short, wealth.

Although money itself is not wealth, from the standpoint of society as a whole, its role in facilitating the production and transfer of wealth is important. The real wealth— the tangible things— that people are entitled to withdraw from a nation's output can instead be redirected toward others through banks and other financial institutions, using money as the means of transfer. Thus wood that could have been used to build furniture, if consumers had chosen to spend their money on that, is instead redirected toward creating paper for printing magazines when those consumers put their money into banks instead of spending it, and the banks then lend it to magazine publishers.

Modern banks, however, do more than simply transfer cash. Such transfers do not change the total demand in the economy but simply change who demands what. The total demand for all goods and services combined is not changed by such transactions, important as these transactions are for other purposes. But what the banking system does, over and beyond what other financial intermediaries do, is affect the total demand in the economy as a whole. The banking system creates credits which, in effect, add to the money supply through what is called "fractional reserve banking." A brief history of how this practice arose may make this process clearer.

Fractional Reserve Banking

Goldsmiths have for centuries had to have some safe place to store the precious metal that they use to make jewelry and other items. Once they had established a vault or other secure storage place, other people often stored their own gold with the goldsmith, rather than take on the cost of creating their own secure storage facilities. In other words, there were economies of scale in storing gold in a vault or other stronghold, so goldsmiths ended up storing other people's gold, as well as their own.

Naturally, the goldsmiths gave out receipts entitling the owners to reclaim their gold whenever they wished to. Since these receipts were redeemable in gold, they were in effect "as good as gold" and circulated as if they were money, buying goods and services as they were passed on from one person to another.

From experience, goldsmiths learned that they seldom had to redeem all the gold that was stored with them at any given time. If a goldsmith felt confident that he would never have to redeem more than one-third of the gold that he held for other people at any given time, then he could lend out the other two-thirds and earn interest on it. Since the receipts for gold and two-thirds of the gold itself were both in circulation at the same time, the goldsmith was, in effect, adding to the total money supply.

In this way, there arose two of the major features of modern banking—(1) holding only a fraction of the reserves needed to cover deposits and (2) adding to the total money supply. Since all the depositors are not going to want their money at one time, the bank lends most of it to other people, in order to earn interest on those loans. Some of this interest they share with the depositors by paying interest on their bank accounts. Again, with the depositors writing checks on their accounts while part of the money in those accounts is also circulating as loans to other people, the banking system is in effect adding to the national money supply, over and above the money printed by the government. Since some of these bank credits are re-deposited in other banks, additional rounds of expansion of the money supply follow, so that the total amount of bank credits in the economy has tended to exceed all the hard cash issued by the government.

One of the reasons this system worked was that the whole banking system has never been called upon to actually supply cash to cover all the checks written by depositors. Instead, if the Acme Bank receives a million dollars' worth of checks from its depositors, who received these checks from people whose accounts are with the Zebra Bank, the Acme bank does not ask the Zebra Bank for the million dollars. Instead, the Acme Bank balances these checks off against whatever checks were written by its own depositors and ended up in the hands of the Zebra Bank. For example, if Acme bank depositors had written a total of $1,200,000 worth of checks to businesses and individuals who then deposited those checks in the Zebra Bank, then the Acme Bank would just pay the difference. This way, only $200,000 is needed to settle more than two million dollars' worth of checks that had been written on accounts in the two banks combined.

Both banks could keep just a fraction of their deposits in cash because all the checks written on all the banks require just a fraction of the total amounts on those checks to settle the differences between banks. Since all depositors would not want their money in cash at the same time, a relatively small amount of hard cash would permit a much larger amount of credits created by the banking system to function as money in the economy.

This system, called "fractional reserve banking," worked fine in normal times. But it was very vulnerable when many depositors wanted hard cash at the same time. While most depositors are not going to ask for their money at the same time under normal conditions, there are special situations where more depositors will ask for their money than the bank can supply from the cash it has kept on hand as reserves. Usually, this would be when the depositors fear that they will not be able to get their money back. At one time, a bank robbery could cause depositors to fear that the bank would have to close and therefore they would all run to the bank at the same time, trying to withdraw their money before the bank collapsed.

If the bank had only one-third as much money available as the total depositors were entitled to, and one-half of the depositors asked for their money, then the bank ran out of money and collapsed, with the remaining depositors losing everything. The money taken by the bank robbers was often far less damaging than the run on the bank that followed.

A bank may be perfectly sound in the sense of having enough assets to cover its liabilities, but these assets cannot be instantly sold to get money to pay off the depositors. A building owned by a bank is unlikely to find a buyer instantly when the bank's depositors start lining up at the tellers' windows, asking for their money. Nor can a bank instantly collect all the money due them on 30-year mortgages. Such assets are not considered to be "liquid" because they cannot be readily turned into cash.

More than time is involved when evaluating the liquidity of assets. You can always sell a diamond for a dime— and pretty quickly. It is the degree to which an asset can be converted to money without losing its value that makes it liquid or not. American Express traveler's checks are liquid because they can be converted to money at their face value at any American Express office. A Treasury bond that is due to mature next month is almost as liquid, but not quite, even though you may be able to sell it as quickly as you can cash a traveler's check, but no one will pay the full face value of that Treasury bond today.

Because a bank's assets cannot all be liquidated at a moment's notice, anything that could set off a run on a bank could cause that bank to collapse. Not only would many depositors lose their savings, the nation's total demand for goods and services could suddenly decline, if this happened to enough banks at the same time. After all, part of the monetary demand consists of credits created by the banking system during the process of lending out money. When that credit disappears, there is no longer enough demand to buy everything that was being produced— at least not at the prices that had been set when the supply of money and credit was larger. This is what happened during the Great Depression of the 1930s, when thousands of banks in the United States collapsed and the total monetary demand of the country (including credits) contracted by one-third.

In order to prevent a repetition of this catastrophe, the Federal Deposit Insurance Corporation was created, guaranteeing that the government would reimburse depositors whose money was in an insured bank when it collapsed. Now there was no longer a reason for depositors to start a run on a bank, so very few banks collapsed, and as a result there was less likelihood of a sudden and disastrous reduction of the nation's total supply of money and credit.

While the Federal Deposit Insurance Corporation is a sort of firewall to prevent bank failures from spreading throughout the system, a more fine-tuned way of trying to control the national supply of money and credit is through the Federal Reserve System. The Federal Reserve is a central bank run by the government to control all the private banks. It has the power to tell the banks what fraction of their deposits must be kept in reserve, with only the remainder being allowed to be lent out. It also lends money to the banks, which the banks can then re-lend to the general public. By setting the interest rate on the money that it lends to the banks, the Federal Reserve System indirectly controls the interest rate that the banks will charge the general public.

All of this has the net effect of allowing the Federal Reserve to control the total amount of money and credit in the economy as a whole, to one degree or another, thereby controlling indirectly the aggregate demand for the nation's goods and services.

Because of the powerful leverage of the Federal Reserve System, public statements by the chairman of the Federal Reserve Board are scrutinized by bankers and investors for clues as to whether "the Fed" is likely to tighten the money supply or ease up. An unguarded statement by the chairman of the Federal Reserve Board, or a statement that is misconstrued by financiers, can set off a panic in Wall Street that causes stock prices to plummet. Or, if the Federal Reserve Board chairman sounds upbeat, stock prices may soar—to unsustainable levels that will ruin many investors when the prices come back down again. Given such drastic repercussions, which can affect financial markets around the world, Federal Reserve Board chairmen over the years have learned to speak in highly guarded and Delphic terms that often leave listeners puzzled as to what they really mean.

What *BusinessWeek* magazine said of Federal Reserve chairman Alan Greenspan could have been said of many of his predecessors in that position: "Wall Street and Washington expend megawatts of energy trying to decipher the delphic pronouncements of Alan Greenspan." In 2004, the following news item appeared in the business section of the *San Francisco Chronicle*:

> Alan Greenspan sneezed Wednesday, and Wall Street caught a chill.
> The Federal Reserve chairman and his colleagues on the central bank's policy-making committee left short-term interest costs unchanged, but issued a statement that didn't repeat the mantra of recent meetings about keeping rates low for a "considerable period."
> Stunned traders took the omission as a signal to unload stocks and bonds.

The Dow Jones average, Nasdaq, and the Standard & Poor's Index all dropped sharply, as did the price of treasury bonds— all because of what was *not* said.

This scrutiny of obscure statements by the Federal Reserve Board was not peculiar to Alan Greenspan's tenure as chairman of that board. Under his successor as chairman, Ben Bernanke, the Federal Reserve was purchasing large amounts of U.S. government bonds, thereby pouring new money into the American economy. But when Chairman Bernanke said in May 2013 that, if the economy improved, the Federal Reserve Board "could in the next few meetings take a step down in our pace of purchases," the reaction was swift and far reaching. The Japanese stock market lost 21 percent of its value in less than a month and total losses in stock markets around the world in that brief time totaled $3 trillion— which is more than the value of the total annual output of France, or of most other nations.

In assessing the role of the Federal Reserve, as well as any other organs of government, a sharp distinction must be made between their stated goals and their actual performance or effect. The Federal Reserve System was established in 1914 as a result of fears of such economic consequences as deflation and bank failures. Yet the worst deflation and the worst bank failures in the country's history occurred *after* the Federal Reserve was established. The financial crises of 1907, which helped spur the creation of the Federal Reserve System, were dwarfed by the financial crises associated with the stock market crash of 1929 and the Great Depression of the 1930s.

BANKING LAWS AND POLICIES

Banks and banking systems vary from one country to another. They differ not only in particular institutional practices but more fundamentally in the general setting and historical experiences of the particular country. Such differences can help illustrate some of the general requirements of a successful banking system and also to evaluate the effects of particular policies.

Requirements for a Banking System

Like so many other things, banking looks easy from the outside— simply take in deposits and lend much of it out, earning interest in the process and sharing some of that interest with the depositors, in order to keep them putting their money into the banks. Yet we do not want to repeat the mistake that Lenin made in grossly under-estimating the complexity of business in general.

At the beginning of the twenty-first century, some post-Communist nations were having great difficulties creating a banking system that could operate in a free market. In Albania and in the Czech Republic, for example, banks were able to receive deposits but were stymied by the problem of how to lend out the money to private businesses in a way that would bring returns on their investment, while minimizing losses from money that was not repaid. The London magazine *The Economist* reported that "the legal infrastructure is so weak" in Albania that the head of a bank there "is afraid to make any loans." Even though another Albanian bank made loans, it discovered that the collateral it acquired from a defaulting borrower was "impossible to sell." An Albanian bank with 83 percent of the country's deposits made no loans at all, but bought government securities instead, earning a low but dependable rate of return.

What this means for the country's economy as a whole, *The Economist* reported, is that "capital-hungry enterprises are robbed of a source of finance." In the post-Communist Czech Republic, lending was more generous— and losses much larger. Here the government stepped in to cover losses and the banks shifted their assets into government securities, as in Albania. Whether such problems will sort themselves out over time— and how much time?— is obviously a question for the Czechs and the Albanians. But it will take time for private enterprises to acquire track records and private bankers to acquire more experience, while the legal system adapts to a market economy after the long decades of a Communist economic and political regime. However, for the rest of us, their experience illustrates again the fact that one of the best ways of understanding and appreciating an economic function is by seeing what happens when that function does not exist or malfunctions.

As with Britain several centuries earlier, foreigners have been brought in to run financial institutions that the people of the former Communist bloc nations were having great difficulty running. As of 2006, foreigners owned more than half of the banking assets in the Czech Republic, Slovakia, Romania, Estonia, Lithuania, Hungary, Bulgaria, Poland and Latvia. The range of the bank assets owned by foreigners was from 60 percent in Latvia to virtually all in Estonia.

In India, a very different problem exists. While the country's rate of saving, as a percent of its economy's output, is much higher than that in the United States, its people are so distrustful of banks that individuals' holdings of gold are the highest in the world. From the standpoint of the country, this means that a substantial part of its wealth does not get used to finance investment to create additional output. Of those savings which do go into India's largely state-dominated banking system, 70 percent are lent to the government or to government-owned enterprises.

In China, where the rate of savings is even higher than in India, 90 percent of those savings go into government-owned banks, where they are lent out at low interest rates, which in effect subsidize government-owned enterprises that typically have either low rates of return on the capital invested in them or are operating at a loss. In short, most of China's savings are *not* allocated to the most efficient and prosperous enterprises, which are in the private sector and may be foreign owned, but are sent to government-owned enterprises by government officials who run the banks.

However much the situations in India and China differ from what is required for the efficient allocation of scarce resources which have alternative uses, it is very convenient for government officials. If private banks were allowed to operate freely in these countries, those banks would obviously lend or invest wherever they could safely get the highest rate of return on their money— which would be in firms and industries that were most prosperous. The private banks would then be able to offer higher interest rates to depositors, thereby attracting savings away from the state-run banks which are paying lower rates of interest.

The net result would tend to be both higher rates of savings, in response to higher rates of interest paid on bank deposits, and the more efficient allocation of those savings to the more successful businesses, leading to higher rates of economic growth for the economy as a whole. But it would also create more headaches for government officials trying to keep government-run banks and government-run enterprises from going bankrupt. While economists might say that these inefficient enterprises should go out of business for the good of the economy, people with careers in government may be unlikely to be so willing to sustain damage to their own careers for the good of others.

Government and Risk

While banks manage money, what they must also manage is risk. Runs on banks are just one of those risks. Making loans that do not get repaid is a more common, if less visibly spectacular, risk. Either risk may not only inflict financial losses but can do so to the point of destroying the institution itself. As already noted, government can do things that either increase or decrease these risks.

Insecure property rights are just one of the things within the control of government that has a major impact on the risks of banking. Because banks are almost invariably regulated by governments around the world, more so than other businesses, because of the potential impact of banking crises on the economy as a whole, the specific nature of that regulation can increase or decrease the riskiness of banking.

One of the most prominent ways of reducing risk in the United States has been the government's Federal Deposit Insurance Corporation. However, there was *state* deposit insurance before there was federal deposit insurance. These state deposit insurance laws were brought on by the increased risks that many states had created by forbidding banks from having branch offices. The purpose of outlawing branch banking was apparently to protect local banks from the competition of bigger and better-known banks headquartered elsewhere. The net effect of such laws made banks more risky because a bank's depositors and borrowers were both concentrated wherever a particular bank's one location might be.

If this was in a wheat-growing area, for example, then a decline in the price of wheat in the world market could reduce the incomes of many of the bank's depositors and borrowers at the same time, reducing both the deposits received and repayments on mortgages and other loans. State deposit insurance thus sought to deal with a risk created by state banking regulation.

But state deposit insurance proved to be inadequate to its task. During the 1920s, and especially during the Great Depression of the 1930s, the thousands of American banks that failed were concentrated overwhelmingly in small communities in states with laws against branch banking. *Federal* deposit insurance, created in 1935, put an end to ruinous bank runs, but it was solving a problem largely created by other government interventions.

In Canada, not a single bank failed during the period when thousands of American banks were failing, even though the Canadian government did not provide bank deposit insurance during that era. But Canada had 10 banks with 3,000 branches from coast to coast. That spread the risks of a given bank among many locations with different economic conditions. Large American banks with numerous branches likewise seldom failed, even during the Great Depression.

Deposit insurance can create risks as well as reducing risk. People who are insured against risks— whether banking risks or risks to automobiles or homes, for example— may engage in more risky behavior than before, now that they have been insured. That is, they might park their car in a rougher neighborhood than they would take it to, if it were not insured against vandalism or theft. Or they might build a home in an area more vulnerable to hurricanes or wildfires than they would live in if they had no financial protection in the event that their home might be destroyed. Financial institutions have even more incentives to engage in risky behavior after having been insured, since riskier investments usually pay higher rates of return than safer investments.

Government restrictions on the activities of banks insured by the Federal Deposit Insurance Corporation seek to minimize such risky investments. But containing the risk does not make the incentives for risk go away. Moreover, the government can misjudge some of the many risks that come and go, and so leave the taxpayers liable for losses that exceed the money collected from the banks as premiums paid for deposit insurance.

As in China, India and other countries where government officials intervene to direct lending to borrowers favored by government officials, rather than to borrowers to whom bank officials were more likely to lend money otherwise, so in the United States the Community Reinvestment

Act of 1977 sought to direct investment into low-income communities, including home mortgages for low or moderate income individuals.

Although more or less dormant for years, the Community Reinvestment Act was re-invigorated during the 1990s in a push to make home-buying affordable to people whose low incomes, substandard credit history or lack of money for a 20 percent down payment made getting a mortgage loan approval unlikely. Under government pressures and threats, banks began to lower mortgage loan approval standards, in order to meet government goals or quotas. The net effect, in the United States as in other countries, was riskier lending and higher rates of default in the early twenty-first century. This contributed to the collapse of banks and other lending institutions, as well as Wall Street firms whose mortgage-based assets' value was ultimately dependent on the monthly mortgage payments that increasingly failed to materialize.

Chapter 18

GOVERNMENT FUNCTIONS

The study of human institutions is always a search for the most tolerable imperfections.

Richard A. Epstein

A modern market economy cannot exist in a vacuum. Market transactions take place within a framework of rules, and require someone with the authority to enforce those rules. Government not only enforces its own rules but also enforces contracts and other agreements and understandings among the numerous parties transacting with one another in the economy. Sometimes government also sets standards, defining what is a pound, a mile, or a bushel. In order to support itself, a government must also collect taxes, which in turn influence economic decision-making by those affected by those taxes.

Beyond these basic functions, which virtually everyone can agree on, governments can play more expansive roles, all the way up to directly owning and operating all the farms and industries in a nation. Controversies have raged around the world, for more than a century, on the role that government should play in the economy. For much of the twentieth century, those who favored a larger role for government were clearly in the ascendancy, whether in democratic or undemocratic countries. The Soviet Union, China, and others in the Communist bloc of nations were at one extreme, but democratic countries like Britain, India, and France also had their governments take over ownership of various industries and tightly control the decisions made in other industries that were allowed to remain privately owned. Wide sections of the political, intellectual and even business communities have often been in favor of this expansive role of government.

During the 1980s, however, the tide began to turn the other way, toward reducing the role of government. This happened first in Britain and the United States. Then such trends spread rapidly through the democratic countries, and even Communist China began to let markets operate more freely. The collapse of Communism in the Soviet bloc led to market economies emerging in Eastern Europe as well. As a 1998 study put it:

> All around the globe, socialists are embracing capitalism, governments are selling off companies they had previously nationalized, and countries are seeking to entice back multinational corporations that they had expelled just two decades earlier.

Experience— often bitter experience— had more to do with such changes than any new theory or analysis.

Despite the wide range of functions which governments can engage in, and have engaged in, here we can examine the basic functions of government that virtually everyone can agree on and explain why those functions are important for the allocation of scarce resources which have alternative uses.

One of the most basic functions of government is to provide a framework of law and order, within which the people can engage in whatever economic and other activities they choose, making such mutual accommodations and agreements among themselves as they see fit. There are also certain activities which generate significant costs or benefits that extend beyond those individuals who engage in those activities. Here government can take account of such costs and benefits when the marketplace does not.

The individuals who work for government in various capacities tend to respond to the incentives facing them, just as people do in corporations, in families, and in other human institutions and activities. Government is neither a monolith nor simply the public interest personified. To understand what it does, its incentives and constraints must be taken into account, just as the incentives and constraints of the marketplace must be for those who engage in market transactions.

LAW AND ORDER

Where government restricts its economic role to that of an enforcer of laws and contracts, some people say that such a policy amounts to "doing nothing" as far as the economy is concerned. However, what is called "nothing" has often taken centuries to achieve— namely, a reliable framework of laws, within which economic activity can flourish, and without which even vast amounts of rich natural resources may fail to be developed into a corresponding level of output and resulting prosperity.

Corruption

Like the role of prices, the role of a reliable framework of laws may be easier to understand by observing what happens in times and places where such a framework does not exist. Countries whose governments are ineffectual, arbitrary, or thoroughly corrupt can remain poor despite an abundance of natural resources, because neither foreign nor domestic entrepreneurs want to risk the kinds of large investments which are required to develop natural resources into finished products that raise the general standard of living. A classic example is the African nation of Congo, rich in minerals but poor in every other way. Here is the scene encountered at the airport in its capital city of Kinshasa:

> Kinshasa is one of the world's poorest cities, so unsafe for arriving crews that they get shuttled elsewhere for overnight stays. Taxiing down the scarred tarmac feels like driving over railroad ties. Managers charge extra to turn on the runway lights at night, and departing passengers can encounter several layers of bribes before boarding.

Bolivia is another Third World country where law and order have broken down:

> The media are full of revelations about police links to drug trafficking and stolen vehicles, nepotism in the force, and the charging of illegal fees for services. Officers on meagre salaries have been found to live in mansions.

In Egypt, when a rich and politically well-connected businessman was sentenced to death for hiring a hit man to kill a former lover, people were "astounded, and pleased," according to the *New York Times*, because he was "a high roller of the type that Egyptians have long assumed to operate beyond the reach of the law."

Whatever the merits or demerits of particular laws, someone must administer those laws— and how efficiently or how honestly that is done can make a huge economic difference. The phrase "the law's delay" goes back at least as far as Shakespeare's time. Such delay imposes costs on those whose investments are idled, whose shipments are held up, and whose ability to plan their economic activities is crippled by red tape and slow-moving bureaucrats. Moreover, bureaucrats' ability to create delay often means an opportunity for them to collect bribes to speed things up— all of which adds up to higher costs of doing business. That in turn means higher prices to consumers, and correspondingly lower standards of living for the country as a whole.

The costs of corruption are not limited to the bribes collected, since these are internal transfers, rather than net reductions of national wealth in themselves. Because scarce resources have alternative uses, the real costs are the foregone alternatives— delayed or aborted economic activity, the enterprises that are *not* started, the investments that are not made, the expansion of output and employment that does *not* take place in a thoroughly corrupt society, as well as the loss of skilled, educated, and entrepreneurial people who leave the country. As *The Economist* magazine put it: "For sound economic reasons, foreign investors and international aid agencies are increasingly taking the level of bribery and corruption into account in their investment and lending."

A study by the World Bank concluded, "Across countries there is strong evidence that higher levels of corruption are associated with lower growth and lower levels of per capita income." The three countries ranked most corrupt were Haiti, Bangladesh, and Nigeria— all poverty-stricken beyond anything seen in modern industrial societies.

During czarist Russia's industrialization in the late nineteenth and early twentieth centuries, one of the country's biggest handicaps was the widespread corruption in the general population, in addition to the corruption that was rampant within the Russian government. Foreign firms that hired Russian workers, and even Russian executives, made it a point *not* to hire Russian accountants. This corruption continued under the Communists and has become an international scandal in the post-Communist era. One study pointed out that the stock of a Russian oil company sold for about one percent of what the stock of a similar oil company would sell for in the United States, because "the market expects that Russian oil companies will be systematically looted by insiders." Similar corruption was common in Russian universities, according to *The Chronicle of Higher Education*'s Moscow correspondent:

> It costs between $10,000 and $15,000 in bribes merely to gain acceptance into well-regarded institutions of higher learning in Moscow, the daily newspaper *Izvestia* has reported. . . At Astrakhan State Technical University, about 700 miles south of Moscow, three professors were arrested after allegedly inducing students to pay cash to ensure good grades on exams. . . . Over all, Russian students and their parents annually spend at least $2 billion— and possibly up to $5 billion— in such "unofficial" educational outlays, the deputy prime minister, Valentina Matviyenko, said last year in an interview.

Corruption can of course take many forms besides the direct bribe. It can, for example, take the form of appointing politicians or their relatives to a company's board of directors, in expectation of receiving more favorable treatment from the government. This practice varies from country to country, like more overt corruption. As *The Economist* put it, "politically linked firms are most common in countries famous for high levels of corruption." Russia has led the way in this practice, in which firms with 80 percent of the country's market capitalization were linked to public officials. The comparable figure for the United States was less than 10 percent, partly due to American laws restricting this practice. Widespread corruption is not something new in Russia. John Stuart Mill wrote about it in the nineteenth century:

> The universal venality ascribed to Russian functionaries, must be an immense drag on the capabilities of economical improvement possessed so abundantly by the Russian empire: since the emoluments of public officers must depend on the success with which they can multiply vexations, for the purpose of being bought off by bribes.

It is not just corruption but also sheer bureaucracy which can stifle economic activity. Even one of India's most spectacularly successful industrialists, Aditya

Birla, found himself forced to look to other countries in which to expand his investments, because of India's slow-moving bureaucrats:

> With all his successes, there were heartbreaks galore. One of them was the Mangalore refinery, which Delhi's bureaucrats took eleven years to clear— a record even by the standards of the Indian bureaucracy. While both of us were waiting for a court to open up at the Bombay Gymkhana one day, I asked Aditya Birla what had led him to invest abroad. He had no choice, he said, in his deep, unaffected voice. There were too many obstacles in India. To begin with, he needed a license, which the government would not give because the Birlas were classified as "a large house" under the MRTP [Monopolies and Restrictive Trade Practices] Act. Even if he did get one miraculously, the government would decide where he should invest, what technology he must use, what was to be the size of his plant, how it was to be financed— even the size and structure of his public issue. Then he would have to battle the bureaucracy to get licenses for the import of capital goods and raw materials. After that, he faced dozens of clearances at the state level— for power, land, sales tax, excise, labor, among others. "All this takes years, and frankly, I get exhausted just thinking about it."

This head of 37 companies with combined sales in the billions of dollars— someone capable of creating many much-needed jobs in India— ended up producing fiber in Thailand, which was converted to yarn in his factory in Indonesia, after which this yarn was sent to Belgium, where it was woven into carpets— which were then exported to Canada. All the jobs, incomes, auxiliary business opportunities, and taxes from which India could have benefitted were lost because of the country's own bureaucracies.

India is not unique, either in government-created business delays or in their negative economic consequences. A survey by the World Bank found that the number of days required to start a new business ranged from less than ten in prosperous Singapore to 155 days in poverty-stricken Congo.

The Framework of Laws

For fostering economic activities and the prosperity resulting from them, laws must be reliable, above all. If the application of the law varies with the whims of kings or dictators, with changes in democratically elected governments, or with the caprices or corruption of appointed officials, then the risks surrounding investments rise, and consequently the amount of investing is likely to be much less than purely economic considerations would produce in a market economy under a reliable framework of laws.

One of the major advantages that enabled nineteenth-century Britain to become the first industrialized nation was the dependability of its laws. Not only could Britons feel confident when investing in their country's economy, without fear that their earnings would be confiscated, or dissipated in bribes, or that the contracts they made would be changed or voided for political reasons, so could foreigners doing business in Britain or making investments there.

For centuries, the reputation of British law for dependability and impartiality attracted investments and entrepreneurs from continental Europe, as well as skilled immigrants and refugees, who helped create whole new industries in Britain. In short, both the physical capital and the human capital of foreigners contributed to the development of the British economy from the medieval era, when it was one of the more backward economies in Western Europe, to a later era, when it became the most advanced economy in the world, setting the stage for Britain's industrial revolution that led the rest of the world into the industrial age.

In other parts of the world as well, a framework of dependable laws has encouraged both domestic and foreign investment, as well as attracting immigrants with skills lacking locally. In Southeast Asia, for example, the imposition of European laws under the colonial regimes of the eighteenth and nineteenth centuries replaced the powers of local rulers and tribes. Under these new frameworks of laws— often uniform across larger geographical areas than before, as well as being more dependable at a given place— a massive immigration from China and a substantial immigration from India brought in people whose skills and entrepreneurship created whole new industries and transformed the economies of countries throughout the region.

European investors also sent capital to Southeast Asia, financing many of the giant ventures in mining and shipping that were often beyond the resources of the Chinese and Indian immigrants, as well as beyond the resources of the indigenous peoples. In colonial Malaya, for example, the tin mines and rubber plantations which provided much of that country's export earnings were financed by European capital and worked by laborers from China and India, while most local commerce and industry were in the hands of the Chinese, leaving the indigenous Malays largely spectators at the modernization of their own economy.

While impartiality is a desirable quality in laws, even laws which are discriminatory can still promote economic development, if the nature of the discrimination is spelled out in advance, rather than taking the form of unpredictably biased and corrupt decisions by judges, juries, and officials. The Chinese and Indians who settled in the European colonial empires of Southeast Asia never had the same legal rights as Europeans there, nor the same rights as the indigenous population. Yet whatever rights they did have could be relied upon, and therefore served as a foundation for the creation of Chinese and Indian businesses throughout the region.

Similarly in the Ottoman Empire, Christians and Jews did not have the same rights as Muslims. Yet, during the flourishing centuries of that empire, the rights which Christians and Jews did have were sufficiently dependable to enable them to prosper in commerce, industry, and banking to a greater extent than the Muslim majority. Moreover, their economic activities contributed to the prosperity of the Ottoman Empire as a whole. Similar stories could be told of the Lebanese minority in colonial West Africa or Indians in colonial Fiji, as well as other minority groups in other countries who prospered under laws that were dependable, even if not impartial.

Dependability is not simply a matter of the government's own treatment of people. It must also prevent some people from interfering with other people, so that criminals and mobs do not make economic life risky and thereby stifle the economic development required for prosperity.

Governments differ in the effectiveness with which they can enforce their laws in general, and even a given government may be able to enforce its laws more effectively in some places than in others. For centuries during the Middle Ages, the borderlands between English and Scottish kingdoms were not effectively controlled by either country and so remained lawless and economically backward. Mountainous regions have often been difficult to police, whether in the Balkans, the Appalachian region of the United States, or elsewhere. Such places have likewise tended to lag in economic development and to attract few outsiders and little outside capital.

Today, high-crime neighborhoods and neighborhoods subject to higher than normal rates of vandalism or riots similarly suffer economically from a lack of law and order. Some businesses simply will not locate there. Those that do may be less efficient or less pleasant than businesses in other neighborhoods, where such substandard businesses would be unable to compete. The costs of additional security devices inside and outside of stores, as well as security guards in some places, all add to the costs of doing business and are reflected in the higher prices of goods and services purchased by people in high-crime areas, even though most people in such areas are not criminals and can ill-afford the extra costs created by those who are.

Property Rights

Among the most misunderstood aspects of law and order are property rights. While these rights are cherished as personal benefits by those fortunate enough to own a substantial amount of property, what matters from the standpoint of economics is how property rights affect the allocation of scarce resources which have alternative uses. What property rights mean to property owners is far less important than what they mean to the economy as a whole. In other words, property rights need to be assessed in terms of their economic effects on the well-being of the population at large. These effects are ultimately an empirical question which cannot be settled on the basis of assumptions or rhetoric.

What is different with and without property rights? One small but telling example was the experience of a delegation of American farmers who visited the Soviet Union. They were appalled at the way various agricultural produce was shipped, carelessly packed and with spoiled fruit or vegetables left to spread the spoilage to other fruits and vegetables in the same sacks or boxes. Coming from a country where individuals owned agricultural produce as their private property, American farmers had no experience with such gross carelessness and waste, which would have caused somebody to lose much money needlessly in the United States, and perhaps go bankrupt. In the Soviet Union, the loss was even more painful, since the country often had trouble feeding itself, but there were no property rights to convey these losses directly to the people handling and shipping produce.

In a country without property rights, or with the food being owned "by the people," there was no given individual with sufficient incentives to ensure that this food did not spoil needlessly before it reached the consumers. Those who handled the food in transit were paid salaries, which were fixed independently of how well they did or did not safeguard the food.

In theory at least, closer monitoring of produce handlers could have reduced the spoilage. But monitoring is not free. The human resources which go into monitoring are themselves among the scarce resources which have alternative uses. Moreover, monitoring raises the further question: Who will monitor the monitors? The Soviets tried to deal with this problem by having Communist Party members honeycombed throughout the society to report on derelictions of duty and violations of law. However, the widespread corruption and inefficiency found even under Stalinist totalitarianism suggest the limitations of official monitoring, as compared to automatic self-monitoring by property owners.

No monitor has to stand over an American farmer and tell him to take the rotten peaches out of a basket before they spoil the others, because those peaches are his private property and he is not about to lose money if he doesn't have to. *Property rights create self-monitoring*, which tends to be both more effective and less costly than third-party monitoring.

Most Americans do not own any agricultural land or crops, but they have more and better food available at more affordable prices than in countries where there are no property rights in agricultural land or its produce, and where much food can spoil needlessly as a result. Since the prices paid for the food that is sold have to cover the costs of all the food produced— including the food that was spoiled and discarded— food prices will be higher where there is more spoilage, even if the cost of producing the food in the first place is the same.

The only animals threatened with extinction are animals not owned by anybody. Colonel Sanders was not about to let chickens become extinct. Nor will McDonald's stand idly by and let cows become extinct. Likewise with inanimate things, it is those things not owned by anybody— air and water, for example— which are polluted. In centuries past, sheep were allowed to graze on unowned land— "the commons," as it was called— with the net result that land on the commons was so heavily grazed that it had little left but patchy ground and the shepherds had hungry and scrawny sheep. But privately owned land adjacent to the commons was usually in far better condition. Similar neglect of unowned land occurred in the Soviet Union. According to Soviet economists, "forested areas that are cut down are not reseeded," though it would be financial suicide for a lumbering company to let that happen on their own property in a capitalist economy.

All these things illustrate, in different ways, the value of private property rights *to the society as a whole*, including people who own virtually no private property, but who benefit from the greater economic efficiency that property rights create, which translates into a higher standard of living for the population at large.

Despite a tendency to think of property rights as special privileges for the rich, many property rights are actually more valuable to people who are not rich— and such property rights have often been infringed or violated for the benefit of the rich.

Although the average rich person, by definition, has more money than the average person who is not rich, in the aggregate the non-rich population often has far more money. This means, among other things, that many properties owned by the rich would be bid away from them by the greater purchasing power of the non-rich, if unrestricted property rights prevailed in a free market. Thus land occupied by mansions located on huge estates can pass through the market to entrepreneurs who build smaller and more numerous homes or apartment buildings on these sites— all for the use of people with more modest incomes, but with more money in the aggregate.

Someone once said, "It doesn't matter whether you are rich or poor, so long as you have money." This was meant as a joke but it has very serious implications. In a free market, the money of ordinary people is just as good as the money of the rich— and in the aggregate, there is often more of it. The individually less affluent need not directly bid against the more affluent. Entrepreneurs or their companies, using their own money or money borrowed from banks and other financial institutions, can acquire mansions and estates, and replace them with middle-class homes and apartment buildings for people of moderate incomes. This would of course change these communities in ways the rich might not like, however much others might like to live in the resulting newly developed communities.

Wealthy people have often forestalled such transfers of property by getting laws passed to *restrict* property rights in a variety of ways. For example, various affluent communities in California, Virginia, and other places have required land to be sold only in lots of one acre or more per house, thereby pricing such land and homes beyond the reach of most people and thus neutralizing the greater aggregate purchasing power of less affluent people.

Zoning boards, "open space" laws, historical preservation commissions and other organizations and devices have also been used to severely limit the sale of private property for use in ways not approved by those who wish to keep things the way they are in the communities where they live— often described as "our community," though no one owns the whole community and each individual owns only that individual's private property. Yet such verbal collectivization is more than just a figure of speech. Often it is a prelude to legal and political actions to negate private property rights and treat the whole community as if it were in fact collectively owned.

By infringing or negating property rights, affluent and wealthy property owners are thus able to keep out people of average or low incomes and, at the same time, increase the value of their own property by ensuring its growing scarcity as population increases in the area.

While strict adherence to property rights would allow landlords to evict tenants from their apartments at will, the economic incentives are for landlords to do just the opposite— that is, to try to keep their apartments as fully rented and as continuously occupied as possible, so long as the tenants pay their rent and create no problems. Only when rent control or other restrictions on their property rights are enacted are landlords likely to do otherwise. Under rent control and tenants' rights laws, landlords have been known to try to harass tenants into leaving, whether in New York or in Hong Kong.

Under stringent rent control and tenants' rights laws in Hong Kong, landlords were known to sneak into their own buildings late at night to vandalize the premises, in order to make them less attractive or even unlivable, so that tenants would move out and the empty building could then be torn down legally, to be replaced by something more lucrative as commercial or industrial property, not subject to rent control laws. This of course was by no means the purpose or intention of those who had passed rent control laws in Hong Kong. But it illustrates again the importance of making a distinction between intentions and effects— and not just as regards property rights laws. In short, incentives matter and property rights need to be assessed economically in terms of the incentives created by their existence, their modifications, or their elimination.

The powerful incentives created by a profit-and-loss economy depend on the profits being private property. When government-owned enterprises in the Soviet Union made profits, those profits were not their private property but belonged to "the people"— or, in more mundane terms, could be taken by the government for whatever purposes higher officials chose to spend them on. Soviet economists Shmelev and Popov pointed out and lamented the adverse effects of this on incentives:

> But what justifies confiscating the larger part— sometimes 90–95 percent— of enterprises' profits, as is being done in many sectors of the economy today? What political or economic right— ultimately what human right— do ministries have to do that? Once again we are taking away from those who work well in order to keep afloat those who do nothing. How can we possibly talk about independence, initiative, rewards for efficiency, quality, and technical progress?

Of course, the country's leaders could continue to *talk* about such things, but destroying the incentives which exist under property rights meant that there was a reduced chance of achieving these goals. Because of an absence of property rights, those who ran enterprises that made profits "can't buy or build anything with the money they have" which represent "just figures in a bank account with no real value whatever without permission from above" to use that money. In other words, success did not automatically lead to expansions of successful enterprises nor failure to the contraction of unsuccessful ones, as it does in a market economy.

Social Order

Order includes more than laws and the government apparatus that administers laws. It also includes the honesty, reliability and cooperativeness of the people themselves. "Morality plays a functional role in the operation of the economic system," as Nobel Prize winning economist Kenneth Arrow put it.

Honesty and reliability can vary greatly between one country and another. As a knowledgeable observer put it: "While it is unimaginable to do business in China without paying bribes, to offer one in Japan is the greatest of faux pas." Losses from shoplifting and employee theft, as a percentage of sales, have been more than twice as high in India as in Germany or Taiwan.

When wallets with money in them were deliberately left in public places as an experiment, the percentage of those wallets returned with the money untouched varied greatly from place to place: in Denmark, for example, nearly all of these wallets were returned with the money still in them. Among United Nations representatives who have diplomatic immunity from local laws in New York City, diplomats from various Middle East countries let numerous parking tickets go unpaid— 246 by Kuwaiti diplomats— while not one diplomat from Denmark, Japan, or Israel had any unpaid parking tickets.

Honesty and reliability can also vary widely among particular groups within a given country, and that also has economic repercussions. Some insular groups rely upon their own internal social controls for doing business with fellow group members whom they can trust. The Marwaris of India are one such group, whose business networks were established in the nineteenth century and extended beyond India to China and Central Asia, and who "transacted vast sums merely on the merchant's word." But, for India as a whole, that is definitely not the case.

Business transactions among strangers are an essential part of a successful modern mass economy, which requires cooperation— including the pooling of vast financial resources from far more people than can possibly know each other personally. As for the general level of reliability among strangers in India, *The Economist* reported:

> If you withdraw 10,000 rupees from a bank, it will probably come in a brick of 100-rupee notes, held together by industrial-strength staples that you struggle to prise open. They are there to stop someone from surreptitiously removing a few notes. On trains, announcements may advise you to crush your empty mineral-water bottles lest someone refill them with tap water and sell them as new. . . . Any sort of business that requires confidence in the judicial system is best left alone.

Where neither the honesty of the general population nor the integrity of the legal system can be relied upon, economic activities are inhibited, if not stifled. At the same time, particular groups whose members can rely on each other, such as the Marwaris, have a great advantage in competition with others, in being able to secure mutual cooperation in economic activities which extend over distance and time— activities that would be far more risky for others in such societies and still more so for foreigners.

Like the Marwaris in India, Hasidic Jews in New York's diamond district often give consignments of jewels to one another and share the sales proceeds on the basis of verbal agreements among themselves. The extreme social isolation of the Hasidic community from the larger society, and even from other Jews, makes it very costly for anyone who grows up in that community to disgrace his family and lose his own standing, as well as his own economic and social relationships, by cheating on an agreement with a fellow Hasidim.

It is much the same story halfway around the world, where the overseas Chinese minority in various Southeast Asian countries make verbal agreements among themselves, without the sanction of the local legal system. Given the unreliability and corruption of some of these post-colonial legal systems, the ability of the Chinese to rely on their own social and economic arrangements gives them an economic advantage over their indigenous competitors, who lack an equally reliable and inexpensive way of making transactions or pooling their money safely. The costs of doing business are thus less for the Chinese than for Malay, Indonesian or other businesses in the region, giving the Chinese competitive advantages.

What economics professor William Easterly of New York University has aptly called "the radius of trust" extends for very different distances among different groups and nations. For some, it extends no further than the family:

> Malagasy grain traders carry out inspections of each lot of grain in person because they don't trust employees. One third of the traders say they don't hire more workers because of fear of theft by them. This limits the grain traders' firm size, cutting short a trader's potential success. In many countries, companies tend to be family enterprises because family members are the only ones felt trustworthy. So the size of the company is then limited by the size of the family.

Even in the same country, the radius of trust can extend very different distances. Although businesses in some American communities must incur the extra expenses of heavy grates for protection from theft and vandalism while closed, and security guards for protection while open, businesses in other American communities have no such expenses and are therefore able to operate profitably while charging lower prices.

Rental car companies can park their cars in lots without fences or guards in some communities, while in other places it would be financial suicide to do so. But, in those places where car thefts from unguarded lots are rare, such rare losses may cost less than paying guards and maintaining fences would cost, so that rental car agencies— and other businesses— can flourish as they operate at lower costs in such communities. Those communities also flourish economically, as a result of attracting enterprises and investments that create jobs and pay local taxes.

In short, honesty is more than a moral principle. It is also a major economic factor. While government can do little to create honesty directly, in various ways it can indirectly either support or undermine the traditions on which honest conduct is based. This it can do by what it teaches in its schools, by the examples set by public officials, or by the laws that it passes. These laws can create incentives toward either moral or immoral conduct. Where laws create a situation in which the only way to avoid ruinous losses is by violating the law, the government is in effect reducing public respect for laws in general, as well as rewarding specific dishonest behavior.

Advocates of rent control, for example, often point to examples of dishonest behavior among landlords to demonstrate an apparent need for both rent control itself and for related tenants' rights legislation. However, rent control laws can widen the difference between the value of a given apartment building to honest owners and dishonest owners. Where the costs of legally mandated services— such as heat, maintenance and hot water— are high enough to equal or exceed the amount of rent permitted under the law, the value of a building to an honest landlord can become zero or even negative. Yet, to a landlord who is willing to violate the law and save money by neglecting required services, or who accepts bribes from prospective tenants during a housing shortage under rent control, the building may still have some value.

Where something has different values to different people, it tends to move through the marketplace to its most valued use, which is where the bids will be highest. In this case, dishonest landlords can easily bid apartment buildings away from honest landlords, some of whom may be relieved to escape the bind that rent control puts them in. Landlords willing to resort to arson may find the building most valuable of all, if they can sell the site for commercial or industrial use after burning the building down, thereby getting rid of both tenants and rent control. As one study found:

> In New York City, landlord arsons became so common in some areas that the city responded with special welfare allowances. For a while, burned-out tenants were moved to the top of the list for coveted public housing. That gave *tenants* an incentive to burn down their buildings. They did, often moving television sets and furniture out onto the sidewalk before starting the fire.

Those who create incentives toward widespread dishonesty by promoting laws which make honest behavior financially impossible are often among the most indignant at the dishonesty— and the least likely to regard themselves as in any way responsible for it. Arson is just one of the forms of dishonesty promoted by rent control laws. Shrewd and unscrupulous landlords have made virtually a science out of milking a rent-controlled building by neglecting maintenance and repairs, defaulting on mortgage payments, falling behind in the payment of taxes, and then finally letting the building become the property of the city by default. Then they move on to repeat the same destructive process with other rent-controlled buildings.

Without rent control, the incentives facing landlords are directly opposite. In the absence of rent control, the incentives are to maintain the quality of the property, in order to attract tenants, and to safeguard it against fire and other sources of dangers to the survival of the building, which is a valuable piece of property to them in a free market. In short, complaints against landlords' behavior by rent control advocates can be valid, even though few of those advocates see any connection between rent control and a declining moral quality in people who become landlords. When honest landlords stand to lose money under rent control, while dishonest landlords can still make a profit, it is virtually inevitable that the property will pass from the former to the latter.

Rent control laws are just one of a number of severe restrictions which can make honest behavior too costly for many people, and which therefore promote widespread dishonesty. It is common in Third World countries for much— sometimes most— economic activity to take place "off the books," which is to say illegally, because oppressive levels of bureaucracy and red tape make legal operation too costly for most people to afford.

In the African nation of Cameroon, for example, setting up a small business has required paying official fees (not counting bribes) that amount to far more money than the average person in Cameroon makes in a year. The legal system imposes similarly high costs on other economic activities:

> To buy or sell property costs nearly a fifth of the property's value. To get the courts to enforce an unpaid invoice takes nearly two years, costs over a third of the invoice's value, and requires fifty-eight separate procedures. These ridiculous regulations are good news for the bureaucrats who enforce them. Every procedure is an opportunity to extract a bribe.

When laws and policies make honesty increasingly costly, then government is, in effect, promoting dishonesty. Such dishonesty can then extend beyond the particular laws and policies in question to a more general habit of disobeying laws, to the detriment of the whole economy and society. As a Russian mother said:

> Now my children tell me I raised them the wrong way. All that honesty and fairness, no one needs it now. If you are honest you are a fool.

To the extent that such attitudes are widespread in any given country, the consequences are economic as well as social.

Despite all the countries which have seen their economic growth rates rise sharply when they went from government-controlled economies to free market economies, Russia saw its output and its standard of living fall precipitously after the dissolution of the Soviet Union and the conversion of state-owned property into property owned by former communist leaders turned capitalists. Rampant corruption can negate the benefits of markets, as it negates the benefits of a rich endowment of natural resources or a highly educated population.

While a market economy operates better in a country where honesty is more widespread, it is also true that free markets tend to punish dishonesty. American investigative journalist John Stossel, who began his career by exposing various kinds of frauds that businesses commit against consumers, found this pattern:

> I did hundreds of stories on such scams but over the years, I came to realize that in the private sector, the cheaters seldom get very rich. It's not because "consumer fraud investigators" catch them and stop them; most fraud never even gets on the government's radar screens. The cheaters get punished by the market. They make money for a while, but then people wise up and stop buying.
>
> There are exceptions. In a multi-trillion-dollar economy with tens of thousands of businesses, there will always be some successful cheaters and Enron-like scams; but the longer I did consumer reporting, the harder it was for us to find serious rip-offs worthy of national television.

Levels of government corruption not only vary greatly among nations, they can vary over time with the same nations. Corrupting an honest government may be easier than trying to change a corrupt way of life into an honest one. But even the latter can be done sometimes. Reporting on economic progress in Africa in 2013, *The Economist* magazine said, "our correspondent visited 23 countries" and "was not once asked for a bribe—inconceivable only ten years ago."

EXTERNAL COSTS AND BENEFITS

Economic decisions made through the marketplace are not always better than decisions that governments can make. Much depends on whether those market transactions accurately reflect both the costs and the benefits that result. Under some conditions, they do not.

When someone buys a table or a tractor, the question as to whether it is worth what it cost is answered by the actions of the purchaser who made the decision to buy it. However, when an electric utility company buys coal to burn to generate electricity, a significant part of the cost of the electricity-generating process is paid by people who breathe the smoke that results from the burning of the coal and whose homes and cars are dirtied by the soot. Cleaning, repainting and medical costs paid by these people are not taken into account in the marketplace, because these people do not participate in the transactions between the coal producer and the utility company.

Such costs are called "external costs" by economists because such costs fall outside the parties to the transaction which creates these costs. External costs are therefore not taken into account in the marketplace, even when these are very substantial costs, which can extend beyond monetary losses to include bad health and premature death. While there are many decisions that can be made more efficiently through the marketplace than by government, this is one of those decisions that can be made more efficiently by government than by the marketplace. Even such a champion of free markets as Milton Friedman acknowledged that there are "effects on third parties for which it is not feasible to charge or recompense them."

Clean air laws can reduce harmful emissions by legislation and regulations. Clean water laws and laws against disposing of toxic wastes where they will harm people can likewise force decisions to be made in ways that take into account the external costs that would otherwise be ignored by those transacting in the marketplace.

By the same token, there may be transactions that would be *beneficial* to people who are not party to the decision-making, and whose interests are therefore not taken into account. The benefits of mud flaps on cars and trucks may be apparent to anyone who has ever driven in a rainstorm behind a car or truck that was throwing so much water or mud onto his windshield as to dangerously obscure vision. Even if everyone agrees that the benefits of mud flaps greatly exceed their costs, there is no feasible way of buying these benefits in a free market, since you receive no benefits from the mud flaps that you buy and put on your own car, but only from mud flaps that other people buy and put on their cars and trucks.

These are "external benefits." Here again, it is possible to obtain collectively through government what cannot be obtained individually through the marketplace, simply by having laws passed requiring all cars and trucks to have mud flaps on them.

Some other benefits are indivisible. Either everybody gets these kinds of benefits or nobody gets them. Military defense is an example. If military defense had to be purchased individually through the marketplace, then those who felt threatened by foreign powers could pay for guns, troops, cannon and all the other means of military deterrence and defense, while those who saw no dangers could refuse to spend their money on such things. However, the level of military security would be the same for both, since supporters and non-supporters of military forces are intermixed in the same society and exposed to the same dangers from enemy action.

Given the indivisibility of the benefits, even some citizens who fully appreciate the military dangers, and who consider the costs of meeting those dangers to be fully justified by the benefits, might still feel no need to voluntarily spend their own money for military purposes, since their individual contribution would have no serious effect on their own individual security, which would depend primarily on how much others contributed. In such a situation, it is entirely possible to end up with inadequate military defense, even if everyone understands the cost of effective defense and considers the benefits to be worth it.

By collectivizing this decision and having it made by government, an end result can be achieved that is more in keeping with what most people want than if those people were allowed to decide individually what to do. Even among free market advocates, few would suggest that each individual should buy military defense in the marketplace.

In short, there are things that government can do more efficiently than individuals because external costs, external benefits, or indivisibilities make individual decisions in the marketplace, based on individual interests, a less effective way of weighing costs and benefits to the whole society.

While external costs and benefits are not automatically taken into account in the marketplace, this is not to say that there may not be some imaginative ways in which they can be. In Britain, for example, ponds or lakes are often privately owned, and these owners have every incentive to keep them from becoming polluted, since a clean body of water is more attractive to fishermen or boaters who pay for its use. Similarly with shopping malls: Although maintaining clean, attractive malls with benches, rest rooms and security personnel costs money that the mall owners do not collect from the shoppers, a mall with such things attracts more customers, and so the rents charged the individual storeowners can be higher because a location in such malls is more valuable than a location in a mall without such amenities.

While there are some decisions which can be made more efficiently by individuals and other decisions which can be made more efficiently through collective action, that collective action need not be that of a national or even a local government, but can be that of individuals spontaneously organizing themselves to deal with external costs or external benefits. For example, back during the pioneering days in the American west, when cattle grazed on the open plains that were not owned by anyone, there was the same danger that more animals would be allowed to graze than the land would support, as with sheep on the commons, since no given cattle owner had an incentive to restrict the number of his own animals that were allowed to graze.

In the American west during the pioneering era, owners of cattle organized themselves into cattlemen's associations that created rules for themselves and in one way or another kept newcomers out, in effect turning the plains into collectively owned land with collectively determined rules, sometimes enforced by collectively hired gunmen.

Modern trade associations can sometimes make collective decisions for an industry more efficiently than individual business owners could, especially when there are externalities of the sort used to justify government intervention in market economies. Such private associations can promote the sharing of information and the standardization of products and procedures, benefitting both themselves and their customers. Railroads can get together and standardize the gauges of their tracks, so that trains can transfer from one line to another, or hotels can standardize their room reservation procedures, in order to make travel reservations for their guests who are traveling on to another community.

In short, while externalities are a serious consideration in determining the role of government, they do not simply provide a blanket justification or a magic word which automatically allows economics to be ignored and politically attractive goals to be pursued without further ado. Both the incentives of the market and the incentives of politics must be weighed when choosing between them on any particular issue.

INCENTIVES AND CONSTRAINTS

Government is of course inseparable from politics, especially in a democratic country, so a distinction must be made and constantly kept in mind between what a government *can* do to make things better than they would be in a free market and what it is in fact *likely* to do under the influence of political incentives and constraints. The distinction between what the government can do and what it is likely to do can be lost when we think of the government as simply an agent of society or even as one integral performer. In reality, the many individuals and agencies within a national government have their own separate interests, incentives, and agendas, to which they may respond far more often than they respond to either the public interest or to the policy agendas set by political leaders.

Even in a totalitarian state such as the Soviet Union, different branches and departments of government had different interests that they pursued, despite whatever disadvantages this might have for the economy or the society. For example, industrial enterprises in different ministries avoided relying on each other for equipment or supplies, if at all possible. Thus an enterprise located in Vladivostok might order equipment or supplies that it needed from another enterprise under the same ministry located in Minsk, thousands of miles away, rather than depend on getting what it needed from another enterprise located nearby in Vladivostok that was under the control of a different ministry. Thus materials might be needlessly shipped thousands of miles eastward on the overburdened Soviet railroads, while the same kinds of materials were also being shipped westward on the same railroads by another enterprise under a different ministry.

Such economically wasteful cross-hauling was one of many inefficient allocations of scarce resources due to the political reality that government is not a monolith, even in a totalitarian society. In democratic societies, where innumerable interest groups are free to organize and influence different branches and agencies of government, there is even less reason to expect that the entire government will follow one coherent policy, much less a policy that would be followed by an ideal government representing the public interest. In the United States, some government agencies have been trying to restrict smoking while other government agencies have been subsidizing the growing of tobacco. Senator Daniel Patrick Moynihan once referred to "the warring principalities that are sometimes known as the Federal government."

Under popularly elected government, the political incentives are to do what is popular, even if the consequences are worse than the consequences of doing nothing, or doing something that is less popular. As an example of what virtually everyone now agrees was a counterproductive policy, the Nixon administration in 1971 created the first peacetime nationwide wage controls and price controls in the history of the United States.

Among those at the meeting where this fateful decision was made was internationally renowned economist Arthur F. Burns, who argued strenuously against the policy being considered— and was over-ruled. Nor were the other people present economically illiterate. The president himself had long resisted the idea of wage and price controls, and had publicly rejected the idea just eleven days before doing an about-face and accepting it. Inflation had created mounting pressures from the public and the media to "do something."

With a presidential election due the following year, the administration could not afford to be seen as doing nothing while inflation raged out of control. However, even aside from such political concerns, the participants in this meeting were "exhilarated by all the great decisions they had made" that day, according to a participant. Looking back, he later recalled that "more time was spent discussing the timing of the speech than how the economic program would work." There was particular concern that, if the president's speech were broadcast in prime time, it would cause cancellation of the very popular television program *Bonanza*, leading to public resentments. Here is what happened:

> Nixon's speech— despite the preemption of *Bonanza*— was a great hit. The public felt that the government was coming to its defense against the price gougers. . . During the next evening's newscasts, 90 percent of the coverage was devoted to Nixon's new policy. The coverage

was favorable. And the Dow Jones Industrial Average registered a 32.9-point gain— the largest one-day increase up to then.

In short, the controls were a complete success politically. As for their economic consequences:

> Ranchers stopped shipping their cattle to the market, farmers drowned their chickens, and consumers emptied the shelves of supermarkets.

In short, artificially low prices led to supplies being reduced while the quantity demanded by consumers increased. For example, more American cattle began to be exported, mostly to Canada, instead of being sold in the price-controlled U.S. market. Thus price controls produced essentially the same results under the Nixon administration as they had produced in the Roman Empire under Diocletian, in Russia under the Communists, in Ghana under Nkrumah, and in numerous other times and places where such policies had been tried before.

Nor was this particular policy unique politically in how it was conceived and carried out. Veteran economic adviser Herbert Stein observed, 25 years after the Nixon administration meeting at which he had been present, "failure to look ahead is extremely common in government policy making."

Another way of saying the same thing is that political time horizons tend to be much shorter than economic time horizons. Before the full negative economic consequences of the wage and price control policies became widely apparent, Nixon had been re-elected with a landslide victory at the polls. There is no "present value" factor to force political decision-makers to take into account the long-run consequences of their current decisions.

One of the important fields neglected as a result of the short political time horizon is education. As a writer in India put it, "No one bothers about education because results take a long time to come." This is not peculiar to India. With fundamental educational reform being both difficult and requiring years to show end results in a better educated population entering adulthood, it is politically much more expedient for elected officials to demonstrate immediate "concern" for education by voting to spend increasing amounts of the taxpayers' money on it, even if that leads only to more expensive incompetence in more showy buildings.

The constraints within which government policy-making operates are as important as the incentives. Important and beneficial as a framework of rules of law may be, what that also means is that many matters must be dealt with categorically, rather than incrementally, as in a market economy. The application of categorical laws prevents the enormous powers of government from being applied at the discretion or whim of individual bureaucratic functionaries, which would invite both corruption and arbitrary oppression.

Since there are many things which require discretionary incremental adjustments, as noted in Chapter 4, for these things categorical laws can be difficult to apply or can produce counterproductive results. For example, while prevention of air pollution and water pollution are widely recognized as legitimate functions of government, which can achieve more economically efficient results in this regard than those of the free market, doing so through categorical laws can create major problems. Despite the political appeal of categorical phrases like "clean water" and "clean air," there are in fact no such things, never have been, and perhaps never will be. Moreover, there are diminishing returns in removing impurities from water or air.

Reducing truly dangerous amounts of impurities from water or air may be done at costs that most people would agree were quite reasonable. But, as higher and higher standards of purity are prescribed by government, in order to eliminate ever more minute traces of ever more remote or more questionable dangers, the costs escalate out of proportion to the benefits. Even if removing 98 percent of a given impurity costs twice as much as eliminating 97 percent, and removing 99 percent costs ten times as much, the political appeal of categorical phrases like "clean water" may be just as potent when the water is already 99 percent pure as when it was dangerously polluted. That was demonstrated back in the 1970s:

> The Council of Economic Advisers argued that making the nation's streams 99 percent pure, rather than 98 percent pure, would have a cost far exceeding its benefits, but Congress was unmoved.

Depending on what the particular impurity is, minute traces may or may not pose a serious danger. But political controversies over impurities in the water are unlikely to be settled at a scientific level when passions can be whipped up in the name of non-existent "clean water." No matter how pure the water becomes, someone can always demand the removal of more impurities. And, unless the public understands the logical and economic implications of what is being said, that demand can become politically irresistible, since no public official wants to be known as being opposed to clean water.

It is not even certain that reducing extremely small amounts of substances that are harmful in larger amounts reduces risks at all. Even arsenic in the water— in extremely minute traces— has been found to have health benefits. An old saying declares: "It is the dose that makes the poison." Similar research findings apply to many substances, including saccharin and alcohol. Although high doses of saccharin have been shown to increase the rate of cancer in laboratory rats, very low doses seem to *reduce* the rate of cancer in these rats. Although a large intake of alcohol shortens people's lifespans in many ways, very modest amounts of alcohol— like one glass of wine or beer per day— tend to reduce life-threatening conditions like hypertension.

If there is some threshold amount of a particular substance required before it becomes harmful, that makes it questionable whether spending vast amounts of money to try to remove that last fraction of one percent from the air or water is necessarily going to make the public safer by even a minute amount. But what politician wants to be known as someone who blocked efforts to remove arsenic from water?

The same principle applies in many other contexts, where minute traces of impurities can produce major political and legal battles— and consume millions of tax dollars with little or no net effect on the health or safety of the public. For example, one legal battle raged for a decade over the impurities in a New Hampshire toxic waste site, where these wastes were so diluted that children could have eaten some of the dirt there for 70 days a year without any significant harm— if there had been any children living or playing there, which there were not.

As a result of spending more than nine million dollars, the level of impurities was reduced to the point where children could have safely eaten the dirt there 245 days a year. Moreover, without anything being done at all, both parties to the litigation agreed that more than half the volatile impurities would have evaporated by the year 2000. Yet hypothetical dangers to hypothetical children kept the issue going and kept money being spent.

With environmental safety, as with other kinds of safety, some forms of safety in one respect create dangers in other respects. California, for example, required a certain additive to be put into all gasoline sold in that state, in order to reduce the air pollution from automobile exhaust fumes. However, this new additive tended to leak from filling station storage tanks and automobile gas tanks, polluting the ground water in the first case and leading to more automobile fires in the second. Similarly, government-mandated air bags in automobiles, introduced to save lives in car crashes, have themselves killed small children.

These are all matters of incremental trade-offs to find an optimal amount and kind of safety, in a world where being categorically safe is as impossible as achieving 100 percent clean air or clean water. Incremental trade-offs are made all the time in individual market transactions, but it can be politically suicidal to oppose demands for more clean air, clean water or automobile safety. Therefore saying that the government *can* improve over the results of individual transactions in a free market is not the same as saying that it *will* in fact do so.

Among the greatest external costs imposed in a society can be those imposed politically by legislators and officials who pay no costs whatever, while imposing billions of dollars in costs on others, in order to respond to political pressures from advocates of particular interests or ideologies.

In the United States, government regulations are estimated to cost about $7,800 per employee in large businesses and about $10,600 per employee in small businesses. Among other things, this suggests that the existence of numerous government regulations tends to give competitive advantages to big business, since there are apparently economies of scale in complying with these regulations.

This is not peculiar to the United States. In some Islamic countries, getting lending practices to comply with the requirements of Islamic law can require more complex and more costly financial arrangements than in Western countries. However, once a financial institution in the Islamic world has had one of these legal documents created at great cost, that same document can be used innumerable times for similar transactions— far more often than a smaller business can, because the smaller business has fewer transactions. As *The Economist* magazine reported:

> Financiers can recycle documentation rather than drawing it up from scratch. The contracts they now use for *sharia*-compliant mortgages in America draw on templates originally drafted at great cost for aircraft leases.

While government regulations may be defended by those who create them by referring to the benefits which such regulations provide, the economically relevant question is whether such benefits are worth the hundreds of billions of dollars in aggregate costs that they impose in the United States. In the marketplace, whoever creates $500 billion in costs will have to be sure to create more than $500 billion in benefits that customers will pay for. Otherwise that producer would risk bankruptcy.

In the government, however, there are seldom any incentives or constraints to force such comparisons. If any new government regulation can plausibly be claimed to solve some problem or create some benefit, then that is usually enough to permit government officials to go forward with that regulation. Since there are also some conceivable benefits that might be created from other government regulations, and costs will be paid by the taxpayers, there are incentives to keep adding more regulations and few constraints on their growth. The number of pages in *The Federal Register*, where government regulations are compiled, almost always keeps increasing. One of the rare times when there was a reduction was during the Reagan administration in the 1980s. But, after the Reagan administration was over, the increase in the number of pages in *The Federal Register* resumed.

Just as we must keep in mind a sharp distinction between the goals of a particular policy and the actual consequences of that policy, so we must keep in mind a sharp distinction between the purpose for which a particular law was created and the purposes for which that law can be used. For example, President Franklin D. Roosevelt took the United States off the gold standard in 1933 under presidential powers created by laws passed during the First World War to prevent trading with enemy nations. Though that war had been over for more than a dozen years and the United States no longer had any enemy nations, the power was still there to be used for wholly different purposes.

Powers do not expire when the crises that created them have passed. Nor does the repeal of old laws have a high priority among legislators. Still less are institutions likely to close up on their own when the circumstances that caused them to be created no longer exist.

When thinking of government functions, we often assume that particular activities are best undertaken by government, rather than by non-governmental institutions, simply because that is the way those activities have been carried out in the past. The delivery of mail is an obvious example. Yet when India allowed private companies to deliver mail, the amount of mail carried by the government's postal service dropped from 16 billion pieces in 1999 to less than 8 billion by 2005. India has also been among the many countries which have had government-owned telephone companies but, after this field was also opened up to private companies these companies have "driven the quality of service up and rates down on everything from local to long-distance to cellular service to Internet connections," according to the *Wall Street Journal*.

Neither particular powers nor particular activities of government should be taken for granted as necessary to be performed by government simply because they have been in the past. Both need to be examined in terms of their incentives, constraints, and track records.

Quite aside from the particular merits or demerits of particular government policies or programs, there are other considerations to take into account when expanding the role of government. These were expressed more than a century ago by John Stuart Mill:

> Every function superadded to those already exercised by the government, causes its influence over hopes and fears to be more widely diffused, and converts, more and more, the active and ambitious part of the public into hangers-on of the government, or of some party which aims at becoming the government. If the roads, the railways, the banks, the insurance offices, the great joint-stock companies, the universities, and the public charities, were all of them branches of government; if, in addition, the municipal corporations and local boards, with all that now devolves on them, became departments of the central administration; if the employés of all these different enterprises were appointed and paid by the

government, and looked to the government for every rise in life; not all
the freedom of the press and popular constitution of the legislature
would make this or any other country free otherwise than in name.

Chapter 19

GOVERNMENT FINANCE

The willingness of government to levy taxes fell distinctly short of its propensity to spend.

Arthur F. Burns

L ike individuals, businesses, and other organizations, governments must have resources in order to continue to exist. In centuries past, some governments would take these resources directly in the form of a share of the crops, livestock or other tangible assets of the population but, in modern industrial and commercial societies, governments take a share of the national output in the form of money. However, these financial transactions have repercussions on the economy that go far beyond money changing hands.

Consumers can change what they buy when some of the goods they use are heavily taxed and other goods are not. Businesses can change what they produce when some kinds of output are taxed and others are subsidized. Investors can decide to put their money into tax-free municipal bonds, or into some foreign country with lower tax rates, when taxes on the earnings from their investments rise— and they can reverse these decisions when tax rates fall. In short, people change their behavior in response to government financial operations. These operations include taxation, the sale of government bonds and innumerable ways of spending money currently, or promising to spend future money, such as by guaranteeing bank deposits or establishing pension systems to cover some or all of the population when they retire.

The government of the United States spent nearly $3.5 trillion in 2013. One of the ways of dealing with the many complications of government financial operations is to break them down into the ways that governments raise money and the ways that they spend money— and then examine each separately, in terms of the repercussions of these operations on the economy as a whole. In fact, the repercussions extend beyond national boundaries to other countries around the world.

Acquiring wealth has long been one of the main preoccupations of governments, whether in the days of the Roman Empire, in the ancient Chinese dynasties or in modern Europe or America. Today, tax revenues and bond sales are usually the largest sources of money for the national government. The choice between financing government activities with current tax revenues or with revenues from the sale of bonds— in other words, going into debt— has further repercussions on the economy at large. As in many other areas of economics, the facts are relatively straightforward, but the words used to describe the facts can lead to needless complications and misunderstandings. Some of the words used in discussing the financial operations of the government— "balanced budget," "deficit," "surplus," "national debt"— need to be plainly defined in order to avoid misunderstandings or even hysteria.

If all current government spending is paid for with money received in taxes, then the budget is said to be balanced. If current tax receipts exceed current spending, there is said to be a budget surplus. If tax revenues do not cover all of the government's spending, some of which is covered by revenues from the sale of bonds, then the government is said to be operating at a deficit, since bonds are a debt for the government to repay in the future. The accumulation of deficits over time adds up to the government's debt, which is called "the national debt." If this term really meant what it said, the national debt would include all the debts in the nation, including those of consumers and businesses. But, in practice, the term "national debt" means simply the debt owed by the national government.

Just as the government's revenues come in from many sources, so government spending goes out to pay for many different things. Some spending is for things to be used during the current year— the pay of civilian and military personnel, the cost of electricity, paper, and other supplies required by the vast array of government institutions. Other spending is for things to be used both currently and in the future, such as highways, bridges, and hydroelectric dams.

Although government spending is often all lumped together in media and political discussions, the particular kind of spending is often related to the particular way money is raised to pay for it. For example, taxes may be considered an appropriate way for current taxpayers to pay for spending on current benefits provided by government, but issuing government bonds may be considered more appropriate to have future generations help pay for things being created for their future use or benefit, such as the highways, bridges and dams already mentioned. In the case of city governments, subways and public libraries are built to serve both the current generation and future generations, so the costs of building them are appropriately shared between current and future generations by paying for their construction with both current tax revenues and money raised by selling bonds that will be redeemed with money from future taxpayers.

GOVERNMENT REVENUES

Government revenues come not only from taxes and the sale of bonds, but also from the prices charged for various goods and services that governments provide, as well as from the sale of assets that the government owns, such as land, old office furniture, or surplus military equipment. Charges for various goods and services provided by local, state or national governments in the United States range from municipal transit fares and fees for using municipal golf courses to charges for entering national parks or for cutting timber on federal land.

The prices charged for goods and services sold by the government are seldom what they would be if the same goods or services were sold by businesses in a free market— and therefore government sales seldom have the same effect on the allocation of scarce resources which have alternative uses. In short, these transactions are not simply transfers of money but, more fundamentally, transfers of tangible resources in ways that affect the efficiency with which the economy operates.

During the pioneering era in America, the federal government of the United States sold to the public vast amounts of land that it had acquired in various ways from the indigenous population or from foreign governments such as those of France, Spain, Mexico and Russia. In centuries past, governments in Europe and elsewhere often also sold monopoly rights to engage in various economic activities, such as selling salt or importing gold. During the late twentieth century, many national governments around the world that had taken over various industrial and commercial enterprises began selling them to private investors, in order to have a more market-directed economy. Another way for governments to get money to spend is simply to print it, as many governments have done at various periods of history. However, the disastrous consequences of the resulting inflation have made this too risky politically for most governments to rely on this as a common practice. Even when the Federal Reserve System of the United States resorted to the creation of more money, as a policy for dealing with a sluggish economy in the early twenty-first century, the Federal Reserve coined a new term— "quantitative easing"— that many people would not understand as readily as they would understand a more straightforward term like "printing money."

Tax Rates and Tax Revenues

"Death and taxes" have long been regarded as inescapable realities. But which of the various ways in which taxes can be collected is actually used, and which particular tax rate is imposed, makes a difference in the way individuals, enterprises, and the national economy as a whole respond. Depending on those responses, a higher tax *rate* may or may not lead to higher tax *revenues*, or a lower tax rate to lower tax revenues.

When tax rates are raised 10 percent, it may be assumed by some that tax revenues will also rise by 10 percent. But in fact more people may move out of a heavily taxed jurisdiction, or buy less of a heavily taxed commodity, so that the revenues received can be disappointingly far below what was estimated. The revenues may, in some cases, go down after the tax rate goes up.

When the state of Maryland passed a higher tax rate on people earning a million dollars a year or more, taking effect in 2008, the number of such people living in Maryland fell from nearly 8,000 to fewer than 6,000. Although it had been projected that the additional tax revenue collected from these people in Maryland would rise by $106 million, instead these revenues *fell* by $257 million. When Oregon raised its income tax rates in 2009 on people earning $250,000 or more, Oregon's income tax revenues likewise *fell* by $50 billion.

Conversely, when the federal tax rate on capital gains was lowered in the United States from 28 percent to 20 percent in 1997, it was assumed that revenues from the capital gains tax would fall below the $54 billion collected under the higher rates in 1996 and below the $209 billion that had been projected to be collected over the next four years, before the tax rate was cut. Instead, tax revenues from the capital gains tax *rose* after the capital gains tax rate was cut and $372 billion were collected in capital gains taxes over the next four years, nearly twice what had been projected under the old and higher tax rates.

People adjusted their behavior to a more favorable outlook for investments by increasing their investments, so that the new and lower tax rate on the returns from these increased investments amounted to more total revenue for the government than that produced by the previous higher tax rate on a smaller amount of investment. Instead of keeping their money in tax-exempt municipal bonds, for example, investors could now find it more advantageous to invest in producing real goods and services with a higher rate of return, now that lower tax rates enabled them to keep more of their gains. Tax-exempt securities usually pay lower rates of return than securities whose returns are subject to taxation.

As a hypothetical example, if tax-exempt municipal bonds are paying 3 percent and taxable corporate bonds are paying 5 percent, then someone who is in an income bracket that pays 50 percent in taxes is better off getting the tax-exempt 3 percent from municipal bonds than to have 2.5 percent left after half of the 5 percent return on corporate bonds has been taxed away. But, if the top tax rate is cut to 30 percent, then it pays someone in that same income bracket to buy the corporate bonds instead, because that will leave 3.5 percent after taxes. Depending on how many people are in that income bracket and how many bonds they buy, the government can end up collecting more tax revenues after cutting the tax rates.

None of this should be surprising. Many a business has become more profitable by charging lower prices, thereby increasing sales and earning higher total profits at a lower rate of profit per sale. Taxes are the prices charged by governments, and sometimes the government too can collect more total revenue at a lower tax rate. It all depends on how high the tax rates are initially and how people react to an increase or a decrease. There are other times, of course, where a higher tax rate leads to a correspondingly higher amount of tax revenues and a lower tax rate leads to a lower amount of tax revenues.

The failure of tax revenues to automatically move in the same direction as tax rates is not peculiar to the United States. In Iceland, as the corporate tax rate was gradually reduced from 45 percent to 18 percent between 1991 and 2001, tax revenues tripled. High-income people in Britain have relocated to avoid impending increases in tax rates, just as such people have in Maryland and Oregon. In 2009, for example, the *Wall Street Journal* reported: "A stream of hedge-fund managers and other financial-services professionals are quitting the U.K., following plans to raise the top personal tax rates to 51%. Lawyers estimate hedge funds managing close to $15 billion have moved to Switzerland in the past year, with more possibly to come."

Although it is common in politics and in the media to refer to government's "raising taxes" or "cutting taxes," this terminology blurs the crucial distinction between tax *rates* and tax *revenues*. The government can change tax rates but the reaction of the public to these changes can result in either a higher or a lower amount of tax revenues being collected, depending on circumstances and responses. Thus references to proposals for a "$500 billion tax cut" or a "$700 billion tax increase" are wholly misleading because all that the government can enact is a change in tax rates, whose actual effects on revenue can be determined only later, after the tax rate changes have gone into effect and the taxpayers respond to the changes.

The Incidence of Taxation

Knowing who is legally required to pay a given tax to the government does not automatically tell us who in fact ultimately bears the burden created by that tax— a burden which in some cases can be passed on to others, and in other cases cannot.

Who pays how much of the taxes collected by the government?

This question cannot be answered simply by looking at tax laws or even at a table of estimates based on those laws. As we have already seen, people may react to tax changes by changing their own behavior, and different people have different abilities to change their behavior, in order to avoid taxes.

While an investor can invest in tax-free bonds at a lower rate of return or in other assets that pay a higher rate of return, but are subject to taxes, a factory worker whose sole income is his paycheck has no such options, and finds whatever taxes the government takes already gone by the time he gets that paycheck. Various complex financial arrangements can spare wealthy people from having to pay taxes on all their income but, since these complex arrangements require lawyers, accountants and other professionals to make such arrangements, people of more modest incomes may not be equally able to escape their tax burden, and can even end up paying a higher percentage of their income in taxes than someone who is in a higher income bracket that is officially taxed at a higher rate.

Since income is not the only thing that is taxed, how much total tax any given individual pays depends also on how many other taxes apply and what that individual's situation is. Obviously, taxes on homes or automobiles fall only on those who own them and, while sales taxes fall on whoever buys any of the many items subject to those taxes, different people spend different proportions of their income on consumer goods. Lower income people tend to spend a higher percentage of their income on consumer goods, while higher income people tend to invest more— sometimes most— of their income.

The net effect is that sales taxes tend to take a higher percentage of the incomes of low-income people than they take from the incomes of higher-income people. This is called a "regressive" tax, as distinguished from a "progressive" tax that subjects higher incomes to a higher percentage rate of taxation. Social Security taxes are likewise regressive, since they apply only to incomes up to some fixed level, with income above that level not being subject to Social Security taxes. Income taxes, on the other hand, exempt incomes below some fixed level. Given the different rules for different kinds of taxation, figuring out what the total incidence of taxation is for different people is not easy in principle, much less in practice.

Issues and controversies about tax rates often discuss the incidence of taxes on "the rich" or "the poor," when in fact the taxes fall on income rather than wealth. A genuinely rich person, someone with enough wealth not to have to work at all, may have a very modest income or no income at all during a given year. Moreover, even during years of high incomes and high rates of taxation on that income, this taxation does not touch the rich individual's accumulated wealth. Most of the people described as "rich" in discussions of tax issues are in fact not rich at all but simply people who have reached their peak earnings years, often having worked their way up to that peak after decades of earning much more modest salaries. Progressive income taxes typically hit such people rather than the genuinely rich.

Since each individual pays a mixture of progressive and regressive taxes, as well as taxes that apply to some goods and not to others, it is by no means easy to determine who is actually paying what share of the country's taxes.

What is even more difficult is to determine who bears the real burden of a given tax by suffering the consequences of changed outcomes. For example, American employers pay half of the taxes that support Social Security and all of the taxes that pay for unemployment compensation. However, as we have seen in Chapter 10, how high an employer is willing to bid for a worker's services is limited by the amount that will be added to the employer's revenue by hiring that worker. But an employee whose output adds $50,000 to a company's sales receipts may not be worth even $45,000, if Social Security taxes, unemployment taxes, and other costs of employment add up to $10,000. In that case, the upper limit to how far an employer would bid for that person's services would be $40,000, not $50,000.

Even though the worker does not directly pay any of that $10,000, if the pay received by that worker is $10,000 less than it would be otherwise, then the burden of these taxes has in effect fallen on the worker, no matter who sends the tax money to the government. It is much the same story when taxes are levied on businesses which then raise their prices to the consumer. Depending on the nature of the tax and the competition in the market, the consumers can end up paying anywhere from none to all of the burden of those taxes. In short, the official legal liability for the direct payment of taxes to the government does not necessarily tell who really bears the economic burden in the end.

Taxes cannot be passed on to consumers when a particular tax falls on businesses or products produced in a particular place, if consumers have the option of buying the same product produced in other places not subject to the same tax. As noted in Chapter 6, if the government of South Africa imposes a tax of $10 an ounce on gold, South African gold cannot be sold in the world market for $10 an ounce more than gold produced in other countries where that tax does not apply, since gold is gold as far as consumers are concerned, regardless of where it was produced. The price of gold produced and sold *within* South Africa could rise by $10 an ounce if the South African government forbad the importation of gold from countries without such a tax. Even in the absence of a ban on the importation of gold, the price of gold could rise somewhat within South Africa if there were transportation costs of, say, $2 an ounce for gold produced in the nearest other gold-producing countries. But, in that case, only $2 an ounce of the tax could be passed on to the South African consumers as a price increase, and South African gold producers would have to absorb the other $8 in tax increases themselves, as well as absorbing the entire $10 for gold that they sell outside South Africa.

Whatever the product and whatever the tax, where the actual burden of that tax falls in practice depends on many economic factors, not just on who is compelled by law to deliver the money to the government.

Inflation can change the incidence of taxation in other ways. Under what is called "progressive taxation," people with higher incomes pay not only a higher amount of taxes but also a higher percentage of their incomes. During periods of substantial inflation, people of modest means find their dollar incomes rising as the cost of living rises, even if on net balance they are unable to purchase any more real goods and services than before. But, because tax laws are written in terms of money, citizens with only average levels of income can end up paying a higher percentage of their incomes in taxes when their money incomes rise to levels once reached by affluent or wealthy people. In short, the combination of inflation and progressive income taxation laws means rising tax rates for a given real income, even when the tax laws remain unchanged. Conversely, a period of deflation means falling tax rates on a given real income.

Where income is in the form of capital gains, the effect of inflation is accentuated because of the years that can elapse between the time when an investment is made and the time when that investment begins to pay a return— or is expected to pay a return, since expectations are by no means always fulfilled. If an investment of a million dollars is made by a business and the price level doubles over the years, that investment will become worth two million dollars *even if it has failed to earn anything*. Because tax laws are based on value expressed in money, that business will now have to pay taxes on the additional million dollars, even though the real value of the investment has failed to grow in the years since it was made.

Whatever the losses sustained by such businesses, the larger and more fundamental question is the effect of inflation on the economy as a whole. Since financial markets make investments— or decline to make investments— on the basis of the anticipated returns, during a period of sustained inflation and substantial tax rates on capital gains, these markets are less willing to make investments at rates of return that would otherwise cause them to invest, because the effective tax rates on real capital gains are higher and taxes may be collected even where there is no real capital gain at all. Declining levels of investment mean declining economic activity in general and declining job opportunities. According to a business economist:

> From the late 1960s to the early 1980s, effective tax rates on capital averaged more than 100%. Perhaps it is no coincidence that real equity values [stock prices adjusted for inflation] collapsed by nearly two-thirds from 1968 to 1982. This period saw sputtering productivity, rising inflation, high unemployment, and an American economy in general decline.

Local Taxation

Taxation of course occurs at both the national and the local levels. In the United States, local property taxes supply much of the revenue used by local governments. Like other governmental units, local governments tend to want to maximize the revenues they receive, which in turn enables local officials to maximize the favorable publicity they receive from spending money in ways that will increase their chances of re-election. At the same time, raising tax *rates* produces adverse political reactions, which can reduce these officials' re-election prospects.

Among the ways used by local officials to escape this dilemma has been one also used by national officials: Issue bonds to pay for much of current spending, thereby producing immediate benefits to dispense and thereby gain votes, while in effect taxing future taxpayers who will have to pay the bondholders when the bonds reach their maturity dates. Since future taxpayers include many who are too young to vote currently— including some who are yet unborn— current deficit spending maximizes the current political benefits to current officials while minimizing effects from current taxpayers and voters.

One of the things that makes deficit spending especially attractive to local politicians is that many municipal and state bonds are tax-exempt. That makes such bonds especially valuable to people with high incomes, when the federal taxes on such incomes are very high. Among the repercussions of this are that large sums of money are often available to finance local projects with tax-exempt bonds, regardless of whether these projects would meet any criterion based on weighing costs against benefits. What the high-income purchaser of these bonds is paying for is exemption of income from federal taxation. Unlike purchasers of bonds or stocks in the private economy, the purchaser of tax-exempt local government securities has no vested interest in whether the particular things financed by these securities achieve whatever their object is. Even if these debt-financed expenditures turn out to be a complete failure in achieving whatever they were supposed to achieve, the taxpayers are nevertheless forced to pay the bondholders.

From the standpoint of the allocation of scarce resources which have alternative uses in the economy, the net result is that these politically chosen projects are able to receive more resources than they would in a private free market, including resources that would be more valuable elsewhere. From the standpoint of government revenue, what is gained by the local government is being able to readily sell its bonds that pay a lower interest rate than private securities whose purchasers have to pay taxes on that interest. What is gained financially by the local government may be a fraction of what is lost financially by the federal government that is unable to tax the income on these local bonds. Finally, what is lost by the local taxpayers— albeit in the future— is having to pay higher taxes because of the ease of financing politically chosen projects with tax-exempt bonds.

Another way of raising local tax revenues without raising local tax rates is to replace low-valued property with higher-valued property, since the latter yields more tax revenue at a given tax rate. This replacement can be achieved by condemning as "blighted" the housing and businesses in low-income or even moderate-income neighborhoods, acquiring the property through the power of eminent domain and then transferring it to other private enterprises that will build upscale shopping malls, hotels, or casinos, for example, which will generate more tax revenue than the existing homeowners and business owners were paying.

The outraged homeowners and business owners, who often receive less in compensation than the market value of their demolished property, are usually a sufficiently small percentage of the voting population that local officials can gain votes on net balance— if they calculate accurately. It is often possible to convince others in the media and in the public that it is these dispossessed tenants, homeowners, and business owners who are "selfish" in opposing "progress" for the whole community.

This apparent progress can be illustrated with pictures taken before and after local "redevelopment," showing newer and more upscale neighborhoods replacing the old. But much of this local progress may be part of a zero-sum process nationally, when things that would have been built in one place are built in another place because confiscated property costs less to the new owners than it would have cost elsewhere in a free market. But the new owners' financial gain is the original owners' financial loss. Even if the original owners were compensated at the full market value of their properties, this may still be less than the property was worth to them, since they obviously had not sold their property before it was taken from them through the power of eminent domain. In this case, there is not simply a zero-sum process but a negative-sum process, in which what is gained by some is exceeded by what is lost by others.

The 2005 U.S. Supreme Court decision in *Kelo v. New London* expanded the powers of governments to take property under the powers of eminent domain for "public purposes," extending beyond the Constitution's authorization of taking private property for "public use" such as building reservoirs, bridges, or highways. This decision confirmed the power already being exercised to transfer private property from one user to another, even if the latter were simply building amusement parks or other recreational facilities.

What this means economically, in terms of the allocation of scarce resources which have alternative uses, is that the alternative uses no longer have to be of higher value than the original uses, since the alternative users no longer have to bid the property away from the original owners. Instead, those who want the property can rely on government officials to simply take it, exercising the power of eminent domain, and then sell it to them for less than they would have had to pay the existing property owners to get the latter to transfer the property to them voluntarily.

Government Bonds

Selling government bonds is simply borrowing money to be repaid from future tax revenues. Government bonds can also be a source of confusion under their other name, "the national debt." These bonds, like all bonds, are indeed a debt but the economic significance of a given amount of debt can vary greatly according to the circumstances. That is as true for the government as it is for an individual.

What would be a huge debt for a factory worker may be insignificant for a millionaire who can easily pay it off at his convenience. Similarly, a national debt that would be crushing when a nation's income is low may be quite manageable when national income is much higher. Thus, although the U.S. national debt held by the public reached a record high in 2004, it was only 37 percent of the country's Gross Domestic Product at that time, while a much smaller debt, decades earlier, was a higher percentage of the GDP back in 1945, when the U.S. national debt was more than 100 percent of the GDP that year.

Like other statistical aggregates, the national debt tends to grow over time as population and the national income grow, and as inflation causes a given number of dollars to represent smaller amounts of real wealth or real liabilities. This presents political opportunities for critics of whatever party is in power to denounce their running up record-breaking debts to be paid by future generations. Depending on the specific circumstances of a particular country at a particular time, this may be a reason for serious concern or the criticisms may be simply political theater.

National debts must be compared not only to national output or national income but also to the alternatives facing a given nation at a given time. For example, the federal debt of the United States in 1945 was $258 billion, at a time when the national income was $182 billion. In other words, the national debt was 41 percent *higher* than the national income, as a result of paying the enormous costs of fighting World War II. The costs of *not* fighting the Nazis or imperial Japan were considered to be so much worse that the national debt seemed secondary at the time.

Even in peacetime, if a nation's highways and bridges are crumbling from a lack of maintenance and repair, that does not appear in national debt statistics, but neglected infrastructure is a burden being passed on to the next generation, just as surely as a national debt would be. If the costs of repairs are worth the benefits, then issuing government bonds to raise the money needed to restore this infrastructure makes sense— and the burden on future generations may be no greater than if the bonds had never been issued, though it takes the form of money owed rather than the form of crumbling and perhaps dangerous infrastructure that may become even more costly to repair in the next generation, due to continued neglect.

Either wartime or peacetime expenditures by the government can be paid for out of tax revenues or out of money received from selling government bonds. Which method makes more economic sense depends in part on whether the money is being spent for a current flow of goods and services, such as electricity or paper for government agencies or food for the military forces, or is instead being spent for adding to an accumulated stock of capital, such as hydroelectric dams or national highways to be used in future years for future generations.

Going into debt to create long-term investments makes as much sense for the government as a private individual's borrowing more than his annual income to buy a house. By the same token, people who borrow more than their annual income to pay for lavish entertainment this year are simply living beyond their means and probably heading for big financial trouble. The same principle applies to government expenditures for current benefits, with the costs being passed on to future generations.

What must also be taken into account when assessing a national debt is to whom it is owed. When a government sells all of its bonds to its own citizens, that is very different from selling all or a substantial part of its bonds to people in other countries. The difference is that an internal debt is held by the same population that is responsible for paying the taxes to redeem the principal and pay the interest. "We owe it to ourselves" is a phrase sometimes used to describe this situation. But, when a significant share of the bonds issued by the U.S. government is bought by people in China or Japan, then the bond-holders and the taxpayers are no longer the same population. Future generations of Chinese and Japanese will be able to collect wealth from future generations of Americans. As of 2011, nearly half the federal debt of the United States— 46 percent— was held by foreigners.

Even when a national debt is held entirely by citizens of the country that issued the bonds, different individuals hold different shares of the bonds and pay different shares of the taxes. Much also depends on how members of future generations acquire the bonds issued to the current generation. If the next generation simply inherits the bonds bought by the current generation, then they inherit both the debt and the wealth required to pay off the debt, so that there is no net burden passed on from one generation to the next. If, however, the older generation sells its bonds to the younger generation— either directly from individual to individual or by cashing in the bonds, which the government pays for by issuing new bonds to new people— then the burden of the debt may be liquidated, as far as the older generation is concerned, and passed on to the next generation.

Financial arrangements and their complications should not obscure what is happening in terms of real goods and services. When the United States fought World War II, running up a huge national debt did not mean that the Americans alive at that time got something for nothing on credit. The tanks, bombers, and other military equipment and supplies used to fight the war came out of the American economy at that time— at the expense of consumer goods that would otherwise have been produced by American industry. These costs were not paid for by borrowing from people in other countries. American consumers simply consumed a smaller share of American output.

Financially, the war was paid for by a mixture of raising taxes and selling bonds. But, whatever the particular mixture, that did not relieve that generation from having to sacrifice their standard of living to fight the war. The burden of paying for World War II could be passed on to a later generation only in the sense that the World War II generation could in later years be reimbursed for their sacrifice by the sale of the bonds they had bought during the war. In reality, however, wartime inflation meant that the real purchasing power of the bonds when they were cashed in was not as much as the purchasing power that had been sacrificed to buy the bonds during the war. The World War II generation was permanently stuck with the losses this entailed.

In general, the government's choice of acquiring money through the collection of taxes or the sale of government bonds does not relieve the current population of its economic burden unless the government sells the bonds to foreigners. Even in that case, however, this merely postpones the burden. The choice may be more significant politically to the government itself, as it may encounter less resistance when it does not raise taxes to cover all current spending but relies on bond sales to supplement its tax revenues. This convenience for the government is a temptation to use bond sales to cover current expenses instead of reserving such sales to cover spending on long-term projects. There are obvious political benefits available to those currently in power by spending money to provide benefits to current voters and passing the costs on to those currently too young to vote, including those who are not yet born.

Although government bonds get paid off when they reach their maturity dates, usually new bonds are issued and sold, so that the national debt is turned over rather than being paid off, though at particular periods of history some countries have paid off their national debts, either partially or completely. This does not mean that selling government bonds is without costs or risks. The cost to the government includes the interest that must be paid on the national debt. The more important cost to the economy is the government's absorption of investment funds that could otherwise have gone into the private sector, where they would have added to the country's capital equipment.

When the national debt reaches a size where investors begin to worry about whether it can continue to be turned over as government bonds mature, without raising interest rates to attract the needed buyers, that can lead to expectations that higher interest rates will inhibit future investment— an expectation that can immediately inhibit current investment. Rising interest rates for government bonds tend to affect other interest rates, which also rise, due to competition for investment funds in the financial markets— and that in turn tends to reduce credit and the aggregate demand on which continuing prosperity depends.

How serious such dangers are depends on the size of the national debt— not absolutely but relative to the nation's income. Professional financiers and investors know this, and so are unlikely to panic even when there is a record-breaking national debt, *if* that is not a large debt relative to the size of the economy. That is why, despite much political rhetoric about the American government's budget deficit and the growing national debt it created in the early twenty-first century, distinguished economist Michael Boskin could say in 2004: "Wall Street yawned when the deficit projections soared." The financiers were vindicated when the size of the deficit in 2005 declined below what it had been in 2004. The *New York Times* reported:

> The big surprise has been in tax revenue, which is running nearly 15 percent higher than in 2004. Corporate tax revenue has soared about 40 percent, after languishing for four years, and individual tax revenue is up as well.

Surprise is in the eye of the beholder. There was nothing unprecedented about rising tax *revenues* without an increase in tax *rates*. Indeed, there have been at various times and places increases in tax revenues following a cut in tax rates.

While the absolute size of the national debt may overstate the economic risks to the economy under some conditions, it may also *understate* the risks under other circumstances. Where the government has large financial liabilities looming on the horizon, but not yet part of the official budget, then the official national debt may be considerably less than what the government owes.

After the financial crises in the housing industry in early twenty-first century America, for example, the Federal Housing Administration had far less money on hand than they were supposed to have, in proportion to the mortgages that they had guaranteed. As more mortgages defaulted, it was only a matter of time before the Federal Housing Administration would have to turn to the Treasury Department for more money. But any such transfer of money from the Treasury would add to the official annual deficit and thus to the national debt, which could be a political embarrassment before an election.

Thus, although the *Wall Street Journal* reported in 2009 that the Federal Housing Administration's "capital reserves have fallen to razor-thin levels, increasing the likelihood the agency will eventually require a taxpayer bailout," that bailout did not come until 2013— the year after the 2012 elections.

When the Treasury Department supplied the FHA with $1.7 billion, only then did the government's financial liability enter the official annual federal deficit and become part of the national debt. Yet it would be politically impossible for any administration to let the FHA default on its mortgage guarantees, so this financial liability was always just as real as anything that was included in the official national debt, even before the Treasury bailout actually occurred.

As the national debt of the United States rose in 2013 to nearly $17 trillion—just over 100 percent of Gross Domestic Product— Wall Street was no longer yawning, as Professor Boskin put it nine years earlier.

It is one thing to have a national debt as large as the Gross Domestic Product, or larger, at the end of a major war, for the return of peace means drastic reductions in military spending, which presents an opportunity to begin paying down that national debt over the ensuing years. But to have a comparable national debt in peacetime presents more grim options, because there is no indication of the kind of reduction of government spending which occurs at the end of a war.

Charges for Goods and Services

As already noted, both local and national governments charge for providing various goods and services. These charges are often quite different from what they would be in a free market because the incentives facing officials who set these charges are different. Therefore the allocation of scarce resources which have alternative uses is also different.

Mass transportation in cities was once provided by private businesses which charged fares that covered both current expenses— fuel, the pay of bus drivers, etc.— and the longer run costs of buying new buses, trolleys, or subway trains to replace those that wore out, as well as paying a rate of return on the capital provided by investors sufficient to keep investors supplying this capital. Over the years, however, many privately owned municipal transit systems became government-owned. Often this was because the fares were regulated by municipal authorities and were not allowed to rise enough to continue to maintain the transit system, especially during periods of inflation. In New York City, for example, the five-cent subway fare remained politically sacred for years, even during periods of high inflation when all other prices were rising, including the prices paid for the equipment, supplies, and labor used to keep the subways running.

Clearly, privately owned subway systems were no longer viable under these money-losing conditions, so the ownership of these systems passed to the city government. While municipal transit was still losing money, the losses were now being made up out of tax revenues.

Incentives to stop the losses, which would have been imperative in a privately owned business faced with financial extinction, were now much weaker, if not non-existent, in a municipally owned transit system whose losses were automatically covered by tax revenues. Thus a service could continue to be provided at costs exceeding the benefits for which passengers were willing to pay. Put differently, resources whose value to people elsewhere in the economy was greater were nevertheless being allocated to municipal transit because of subsidies extracted from taxpayers.

Incentives to price government-provided goods and services at lower levels than in a private business are by no means confined to municipal transit. Since lower prices mean more demanded than at higher prices, those who set prices for government-provided goods and services have incentives to assure a sufficient continuing demand for the goods and services they sell and therefore continuing jobs for themselves. Moreover, since lower prices are less likely to provoke political protests and pressures than are higher prices, the jobs of those controlling the sales of government-provided goods and services are easier, as well as more secure and less stressful when prices are kept below the level that would prevail in a free market, where costs must be covered by sales revenues.

In situations where the money paid by those people who are using the goods and services goes into the general treasury, rather than into the coffers of the particular government agency which is providing these goods and services, there is even less incentive to make the charges cover the costs of providing the goods and services. For example, the fees collected for entering Yosemite, Yellowstone, or other national parks go into the U.S. government's treasury and the costs of maintaining these parks are paid from the treasury, which is to say, from general tax revenues. There is therefore no incentive for officials who run national parks to charge fees that will cover the costs of running those parks.

Even where a national park is considered to be overcrowded and its facilities deteriorating from heavy use, there is still no incentive to raise the entry fees, when what matters is how much money Congress will authorize to be paid out of general tax revenues. In short, the normal function provided by prices of causing consumers to ration themselves and producers to keep costs below what consumers are willing to pay is non-existent in these situations.

The independence of prices from costs offers political opportunities for elected or appointed officials to cater to particular special interests by offering lower prices to the elderly, for example. Thus senior citizens are charged a one-time $10 fee for a pass that entitles the holders to enter any national park free for the rest of their lives, while others may be charged $25 each time they enter any national park. The fact that the elderly usually have greater net worth than the general population may carry less weight politically than the fact that the elderly are more likely to vote.

Although there are many contexts in which government-provided goods and services are priced below cost, there are other contexts in which these services are priced well above their costs. Bridges, for example, are often built with the idea that the tolls collected from bridge users over the years will eventually cover the cost of building it. However, it is not uncommon for the tolls to continue to be collected long after the original cost has been covered several times over, and when the tolls necessary to cover maintenance and repairs are a fraction of the money that continues to be charged to cross the bridge.

Where the particular government agency in charge of a bridge is allowed to keep the tolls it collects, there is every incentive to use that money to undertake other projects— that is, to expand the bureaucratic empire controlled by those in charge of the agency. The bridge authority may decide, for example, to initiate or subsidize ferry service across the same waterway spanned by the bridge, in order to meet an "unmet need" of commuters. As already noted in the first chapter, there are always "unmet needs" in any economy and, at a sufficiently low fare on the ferries, there will be people using those ferries— politically demonstrating that "need"— even if what they pay does not come close to covering the cost of the ferry service.

In short, resources will be allocated to the ferry that would never be allocated there if both the bridge and the ferry were independent operations in a free market, and therefore each had to cover its costs from the prices charged. More important, ferries can be allocated resources whose value is greater in alternative uses.

In California, for example, the two million ferry rides annually from San Francisco to Sausalito and to Larkspur are subsidized by about $15 per ride, or about $30 million total. On the ferry service from South San Francisco to Oakland and Alameda that began in 2012, the average fare charged per round trip was set at $14, with the subsidy from taxpayers and toll payers combined being $94 per round trip. No doubt this new ferry provides a service that benefits the riders. But the relevant question economically is whether these benefits cover the costs— $108 per round trip in this case, of which only $14 is paid by the riders. The only way to determine whether the benefits are really worth the cost of $108 per round trip is to charge $108 per round trip. But there are no incentives for the officials who run the ferry service to do that, when subsidies are readily available from taxpayers and bridge users.

Sometimes taxpayer-provided subsidies for some government-provided goods and services are said to be justified because otherwise "the poor" would be unable to obtain these goods and services. Putting aside for the moment the question whether most of "the poor" are a permanent class or simply people transiently in low income brackets (including young people living with middle-class or affluent parents), and even accepting for the sake of argument that it is somehow imperative that "the poor" use the particular goods and services in question, subsidizing *everybody* who uses those goods and services in order to help a fraction of the population seems less efficient than directly helping "the poor" with money or vouchers and letting the others pay their own way.

The same principle applies when considering cross-subsidies provided, not by the taxpayers, but by excessive charges on some people (such as toll bridge users) to subsidize others (such as ferry boat riders). The weakness of the rationale based on subsidizing "the poor" is shown also by how often taxpayer subsidies are used to finance things seldom used by "the poor," such as municipal golf courses or symphony orchestras.

In general, government charges for goods and services are not simply a matter of transferring money but of redirecting resources in the economy, usually without much concern for the allocation of those resources in ways that maximize net benefits to the population at large.

GOVERNMENT EXPENDITURES

The government spends both voluntarily and involuntarily. Officials may voluntarily decide to create a new program or department, or to increase or decrease their appropriations. Alternatively, the government may be forced by pre-existing laws to pay unemployment insurance when a downturn in the economy causes more people to lose their jobs. Government spending may also go up automatically when farmers produce such a bumper crop that it cannot all be sold at the prices guaranteed under agricultural subsidy laws, and so the government is legally obligated to buy the surplus. Unemployment compensation and agricultural subsidies are just two of a whole spectrum of "entitlement" programs whose spending is beyond the control of any given administration, once these programs have been enacted into law. Only repeal of existing entitlement legislation can stop the spending— and that means offending all the existing beneficiaries of such legislation, who may be more numerous than those whose support made that legislation possible in the first place.

In short, although government spending and the annual deficits and accumulated national debts which often result from that spending are often blamed on those officials who happen to be in charge of the government at a given time, much of the spending is not at their discretion but is mandated by pre-existing laws. In the U.S. budget for fiscal year 2008, for example, even the military budget for a country currently at war was exceeded by non-discretionary spending on Medicare, Medicaid and Social Security.

Government spending has repercussions on the economy, just as taxation does— and both the spending going out and the tax revenues coming in are to some extent beyond the existing administration's control. When production and employment go down in the economy, the tax revenues collected from businesses and workers tend to go down as well. Meanwhile, unemployment compensation, farm subsidies and other outlays tend to go up. This means that the government is spending more money while receiving less. Therefore, on net balance, government is adding purchasing power to the economy during a downturn, which tends to cushion the decline in output and employment.

Conversely, when production and employment are booming, more tax revenues come in and there are fewer individuals or enterprises receiving government financial help, so the government tends to be removing purchasing power from the economy at a time when there might otherwise be inflation. These institutional arrangements are sometimes called "automatic stabilizers," since they counter upward or downward movements in the economy without requiring any given administration to make any decisions.

Sometimes more is claimed for government spending than the reality will support. Many government programs, whether at local or national levels, are often promoted by saying that, in addition to whatever other benefits are claimed, the money will be spent and respent, creating some multiple of the wealth represented by the initial expenditure. In reality, any money— government or private— that is spent will be respent again and again. In so far as the government takes money from one place— from taxpayers or from those who buy government bonds— and transfers it somewhere else, the loss of purchasing power in one place offsets the gain in purchasing power elsewhere. Only if, for some reason, the government is more likely to spend the money than those from whom it was taken, is there a net increase in spending for the country as a whole. John Maynard Keynes' historic contribution to economics was to spell out the conditions under which this was considered likely, but Keynesian economics has been controversial on this and other grounds.

The Keynesian policy prescription for getting an economy out of a recession or depression is for the government to spend more money than it receives in tax revenue. This deficit spending adds to the aggregate monetary demand in the economy, according to Keynesian economists, leading to more purchases of goods and services, thereby requiring more hiring of workers, and thus reducing unemployment. Dissenters and critics of Keynesian policies have argued that markets can restore employment better through the normal adjustment processes than government intervention can. But neither Keynesian economists nor economists of the rival Chicago School represented by Milton Friedman have advocated the kind of ad hoc government interventions in markets actually followed by both the Republican administration of Herbert Hoover and the Democratic administration of Franklin D. Roosevelt during the Great Depression of the 1930s.

Costs vs. Expenditures

When discussing government policies or programs, the "cost" of those policies or programs is often spoken of without specifying whether that means the cost to the government or the cost to the economy. For example, the cost to the government of forbidding homes or businesses to be built in certain areas is only the cost of running the agencies in charge of controlling such things, which can be a very modest cost, especially after knowledge of the law or policy becomes widespread and few people would consider incurring legal penalties for trying to build in the forbidden areas. But, although such a ban on building may cost the government very little, it can cost the economy many billions of dollars by forbidding the creation of valuable assets.

Conversely, it may cost the government large sums of money to build and maintain levees along the banks of a river but, if the government did not spend this money, the people could suffer even bigger losses from floods.

When the cost of any given policy is considered, it is important to be very clear as to *whose costs* are being discussed or considered— the cost to the government or the cost to the economy.

One of the objections to building more prisons to lock up more criminals for longer periods of time is that it costs the government a large amount of money per criminal per year to keep them behind bars. Sometimes a comparison is made between the cost of keeping a criminal in prison versus the cost of sending someone to college for the same period of time. However, the relevant alternative to the costs of incarceration is the costs sustained by the public when career criminals are outside of prison. In early twenty-first century Britain, for example, the financial costs of crime have been estimated at £60 billion, while the total costs of prisons were less than £3 billion. Government officials are of course preoccupied with the prison costs that they have to cover rather than the £60 billion that others must pay. In the United States, it has been estimated that the cost of keeping a career criminal behind bars is at least $10,000 a year *less* than the cost of having him at large.

Another area where government expenditures are a grossly misleading indicator of the costs to the country are land acquisition costs under either "redevelopment" programs or "open space" policies. When local government officials merely begin discussing publicly the prospect of "redeveloping" a particular neighborhood by tearing down existing homes and businesses there, under the power of eminent domain, that alone is enough to discourage potential buyers of homes or businesses in that neighborhood, so that the present values of those homes and businesses begin declining long before any concrete action is taken by the government.

By the time the government acts, which may be years later, the values of properties in the affected neighborhood may be far lower than before the redevelopment plan was discussed. Therefore, even if the property owners are paid "just compensation," as required by law, what they are compensated for is the reduced value of their property, not its value before government officials began discussing plans to redevelop the area. Therefore government compensation expenditures may be far less than the actual costs to the society of losing these particular resources.

It is much the same principle when land use restrictions in the name of "open space" or "smart growth" reduce the value of land because home builders and others are now prevented from using the land and no longer bid for it. The owners of that land now have few, if any, potential buyers besides some local government agency or some non-profit group that wants the land kept as "open space." In either case, the money spent to acquire this land can completely understate the cost to the society of no longer having this resource available for alternative uses. As elsewhere, the real costs of any resources, under any economic policy or system, are the alternative uses of those resources. The prices at which the artificially devalued land is transferred completely understate the value of its alternative uses in a free market.

Benefits vs. Net Benefits

The weighing of costs against benefits, which is part of the allocation of scarce resources which have alternative uses, can be greatly affected by government expenditures.

While there are some goods and services which virtually everyone considers desirable, different people may consider them desirable to different degrees and are correspondingly willing to pay for them to different degrees. If some Product X costs ten dollars but the average person is willing to pay only six dollars for it, then that product will obviously be purchased by only a minority, even if the vast majority regard Product X as desirable to some extent. Such situations provide political opportunities to those holding, or seeking to be elected to, government offices.

What is a common situation from an economic standpoint can be redefined politically as a "problem"— namely that most people want something that costs more than they feel like paying for it. The proposed solution to this problem is often that the government should in one way or another make this widely desired product more "affordable" to more people. Price control is likely to reduce the supply, so the more viable options are government subsidies for the production of the desired product or government subsidies for its purchase. In either case, the public now pays for the product through both the prices paid directly by the purchasers and the taxes paid by the population at large.

For the price of this particular ten-dollar product to become "affordable"— that is, to cost what most people are willing to pay— that price can be no higher than six dollars. Therefore a government subsidy of at least four dollars must make up the difference, and taxes or bond sales must provide that additional money. The net result, under these conditions, is that millions of people will be paying ten dollars— counting both taxes and the price of the commodity— for something that is worth only six dollars to them. In short, government finance in such cases creates a misallocation of scarce resources which have alternative uses.

A more realistic scenario would be that the costs of running the government program must be added to the costs of production, so that the total cost of the product would rise above the initial ten dollars, making the misallocation of resources greater. Moreover, it is unlikely that the price would be reduced only to that level which the average person was willing to pay, since that would still leave half the population unable to buy the product at a price that they are willing to pay. A more politically likely scenario would be that the price would be reduced below six dollars and the cost rise above ten dollars.

Many government expenditure patterns that would be hard to explain in terms of the costs and benefits to the public are by no means irrational in terms of the incentives and constraints facing elected officials responsible for these patterns. It is, for example, not uncommon to find governments spending money on building a sports stadium or a community center at a time when the maintenance of roads, highways, and bridges is neglected.

The cost of damage done to all the cars using roads with potholes may greatly exceed the cost of repairing the potholes, which in turn may be a fraction of the cost of building a shiny new community center or an impressive sports stadium. Such an expenditure pattern is irrational only if government is conceived of as the public interest personified, rather than as an organization run by elected officials who put their own interests first, as people do in many other institutions and activities.

The top priority of an elected official is usually to get re-elected, and that requires a steady stream of favorable publicity to keep the official's name before the public in a good light. The opening of any major new facility, whether urgently needed or not, creates such political opportunities by attracting the media to ribbon-cutting ceremonies, for example. Filling potholes, repairing bridges, or updating the equipment at a sewage treatment plant creates no ribbon-cutting ceremonies or occasions for speeches by politicians. The pattern of government expenditures growing out of such incentives and constraints is not new or limited to particular countries. Adam Smith pointed out a similar pattern back in eighteenth century France:

> The proud minister of an ostentatious court may frequently take pleasure in executing a work of splendour and magnificence, such as a great highway, which is frequently seen by the principal nobility, whose applauses not only flatter his vanity, but even contribute to support his interest at court. But to execute a great number of little works, in which nothing that can be done can make any great appearance, or excite the smallest degree of admiration in any traveller, and which, in short, have nothing to recommend them but their extreme utility, is a business which appears in every respect too mean and paultry to merit the attention of so great a magistrate.

GOVERNMENT BUDGETS

Government budgets, including both taxes and expenditures, are *not* records of what has already happened. They are plans or predictions about what is going to happen. But of course no one really knows what is going to happen, so everything depends on how projections about the future are made. In the United States, the Congressional Budget Office projects tax receipts without fully taking into account how tax rates tend to change economic behavior— and how changed economic behavior then changes tax receipts. For example, the Congressional Budget Office advised Congress that raising the capital gains tax rate from 20 percent to 28 percent in 1986 would increase the revenue received from that tax— but in fact the *revenues* from this tax fell after the tax *rate* was raised. Conversely, cuts in the capital gains tax rate in 1978, 1997, and 2003 all led to increased revenues from that tax.

Undaunted, the Congressional Budget Office estimated that an extension of a temporary reduction in the capital gains tax to 15 percent would cost the Treasury $20 billion in lost revenues— even though this temporary tax cut had already resulted in tens of billions of dollars in *increased* revenues. From 2003 through 2007, the disparities between the Congressional Budget Office's estimates of tax receipts were off by growing amounts— under-estimating tax receipts by $13 billion in 2003 and by $147 billion in 2007. Many in the media reason the same way the Congressional Budget Office reasons— and are caught by surprise when tax revenues do not follow those beliefs. "An unexpectedly steep rise in tax revenues from corporations and the wealthy is driving down the projected budget deficit this year," the *New York Times* reported in 2006.

A year later, the deficit had fallen some more and was now just over one percent of the Gross Domestic Product. Moreover, a growing proportion of all the federal tax revenues came from the highest income earners, despite widespread use of the phrase "tax cuts for the rich." Back in 1980, when the highest marginal tax rate was 70 percent on the top income earners, before the series of tax cuts that began in the Reagan administration, 37 percent of all income tax revenues came from the top 5 percent of income earners. After a series of "tax cuts for the rich" over the years had reduced the highest marginal tax rate to 35 percent by 2004, now more than half of all income tax revenues came from the top 5 percent.

Nevertheless the phrase "tax cuts for the rich" has continued to flourish in politics and in the media. As Justice Oliver Wendell Holmes once said, catchwords can "delay further analysis for fifty years." When it comes to tax policy, such catchwords have delayed analysis even longer.

Neither the Congressional Budget Office nor anyone else can predict with certainty the consequences of a given tax rate increase or decrease. It is not just that the exact amount of revenue cannot be predicted. Whether revenue will move in one direction or in the opposite direction is not a foregone conclusion. The choice is among alternative educated guesses— or, what is worse, mechanically calculating how much revenue will come in if no one's behavior changes in the wake of a tax change. Behavior has changed too often, and too dramatically, to proceed on that assumption. As far back as 1933, John Maynard Keynes observed that "taxation may be so high as to defeat its object," and that, "given sufficient time to gather the fruits, a reduction of taxation will run a better chance, than an increase, of balancing the Budget."

Since budgets are *not* records of what has already happened, but projections of what is supposed to happen in the future, everything depends on what assumptions are made— and by whom. While the Congressional Budget Office issues projections of what future costs and payments are expected to be, the assumptions from which they derive these projections are provided by Congress. If Congress assumes an unrealistically high rate of economic growth, and therefore a far higher intake of tax revenues, the Congressional Budget Office is required to make its projections of future budget deficits or surpluses based on Congress' assumptions, whether those assumptions are realistic or unrealistic. The media or the public may treat the Congressional Budget Office's estimates as the product of a non-partisan group of economists and statisticians, but the assumptions provided by politicians are what ultimately determines the end results.

A similar situation exists at the state level, whether the assumptions provided by politicians are about growth rates, rates of return on the government's investments or any of the many other factors that go into making estimates of the government's finances.

When the state of Florida estimated in 2011 how far the money it had set aside to pay its employees' pensions fell short of what was needed to pay those pensions, it proceeded on the arbitrary assumption that it would receive an annual rate of return of 7.75 percent on the investments it made with that money. But if in fact it turned out to receive only 7 percent, this difference of less than one percentage point would translate into being nearly $14 billion deeper in debt.

If Florida received only a 5 percent rate of return on its investment of the money set aside to pay these pensions, that would produce a shortfall nearly five times what the state officially estimated, based on a 7.75 percent rate of return. Because Florida had in fact received only a 2.6 percent rate of return on this investment in the previous ten years, these comparisons show the enormous potential for deception when preparing government budgets, simply by changing the arbitrary assumptions on which those budget projections are based.

Florida was not unique. As the British magazine *The Economist* put it, "nearly all states apply an optimistic discount rate to their obligations, making the liabilities seem smaller than they are." Among the reasons: "Governors and mayors have long offered fat pensions to public servants, thus buying votes today and sending the bill to future taxpayers."

Chapter 20

SPECIAL PROBLEMS IN THE NATIONAL ECONOMY

Demagoguery beats data in making public policy.

Congressman Dick Armey

Economic decisions affect more than the economy. They affect the scope of government power and the growth of government financial obligations, including— but not limited to— the national debt. There are also sometimes misconceptions of the nature of government, leading to unrealistic demands being made on it, followed by hasty denunciations of the "stupidity" or "irrationality" of government officials when those demands are not met. To understand many issues in the national economy requires some understanding of political processes as well as economic processes.

THE SCOPE OF GOVERNMENT

While some decisions are clearly political decisions and others are clearly economic decisions, there are large areas where choices can be made through either process. Both the government and the marketplace can supply housing, transportation, education and many other things. For those decisions that can be made either politically or economically, it is necessary not only to decide which particular outcome would be preferred but also which process offers the best prospect of actually reaching that outcome. This in turn requires understanding how each process works in practice, under their respective incentives and constraints, rather than how they should work ideally.

The public can express their desires either through choices made in the voting booth or choices made in the marketplace. However, political choices are offered less often and are usually binding until the next election. Moreover, the political process offers "package deal" choices, where one candidate's whole spectrum of positions on economic, military, environmental, and other issues must be accepted or rejected as a whole, in comparison with another candidate's spectrum of positions on the same range of issues. The voter may prefer one candidate's position on some of these issues and another candidate's position on other issues, but no such choice is available on election day. By contrast, consumers make their choices in the marketplace every day and can buy one company's milk and another company's cheese, or ship some packages by Federal Express and other packages by United Parcel Service. Then they can change their minds a day or a week later and make wholly different choices.

As a practical matter, virtually no one puts as much time and close attention into deciding whether to vote for one candidate rather than another as is usually put into deciding what job to take or where to rent an apartment or buy a house. Moreover, the public usually buys finished products in the marketplace, but can choose only among competing promises in the political arena. In the marketplace, the strawberries or the car that you are considering buying are right before your eyes when you make your decision, while the policies that a candidate promises to follow must be accepted more or less on faith— and the eventual consequences of those policies still more so. Speculation is just one aspect of a market economy but it is the essence of elections.

On the other hand, each voter has the same single vote on election day, whereas consumers have very different amounts of dollars with which to express their desires in the marketplace. However, these dollar differences may even out somewhat over a lifetime, as the same individual moves from one income bracket to another over the years, although the differences are there as of any given time.

The influence of wealth in the marketplace makes many prefer to move decisions into the political arena, on the assumption that this is a more level playing field. However, among the things that wealth buys is more and better education, as well as more leisure time that can be devoted to political activities and the mastering of legal technicalities. All this translates into a disproportionate influence of wealthier people in the political process, while the fact that those who are not rich often have more money in the aggregate than those who are may give ordinary people more weight in the market than in the political or legal arena, depending on the issue and the circumstances.

Too often there has been a tendency to regard government as a monolithic decision-maker or as the public interest personified. But different elements within the government respond to different outside constituencies and are often in opposition to one another for that reason, as well as because of jurisdictional frictions among themselves. Many things done by government officials in response to the particular incentives and constraints of the situations in which they find themselves may be described as "irrational" by observers but are often more rational than the assumption that these officials represent the public interest personified.

Politicians like to come to the rescue of particular industries, professions, classes, or racial or ethnic groups, from whom votes or financial support can be expected— and to represent the benefits to these groups as net benefits to the country. Such tendencies are not confined to any given country but can be found in modern democratic states around the world. As a writer in India put it:

> Politicians lack the courage to privatize the huge, loss-making public sector because they are afraid to lose the vote of organized labor. They resist dismantling subsidies for power, fertilizers, and water because they fear the crucial farm vote. They won't touch food subsidies because of the massive poor vote. They will not remove thousands of inspectors in the state governments, who continuously harass private businesses, because they don't want to alienate government servants' vote bank. Meanwhile, these giveaways play havoc with state finances and add to our disgraceful fiscal deficit. Unless the deficit comes under control, the nation will not be more competitive; nor will the growth rate rise further to 8 and 9 percent, which is what is needed to create jobs and improve the chances of the majority of our people to actualize their capabilities in a reasonably short time.

While such problems may be particularly acute in India, they are by no means confined to India. In 2002, the Congress of the United States passed a farm subsidy bill— with bipartisan support— that has been estimated to cost the average American family more than $4,000 in inflated food prices over the following decade. Huge financial problems have been created in Brazil by such generous pensions to government employees that they can retire in a better economic condition than when they were working.

One of the pressures on governments in general, and elected governments in particular, is to "do something"— even when there is nothing they can do that is likely to make things better and much that they can do that will risk making things worse. Economic processes, like other processes, take time but politicians may be unwilling to allow these processes the time to run their course, especially when their political opponents are advocating quick fixes, such as wage and price controls during the Nixon administration or restrictions on international trade during the Great Depression of the 1930s.

In the twenty-first century, it is virtually impossible politically for any American government to allow a recession to run its course, as American governments once did for more than 150 years prior to the Great Depression, when both Republican President Herbert Hoover and then Democratic President Franklin D. Roosevelt intervened on an unprecedented scale. Today, it is widely assumed as axiomatic that the government must "do something" when the economy turns down. Very seldom does anyone compare what actually happens when the government does something with what has happened when the government did nothing.

The Great Depression

While the stock market crash of October 1929 and the ensuing Great Depression of the 1930s have often been seen as examples of the failure of market capitalism, it is by no means certain that the stock market crash made mass unemployment inevitable. Nor does history show better results when the government decides to "do something" compared to what happens when the government does nothing.

Although unemployment rose in the wake of the record-setting stock market crash of 1929, the unemployment rate peaked at 9 percent two months after the crash, and then began a trend generally downward, falling to 6.3 percent in June 1930. Unemployment never reached 10 percent for any of the 12 months following the stock market crash of 1929. But, after a series of major and unprecedented government interventions, the unemployment rate soared over 20 percent for 35 consecutive months.

These interventions began under President Herbert Hoover, featuring the Smoot-Hawley tariffs of 1930— the highest tariffs in well over a century— designed to reduce imports, so that more American-made products would be sold, thereby providing more employment for American workers. It was a plausible belief, as so many things done by politicians seem plausible. But a public statement, signed by a thousand economists at leading universities around the country, warned against these tariffs, saying that the Smoot-Hawley bill would not only fail to reduce unemployment but would be counterproductive.

None of this, however, dissuaded Congress from passing this legislation or dissuaded President Hoover from signing it into law in June 1930. Within five months, the unemployment rate reversed its decline and rose to double digits for the first time in the 1930s— and it never fell below that level for any month during the entire remainder of that decade, as one massive government intervention after another proved to be either futile or counterproductive.

What of the track record when the government refused to "do something" to counter a downturn in the economy? Since the massive federal intervention under President Hoover was unprecedented, the whole period between the nation's founding in 1776 and the 1929 stock market crash was essentially a "do nothing" era, as far as federal intervention to counter a downturn.

No downturn during that long era was as catastrophic as the Great Depression of the 1930s became, after massive government intervention under both the Hoover administration and the Roosevelt administration that followed. Yet there was a downturn in the economy in 1921 that was initially more severe than the downturn in the twelve months immediately following the stock market crash of October 1929. Unemployment in the first year of President Warren G. Harding's administration was 11.7 percent. Yet Harding did nothing, except reduce government spending as tax revenues declined— the very opposite of what would later be advocated by

Keynesian economists. The following year unemployment fell to 6.7 percent, and the year after that to 2.4 percent.

Even after it became a political axiom, following the Great Depression of the 1930s, that the government had to intervene when the economy turned down, that axiom was ignored by President Ronald Reagan when the stock market crashed in 1987, breaking the record for a one-day decline that had been set back in 1929. Despite outraged media reaction at his failure to act, President Reagan let the economy recover on its own. The net result was an economy that in fact recovered on its own, followed by what *The Economist* later called 20 years of "an enviable combination of steady growth and low inflation."

These were not controlled experiments, of course, so any conclusions must be suggestive rather than definitive. But, at the very least, the historical record calls into question whether a stock market crash must lead to a long and deep depression. It also calls into question the larger issue whether it was the market or the government that failed in the 1930s— and whether a "do something" policy must produce a better result than a "do nothing" policy.

Monetary Policy

Even a nominally independent agency like the Federal Reserve System in the United States operates under the implicit threat of new legislation that can both counter its existing policies and curtail its future independence. In 1979, the distinguished economist Arthur F. Burns, a former chairman of the Federal Reserve System, looked back on the efforts of the Federal Reserve under his chairmanship to try to cope with a growing inflation. As the Federal Reserve "kept testing and probing the limits of its freedom," he said, "it repeatedly evoked violent criticism from both the Executive establishment and the Congress and therefore had to devote much of its energy to warding off legislation that could destroy any hope of ending inflation."

More fundamental than the problems that particular monetary policies may cause is the difficulty of crafting any policies with predictable outcomes in complex circumstances, when the responses of millions of other people to their perception of a policy can have consequences as serious as the policy itself. Economic problems that are easy to solve as theoretical exercises can be far more challenging in the real world. Merely estimating the changing dimensions of the problem is not easy. Federal Reserve forecasts of inflation during the 1960s and 1970s under-estimated how much inflation was developing, under the chairmanship of both William McChesney Martin and Arthur F. Burns. But during the subsequent chairmanships of Paul Volcker and Alan Greenspan, the Federal Reserve over-estimated what the rate of inflation would be.

Even a successful monetary policy is enveloped in uncertainties. Inflation, for example, was reduced from a dangerous 13 percent per year in 1979 to a negligible 2 percent by 2003, but this was done through a series of trial-and-error monetary actions, some of which proved to be effective, some ineffective— and all with painful repercussions on the viability of businesses and on unemployment among workers. As the Federal Reserve tightened money and credit in the early 1980s, in order to curb inflation, unemployment rose while bankruptcies and business failures rose to levels not seen in decades.

During this process, Federal Reserve System chairman Paul Volcker was demonized in the media and President Ronald Reagan's popularity plummeted in the polls for supporting him. But at least Volcker had the advantage that Professor Burns had not had, of having support in the White House. However, not even those who had faith that the Federal Reserve's monetary policy was the right one for dealing with rampant inflation had any way of knowing how long it would take— or whether Congress' patience would run out before then, leading to legislation restricting the Fed's independent authority. One of the governors of the Federal Reserve System during that time later reported his own reactions:

> Did I get sweaty palms? Did I lie awake at night? The answer is that I did both. I was speaking before these groups all the time, home builders and auto dealers and others. It's not so bad when some guy gets up and yells at you, "You SOB, you're killing us." What really got to me was when this fellow stood up and said in a very quiet way, "Governor, I've been an auto dealer for thirty years, worked hard to build up that business. Next week, I am closing my doors." Then he sat down. That really gets to you.

The tensions experienced by those who had the actual responsibility for dealing with the real world problem of inflation were in sharp contrast with the serene self-confidence of many economists in previous years, who believed that economics had reached the point where economists could not merely deal in a general way with recession or inflation problems but could even "fine tune" the economy in normal times. The recommendations and policies of such confident economists had much to do with creating the inflation that the Federal Reserve was now trying to cope with. As a later economist and columnist, Robert J. Samuelson, put it:

> As we weigh our economic prospects, we need to recall the lessons of the Great Inflation. Its continuing significance is that it was a self-inflicted wound: something we did to ourselves with the best of intentions and on the most impeccable of advice. Its intellectual godfathers were without exception men of impressive intelligence. They were credentialed by some of the nation's outstanding universities: Yale, MIT, Harvard, Princeton. But their high intellectual standing did not make their ideas any less impractical or destructive. Scholars can have tunnel vision, constricted by their own political or personal agendas. Like politicians, they can also yearn for the power and celebrity of the public arena. Even if their intentions are pure, their ideas may be mistaken. Academic pedigree alone is no guarantor of useful knowledge and wisdom.

GOVERNMENT OBLIGATIONS

In addition to what the government currently spends, it has various legal obligations to make future expenditures. These obligations are specified and quantified in the case of government bonds that must be redeemed for various amounts of money at various future dates. Other obligations are open-ended, such as legal obligations to pay whoever qualifies for unemployment compensation or agricultural subsidies in the future. These obligations are not only open-ended but difficult to estimate, since they depend on things beyond the government's control, such as the level of unemployment and the size of farmers' crops.

Other open-ended obligations that are difficult to estimate are government "guarantees" of loans made by others to private borrowers or guarantees to those who lend to foreign governments. These guarantees appear to cost nothing, so long as the loans are repaid— and the fact that these guarantees cost the taxpayers nothing is likely to be trumpeted in the media by the advocates of such guarantees, who can point out how businesses and jobs were saved, without any expense to the government. But, at unpredictable times, the loans do not get paid and then huge amounts of the taxpayers' money get spent to cover one of these supposedly costless guarantees.

When the U.S. government guaranteed the depositors in savings and loan associations that their deposits would be covered by government insurance, this appeared to cost nothing until these savings and loan associations ran up losses of more than $500 billion— the kind of costs incurred in fighting a war for several years— and their depositors were reimbursed by the federal government after these enterprises collapsed.

Among the largest obligations of many governments are pensions that have been promised to future retirees. These are more predictable, given the size of the aging population and their mortality rates, but the problem here is that very often there is not enough money put aside to cover the promised pensions. This problem is not peculiar to any given country but is widespread among countries around the world, since elected officials everywhere benefit at the polls by promising pensions to people who vote, but stand to lose votes by raising tax rates high enough to pay what it would cost to redeem those promises. It is easier to leave it to future government officials to figure out how to deal with the later financial shortfall when the time comes to actually pay the promised pensions.

The difference between political incentives and economic incentives is shown by the difference between government-provided pensions and annuities provided by insurance companies. Government programs may be analogized to the activities of insurance companies by referring to these programs as "social insurance," but without in fact having either the same incentives, the same legal obligations or the same results as private insurance companies selling annuities. The most fundamental difference between private annuities and government pensions is that the former create real wealth by investing premiums, while the latter create no real wealth but simply use current premiums from the working population to pay current pensions to the retired population.

What this means is that a private annuity invests the premiums that come in— creating factories, apartment buildings, or other tangible assets whose earnings will later enable the annuities to be paid to those whose money was used to create these assets. But government pension plans, such as Social Security in the United States, simply spend the premiums as they are received. Much of this money is used to pay pensions to current retirees, but the rest of the money can be used to finance other government activities, ranging from fighting wars to paying for Congressional junkets. There is no wealth created in this process to be used in the future to pay the pensions of those who are currently paying into the system. On the contrary, part of the wealth paid into these systems by current workers is siphoned off to finance whatever other government spending Congress may choose.

The illusion of investment is maintained by giving the Social Security trust fund government bonds in exchange for the money that is taken from it and spent on other government programs. But these bonds likewise represent no tangible assets. They are simply promises to pay money collected from future taxpayers. The country as a whole is not one dollar richer because these bonds were printed, so there is no analogy with private investments that create tangible wealth. If there were no such bonds, then future taxpayers would still have to make up the difference when future Social Security premiums are insufficient to pay pensions to future retirees. That is exactly the same as what will have to happen when there are bonds. Accounting procedures may make it seem that there is an investment when the Social Security system holds government bonds, but the economic reality is that neither the government nor anyone else can spend and save the same money.

What has enabled Social Security— and similar government pension plans in other countries— to postpone the day of reckoning is that a relatively small generation in the 1930s was followed by a much larger "baby boom" generation of the 1940s and 1950s. Because the baby boom generation earned much higher incomes, and therefore paid much larger premiums into the Social Security system, the pensions promised to the retirees from the previous generation could easily be paid. Not only could the promises made to the 1930s generation be kept, additional benefits could be voted for them, with obvious political advantages to those awarding these additional benefits.

With the passage of time, however, a declining birthrate and an increasing life expectancy reduced the ratio of people paying into the system to people receiving money from the system. Unlike a private annuity, where premiums paid by each generation create the wealth that will later pay for its own pensions, government pensions pay the pensions of the retired generation from the premiums paid by the currently working generation. That is why private annuities are not jeopardized by the changing demographic makeup of the population, but government pension plans are.

Government pension plans enable current politicians to make promises which future governments will be expected to keep. These are virtually ideal political conditions for producing generous pension benefits— and future financial crises resulting from those generous benefits. Nor are such incentives and results confined to the United States. Countries of the European Union likewise face huge financial liabilities as the size of their retired populations continues to grow, not only absolutely but also relative to the size of the working populations whose taxes are paying their pensions. Moreover, the pensions in European Union countries tend to be more readily available than in the United States.

In Italy, for example, working men retire at an average age of 61 and those working in what are defined as "arduous" occupations— miners, bus drivers, and others— retire at age 57. The cost of this generosity consumes 15 percent of the country's Gross Domestic Product, and Italy's national debt in 2006 was 107 percent of the country's GDP. Belatedly, Italy *raised* the minimum retirement age to 59. As France, Germany and other European countries began to scale back the generosity of their government pension policies, political protests caused even modest reforms to be postponed or trimmed back. But neither the financial nor the political costs of these government pensions were paid by the generation of politicians who created these policies, decades earlier.

Local governments operate under much the same set of political incentives as national governments, so it is not surprising that employees of local governments, and of enterprises controlled or regulated by local governments, often have very generous pensions. Not only may employees of New York's Long Island Rail Road, run by the Metropolitan Transportation Authority, retire in their fifties, the vast majority of these retirees also receive disability payments in addition to their pensions, even though most made no disability claims while working, but only after retiring. In 2007, for example, "94 percent of career employees who retired from the Long Island Rail Road after age 50 then received disability benefits," according to the *New York Times*. Far from reflecting work hazards, these post-retirement disability claims are part of a whole web of arcane work rules under union contracts that permit employees to collect two days' pay for one day's work and permitted one engineer to collect "five times his base salary" one year and later be classified as disabled after retirement, according to the *New York Times*.

In Brazil, government pensions are already paying out more money than they are taking in, with the deficits being especially large in the pensions for unionized government employees. In other words, the looming financial crisis which American and European governments are dreading and trying to forestall has already struck in Brazil, whose government pensions have been described as "the most generous in the world." According to *The Economist*:

> Civil servants do not merely retire on full salary; they get, in effect, a pay rise because they stop paying contributions into the system. Most women retire from government service at around 50 and men soon afterwards. A soldier's widow inherits his pension, and bequeaths it to her daughters.

Given that Brazil's civil servants are an organized and unionized special interest group, such generosity is understandable politically. The question is whether the voting public in Brazil and elsewhere will understand the economic consequences well enough to be able to avoid the financial crises to which such unfunded generosity can lead— in the name of "social insurance." Such awareness is beginning to dawn on people in some countries. In New Zealand, for example, a poll found that 70 percent of New Zealanders under the age of 45 believe that the pensions they have been promised will not be there for them when they retire.

In one way or another, the day of reckoning seems to be approaching in many countries for programs described as "social insurance" but which were in fact never insurance at all. Such programs not only fail to create wealth, the more generous retirement plans may in fact lessen the rate at which wealth is created, by enabling people to retire while they are still quite capable of working and thus adding to the nation's output. For example, while 62 percent of the people in the 55 to 64 year old bracket in Japan are still working and 60 percent in the United States, only 41 percent of the people in that age bracket are still working in the countries of the European Union.

It is not just the age at which people retire that varies from country to country. How much their pensions pay, compared to how much they made while working, also varies greatly from one country to another. While pensions in the United States pay about 40 percent of pre-retirement earnings and those in Japan less than 40 percent, pensions in the Netherlands and Spain pay about 80 percent and, in Greece, 96 percent. No doubt that has something to do with when people choose to stop working. It also has something to do with the financial crises that struck some European Union countries in the early twenty-first century.

While the United States has long lagged behind European industrial nations in government-provided or government-mandated benefits, it has in more recent years been increasing such benefits rapidly. Unemployment insurance benefits, which used to end after 26 weeks in the United States, have been extended to 99 weeks. Other alternatives to working have also increased in their utilization— disability pay under Social Security "insurance," for example:

> Barely three million Americans received work-related disability checks from Social Security in 1990, a number that had changed only modestly in the preceding decade or two. Since then, the number of people drawing disability checks has soared, passing five million by 2000, 6.5 million by 2005, and rising to nearly 8.6 million today.

MARKET FAILURE AND

GOVERNMENT FAILURE

The imperfections of the marketplace— including such things as external costs and benefits, as well as monopolies and cartels— have led many to see government interventions as necessary and beneficial. Yet the imperfections of the market must be weighed against the imperfections of the government whose interventions are prescribed. Both markets and governments must be examined in terms of their incentives and constraints.

The incentives facing government enterprises tend to result in very different ways of carrying out their functions, compared to the way things are done in a free market economy. After banks were nationalized in India in 1969, for example, uncollectible debts rose to become 20 percent of all loans outstanding. Efficiency also suffered: An Indian entrepreneur reported that "it takes my wife half an hour to make a deposit or withdraw money from our local branch." Moreover, government ownership and control led to political influence in deciding to whom bank loans were to be made:

> I once chanced to meet the manager of one of the rural branches of a nationalized bank... He was a sincere young man, deeply concerned, and he wanted to unburden himself about his day-to-day problems. Neither he nor his staff, he told me, decided who qualified for a loan. The local politicians invariably made this decision. The loan takers were invariably cronies of the political bosses and did not intend to repay the money. He was told that such and such a person was to be treated as a "deserving poor." Without exception, they were rich.

The nationalization of banks in India was not simply a matter of transferring ownership of an enterprise to the government. This transfer changed all the incentives and constraints from those of the marketplace to those of politics and bureaucracy. The proclaimed goals, or even the sincere hopes, of those who created this transfer often turned out to mean much less than the changed incentives and constraints. These incentives and constraints were changed again after India began to allow private banks to operate. As the *Wall Street Journal* reported, "the country's growing middle class is taking most of its business to the high-tech private banks," thereby "leaving the state banks with the least-profitable businesses and worst borrowers." The people in the private sector may not have been much different from those in government but they operated under very different incentives and constraints.

In the United States, political control of banks' investment decisions has been less pervasive but has nevertheless changed the directions that investments have taken from what they would take in a free market. As the *Wall Street Journal* reported:

Regulators whose approval is needed for mergers are taking a harder line on banks' and savings-and-loans' performance under the Community Reinvestment Act, a law that requires them to lend in every community where they take deposits. A weak lending record can slow or even derail a deal, while a strong one can speed approval and head off protests by community groups.

In other words, people with neither expertise nor experience in financial institutions— politicians, bureaucrats, and community activists— are enabled to influence where investments are to go. Yet, when financial institutions began to have huge losses in 2007 and 2008 on "subprime" loans— Citigroup losing more than $40 billion— politicians were seldom blamed for having pushed these institutions to lend to people whose credit was below par. On the contrary, precisely those same politicians who had been most prominent in pushing lenders to take chances were now most prominent in fashioning "solutions" to the resulting crises, based on their experience on Congressional banking committees and therefore presumed expertise in dealing with financial matters.

As an entrepreneur in India put it: "Indians have learned from painful experience that the state does not work on behalf of the people. More often than not, it works on behalf of itself." So do people in other walks of life and in other countries around the world. The problem is that this fact is not always recognized when people look to government to right wrongs and fulfill desires to an extent that may not always be possible.

Whatever the merits or demerits of particular government economic policies, the market alternative is very new as history is measured, and the combination of democracy and a free market still newer and rarer. As an observer in India put it:

> We tend to forget that liberal democracy based on free markets is a relatively new idea in human history. In 1776 there was one liberal democracy— the United States; in 1790 there were 3, including France; in 1848 there were only 5; in 1975 there were still only 31. Today 120 of the world's 200 or so states claim to be democracies, with more than 50 percent of the world's population residing in them (although Freedom House, an American think tank, counts only 86 countries as truly free).

Where there are elected governments, their officials must be concerned about being re-elected— which is to say that mistakes cannot be admitted and reversed as readily as they must be by a private business operating in a competitive market, in order for the business to survive financially. No one likes to admit being mistaken but, under the incentives and constraints of profit and loss, there is often no choice but to reverse course before financial losses threaten bankruptcy. In politics, however, the costs of the government's mistakes are often paid by the taxpayers, while the costs of admitting mistakes are paid by elected officials.

Given these incentives and constraints, the reluctance of government officials to admit mistakes and reverse course is perfectly rational from those officials' standpoint. For example, when supersonic passenger jet planes were first contemplated, by both private plane manufacturers like Boeing and by the British and French governments who proposed building the Concorde, it became clear early on that the costs of fuel-guzzling supersonic passenger jets would be so high that there would be little hope of recovering those costs from fares that passengers would be willing to pay. Boeing dropped the whole idea, absorbing the losses of its early efforts as a lesser evil than continuing on and absorbing even bigger losses by completing the project. But the British and French governments, once publicly committed to the idea of the Concorde, continued on instead of admitting that it was a bad idea.

The net result was that British and French taxpayers for years subsidized a commercial venture used largely by very affluent passengers, because fares on the Concorde were far higher than fares on other jets flying the same routes, even though these very expensive fares still did not fully cover the costs. Eventually, as Concordes aged, the plane was discontinued because its huge losses were now so widely known that it would have been politically difficult, if not impossible, to get public support for more government spending to replace planes that had never been economically viable.

Although we often speak of "the government" as if it were a single thing, it is not only fragmented into differing and contending interests at any given time, its leadership consists of entirely different people over time. Thus those who put an end to the costly Concorde experiment were not the same as those who had launched this experiment in the first place. It is always easier to admit someone else's mistakes— and to take credit for correcting them.

In a competitive market, by contrast, the costs of mistakes can quickly become so high that there is no choice but to admit one's own mistakes and change course before bankruptcy looms on the horizon. Because the day of reckoning comes earlier in markets than in government, there is not only more pressure to admit mistakes in the private sector, there is more pressure to avoid making mistakes in the first place. When proposals for new ventures are made in these different sectors, proposals made by government officials need only persuade enough people, in order to be successful within the time horizon that matters to those officials— usually the time until the next election. In a competitive market, however, proposals must convince those particular people whose own money is at stake and who therefore have every incentive to marshal the best available expertise to assess the future before proceeding.

It is hardly surprising that these two processes can produce very different conclusions about the very same situations. Thus when the proposal for building a tunnel under the English Channel was being considered, the British and French governments projected costs and earnings that made it look like a good investment, at least to enough of the British and French public to make the venture politically viable. Meanwhile, companies running ferry service across the English Channel obviously thought otherwise, for they proceeded to invest in more and bigger ferries, which could have been financial suicide if the tunnel under the channel had turned out to be the kind of success that was projected by political officials, for that would lead people to take the underwater route across the channel, instead of ferries.

Only after years of building and more years of operation did the economic outcome of the tunnel project become clear— and the British and French officials initially responsible for this venture were long gone from the political scene by then. In 2004 *The Economist* reported:

> "Without a doubt, the Channel Tunnel would not have been built if we'd known about these problems," Richard Shirrefs, the chief executive of Eurotunnel, said this week. Too few people are using the ten-year-old undersea link between Britain and France to repay even the interest on its bloated construction costs, which have left Eurotunnel with [$11.5 billion] in debt. So, just as happened with supersonic Concorde,

taxpayers are being asked to bail out another Anglo-French transport fiasco. . . . None of this will come as a surprise to tunnel-sceptics— who, like Concorde's, were mostly ignored.

While these examples involved the British and French governments, similar incentives and constraints— and similar results— apply to many governments around the world.

Sometimes, however, the short memory of the voting public can spare elected officials the consequences of having advocated a policy that has either failed or has quietly been abandoned. For example, in the United States, both individual states and the federal government have imposed gasoline taxes dedicated to the building and maintenance of highways— and both have later diverted these taxes to other things. In 2008, Congress passed a bill to spend hundreds of billions of dollars for the purpose of preventing financial institutions from collapsing. Yet, before the year was out, those Treasury Department officials in charge of dispersing this money openly admitted that much of it was diverted to bailing out other firms in other industries.

None of this is new or peculiar to the United States. As far back as 1776, Adam Smith warned that a fund set aside by the British government for paying off the national debt was "an obvious and easy expedient" to be "misapplied" to other purposes.

PART VI:

THE INTERNATIONAL

ECONOMY

Chapter 21

INTERNATIONAL TRADE

*Facts are stubborn things; and whatever may be our
wishes, our inclinations, or the dictates of our passions,
they cannot alter the state of facts and evidence.*

John Adams

When discussing the historic North American Free Trade Agreement of 1993 (NAFTA), the *New York Times* said:

> Abundant evidence is emerging that jobs are shifting across borders too rapidly to declare the United States a job winner or a job loser from the trade agreement.

Posing the issue in these terms committed the central fallacy in many discussions of international trade— assuming that one country must be a "loser" if the other country is a "winner." But international trade is not a zero-sum contest. Both sides must gain or it would make no sense to continue trading. Nor is it necessary for experts or government officials to determine whether both sides are gaining. Most international trade, like most domestic trade, is done by millions of individuals, each of whom can determine whether the item purchased is worth what it cost and is preferable to what is available from others.

As for jobs, before the NAFTA free-trade agreement among the United States, Canada, and Mexico went into effect, there were dire predictions of "a giant sucking sound" as jobs would be sucked out of the United States to Mexico because of Mexico's lower wage rates. In reality, the number of American jobs *increased* after the agreement, and the unemployment rate in the

United States fell over the next seven years from more than seven percent down to four percent, the lowest level seen in decades. In Canada, the unemployment rate fell from 11 percent to 7 percent over the same seven years.

Why was what happened so radically different from what was predicted? Let's go back to square one. What happens when a given country, in isolation, becomes more prosperous? It tends to buy more because it has more to buy with. And what happens when it buys more? There are more jobs created for workers producing the additional goods and services.

Make that two countries and the principle remains the same. Indeed, make it any number of countries and the principle remains the same. Rising prosperity usually means rising employment.

There is no *fixed* number of jobs that countries must fight over. When countries become more prosperous, they all tend to create more jobs. The only question is whether international trade tends to make countries more prosperous.

Mexico was considered to be the main threat to take jobs away from the United States when trade barriers were lowered, because wage rates are much lower in Mexico. In the post-NAFTA years, jobs did in fact increase by the millions in Mexico— at the same time when jobs were increasing by the millions in the United States. Both countries saw an increase in their international trade, with especially sharp increases in those goods covered by NAFTA.

The basic facts about international trade are not difficult to understand. What is difficult to untangle are all the misconceptions and jargon which so often clutter up the discussion. The great U.S. Supreme Court Justice Oliver Wendell Holmes said, "we need to think things instead of words." Nowhere is that more important than when discussing international trade, where there are so many misleading and emotional words used to describe and confuse things that are not very difficult to understand in themselves.

For example, the terminology used to describe an export surplus as a "favorable" balance of trade and an import surplus as an "unfavorable" balance of trade goes back for centuries. At one time, it was widely believed that importing more than was exported impoverished a nation because the difference between imports and exports had to be paid in gold, and the loss of gold was seen as a loss of national wealth. However, as early as 1776, Adam Smith's classic *The Wealth of Nations* argued that the real wealth of a nation consists of its goods and services, not its gold supply.

Too many people have yet to grasp the full implications of that, even in the twenty-first century. If the goods and services available to the American people are greater as a result of international trade, then Americans are wealthier, not poorer, regardless of whether there is a "deficit" or a "surplus" in the international balance of trade.

Incidentally, during the Great Depression of the 1930s, the United States had an export surplus— a "favorable" balance of trade— in every year of that disastrous decade. But what may be more relevant is that both imports and exports were sharply lower than they had been during the prosperous decade of the 1920s. This reduction in international trade was a result of rising tariff barriers in countries around the world, as nations attempted to save jobs in their own domestic economies, during a period of widespread unemployment, by keeping out international trade.

Such policies have been regarded by many economists as needlessly worsening and prolonging the worldwide depression. The last thing needed when real national income is going down is a policy that makes it go down faster, by denying consumers the benefits of being able to buy what they want at the lowest price available.

Slippery words can make bad news look like good news and vice versa. For example, the much-lamented international trade deficit of the United States narrowed by a record-breaking amount in the spring of 2001, as *BusinessWeek* magazine reported under the headline: "A Shrinking Trade Gap Looks Good Stateside." However, this happened while the stock market was falling, unemployment was rising, corporate profits were down, and the total output of the American economy declined. The supposedly "good" news on international trade was due to reduced imports during shaky economic times. Had the country gone into a deep depression, the international trade balance might have disappeared completely, but fortunately Americans were spared that much "good" news.

Just as the United States had a "favorable" balance of trade in every year of the Great Depression of the 1930s, it became a record-breaking "debtor nation" during the booming prosperity of the 1990s. Obviously, such words cannot be taken at face value as indicators of the economic well-being of a country. We will need to examine more closely what such words mean in context.

THE BASIS FOR INTERNATIONAL TRADE

While international trade takes place for the same reason that other trades take place— because both sides gain— it is necessary to understand just why both countries gain, especially since there are so many politicians and journalists who muddy the waters with claims to the contrary.

The reasons why countries gain from international trade are usually grouped together by economists under three categories: absolute advantage, comparative advantage, and economies of scale.

Absolute Advantage

It is obvious why Americans buy bananas grown in the Caribbean. Bananas can be grown much more cheaply in the tropics than in places where greenhouses and other artificial means of maintaining warmth would be necessary. In tropical countries, nature provides free the warmth that people have to provide by costly means in cooler climates, such as that of the United States. Therefore it pays Americans to buy bananas grown in the tropics, rather than grow them at higher costs within the United States.

Sometimes the advantages that one country has over another, or over the rest of the world, are extreme. Growing coffee, for example, requires a peculiar combination of climatic conditions— warm but not too hot, nor with sunlight beating down on the plants directly all day, nor with too much moisture or too little moisture, and in some kinds of soils but not others. Putting together these and other requirements for ideal coffee-growing conditions drastically reduces the number of places that are best suited for producing coffee.

In the early twenty-first century, more than half the coffee in the entire world was grown in just three countries— Brazil, Vietnam, and Colombia. This does not mean that other countries were completely incapable of growing coffee. It is just that the amount and quality of coffee that most countries could produce would not be worth the resources it would cost, when coffee can be bought from these three countries at a lower cost.

Sometimes an absolute advantage consists simply of being located in the right place or speaking the right language. In India, for example, the time is about 12 hours different from the time in the United States, which means that an American company which wants round-the-clock computer services can engage a computer company in India to have Indian technicians available when it is night in the United States and day in India. Since many educated people in India speak English and India has 30 percent of all the computer software engineers in the world, this combination of circumstances gives India a large advantage in competing for computer services in the American market. Similarly, South American countries supply fruits and vegetables to North American countries when it is winter in the northern hemisphere and summer in the southern hemisphere.

These are all examples of what economists call "absolute advantage"— one country, for any of a number of reasons, can produce some things cheaper or better than another. Those reasons may be due to climate, geography, or the mixture of skills in their respective populations. Foreigners who buy that country's products benefit from the lower costs, while the country itself obviously benefits from the larger market for its products or services, and sometimes from the fact that part of the inputs needed to create the product are free, such as warmth in the tropics or rich nutrients in the soil in various places around the world.

There is another more subtle, but at least equally important, reason for international trade. This is what economists call "comparative advantage."

Comparative Advantage

To illustrate what is meant by comparative advantage, suppose that one country is so efficient that it is capable of producing *anything* more cheaply than a neighboring country. Is there any benefit that the more efficient country can gain from trading with its neighbor?

Yes.

Why? Because being able to produce *anything* more cheaply is not the same as being able to produce *everything* more cheaply. When there are scarce resources which have alternative uses, producing more of one product means producing less of some other product. The question is not simply how much it costs, in either money or resources, to produce chairs or television sets in one country, compared to another country, but how many chairs it costs to produce a television set, when resources are shifted from producing one product to producing the other.

If that trade-off is different between two countries, then the country that can get more television sets by foregoing the production of chairs can benefit from trading with the country that gets more chairs by not producing television sets. A numerical example can illustrate this point.

Assume that an average American worker produces 500 chairs a month, while an average Canadian worker produces 450, and that an American worker can produce 200 television sets a month while a Canadian worker produces 100. The following tables illustrate what the output would be under these conditions if both countries produced both products versus each country producing only one of these products. In both tables we assume the same respective outputs per worker and the same total number of workers— 500— devoted to producing these products in each country:

PRODUCTS	AMERICAN WORKERS	AMERICAN OUTPUT	CANADIAN WORKERS	CANADIAN OUTPUT
chairs	200	100,000	200	90,000
TV sets	300	60,000	300	30,000

With both countries producing both products, under the conditions specified, their combined output would come to a grand total of 190,000 chairs and 90,000 television sets per month from a grand total of a thousand workers.

What if the two countries specialize, with the United States putting all its chair-producing workers into the production of television sets instead, and Canada doing the reverse? Then *with the very same output per worker* as before in each country, they can now produce a larger grand total of the two products from the same thousand workers:

PRODUCTS	AMERICAN WORKERS	AMERICAN OUTPUT	CANADIAN WORKERS	CANADIAN OUTPUT
chairs	0	0	500	225,000
TV sets	500	100,000	0	0

Without any change in the productivity of workers in either country, the total output is now greater from the same number of workers, that output now being 100,000 television sets instead of 90,000 and 225,000 chairs instead of 190,000. That is because each country now produces where it has a comparative advantage, whether or not it has an absolute advantage.

Economists would say that the United States has an "absolute advantage" in producing both products but that Canada has a "comparative advantage" in producing chairs. That is, Canada sacrifices fewer television sets by shifting resources to the production of chairs than the United States would by such a shift. Under these conditions, Americans can get more chairs by producing television sets and trading them with Canadians for chairs, instead of by producing their own chairs directly. Conversely, Canadians can get more television sets by producing chairs and trading them for American-made television sets, rather than producing television sets themselves.

Only if the United States produced everything more efficiently than Canada *by the same percentage for each product* would there be no gain from trade because there would then be no comparative advantage. Such a situation is virtually impossible to find in the real world.

Similar principles apply on a personal level in everyday life. Imagine, for example, that you are an eye surgeon and that you paid your way through college by washing cars. Now that you have a car of your own, should you wash it yourself or should you hire someone else to wash it— even if your previous experience allows you to do the job in less time than the person you hire? Obviously, it makes no sense to you financially, or to society in terms of over-all well-being, for you to be spending your time sudsing down an automobile instead of being in an operating room saving someone's eyesight. In other words, even though you have an "absolute advantage" in both activities, your comparative advantage in treating eye diseases is far greater.

The key to understanding both individual examples and examples from international trade is the basic economic reality of scarcity. The surgeon has only 24 hours in the day, like everyone else. Time that he is spending doing one thing is time taken away from doing something else. The same is true of countries, which do not have an unlimited amount of labor, time, or other resources, and so must do one thing at the cost of not doing something else. That is the very meaning of economic costs— *foregone alternatives*, which apply whether the particular economy is capitalist, socialist, feudal, or whatever— and whether the transactions are domestic or international.

The benefits of comparative advantage are particularly important to poorer countries. Someone put it this way:

> Comparative advantage means there is a place under the free-trade sun for every nation, no matter how poor, because people of every nation can produce some products relatively more efficiently than they produce other products.

Comparative advantage is not just a theory but a very important fact in the history of many nations. It has been more than a century since Great Britain produced enough food to feed its people. Britons have been able to get enough to eat only because the country has concentrated its efforts on producing those things in which it has had a comparative advantage, such as manufacturing, shipping, and financial services— and using the proceeds to buy food from other countries. British consumers ended up better fed and with more manufactured goods than if the country grew enough of its own food to feed itself.

Since the real costs of anything that is produced are the other things that could have been produced with the same efforts, it would cost the British too much industry and commerce to transfer enough resources into agriculture to become self-sufficient in food. They are better off getting food from some other country whose comparative advantage is in agriculture, *even if that other country's farmers are not as efficient as British farmers.*

Such a trade-off is not limited to industrialized nations. When cocoa began to be grown on farms in West Africa, which ultimately produced over half of the world's supply, African farmers reduced the amount of food they grew, in order to earn more money by planting cocoa trees on their lands, instead of food crops. As a result, their increased earnings enabled them to live off food produced elsewhere. This food included not only meat and vegetables grown in the region, but also imported rice and canned fish and fruit, the latter items being considered to be luxuries at the time.

Economies of Scale

While absolute advantage and comparative advantage are the key reasons for benefits from international trade, they are not the only reasons. Sometimes a particular product requires such huge investment in machinery, in the engineering required to create the machinery and the product, as well as in developing a specialized labor force, that the resulting output can be sold at a low enough price to be competitive only when some enormous amount of output is produced, because of economies of scale, as discussed in Chapter 6.

It has been estimated that the minimum output of automobiles needed to achieve an efficient cost per car is somewhere between 200,000 and 400,000 automobiles per year. Producing in such huge quantities is not a serious problem in a country of the size and wealth of the United States, where each of the big three domestic automakers— Ford, General Motors, and Chrysler— has had at least one vehicle with sales of more than 400,000, as did Toyota, while the Ford F-Series pickup truck has had more than 800,000 annual sales. But, in a country with a much smaller population— Australia, for example— there is no way to sell enough cars within the country to be able to cover the high costs of developing automobiles from scratch to sell at prices low enough to compete with automobiles produced in much larger quantities in the United States or Japan.

The largest number of cars of any given make sold in Australia is only about half of the quantity needed to reap all the cost benefits of economies of scale. While the number of automobiles owned per capita is higher in

Australia than in the United States, there are more than a dozen times as many Americans as there are Australians.

Even those cars which have been manufactured in Australia have been developed in other countries— Toyotas and Mitsubishis from Japan, and Ford and General Motors cars from the United States. They are essentially Australian-built Japanese or American cars, which means that companies in Japan and the United States have already paid the huge engineering, research, and other costs of creating these vehicles. But the Australian market is not large enough to achieve sufficient economies of scale to produce original Australian automobiles from scratch at a cost that would enable them to compete in the market with imported cars.

Although Australia is a modern prosperous country, with output per person higher than that of Great Britain, Canada or the United States, its small population limits its total purchasing power to one-fifth that of Japan and one-seventeenth that of the United States.

Exports enable some countries to achieve economies of scale that would not be possible from domestic sales alone. Some business enterprises make most of their sales outside their respective countries' borders. For example, Heineken does not have to depend on the small Holland market for its beer sales, since it sells beer in 170 other countries. Nokia sells its phones around the world, not just in its native Finland. The distinguished British magazine *The Economist* sells three times as many copies in the United States as in Britain. Toyota, Honda, and Nissan all earn most of their profits in North America, and Japanese automakers as a whole began in 2006 to manufacture more cars outside of Japan than in Japan itself. Small countries like South Korea and Taiwan depend on international trade to be able to produce many products on a scale far exceeding what can be sold domestically.

In short, international trade is necessary for many countries to achieve economies of scale that will enable them to sell at prices that can compete with the prices of similar products in the world market. For some products requiring huge investments in machinery and research, only a very few large and prosperous countries could reach the levels of output needed to repay all these costs from domestic sales alone. International trade creates greater efficiency by allowing more economies of scale around the world, even in countries whose domestic markets are not large enough to absorb all the output of mass production industries, as well as by taking advantage of each country's absolute or comparative advantages.

As in other cases, we can sometimes understand the benefits of a particular way of doing things by seeing what happens when they are done differently. For many years, India encouraged small businesses and maintained barriers against imports that could compete with them. However, the lifting of import restrictions at the end of the twentieth century and the beginning of the twenty-first century changed all that. As the *Far Eastern Economic Review* put it:

> The nightmare of the Indian toy industry comes in the form of a pint-sized plastic doll. It's made in China, sings a popular Hindi film song, and costs about 100 rupees ($2). Indian parents have snapped it up at markets across the country, leaving local toy companies petrified. Matching the speed, scale and technology involved in the doll's production— resulting in its rock-bottom price— is beyond their abilities. . . . In areas such as toys and shoes, China has developed huge economies of scale while India has kept its producers artificially small.

The economic problems of toy manufacturers in India under free trade are overshadowed by the far more serious problems created by previous import restrictions which forced hundreds of millions of people in a very poor country to pay needlessly inflated prices for a wide range of products because of policies protecting small-scale producers from the competition of larger producers at home and abroad. Fortunately, decades of such policies were finally ended in India in the last decade of the twentieth century.

INTERNATIONAL TRADE RESTRICTIONS

While there are many advantages to international trade for the world as a whole and for countries individually, like all forms of greater economic efficiency, whether at home or abroad, it displaces less efficient ways of doing things. Just as the advent of the automobile inflicted severe losses on the horse-and-buggy industry and the spread of giant supermarket chains drove many small neighborhood grocery stores out of business, so imports of things in which other countries have a comparative advantage create losses of revenue and jobs in the corresponding domestic industry.

Despite offsetting economic gains that typically far outweigh the losses, politically it is almost inevitable that there will be loud calls for government protection from foreign competition through various restrictions against imports. Many of the most long-lived fallacies in economics have grown out of attempts to justify these international trade restrictions. Although Adam Smith refuted most of these fallacies more than two centuries ago, as far as economists are concerned, such fallacies remain politically alive and potent today.

Some people argue, for example, that wealthy countries cannot compete with countries whose wages are much lower. Poorer countries, on the other hand, may say that they must protect their "infant industries" from competition with more developed industrial nations until the local industries acquire the experience and know-how to compete on even terms. In all countries, there are complaints that other nations are not being "fair" in their laws regarding imports and exports. A frequently heard complaint of unfairness, for example, is that some countries "dump" their goods on the international market at artificially low prices, losing money in the short run in order to gain a larger market share that they will later exploit by raising prices after they achieve a monopolistic position.

In the complexities of real life, seldom is any argument right 100 percent of the time or wrong 100 percent of the time. When it comes to arguments for international trade restrictions, however, most of the arguments are fallacious most of the time. Let us examine them one at a time, beginning with the high-wage fallacy.

The High-Wage Fallacy

In a prosperous country such as the United States, a fallacy that sounds very plausible is that American goods cannot compete with goods produced by low-wage workers in poorer countries, some of whom are paid a fraction of what American workers receive. But, plausible as this may sound, both history and economics refute it. Historically, high-wage countries have been exporting to low-wage countries for centuries. The Dutch Republic was a leader in international trade for nearly a century and a half— from the 1590s to the 1740s— while having some of the highest-paid workers in the world. Britain was the world's greatest exporter in the nineteenth century and its wage rates were much higher than the wage rates in many, if not most, of the countries to which it sold its goods.

Conversely, India has had far lower wage rates than those in more industrialized countries like Japan and the United States, but for many years India restricted imports of automobiles and other products made in Japan and the United States, because India's domestic producers could not compete in price or quality with such imported products. After an easing of restrictions on international trade, even the leading Indian industrial firm, Tata, has had to be concerned about imports from China, despite the higher wages of Chinese workers compared to workers in India:

> . . .the Tata group set up a special office to educate the different parts of its sprawling business empire on the possible fallout from the removal of import restrictions. Jiban Mukhopadhyay, economic adviser to the group's chairman, heads the operation. In his desk drawer, he keeps a silk tie bought on a trip to China. Managers who attend the company's WTO [World Trade Organization] workshops are asked to guess its price. "It's only 85 rupees," he points out. "A similar tie made in India would cost 400 rupees."

Economically, the key flaw in the high-wage argument is that it confuses wage rates with labor costs— and labor costs with total costs. Wage rates are measured per hour of work. Labor costs are measured per unit of output. Total costs include not only the cost of labor but also the cost of capital, raw materials, transportation, and other things needed to produce output and bring the finished product to market.

When workers in a prosperous country receive wages twice as high as workers in a poorer country and produce three times the output per hour, then it is the high-wage country which has the lower labor costs per unit of output. That is, it is cheaper to get a given amount of work done in the more prosperous country simply because it takes less labor, even though individual workers are paid more for their time. The higher-paid workers may be more efficiently organized and managed, or have more or better machinery to work with, or work in companies or industries with greater economies of scale. Often transportation costs are lower in the more developed country, so that total costs of delivering the product to market are less.

There are, after all, reasons why one country is more prosperous than another, in the first place— and often that reason is that they are more efficient at producing and delivering output, for any of a number of reasons. In short, higher wage rates per unit of time are not the same as higher costs per unit of output. It may not even mean higher labor costs per unit of output— and of course labor costs are not the only costs.

An international consulting firm determined that the average labor productivity in the modern sectors in India is 15 percent of labor productivity in the United States. In other words, if you hired an average Indian worker and paid him one-fifth of what you paid an average American worker, it would cost you *more* to get a given amount of work done in India than in the United States. Paying 20 percent of what an American worker makes to someone who produces only 15 percent of what an American worker produces would increase your labor costs.

None of this means that no low-wage country can ever gain jobs at the expense of a high-wage country. Where the difference in productivity is less than the difference in wage rates, as with India's well-trained and English-speaking computer programmers, then much American computer programming will be done in India. All other forms of comparative advantage will also mean a shift of jobs to countries with particular advantages in doing particular things. But this does not imply a *net* loss of jobs in the economy as a whole, any more than other forms of greater efficiency, domestically or internationally, imply a net loss of jobs in the economy. The job losses are quite real to those who suffer them, whether due to domestic or international competition, but restrictions on either domestic or international markets usually cost jobs on net balance because such restrictions reduce the prosperity on which the demand for goods and labor depends.

Labor costs are only part of the story. The costs of capital and management are a considerable part of the cost of many products. In some cases, capital costs exceed labor costs, especially in industries with high fixed costs, such as electric utilities and railroads, both of which have huge investments in infrastructure. A prosperous country usually has a greater abundance of capital and, because of supply and demand, capital tends to be cheaper there than in poorer countries where capital is more scarce and earns a correspondingly higher rate of return.

The history of the beginning of the industrialization of Russia under the czars illustrates how the supply of capital affects the cost of capital. When Russia began a large-scale industrialization program in the 1890s, foreign investors could earn a return of 17.5 percent per year on their investments— until so many invested in Russia that the rate of return declined over the years and fell below 5 percent by 1900. Poorer countries with high capital costs would have difficulty competing with richer countries with lower capital costs, even if they had a real advantage in labor costs, which they often do not.

At any given time, it is undoubtedly true that some industries will be adversely affected by competing imported products, just as they are adversely affected by every other source of cheaper or better products, whether domestic or foreign. These other sources of greater efficiency are at work all the time, forcing industries to modernize, downsize or go out of business. Yet, when this happens because of foreigners, it can be depicted politically as a case of our country versus theirs, when in fact it is the old story of domestic special interests versus consumers.

Saving Jobs

During periods of high unemployment, politicians are especially likely to be under great pressure to come to the rescue of particular industries that are losing money and jobs, by restricting imports that compete with them. One of the most tragic examples of such restrictions occurred during the worldwide depression of the 1930s, when tariff barriers and other restrictions went up around the world. The net result was that world exports in 1933 were only one-third of what they had been in 1929. Just as free trade provides economic benefits to all countries simultaneously, so trade restrictions reduce the efficiency of all countries simultaneously, lowering standards of living, without producing the increased employment that was hoped for.

These trade restrictions around the world were set off by passage of the Smoot-Hawley tariffs in the United States in 1930, which raised American tariffs on imports to record high levels. Other countries retaliated with severe restrictions on their imports of American products. Moreover, the same political pressures at work in the United States were at work elsewhere, since it seems plausible to many people to protect jobs at home by reducing imports from foreign countries. The net result was that severe international trade restrictions were applied by many countries to many other countries, not just to the United States. The net economic consequences were quite different from what was expected— but were precisely what had been predicted by more than a thousand economists who signed a public appeal against the tariff increases, directed to Senator Smoot, Congressman Hawley and President Herbert Hoover. Among other things, they said:

> America is now facing the problem of unemployment. The proponents of higher tariffs claim that an increase in rates will give work to the idle. This is not true. We cannot increase employment by restricting trade.

These thousand economists— including many leading professors of economics at Harvard, Columbia, and the University of Chicago— accurately predicted "retaliatory" tariffs against American goods by other countries. They also predicted that "the vast majority" of American farmers, who were among the strongest supporters of tariffs, would lose out on net balance, as other countries restricted their imports of American farm products. All these predictions were fulfilled: Unemployment grew worse and U.S. farm exports plummeted, along with a general decline in America's international trade.

The unemployment rate in the United States was 6 percent in June 1930, when the Smoot-Hawley tariffs were passed— down from its peak of 9 percent in December 1929. A year later, unemployment was 15 percent, and a year after that it was 26 percent. All of this need not be attributed to the tariffs. But the whole point of those tariffs was to reduce unemployment.*

---

* A case could be made that the Smoot-Hawley tariffs had more to do with the massive unemployment of the 1930s than did the stock market crash in 1929 which has often been blamed. While the unemployment rate rose after the stock market crash, the unemployment rate did not reach 10 percent during any of the 12 months following that crash. But, unemployment reached 11.6 percent just five months after the Smoot-Hawley tariff— on its way up to still higher levels, and never got down to 11.6 percent until more than eight years later. Richard K. Vedder and Lowell E. Gallaway, *Out of Work*, 1993 edition, p. 77.

At any given time, a protective tariff or other import restriction may provide immediate relief to a particular industry and thus gain the political and financial support of corporations and labor unions in that industry. But, like many political benefits, it comes at the expense of others who may not be as organized, as visible, or as vocal.

When the number of jobs in the American steel industry fell from 340,000 to 125,000 during the decade of the 1980s, that had a devastating impact and was big economic and political news. It also led to a variety of laws and regulations designed to reduce the amount of steel imported into the country that competed with domestically produced steel. Of course, this reduction in supply led to higher steel prices within the United States and therefore higher costs for all other American industries that were manufacturing products made of steel, which range from automobiles to oil rigs.

All these products made of steel were now at a disadvantage in competing with similar foreign-made products, both within the United States and in international markets. It has been estimated that the steel tariffs produced $240 million in additional profits to the steel companies and saved 5,000 jobs in the steel industry. At the same time, those American industries that manufacture products made from this artificially more expensive steel lost an estimated $600 million in profits and 26,000 jobs as a result of the steel tariffs. In other words, both American industry and American workers as a whole were worse off, on net balance, as a result of the import restrictions on steel.

Similarly, a study of restrictions on the importation of sugar into the United States indicated that, while it saved jobs in the sugar industry, it cost three times as many jobs in the confection industry, because of the high cost of the sugar used in making confections. Some American firms relocated to Canada and Mexico because sugar costs were lower in both these countries. In 2013 the *Wall Street Journal* reported, "Atkinson Candy Co. has moved 80% of its peppermint-candy production to a factory in Guatemala that opened in 2010." From 2000 to 2012, the average price of sugar in the United States was more than double its price in the world market, according to the *Wall Street Journal*.

International trade restrictions provide yet another example of the fallacy of composition, the belief that what is true of a part is true of the whole. There is no question that a particular industry or occupation can be benefitted by international trade restrictions. The fallacy is in believing that this means the economy as a whole is benefitted, whether as regards jobs or profits.

"Infant Industries"

One of the arguments for international trade restrictions that economists have long recognized as valid, in theory at least, is that of protecting "infant industries" *temporarily* until they can develop the skills and experience necessary to compete with long-established foreign competitors. Once this point is reached, the protection (whether tariffs, import quotas, or whatever) can be taken away and the industry allowed to stand or fall in the competition of the marketplace.

In practice, however, a new industry in its infancy seldom has enough political muscle— employees' votes, employers' campaign contributions, local governments dependent on their taxes— to get protection from foreign competition. On the other hand, an old, inefficient industry that has seen better days may well have some political muscle left and obtain enough protectionist legislation or subsidies from the government to preserve itself from extinction— at the expense of the consumers, the taxpayers, or both.

National Defense

Even the greatest advocates of free trade are unlikely to want to depend on imports of military equipment and supplies from nations that could turn out at some future time to be enemy nations. Therefore domestic supplies of munitions and weapons of war have long been supported in one way or another, in order to assure that those suppliers will be available in the event that they are needed to provide whatever is required for national defense.

One of the rare cases in history where a people did depend on potential enemies for military supplies occurred in colonial America, where the indigenous American Indians obtained guns and ammunition from the European settlers. When warfare broke out between them, the Indians could win most of the battles and yet lose the war when they began to run out of bullets, which were available only from the white settlers. Since guns and bullets were products of European civilization, the Indians had no choice but to rely on that source. But countries that do have a choice almost invariably prefer having their own domestic suppliers of the things that are essential to their own national survival.

Unfortunately, the term "essential to national defense" can be— and has been— stretched to include products only remotely, tangentially, or fictitiously, related to military defense. Such products can acquire protection from international competition under a national defense label for purely self-serving reasons. In short, while the argument for international trade restrictions for the sake of national defense can be valid, whether it is or is not valid for a particular industry in a particular country at a particular time depends on the actual circumstances of that industry, that country, and that time.

Different foreign countries can represent different probabilities of becoming future enemies, so that the dangers of relying on foreign suppliers of military equipment vary with the particular countries involved. In 2004, for example, Canada was the largest foreign recipient of Pentagon contracts— $601 million worth— followed by Britain and Israel, none of these three countries being likely to be at war with the United States.

Sometimes it is not the import of physical goods themselves, but the export of technology embodied in goods, which represents a military threat. In the 1990s, bans on selling American products using advanced computer technology were lifted for sales to China, over the objections of U.S. military authorities. The military wished to keep such restrictions because this advanced technology would enable the Chinese military to acquire the ability to more accurately aim nuclear missiles at American cities. It was not economists but politicians who favored lifting such international trade restrictions. Economists have long recognized the national defense exception to free trade as valid where it applies, even though the national defense rationale has been used in many cases where it did not apply.

"Dumping"

A common argument for government protection against a competitor in other countries is that the latter is not competing "fairly" but is instead "dumping" its products on the market at prices below their costs of production. The argument is that this is being done to drive the domestic producers out of business, letting the foreign producer take over the market, after which prices will be raised to monopolistic levels. In response to this argument, governments have passed "anti-dumping" laws, which ban, restrict, or heavily tax the importation of products from foreign companies declared to be guilty of this practice.

Everything in this argument depends on whether or not the foreign producer is in fact selling goods below their costs of production. As already noted in Chapter 6, determining production cost is not easy in practice, even for a firm operating within the same country as the government agencies that are trying to determine its costs. For government officials in Europe to try to determine the production costs of a company located in Southeast Asia is even more problematical, especially when they are simultaneously investigating many dumping charges involving many other companies scattered around the world. All that is easy is for domestic producers to bring such charges when imports are taking away some of their customers.

Given the uncertainties of determining cost, the path of least resistance for officials ruling on "dumping" charges is to accept such charges. Authorities in the European Union, for example, declared that a producer of mountain bikes in Thailand was exporting these bikes to Europe below their cost of production, because he was charging less for the bikes in Europe than such bikes had been selling for in Thailand. However, since there are economies of scale, the Thai producer's costs when selling huge numbers of mountain bikes in Europe were unlikely to be as high as the costs of other producers selling much smaller numbers of mountain bikes within Thailand, where there was far less demand for such a luxury item from a poorer and smaller population.

Indeed, this Thai producer's own costs of selling small numbers of mountain bikes in Thailand were likely to be higher per bike than the costs of selling vast numbers of them in large orders to Europe. To sell bikes in Europe for less than bicycle producers charged in Thailand did not necessarily mean selling below the cost of producing bikes for the huge European market.

This situation was not unique. The European Union has applied anti-dumping laws against bed linen from Egypt, antibiotics from India, footwear from China, microwave ovens from Malaysia, and monosodium glutamate from Brazil, among other products from other places. Nor is the

European Union unique. The United States has applied anti-dumping laws to steel from Japan, aluminum from Russia, and golf carts from Poland, among other products. Without any serious basis for determining the costs of producing these things, U.S. government agencies rely on the "best information available"— which is often supplied by those American businesses that are trying to keep out competing foreign products.

Whatever the theory behind anti-dumping laws, in practice they are part of the arsenal of protectionism for domestic producers, at the expense of domestic consumers. Moreover, even the theory is not without its problems. Dumping theory is an international version of the theory of "predatory pricing," whose problems were discussed in Chapter 8. Predatory pricing is a charge that is easy to make and hard to either prove or disprove, whether domestically or internationally. Where the political bias is toward accepting the charge, it does not have to be proven.

Kinds of Restrictions

Tariffs are taxes on imports which serve to raise the prices of those imports, and thus enable domestic producers to charge higher prices for competing products than they could in the face of cheaper foreign competition. Import quotas likewise restrict foreign companies from competing on even terms with domestic producers. Although tariffs and quotas may have the same economic end results, these effects are not equally obvious to the public. Thus, while a $10 tariff on imported widgets may enable the domestic producers of widgets to charge $10 more than they could otherwise, without losing business to foreign producers, a suitable quota limitation on the number of imported widgets can also drive up the price of widgets by $10 through its effect on supply and demand. In the latter case, however, it is by no means as easy for the voting public to see and quantify the effects. What that can mean politically is that a quota restriction which raises the price of widgets by $15 may be as easy for elected officials to pass as a tariff of $10.

Sometimes this approach is buttressed by claims that this or that foreign country is being "unfair" in its restrictions on imports from the United States. But the sad fact is that virtually all countries impose "unfair" restrictions on imports, usually in response to internal special interests.

However, here as elsewhere, choices can only be made among alternatives actually available. Other countries' restrictions deprive both them and us of some of the benefits of international trade. If we do the same in response, it will deprive both of us of still more benefits. If we let them "get away with it," this will minimize the losses on both sides.

Even more effective disguises for international trade restrictions are health and safety rules applied to imports— rules which often go far beyond what is necessary for either health or safety. Mere red tape requirements can also grow to the point where the time needed to comply adds enough costs to be prohibitive, especially for perishable imports. If it takes a week to get your strawberries through customs, you may as well not ship them. All these measures, which have been engaged in by countries around the world, share with import quotas the political advantage that it is hard to quantify precisely their effect on consumer prices, however large that effect may be.

CHANGING CONDITIONS

Over time, comparative advantages change, causing international production centers to shift from country to country. For example, when the computer was a new and exotic product, much of its early development and production took place in the United States. But, after the technological work was done that turned computers into a widely used product that many people knew how to produce, the United States retained its comparative advantage in the development of computer software design, but the machines themselves could now be easily assembled in poorer countries overseas— and were. Even computers sold within the United States under American brand names were often manufactured in Asia. By the early twenty-first century, *The Economist* magazine reported, "Taiwan now makes the vast majority of the world's computer components." This pattern extended beyond the United States and Taiwan, as the *Far Eastern Economic Review* reported: "Asian firms heavily rely on U.S., Japanese and European firms as the dominant sources of new technology," while the Asian manufacturers make "razor-thin profit margins due to the hefty licensing fees charged by the global brand firms."

The computer software industry in the United States could not have expanded so much and so successfully if most American computer engineers and technicians were tied down with the production of machines that could have been just as easily produced in some other country. Since the same American labor cannot be in two places at one time, it can move to where its comparative advantage is greatest only if the country "loses jobs" where it has no comparative advantage. That is why the United States could have unprecedented levels of prosperity and rapidly growing employment at the very times when media headlines were regularly announcing lay-offs by the tens of thousands in some American industries and by the hundreds of thousands in others.

Regardless of the industry or the country, if a million new and well-paying jobs are created in companies scattered all across the country as a result of international free trade, that may carry less weight politically than if half a million jobs are lost in one industry where labor unions and employer associations are able to raise a clamor. When the million new jobs represent a few dozen jobs here and there in innumerable businesses scattered across the nation, there is not enough concentration of economic interest and political clout in any one place to make it worthwhile to mount a comparable counter-campaign. Therefore laws are often passed restricting international trade for the benefit of some concentrated and vocal constituency, even though these restrictions may cause far more losses of jobs nationwide.

The direct transfer of particular jobs to a foreign country—"outsourcing"— arouses much political and media attention, as when American or British telephone-answering jobs are transferred to India, where English-speaking Indians answer calls made to Harrod's department store in London or calls to American computer companies for technical information are answered by software engineers in India. There is even a company in India called TutorVista which tutors American students by phone, using 600 tutors in India to handle 10,000 subscribers in the United States.

Those who decry the numbers of jobs transferred to another country almost never state whether these are *net* losses of jobs. While many

American jobs have been "outsourced" to India and other countries, many other countries "outsource" jobs to the United States. The German company Siemens employs tens of thousands of Americans in the United States and so do Japanese automakers Honda and Toyota. As of 2006, 63 percent of the Japanese brand automobiles sold in the United States were manufactured in the United States. The total number of Americans employed by foreign multinational companies runs into the millions.

How many jobs are being outsourced in one direction, compared to how many are being outsourced in the other direction, changes with the passage of time. During the period from 1977 to 2001 the number of jobs created in the United States by foreign-owned multinational companies grew by 4.7 million, while the number of jobs created in other countries by American-owned multinational companies grew by just 2.8 million. However, during the last decade of that era, more American jobs were sent abroad by American multinational companies than there were jobs created in the United States by foreign multinationals. Not only is the direction of outsourcing volatile and unpredictable, the net difference in numbers of jobs is small compared to the country's total employment. Moreover, such comparisons leave out the jobs created in the economy as a whole as a result of greater efficiency and wealth created by international transactions.

Even a country which is losing jobs to other countries, on net balance, through outsourcing may nevertheless have more jobs than it would have had without outsourcing. That is because the increased wealth from international transactions means increased demand for goods and services in general, including goods and services produced by workers in purely domestic industries.

Free trade may have wide support among economists, but its support among the public at large is considerably less. An international poll conducted by *The Economist* magazine found more people in favor of protectionism than of free trade in Britain, France, Italy, Australia, Russia, and the United States. Part of the reason is that the public has no idea how much protectionism costs and how little net benefit it produces. It has been estimated that all the protectionism in the European Union countries put together saves no more than a grand total of 200,000 jobs— at a cost of $43 billion. That works out to about $215,000 a year for each job saved.

In other words, if the European Union permitted 100 percent free international trade, every worker who lost his job as a result of foreign competition could be paid $100,000 a year in compensation and the European Union countries would still come out ahead. Alternatively, of course, the displaced workers could simply go find other jobs. Whatever losses they might encounter in the process do not begin to compare with the staggering costs of keeping them working where they are. That is because the costs are not simply their salaries, but the even larger costs of producing in less efficient ways, using up scarce resources that would be more productive elsewhere. In other words, what the consumers lose greatly exceeds what the workers gain, making the society as a whole worse off.

Another reason for public support for protectionism is that many economists do not bother to answer either the special interests or those who oppose free trade for ideological reasons. The arguments of both have essentially been refuted centuries ago and are now regarded within the economics profession as beneath consideration. For example, as far back as 1828, British economist Nassau W. Senior wrote, "high wages instead of preventing our manufacturers from competing with foreign countries, are, in fact, a necessary consequence of the very cause which enables us to compete with them. . . namely, the superior productiveness of English labour." But economists' disdain for long-refuted fallacies has only allowed vehement and articulate spokesmen to have a more or less free hand to monopolize public opinion, which seldom hears more than one side of the issue.

One of the few leading contemporary economists to bother answering protectionist arguments has been internationally renowned economist Jagdish Bhagwati, who agreed to a public debate against Ralph Nader. Here was his experience:

> Faced with the critics of free trade, economists have generally reacted with contempt and indifference, refusing to get into the public arena to engage the critics in battle. I was in a public debate with Ralph Nader on the campus of Cornell University a couple of years ago. The debate was in the evening, and in the afternoon I gave a technical talk on free trade to the graduate students of economics. I asked, at its end, how many were

going to the debate, and not one hand went up. Why, I asked. The typical
reaction was: why waste one's time? As a consequence, of the nearly
thousand students who jammed the theater where the debate was held,
the vast majority were anti-free traders, all rooting for Mr. Nader.

Because the buzzword "globalization" has been coined to describe the
growing importance of international trade and global economic
interdependence, many tend to see international trade and international
financial transactions as something new— allowing both special interests and
ideologues to play on the public's fear of the unknown. However, the term
"globalization" also covers more than simple free trade among nations. It
includes institutional rules governing the reduction of trade barriers and the
movements of money. Among the international organizations involved in
creating these rules are the World Bank, the International Monetary Fund,
and the World Trade Organization. These rules are legitimate subjects of
controversy, though these are not all controversies about free trade.

Chapter 22

INTERNATIONAL

TRANSFERS OF WEALTH

*The financial industry is the most cosmopolitan in the
world because its product, money, is more portable and
more widely utilized than any other.*

Michael Mandelbaum

Transfers of wealth among nations take many forms. Individuals and
businesses in one country may invest directly in the business
enterprises of another country. Americans, for example, invested $329
billion directly in other countries and foreigners invested $168 billion in the
United States in 2012, which is both the source and the recipient of more
foreign investment than any other country. Citizens of a given country may
also put their money in another country's banks, which will in turn make
loans to individuals and enterprises, so that this is indirect foreign
investment. Yet another option is to buy the bonds issued by a foreign
government. Forty-six percent of the publicly held bonds issued by the U.S.
government are held by people in other countries.

In addition to investments of various kinds, there are remittances from
people living in foreign countries sent back to family members in their
countries of origin. In 2012, 250 million migrants around the world sent
remittances of $410 billion. In 2011, a survey in Mexico found that one-fifth
of the 112 million people in that country received money from family
members in the United States, for a total of nearly $23 billion. Nor is this a
new phenomenon or one confined to Mexicans. Emigrants from India sent
$64 billion and emigrants from China sent $62 billion back to their respective

countries in 2011. As with money sent back to other poor countries, this has a significant economic impact. As the *Wall Street Journal* reported:

> Money sent home from abroad accounts for about 60% of the income of the poorest households in Guatemala, and has helped reduce the number of people living in poverty by 11 percentage points in Uganda and six percentage points in Bangladesh, according to World Bank studies.

Money sent back to Lebanon equals 22 percent of that country's Gross Domestic Product. Remittances to Moldova equal 23 percent of that country's Gross Domestic Product and, for Tajikistan 35 percent. International remittances have long played an especially important role for poor people in poor countries. Back in the 1840s, remittances from Irish immigrants in America to members of their families in Ireland enabled many of these family members not only to survive in famine-stricken Ireland but also to immigrate to the United States.

Other international transfers of wealth have not been so benign. In centuries past, imperial powers simply transferred vast amounts of wealth from the nations they conquered. Alexander the Great looted the treasures of the conquered Persians. Spain took gold and silver by the ton from the conquered indigenous peoples of the Western Hemisphere and forced some of these indigenous peoples into mines to dig up more. Julius Caesar was one of many Roman conquerors to march in triumph through the eternal city, displaying the riches and slaves he was bringing back from his victories abroad. In more recent times, both prosperous nations and international agencies have transferred part of their wealth to poorer countries under the general heading of "foreign aid."

None of this is very complicated— so long as we remember Justice Oliver Wendell Holmes' admonition to "think things instead of words." When it comes to international trade and international transfers of wealth, the things are relatively straightforward, but the words are often slippery and misleading.

INTERNATIONAL INVESTMENTS

Theoretically, investments might be expected to flow from where capital is abundant to where it is in short supply, much like water seeking its own level. In a perfect world, wealthy nations would invest much of their capital in poorer nations, where capital is more scarce and would therefore offer a higher rate of return. However, in the highly imperfect world that we live in, that is by no means what usually happens. For example, out of a worldwide total of about $21 trillion in international bank loans in 2012, only about $2.5 trillion went to poor countries— *less than twelve percent.* Out of nearly $6 trillion in international investment securities, less than $400 billion went to poor countries, less than 7 percent. In short, rich countries tend to invest in other rich countries.

There are reasons for this, just as there are reasons why some countries are rich and others poor in the first place. The biggest deterrent to investing in any country is the danger that you will never get your money back. Investors are wary of unstable governments, whose changes of personnel or policies create risks that the conditions under which the investment was made can change— the most drastic change being outright confiscation by the government, or "nationalization" as it is called politically. Widespread corruption is another deterrent to investment, as it is to economic activity in general. Countries high up on the international index of corruption, such as Nigeria or Russia, are unlikely to attract international investments on a scale that their natural resources or other economic potential might justify. Conversely, the top countries in terms of having low levels of corruption are all prosperous countries, mostly European or European-offshoot nations plus Japan and Singapore. As noted in Chapter 18, the level of honesty in a country has serious economic implications.

Even aside from confiscation and corruption, many poorer countries "do not let capital come and go freely," according to *The Economist*. Where capital cannot get out easily, it is less likely to go in, in the first place. It is not these countries' poverty, as such, that deters investments. When Hong Kong was a British colony, it began very poor and yet grew to become an industrial powerhouse, at one time having more international trade than a vast country like India. Massive inflows of capital helped develop Hong Kong, which operated under the security of British laws, had low tax rates, and allowed some of the freest flows of capital and trade anywhere in the world.

Likewise, India today remains a very poor country but, since the loosening of government controls over the Indian economy, investment has poured in, especially for the Bangalore region, where a concentrated supply of computer software engineers has attracted investors from California's Silicon Valley, creating in effect the beginnings of a new Silicon Valley in India.

Simple and straightforward as the basic principles of international transfers of wealth may be, words and accounting rules can make it seem more complicated. If Americans buy more Japanese goods than the Japanese buy American goods, then Japan gets American dollars to cover the difference. Since the Japanese are not just going to collect these dollars as souvenirs, they usually turn around and invest them in the American economy. In most cases, the money never leaves the United States. The Japanese simply buy investment goods— Rockefeller Center, for example— rather than consumer goods. American dollars are worthless to the Japanese if they do not spend them on something.

In gross terms, international trade has to balance. But it so happens that the conventions of international accounting count imports and exports in the "balance of trade," but not things which don't move at all, like Rockefeller Center. However, accounting conventions and economic realities can be very different things.

In some years, the best-selling car in America has been a Honda or a Toyota, but no automobile made in Detroit has been the best-selling car in Japan. The net result is that Japanese automakers receive billions of dollars in American money and Japan usually has a net surplus in its trade with the United States. But what do the makers of Hondas and Toyotas do with all that American money? One of the things they do is build factories in the United States, employing thousands of American workers to manufacture their cars closer to their customers, so that Honda and Toyota do not have to pay the cost of shipping cars across the Pacific Ocean.

Their American employees have been paid sufficiently high wages that they have repeatedly voted against joining labor unions in secret ballot elections. On July 29, 2002, the ten millionth Toyota was built in the United States. Looking at *things*, rather than words, there is little here to be alarmed about. What alarms people are the words and the accounting rules which produce numbers to fit those words.

A country's total output consists of both goods and services— houses and haircuts, sausages and surgery— but the international trade balance consists only of physical goods that move. The American economy produces more services than goods, so it is not surprising that the United States imports more goods than it exports— and exports more services than it imports. American know-how and American technology are used by other countries around the world, and these countries of course pay the U.S. for these services. For example, most of the personal computers in the world run on operating systems created by the Microsoft Corporation. But foreign payments to Microsoft and other American companies for their services are not counted in the international balance of trade, since trade includes only goods, not services.

This is just an accounting convention. Yet the American "balance of trade" is reported in the media as if this partial picture were the whole picture, and the emotionally explosive word "deficit" sets off alarms. Yet there is often a substantial surplus earned by the United States from its services, which are of course omitted from the trade balance. In 2012, for example, the United States earned $124 billion from royalty and license fees alone, and more than $628 billion from all the services it supplied to other countries. The latter was more than double the Gross Domestic Product of Egypt or Malaysia.

The *Wall Street Journal*'s comment on the trade deficit was:

> On the list of economic matters to worry about, "the trade deficit" is about 75th— unless politicians react to it by imposing new trade barriers or devaluing the currency.

With trade deficits, as with many other things, what matters is not the absolute size but the size relative to the size of the economy as a whole. While the United States has the world's largest trade deficit, it also has the world's largest economy. The American trade deficit was just under 5 percent of the country's Gross Domestic Product in 2011— less than half that of Turkey and less than one-fourth that of Macedonia.

When you count all the money and resources moving in and out of a country for all sorts of reasons, then you are no longer talking about the "balance of trade" but about the "balance of payments"— regardless of whether the payments were made for goods or services. While this is not as misleading as the balance of trade, it is still far from being the whole story, and it has no necessary connection with the health of the economy. Ironically, one of the rare balance of payments surpluses for the United States in the late twentieth century was followed by the 1992 recession. Germany has regularly run export surpluses, but at the same time its economy has had slower growth rates and higher unemployment rates than those of the United States. Nigeria has often had years of international trade surpluses and is one of the poorest countries in the world.

This is not to say that countries with trade surpluses or payments surpluses are at an economic disadvantage. It is just that these numbers, by themselves, do not necessarily indicate either the prosperity or the poverty of any economy.

Data on foreign investments can also produce misleading words. According to the accounting rules, when people in other countries invest in the United States, that makes the U.S. a "debtor" to those people, because Americans owe them the money that they sent to the U.S., since it was not sent as a gift. When people in many countries around the world feel more secure putting their money in American banks or investing in American corporations, rather than relying on their own banks and corporations, then vast sums of money from overseas find their way to the United States.

Foreigners invested $12 billion in American businesses in 1980 and this rose over the years until they were investing more than $200 billion annually by 1998. By the early twenty-first century, the United States received more than twice as much foreign investment as any other country in the world. As of 2012, foreigners bought $400 billion more assets in the United States than Americans acquired abroad. That exceeds the Gross Domestic Product of many countries. Most of this money (60 percent) comes from Europe and another 9 percent from Canada— together adding up to more than two-thirds of all foreign investment in the United States. Prosperous countries tend to invest in other prosperous countries.

Looked at in terms of *things*, there is nothing wrong with this. By creating more wealth in the United States, such investments created more jobs for American workers and created more goods for American consumers, as well as providing income to foreign investors. Looked at in terms of *words*, however, this was a growing debt to foreigners.

The more prosperous and secure the American economy is, the more foreigners are likely to want to send their money to the United States, and the higher the annual American balance of payments "deficits" and accumulated international "debt" rises. Hence it is not at all surprising that the long prosperity of the U.S. economy in the 1990s was accompanied by record levels of international deficits and debts. The United States was where the action was and this was where many foreigners wanted their money to be, in order to get in on the action. This is not to say that things cannot be different for other countries with different circumstances.

Some other prosperous countries invest more abroad than foreign countries invest in them. France, Britain, and Japan, for example, invest hundreds of billions of dollars more in other countries than other countries invest in them. There is nothing intrinsically wrong with being a creditor nation, any more than there is anything intrinsically wrong with being a debtor nation. Everything depends on the particular circumstances, opportunities, and constraints facing each country. Switzerland, for example, has had a net investment in other countries larger than the Swiss Gross Domestic Product. Vast sums of money come into Switzerland as a major international financial center and, if the Swiss cannot find enough good investment opportunities within their own small country for all this money, it makes perfect sense for them to invest much of the money in other countries.

The point here is that neither international deficits nor surpluses are inevitable consequences of either prosperity or poverty and neither word, by itself, tells much about the condition of a country's economy. The word "debt" covers very different kinds of transactions, some of which may in fact present problems and some of which do not. Every time you deposit a hundred dollars in a bank, that bank goes a hundred dollars deeper into debt, because it is still your money and they owe it to you. Some people might become alarmed if they were told that the bank in which they keep their life's savings was going deeper and deeper into debt every month. But such worries would be completely uncalled for, if the bank's growing debt means only that many other people are also depositing their paychecks in that same bank.

On the other hand, if you are simply buying things on credit, then that is a debt that you are expected to pay— and if you run up debts that are beyond your means of repayment, you can be in big trouble. However, a bank is in no trouble if someone deposits millions of dollars in it, even though that means going millions of dollars deeper in debt. On the contrary, the bank officials would probably be delighted to get millions of dollars, from which they can make more loans and earn more interest.

For most of its history, the United States has been a debtor nation— and has likewise had the highest standard of living in the world for most of its history. One of the things that helped develop the American economy and changed the United States from a small agricultural nation to an industrial giant was an inflow of capital from Western Europe in general and from Britain in particular. These vast resources enabled the United States to build canals, factories and transcontinental railroads to tie the country together economically. As of the 1890s, for example, foreign investors owned about one-fifth of the stock of the Baltimore & Ohio Railroad, more than one-third of the stock of the New York Central, more than half the stock of the Pennsylvania Railroad, and nearly two-thirds of the stock of the Illinois Central.

Even today, when American multinational corporations own vast amounts of assets in other countries, foreigners have owned more assets in the United States than Americans owned abroad for more than a quarter of a century, beginning in 1986.

Obviously, foreign investors would never have sent their money to America unless they expected to get it back with interest and dividends. Equally obviously, American entrepreneurs would never have agreed to pay interest and dividends unless they expected these investments to produce big enough returns to cover these payments and still leave a profit for the American enterprises. These investments usually worked out largely as planned, for generations on end. But this meant that the United States was officially a debtor nation for generations on end. Only as a result of lending money to European governments during the First World War did the United States become a creditor nation. Since then, the U.S. has been both, at one time or another. But these have been accounting details, not determinants of American prosperity or economic problems.

While foreign investments played a major role in the development of particular sectors of the American economy, especially in the early development of industry and infrastructure, there is no need to exaggerate their over-all importance, even in the nineteenth century. For the American economy as a whole, it has been estimated that foreign investment financed about 6 percent of all capital formation in the United States in the nineteenth century. Railroads were exceptional and accounted for an absolute majority of foreign investments in the stocks and bonds of American enterprises.

In various other countries, the role of foreign investors has been much greater than in the United States, even though the large American economy has received more foreign investments in absolute amounts. In the early twentieth century, for example, overseas investors owned one-fifth of the Australian economy and one-half that of Argentina.

Neither the domestic economy nor the international economy is a zero-sum process, where some must lose what others win. Everyone can win when investments create a growing economy. There is a bigger pie, from which everyone can get bigger slices. Massive infusion of foreign capital contributed to making the United States the world's leading industrial nation by 1913, when Americans produced more than one-third of all the manufactured goods in the world.

Despite fears in some countries that foreign investors would carry off much of their national wealth, leaving the local population poorer, there is probably no country in history from which foreigners have carried away more vast amounts of wealth than the United States. By that reasoning, Americans ought to be some of the poorest people in the world, instead of consistently having one of the world's highest standards of living. The reason for that prosperity is that economic transactions are not a zero-sum activity. They create wealth.

In some less fortunate countries, the same words used in accounting— especially "debt"— may have a very different economic reality behind them.

For example, when exports will not cover the cost of imports and there is no high-tech know-how to export, the government may borrow money from some other country or from some international agency, in order to cover the difference. These are genuine debts and causes for genuine concern. But the mere fact of a large trade deficit or a large payments deficit does not by itself create a crisis, though political and journalistic rhetoric can turn it into something to alarm the public.

Lurking in the background of much confused thinking about international trade and international transfers of wealth is an implicit assumption of a zero-sum contest, where some can gain only if others lose. Thus, for example, some have claimed that multinational corporations profit by "exploiting" workers in the Third World. If so, it is hard to explain why the vast majority of American investments in other countries go to richer countries, where high wage rates must be paid, not poorer countries whose wage rates are a fraction of those paid in more prosperous nations.

Over the period from 1994 to 2002, for example, more U.S. direct investment in foreign countries went to Canada and to European nations than to the entire rest of the world combined. Moreover, U.S. investments in truly poverty-stricken areas like sub-Saharan Africa and the poorer parts of Asia have been about one percent of worldwide foreign investment by Americans. Over the years, a majority of the jobs created abroad by American multinational companies have been created in high-wage countries.

Just as Americans' foreign investments go predominantly to prosperous nations, so the United States is itself the world's largest recipient of international investments, despite the high wages of American workers. India's Tata conglomerate bought the Ritz-Carlton Hotel in Boston and Tetley Tea in Britain, among its many international holdings, even though these holdings in Western nations require Tata Industries to pay far higher wages than it would have to pay in its native India.

Why are profit-seeking companies investing far more where they will have to pay high wages to workers in affluent industrial nations, instead of low wages to "sweatshop" labor in the Third World? Why are they passing up supposedly golden opportunities to "exploit" the poorest workers? Exploitation may be an intellectually convenient, emotionally satisfying, and politically expedient explanation of income differences between nations or between groups within a given nation, but it does not have the additional feature of fitting the facts about where profit-seeking enterprises invest most of their money, either internationally or domestically. Moreover, even within poor countries, the very poorest people are typically those with the least contact with multinational corporations, often because they are located away from the ports and other business centers.

American multinational corporations alone have provided employment to more than 30 million people worldwide. But, given their international investment patterns, relatively few of those jobs are likely to be in the poorest countries where they are most needed. In some cases, a multinational corporation may in fact invest in a Third World country, where the local wages are sufficiently lower to compensate for the lower productivity of the workers and/or the higher costs of shipping in a less developed transportation system and/or the bribes that have to be paid to government officials to operate in many such countries.

Various reformers or protest movements of college students and others in the affluent countries may then wax indignant over the low wages and "sweatshop" working conditions in these Third World enterprises. However, if these protest movements succeed politically in forcing up the wages and working conditions in these countries, the net result can be that even fewer foreign companies will invest in the Third World and fewer Third World workers will have jobs. Since multinational corporations typically pay about double the local wages in poor countries, the loss of these jobs is likely to translate into more hardship for Third World workers, even as their would-be benefactors in the West congratulate themselves on having ended "exploitation."

REMITTANCES AND HUMAN CAPITAL

Even in an era of international investments in the trillions of dollars, other kinds of transfers of wealth among nations remain significant. These include remittances, foreign aid, and transfers of human capital in the form of the skills and entrepreneurship of emigrants.

Remittances

Emigrants working in foreign countries often send money back to their families to support them. During the nineteenth and early twentieth centuries, Italian emigrant men were particularly noted for enduring terrible living conditions in various countries around the world, and even skimping on food, in order to send money back to their families in Italy. Most of the people fleeing the famine in Ireland during the 1840s traveled across the Atlantic with their fares paid by remittances from members of their families already living in the United States. The same would be true of Jewish emigrants from Eastern Europe to the United States in later years.

In the twenty-first century, remittances are among the main sources of outside money flowing into poorer countries. In 2009, for example, the worldwide remittances to these countries were more than two and a half times the value of all foreign aid.

At one time, overseas Chinese living in Malaysia, Indonesia and other Southeast Asian nations were noted for sending money back to their families in China. Politicians and journalists in these countries often whipped up hostility against the overseas Chinese by claiming that such remittances were impoverishing the host countries for the benefit of China. In reality, the Chinese created many of the enterprises— and sometimes whole industries— in these Southeast Asian nations. What they were sending back to China was a fraction of the wealth they had created and added to the wealth of the countries where they were now living.

Similar charges were made against the Lebanese in West Africa, the Indians and Pakistanis in East Africa, and other groups around the world. The underlying fallacy in each case was due to ignoring the wealth created by these groups, so that the countries to which they immigrated had more wealth— not less— as a result of these groups being there. Sometimes the hostility generated against such groups has led to their leaving these countries or being expelled, often followed by economic declines in the countries they left.

Emigrants and Immigrants

People are one of the biggest sources of wealth. Whole industries have been created and economies have been transformed by immigrants.

Historically, it has not been at all unusual for a particular ethnic or immigrant group to create or dominate a whole industry. German immigrants created the leading beer breweries in the United States in the nineteenth century, and most of the leading brands of American beer in the twenty-first century are still produced in breweries created by people of German ancestry. China's most famous beer— Tsingtao— was also created by Germans and there are German breweries in Australia, Brazil, and Argentina. There were no watches manufactured in London until Huguenots fleeing France took watch-making skills with them to England and Switzerland, making both these nations among the leading watch-makers in the world. Conversely, France faced increased competition in a number of industries which it had once dominated, because the Huguenots who had fled persecution in France created competing businesses in surrounding countries.

Among the vital sources of the skills and entrepreneurship behind the rise of first Britain, and later the United States, to the position of the leading industrial and commercial nation in the world were the numerous immigrant groups who settled in these countries, often to escape persecution or destitution in their native lands. The woolen, linen, cotton, silk, paper, and glass industries were revolutionized by foreign workers and foreign entrepreneurs in England, while the Jews and the Lombards developed British financial institutions. The United States, as a country populated overwhelmingly by immigrants, had even more occupations and industries created or dominated by particular immigrant groups. The first pianos built in colonial America were built by Germans— who also pioneered in building pianos in czarist Russia, England, and France— and firms created by Germans continued to produce the leading American pianos, such as Steinway, in the twenty-first century.

Perhaps to an even greater degree, the countries of Latin America have been dependent on immigrants— especially immigrants from countries other than the conquering nations of Spain and Portugal that created these Latin American nations. According to the distinguished French historian Fernand

Braudel, it was these immigrants who "created modern Brazil, modern Argentina, modern Chile." Among the foreigners who have owned or directed more than half of particular industries in particular countries have been the Lebanese in West Africa, Greeks in the Ottoman Empire, Germans in Brazil, Indians in Fiji, Britons in Argentina, Belgians in Russia, Chinese in Malaysia, and many others. Nor is this all a thing of the past. Four-fifths of the doughnut shops in California are owned by people of Cambodian ancestry.

Throughout history, national economic losses from emigration have been as striking as gains from receiving immigrants. After the Moriscos were expelled from Spain in the early seventeenth century, a Spanish cleric asked: "Who will make our shoes now?" This was a question that might better have been asked *before* the Moriscos were expelled, especially since this particular cleric had supported the expulsions. Some countries have exported human capital on a large scale— for example, when their educated young people emigrate because other countries offer better opportunities. *The Economist* reported that more than 60 percent of the college or university graduates in Fiji, Trinidad, Haiti, Jamaica and Guyana have gone to live in countries belonging to the Organisation for Economic Co-Operation and Development. For Guyana, 83 percent did so.

Although it is not easy to quantify human capital, emigration of educated people on this scale represents a serious loss of national wealth. One of the most striking examples of a country's losses due to those who emigrated was that of Nazi Germany, whose anti-Semitic policies led many Jewish scientists to flee to America, where they played a major role in making the United States the first nation with an atomic bomb. Thus Germany's ally Japan then paid an even bigger price for policies that led to massive Jewish emigration from Nazi-dominated Europe.

It would be misleading, however, to assess the economic impact of immigration solely in terms of its positive contributions. Immigrants have also brought diseases, crime, internal strife, and terrorism. Nor can all immigrants be lumped together. When only two percent of immigrants from Japan to the United States go on welfare, while 46 percent of the immigrants from Laos do, there is no single pattern that applies to all immigrants. There are similar disparities in crime rates and in other both negative and positive factors that immigrants from different countries bring to the United States and to other countries in other parts of the world. Russia and Nigeria are usually ranked among the most corrupt countries in the world and immigrants from Russia and Nigeria have become notorious for criminal activities in the United States.

Everything depends on which immigrants you are talking about, which countries you are talking about and which periods of history.

Imperialism

Plunder of one nation or people by another has been all too common throughout human history.

Although imperialism is one of the ways in which wealth can be transferred from one country to another, there are also non-economic reasons for imperialism which have caused it to be persisted in, even when it was costing the conquering country money on net balance. Military leaders may want strategic bases, such as the British base at Gibraltar or the American base at Guantanamo Bay in Cuba. Nineteenth century missionaries urged the British government toward acquiring control of various countries in Africa where there was much missionary work going on— such urgings often being opposed by chancellors of the exchequer, who realized that Britain would never get enough wealth out of these poor countries to repay the costs of establishing and maintaining colonial regimes there.

Some private individuals like Cecil Rhodes might get rich in Africa, but the costs to the British taxpayers exceeded even Rhodes' fabulous fortune. Modern European imperialism in general was much more impressive in terms of the size of the territories controlled than in terms of the economic significance of those territories. When European empires were at their zenith in the early twentieth century, Western Europe was less than 2 percent of the world's land area but it controlled another 40 percent in overseas empires. However, most major industrial nations sent only trivial percentages of their exports or investments to their conquered colonies in the Third World and received imports that were similarly trivial compared to what these industrial nations produced themselves or purchased as imports from other industrial countries.

Even at the height of the British Empire in the early twentieth century, the British invested more in the United States than in all of Asia and Africa put together. Quite simply, there is more wealth to be made from rich countries than from poor countries. For similar reasons, throughout most of the twentieth century the United States invested more in Canada than in all of Asia and Africa put together. Only the rise of prosperous Asian industrial nations in the latter part of the twentieth century attracted more American investors to that part of the world. After the world price of oil skyrocketed in the early twenty-first century, foreign investments poured into the oil-producing countries of the Middle East. As the *Wall Street Journal* reported: "Overall, foreign direct investment in the Arab Middle East reached $19 billion last year [2006], up from $4 billion in 2001." International investment in general continues to go where wealth exists already.

Perhaps the strongest evidence against the economic significance of colonies in the modern world is that Germany and Japan lost all their colonies and conquered lands as a result of their defeat in the Second World War— and both countries rebounded to reach unprecedented levels of prosperity thereafter. A need for colonies was a particularly effective political talking point in pre-war Japan, which has had very few natural resources of its own. But, after its dreams of military glory ended with its defeat and devastation, Japan simply bought whatever natural resources it needed from those countries that had them, and prospered doing so.

Imperialism has often caused much suffering among the conquered peoples. But, in the modern industrial world at least, imperialism has seldom been a major source of international transfers of wealth.

While investors have tended to invest in more prosperous nations, making both themselves and these nations wealthier, some people have depicted investments in poor countries as somehow making the latter even poorer. The Marxian concept of "exploitation" was applied internationally in Lenin's book *Imperialism*, where investments by industrial nations in non-industrial countries were treated as being economically equivalent to the looting done by earlier imperialist conquerors. Tragically, however, it is in precisely those less developed countries where little or no foreign investment has taken place that poverty is at its worst.

Similarly, those poor countries with less international trade as a percentage of their national economies have usually had lower economic growth rates than poor countries where international trade plays a larger economic role. Indeed, during the decade of the 1990s, the former countries had declining economies, while those more "globalized" countries had growing economies.

Wealthy individuals in poor countries often invest in richer countries, where their money is safer from political upheavals and confiscations. Ironically, poorer countries are thus helping richer industrial nations to become still richer. Meanwhile, under the influence of theories of economic imperialism which depicted international investments as being the equivalent of imperialist looting, governments in many poorer countries pursued policies which discouraged investments from being made there by foreigners.

By the late twentieth century, however, the painful economic consequences of such policies had become sufficiently apparent to many people in the Third World that some governments— in Latin America and India, for example— began moving away from such policies, in order to gain some of the benefits received by other countries which had risen from poverty to prosperity with the help of investments made in their countries by enterprises in other countries.

Economic realities finally broke through ideological visions, though generations had suffered needless deprivations before basic economic facts and principles were finally accepted. Once markets in these countries were opened to foreign goods and foreign investments, both poured in. However small the investments of prosperous countries in poor countries might seem in comparison with their investments in other prosperous countries, those investments have loomed large within the Third World, precisely because of the poverty of these countries. As of 1991, foreign companies owned 27 percent of the businesses in Latin America and, a decade later, owned 39 percent.

Many economic fallacies are due to conceiving of economic activity as a zero-sum contest, in which what is gained by one is lost by another. This in turn is often due to ignoring the fact that wealth is *created* in the course of economic activity. If payments to foreign investors impoverished a nation, then the United States would be one of the most impoverished nations in the world, because foreigners took $543 billion out of the American economy in 2012— which was more than the Gross Domestic Product of Argentina or Norway. Since most of this money consisted of earnings from assets that foreigners owned in the United States, Americans had already gotten the benefits of the additional wealth that those assets had helped create, and were simply sharing part of that additional wealth with those abroad who had contributed to creating it.

A variation on the theme of exploitation is the claim that free international trade increases the inequality between rich and poor nations. Evidence for this conclusion has included statistical data from the World Bank showing that the ratio of the incomes of the twenty highest-income nations to that of the twenty lowest-income nations increased from 23-to-one in 1960 to 36-to-one by 2000. But such statistics are grossly misleading because neither the top twenty nations nor the bottom twenty nations were the same in 2000 as in 1960. Comparing the *same* twenty nations in 1960 and in 2000 shows that the ratio of the income of the most prosperous nations to that of the most poverty-stricken nations *declined* from 23-to-one to less than ten-to-one. Expanded international trade is one of the ways poor nations have risen out of the bottom twenty.

It is of course also possible to obtain foreign technology, machinery, and expertise by paying for these things with export earnings. The poorer a country is, the more that means domestic hardships as the price of economic development. "Let us starve but export," declared a czarist minister— who was very unlikely to do any starving himself. The very same philosophy was employed later, though not announced, during the era of the Soviet Union, when the industrialization of the economy was heavily dependent on foreign imports financed by exports of food and other natural resources. According to two Soviet economists, writing many years later:

> During the first Five-Year Plan, 40 percent of export earnings came from grain shipments. In 1931 one third of the machinery and equipment imported in the world was purchased by the U.S.S.R. Of all the equipment put into operation in Soviet factories during this period, 80 to 85 percent was purchased from the West.

At the time, however, the growth of the state-run Soviet industrial complex was proclaimed a triumph of communism, though in fact it represented an importation of capitalist technology, while skimping on food in the Soviet Union. The alternative of allowing foreign investment was not permitted in a government-run economy founded on a rejection of capitalism.

Foreign Aid

What is called "foreign aid" are transfers of wealth from foreign governmental organizations, as well as international agencies, to the governments of poorer countries. The term "aid" assumes *a priori* that such transfers will in fact aid the poorer countries' economies to develop. In some cases it does, but in other cases foreign aid simply enables the existing politicians in power to enrich themselves through graft and to dispense largess in politically strategic ways to others who help to keep them in power. Because it is a transfer of wealth to governments, as distinguished from investments in private enterprises, foreign aid has encouraged many countries to set up government-run enterprises that have failed, or to create palaces, plazas or other things meant to impress on-lookers rather than produce things that raise the material standard of living in the recipient country.

Perhaps the most famous foreign aid program was the Marshall Plan, which transferred wealth from the United States to various countries in Western Europe after the end of World War II. The Marshall Plan was far more successful than many later attempts to imitate it by sending foreign aid to Third World countries. Western Europe's economic distress was caused by the physical devastations of the war. Once the people were fed and the infrastructure rebuilt, Western Europe simply resumed the industrial way of life which they had achieved before— indeed, which they had pioneered before.

That was wholly different from trying to create all the industrial skills that were lacking in poorer, non-industrial nations. What needed to be rebuilt in Europe was physical capital. What needed to be created in much of the Third World was more human capital. The latter proved harder to do, just as the vast array of skills needed in a modern economy had taken centuries to develop in Europe.

Even massive and highly visible failures and counterproductive results from foreign aid have not stopped its continuation and expansion. The vast sums of money dispensed by foreign aid agencies such as the International Monetary Fund and the World Bank give the officials of these agencies enormous influence on the governments of poorer countries, regardless of the success or failure of the programs they suggest or impose as preconditions for receiving money. In short, there is no economic bottom line constraining aid dispensers to determine which actions, policies, organizations or individuals could survive the weeding out process that takes place through competition in the marketplace.

In addition to the "foreign aid" dispensed by international agencies, there are also direct government-to-government grants of money, shipments of free food, and loans which are made available on terms more lenient than those available in the financial markets, and which are from time to time "forgiven," allowed to default, or "rolled over" by being repaid from the proceeds of new and larger loans. Thus American government loans to the government of India and British government loans to a number of Third World governments have been simply cancelled, converting these loans into gifts.

Sometimes a richer country takes over a whole poor society and heavily subsidizes it, as the United States did in Micronesia. So much American aid poured in that many Micronesians abandoned economic activities on which they had supported themselves before, such as fishing and farming. If and when Americans decide to end such aid, it is not at all certain that the skills and experience that Micronesians once had will remain widespread enough in later generations to allow them to become self-sufficient again.

Beneficial results of foreign aid are more likely to be publicized by the national or international agencies which finance these ventures, while failures are more likely to be publicized by critics, so the net effect is not immediately obvious. One of the leading development economists of his time, the late Professor Peter Bauer of the London School of Economics, argued that, on the whole, "official aid is more likely to retard development than to promote it." Whether that controversial conclusion is accepted or rejected, what is more fundamental is that terms like "foreign aid" not be allowed to insinuate a result which may or may not turn out to be substantiated by facts and analysis.

Another phrase that presupposes an outcome which may or may not in fact materialize is the term "developing nations" for poorer nations, who may or may not be developing as fast as more prosperous nations, and in a number of cases have actually retrogressed economically over the years.

Many Third World countries have considerable internal sources of wealth which are not fully utilized for one reason or another— and this wealth often greatly exceeds whatever foreign aid such countries have ever received. In many poorer countries, much— if not most— economic activity takes place "off the books" or in the "underground economy" because the costs of red tape, corruption, and bureaucratic delays required to obtain legal permission to run a business or own a home put legally recognized economic activities beyond the financial reach of much of the population. These people may operate businesses ranging from street vending to factories, or build homes for themselves or others, without having any of this economic activity legally recognized by their governments.

According to *The Economist* magazine, in a typical African nation, only about one person in ten works in a legally recognized enterprise or lives in a house that has legally recognized property rights. In Egypt, for example, an estimated 4.7 million homes have been built illegally. In Peru, the total value of all the real estate that is not legally covered by property rights has been estimated as more than a dozen times larger than all the foreign direct investments ever made in the country in its entire history. Similar situations have been found in India, Haiti, and other Third World countries. In short, many poor countries have already created substantial amounts of physical wealth that is not legally recognized, and therefore cannot be used to draw upon the financial resources of banks or other lenders and investors, as existing physical wealth can be used to build more wealth-creating enterprises in nations with better functioning property rights systems.

The economic consequences of legal bottlenecks in many poor countries can be profound because they prevent many existing enterprises, representing vast amounts of wealth in the aggregate, from developing beyond the small scale in which they start. Many giant American corporations began as very small enterprises, not very different from those which abound in Third World countries today. Founders of Levi's, Macy's, Saks, and Bloomingdale's all began as peddlers, for example.

While such businesses may get started with an individual's own small savings or perhaps with loans from family or friends, eventually their expansion into major corporations usually requires the mobilization of the money of innumerable strangers who are willing to become investors. But the property rights system which makes this possible has not been as accessible to ordinary people in Third World countries as it has been to ordinary people in the United States.

An American bank that is unwilling to invest in a small business may nevertheless be willing to lend money to its owner in exchange for a mortgage on his home— but the home must first be legally recognized as the property of the person seeking the loan. After the business becomes a major success, other strangers may then lend money on its growing assets or invest directly as stockholders. But all of this hinges on a system of dependable and accessible property rights, which is capable of mobilizing far more wealth within even a poor country than is ever likely to be transferred from other nations or from international agencies like the World Bank or the International Monetary Fund.

Many people judge how much help is being given to poorer countries by either the absolute amount of a donor nation's government transfer of wealth to poorer countries, or by the percentage share of that national income that is sent in the form of government-to-government transfers as "foreign aid." But an estimated 90 percent of the wealth transfers to poorer nations from the United States takes the form of private philanthropic donations, business investments or remittances from citizens from Third World countries living in the United States. As of 2010, for example, official development assistance from the United States to Third World nations was $31 billion but American private philanthropy alone sent $39 billion to those nations, while American private capital flows to the Third World were $108 billion, and remittances from the United States to those countries were $100 billion.

People who measure a donor nation's contributions to poorer countries solely by the amount of official "foreign aid" sometimes point out that, although "foreign aid" from the United States is the largest in the world, it is also among the smallest as a percentage of Americans' income. But that ignores the vastly larger amount of American transfers of wealth to poor countries in non-governmental forms. Since the beginning of the twenty-first century, most of the transfers of wealth from prosperous countries in general to poorer countries have been in forms other than what is called "foreign aid."

A much larger question is the extent to which these international transfers of hundreds of billions of dollars have actually benefitted the countries receiving them. That is a much harder question to answer. However, given the differing incentives of those sending wealth in different forms, official "foreign aid" may have the fewest incentives to ensure that the wealth received will be used to increase output in the recipient country and thus raise the standard of living of the general population of these nations.

THE INTERNATIONAL MONETARY SYSTEM

Wealth may be transferred from country to country in the form of goods and services, but by far the greatest transfers are made in the form of money. Just as a stable monetary unit facilitates economic activity within a country, so international economic activity is facilitated when there are stable relationships between one country's currency and another's. It is not simply a question of the ease or difficulty of converting dollars into yen or euros at a given moment. A far more important question is whether an investment made in the United States, Japan, or France today will be repaid a decade or more from now in money of the same purchasing power.

When currencies fluctuate relative to one another, anyone who engages in any international transactions becomes a speculator. Even an American tourist who buys souvenirs in Mexico will have to wait until the credit card bill arrives to discover how much the item they paid 30 pesos for will cost them in U.S. dollars. It can turn out to be either more or less than they thought. Where millions of dollars are invested overseas, the stability of the various currencies is urgently important. It is important not simply to those whose money is directly involved, it is important in maintaining the flows of trade and investment which affect the material well-being of the general public in the countries concerned.

During the era of the gold standard, which began to break down during the First World War and ended during the Great Depression of the 1930s, various nations made their national currencies equivalent to a given amount of gold. An American dollar, for example, could always be exchanged for a fixed amount of gold from the U.S. government. Both Americans and foreigners could exchange their dollars for a given amount of gold. Therefore any foreign investor putting his money into the American economy knew in advance what he could count on getting back if his investment worked out. No doubt that had much to do with the vast amount of capital that poured into the United States from Europe and helped develop it into the leading industrial nation of the world.

Other nations which made their currency redeemable in fixed amounts of gold likewise made their economies safer places for both domestic and foreign investors. Moreover, their currencies were also automatically fixed relative to the dollar and other currencies from other countries that used the gold standard. As Nobel Prizewinning monetary economist Robert Mundell put it, "currencies were just names for particular weights of gold." During that era, famed financier J.P. Morgan could say, "money is gold, and nothing else." This reduced the risks of buying, selling, or investing in those foreign countries that were on the gold standard, since exchange rate fluctuations were not the threat that they were in transactions with other countries.

The end of the gold standard led to various attempts at stabilizing international currencies against one another. Some nations have made their currencies equivalent to a fixed number of dollars, for example. Various European nations have joined together to create their own international currency, the euro, and the Japanese yen has been another stable currency widely accepted in international financial transactions. At the other extreme have been various South American countries, whose currencies have fluctuated wildly in value, with annual inflation rates sometimes reaching double or even triple digits.

These monetary fluctuations have had repercussions on such real things as output and employment, since it is difficult to plan and invest when there is much uncertainty about what the money will be worth, even if the investment is successful otherwise. The economic problems of Argentina and Brazil have been particularly striking in view of the fact that both countries are richly endowed with natural resources and have been spared the destruction of wars that so many other countries on other continents suffered in the course of the twentieth century.

With the spread of electronic transfers of money, reactions to any national currency's change in reliability can be virtually instantaneous. Any government that is tempted toward inflation knows that money can flee from their economy literally in a moment. The discipline this imposes is different from that once imposed by a gold standard, but whether it is equally effective will only be known when future economic pressures put the international monetary system to a real test.

As in other areas of economics, it is necessary to be on guard against emotionally loaded words that may confuse more than they clarify. Among the terms widely used in discussing the relative values of various national currencies are "strong" and "weak." Thus, when the euro was first introduced as a monetary unit in the European Union countries, its value fell from $1.18 to 83 cents and it was said to be "weakening" relative to the dollar. Later it rose again, to reach $1.16 in early 2003, and was then said to be "strengthening." Words can be harmless if we understand what they do and don't mean, but misleading if we take their connotations at face value.

One thing that a "strong" currency does *not* mean is that the economies which use that currency are necessarily better off. Sometimes it means the opposite. A "strong" currency means that the prices of exports from countries which use that currency have risen in price to people in other countries. Thus the rise in value of the euro in 2003 has been blamed by a number of European corporations for falling exports to the United States, as the prices of their products rose in dollars, causing fewer Americans to buy them. Meanwhile, the "weakening" of Britain's pound sterling had opposite effects. *BusinessWeek* magazine reported:

> Britain's hard-pressed manufacturers love a falling pound. So they have warmly welcomed the 11% slide in sterling's exchange rate against the euro over the past year. ... As the pound weakens against the euro, it makes British goods more competitive on the Continent, which is by far their largest export market. And it boosts corporate profits when earnings from the euro zone are converted into sterling.

Just as a "strong" currency is not always good, it is not always bad either. In the countries that use the euro, businesses that borrow from Americans find the burden of that debt to be less, and therefore easier to repay, when fewer euros are needed to pay back the dollars they owe. When Norway's krone rose in value relative to Sweden's krona, Norwegians living near the border of Sweden crossed over the border and saved 40 percent buying a load of groceries in Sweden. The point here is simply that words like "strong" and "weak" currencies by themselves tell us little about the economic realities, which have to be looked at directly and specifically, rather than by relying on the emotional connotations of words.

It should also be noted that a given currency can be both rising and falling at the same time. For example, over the period from December 2008 to April 2009, the American dollar was rising in value relative to the Swedish krona and the Swiss franc while falling in value relative to the British pound and the Australian dollar.

Chapter 23

INTERNATIONAL

DISPARITIES

IN WEALTH

Everywhere in the world there are gross inequities of income and wealth. They offend most of us. Few can fail to be moved by the contrast between the luxury enjoyed by some and the grinding poverty suffered by others.

Milton and Rose Friedman

Any study of international economic activities inevitably encounters the fact of vast differences among nations in their incomes and wealth. In the early nineteenth century, for example, there were four Balkan countries where the average income per capita was only one-fourth that in the industrialized countries of Western Europe. Two centuries later, there were still economic differences of a similar magnitude between the countries of Western Europe and various countries in the Balkans and Eastern Europe. The per capita Gross Domestic Product (GDP) of Albania, Moldova, Ukraine and Kosovo were each less than one-fourth of the per capita GDP of Holland, Switzerland, or Denmark— and less than one-fifth of the per capita GDP of Norway.

Similar disparities are common in Asia, where the per capita GDP of China is less than one-fourth that of Japan, while that of India is barely more than ten percent of the per capita GDP of Japan. The per capita GDP

527

of sub-Saharan Africa is less than ten percent of the per capita GDP of the nations of the Euro zone.

Many find such disparities both puzzling and troubling, especially when contemplating the fate of people born in such dire poverty that their chances of a fulfilling life seem very remote. Among the many explanations that have been offered for this painful situation, there are some that are more emotionally satisfying or politically popular than others. But a more fundamental question might be: Was there ever any realistic chance that the nations of the world would have had similar prospects of economic development?

Innumerable factors go into economic development. For all the possible combinations and permutations of these factors to work out in such a way as to produce even approximately equal results for all countries around the world would be a staggering coincidence. We can, however, examine some of these factors, in order to get some insight into some of the causes of these differences.

GEOGRAPHIC FACTORS

Whether human beings are divided into countries, races or other categories, geography is just one of the reasons why they have never had either the same direct economic benefits or the same opportunities to develop their own human capital. Virtually none of the geographic factors that promote economic prosperity and human development is equally available in all parts of the world.

To begin with the most basic, land is not equally fertile everywhere. The unusually fertile soils that scientists call Mollisols are distributed around the world in a very uneven pattern. Large concentrations of these rich soils are found in the American upper midwestern and plains states, extending into parts of Canada, and a vast swath of these soils spreads all the way across the Eurasian land mass, from the southern part of Eastern Europe to northeastern China. A smaller concentration of these soils is found in the temperate zone of South America, in southern Argentina, southern Brazil and Uruguay.

While such soils are found in various parts of the temperate zones of both the Northern Hemisphere and the Southern Hemisphere, they are seldom found in the tropics. The soils of sub-Saharan Africa have multiple and severe deficiencies, leading to crop yields that are a fraction of those in China or the United States. In many parts of Africa, the topsoil is shallow, allowing little space for the roots of plants to go down and collect nutrients and water. The dryness of much of Africa inhibits the use of fertilizers to supply the nutrients missing in the soil, because fertilizers used without adequate water can inhibit, rather than enhance, the growth of crops. Where there are wetlands in Africa of a sort that are cultivated successfully in Asia, these wetlands are less often cultivated in tropical Africa, where wetlands breed such dangerous diseases as malaria and river blindness.

Even within a given country, such as China, there are very different varieties of soils— predominantly rich, black soils in the northeast and less fertile red soil in the southeast, soil of a sort often found in tropical and subtropical regions of the world. Not only does the fertility of the land vary greatly in different regions of the world, it has also varied over time. Heavy soils in parts of Europe *became* fertile after ways of harnessing horses and oxen to pull the plow were developed, but these soils were far less fertile in earlier centuries, when more primitive methods were used that were effective in lighter soils. It was much the same story in Asia: "Japanese croplands were originally much inferior to those in Northern India; they are greatly superior today."

The rain that falls on the land is not equal in amount or reliability in different regions of the world, nor does all land absorb and hold rain water equally. Loess soil, such as that in northern China, can absorb and hold much more of the rain that falls on it than can the limestone soils in parts of the Balkans, through which the water drains more quickly, leaving less moisture behind to help crops grow. Of course the deserts of the world get little rainfall in the first place. In some places, such as Western Europe, the rain falls more or less evenly throughout the year, whereas in other places, such as sub-Saharan Africa, there are long dry spells followed by torrential downpours that can wash away topsoil.

During the many centuries when agriculture was the most important economic activity in countries around the world, there was no way that this crucial activity could produce similar economic results everywhere— whether in terms of a general standard of living or in terms of an ability to develop and sustain major urban communities dependent on local agriculture for their food. Given the large role of cities in economic progress and the development of a wide range of skills, a dearth of cities can adversely affect not only current economic conditions but also future economic progress.

Such fundamental things as sunshine and rain vary greatly from one place to another. The average annual hours of sunshine in Athens are nearly double that in London, and the annual hours of sunshine in Alexandria are more than double. Even within the same country, different places can have much different amounts of rain. In Spain, for example, the annual rainfall ranges from under 300mm to just over 1,500mm.

Sunlight has both positive and negative effects on agriculture, directly promoting photosynthesis and at the same time evaporating the water that plants need to survive. In various lands around the Mediterranean, abundant summer sunshine evaporates more water than falls as the meager summer rain in that region. Thus irrigation may be necessary for agriculture in places that would not be considered arid if judged solely by the amount of annual rainfall, because most of that rain falls in the winter in this part of the world. In other parts of the world, there is far more rain in the summer than in the winter. In both situations, this limits which kinds of crops can be grown successfully in particular places.

The larger point here is that the effect of different geographic factors, such as sunshine and rain, cannot be considered in isolation, because their interactions are crucial and their timing is crucial. The possible combinations and permutations of these factors are exponentially greater than the number of factors considered in isolation, leading to great variations in economic outcomes in places that may seem to be similar, when the interaction of factors is not taken into account. This applies not only to variations in the land but also to variations in waterways, and not only to effects in agriculture but also to effects on cities, industries and commerce.

None of the valuable natural resources in the land— whether iron ore, coal, petroleum or many others— is spread evenly over the planet. Not only do particular natural resources tend to be concentrated in particular places, such as oil in the Middle East, the knowledge of how to extract and process such resources develops in different eras, so that a particular material thing becomes a valuable resource in different countries and at different periods of history. While there have been large petroleum deposits in the Middle East for thousands of years, petroleum became a valuable resource only after science and technology developed to the point that made it indispensable to the industrial nations of the world, and thus brought large amounts of wealth from these nations to the Middle East to pay for its oil.

In addition to natural resources such as land and the minerals in it, which can contribute directly to economic prosperity and development, there are other geographic factors which contribute indirectly but importantly, by facilitating various economic activities. Among these are navigable waterways and animals that facilitate both travel and agriculture.

Navigable Waterways

There are economic reasons why most cities around the world are located on waterways, whether rivers, harbors or lakes. Some of the most famous cities are located at or near the terminus of great rivers that empty into the open seas (New York, London, Shanghai, Rotterdam), some are located beside huge lakes or inland seas (Geneva, Chicago, Odessa, Detroit) and some are located on great harbors emptying into the open seas (Sydney, San Francisco, Tokyo, Rio de Janeiro).

Among the economic reasons for these locations are transportation costs. Land transport has cost far more than water transport, especially in the millennia before self-propelled vehicles appeared, less than two centuries ago. Even today, it can cost more to ship cargo a hundred miles by land than to ship it a thousand miles by water. In 1830, a cargo that cost more than thirty dollars to ship 300 miles over land could be shipped 3,000 miles across the Atlantic Ocean for just ten dollars. Given the vast amounts of things that have to be constantly transported into cities, such as food and fuel, and the huge volume of a city's output that must be transported out to sell elsewhere, it is not surprising that so many cities are located on navigable waterways.

The benefits of navigable waterways are by no means evenly distributed around the world, whether in terms of the number of rivers and harbors or the suitability of those rivers and harbors for transporting cargoes. The navigability of rivers is limited by the shape of the lands through which they flow. Western Europe, for example, is criss-crossed with rivers flowing gently across wide and level coastal plains into the open seas, which provide access to countries around the world. By contrast, most of sub-Saharan Africa, except for narrow coastal plains, is more than 1,000 feet in elevation and much of it is more than 2,000 feet high. Africa's narrow coastal plains are often backed by steep escarpments that block the penetration of the interior by vessels coming in from the sea, and prevent boats from the interior from reaching the coast.

Because of the physical shape of the land, rivers in sub-Saharan Africa plunge from a height of a thousand feet or more, down through cascades and waterfalls on their way to the sea. The huge Zaire River, for example, begins 4,700 feet above sea level, and so must fall nearly a mile before it finally flows out into the Atlantic. Such rivers are navigable only for limited level stretches, usually navigable for boats of only limited sizes, and often for only limited times of the year, given the more sporadic rainfall patterns in sub-Saharan Africa, compared to the more even rainfall patterns in Western Europe. During the dry season, even a major African river like the Niger, draining water from an area larger than Texas, is at some point less than three feet deep. Yet, during the height of the rainy season, the Niger has been characterized as "a 20-mile-wide moving lake."

Although the Zaire River empties more water into the sea than does the Mississippi, the Yangtze, the Rhine or many other great commercial waterways of the world, the thousands of feet that the Zaire must come down on its way to the sea, through rapids, cascades and waterfalls, preclude any comparable volume of cargo traffic. Ships coming in from the Atlantic on the Zaire River cannot get very far inland before they are stopped by a series of cataracts. Neither the length of a river nor even its volume of water says anything about its economic value as an artery of transportation.

Like other African rivers, the Zaire provides many miles of local transportation, but these are not necessarily long *continuous* miles that would connect the interior of Africa by water with the open seas and international trade. The extent to which African rivers connect different communities within the continent with each other is also limited by the many cascades and waterfalls which determine how far a given vessel can go.

Sometimes canoes may be emptied of their cargoes and carried around a cascade or waterfall, to be reloaded for the next portion of the journey. But this not only limits the size of the vessels used, and therefore the size of the cargoes, but also increases the cost of the additional time and labor required to get a cargo to its destination. The net result is that only cargoes with a very high value in a small physical size are economically viable to transport. By contrast, in parts of the world where rivers flow continuously for hundreds of miles through level plains, large cargoes of relatively low value in proportion to their bulk and weight— such as wood, wheat or coal— are economically viable to ship.

Harbors are likewise neither as common nor as useful in some parts of the world as in others. Although Africa is more than twice the size of Europe, the African coastline is shorter than the European coastline. This is possible only because the European coastline twists and turns far more, creating many more harbors where ships can dock, sheltered from the rough waters of the open seas.

Moreover, the deep waters in many European harbors mean that large, ocean-going ships can often dock right up against the land, as in Stockholm or Monaco, whereas the shallow coastal waters in much of sub-Saharan Africa mean that large ships have had to anchor offshore, and unload their cargoes onto smaller vessels that can travel in these shallow waters— a far more expensive process, and one that has often been prohibitively expensive. For centuries, trade between Europe and Asia took place in ships that sailed around Africa, usually without stopping.

Even within Europe, the rivers and harbors of Eastern Europe are not the same as the rivers and harbors of Western Europe. Because Western Europe is warmed by the Gulf Stream flowing through the Atlantic Ocean, Western Europe's rivers and harbors are not frozen as often or as long in winter as the rivers and harbors of Eastern Europe. But, even when the rivers in both parts of Europe are flowing, those in Western Europe are more often flowing into the open seas, providing ships with access to every continent in the world, while many rivers in Eastern Europe flow into lakes or inland seas, or into the Arctic Ocean, which is more distant from the rest of the world, even when the Arctic Ocean is not encumbered by ice.

In Western Europe the Rhine, for example, flows northward from Switzerland through Germany, France and Holland, and out into the North Sea, which is part of the same vast, continuous expanse of water as the Atlantic Ocean. But the Danube flows generally southeastward through Eastern Europe into the Black Sea, an inland sea far distant from the Atlantic Ocean, which can be reached only by sailing westward across the entire length of the Mediterranean Sea before finally getting out into the Atlantic to gain access to the rest of the world. Economically, the rivers of Eastern Europe and Western Europe are obviously not equivalent for purposes of overseas trade, however valuable the Danube may be for trade among those parts of Europe that it flows through.

Nor are the rivers that flow from Southern Europe into the Mediterranean the economic equivalent of rivers to the north. As a distinguished geographer put it: "The rivers which flowed north of the Alps were incomparably more useful than those of the Mediterranean basin. Their flow was more regular; they were deeper, and low water and ice rarely interrupted navigation for more than short periods." He also said of Europe's waterways:

> Only in southern Europe was river navigation of little or no importance. There were exceptions, like the Po and Guadalquivir, but most Mediterranean rivers were torrents in winter and almost dry in summer.

When one considers the depths of rivers, there are still more inequalities that are economically relevant. Although the Nile is the longest river in the world, its depth was not great enough for the largest ships in the days of the Roman Empire, much less for the aircraft carriers and other giant ships of today. Yet an aircraft carrier can sail up the Hudson River and dock right up against the land in midtown Manhattan. Some of the rivers in Angola are navigable only by boats requiring no more than 8 feet of water. During the dry season, even a major West African river like the Niger will carry barges weighing no more than 12 tons. By contrast, ships weighing 10,000 tons have been able to go hundreds of miles up the Yangtze River in China, and smaller vessels another thousand miles beyond that.

China has had an "immense network— unique in the world— of navigable waterways formed by the Yangtze and its tributaries," as well as an "indented coastline," full of harbors. These navigable waterways contributed to China's development as a nation, including during many centuries when it was the world's most advanced nation.

Rivers in Japan, however, have smaller and steeper drainage areas, making these rivers less navigable, because their waters are flowing more steeply down to the sea. Japan was for centuries a poor and underdeveloped country before it began, in the second half of the nineteenth century, to import modern technology from countries more favorably situated geographically in Europe or from the United States. As of 1886, the per capita purchasing power in Japan was one-fortieth of that in the United Kingdom, though by 1898 this had risen to one-sixth. Only in the twentieth century did Japan rise to the level of being one of the most technologically advanced and economically prosperous nations in the world.

Japan lacked the geographical advantages— such as natural resources and networks of navigable rivers flowing over vast level plains— that enabled first China, and later Western Europe, to become the most technologically and economically advanced region of the world in their respective eras. Without these geographic advantages, Japan had little opportunity to pioneer the kind of epoch-making technological advances that marked early Chinese, and later Western European, civilizations. But the ability of the Japanese to incorporate the industrial revolution that had originated elsewhere, master its requirements and then exploit its opportunities, enabled Japan to become the technological equal of Western nations and to surpass a China that had, over the centuries, eventually lost its technological lead and dynamism.

Given the dependence of cities on waterways, it can hardly be surprising that Western Europe became one of the most urbanized regions of the world, and sub-Saharan Africa remained one of the least urbanized. In the Middle Ages, China had larger cities than any in Europe. What urbanization means in terms of people, and the range of their knowledge, skills and experience— their human capital— is that first the Chinese, and later Western Europeans, had opportunities to develop urban industrial, commercial and financial skills and orientations far more often, and far longer, than the peoples of the Balkans or of sub-Saharan Africa. For centuries, in countries around the world, achievements and advances in many fields of endeavor have been far greater in cities than among a similar number of people scattered in the hinterlands.

To the direct economic benefits created by low transport costs on navigable waterways must be added the value of greater human capital resulting from exposure to a wider cultural universe that includes the products, technology and ideas of countries around the world. The economic benefits of this exposure to a wider cultural universe may well equal or exceed that of the direct economic benefits of international trade.

In addition to being arteries of transportation, waterways can also supply the drinking water necessary to sustain both human and animal life, as well as the water needed to irrigate crops in arid regions. Waterways also supply food directly, in the form of fish and other marine life. In none of these roles are waterways the same in different places and times.

Waters around the world contain very different amounts of fish and other marine life, so that fishing has long been a far more flourishing enterprise in some places than in others. Most of the Mediterranean countries, for example, have had far less productive opportunities for fishing than in the Newfoundland Banks or other places on the Atlantic coasts of North America or Europe. The continental shelf that goes far out into the Atlantic Ocean creates an environment more conducive to abundant marine life, compared to the Mediterranean Sea, where such a shelf is lacking. In short, the waters of the world differ from each other, like the lands, and they differ in many different aspects, adding to the factors that make equal economic outcomes unlikely.

Mountains

Mountains, like waterways, have had both direct economic effects on people's lives and, indirectly, effects on how those people themselves developed. But, unlike waterways, these direct and indirect effects of mountains have tended to be negative on those living in these mountains. As distinguished French historian Fernand Braudel pointed out: "Mountain life persistently lagged behind the plain."

This pattern of both economic and cultural lags among people living in the mountains, compared with their contemporaries on the land below, has been as common in America's Appalachian Mountains as in the Rif Mountains of Morocco or the Pindus Mountains of Greece. In times past, there was a similar contrast between the people living in the highlands of colonial Ceylon and people of the same race living on the land below, just as a similar contrast existed between Scottish highlanders and Scottish lowlanders. Moreover, the economic and cultural contrast between Scottish highlanders and Scottish lowlanders persisted, even after both had immigrated to Australia or to the United States— the lowlanders being much more economically successful and more socially integrated in both countries. Cultural differences that developed over the centuries do not vanish overnight when people move from one environment to another, or when the environment around them at a given place changes.

In the ages before modern transportation and communication, mountain communities tended to be especially isolated, both from lowland communities and from each other. While these communities were not hermetically sealed off from the whole world, the culture of the lowlands tended to reach the highlands only very belatedly. Thus the Vlach language survived in the Pindus mountains of Greece for centuries after the people in lower elevations were speaking Greek, just as the Scottish highlanders continued to speak Gaelic after the Scottish lowlanders were speaking English. Islam became the religion of people living in the Rif Mountains of Morocco centuries after the people living below had already become Muslims.

Technological, economic and other developments likewise tended to reach the mountains long after they had spread across the lowlands, so that mountain peoples have long been known for their poverty and backwardness— whether in the Himalayas, the Appalachians or the mountains of Albania, Morocco or other places around the world.

Villages in the Pindus mountains of Greece have had populations of fewer than a thousand people each in the past and, in more recent times, the average permanent population of these villages has usually been fewer than two hundred people. The Vlach language had still not yet completely died out in these mountains in the 1990s, though by then it was usually spoken by old people, while the younger generation was now educated in Greek and identified themselves as Greeks. In these mountain villages, there were places where travel was very slow because it was limited to travel by mule or on foot, as distinguished from using wheeled vehicles, and a few villages could be reached only on foot. Many villages in the Pindus Mountains have, from time to time, been cut off from the outside world by snow or landslides.

Such severe geographic limitations have not been peculiar to the Pindus Mountains. Similar conditions have existed in other mountains around the world. But, as a geographic study of mountains put it, "In gentler environments, such as northwestern Europe or eastern North America, such tight constraints have never existed." Peoples living in isolated mountain settings have never had the same opportunities for either economic prosperity or self-development as peoples living in those "gentler environments." Nor has resettlement of mountain peoples on the more promising land below always been a viable option, given their lack of the skills, sometimes the language, or even an understanding of a very different way of life in the lower elevations.*

Neither geographic isolation nor its economic and cultural handicaps have been confined to people living in mountains, however. Similar effects have been seen where isolation has been due to islands located far from the nearest mainland. When the Spaniards discovered the Canary Islands in the fifteenth century, for example, they found people of a Caucasian race living at a stone age level.

What mountains often create are cultural "islands" on land, where people in one mountain valley have had little communication with people living in other mountain valleys, perhaps not far away as the crow flies, but not very accessible across rugged mountain terrain. Deserts, jungles, rift valleys and other geographic barriers can likewise create the equivalent of "islands" on land, where people are isolated from the progress of the rest of the world, and live deprived of both the economic benefits of that progress and of opportunities to develop themselves as individuals and societies by learning how things are done elsewhere.

---

* See, for example, the discussion of "urban hillbillies" in Michael Harrington, *The Other America*, 1962 edition, pp. 96–100.

The poverty of many mountain peoples has often led them to put their children to work at an early age, depriving them of education that could at least partially break through their physical isolation from the rest of the world. Most of the people living in various mountain communities around the Mediterranean remained illiterate on into the nineteenth and early twentieth centuries. Thus lower levels of human capital have been added to the other, more direct handicaps of isolated mountain communities, such as high transportation costs and high costs per capita of building water supply systems, sewage systems, electrical systems, railroads and highways in distant and sparsely populated communities.

Mountains play a major economic role, not only in the lives of people living in those mountains, but also in the lives of others who are affected indirectly by the presence of mountain ranges. For example, the melting of snow on mountainsides supplies rivers, streams and lakes with water, so that these waterways are not wholly dependent on rainfall. But where there are no mountain ranges, as in sub-Saharan Africa, the waterways are in fact wholly dependent on rainfall— and that rainfall is itself undependable in tropical Africa, so that rivers and streams can shrink or even dry up for months until the next rainy season comes.

While mountains have often kept the people living in them mired in poverty and backwardness, these mountains have at the same time often brought prosperity to people living on the land below, by supplying water to otherwise arid regions. The Sierra Nevada in Spain and the Taurus Mountains in Turkey both supply the water that makes a flourishing irrigated agriculture possible in the lowlands, where rainfall alone would not be sufficient. This water comes not only from melting snows on the mountainsides but also from the drainage of rain water from vast mountainous areas— trickles of water joining together as they pour down the mountainsides to become streams and the streams joining together to become rivers that can be put to use by farmers and others below.

Animals

Although much of the Western Hemisphere seems geographically similar to Europe, in terms of land, climate and waterways, it was a profoundly different economic setting for the indigenous peoples of North and South America before the Europeans arrived. What was totally lacking throughout the Western Hemisphere when the Europeans arrived were horses, oxen or other heavy-duty beasts of burden.

The whole economic way of life that existed in Europe for centuries would have been impossible without horses— and was impossible in the Western Hemisphere before the Europeans brought horses across the Atlantic. Severely constrained transportation options meant that the cultural universe in the Western Hemisphere was for millennia much smaller than the cultural universe available to the people living in much of Europe, Asia or North Africa. Advances made in Asia, such as gunpowder in China or so-called Arabic numerals in India,* could find their way across thousands of miles into Europe. But the indigenous peoples living on the east coast of North America had no way of even knowing of the existence of indigenous peoples living on the west coast, much less acquiring knowledge of the skills or technology developed in their different cultures.

Large, ocean-going ships also facilitated trade in goods and knowledge between Europeans and Asians. But the loading and unloading of large cargo ships was by no means as economically feasible when there were no heavy-duty beasts of burden to carry these cargoes to or from a wide enough area on land to either supply or carry away cargoes large enough to fill a ship. Accordingly, water transport in the Western Hemisphere was in smaller vessels such as canoes, whose economically viable range and cargo capacity in the pre-Columbus era were by no means comparable to that of the ships in Europe or the even larger ships in China at that time.

When the invaders from Europe encountered the indigenous peoples of the Western Hemisphere, it was an encounter between races with cultural universes of vastly different sizes. The Europeans were able to navigate across the Atlantic, in the first place, by drawing upon information and technologies derived over the centuries from Asia, the Middle East and North Africa. Western Europeans' knowledge was preserved in letters created by the Romans, written on paper invented by the Chinese. They

* Westerners called them Arabic numerals because Europeans first encountered these numbers in use among the Arabs, who got them from India.

made navigational calculations at sea using a numbering system that originated in India, and were able when they landed to prevail in armed conflicts as a result of gunpowder, invented in Asia.

When the British confronted the Iroquois or the Spaniards confronted the Incas, it was by no means a confrontation based solely on what each culture had developed within itself. The Iroquois had no way of knowing of the very existence of the Incas or the Mayans, much less drawing upon features of Inca's or Mayan's culture to advance their own.

Australia likewise had no heavy-duty beasts of burden before the Europeans arrived. Nor were there farm animals like cows or goats, or herd animals like sheep or cattle. Given this vast island continent, isolated in the South Pacific, much of the land a desert and therefore sparsely populated, it can hardly be surprising that the Australian aborigines were long regarded as among the world's most backward peoples. Rainfall patterns in the arid interior were at least as unreliable as in parts of tropical Africa. As a National Geographic Society publication put it: "Years without rain may be followed by summer deluges." These are clearly not conditions for agriculture, or even for much spontaneous growth of vegetation.

Much of the soil in Australia is of low fertility. However, Australia has an abundance of valuable natural resources and has been the world's largest exporter of titanium ore. However, this and other mining products *became* natural resources only after the British arrived and applied modern science and technology. Such resources were of little or no value to the aborigines.

The coastal fringe of Australia, where most of the country's population lives today, had better land and climate. But, even there, it was only after the British settled in Australia, and brought Western technology, that agriculture and cattle raising were introduced to replace the hunter-gatherer societies of the aborigines. Here as elsewhere, the Europeans came armed with knowledge and technologies gathered from a vastly wider cultural universe. Geography alone was enough to keep the aborigines from having equal economic or other advances.

Location

Location, as such, can affect the fate of whole peoples and nations, even aside from the particular geographic characteristics of a particular location.

Something as simple as the fact that "Russian rivers run north-south, and most traffic moved east-west" means that the economic value of those rivers as transportation arteries was greatly reduced. Differences in location can also mean differences in climate that affect how much a particular waterway is subject to being frozen, and therefore unable to carry any cargo. In the south of Russia, "waterways remained open nine months of the year; in the north, only six weeks." Most of the water in Russian rivers drains into the Arctic Ocean.

Although the Volga is Russia's most important river economically, in terms of the cargo it carries, there are two other Russian rivers which each have more than twice as much water as the Volga. But the Volga happens to be located near centers of population, industry and farmland, and the others are not. Location can matter more than the physical characteristics of a river— or of mountains or other geographic features.

Agriculture— perhaps the most life-changing innovation in the history of the human species— came to Europe from the Middle East in ancient times, so that Europeans who happened to be located in the eastern Mediterranean, closer to the Middle East, received this epoch-making advance, moving them beyond the era of hunter-gatherers, centuries before those Europeans living in northern Europe. Agriculture greatly reduced the amount of land required to provide food to sustain a given number of people, and thus made cities possible.

Cities were common in ancient Greece but very uncommon in northern Europe or in many other parts of the world at that time. From these ancient Greek cities came Socrates, Plato, Aristotle and others who helped lay the intellectual foundations of Western thought and civilization.* The ancient

---

* While geographic location alone cannot create genius, different geographic settings can provide very different opportunities for genius to emerge and develop. Few, if any, individuals with recognized historic achievements have developed in isolated mountain villages. On the contrary, historic achievements have been highly concentrated geographically as of a given time, even though these concentrations have changed over the centuries— but, again, seldom coming from geographically isolated places.

Greeks were producing philosophy, literature, geometry and architecture at a time when other Europeans tended to lag further behind the Greeks in cultural and technological development the farther away from Greece they were located. As a scholarly study of the evolution of Europe put it, in the fifth century B.C., "in the Baltic and Scandinavian regions and on the outermost fringes of the British Isles, Stone Age peoples were beginning to learn the rudiments of agriculture." Even farther north, "hunters and herders still practiced a culture which had ended ten thousand years earlier in southern Europe."

In a later era, people located in Western Europe received the benefits of Roman civilization that people in various other parts of Europe did not. Roman letters, for example, enabled Western European languages to develop written versions, centuries before the languages of Eastern Europe did the same. In other parts of the world as well, the happenstance of being located near an advanced civilization, such as that of ancient China, enabled some races or nations to advance far beyond other races or nations not situated near comparable sources of progress. Thus Koreans and Japanese were able to adapt Chinese writing to their own languages, becoming literate long before other Asian peoples who lived in regions remote from China. Literacy obviously opens up wider economic and other prospects denied to those who remain illiterate.

The happenstance of being in the right place at the right time has made a huge difference in the economic fate of whole peoples. Moreover, what was the right place has varied greatly at different periods of history. After many centuries, the peoples of northern Europe would eventually surpass the peoples of southern Europe economically and technologically— as the people of Japan would likewise surpass the people of China who had for centuries been far more advanced than the Japanese. Economic inequalities between peoples or nations have been pervasive in both ancient times and modern times, though the particular patterns of those inequalities have changed drastically over the centuries.

CULTURES

Whether human beings are divided into countries, tribes, races or other categories, geography is just one of the reasons why they have never had either the same direct economic benefits or the same opportunities to develop their own human capital. Cultures are another reason. Places blessed with beneficial climates, waterways and other natural advantages can nevertheless remain poverty-stricken if the culture of the people living there presents many obstacles to their developing the resources that nature has provided. What has sometimes been called "living in harmony with nature" can also be called stagnating in poverty amid potential wealth. Other peoples from other cultures often move into the same geographic setting and thrive by developing its resources.

Cultures that promote the rule of law, rather than arbitrary powers exercised by leaders, have increasingly been recognized as major factors promoting economic development. So too are cultures where honesty is highly valued in both principle and practice. International studies of nations ranked high and low in honesty repeatedly show that the most corrupt nations are almost invariably ranked among the poorest, even when they have rich natural resources, because pervasive corruption can make it too risky to make the large investments required to develop natural resources.

Cultural attitudes toward work also affect economic development, and these attitudes have also varied, for centuries, even within the same European civilization, where the attitudes of the elite in England during the reign of the Tudors differed considerably from the attitudes among the elites in continental European nations at that time:

> The younger son of the Tudor gentleman was not permitted to hang idle about the manor-house, a drain on the family income like the empoverished nobles of the Continent who were too proud to work. He was away making money in trade or in law.

Sometimes economic progress depends on whether people in a particular culture are seeking progress, rather than being contented with doing things the way things have always been done. The proportions of the population who seek progress and the proportions who are satisfied with doing things in familiar ways can differ between societies and within societies, thereby affecting economic differences among regions and nations. In the United States, for example, the antebellum South tended not to advance as fast as other parts of the country:

> Techniques of Southern agriculture changed slowly, or not at all. So elementary a machine as the plow was adopted only gradually and only in scattered places; as late as 1856, many small farmers in South Carolina were still using the crude colonial hoe. There was little change in the cotton gin, gin house, or baling screw between 1820 and the Civil War.

The cotton gin, a crucial economic factor in the antebellum South, was invented by a Northerner. When it came to inventions, only 8 percent of the U.S. patents issued in 1851 went to residents of the Southern states, whose white population was approximately one-third of the white population of the country. Even in agriculture, the main economic activity of the region, only 9 out of 62 patents for agricultural implements went to Southerners. Differences in habits and attitudes are differences in human capital, which can mean differences in economic outcomes. As of the Civil War era, the North produced 14 times as much textiles as the South, despite the South's virtual monopoly of growing cotton, and the North also produced 15 times as much iron as the South, 25 times the merchant ship tonnage and 32 times as many firearms.

The advantages of a larger cultural universe do not end with the particular products, technologies or ideas that come from other cultures. Repeatedly seeing how things are done differently in other societies, with better results in particular cases, not only brings those particular foreign products, technologies and ideas, but also counters the normal human tendency toward inertia that keeps individuals and societies doing things in the same old familiar ways. In other words, a particular culture may develop *its own original new ways* of doing things, as a result of seeing repeatedly how others have done other things differently. Conversely, a society isolated from the outside world has fewer spurs toward rethinking their own traditional ways.

Human Capital

Physical wealth may be highly visible, but human capital, invisible inside people's heads, is often more crucial to the long-run prosperity of a nation or a people. John Stuart Mill used this fact to explain why nations often recover, with surprising speed, from the physical devastations of war: "What the enemy have destroyed, would have been destroyed in a little time by the inhabitants themselves" in the normal course of their consumption, and would require replenishing. Given the wear and tear on capital equipment, constant reproduction of new equipment would likewise be required. What the war does *not* destroy is the human capital that created the physical capital in the first place.

Even the massive physical devastations of World War II, from bombings and widely destructive ground battles, were followed by a rapid economic recovery in postwar Western Europe. Aid from the United States under the Marshall Plan has often been credited with this recovery, but the later sending of foreign aid to many Third World countries produced no such dramatic economic growth.

The difference is that industrialized Western Europe had already developed the human capital which had produced modern industrial societies there before the war began, but Third World countries had yet to develop that human capital, without which the physical capital was often of little or no use when it was donated as foreign aid. The Marshall Plan eased the transition to peacetime economic recovery in Western Europe, but foreign aid could not create the necessary scale of human capital where that human capital did not already exist.

Confiscations of physical capital have likewise seldom produced any major or lasting enrichment of those who do the confiscating— whether these are Third World governments confiscating ("nationalizing") foreign investments or urban rioters looting stores in their neighborhoods. What they cannot confiscate is the human capital that created the physical things that are taken. However serious the losses suffered by those who have been robbed, whether by governments or by mobs, the physical things have a limited duration. Without the human capital required to create their replacements, the robbers are unlikely to prosper in future years as well as those who were robbed.

Human capital may also play a role in the fact that has often been pointed out, that many of the poorest societies have been located in the tropics, and many of the most prosperous have been located in temperate zones. Yet many peoples from temperate zones who have gone to live in the tropics have often prospered there, as the Chinese have in Malaysia and the Lebanese have in West Africa, far more so than people indigenous to those regions. Here, as elsewhere, the effects of a particular geographic setting can be both direct and indirect— presenting objective opportunities and either extending or restricting the development of the human capital necessary to make the most of those opportunities.

Sometimes the very advantages of a given geographic setting can make it unnecessary for the people indigenous in that setting to have to develop their human capital to the fullest. For example, a tropical land capable of producing crops the year round can make it unnecessary for the people there to develop the same sense of urgency about time, and the resulting habits of economic self-discipline, that are necessary for sheer physical survival in a climate where people must begin plowing the land soon after it thaws in the spring, if they are to raise a crop during the limited growing season in the temperate zone that will enable them to feed themselves throughout the long winter months. This was especially so during the millennia before modern transportation made it economically feasible to draw vast amounts of food from other lands around the world.

The unavoidable necessity of storing food to live on during the winter means that, for centuries, ingrained habits of saving were also essential for survival among peoples in the temperate zones. But, in the tropics, the development of such habits is by no means always so urgent. Moreover, the ability to store grain or potatoes to eat during the winter is much greater in temperate climates than the ability to store bananas, pineapples or other tropical foods in hot climates.* Human capital includes not only information

---

* The imperative to store food, in order to survive in winter, also provides incentives to turn a perishable product like milk into a storable product like cheese.

but *habits*, and the habits necessary for survival in some geographic settings are by no means the same as in other geographic settings.

Like many other things, natural abundance can have both positive and negative effects. The saying among the Thais, "Rice on the land and fish in the water" expressed a confidence in the abundance of nature that was foreign to people struggling to survive in the very different geographic setting of southern China, where hunger and starvation were perils for centuries, forcing the people there to become frugal, hard-working and resourceful, under threat of extinction. When people from southern China migrated into more promising geographic environments in Thailand, Malaysia or the United States, these qualities— these *habits*, this human capital— enabled them to thrive, even when they began as destitute immigrants and later became more prosperous than the people who were living in the same environment before them.

Much the same story could be told of the Lebanese, the Jews and others who arrived in many places around the world as immigrants with very little money, but with much human capital that they had developed in other, more challenging settings. Many other groups have had similar patterns as migrants within their own countries:

> Conspicuous among advanced groups are some whose home region is infertile and overpopulated. The Tamils of Sri Lanka, the Bamiléké of Cameroon, the Kabyle Berbers of Algeria, the Kikuyu of Kenya, the Toba Batak of Indonesia, the Ilocano of the Philippines, the Malayalees of Kerala in India, and the Ibo of Nigeria all come from regions too poor to support their populations, and all have unusually high rates of migration to areas outside their home regions, where they have taken up a variety of opportunities in the modern sector.

The era of European colonialism put Western education and Western industrial, commercial and administrative skills within reach for groups previously among the poorer indigenous people such as the Ibos in Nigeria and the Tamils in Sri Lanka, who then rose to become more prosperous than others who had been more prosperous before. The resentments of their rise, and the politicized polarizations that followed, led to bloody civil wars in both countries.

Cultural Isolation

One of the aspects of a culture that can be very important in its economic consequences is a willingness, or unwillingness, to learn from other cultures. This can vary greatly from one culture to another. Both Britain and Japan, for example, rose from being island nations lagging economically for centuries behind their respective continental neighbors, before eventually catching up and then surging ahead of them, largely as a result of absorbing the cultural and economic advances of other nations and then carrying these advances further themselves. The otherwise very different cultures of Britain and Japan were alike in their receptivity to incorporating features of other cultures into their own. This receptivity to advances made elsewhere is at least part of the answer to a question about Britain posed by an Italian scholar: "How, in the first place, did a peripheral island rise from primitive squalor to world domination?"

By way of contrast, the Arab Middle East— once a culture more advanced than that in Europe— became resistant to learning from others, lost its lead, and then fell behind other nations that were advancing faster. In today's Arab world— about 300 million people in 22 countries— the number of books translated from other languages has been just one-fifth of the number translated by Greece alone, for a population of 11 million. A United Nations study showed that the number of books translated in the Arab world during a five-year period was less than one book for every million Arabs, while in Hungary there were 519 books translated for every million people, and in Spain 920 books per million people.

Put differently, Spain translates as many books into Spanish annually as the Arabs have translated into Arabic in a thousand years. Cultural isolation can be a factor in wealth differences among nations, just as geographic isolation can be.* While highly educated people in the Arab world may not require translations to be able to understand what is written in other languages, the same is not true for the less fortunate masses of people.

---

* Since many of the elites in Arab countries speak English or other languages, these elites have access to a vastly larger cultural universe than the masses. The absence of translated writings would therefore tend to increase the economic and other inequalities within these countries, as well as increase the economic inequalities between these countries and the Western world.

Sometimes cultural isolation has been the result of a government decision, as in fifteenth-century China, when that country was far more advanced than many other nations. China's rulers deliberately chose to isolate China from what they saw as foreign barbarians. In the seventeenth century, the rulers of Japan likewise chose to isolate their country from the rest of the world. In later centuries, both countries were shocked to discover that some other nations had far surpassed them technologically, economically and militarily during their self-imposed isolation.

Among the other ways in which cultures handicap themselves is in limiting which segments of their populations are allowed to play which roles in the economy or society. If only people from certain pre-selected groups—whether defined by class, caste, tribe, race, religion or sex— are allowed to have particular careers, this cultural distribution of economic roles can differ greatly from the individual distribution of inborn talents. The net result can be that, by forfeiting the potentialities of many of its own people, such a society ends up with a less productive economy than in other societies without such self-imposed restrictions on the development and use of their people's talents and potentialities.

History is full of examples of societies whose cultural norms confined particular segments of their population to particular roles, or even drove some of their most productive groups out of the country, because the prosperity of those groups made them targets of resentments that resulted in persecution, mob violence or outright expulsions. Other societies whose cultures were less restrictive or repressive often benefitted economically from the arrival of refugees with valuable skills and talents, even if these refugees had little money with them when they arrived.

Seventeenth century England, for example, benefitted from the arrival of tens of thousands of Huguenots fleeing persecution in France. Huguenots created the watch industry in London, as other refugees created other enterprises and industries in Britain. Similarly, Spain's mass expulsions of Jews in 1492— forcing them to leave most of their wealth behind— led many to settle in Holland, where the human capital that they retained helped make themselves prosperous again, and helped make Amsterdam one of the world's great commercial ports.

Over the centuries, tens of millions of people fled from various parts of Europe to the United States, whether to escape persecution or just to seek wider economic opportunities than were available to ordinary people in Europe. Many American industries were created, or greatly advanced, by immigrants who had been people of no real wealth or distinction in Europe, but who became economic titans in America, while transforming the United States from a predominantly agricultural country into the leading industrial nation of the world.

Cultural isolation takes many forms, creating economic and other handicaps that differ from group to group and from one society, nation or civilization to another. Differing levels of cultural isolation within and between societies add to geographic and other factors making economic equality unlikely among groups, societies, nations or civilizations.

Cultural Development

Because not all cultures developed written versions of their languages at the same time, there has been vastly larger and more varied written knowledge available in one language than in another language, at a particular period of history. Thus, in the nineteenth century, Czechs, Estonians or Latvians who wanted to become doctors or scientists, or to work in other professions that required advanced education, could more readily find the appropriate books and courses available in the German language than in their own languages.

Although there was a written version of the indigenous language in Estonia before the nineteenth century, most of the publications in the Estonian language "remained religiously oriented" before 1850, and "the working language of all educated persons was German." Educated people in adjoining Latvia, and in the Habsburg Empire's province of Bohemia — among other places in Eastern Europe and the Baltic— were likewise educated in German.

German was the language of the educated classes in Prague, whether those educated individuals were ethnically German, Czech or Jewish. Similarly in the Baltic port city of Riga in the Russian Empire, most of the education in that city in the nineteenth century was conducted in German, even though

Germans were no more than one-fourth of the city's population. When the czarist government opened a university in Estonia in 1802, most of its faculty and students were German, and this remained so for most of the nineteenth century. It was not just in formal education, but also in many different craft skills, that Germans were more advanced than many of the peoples of Eastern Europe. German farm settlements along the Volga and in the Black Sea region of the Russian Empire were more productive and more prosperous than the farms of the indigenous population.

There was a history behind such patterns. As already noted, Western European languages developed written versions centuries before Eastern European languages, as a result of Western Europe's having been conquered by the Romans and having acquired Latin letters. During the Middle Ages, it was not uncommon for Western Europeans to be a majority of the population in various Eastern European cities. These urban Western Europeans were often Germans, though there were some Jews and other Western Europeans as well. Even when the Germans were not a majority of the urban inhabitants, they were often a majority of the economic elites, as in Prague in the Habsburg Empire or in Riga, Tallinn and other Baltic cities in the Russian Empire.

While Slavs were usually an overwhelming majority of the people in the Eastern European countrysides, there were also enclaves of German farming communities in Eastern Europe, often deliberately recruited by Eastern European rulers, who were anxious to bring people with more advanced skills into their domains, so as to increase the wealth and power of the lands they ruled. Not only did this transplant more advanced knowledge, technology and experience into Eastern Europe, it also opened the possibility of indigenous individuals in Eastern Europe acquiring some of the cultural advances from Western Europe.

From a purely economic standpoint, these infusions of human capital into Eastern Europe contributed to greater opportunities for members of the indigenous population to advance economically by rising, as many did, through the acquisition of the German language and culture. However, from a social and political standpoint, a situation in which the German minority dominated the business and professional elites— when German families in

Prague often had Czech servants but few, if any, Germans were servants—was a situation provoking ethnic resentments and eventually ethnic identity movements expressing those resentments politically. Similar tensions and polarizations have been common in other countries, where an immigrant group brought more human capital than that of the indigenous population, and was conspicuously more prosperous as a result— the Chinese in Southeast Asia, Lebanese in West Africa, Japanese in Peru and Indians in Fiji, among many others.

Within nations, as well, particular groups have migrated from one part of their country to another, bringing economic benefits while provoking social and political backlashes because of others' resentments of their higher economic achievements. However these conflicts turned out— and some have turned out tragically— from a purely economic standpoint these are among the many complicating factors which prevent regions, races and nations from having either equal outcomes or even the same pattern of inequalities over time.

Leaders and spokesmen for lagging groups have often tended to blame others for their lags, sometimes depicting qualifications standards for admissions to educational institutions or for employment as arbitrary barriers. This view was epitomized by an ethnic spokesman in India who asked, "Are we not entitled to jobs just because we are not as qualified?" and by an ethnic spokesman in Nigeria who decried "the tyranny of skills." Very similar political responses to achievement differences have been common in other countries, with the German minority being blamed for the lags of Czechs in nineteenth century Bohemia or Latvians in Latvia, just as Fijians in Fiji blamed the Indian minority there and the peoples of various countries in Southeast Asia tended to blame the Chinese minority there.*

In other words, ethnic leaders have often turned their people against the cultures that could help advance them, and dissipated their energies in opposing both such cultures and the people who had the advantages of those cultures. These were not necessarily irrational actions on the part of ethnic

---

* The very concept of blame seems questionable in this context, when no one can choose what culture to be born into, nor in which geographic setting or in which period of history.

leaders, whose promotion of an "us against them" attitude advanced the ethnic leaders' careers, even when it was detrimental to the economic interests of the people they led. This pattern has been common at various times and places on every inhabited continent.

It was the exception, rather than the rule, when the great philosopher David Hume urged his fellow eighteenth century Scots to learn the English language for the sake of their own advancement— which they did, and rose rapidly in many fields. Ultimately the Scots surpassed the English in engineering and medicine. That too was the exception, rather than the rule. The nineteenth century Japanese were another exception. Once their isolation was ended, the Japanese openly acknowledged their long lag behind Western nations, and proceeded to bring in experts from Europe and America to introduce Western technology into Japan.

In the twentieth century, Japan caught up to the West in many areas and surpassed the West in others. But, as of the time when Commodore Perry's American naval forces pressured the Japanese government to open their country to the outside world in 1853, the backwardness of the Japanese was demonstrated in their reaction to a train that Perry presented as a gift:

> At first the Japanese watched the train fearfully from a safe distance, and when the engine began to move they uttered cries of astonishment and drew in their breath.
> Before long they were inspecting it closely, stroking it, and riding on it, and they kept this up throughout the day.

Yet from such levels of technological backwardness, Japan began a massive importation of European and American technology and engineers, and a widespread learning of the English language to directly acquaint themselves with the science and technology of the West. Slowly at first, but more rapidly as they acquired more experience, the Japanese rose in the following century to the forefront of world technology in many fields, producing trains that surpassed any produced in the United States.

As a country with a population almost entirely of one race and with no history of being a conquered people before 1945, there was little basis on which nineteenth century Japan could blame others for their lags. Nor did they or their leaders attempt to do so. But, again, Scotland and Japan were rare exceptions, and so was their spectacular rise to economic success. Both countries had meager natural resources and were in previous centuries poor and backward. Neither had the same geographic prerequisites for originating an industrial revolution as some other countries did. But the fact that both acquired knowledge of the advances already made by other people, who lived in more fortunate environments, enabled them to transcend the geographic handicaps of their own environment and move to the forefront of human achievement.

Because nations that are culturally and economically more advanced are not necessarily more advanced militarily as well, their prosperity and the culture that created it can be destroyed by militarily more powerful peoples who may not be as advanced otherwise. When invading barbarians destroyed the Roman Empire, they destroyed most of the institutions that had perpetuated Roman culture, leaving the peoples of the former Roman Empire both economically and technologically living below the level their forebears had achieved under Roman rule.

Artifacts from medieval Europe reveal that the quality of their workmanship had declined significantly since the days of the Roman Empire. Central heating, which was introduced into Britain in Roman times, became rare or non-existent, even among the nobility, in the centuries after the Romans withdrew. Medieval cities in Europe, including Rome itself, had much smaller populations and fewer amenities than in Roman times. As late as the early nineteenth century, no European city had as dependable a water supply as many Roman cities once had, more than a thousand years earlier. History does not always move in an upward line of progress. Sometimes the retrogressions can be deep and long lasting.

POPULATION

Populations can affect economic outcomes by their size, their demographic characteristics or their mobility, among other factors. The concentration or dispersion of a population can also greatly affect economic progress, which often varies with the degree of urbanization. Either the physical or the social separation of different segments of a country's population can also affect the extent of their cooperation and coordination in economic activities.

Population Size

The danger of "overpopulation" has long been a recurrent concern, even before Malthus raised his historic alarm at the end of the eighteenth century that the number of human beings threatened to exceed the number for which there was an adequate food supply. At various places and times throughout history, famines have been monumental tragedies that some have regarded as confirmation of Malthus' theory.

As late as the twentieth century, a famine in the Soviet Union under Stalin took millions of lives and, in China under Mao, tens of millions. But even catastrophes of this almost unimaginable magnitude do not prove that the world's food supply is inadequate to feed the world's population. Famines in particular countries or regions are often due to factors at work in those particular countries and regions at the time, such as a local crop failure or the disruption of transportation due to war, weather or other causes. In the case of the Soviet Union, the famine was concentrated in a region— the Ukraine— that was before, and is again today, a major producer and exporter of wheat.

Crop failures are not sufficient, by themselves, to bring on famine, unless food from other parts of the world cannot reach the stricken areas in time, and on a scale sufficient to head off mass starvation or the diseases to which undernourished people become vulnerable. Poor countries lacking transportation networks capable of moving vast amounts of food in a short time have been especially susceptible to famines. The modern transportation revolution has reduced such conditions over most of the world. But a country or region isolated for political reasons can remain susceptible to famine, as in the Soviet Union under Stalin and China under Mao. After radical changes in China's economic system in the decades following the death of Mao, an estimated one-fourth of China's adults were overweight by the early twenty-first century.

Contrary to Malthusian theory, few— if any— countries have had a higher standard of living when their population was half of what it is today.

Studies based on empirical evidence show results very different from those projected by advocates of "overpopulation" theories. For example:

> Between the 1890s and 1930s the sparsely populated area of Malaysia, with hamlets and fishing villages, was transformed into a country with large cities, extensive agricultural and mining operations and extensive commerce. The population rose from about one and a half to about six million. . . The much larger population had much higher material standards and lived longer than the small population of the 1890s. Since the 1950s rapid population increase in densely-populated Hong Kong and Singapore has been accompanied by large increases in real income and wages. The population of the Western world has more than quadrupled since the middle of the eighteenth century. Real income per head is estimated to have increased by a factor of five or more.

Nevertheless, "overpopulation" theories of poverty have endured and have had sporadic resurgences in the media and in politics, much like theories that we are running out of various natural resources. Moreover, the arguments are similar in both cases. The indisputable fact that there are finite limits to the amount of each natural resource has led to the *non sequitur* that we are nearing those limits. Similarly, the indisputable fact that there are finite limits to the number of people that the planet can feed has led to the *non sequitur* that we are nearing those limits.

Poverty and famine in various parts of the world have been taken as evidence of "overpopulation." But poverty and famine have been far more common in such thinly populated regions as sub-Saharan Africa than in densely populated Western Europe or Japan, which each have several times as many people per square mile as in sub-Saharan Africa. Travelers in Eastern Europe during the Middle Ages often commented on the large amount of land that was unused in this poorer part of Europe. While today there are densely populated poor countries like Bangladesh, there are also sparsely populated poor countries like Guyana, whose population density is the same as that of Canada, which has several times as large an output per capita and one of the highest standards of living in the world.

In short, neither high population density nor low population density automatically makes a country rich or poor. What seems to matter more is not the number of people but the productivity of those people, which is dependent on many factors, including their own habits, skills, and experience. To the extent that population density, as in urban communities, can facilitate the development of human capital, people in small isolated societies have tended to lag behind the general progress of others.

Population Movements

While peoples in different regions of the world might live, and their cultures and societies evolve, in their own respective regions for millennia, at various times they have also moved to other regions of the world, whether as conquerors, immigrants or slaves. Some have migrated singly or in families, and others have migrated *en masse*, whether settling among existing inhabitants or driving the existing inhabitants out and displacing them, as invaders from Asia in centuries past set off chain reactions of population displacements in Eastern Europe and the Balkans, or as invaders from Europe would later displace indigenous populations in North America.

In the early years of the industrial revolution, when technology advanced through the direct practical work of people in factories, mines and other productive facilities, rather than through the application of science as in later times, the movement of migrants was the principal means of diffusion of technology from its sources to other nations and regions. Thus British technological advances could spread more readily to an English-speaking country like the United States than to nearer countries on the continent of Europe. The government of Britain, where the industrial revolution began, tried to restrict the movement of British workers to other countries, in order to protect Britain's technological advantages. However, as technological advances became more and more a matter of applying science, knowledge could more readily be spread on paper, rather than requiring the actual movement of people.

Improvements in transportation and communications during the nineteenth century also sped up the diffusion of technological advances. By 1914 British advances in technology had spread not only to nearby countries but across the continent of Europe.

In countries around the world, the movement of peoples is also a movement of their cultures. This can result in a displacement of existing cultures at their destination, a planting of a new culture in the midst of one already in place, or an assimilation to the destination culture by the migrants. These varied prospects add more combinations and permutations to the possibilities affecting economic and social development— making equal development among regions, races and nations even less likely than with geographic or cultural differences alone.

Sometimes the newcomers end up adopting the culture of the surrounding society, beginning with the language, as most of the millions of immigrants to the United States did in the nineteenth and early twentieth centuries. In other cases, however, such as the settlement of Western Europeans in Eastern Europe during the Middle Ages, the migrants retained their own language and culture for centuries and, to some extent, assimilated members of the indigenous population to the transplanted cultures. This was especially so when the transplanted peoples were more prosperous, more highly skilled and better educated.

Peoples who may be very poor in their native lands can sometimes prosper in some other lands which have more promising geographic or other advantages that the migrants have the human capital to benefit from, often more so than indigenous inhabitants. For generations, it was a paradox that the Chinese and the Indians prospered almost everywhere around the world, except in China and India. As late as 1994, 57 million overseas Chinese produced as much wealth as the one billion Chinese in China. However, major economic reforms in China and India, beginning in the late twentieth century, brought much higher economic growth rates in both countries, suggesting that their domestic populations, as well as their overseas offshoots, had potentialities that required only a better setting in which to reach fruition.

IMPERIALISM

Conquests have transferred wealth, as well as cultures, among nations and peoples. During the height of the Spanish empire, more than 200 tons of gold were shipped from the Western Hemisphere to Spain, and more than 18,000 tons of silver. King Leopold of Belgium likewise took vast riches from the

Belgian Congo. In both cases— and others— imperial powers extracted huge amounts of wealth from some conquered peoples, often through the forced labor of those peoples. As John Stuart Mill put it, conquerors have often treated the conquered peoples as "mere dirt under their feet." This was true not only of European conquests in the Western Hemisphere, Africa and Asia, it was equally true of indigenous conquerors of other indigenous peoples in all those places— and of Asian, Middle Eastern and North African conquerors who invaded Europe in the centuries preceding Europeans' invasions of other lands.

From a purely economic standpoint, putting aside the painful implications of such behavior for human nature in general, the question is: How much do these conquests and enslavements of the past explain economic disparities among nations and peoples in the present?

There is no question that, during the centuries when Spain was the leading conqueror in the world, it destroyed whole civilizations— such as those of the Incas and the Mayans— and impoverished whole peoples, in the process of enriching itself. Spain's empire in the Western Hemisphere extended continuously from the southern tip of South America all the way up to the San Francisco Bay, and also included Florida, among other places, while there were also parts of Europe ruled by Spain and, in Asia, the Philippines. But there is also no question that Spain is today one of the poorer countries in Western Europe. Meanwhile, European countries that have never had empires, such as Switzerland and Norway, have higher standards of living than Spain.

While the vast wealth that poured into Spain from its colonies could have been invested in building up the commerce and industry of the country, and building up the literacy and occupational skills of its people, this wealth was in fact largely dissipated in the consumption of imported luxuries and military adventures during the "golden age" of Spain in the sixteenth century. Both luxuries and war were primarily for the benefit of the ruling elite, rather than for the advancement of the Spanish people at large. As late as 1900, more than half the population of Spain remained illiterate. By contrast, in the United States that same year a majority of the black population could read and write, despite having been free for less than 50 years. A century later, the real per capita income in Spain was slightly lower than the real per capita income of black Americans.

Like many conquering peoples, the Spaniards in their "golden age" disdained commerce, industry and labor— and their elites reveled in leisurely and luxurious living. This led to a large and continuous drain of precious metals from Spain to other countries, to pay for imports. Silver could thus become in short supply within Spain just weeks after the arrival of ships laden with silver from its Western Hemisphere colonies. The Spaniards themselves spoke of gold as pouring down on Spain like rain on a roof, flowing on away immediately.

Nor were Spaniards unique among great conquering peoples in having little to show economically in later centuries for their earlier historic conquests and exploitations of other peoples. The descendants of Genghis Khan's vast conquering hordes in Central Asia are today among the poorer peoples of the world. So are the many peoples in the Middle East who were once part of a triumphant Ottoman Empire that ruled conquered lands in Europe, North Africa and the Middle East. Nor have the descendants of the peoples of the Mogul Empire or the Russian empire been particularly prosperous.

Britain might seem to be an exception, in that it once had the largest empire of all— encompassing one-fourth of the land area of the Earth and one-fourth of the human race— and today has a high standard of living. However, it is questionable whether the British Empire had a net profit over the relatively brief span of history in which it was at its ascendancy. Individual Britons such as Cecil Rhodes grew rich in the empire, but the British taxpayers bore the heavy costs of conquering and maintaining the empire, including the world's largest burden of military expenditures per capita.

Britain also had at one time the world's largest slave trade in its empire. But, even if all the profits from slavery had been invested in British industry, this would have amounted to less than 2 percent of Britain's domestic investments during that era.

The economic record of slavery in general as a source of lasting economic development is unimpressive. Slavery was concentrated in the southern part of the United States and in the northern part of Brazil— and, in both cases, these remained the less prosperous and less technologically advanced regions of these countries. Similarly in Europe, where slavery persisted in Eastern Europe long after it had died out in Western Europe, the latter being for centuries the faster growing and more prosperous part of the continent, right up to the present day. Slavery continued to exist in the Middle East and in parts of sub-Saharan Africa long after it was banished from the rest of the world, but the Middle East and sub-Saharan Africa are today places noted more for poverty than for economic achievements.

In short, forcible transfers of wealth from some nations or peoples to other nations or peoples, whether through conquest or enslavement, can be large without producing lasting economic development. A vast amount of human suffering may produce little more than the transient enrichment of contemporary elites, who live in luxury and invest little or nothing for the benefit of future generations. What was said of serfdom in Russia, that it simply put "much wealth in the hands of a spendthrift nobility," would apply to other systems of oppression elsewhere that contributed little or nothing to economic development.

By and large, imperialism cannot be said unequivocally to have been a net economic benefit or a net economic loss to those who were conquered. In some cases, it was clearly one rather than the other. But even where there were long-run benefits to the descendants of the conquered peoples, as in Western European nations conquered by the Romans, the generations that were conquered and lived under Roman oppression were by no means necessarily better off. However, even such a British patriot as Winston Churchill said, "We owe London to Rome," because the ancient Britons created nothing comparable themselves. Yet the sufferings and humiliations inflicted on the ancient Britons provoked a mass uprising that was put down by the Romans with a merciless slaughter of thousands.

What can be said from an economic standpoint is that there is little compelling evidence that current economic disparities between nations in income and wealth can be explained by a history of imperial exploitation. There were usually large economic or other disparities *before* these conquests, and these pre-existing disparities facilitated worldwide conquests by relatively modest-sized nations like Spain and Britain, each of which conquered vastly larger lands and populations than their own.

IMPLICATIONS

Trying to assign relative weights to the various factors behind economic differences would be an ambitious and hazardous undertaking. Even a sketch of just some of the individual factors involved in economic advancement suggests that equal economic outcomes for different regions, races, nations or civilizations have been unlikely in principle and rare empirically. When the various interactions of these factors are considered, the chances of equal outcomes become even more remote, as the number of combinations and permutations increase exponentially. For example, regions with similar rivers are unlikely to have similar economic outcomes if the lands through which the rivers flow are different, or the cultures of the people living on those lands are different, or the waterways into which the rivers empty are different in proximity to markets or in other ways.

Interactions are crucial. Despite the importance of geographic settings in limiting or extending opportunities for economic development, there can be no geographic determinism, since it is the *interactions* of the physical world with changing human knowledge and varied human cultures which help determine economic outcomes. Most of the substances found in nature that are natural resources for us today were not natural resources for the caveman, because human knowledge had not yet reached the level required to use those substances for human purposes. Only as the frontiers of knowledge advanced did more and more substances *become* natural resources, in unpredictable times and places, changing the relative geographic advantages and disadvantages of different regions. Even when geography is unchanging, its economic consequences are not.

Nevertheless the effect of geographic influences can be considerable in a sequence of events involving many other factors. Peoples isolated geographically for centuries— whether in the Balkan mountains or in the rift valleys of Africa— tend to be culturally fragmented as well. They may also tend to have highly localized loyalties ("tribalism" or "Balkanization") that make it more difficult for them to combine with others to form larger political units like nation-states. In turn their individually small societies may for centuries be vulnerable to marauding enslavers or imperial conquerors.

Nor do cultures which originated in places that were geographically isolated for centuries quickly vanish when modern transportation and communications penetrate that isolation. Some people define environment as the physical, geographic or socioeconomic surroundings as of a given time and place. But this leaves out the cultural patterns inherited from the past, which can differ greatly among groups who are all currently living in the same setting, with the same opportunities, but leading to very different economic outcomes among these groups. Although the children of Italian and Jewish immigrants to the United States in the early twentieth century lived in very similar surroundings, and often attended the same neighborhood schools, they came from cultures that put very different emphasis on education, and these children performed very differently in school, leading to different economic patterns as adults.

Even the relatively few individual factors sketched here show many complications when examined in greater detail*— which is to say that the variables at work increase exponentially for each of these factors, making equal outcomes ever more unlikely. Other factors not explored here— such as demographic differences among regions, races, nations and civilizations— simply add to the complications and the inequalities. When the difference in median age between nations, or between racial or ethnic groups within a given nation, can be ten or twenty years, the likelihood that different peoples would

---

* Even though the advent of agriculture was an epoch-making advance in the social evolution of the human species, opening up the possibility of larger and more complex societies than would have been possible for hunter-gatherers, the need for replenishing the soil nutrients used up by agriculture was by no means immediately obvious to the first farmers. But those farmers who happened to be located where rivers flooded the land annually— automatically replenishing the nutrients at a given location with nutrients washed down from other locations— prospered for reasons the farmers did not even need to understand.

The agricultural methods available at that time made permanent settlement of relatively large populations impossible in most parts of the earth. Only in some river valleys where annual floods fertilized the fields could the land be farmed continuously over the years. These rare conditions were found in the valley of the Tigris and Euphrates rivers in what is today Iraq. This created great economic inequalities between those fortunate enough to live in that part of the world at that time and most people in most other places, until farmers elsewhere realized the need for applying fertilizer to the land. This then made sedentary agriculture possible elsewhere— and this meant that sedentary societies, including cities, became possible around the world.

have even approximately equal economic outcomes, despite their many years' differences in adult economic experience, is reduced to the vanishing point.

While there are discernible geographic, cultural and other patterns behind many economic inequalities among peoples and nations, there are also sheer happenstances that can play major roles. Wise decisions or foolish mistakes made by those who happened to be political or military leaders of particular peoples at crucial junctures in history can determine the fate of nations, empires and generations yet unborn. The decision of China's leaders, when that was the most advanced nation in the world, to seal off their country from the rest of the world, forfeited China's preeminence in the centuries that followed.

The role of chance when closely matched armies clash on chaotic battlefields can make the difference between victory and defeat "a near run thing," as the Duke of Wellington said of the battle of Waterloo, which he won against Napoleon— and which determined the fate of Europe for generations to come. Had the battle of Tours in 732 or the siege of Vienna in 1529 gone the other way, this could be culturally a very different world today, with very different economic patterns.

Other happenstances include the great biological vulnerability of the indigenous peoples of the Western Hemisphere to the diseases brought by Europeans, which diseases often decimated the native populations more than the European weapons did. Because the Europeans were far less vulnerable to the diseases of the Western Hemisphere, the outcomes of many of the struggles between the two races were essentially predetermined by microorganisms that neither of these races knew existed at the time.* It

---

* The far larger cultural universe of the Europeans was matched by a far larger disease universe, since diseases from Asia could travel thousands of miles to Europe by land or sea, just as merchandise did. Plagues from Asia, the Middle East or North Africa could kill many people in Europe, but the survivors would build up biological resistance to these diseases from vast regions of the Earth. Just as Europeans who moved to the Western Hemisphere came equipped with many cultural features that originated outside of Europe, so they came carrying diseases from vast regions both inside and outside of Europe. Meanwhile, the indigenous peoples of the Western Hemisphere had much smaller disease environments from which to gain biological resistance, and were decimated by many of the diseases that Europeans transmitted, even when the Europeans were not personally suffering from those diseases.

was said of a kindly Spanish priest who went among the native peoples in friendship, as a missionary, that he was probably responsible for more deaths among them than even the most brutal *Conquistador*.

Taking into account both discernible geographic, cultural and other patterns that present either wide or narrow opportunities for different peoples in different places and times, and unpredictable happenstances that can disrupt existing patterns of life or even change the course of history, suggests that neither equality of economic outcomes nor the indefinite persistence of a particular pattern of inequalities can be assumed.

What the centuries ahead will be like, no one can know. But much may depend on how well the many peoples and their leaders around the world understand what factors promote economic growth and what factors impede it.

PART VII:

SPECIAL ECONOMIC ISSUES

Chapter 24

MYTHS ABOUT MARKETS

Many a man has cherished for years as his hobby some vague shadow of an idea, too meaningless to be positively false.

Charles Sanders Peirce

Perhaps the biggest myth about markets comes from the name itself. We tend to think of a market as a *thing* when in fact it is *people* engaging in economic transactions among themselves on whatever terms their competition and mutual accommodations lead to. A market in this sense can be contrasted with central planning or government regulation. Too often, however, when a market is conceived of as a thing, it is regarded as an impersonal mechanism, when in fact it is as personal as the people in it. This misconception allows third parties to seek to take away the freedom of individuals to transact with one another on mutually agreeable terms, and to depict this restriction of their freedom as rescuing people from the "dictates" of the impersonal market, when in fact this would be subjecting them to the dictates of third parties.

There are so many myths about markets that only a sample can be presented here. For example, it is common to hear that the same thing is being sold at very different prices by different sellers, apparently contradicting the economics of supply and demand. Usually such statements involve defining things as being "the same" when in fact they are not. Other common misconceptions involve the role of brand names and of non-profit organizations. While these are only a small sample of myths about prices and markets, looking at these myths closely may illustrate how easy it is to create a plausible-sounding notion and get it accepted by many otherwise intelligent people, who simply do not bother to scrutinize the logic or the evidence— or even to define the words they use.

One of the reasons for the survival of economic myths is that many professional economists consider such beliefs to be too superficial, or even downright silly, to bother to refute them. But superficial and even silly beliefs have sometimes been so widespread as to become the basis for laws and policies with serious and even catastrophic consequences. Leaving myths unchallenged is risky, so scrutinizing silly notions can be a very serious matter.

PRICES

There seem to be almost as many myths about prices as there are prices. Most involve ignoring the role of supply and demand but some involve confusing prices with costs.

The Role of Prices

The very reasons for the existence of prices and the role they play in the economy have often been misunderstood. One of the oldest and most consequential of these myths is a notion summarized this way:

> Prices have been compared to tolls levied for private profit or to barriers which, again for private profit, keep the potential stream of commodities from the masses who need them.

Crude as this notion might seem after examining the many economic activities coordinated by prices, it is an idea which has inspired political movements around the world, movements that have in some cases changed the history of whole nations. These movements— socialist, communist, and other— have been determined to end what they have seen as the gratuitous payment of profits that needlessly add to the prices of goods and correspondingly restrict the standard of living of the people.

Implicit in this vision is the assumption that what entrepreneurs and investors receive as income from the production process exceeds the value of any contribution they may have made to that process. The plausibility of this belief and the conviction that it was true inspired people from many walks of life to dedicate their lives— sometimes risking or even sacrificing their lives— to the cause of ending "exploitation." But their own political success in replacing price-coordinated economies with economies coordinated by collective political decisions took the issue beyond the realm of beliefs and into the realm of empirical evidence. During the course of the twentieth century, that evidence increasingly made it painfully clear that eliminating price coordination and profits did not raise living standards but tended to make them lower than in countries where prices remained the prevailing method of allocating resources.

For decades, and even generations, many nations clung to their original assumption and the policies based on it, despite economic setbacks that were often attributed to short run "growing pains" of a new economic system or to isolated individual mistakes, rather than to problems inherent in collective decision-making by third parties. However, by the end of the twentieth century, even socialist and communist countries began abandoning government-owned economic enterprises, and all but a few die-hard countries had begun allowing prices to function more freely in their economies. A very elementary lesson about prices had been learned at a very high cost to hundreds of millions of human beings.

No one would say that wages were just arbitrary charges added to the prices of goods for the financial benefit of workers, since it is obvious that there would be no production without those workers, and that they would not contribute to production unless they were compensated. Yet it took a very long time for the same thing to be realized about those who manage economic enterprises or those whose investments pay for the structures and equipment used in such enterprises. Whether the payments received by those who contributed in these ways were unnecessarily large is a question answered by whether those same contributions are available from others at a lower cost. That question is one which those who are doing the paying have every incentive to have answered by hard facts before they pay out their own hard cash.

Different Prices for the "Same" Thing

Physically identical things are often sold for different prices, usually because of accompanying conditions that are quite different. Goods sold in attractively decorated stores with pleasant, polished and sophisticated sales staffs, as well as easy return policies, are likely to cost more than physically identical products sold in a stark warehouse store with a no-refund policy. Christmas cards can usually be bought for much lower prices on December 26th than on December 24th, even though the cards are physically identical to what they were when they were in great demand before Christmas.

A consumer magazine in northern California compared the total cost of buying the identical set of food items, of the same brands, in various grocery stores in their area. These total costs ranged from $80 in the least expensive store to $125 in the most expensive. Indeed, they ranged from $98 to $103 at three different Safeway supermarkets.

Part of the reason for the variations in price was the variation in the cost of real estate in different communities— the store with the lowest prices being located in less expensive Fremont and the one with the highest prices being located in San Francisco, whose real estate prices have been among the highest of any major city in the country. The cost of the land on which the stores sat was different, and these costs had to be recovered from the prices charged the stores' customers.

Another reason for price differences is the cost of inventory. The cheapest store had only 49 percent of the items on the shopping list in stock at a given time, while all three Safeway stores had more than three-quarters of the items in stock. Price differences reflected differences in the costs of maintaining a larger inventory, even when the particular commodities were physically the same.

Customers' costs, measured in the time spent shopping, also varied. It varied both in the time that a customer would have to spend going from store to store to find all the items on a shopping list and in the time spent in checkout lines. One upscale supermarket was rated "superior" in the speed of its checkout line by 90 percent of its customers but one of the low-price warehouse stores received a similar rating from only 12 percent of its customers. Consumers pay in both money and time, and those who value their time more highly are often willing to pay more money in order to save that time and the exasperation of waiting in long lines or having to go from store to store to buy the all the items on their shopping lists. In short, people shopping at different supermarkets were paying different prices for different things, although superficially these might be called the "same" things, based solely on their physical characteristics.

"Reasonable" or "Affordable" Prices

A long-standing staple of political rhetoric has been the attempt to keep the prices of housing, medical care, or other goods and services "reasonable" or "affordable." But to say that prices should be reasonable or affordable is to say that economic realities have to adjust to our budget, or to what we are willing to pay, because we are not going to adjust to the realities. Yet the amount of resources required to manufacture and transport the things we want are wholly independent of what we are willing or able to pay. It is completely unreasonable to expect reasonable prices. Price controls can of course be imposed by government but we have already seen in Chapter 3 what the consequences are. Subsidies can also be used to keep prices down, but that does not change the costs of producing goods and services in the slightest. It just means that part of those costs are paid in taxes.

Often related to the notion of reasonable or affordable prices is the idea of keeping "costs" down by various government policies. But prices are not costs. Prices are what pay for costs. Where the costs are not covered by the prices that are legally allowed to be charged, the supply of the goods or services simply tends to decline in quantity or quality, whether these goods are apartments, medicines, or other things.

The cost of medical care is not reduced in the slightest when the government imposes lower rates of pay for doctors or hospitals. There are still just as many resources required as before to build and equip a hospital or to train a medical student to become a doctor. Countries which impose lower prices on medical treatment have ended up with longer waiting lists to see doctors and less modern equipment in their hospitals.

Refusing to pay all the costs is not the same as lowering the costs. It usually leads to a reduction of either the quantity or the quality of the goods and services provided, or both.

BRAND NAMES

Brand names are often thought to be just ways of being able to charge a higher price for the same product by persuading people through advertising that there is a quality difference, when in fact there is no such difference. In other words, some people consider brand names to be useless from the standpoint of the consumer's interests. India's first Prime Minister, Jawaharlal Nehru, once asked, "Why do we need nineteen brands of toothpaste?"

In reality, brand names serve a number of purposes from the standpoint of the consumer. Brands are a way of economizing on scarce knowledge, and of forcing producers to compete in quality as well as price.

When you drive into a town you have never seen before and want to get some gasoline for your car or to eat a hamburger, you have no direct way of knowing what is in the gasoline that some stranger at the filling station is putting into your tank or what is in the hamburger that another stranger is cooking for you to eat at a roadside stand that you have never seen before. But, if the filling station's sign says Chevron and the restaurant's sign says McDonald's, then you don't worry about it. At worst, if something terrible happens, you can sue a multi-billion-dollar corporation. You know it, the corporation knows it, and the local dealer knows it. That is what reduces the likelihood that something terrible will happen.

On the other hand, imagine if you pull into a no-name filling station in some little town and the stranger there puts something into your tank that messes up your engine or— worse yet— if you eat a no-name hamburger that sends you to the hospital with food poisoning. Your chances of suing the local business owner successfully (perhaps before a jury of his friends and neighbors) may be considerably less. Moreover, even if you should win, the chances of collecting enough money to compensate you for all the trouble you have been put through is more remote than if you were suing a big corporation.

In an increasingly global economy, Europeans and Americans might be very hesitant to buy telecommunications equipment made halfway around the world in South Korea. But, once the Samsung brand acquired a track record, people in Berlin or Chicago would just as soon buy Samsung products as buy competing products manufactured down the street. Asian companies in general have only in relatively recent history begun investing much time and money in making their brand names widely known, and still they spend less on this than other multinational companies. However, brand names like Toyota, Honda, and Nikon are recognized around the world, and the Cathay Pacific airline and the Shangri-La hotel chain are also becoming better known internationally.

Brand names are not guarantees. But they do reduce the range of uncertainty. If a hotel sign says Ritz-Carlton, chances are you will not have to worry about whether the bed sheets in your room were changed since the last person slept there. Even if you stop at a dingy and run-down little store in a strange town, you are not afraid to drink a soda they sell you, if it is a bottle or can of Coca-Cola or Seven Up. Imagine, however, if the owner of this unsavory little place mixed you a soda at his own soda fountain. Would you have the same confidence in drinking it?

Like everything else in the economy, brand names have both benefits and costs. A hotel with a Ritz-Carlton sign out front may charge you more for the same size and quality of room, and accompanying service, than you would pay in some comparable, locally-run, independent hotel *if you knew where to look*. Someone who regularly stops in this town on business trips might well find a locally-run hotel that is a better deal. But it is just as rational for you to look for a brand name when passing through for the first time as it is for the regular traveler to go back where he knows he can get the same things for less.

Since brand names are a substitute for specific knowledge, how valuable they are depends on how much knowledge you already have about the particular product or service. Someone who is very knowledgeable about photography might be able to safely get a bargain on an off-brand camera or lens, or even a second-hand camera or lens. But someone whose knowledge of stereo equipment is far less than that same person's knowledge of photography might be well advised to purchase only well-known brands of new stereo equipment.

Many critics of brand names argue that the main brands "are all alike." Even when that is so, the brand names still perform a valuable function. The question is not whether Campbell's soup is better than some other brand of soup but whether both are better than they would be if both were sold under anonymous or generic labels. If Campbell's soup were identified on the label only as "Tomato Soup," "Clam Chowder," or "Minestrone," with no brand name on the label— the pressures on all canned soup producers to maintain both safety and quality would be less.

Brands have not always existed. They came into existence and then survived and spread for a reason. In eighteenth century England, for example, only a few luxury goods, such as Chippendale furniture, were known by their manufacturer's brand name. It was an innovation when Josiah Wedgwood put his name on chinaware that he sold and which ultimately became world famous for its quality and appearance. In the United States, brand names began to flourish around the time of the Civil War. In nineteenth century America, most food processors did not put brand names on the food that they sold— a situation which allowed adulteration of food to flourish. When Henry Heinz entered this business and sold unadulterated processed food, he identified his products with his name, reaping the benefits of the reputation he established among consumers, which allowed his company to expand rapidly, and an array of new processed foods bearing his name to be readily accepted by the public from the outset.

In short, the rise of brands promoted better quality by allowing consumers to distinguish and choose, and by forcing producers to take responsibility for what they made, reaping rewards when it was good and losing customers when it was not. Quality standards for hamburgers, milk shakes and French fries were all revolutionized in the 1950s and 1960s by McDonald's, whose methods and machinery were later copied by some of its leading competitors. But the whole industry's standards became higher than before because McDonald's spent millions of dollars researching the growing, storage and processing of potatoes. Moreover, McDonald's established a policy of making unannounced visits to its potato suppliers, as it did to its suppliers of hamburger meat, in order to ensure that its quality specifications were being followed, and it forced dairies to supply a higher quality of milk shake mix.

McDonald's competitors were of course forced to do similar things, in order to remain in business. Afterwards, some might say in later years that leading hamburger chains were "all alike," but they were all better because

McDonald's could first reap the rewards of having its brand name identified in the public mind with higher quality products than they had previously been used to in hamburger stands.

Even when the various brands of a product are made to the same formula by law, as with aspirin, quality control is promoted when each producer of each bottle of aspirin is identified than when the producer is anonymous. Moreover, the best-known brands have the most to lose if some impurity gets into the aspirin during production and causes anyone illness or death. This is especially important with foods and medicines.

Like many other things, the importance of brand names can be seen more clearly by seeing what happens in their absence. In countries where there are no brand names, or where there is only one producer created or authorized by the government, the quality of the product or service tends to be lower. During the days of the Soviet Union, that country's only airline, Aeroflot, became notorious for bad service and rudeness to passengers. After the dissolution of the Soviet Union, a new privately financed airline began to have great success, in part because its passengers appreciated being treated like human beings for a change. The management of the new airline declared that its employment policy was that it would not hire anyone who had ever worked for Aeroflot.

When it came to consumer products, Soviet consumers tried to make up for a lack of brands by developing their own methods of trying to figure out where a given product was made. As *The Economist* reported:

> In the old Soviet Union, where all products were supposed to be the same, consumers learnt how to read barcodes as substitutes for brands in order to identify goods that came from reliable factories.

In effect, Soviet consumers created brands *de facto* for their own benefit, where none existed, indicating that brands have value to consumers as well as producers.

Among a business' assets— its money, machinery, real estate, inventory and other tangible assets— its brand name may be its largest asset, though intangible. It has been estimated that the market value of the Coca-Cola company exceeds the value of its tangible assets by more than $100 billion and that $70 billion of that is due to the value of its brand. That is a very large incentive for them to maintain quality and safety, in order to maintain the financial value of that asset.

NON-PROFIT ORGANIZATIONS

We have seen that the role of profit-seeking businesses is better understood when they are recognized as profit-and-loss businesses, with all the pressures and incentives created by these dual potentialities, which force these enterprises to respond to feedback from those who use their goods or services, as well as feedback from those who invested the capital that made the business possible and whose continuing investments are necessary for its continued existence and prosperity. By the same token, what are called "non-profit organizations" can be better understood when they are seen as institutions which are insulated, to varying degrees, from a need to respond to feedback from those who use their goods and services, or those whose money enabled them to be founded and to continue operating.

The tendency of those who run any organization— whether profit-seeking or non-profit, military, religious, educational or other— is to use the resources of the organization to benefit themselves in one way or another, even at the expense of the ostensible goals of the organization. How far this tendency can go can be limited by powerful outside interests on which the organization depends for its existence, such as investors who will either get a satisfactory return on their investment or take their money elsewhere, and customers who will either get a product or service that they want at a price they are willing to pay or likewise take their money elsewhere. These outside interests are not as decisive in the case of non-profit organizations.

This does not mean that non-profit organizations have unlimited money or that they do not need to worry about spending more than they take in. It does mean, however, that with whatever money they do have, non-profit organizations are under very little pressure to achieve their institutional goals to the maximum extent possible with the resources at their disposal. Those who supply those resources include the general public, who cannot closely monitor what happens to their donations, and neither can those whose money provided the endowments which help finance non-profit institutions. Much, or sometimes most, of those endowments were left by people who are now dead and so cannot monitor at all.

Non-profit organizations have additional sources of income, including fees from those who use their services, such as visitors to museums and audiences for symphony orchestras. These fees are in fact the main source of the more than two trillion dollars in revenue received annually by non-profit organizations in the United States. However, these fees do not cover the full costs of the goods and services being supplied.

In other words, the recipients are receiving goods and services which cost more to produce than these recipients are paying, and some are receiving them free. Such subsidized beneficiaries cannot exert the same kind of influence or pressure on a non-profit organization that can be exerted by the customers of a profit-and-loss business, since these latter customers are paying the full cost of everything they get— and will continue to do so only when they find what they receive to be worth what it costs them, compared to what they can get for the same money elsewhere.

A non-profit organization's goods or services may be worth what it costs the recipients— sometimes nothing— without being worth what it cost to produce. In other words, while an enterprise constrained by profit and loss considerations cannot continue to use resources which have a greater value in alternative uses elsewhere in the economy, a non-profit organization can, since it need not recover the full costs of the resources it uses from the recipients of the goods and services it provides. Where non-profit organizations are making grants of money, the recipients of that money are in no position to influence the way the non-profit organization operates, as customers of profit-seeking organizations can and do.

In the case of non-profit organizations that serve as intermediaries in the transfer of human organs such as livers and kidneys donated to be transplanted to ill patients, these non-profit organizations can impose arbitrary rules which neither doctors nor patients are in much position to challenge.

In general, those who run non-profit organizations are in a position vis-à-vis those who use their goods and services very similar to that of a landlord during a shortage of housing: There is a surplus of applicants. Under these conditions, where neither the desires of the current users of the non-profit organization's goods and services nor the original desires of those who supplied their endowments in the past have the kind of leverage that both customers and investors have on a profit-seeking enterprise, those individuals who happen to be in charge of a non-profit institution at a given time can substitute their own goals for the institution's ostensible goals or the goals of their founders.

It has been said, for example, that Henry Ford and John D. Rockefeller would turn over in their graves if they knew what kinds of things are being financed today by the foundations which bear their names. While that is ultimately unknowable, what is known is that Henry Ford II resigned from the board of the Ford Foundation in protest against what the foundation was doing with the money left by his grandfather. More generally, it is now widely recognized how difficult it is to establish a foundation to serve a given purpose and expect it to stick to that purpose after the money has been contributed, and especially after the original donors are dead. Much money can be dissipated in creating luxurious surroundings in the organization's workplace or arranging showy conferences in posh hotels and resorts, held in upscale locations around the country or overseas.

The aims of the organization can be bent to the aims of its current officials or to decisions and activities that will gain them public visibility and applause, whether or not any of this serves the original purpose for which the non-profit organization was founded or even its current ostensible purpose. British writer Peter Hitchens observed that the government-established Church of England "was more and more being run for the benefit of its own employees" rather than for the benefit of churchgoers or the country. Adam Smith made similar charges against endowed universities in the eighteenth century.

Smith pointed out how academics running colleges and universities financed by endowments can run them in self-serving ways, being "very indulgent to one another," so that each academic would "consent that his neighbour may neglect his duty, provided he himself is allowed to neglect his own." Widespread complaints today that professors neglect teaching in favor of research, and sometimes neglect both in favor of leisure or other activities, suggest that the underlying principle has not changed much in more than two hundred years. Tenure guaranteeing lifetime appointments is common in non-profit colleges and universities, but is virtually unknown in businesses that must meet the competition of the marketplace, including profit-seeking educational institutions such as the University of Phoenix.

Academic institutions, hospitals and foundations are usually non-profit organizations in the United States. However, non-profit institutions cover a wide range of endeavors and can also engage in activities normally engaged in by profit-seeking enterprises, such as selling Sunkist oranges or publishing *The Smithsonian* magazine. In whatever activities they engage, non-profit organizations are not under the same pressures to get "the most bang for the buck" as are enterprises in which profit and loss determine their survival. This affects efficiency, not only in the narrow financial sense, but also in the broader sense of achieving the avowed purposes of institutions. Colleges and universities, for example, can become disseminators of particular ideological views that happen to be in vogue ("political correctness") and restrictors of alternative views, even though the goals of education might be better served by exposing students to a wider range of contrasting and contending ideas.*

Employment policies of non-profit organizations have more latitude than those of enterprises which operate in the hope of profit and under the threat of losses. Before World War II, hospitals were among the most racially discriminatory of American employers, even though their avowed purposes would have been better served by hiring the best-qualified doctors, even when those doctors happened to be black or Jewish. Non-profit foundations were also among the most racially discriminatory institutions at that time.

The same was true of the non-profit academic world, where the first black professor did not receive tenure at a major university until 1948. Yet there were hundreds of black chemists working for profit-seeking chemical companies,

---

* John Stuart Mill pointed this out in his essay *On Liberty* in 1859: "He who knows only his own side of the case, knows little of that. . . Nor is it enough that he should hear the arguments of adversaries from his own teachers, presented as they state them, and accompanied by what they offer as refutations. That is not the way to do justice to the arguments, or bring them into real contact with his own mind. He must be able to hear them from persons who actually believe them; who defend them in earnest, and do their very utmost for them. He must know them in their most plausible and persuasive form. . ."

years before blacks were hired to teach chemistry at non-profit colleges. Similarly, both black and Jewish doctors had flourishing private practices long before they could practice medicine in many non-profit hospitals.

Regardless of the purposes for which money has been donated to non-profit organizations, it is spent at the discretion of people who can use it for their own perks, prejudices, or politics.

The performances of non-profit organizations shed light on the role of profit when it comes to efficiency. If those who conceive of profit as simply an unnecessary charge added on to the cost of production of goods and services are correct, then non-profit organizations should be able to produce those goods and services at a lower cost and sell them at a lower price. Over the years, this should lead to non-profit enterprises taking away the customers of profit-seeking enterprises and increasingly replacing them in the economy.

Not only have non-profit organizations not usually taken away the customers of profit-seeking enterprises, increasingly the direct opposite has happened: Non-profit organizations have seen more and more of their own economic activities taken over by profit-seeking businesses. Colleges and universities are just one example. Over the years, more and more activities once run by non-profit academic institutions themselves— college bookstores, dining halls, and other auxiliary services— have been increasingly turned over to profit-seeking businesses that can do the job cheaper or better, or both. As *The Chronicle of Higher Education* reported:

> Follet runs the Stanford Bookstore. Aramark prepares the meals at Yale University. And Barnes & Noble manages the Harvard Coop.
> The nation's most prestigious universities— and many others in academe— increasingly contract out portions of their campus operations.

According to *The Chronicle of Higher Education*, "Money is the No. 1 reason that colleges contract out an operation." In other words, commercial businesses not only run such services at lower costs, they make enough profit to pay the colleges more than these non-profit organizations could make from the same operations on their own campuses. For example, the University of South Carolina "rarely netted as much as $100,000 per year" from its college bookstore but Barnes & Noble paid them $500,000 a year to run the same bookstore. This implies that Barnes & Noble must have made even more money in order to pay the University of South Carolina more than the university ever made for itself from the same bookstore.

Sometimes the reason many campus operations are more profitable under commercial business management is that profit-seeking enterprises reduce such waste as hiring year-round employees for highly seasonal businesses like college bookstores, where large sales of textbooks are concentrated at the beginning of each academic term. Other reasons include more experience at marketing. At the University of Georgia's bookstore, for example, 70 percent of the books were stored in inventory when the university ran its own bookstore but, after Follet took over, 70 percent of the books were put on display, where they were more likely to be bought.

In the Middle East, the first kibbutz was founded in 1910 as a non-profit community of individuals providing each other with goods and services, and sharing their output on an egalitarian basis. That first kibbutz voted to stop being non-profit and egalitarian in 2007— and, by that time, so had 61 percent of the kibbutzim in Israel. One factor in that first kibbutz's decision to change was that young people tended to leave and go live in the market-oriented sector of the economy. In short, even people raised in the philosophy of a non-profit institution like the kibbutz nevertheless voted with their feet to go join the market economy.

Despite a tendency in the media to treat non-profit institutions as disinterested sources of information, those non-profit organizations which depend on continuing current donations from the public have incentives to be alarmists, in order to scare more money out of their donors. For example, one non-profit organization which regularly issues dire warnings about health risks in the environment has admitted to not having a single doctor or scientist on its staff. Other non-profit organizations that are financially dependent on current contributions, as distinguished from large endowments, have similar incentives to alarm their respective constituencies over various social, political, or other issues, and few constraints to confine themselves to accurate or valid bases for those alarms.

Chapter 25

"NON-ECONOMIC" VALUES

Beware the people who moralize about great issues;
moralizing is easier than facing hard facts.

John Corry

While economics offers many insights, and makes it easier to see through some popular notions that sound good but will not stand up under scrutiny, economics has also acquired the name "the dismal science" because it pours cold water on many otherwise attractive and exciting— but fallacious— notions about how the world can be arranged. One of the last refuges of someone whose pet project or pet theory has been exposed as economic nonsense is to say: "Economics is all very well, but there are also *non-economic* values to consider." Presumably, these are supposed to be higher and nobler concerns that soar above the level of crass materialism.

Of course there are non-economic values. In fact, there are *only* non-economic values. Economics is not a value in and of itself. It is only a way of weighing one value against another. Economics does not say that you should make the most money possible. Many professors of economics could themselves make more money in private industry. Many people with a knowledge of firearms could probably make more money working as hit men for organized crime. But economics does not urge you toward such choices.

Adam Smith, the father of *laissez-faire* economics, gave away substantial sums of his own money to less fortunate people, though he did so with such discretion that this fact was discovered only after his death, when his personal records were examined. Henry Thornton, one of the leading monetary economists of the nineteenth century and a banker by trade, regularly gave away more than half his annual income before he got married and had a family to support— and he continued to give large donations to humanitarian causes afterwards, including the anti-slavery movement.

The first public libraries in New York City were not established by the government but by industrial entrepreneur Andrew Carnegie, who also established the foundation and the university that bear his name. John D. Rockefeller likewise established the foundation that bears his name and the University of Chicago, as well as creating many other philanthropic enterprises. Halfway around the world, the Tata Institute in Mumbai was established by India's leading industrialist, J.R.D. Tata, as a scholarly enterprise, while another leading entrepreneurial family, the Birlas, established numerous religious and social institutions across India.

The United States, which has come to epitomize capitalism in the eyes of many people around the world, is unique in having hundreds of colleges, hospitals, foundations, libraries, museums and other institutions created by the donations of private individuals, many of these being people who earned money in the marketplace and then devoted much of it— sometimes most of it— to helping others. *Forbes* magazine in 2007 listed half a dozen Americans who had donated multiple billions of dollars each to philanthropy. The largest of these donations was $42 billion by Bill Gates— 42 percent of his total wealth. The largest percentage of his wealth donated by an American billionaire was 63 percent by Gordon Moore. For the American population as a whole, the amount of private charitable donations per person is several times what it is in Europe. The percentage of the country's output that is donated to philanthropic causes is more than three times that in Sweden, France or Japan.

The market as a mechanism for the allocation of scarce resources among alternative uses is one thing; what one chooses to do with the resulting wealth is another.

What lofty talk about "non-economic values" often boils down to is that some people do not want their own particular values weighed against anything. If they are for saving Mono Lake or preserving some historic building, then they do not want that weighed against the cost— which is to say, ultimately, against all the other things that might be done instead with the same resources. For such people, there is no point considering how many Third World children could be vaccinated against fatal diseases with the money that is spent saving Mono Lake or preserving a historic building. We should vaccinate those children *and* save Mono Lake *and* preserve the historic building— as well as doing innumerable other good things, according to this way of looking at the world.

To people who think— or rather, react— in this way, economics is at best a nuisance that obstructs them from doing what they have their hearts set on doing. At worst, economics is seen as a needlessly narrow, if not morally warped, way of looking at the world. Such condemnations of economics are due to the fundamental fact that economics is a study of the use of scarce resources which have alternative uses. We might all be happier in a world where there were no such constraints to force us into choices and trade-offs that we would rather not face. But that is not the world that human beings live in— or have ever lived in, during thousands of years of recorded history.

Politics has sometimes been called "the art of the possible," but that phrase applies far more accurately to economics. Politics allows people to vote for the impossible, which may be one reason why politicians are often more popular than economists, who keep reminding people that there is no free lunch and that there are no "solutions" but only trade-offs. In the real world that people live in, and are likely to live in for centuries to come, trade-offs are inescapable. Even if we refuse to make a choice, circumstances will make choices for us, as we run out of resources for many important things that we could have had, if only we had taken the trouble to weigh alternatives.

SAVING LIVES

Perhaps the strongest arguments for "non-economic values" are those involving human lives. Many highly costly laws, policies, or devices designed to safeguard the public from lethal hazards are defended on grounds that "if it saves just one human life" it is worth whatever it costs. Powerful as the moral and emotional appeal of such pronouncements may be, they cannot withstand scrutiny in a world where scarce resources have alternative uses.

One of those alternative uses is saving other human lives in other ways. Few things have saved as many lives as simply the growth of wealth. An earthquake powerful enough to kill a dozen people in California will kill hundreds of people in some less affluent country and thousands in a Third World nation. Greater wealth enables California buildings, bridges, and other structures to be built to withstand far greater stresses than similar structures can withstand in poorer countries. Those injured in an earthquake in California can be rushed far more quickly to far more elaborately equipped hospitals with larger numbers of more highly trained medical personnel. This is just one of innumerable ways in which wealth saves lives.

Natural disasters of all sorts occur in rich and poor countries alike— the United States leads the world in tornadoes, for example— but their consequences are very different. The Swiss Reinsurance Company reported that the biggest financial costs of natural disasters in 2013 were in Germany, the Czech Republic and France. But that same year the biggest costs of natural disasters in human lives were all in Third World countries— the Philippines and India. Given the high cost of medical care and of such preventive measures against disease as water treatment plants and sewage disposal systems, Third World countries likewise suffer far more from diseases, including diseases that have been virtually wiped out in affluent countries. The net result is shorter lifespans in poorer countries.

There have been various calculations of how much of a rise in national income saves how many lives. Whatever the correct figure may be— X million dollars to save one life— anything that prevents national income from rising that much has, in effect, cost a life. If some particular safety law, policy, or device costs $5X$ million dollars, either directly or by its inhibiting effect on economic growth, then it can no longer be said to be worth it "if it saves just one human life" because it does so at the cost of 5 other human lives. There is no escaping trade-offs, so long as resources are scarce and have alternative uses.

More is involved than saving lives in alternative ways. There is also the question of how much life is being saved and at how much cost. Some might say that there is no limit on how much value should be placed on a human life. But, however noble such words may sound, in the real world no one would favor spending half the annual output of a nation to keep one person alive 30 seconds longer. Yet that would be the logical implication of a claim that a life is of infinite value.

When we look beyond words to behavior, people do not behave as if they regard even their own lives as being of infinite value. For example, people take life-threatening jobs as test pilots or explosives experts when such jobs pay a high enough salary for them to feel compensated for the risk. They even risk their lives for purely recreational purposes, such as skydiving, white-water rafting, or mountain climbing.

Using various indicators of the value that people put on their own lives in various countries, a study at the Harvard Law School estimated that the average American puts a value of $7 million on his or her life, while Canadians put a value of $4 million each on their lives and people in Japan put a value of nearly $10 million. Whatever the validity or accuracy of these particular numbers, the general results seem to indicate that people do not in fact behave as if their own lives are of infinite value— and presumably they value their own lives at least as much as they value the lives of other people.

How much it costs to save one life varies with the method used. Vaccinating children against deadly diseases in Third World countries costs very little per child and saves many lives, including decades of life per child. Meanwhile, a heart transplant on an eighty-year-old man is enormously expensive and can yield only a limited amount of additional life, even if the transplant surgery is completely successful, since the life expectancy of an octogenarian is not very great in any case.

If a life is not of infinite value, then it cannot be true that "if it saves just one life" some device, law or policy is worth whatever it may cost. Certainly it cannot be true if the cost of saving one life is sacrificing other lives.

MARKETS AND VALUES

Often the market is blamed for obstructing moral or social values. For example, writers for the *San Francisco Chronicle* referred to "how amoral the marketplace can be" when explaining why the water supply owned by the city of Stockton, California, could not be entrusted to private enterprise.

"Water is too life-sustaining a commodity to go into the marketplace with," the *Chronicle* quoted the mayor of Stockton as saying. Yet, every day, life-sustaining food is supplied through private enterprises. Moreover, most new life-saving medicines are developed in market economies, notably that of the United States, rather than in government-run economies.

As for privately run water systems, they already exist in Argentina. *The Economist* magazine reported on the results of this privatization:

> Connections to the water and sewerage networks rose, especially among poorer households: most richer households and families in the city centre were already hooked up. . . . Before privatisation really got under way, in 1995, child mortality rates were falling at much the same pace in municipalities that eventually privatised and those that did not. After 1995, the fall accelerated in privatising municipalities. . .The fall was concentrated in deaths from infectious and parasitic diseases, the sort most likely to be affected by water quality and availability. Deaths from other causes did not decline.

In Britain as well, the privatized water supply in England has meant lower water bills, higher quality drinking water, less leakage, and a sewage disposal system that complies with environmental regulations a higher percentage of the time than that in Scotland, where the government runs the water system. This evidence may be suggestive, rather than conclusive, but those who argue for political control of the water supply seldom see a need for any evidence at all. To many people, empirical consequences often matter less than deeply ingrained beliefs and attitudes. Whether in urgent or less urgent matters, many believe that those with political power are better qualified to make moral decisions than are the private parties directly concerned.

Such attitudes are international. An entrepreneur in India reported his experience with a government minister there:

> I had argued that lowering the excise duty would lower consumer prices of shampoos, skin creams, and other toiletries, which in turn would raise their demand. The tax revenues would thus rise, although the tax rate might be lower. Indian women did not need lipsticks and face creams, felt the minister. I replied that all women wanted to look pretty.
> "A face cream won't do anything for an ugly face. These are luxuries of the rich," he said. I protested that even a village girl used a paste of haldi so that she could look pretty.

"No, it's best to leave a face to nature," he said impatiently.

"Sir," I pleaded, "how can you decide what she wants? After all, it is her hard-earned money."

"Yes, and I don't want her wasting it. Let her buy food. I don't want multinational companies getting rich selling face creams to poor Indians."

The idea that third party observers can impose morally better decisions often includes the idea that they can define what are "luxuries of the rich," when it is precisely the progress of free market economies which has turned many luxuries of the rich into common amenities of people in general, including the poor. Within the twentieth century alone, automobiles, telephones, refrigerators, television sets, air-conditioners, and personal computers all went from being luxuries of the rich to being common items across the spectrum of Americans and among millions of people in many other market economies. The first videocassette recorders sold for $30,000 each before technological progress, trial and error experience, and economies of scale brought the price down within the budget of most Americans.

In past centuries, even such things as oranges, sugar, and cocoa were luxuries of the rich in Europe. Not only do third party definitions of what is a luxury of the rich fail to account for such changes, the stifling of free markets by third parties can enable such things to remain exclusive luxuries longer than they would otherwise.

Markets and Greed

Those who condemn greed may espouse "non-economic values." But lofty talk about "non-economic values" too often amounts to very selfish attempts to have one's own values subsidized by others, obviously at the expense of those other people's values. A typical example of this appeared in a letter to the newspaper trade magazine *Editor & Publisher*. This letter was written by a newspaper columnist who criticized "the annual profit requirements faced by newspapers" due to "the demands of faceless Wall Street financial analysts who seem, from where I sit, insensitive to the vagaries of newspaper journalism."

Despite the rhetorical device of describing some parties to a transaction in less than human terms ("faceless Wall Street financial analysts"), they are all people and they all have their own interests, which must be mutually reconciled in one way or another, if those who supply the money that enables newspapers to operate are to be willing to continue to do so. Although people who work on Wall Street may control millions of dollars each, this is not all their own personal money by any means. Much of it comes from the savings, or the money paid into pension funds, by millions of other people, many of whom have very modest incomes.

If "the vagaries of newspaper journalism"— however defined— make it difficult to earn as high a return on investments in newspapers or newspaper chains as might be earned elsewhere in the economy, why should workers whose pension funds will be needed to provide for their old age subsidize newspaper chains by accepting a lower rate of return on money invested in such corporations? Since many editors and columnists earn much more money than many of the people whose payments into pension funds supply newspapers with the money to operate, it would seem especially strange to expect people with lower incomes to be subsidizing people with higher incomes— teachers and mechanics, for example, subsidizing editors and reporters.

Why should financial analysts, as the intermediaries handling pension funds and other investments from vast numbers of people, betray those people, who have entrusted their savings to them, by accepting less of a return from newspapers than what is available from other sectors of the economy? If good journalism, however defined, results in lower rates of return on the money invested in newspaper chains, whatever special costs of newspaper publishing are responsible for this can be borne by any of a number of people who benefit from newspapers. Readers can pay higher prices for papers; columnists, editors and reporters can accept lower salaries; or advertisers can pay higher rates, for example.

Why should the sacrifice be forced on mechanics, nurses, teachers, etc., around the country whose personal savings and pension funds provide the money that newspaper chains acquire by selling corporate stocks and bonds? Why should other sectors of the economy that are willing to pay more for the use of these funds be deprived of such resources for the sake of one particular sector?

The point here is not how to solve the financial problems of the newspaper industry. The point is to show how differently things look when considered from the standpoint of allocating scarce resources which have alternative uses. This fundamental economic reality is obscured by emotional rhetoric that ignores the interests and values of many people by summarizing them via unsympathetic intermediaries such as "insensitive" financial analysts, while competing interests are expressed in idealistic terms, such as journalistic quality. Financial analysts may be as sensitive to the people they are serving as others are to the very different constituencies they represent.

Often what critics of the market want are special dispensations for particular individuals or groups, whether these are newspapers, ethnic groups, social classes or others— without acknowledging that these dispensations will inevitably be at the expense of other individuals or groups, who are either arbitrarily ignored or summarized in impersonal terms as "the market." For example, a *New York Times* reporter writing about the problems of a middle-aged, low-income woman said, "if the factory had just let Caroline work day shifts, her problem would have disappeared." But, he lamented: "Wages and hours are set by the marketplace, and you cannot expect magnanimity from the marketplace."

Here again, the inescapable conflict between what one person wants and what another person wants is presented in words that recognizes only one side of this equation as human. Most people prefer working day shifts to working night shifts but, if Caroline were transferred to the day shift, someone else would have to be transferred to the night shift. As for "magnanimity," what would that mean except forcing someone else to bear this woman's costs? What is magnanimous about someone who is paying no cost whatsoever— in this case, the *New York Times* reporter— demanding that someone else be saddled with those costs?

Both in the private sector and in the government sector, there are always values that some people think worthy enough that other people should have to pay for them— but not worthy enough that they should have to pay for them themselves. Nowhere is the weighing of some values against other values obscured more often by rhetoric than when discussing government policies. Taxing away what other people have earned, in order to finance one's own moral adventures via social programs, is often depicted as a humanitarian endeavor. But allowing others the same freedom and dignity as oneself, so that they can make their own choices with their own earnings, is considered to be pandering to "greed." Greed for power is no less dangerous than greed for money, and has historically shed far more blood in the process.

Markets and Morality

Whether assessing the effects of market economies or of government or other institutions, it is a challenge to make a clear distinction between results that emerge from those institutions and results caused by those institutions. Because a given institution or process *conveys* a certain outcome does not mean that it *caused* that outcome. As we have seen in Chaper 4, stores in low-income neighborhoods often charge higher prices than in other neighborhoods, but the causes of those higher prices are higher costs of doing business in those neighborhoods, not higher rates of profits resulting from arbitrary price increases by the stores. Many businesses and professions in fact avoid low-income neighborhoods because earnings prospects are usually not as good there.

The same principle applies to many other institutions, whether in a market economy, a socialist economy, a government agency or others. Some hospitals have higher death rates than others precisely because they have the finest doctors and the most advanced medical technology— and therefore treat patients with the most difficult, life-threatening medical problems that other hospitals are simply not equipped to handle. A hospital that treats mostly people with routine infections or broken arms may well have a lower death rate than a hospital that performs operations like brain surgery or heart transplants. Higher death rates at more advanced hospitals convey a reality that they did not *cause*.

Similarly, everything that happens in a market economy, or a socialist economy, or in a government agency, is not necessarily caused by those institutions. Everything depends on the particular facts of the particular situation. This affects not only questions about causation but also moral questions. Income differences, for example, may be a result of barriers created against some groups or a result of factors internal to the groups themselves, such as average age, years of education and other factors that vary from one group to another.

Most people, in the Western world at least, would probably consider arbitrary barriers against particular groups to be morally wrong, and something that should be eliminated. But such a consensus is not equally likely if income differences are due to age differences— a factor that evens out over a lifetime, since all of us spend the same amount of time being 20 years old, 30 years old or 40 years old, even if we are not all *simultaneously* at the same ages when statistics are collected. Nor is such a consensus likely if income differences are a result of differences in individuals' chosen behavior, such as dropping out of school or going on drugs, since many people feel no obligation to subsidize such behavior.

In short, moral decisions depend on factual realities. However, people with different moral values can make different decisions about the same facts. Therefore the policy question often comes down to whether some people feel that their moral values should be imposed on other people with different moral values through the power of government. Market economies permit individuals to make decisions for themselves, based on their own moral values or other personal considerations— and at the same time the market forces them to pay the costs that their decisions create. The question is therefore not whether moral values should guide market economies, but *whose* moral values, if any, should be imposed on others or subsidized by others.

Many whose sense of morality is offended by large economic disparities among individuals, groups and nations tend to see the causes of these differences as "advantages" or "privileges" that some people have over others. But it is crucial to make a distinction between achievements and privileges. This is not simply a matter of semantics. Privileges come at the expense of others, but achievements add to the benefits of others.

Few of us may have had whatever combination of factors enabled Thomas Edison to make electricity a major part of millions of people's lives. But vast numbers of people around the world benefitted from Edison's achievements, both in his own time and in generations that followed. Whatever the sources of Edison's achievements, we have all benefitted from those achievements, as we have benefitted from the achievements of the Wright brothers and of others who added whole new dimensions to human life.

Similarly for the scientists whose work led to cures or preventatives for crippling diseases like polio or lethal diseases like malaria. Even business leaders who simply found ways to produce goods and services better, or to deliver them to consumers at lower cost, contributed to rising standards of living around the world.

All these things, and more, create economic disparities among individuals, groups and nations with different achievements. That may seem morally offensive to some observers. But, here again, moral decisions require an accurate understanding of facts and causes, as well as a clear distinction between privileges and achievements. Moral decisions, and policies based on those decisions, cannot be made on the simple basis of statistics, visions and rhetoric— not if the purpose is to make human life better, either materially or otherwise, rather than to indulge one's emotions in disregard of the actual consequences for others.

The moral judgment that life is not "fair" to individuals, groups or nations in the sense of providing them all with the same factors that promote economic prosperity or other benefits, is one that can be shared by people with very different moral or ideological values.

As already noted in Chapter 23, neither geography nor culture nor history has presented equal opportunities to all individuals, groups or nations. Nor have such other factors as demography or politics. In the words of distinguished economic historian David S. Landes, "nature like life is unfair." But not all sources of unfairness— in the sense of very different life chances— have moral dimensions: "No one can be praised or blamed for the temperature of the air, or the volume and timing of rainfall, or the lay of the land."

There are of course decisions and actions for which human beings can be judged morally or held responsible legally. But just looking at the bare facts of statistical disparities does not tell us which those are, much less what actions taken now can or will be effective. For that we need not only facts but analysis, whether of economics, history, politics or human nature.

We also need to keep in mind a clear moral distinction between doing things that let us vent our pent-up feelings and doing things likely to actually help those who have been unfortunate in the circumstances into which they were born. Transferring income or wealth is relatively easy. But developing human capital among those who lag is far more effective, even if it is also far more difficult. After all, the income or wealth that is transferred has a limited time before it is gone, and continued economic progress depends on having the human capital to replenish this income and wealth as it is used up. Moral decisions cannot be divorced from the consequences they create.

Morality is not a luxury but a necessity, because no society can be held together solely by force. Even totalitarian dictatorships promote an ideology with their particular kind of morality because not even a government apparatus with pervasive and ruthless powers of repression and terror is sufficient by itself to create or sustain a functioning society. But, while moral principles are necessary for any society, they are seldom sufficient. To apply moral principles to an economy requires knowledge and understanding of that economy— and an ability to "think things, not words," as Justice Oliver Wendell Holmes once said.

Otherwise, attempts to help "the poor," for example, may not merely fail but be counterproductive, if we cannot distinguish people who are genuinely and enduringly poor from people who are simply young and beginning their careers in entry-level jobs that they will soon outgrow, as they acquire human capital that is valuable to themselves and to the society. Making blanket benefits available to "the poor" can short-circuit this process by making it unnecessary for many people to work, and minimum wage laws can make it harder for the young to find work, costing them both current pay and the acquisition of human capital for the future. Similarly, the need to "think things, not words" makes the distinction between privilege and achievement not simply a matter of semantics, but an urgent need for clarity when making moral decisions. Privileges, which harm others, must be distinguished from achievements, which benefit others and advance society as a whole.

Chapter 26

THE HISTORY OF
ECONOMICS

I am sure that the power of vested interests is vastly exaggerated compared with the gradual encroachment of ideas.

John Maynard Keynes

People have been talking about economic issues, and some writing about them, for thousands of years, so it is not possible to put a specific date on when the study of economics began as a separate field. Modern economics is often dated from 1776, when Adam Smith wrote his classic, *The Wealth of Nations*, but there were substantial books devoted to economics at least a century earlier, and there was a contemporary school of French economists called the Physiocrats, some of whose members Smith met while traveling in France, years before he wrote his own treatise on economics. What was different about *The Wealth of Nations* was that it became the foundation for a whole school of economists who continued and developed its ideas over the next two generations, including such leading figures as David Ricardo (1772–1823) and John Stuart Mill (1806–1873), and the influence of Adam Smith has to some extent persisted on to the present day. No such claim could be made for any previous economist, despite many people who had written knowledgeably and insightfully on the subject in earlier times.

More than two thousand years ago, Xenophon, a student of Socrates, analyzed economic policies in ancient Athens. In the Middle Ages, religious conceptions of a "fair" or "just" price, and a ban on usury, led Thomas

Aquinas to analyze the economic implications of those doctrines and the exceptions that might therefore be morally acceptable. For example, Aquinas argued that selling something for more than was paid for it could be done "lawfully" when the seller has "improved the thing in some way," or as compensation for risk, or because of having incurred costs of transportation. Another way of saying the same thing is that much that looks like sheer taking advantage of other people is often in fact compensation for various costs and risks incurred in the process of bringing goods to consumers or lending money to those who seek to borrow.

However far economists have moved beyond the medieval notion of a fair and just price, that concept still lingers in the background of much present-day thinking among people who speak of things being sold for more or less than their "real" value and individuals being paid more or less than they are "really" worth, as well as in such emotionally powerful but empirically undefined notions as price "gouging."

From more or less isolated individuals writing about economics there evolved, over time, more or less coherent schools of thought, people writing within a common framework of assumptions— the medieval scholastics, of whom Thomas Aquinas was a prominent example, the mercantilists, the classical economists, the Keynesians, the "Chicago School," and others. Individuals coalesced into various schools of thought even before economics became a profession in the nineteenth century.

THE MERCANTILISTS

One of the earliest schools of thought on economics consisted of a group of writers called the mercantilists, who flourished from the sixteenth through the eighteenth centuries. In a motley collection of writings, ranging from popular pamphlets to a multi-volume treatise by Sir James Steuart in 1767, the mercantilists argued for policies enabling a nation to export more than it imports, causing a net inflow of gold to pay for the difference. This gold they equated with wealth. From this school of thought have come such present-day practices as referring to an export surplus as a "favorable" balance of trade and a surplus of imports as an "unfavorable" balance of trade— even though, as we have seen in earlier chapters, there is nothing inherently more beneficial about one than the other, and everything depends on the surrounding circumstances.

The inevitable gropings of pioneers include inevitable ambiguities and errors— and economics was no exception. Some of the errors of the mercantilists, which have been largely expunged from the work of modern economists, still live on in popular beliefs and political rhetoric. However, there is a coherence in the writings of the mercantilists, if we understand their purposes, as well as their conceptions of the world.

The purposes of the mercantilists were not the same as those of modern economists. Mercantilists were concerned with increasing the power of their own respective nations relative to that of other nations. Their goal was *not* the allocation of scarce resources in a way that would maximize the standard of living of the people at large. Their goal was gaining or maintaining a national competitive advantage in aggregate wealth and power over other nations, so as to be able to prevail in war, if war occurred, or to deter potential enemies by one's obvious wealth that could be turned to military purposes. A hoard of gold was ideal for their purposes.

In a typical mercantilist writing in 1664, Thomas Mun's book *England's Treasure by Forraign Trade* declared the cardinal rule of economic policy to be "to sell more to strangers yearly than wee consume of theirs in value." Conversely, the nation must try to produce at home "things which now we fetch from strangers to our great impoverishing." Mercantilists focused on the relative power of national governments, based on the wealth available to be used by their respective rulers.

Mercantilists were by no means focused on the average standard of living of the population as a whole. Thus the repression of wages by imposing government control was considered by them to be a way of lowering the costs of exports, creating a surplus of exports over imports, which would bring in gold. The promotion of imperialism and even slavery was acceptable to some mercantilists for the same reason. The "nation" to them did not mean a country's whole population. Thus Sir James Steuart could write in 1767 of "a whole nation fed and provided for gratuitously" by means of slavery. Although slaves were obviously part of the population, they were not considered to be part of the nation.

CLASSICAL ECONOMICS

Adam Smith

Within a decade after Sir James Steuart's multi-volume mercantilist treatise, Adam Smith's *The Wealth of Nations* was published and dealt a historic blow against mercantilist theories and the whole mercantilist conception of the world. Smith conceived of the nation as all the people living in it. Thus you could not enrich a nation by keeping wages down in order to export. "No society can surely be flourishing and happy, of which the far greater part of the members are poor and miserable," Smith said. He also rejected the notion of economic activity as a zero-sum process, in which one nation loses what another nation gains. To him, all nations could advance at the same time in terms of the prosperity of their respective peoples, even though military power— a major concern of the mercantilists— was of course relative and a zero-sum competition.

In short, the mercantilists were preoccupied with the *transfer* of wealth, whether by export surpluses, imperialism, or slavery— all of which benefit some at the expense of others. Adam Smith was concerned with the *creation* of wealth, which is not a zero-sum process. Smith rejected government intervention in the economy to help merchants— the source of the name "mercantilism"— and instead advocated free markets along the lines of the French economists, the Physiocrats, who had coined the term *laissez faire*. Smith repeatedly excoriated special-interest legislation to help "merchants and manufacturers," whom he characterized as people whose political activities were designed to deceive and oppress the public. In the context of the times, *laissez faire* was a doctrine that opposed government favors to business.

The most fundamental difference between Adam Smith and the mercantilists was that Smith did not regard gold as being wealth. The very title of his book— *The Wealth of Nations*— raised the fundamental question of what wealth consisted of. Smith argued that wealth consisted of the goods and services which determined the standard of living of the people— the whole people, who to Smith constituted the nation. Smith rejected both imperialism and slavery— on economic grounds as well as moral grounds, saying that the "great fleets and armies" necessary for imperialism "acquire nothing which can compensate the expence of maintaining them." *The Wealth of Nations* closed by urging Britain to give up dreams of empire. As for slavery, Smith considered it economically inefficient, as well as morally repugnant, and dismissed with contempt the idea that enslaved Africans were inferior to people of European ancestry.

Although Adam Smith is today often regarded as a "conservative" figure, he in fact attacked many of the dominant ideas and interests of his own times. Moreover, the idea of a spontaneously self-equilibrating system— the market economy— first developed by the Physiocrats and later made part of the tradition of classical economics by Adam Smith, represented a radically new departure, not only in analysis of social causation but also in seeing a reduced role for political, intellectual, or other elites as guides or controllers of the masses.

For centuries, landmark intellectual figures from Plato onward had discussed what policies wise leaders might impose for the benefit of society in various ways. But, in the economy, Smith argued that governments were giving "a most unnecessary attention" to things that would work out better if left alone to be sorted out by individuals interacting with one another and making their own mutual accommodations. Government intervention in the economy, which mercantilist Sir James Steuart saw as the role of a wise "statesman," Smith saw as the notions and actions of "crafty" politicians, who created more problems than they solved.

While *The Wealth of Nations* was not the first systematic treatise on economics, it became the foundation of a tradition known as classical economics, which built upon Smith's work over the next century. Not all earlier treatises were mercantilist by any means. Books by Richard Cantillon in the 1730s and by Ferdinando Galiani in 1751, for example, presented sophisticated economic analyses, and François Quesnay's *Tableau Économique* in 1758, contained insights that inspired the transient but significant school of economists called the Physiocrats. But, as already noted, these earlier pioneers created no enduring school of leading economists in later generations who based themselves on their work, as Adam Smith did.

Here and there in history there have been a number of individual economists who produced work well in advance of their times, but who attracted little attention and had few followers— and who faded into obscurity until they were rediscovered by later generations of scholars as pioneers in their field. French mathematician Augustin Cournot, for example, produced mathematical analyses of economic principles in 1838 that did not become part of the analytical tools of economists until nearly a century later, when they were developed independently by economists of that later era.

One of the consequences of Adam Smith's economic theories, developed in opposition to the theories of the mercantilists, was an emphasis on downplaying the role of money in the economy. This emphasis persisted throughout the era of classical economics, which lasted nearly a century. Understandable as this opposition to the mercantilists was, in light of the mercantilists' over-emphasis on the role of gold, which was money in many economies, the classical economists' statements that money was only a "veil"— obscuring but not essentially changing the underlying real economic activities— were often misunderstood by those who read them. The leading classical economists understood that contractions in the money supply could create reduced production, and correspondingly increased unemployment, at a given time.* But this was not always clear to their readers, and the classical economists' own attention was seldom focused in that direction.

David Ricardo

Among the followers of Adam Smith was the great classical economist David Ricardo, the leading economist of the early nineteenth century who, among other things, developed the theory of comparative advantage in international trade. In addition to his substantive contributions to economic analysis, Ricardo created a new approach and style in writing about economics. Adam Smith's *The Wealth of Nations* was full of social commentary

---

* This point is elaborated on pages 34 to 42 of my book *On Classical Economics*.

and philosophical observations, and closed with a strong suggestion that Britain should not try to hold on to its American colonies that were in rebellion the same year that his treatise was published. By contrast, David Ricardo's *Principles of Political Economy* in 1817 was the first of the great classic works in economics to be devoted to analysis of enduring principles of economics, divorced from social, political and philosophical commentary, and emphasizing those principles more so than immediate policy issues.

This is not to say that Ricardo had no interest in social or moral issues. Some of his analysis was inspired by the particular economic problems faced by Britain in the wake of the Napoleonic wars but the principles he derived were not confined to those problems or that era, any more than Newton's law of gravity was confined to falling apples. Contemporary policy issues were simply not what his *Principles of Political Economy* was about. What Ricardo brought to economics was a more narrowly focused system of analysis, using more sharply defined terms and more tightly reasoned analysis.

David Ricardo was not simply a reasoning machine, however. In his personal actions and private correspondence, Ricardo showed himself to be a man of very high moral standards and social concerns. When he became a member of Parliament, Ricardo wrote to a friend:

> I wish that I may never think the smiles of the great and powerful a sufficient inducement to turn aside from the straight path of honesty and the convictions of my own mind.

As a member of Parliament, Ricardo lived up to his ideals. He voted repeatedly against the interests of wealthy landowners, though he himself was one, and he voted for election reforms which would have cost him his seat in Parliament.*

What we today call "economics" was once called "political economy" up through much of the nineteenth century. When the classical economists referred to "political economy," they meant the economics of the country as a whole— the polity— as distinguished from the economics of the

---

* But, however much he exemplified moral principles in his actions, Ricardo was "above the unctuous phrases that cost so little and yield such ample returns." J.A. Schumpeter, *History of Economic Analysis*, p. 471n.

household, or what might today be called "home economics." The term "political economy" did *not* imply an amalgamation of economics and politics, as some have used that term in more recent times.

The principles of economics did not spring forth, ready-made, in a flash of inspiration or genius. Instead, profound and conscientious thinkers in successive generations groped toward some kind of understanding of both the real world of economic activity and the intellectual concepts that would make it possible to study such things systematically. The supply and demand analysis that can be taught to today's beginning students in a week took at least a century to emerge from the controversies among early nineteenth-century thinkers like David Ricardo, Thomas Malthus, and Jean-Baptiste Say.

In one of many letters between Ricardo and his friend Malthus, discussing economic issues over the years, Ricardo said in 1814: "I sometimes suspect that we do not attach the same meaning to the word demand." He was right; they did not.* It would be decades after both men had passed from the scene before the term could be clarified and defined precisely enough to mean what it means to economists today. What may seem like small steps in logic, after the fact, can be a long, time-consuming process of trial and error groping, while creating and refining concepts and definitions to express ideas in clear and unmistakable terms which allow substantive issues to be debated in terms that opposing parties can agree on, so that they can at least disagree on substance, rather than be frustrated by semantics.

Say's Law

One of the fundamental concepts of economics, over which controversies raged in the early nineteenth century and were re-ignited by John Maynard Keynes in 1936, was what has been called Say's Law. Named for French economist Jean-Baptiste Say (1767–1832), though other economists had a role in its development, Say's Law began as a relatively simple principle whose corollaries and extensions grew ever more complex in the hands of both its advocates and its critics, during the controversies between the two in both the nineteenth and twentieth centuries.

---

* For a clarification of the differences, see pages 69–71 of my *On Classical Economics*.

At its most basic, Say's Law was an answer to perennial popular fears that the growing output of an economy could reach the point where it would exceed the ability of the people to buy it, leading to unsold goods and unemployed workers. Such fears were expressed, not only before the time of Jean-Baptiste Say, but also long afterward. As we have seen in Chapter 16, a best-selling writer of the 1960s warned of "a threatened overabundance of the staples and amenities and frills of life" which have become "a major national problem." What Say's Law, in its most basic sense, argued was that the production of output, and the generation of real income for those producing that output, were not processes independent of each other. Therefore, whether a nation's output was large or small, the incomes generated in producing it would be sufficient to buy it. Say's Law has often been expressed as the proposition that "supply creates its own demand." In other words, there is no inherent limit to how much output an economy can produce and purchase.

Say himself asked: "Otherwise, how could it be possible that there should now be bought and sold in France five or six times as many commodities, as in the miserable reign of Charles VI?" A similar idea had been expressed even earlier by one of the Physiocrats, that aggregate demand "has no known limits." This, of course, did not preclude the possibility that, as of any given time, consumers or investors might not choose to exercise all the aggregate demand that was in their power. What Say's Law did preclude was the recurrent popular fear that the sheer rapid growth of output, with the rise of modern industry, would reach a point where output would become so great that it would be impossible to buy it all.

As often happens in the history of ideas, an initially very straightforward concept became extended in so many directions by its advocates, and embroiled in so many controversies by its opponents, that meanings and distortions proliferated, even when the economists on both sides— which included virtually all the leading economists of the early nineteenth century— were earnest and intelligent thinkers who simply talked past each other. That was, in part, because economics had not yet reached the stage where the terms in which they spoke ("demand," for example) had rigorous definitions agreed to by all.* However tedious the students of a later time might find the process of rigorous definition, the history of economics— and of other fields— makes painfully clear the confusing consequences of trying to discuss substantive issues without having clear-cut terms that mean the same thing to all those who use those terms.

MODERN ECONOMICS

Today we think of economics as a profession with academic departments, scholarly journals, and professional organizations like the American Economic Association. But these are relatively late developments, as history is measured.

It was centuries before economics became a separate subject, even though philosophers from Aristotle to David Hume wrote knowledgeably about economic matters, as did theologians like Thomas Aquinas and members of the nobility like Sir James Steuart. But, even after some writers began to specialize in economics, they did not immediately begin to earn their livings as economists. Adam Smith, for example, was a professor of philosophy, and achieved renown for his book *Theory of Moral Sentiments* nearly twenty years before achieving lasting fame for *The Wealth of Nations*. David Ricardo was an independently wealthy retired stockbroker when his writings made him the leading economist of his times. When Thomas R. Malthus was appointed a professor of history and political economy in 1805, he became the first academic economist in Britain and probably in the world. Britain at that point produced most of the leading economists in the world, and would continue to do so for the remainder of the nineteenth century.

Aside from Malthus, most of the leading British economists of the first half of the nineteenth century did not derive a major part of their income from teaching or writing about economics. Economics was a specialty but not yet a career. Nor was it yet enough of a specialty to have its own professional journals. Most leading analytical articles on economics during

---

* A more extended discussion of these controversies can be found in Thomas Sowell, *On Classical Economics* (New Haven: Yale University Press, 2006), pp. 23–34.

the first half of the nineteenth century were published in the intellectual periodicals of that era, such as the *Edinburgh Review*, the *Quarterly Review* or the *Westminster Review* in Britain or the *Revue Encyclopédique* or the *Annales de Législation et d'Économie Politique* in France. The first scholarly journal devoted exclusively to economics was the *Quarterly Journal of Economics*, first published at Harvard in 1886. Many more such journals were then created in many countries in the twentieth century. Those who wrote for these journals were overwhelmingly academic economists, with Americans now joining British, Austrian and other economists among the leaders of the profession. The first professor of economics in the United States was appointed by Harvard in 1871 and the first Ph.D. in economics was awarded by the same institution four years later.

From the time of Alfred Marshall's *Principles of Economics* in 1890 onward, economics began increasingly to be expressed to the profession and taught to students with graphs and equations, though purely verbal presentations have not completely died out even today. It was in the second half of the twentieth century that mathematical analyses in economics began to supersede wholly verbal analyses in the leading academic journals and scholarly books. While predominantly mathematical economic analysis can be found as far back as Augustin Cournot in the 1830s, Cournot was one of those pioneers whose work made no impact on the dominant economists of his time, so that much of what he said had to be rediscovered, generations later, as if Cournot had never existed.

The "Marginalist" Revolution

One of the watersheds in the development of economic analysis in the nineteenth century was the widespread acceptance among economists of a price theory based on the demands of consumers, rather than just on the costs of producers. It was revolutionary not only as a theory of price but also in introducing new concepts and new methods of analysis that spread into other branches of economics.

Classical economics had regarded the amount of labor and other inputs as crucial factors determining the price of the resulting output. Karl Marx had taken this line of thinking to its logical extreme with his theory of the exploitation of labor, which was seen as the ultimate source of wealth, and therefore as the ultimate source of the income and wealth of the non-working classes, such as capitalists and landowners.*

Although the cost-of-production theory of value had prevailed in England since the time of Adam Smith, an entirely different theory had prevailed in continental Europe, where value was considered to be determined by the utility of goods to consumers, which was what would determine their demand. Smith, however, disposed of this theory by saying that water was obviously more useful than diamonds, since one could not live without water but many people lived without diamonds— and yet diamonds sold for far more than water. But, in the 1870s, a new conception emerged from Carl Menger in Austria and W. Stanley Jevons in England, both basing prices on the utility of goods to consumers— and, more important, refining and more sharply defining the terms of the debate, while introducing new concepts into economics in general.

What Adam Smith had been comparing was the *total* utility of water versus the *total* utility of diamonds. In other words, he was asking whether we would be worse off with *no* water or *no* diamonds. In that sense, the total utility of water obviously greatly exceeded the total utility of diamonds, since water was a matter of life and death. But Menger and Jevons conceived of the issue in a new way— a way that could be applied to many other analyses in economics besides price theory.

First of all, Menger and Jevons conceived of utility as entirely subjective. That is, there was no point in third party observers declaring one thing to be more useful than another, because each consumer's demand was based on what that particular consumer considered useful— and consumer demand was what affected prices. More fundamentally, *utility varies*, even for the same consumer, depending on how much of particular goods and services that consumer already has.

---

* However major a figure Karl Marx was in the history of the world and however great his intellectual as well as political influence on the twentieth century, his work in economics has left little trace on the development of that discipline. Even those economists who are Marxists typically use other economic concepts in their professional work.

Carl Menger pointed out that an amount of food necessary to sustain life is enormously valuable to everyone. Beyond the amount of food necessary to avoid starving to death, there was still value to additional amounts necessary for health, even though not as high a value as to the amount required to avoid death, and there was still some value to food to be eaten just for the pleasure of eating it. But eventually "satisfaction of the need for food is so complete that every further intake of food contributes neither to the maintenance of life nor to the preservation of health— nor does it even give pleasure to the consumer." In short, what mattered to Menger and Jevons was the *incremental* utility, what Alfred Marshall would later call the "marginal" utility of additional units consumed.

Returning to Adam Smith's example of water and diamonds, the relative utilities that mattered were the *incremental* or marginal utility of having another gallon of water compared to another carat of diamonds. Given that most people were already amply supplied with water, the marginal utility of another carat of diamonds would be greater— and this would account for a carat of diamonds selling for more than a gallon of water. This ended the difference between the cost-of-production theory of value in England and the utility theory of value in continental Europe, as economists in both places now accepted the marginal utility theory of value, as did economists in other parts of the world.

Essentially the same analysis and conclusions that Carl Menger reached in Austria in his 1871 book *Principles of Economics* appeared at the same time in England in W. Stanley Jevons' book *The Theory of Political Economy*. What Jevons also saw, however, was how the concept of *incremental* utility was readily expressed in graphs and differential calculus, making the argument more visibly apparent and more logically rigorous than in Menger's purely verbal presentation. This set the stage for the spread of incremental or marginal concepts to other branches of economics, such as production theory or international trade theory, where graphs and equations could more compactly and more unambiguously convey such concepts as economies of scale or comparative advantage.

This has been aptly called "the marginalist revolution," which marked a break with both the methods and the concepts of the classical economists.

This marginalist revolution facilitated the increased use of mathematics in economics to express cost variations, for example, in curves and to analyze rates of change of costs with differential calculus. However, mathematics was not necessary for understanding the new utility theory of value, for Carl Menger did not use a single graph or equation in his *Principles of Economics*.

Although Menger and Jevons were the founders of the marginal utility school in economics, and pioneers in the introduction of marginal concepts in general, it was Alfred Marshall's monumental textbook *Principles of Economics*, published in 1890, which systematized many aspects of economics around these new concepts and gave them the basic form in which they have come down to present-day economics. Jevons had been especially at pains to reject the notion that value depends on labor, or on cost of production in general, but insisted that it was utility which was crucial. Alfred Marshall, however, said:

> We might as reasonably dispute whether it is the upper or the under blade of a pair of scissors that cuts a piece of paper, as whether value is governed by utility or cost of production.

In other words, it was the *combination* of supply (dependent on the cost of production) and demand (dependent on marginal utility) which determined prices. In this and other ways, Marshall reconciled the theories of the classical economists with the later marginalist theories to produce what became known as neo-classical economics. His *Principles of Economics* became the authoritative text and remained so on into the first half of the twentieth century, going through eight editions in his lifetime.*

That Alfred Marshall was able to reconcile much of classical economics with the new marginal utility concepts was not surprising. Marshall was highly trained in mathematics and first learned economics by reading Mill's *Principles of Political Economy*. In 1876, he called it "the book by which most living English economists have been educated." Before that, Alfred Marshall had been a student of philosophy, and was critical of the economic inequalities in society, until someone told him that he needed to understand

---

* Marshall's *Principles of Economics* was still being used as a textbook in economics when I was a graduate student at Columbia University in academic year 1958–59.

economics before making such judgments. After doing so, and seeing circumstances in a very different light, his continuing concern for the poor then led him to change his career and become an economist. He afterwards said that what social reformers needed were "cool heads" as well as "warm hearts." As he was deciding what career to pursue, "the increasing urgency of economic studies as a means towards human well-being grew upon me."

Equilibrium Theory

The increased use of graphs and equations in economics made it easier to illustrate such things as the effects of shortages and surpluses in causing prices to rise or fall. It also facilitated analyses of the conditions in which prices would neither rise nor fall— what have been called "equilibrium" conditions. Moreover, the concept of "equilibrium" applied to many things besides prices. There could be equilibrium in particular firms, whole industries, the national economy or international trade, for example.

Many people unfamiliar with economics have regarded these equilibrium conditions as unrealistic in one way or another, because they often seem different from what is usually observed in the real world. But that is not surprising, since the real world is seldom in equilibrium, whether in economics or in other fields. For example, while it is true that "water seeks its own level," that does not mean that the Atlantic Ocean has a glassy smooth surface. Waves and tides are among the ways in which water seeks its own level, as are waterfalls, and all these things are in motion at all times. Equilibrium theory allows you to analyze what that motion will be like in various disequilibrium situations found in the real world.

Similarly, students in medical school study the more or less ideal functioning of various body parts in healthy equilibrium, but not because body parts always function ideally in healthy equilibrium— since, if that were true, there would then be no reason to have medical schools in the first place. In other words, the whole point of studying equilibrium is to understand what happens when things are *not* in equilibrium, in one particular way or in some other way.

In economics, the concept of equilibrium applies not only in analyses of particular firms, industries or labor markets, but also in the economy as a whole.

In other words, there are not only equilibrium prices or wages but also equilibrium national income and equilibrium in the balance of trade. The analysis of equilibrium and disequilibrium conditions in particular markets has become known as "microeconomics," while analyses of changes in the economy as a whole— such as inflation, unemployment or rises and falls in total output— became known as "macroeconomics." However, this convenient division overlooks the fact that all these elements of an economy affect one another. Ironically, it was two Soviet economists, living in a country with a non-market economy, who saw a crucial fact about market economies when they said: "Everything is interconnected in the world of prices, so that the smallest change in one element is passed along the chain to millions of others."

For example, when the Federal Reserve System raises the interest rate on borrowed money, in order to reduce the danger of inflation, that can cause home prices to fall, savings to rise, and automobile sales to decline, among many other repercussions spreading in all directions throughout the economy. Following all these repercussions in practice is virtually impossible, and even analyzing it in theory is such a challenge that economists have won Nobel Prizes for doing so. The analysis of these complex interdependencies— whether microeconomic or macroeconomic— is called "general equilibrium" theory. It is what J.A. Schumpeter's *History of Economic Analysis* called a recognition of "this all-pervading interdependence" that is the "fundamental fact" of economic life.

The landmark figure in general equilibrium theory was French economist Léon Walras (1834–1910), whose complex simultaneous equations essentially created this branch of economics in the nineteenth century. Back in the eighteenth century, however, another Frenchman, François Quesnay (1694–1774), was groping toward some notion of general equilibrium with a complex table intersected by lines connecting various economic activities with one another. Karl Marx, in the second volume of *Capital*, likewise set forth various equations showing how particular parts of a market economy affected numerous other parts of that economy. In other words, Walras had predecessors, as most great discoverers do, but he was still the landmark figure in this field.

While general equilibrium theory is something that can be left for advanced students of economics, it has some practical implications that can be understood by everyone. These implications are especially important because politicians very often set forth a particular economic "problem" which they are going to "solve," without the slightest attention to how the repercussions of their "solution" will reverberate throughout the economy, with consequences that may dwarf the effects of their "solution."

For example, laws setting a ceiling on the interest rate that can be charged on particular kinds of loans, or on loans in general, can reduce the amount of loans that are made, and change the mixture of people who can get loans— lower income people being particularly disqualified— as well as affecting the price of corporate bonds and the known reserves of natural resources,* among other things. Virtually no economic transaction takes place in isolation, however much it may be seen in isolation by those who think in terms of creating particular "solutions" to particular "problems."

Keynesian Economics

The most prominent new developments in economics in the twentieth century were in the study of the variations in national output from boom times to depressions. The Great Depression of the 1930s and its tragic social consequences around the world had as one of its major and lasting impacts an emphasis on trying to determine how and why such calamities happened and what could be done about them.** John Maynard Keynes' 1936 book, *The General Theory of Employment Interest and Money*, became the most famous and most influential economics book of the twentieth century. By mid-century, it was the prevailing orthodoxy in the leading economics departments of the world— with the notable exception of the University of Chicago and a few other economics departments in other universities largely staffed or dominated by former students of Milton Friedman and others in the "Chicago School" of economists.

---

* As discussed in Chapter 13 of *Basic Economics*.
** John Maynard Keynes wrote in 1930: "The world has been slow to realise that we are living this year in the shadow of one of the greatest economic catastrophes of modern history." John Maynard Keynes, *Essays in Persuasion*, 1952 edition, p. 135.

To the traditional concern of economics with the allocation of scarce resources which have alternative uses, Keynes added as a major concern those periods in which substantial proportions of a nation's resources— including both labor and capital— are not being allocated at all. This was certainly true of the time when Keynes' *General Theory* was written, the Great Depression of the 1930s, when many businesses produced well below their normal capacity and as many as one-fourth of American workers were unemployed.

While writing his magnum opus, Keynes said in a letter to George Bernard Shaw: "I believe myself to be writing a book on economic theory which will largely revolutionize— not, I suppose, at once but in the course of the next ten years— the way the world thinks about economic problems." Both predictions proved to be accurate. However, the contemporary New Deal policies in the United States were based on ad hoc decisions, rather than on anything as systematic as Keynesian economics. But, within the economics profession, Keynes' theories not only triumphed but became the prevailing orthodoxy.

Keynesian economics offered not only an economic explanation of changes in aggregate output and employment, but also a rationale for government intervention to restore an economy mired in depression. Rather than wait for the market to adjust and restore full employment on its own, Keynesians argued that government spending could produce the same result faster and with fewer painful side-effects. While Keynes and his followers recognized that government spending entailed the risk of inflation, especially when "full employment" became an official policy, it was a risk they found acceptable and manageable, given the alternative of unemployment on the scale seen during the Great Depression.

Later, after Keynes' death in 1946, empirical research emerged suggesting that policy-makers could in effect choose from a menu of trade-offs between rates of unemployment and rates of inflation, in what was called the "Phillips Curve," in honor of economist A.W. Phillips of the London School of Economics, who had developed this analysis.

Post–Keynesian Economics

The Phillips Curve was perhaps the high-water mark of Keynesian economics. However, the Chicago School began chipping away at the

Keynesian theories in general and the Phillips Curve in particular, both analytically and with empirical studies. In general, Chicago School economists found the market more rational and more responsive than the Keynesians had assumed— and the government less so, at least in the sense of promoting the national interest, as distinguished from promoting the careers of politicians. By this time, economics had become so professionalized and so mathematical that the work of its leading scholars was no longer something that most people, or even most scholars outside of economics, could follow. What could be followed, however, was the slow erosion of the Keynesian orthodoxy, especially after the simultaneous rise of inflation and unemployment to high levels during the 1970s undermined the notion of the government making a trade-off between the two, as suggested by the Phillips Curve.

When Professor Milton Friedman of the University of Chicago won a Nobel Prize in economics in 1976, it marked a growing recognition of non-Keynesian and anti-Keynesian economists, such as those of the Chicago School. By the last decade of the twentieth century, a disproportionate share of the Nobel Prizes in economics were going to economists of the Chicago School, whether located on the University of Chicago campus or at other institutions. The Keynesian contribution did not vanish, however, for many of the concepts and insights of John Maynard Keynes had now become part of the stock in trade of economists in all schools of thought. When John Maynard Keynes' picture appeared on the cover of the December 31, 1965 issue of *Time* magazine, it was the first time that someone no longer living was honored in this way. There was also an accompanying story inside the magazine:

> *Time* quoted Milton Friedman, our leading non-Keynesian economist, as saying, "We are all Keynesians now." What Friedman had actually said was: "We are all Keynesians now and nobody is any longer a Keynesian," meaning that while everyone had absorbed some substantial part of what Keynes taught no one any longer believed it all.

While it is tempting to think of the history of economics as the history of a succession of great thinkers who advanced the quantity and quality of analysis in this field, seldom did these pioneers create perfected analyses. The gaps, murkiness, errors and shortcomings common to pioneers in many fields were also common in economics. Clarifying, repairing and more rigorously systematizing what the giants of the profession created required the dedicated work of many others, who did not have the genius of the giants, but who saw many individual things more clearly than did the great pioneers.

David Ricardo, for example, was certainly far more of a landmark figure in the history of economics than was his obscure contemporary Samuel Bailey, but there were a number of things that Bailey expressed more clearly in his analysis of Ricardian economics than did Ricardo himself. Similarly, in the twentieth century, Keynesian economics began to be developed and presented with concepts, definitions, graphs and equations found nowhere in the writings of John Maynard Keynes, as other leading economists extended the analysis of Keynesian economics to the profession in scholarly writings, and its presentation to students in textbooks, using devices that Keynes himself never used or conceived.

THE ROLE OF ECONOMICS

Among the questions often raised about the history of economic analysis are: (1) Is economics scientific or is it just a set of opinions and ideological biases? and (2) Do economic ideas reflect surrounding circumstances and events and change with those circumstances and events?

Scientific Analysis

There is no question that economists as individuals have their own respective preferences and biases, as do all individuals, including mathematicians and physicists. But the reason mathematics and physics are not considered to be mere subjective opinions and biased notions is that there are accepted *procedures* for testing and proving beliefs in these disciplines. It is precisely because individual scientists are likely to have biases that scientists in general seek to create and agree upon scientific methods and procedures that are unbiased, so that individual biases may be deterred or exposed.

In economics, the preferences of Keynesian economists for government intervention and of University of Chicago economists for relying on markets instead of government, may well have influenced their respective initial reactions to the analysis and data of the Phillips Curve, for example. But the fact that both Keynesian economists and economists of the Chicago School shared a common set of analytical and empirical procedures in their professional work enabled them to reach common conclusions as more data came in over time, undermining the Phillips Curve.

Controversies have raged in science, but what makes a particular field scientific is not automatic unanimity on particular issues but a commonly accepted set of procedures for resolving differences about issues when there are sufficient data available. Einstein's theory of relativity was not initially accepted by most physicists, nor did Einstein want it accepted without some empirical tests. When the behavior of light during an eclipse of the sun provided a test of his theory, the unexpected results convinced other scientists that he was right. A leading historian of science, Thomas Kuhn, has argued that what distinguishes science from other fields is that mutually contradictory theories cannot co-exist indefinitely in science but that one or the other must prevail, and the others disappear, when enough of the right data become available.

Thus the phlogiston theory of combustion gave way to the oxygen theory of combustion and the Ptolemaic theory of astronomy gave way to the Copernican theory. The history of ideologies, however, is quite different from the history of science. Mutually contradictory ideologies can co-exist for centuries, with no resolution of their differences in sight or perhaps even conceivable.*

What scientists share is not simply agreement on various conclusions but, more fundamentally, agreement about the ways of testing and verifying conclusions, beginning with a careful and strict definition of the terms being used. The crucial importance of definitions in economics has been demonstrated, for example, by the fallacies that result when popular discussions of economic policies use a loose term like "wages" to refer to such different things as wage rates per unit of time, aggregate earnings of workers, and labor

---

* This theme is explored in my book *A Conflict of Visions*.

costs per unit of output.* As noted in Chapter 21, a prosperous country with higher wage rates per unit of time may have lower labor costs per unit of output than a Third World country where workers are not paid nearly as much.

Mathematical presentations of arguments, whether in science or economics, not only make these arguments more compact and their complexities easier to follow than a longer verbal presentation would be, but can also make their implications clearer and their flaws harder to hide. For example, when preparing a landmark 1931 scholarly article on economics, one later reprinted for decades thereafter, Professor Jacob Viner of the University of Chicago instructed a draftsman on how he wanted certain complex cost curves constructed. The draftsman replied that one of the set of curves with which Professor Viner wanted to illustrate the analysis in his article was impossible to draw with all the characteristics that Viner had specified.

As Professor Viner later recognized, he had asked for something that was "technically impossible and economically inappropriate," because some of the assumptions in his analysis were incompatible with some of his other assumptions. That flaw became apparent in a mathematical presentation of the argument, whereas mutually incompatible assumptions may co-exist indefinitely in an imprecise verbal presentation.

Systematic analysis of carefully defined terms and the systematic testing of theories against empirical evidence are all part of a scientific study in many fields. Clearly, economics has advanced in this direction in the centuries since its beginnings. However, economics is scientific only in the sense of having some of the procedures of science. But the inability to conduct controlled experiments prevents its theories from having the precision and repeatability often associated with science. On the other hand,

---

* As we have seen in Chapter 17, during the Great Depression of the 1930s successive American administrations of both political parties sought to maintain high wage rates per unit of time as a way of maintaining labor's "purchasing power"— which depends on the aggregate earnings of workers. But, among economists, both Keynesian and non-Keynesian, it was understood that the number of workers employed was affected by the wage rate per unit of time, so that higher wage rates could mean fewer people employed— and those earning no income reduce purchasing power. A common fallacy in popular discussions of international trade is that countries with high "wages"— that is, wage rates per unit of time— cannot compete with countries that have low "wages," on the assumption that the high-wage countries will have higher production costs.

there are other fields with a recognized scientific basis which also do not permit controlled experiments, astronomy being one example and meteorology being another. Moreover, there are different degrees of precision among these fields.

In astronomy, for example, the time when eclipses will occur can be predicted to the second, even centuries ahead of time, while meteorologists have a high error rate when forecasting the weather a week ahead.

Although no one questions the scientific principles of physics on which weather forecasting is based, the uncertainty as to how the numerous combinations of factors will come together at a particular place on a particular day makes *forecasting* a particular event that day much more hazardous than *predicting* how those factors will interact if they come together.

Presumably, if a meteorologist knew in advance exactly when a warm and moisture-laden air mass moving up from the Gulf of Mexico would encounter a cold and dry air mass moving down from Canada, that meteorologist would be able to predict rain or snow in St. Louis to a certainty, since that would be nothing more than the application of the principles of physics to these particular circumstances. It is not those principles which are uncertain but all the variables whose behavior will determine which of those principles will apply at a particular place at a particular time.

What is scientifically known is that the collision of cold dry air and warm moist air does not produce sunny and calm days. What is unknown is whether these particular air masses will arrive in St. Louis at the same time or pass over it in succession— or both miss it completely. That is where statistical probabilities are calculated as to whether they will continue moving at their present speeds and without changing direction.

In principle, economics is much like meteorology. There is no example in recorded history in which a government increased the money supply ten-fold in one year without prices going up. Nor does anyone expect that there ever will be. The effects of price controls in creating shortages, black markets, product quality decline, and a reduction in auxiliary services, have likewise been remarkably similar, whether in the Roman Empire under Diocletian, in Paris during the French Revolution or in the New York housing market under rent control today. Nor has there been any fundamental difference whether the price being controlled was that of housing, food, or medical care.

Controversies among economists make news, but that does not mean that there are no established principles in this field, any more than controversies among scientists mean that there is no such thing as established principles of chemistry or physics. In both cases, these controversies seldom involve predicting what *would* happen under given circumstances but forecasting what *will* in fact happen in circumstances where there are too many combinations and permutations of factors for the outcome to be completely foreseen. In short, these controversies usually do not involve disagreement about fundamental principles of the field but about how all the trends and conditions will come together to determine which of those principles will apply or predominate in a particular set of circumstances.

Assumptions and Analysis

Among the many objections made against economics have been claims that it is "simplistic," or that it assumes too much self-interested and materialistic rationality, or that the assumptions behind its analyses and predictions are not a true depiction of the real world.

Some of the problems of declaring something "simplistic" have already been dealt with in Chapter 4. Implicit in the term "simplistic" is that a particular explanation is not just simple but *too* simple. That only raises the question: Too simple for what? If the facts consistently turn out the way the explanation predicts, then it has obviously not been too simple for its purpose— especially if the facts do *not* turn out the way a more complicated or more plausible-sounding explanation predicts. In short, whether or not any given explanation is too simple is an empirical question that cannot be decided in advance by how plausible, complex, or nuanced an explanation seems on the face of it, but can only be determined after examining hard evidence on how well its predictions turn out.*

---

* There was consternation among wine connoisseurs when economist Orley Ashenfelter said that he could predict the prices of particular wines using data on the weather during the season in which its grapes were grown, without either tasting the wine or paying any attention to the opinions of experts who had tasted it. But his methods turned out to predict prices more accurately than the opinions of experts who had tasted the wine.

A related attempt to determine the validity of a theory by how plausible it looks, rather than how well it performs when put to the test, is the criticism that economic analysis depicts people as thinking or acting in a way that most people do not think or act. But economics is ultimately about systemic *results*, not personal *intentions* or individual acts.

Economists on opposite ends of the ideological spectrum have understood this. Karl Marx said that capitalists lower their prices when technological advances lower their costs of production, not because they *want* to, but because market competition forces them to. Adam Smith likewise said that the benefits of a competitive market economy are "no part" of capitalists' intentions. As already noted in Chapter 4, Marx's collaborator Engels said, "what each individual wills is obstructed by everyone else, and what emerges is something that no one willed." It is "what emerges" that economics tries to predict and its success or failure is measured by that, not by how plausible its analysis looks at the outset.

Bias and Analysis

Personal bias is another fundamental question that has long been raised about economics and its claim to scientific status. J.A. Schumpeter, whose massive *History of Economic Analysis* remains unequalled for its combination of breadth and depth, dealt with the much-discussed question of the effect of personal bias on economic analysis. He found ideological bias common among economists, ranging from Adam Smith to Karl Marx— but what he also concluded was how little effect these biases had on these economists' analytical work, which can be separated out from their ideological comments or advocacies.

In a scholarly journal as well, Schumpeter singled out Adam Smith in particular: "In Adam Smith's case the interesting thing is not indeed the absence but the harmlessness of ideological bias."

Smith's unrelievedly negative picture of businessmen was, to Schumpeter, an ideological bias deriving from Smith's background in a family which "did *not* belong to the business class" and his intellectual immersion in the work of "similarly conditioned" intellectuals. But "all this ideology, however strongly held, really did not much harm to his scientific achievement" in producing "sound factual and analytic teaching." Similarly with Karl Marx, whose ideological vision of social processes was formed before he began to study economics, but "as his analytic work matured, Marx not only elaborated many pieces of scientific analysis that were neutral to that vision but also some that did not agree with it well," even though Marx continued to use "vituperative phraseology that does not affect the scientific elements in an argument." Ironically, Marx's view of businessmen was not quite as totally negative as that of Adam Smith.*

According to Schumpeter, "*in itself* scientific performance does not require us to divest ourselves of our value judgments or to renounce the calling of an advocate of some particular interest." More bluntly, he said, "advocacy does not imply lying," though sometimes ideologies "crystallize" into "creeds" that are "impervious to argument." But among the hallmarks of a scientific field are "rules of procedure" which can "crush out ideologically conditioned error" from an analysis. Moreover, having "something to formulate, to defend, to attack" provides an impetus for factual and analytical work, even if ideology sometimes interferes with it. Therefore "though we proceed slowly because of our ideologies, we might not proceed at all without them."

Events and Ideas

Does economics influence events and do events influence economics? The short answer to both questions is "yes" but the only meaningful question is— to what extent and in what particular ways? John Maynard Keynes' answer to the first question was this:

> . . .the ideas of economists and political philosophers, both when they are right and when they are wrong, are more powerful than is commonly understood. Indeed the world is ruled by little else. Practical men, who

---

* In *Capital*, Marx said, "I paint the capitalist and the landlord in no sense *couleur de rose*. But here individuals are dealt with only in so far as they are the personifications of economic categories. . . My stand-point. . .can less than any other make the individual responsible for relations whose creature he socially remains, however much he may subjectively raise himself above them." Contrary to many others on the left, Marx did not see capitalists as controlling the economy but just the opposite: "Free competition brings out the inherent laws of capitalist production, in the shape of external coercive laws having power over every individual capitalist." Karl Marx, *Capital*, Vol. I, pp. 15, 297.

believe themselves to be quite exempt from any intellectual influences, are usually the slaves of some defunct economist. Madmen in authority, who hear voices in the air, are distilling their frenzy from some academic scribbler of a few years back. I am sure that the power of vested interests is vastly exaggerated compared with the gradual encroachment of ideas.

In other words, it was not by direct influence over those who hold power at a particular point in time that economists influence the course of events, according to Keynes. It was by generating certain general beliefs and attitudes which provide the context within which opinion-makers think and politicians act. In that sense, the mercantilists are still an influence on beliefs and attitudes in the world today, centuries after they were refuted decisively within the economics profession by Adam Smith.

The question whether economics is shaped by events is more controversial. At one time, it was widely believed that ideas are shaped by surrounding circumstances and events, and that economic ideas were no exception. No doubt something in the real world starts people thinking about economic ideas, as is no doubt true of ideas in other fields, including science and mathematics. Trigonometry was given an impetus, in ancient times, by the need to re-survey land in Egypt after recurring floods along the Nile wiped out boundaries between different people's properties.

That is one kind of influence. A more immediate and direct influence has been assumed by those who believed that the Great Depression of the 1930s spawned Keynesian economics. But even if the Great Depression inspired Keynes' thinking and the widespread acceptance of that thinking among economists around the world, how typical was that of the way that economics has evolved historically, much less how ideas in other fields have evolved historically?

Were more things falling down, or was their falling creating more social problems, when Newton developed his theory of gravity? Certainly there were not more free markets when Adam Smith wrote *The Wealth of Nations*, which advocated freer markets precisely because of his dissatisfaction with the effects of various kinds of government intervention that were pervasive at the time.* The great shift within nineteenth century economics from a

---

* No one writes a 900-page book to say how happy he is with the way things are going.

theory of price determined by production costs to a theory of price determined by consumer demand was not in response to changes in either production costs or consumer demand. It was simply the unpredictable emergence of a new intellectual insight as a way of resolving ambiguities and inconsistencies in existing economic theory. As for depressions, there had been depressions before the 1930s without producing a Keynes.

Nobel Prize-winning economist George Stigler pointed out that momentous events in the real world may have no intellectual consequences: "A war may ravage a continent or destroy a generation without posing new theoretical questions," he said. The tragic reality is that wars have spread ruination and devastation across continents many times over the centuries, so that there need be no new issue to confront intellectually, even in the midst of an overwhelming catastrophe.

Whatever its origins or its ability to influence or be influenced by external events, economics is ultimately a study of an enduring part of the human condition. Its value depends on its contribution to our understanding of a particular set of conditions involving the allocation of scarce resources which have alternative uses. Unfortunately, little of the knowledge and understanding within the economics profession has reached the average citizen and voter, leaving politicians free to do things that would never be tolerated if most people understood economics as well as Alfred Marshall understood it a century ago or David Ricardo two centuries ago.

As for what economists today can offer, there have been some very different assessments within the profession. Economics had long been christened "the dismal science" by those unhappy with all the promising-sounding social theories and policy proposals that economists punctured as counterproductive. However, in the wake of John Maynard Keynes' economic theories, which proposed useful roles for government intervention, there was in many quarters a sense that economists could do much more than provide insights on particular problems or issue warnings against more ambitious but unsound policies. By the 1960s, there were Keynesian economists who spoke of their ability to "fine-tune" the economy. One of these was Walter Heller, Chairman of the Council of Economic Advisors under President John F. Kennedy:

Economics has come of age in the 1960's. . . . the Federal government has an overarching responsibility for the nation's economic stability and growth. And we have at last unleashed fiscal and monetary policy for the aggressive pursuit of those objectives. . . .Interwoven with the growing Presidential reliance on economists has been a growing political and popular belief that modern economics can, after all, deliver the goods.

The simultaneous rise of unemployment and inflation during the 1970s dealt a blow to Keynesian economics in general and to the idea that the government could fine-tune the economy in particular. Milton Friedman expressed a view that was the direct opposite of that expressed earlier by Walter Heller:

A major problem of our time is that people have come to expect policies to produce results that they are incapable of producing. . . . we economists in recent years have done vast harm— to society at large and to our profession in particular— by claiming more than we can deliver. We have thereby encouraged politicians to make extravagant promises, inculcate unrealistic expectations in the public at large, and promote discontent with reasonably satisfactory results because they fall short of the economists' promised land.

Chapter 27

PARTING THOUGHTS

*We shall not grow wiser before we learn that much that
we have done was very foolish.*

F. A. Hayek

Sometimes the whole is greater than the sum of its parts. In addition to whatever you may have learned in the course of this book about particular things such as prices, investment, or international trade, you may also have acquired a more general skepticism about many of the glittering words and fuzzy phrases that are mass produced by the media, by politicians and by others.

You may no longer be as ready to uncritically accept statements and statistics about "the rich" and "the poor." Nor should you find it mysterious that so many places with rent control laws have also had housing shortages, or that attempts to control the price of food have often led to hunger or even starvation.

However, no listing of economic fallacies can be complete, because the fertility of the human imagination is virtually unlimited. New fallacies are being conceived, or misconceived, while the old ones are still being refuted. The most that can be hoped for is to reveal some of the more common fallacies and promote both skepticism and an analytical approach that goes beyond the emotional appeals which sustain so many harmful and even dangerous economic fallacies in politics and in the media.

This should include a more careful use and definition of words, so that statements about how countries with high wages cannot compete in international trade with countries which have low wages do not escape scrutiny because of confusing high *wage rates per unit of time* with high *labor costs per unit of output*. Similar confusion between *tax rates per dollar of income* and *total tax revenues* received by the government has often made rational discussion of tax policies virtually impossible.

Many economic fallacies depend upon (1) thinking of the economy as a set of zero-sum transactions, (2) ignoring the role of competition in the marketplace, or (3) not thinking beyond the initial consequences of particular policies.

If economic transactions could benefit one party to those transactions only at the expense of the other party, then it would be understandable to believe that government intervention to change the transactions terms would produce a net benefit to a particular party, such as tenants or employees. But, if economic transactions benefit both parties, then changing the transactions terms to favor one side tends to reduce the number of transactions that the other side is willing to engage in. In a world of positive-sum transactions, it is understandable why rent control laws lead to housing shortages and minimum wage laws increase unemployment. Few people are likely to explicitly say that economic transactions benefit only one party to those transactions, but many fallacies persist because of implicit assumptions that people do not bother to spell out, even to themselves.

Seldom do people think things through foolishly. More often, they do not bother to think things through at all, so that even highly intelligent individuals can reach untenable conclusions because their brainpower means little if it is not deployed and applied.

The central role that competition plays in free market economies often gets overlooked by those who do not spell out their assumptions. One of the attractions of central planning, especially before it was put into operation and its consequences experienced, was that the alternative seemed to be a chaos of uncoordinated activity in an uncontrolled market.

Many have also believed that labor unions can increase labor's share of an industry's income simply by reducing the share going to investors in that industry. But this ignores the competition for investment, which is attracted to industries where the returns are higher and repelled from industries where it is lower, thereby changing employment prospects in both places. Where there is competition between unionized and non-union companies in the same industry, as in American automobile manufacturing, it is hardly surprising to see General Motors drastically reducing the number of workers on its payroll while Toyota is increasing its hiring in the United States.

Not thinking beyond the initial consequences of economic decisions, including government policies, is a special example of not bothering to think things through. Restricting the importation of foreign steel into the United States did indeed save jobs in the domestic steel industry, but its repercussions on the prices and sales of other domestic products made with higher-priced domestic steel cost far more jobs than those that were saved in the steel industry. None of this is rocket science but it does require stopping to think. The particular examples here or elsewhere in this book are not nearly as important as keeping in mind the economic principles they illustrate.

Much confusion comes from judging economic policies by the goals they proclaim rather than the incentives they create. In wartime, for example, when military forces absorb many resources that would normally go into producing civilian products, there is often an understandable desire to ensure that such basic things as food continue to be available to the civilian population, especially those with low incomes. Thus price controls may be imposed on bread and butter, but not on champagne and caviar. However right this might seem, when you look only at the goal or the initial consequences, the picture changes drastically when you follow the subsequent repercussions from the incentives created.

If the prices of bread and butter are kept lower than they would be if determined by supply and demand in a free market, then producers of bread and butter tend to end up with lower rates of profit than producers of champagne and caviar, who remain free to charge "whatever the traffic will bear," since no one regards these things as essential. However, because all producers compete for labor and other scarce resources, this means that the higher profits from champagne and caviar enable their producers to bid away more resources, at the expense of producers of bread and butter, than they would have been able to in a free market without price controls. Shifting resources from the production of bread and butter to the production of champagne and caviar is one of the repercussions that escapes notice when we fail to think beyond the initial stage of consequences of economic policies. For similar reasons, rent control tends to shift resources from the production of ordinary housing for moderate-income people toward the building of luxury housing for the affluent and wealthy.

The importance of economic principles extends beyond things that most people think of as economics. For example, those who worry about the exhaustion of petroleum, iron ore, or other natural resources often assume that they are discussing the amount of physical stuff on the planet. But that assumption changes radically when you realize that statistics on "known reserves" of these resources may tell us more about costs of exploration, and about the interest rate on the money that finances this exploration, than about how much of the resource remains on Earth. Nor is the amount of physical stuff necessarily what matters, without knowing how much of it can be extracted and processed at what costs.

Many other decisions that are not usually thought of as economic, may in fact have serious economic repercussions. For example, some communities may decide to restrict how tall local buildings will be allowed to be built, without any thought that this has economic implications which can result in much higher rents being charged.* These are just some of a whole range of problems and issues which, on the surface, might not seem to be economic matters, but which nevertheless look very different after understanding basic economic principles and applying them.

The importance of the distinction between policy *goals* versus the *incentives* created by those policies extends beyond the particular things discussed in this book— and, indeed, beyond economics. Nothing is easier than to proclaim a wonderful goal. The "Law to Relieve the Distress of the People and Reich" during the Great Depression of the 1930s gave dictatorial powers to Adolf Hitler, leading to World War II, which created more distress and disaster than the German people— and many other peoples— had ever experienced before.

What must be asked about any goal is: What specific things are going to be done in the name of that goal? What does the particular legislation or

---

* When laws prevent the building of ten-story apartment buildings, a five-story apartment building on the same land now has higher costs per apartment because the cost of the land— which can be higher than the cost of the building in some places— has to be recovered in the rent charged to only half as many people.

policy reward and what does it punish? What constraints does it impose? Looking to the future, what are the likely consequences of such incentives and constraints? Looking back at the past, what have been the consequences of similar incentives and constraints in other times and places? As the distinguished British historian Paul Johnson put it:

> The study of history is a powerful antidote to contemporary arrogance. It is humbling to discover how many of our glib assumptions, which seem to us novel and plausible, have been tested before, not once but many times and in innumerable guises; and discovered to be, at great human cost, wholly false.

We have seen some of those great human costs— people going hungry in Russia, despite some of the richest farmland on the continent of Europe, people sleeping on cold sidewalks during winter nights in New York, despite far more boarded-up housing units in the city than it would take to shelter them all.

Some of the economic policies which have led to counterproductive or even catastrophic consequences in various countries and in various periods of history might suggest that there was unbelievable stupidity on the part of those making these decisions— which, in democratic countries, might also imply unbelievable stupidity on the part of those who voted for them. But this is not necessarily so. While the economic analysis required to understand these issues may not be particularly difficult to grasp, one must first stop and think about the issues in an economic framework. When people do not stop and think through the issues, it does not matter whether those people are geniuses or morons, because the quality of the thinking that they *would have* done is a moot point.

In addition to the role of incentives and constraints, one of our other central themes has been the role of *knowledge*. In free market economies, we have seen giant multi-billion-dollar corporations fall from their pinnacles, some all the way to bankruptcy and extinction, because their knowledge of changing circumstances, and the implications of those changes, lagged behind that of upstart rivals.

While facts are important, understanding the *implications* of those facts is even more important, and that is what an understanding of economics seeks to provide. For example, the Eastman Kodak Company was the international colossus of the photographic industry for more than a century— and yet it was devastated economically by the rise of digital cameras, which destroyed the market for many Kodak products built around the now obsolete technology of film. Yet what Kodak lacked was not knowledge of digital cameras, *which were invented by Kodak*, but a failure to see the *implications* of this radically new technology as well as other companies which developed the potentialities of this technology to the point where Eastman Kodak was forced into bankruptcy. These other companies included not only traditional camera makers like Nikon and Canon but also companies outside the photographic industry, like Sony and Samsung, which began producing digital cameras.

What is important is not that particular companies succumbed to competing companies, whether in the photographic industry or elsewhere, but that knowledge and insights proved decisive in market competition. The public benefitted because some business decisions were based on a clearer understanding of the economic realities of the times and circumstances— and these were the businesses that survived to use scarce resources that had alternative uses.

In centrally planned economies, we have seen the planners overwhelmed by the task of trying to set literally millions of prices— and keep changing those prices in response to innumerable and often unforeseeable changes in circumstances. It was not remarkable that they failed so often. What was remarkable was that anyone had expected them to succeed, given the vast amount of knowledge that would have had to be marshaled and mastered in one place by one set of people at one time, in order to make such an arrangement work. Lenin was only one of many theorists over the centuries who imagined that it would be easy for government officials to run economic activities— and the first to encounter directly the economic and social catastrophes to which that belief led, as he himself admitted, after just a few years in power.

Given the decisive advantages of knowledge and insight in a market economy, even when this knowledge and insight are in the minds of people born and raised in poverty, such as J.C. Penney or F.W. Woolworth, we can see why market economies have so often outperformed other economies that depend on ideas originating solely within a narrow elite of birth or ideology. While market economies are often thought of as money economies, they are still more so knowledge economies, for money can always be found to back new insights, technologies and organizational methods that work, even when these innovations were created by people initially lacking in money, whether Henry Ford, Thomas Edison, David Packard, or others. Capital is always available under capitalism, but knowledge and insights are rare and precious under any economic system.

Knowledge should not be narrowly conceived as the kind of information in which intellectuals and academics specialize. We should not be like the depiction of the famous scholar Benjamin Jowett, master of Balliol College at Oxford, who inspired this verse:

> My name is Benjamin Jowett.
> If it's knowledge, I know it.
> I am the master of this college,
> What I don't know isn't knowledge.

In reality, there is much that the intelligentsia do not know that is knowledge vital to the functioning of an economy. It may be easy to disdain the kinds of highly specific mundane knowledge and its implications which are often economically decisive by asking, for example: "How much knowledge does it take to fry a hamburger?" Yet McDonald's did not become a multi-billion-dollar corporation, with thousands of outlets around the world, for no reason— not with so many rivals trying desperately and unsuccessfully to do the same thing, and some of them failing even to make enough money to stay in business. Anyone who studies the history of this franchise chain* will be astonished at the amount of detailed knowledge, insights, organizational and technological innovation, financial improvisation, all-out efforts and desperate sacrifices that went into creating an enormous economic success from selling just a few common food products.

---

* For example, John F. Love, *McDonald's: Behind the Arches*.

Nor was McDonald's unique. All sorts of businesses— from Sears to Intel and from Honda to the Bank of America— had to struggle upward from humble beginnings to ultimately achieve wealth and security. In all these cases, it was the knowledge and insight that was built up over the years— the human capital— which ultimately attracted the financial capital to make ideas become a reality. The other side of this is that, in countries where the mobilization of financial resources is made difficult by unreliable property rights laws, those at the bottom have fewer ways of getting the capital needed to back their entrepreneurial endeavors. More important, the whole society loses the benefits it could gain from what these stifled entrepreneurs could have contributed to the economic rise of the nation.

Success is only part of the story of a free market economy. Failure is at least as important a part, though few want to talk about it and none want to experience it. When the same resources— whether land, labor or petroleum— can be used by different firms and different industries to produce different products, the only way for the successful ideas to become realities is to take resources away from other uses that turn out to be unsuccessful, or which have become obsolete after having had their era of success. Economics is not about "win-win" options, but about often painful choices in the allocation of scarce resources which have alternative uses. Success and failure are not isolated good fortunes and misfortunes, but inseparable parts of the same process.

All economies— whether capitalism, socialism, feudalism or whatever— are essentially ways of cooperating in the production and distribution of goods and services, whether this is done efficiently or inefficiently, voluntarily or involuntarily. Naturally, individuals and groups want their own particular contributions to the process to be better rewarded, but their complaints or struggles over this are a sideshow to the main event of complementary efforts which produce the output on which all depend. Yet invidious comparisons and internecine struggles are the stuff of social melodrama, which in turn is the lifeblood of the media and politics, as well as portions of the intelligentsia.

By portraying cooperative activities as if they were zero-sum contests— whether in employer-employee relations or in international trade or other cooperative endeavors— those with the power to impose their misconceptions on others through words or laws can create a negative-sum contest, in which all are worse off. A young worker who is destitute of both knowledge and money would today find it virtually impossible to purchase the knowledge that was vital to a future career by working long hours for no pay, as many did in times past— including F. W. Woolworth, who by this means rose from dire poverty to become one of the richest men of his era in retailing.

Those with a zero-sum vision who have seen property rights as mere special privileges for the affluent and the rich have helped erode or destroy such rights, or have made them practically inaccessible to the poor in Third World countries, thereby depriving the poor of one of the mechanisms by which people from backgrounds like theirs have risen to prosperity in other times and places.

However useful economics may be for understanding many issues, it is not as emotionally satisfying as more personal and melodramatic depictions of these issues often found in the media and in politics. Dry empirical questions are seldom as exciting as political crusades or ringing moral pronouncements. But empirical questions are questions that must be asked, if we are truly interested in the well-being of others, rather than in excitement or a sense of moral superiority for ourselves. Perhaps the most important distinction is between what sounds good and what works. The former may be sufficient for purposes of politics or moral preening, but not for the economic advancement of people in general or the poor in particular. For those who are willing to stop and think, basic economics provides some tools for evaluating policies and proposals in terms of their logical implications and empirical consequences.

If this book has contributed to that end, then it has succeeded in its mission.

QUESTIONS

QUESTIONS

The pages in parentheses are where answers to these questions can be found.

PART I: PRICES AND MARKETS

1. Can there be a growing scarcity without a growing shortage— or a growing shortage without a growing scarcity? Explain with examples. (pages 38, 47–48)

2. Can a decision be economic, if there is no money involved? Why or why not? (pages 6–7)

3. Can there be surplus food in a society where people are hungry? Explain why or why not. (pages 54–55)

4. When a housing shortage suddenly disappears, within a time period too short for any new housing to have been built, and yet people no longer have any trouble finding a vacant home or apartment, what has probably happened? What will probably happen in the longer run? Explain. (page 39)

5. Which of the following are— or are not— affected by price controls that limit how high the product's price can go: (a) the quantity supplied, (b) the quantity demanded, (c) the quality of the product, (d) a black market for the product, (e) hoarding of the product, (f) the supply of auxiliary services that usually go with the product, or (g) efficiency in the allocation of resources? Explain in each case. (a: pages 41–44; b: pages 39–41; c: pages 49–50, 51–53; d: pages 50–51, 53; e: pages 48–49; f: page 42; g: pages 52–53, 64–65)

6. Building ordinary housing and building luxury housing involves using many of the same resources, such as bricks, pipes, and construction labor. How does the allocation of these resources between ordinary housing and luxury housing tend to change after rent control laws are passed? (pages 43, 47)

7. Are prices usually higher or lower in low–income neighborhoods? Why? Include among prices the interest rate on money borrowed and the cost of getting paychecks cashed. (pages 66–68)

8. When a government institution or program produces counterproductive results, is that necessarily a sign of irrationality or incompetence on the part of those who run that particular institution or program? Explain with examples. (pages 70–72)

9. We all consider some things more important than others. Why then can there be a problem when some official government policy establishes "national priorities"? (pages 77–78)

10. We tend to think of costs as the money we pay for things. But does that mean that there would be no costs in a primitive society that did not yet use money or in a modern cooperative community, where people collectively produce the goods and services they use and do not charge each other for them? (pages 22, 28)

11. How does rent control affect the average number of persons per apartment and the average amount of time that the same persons stay in the same apartment? (pages 39–41)

12. Back in the days of the Soviet Union, the government owned and operated most of the enterprises in the economy. Most prices were set by central planners, rather than by supply and demand, and the success or failure of Soviet enterprises was judged primarily by how well they met the numerical targets for production, which were set by the central planners. Specify five ways in which this arrangement produced different economic end results from those in market economies. (pages 17, 22–23, 27, 71, 73–74)

13. How can the price of baseball bats be affected by the demand for paper or the price of catchers' mitts be affected by the demand for cheese? (page 20)

14. Why are price controls likely to cause more of a shortage of gasoline than of strawberries? (page 49)

15. How does rent control affect the quality of housing and the average age of housing? (pages 41–42)

PART II: INDUSTRY AND COMMERCE

1. Why would a big corporation pay millions of dollars in severance money to an executive who has been a complete failure, who has turned corporate profits into corporate losses? (page 145)

2. Why has Toyota manufactured cars with only enough inventory of parts to last a few hours? Why did Soviet industries have nearly enough inventory to last for a year? (page 136)

3. Why do American manufacturers of computers or television sets tend to have them transported by others while Chinese manufacturers tend to transport them themselves? (page 135)

4. How did the movement of population from rural to urban America affect the economics of retail selling in the early twentieth century? How did the later movement of population from urban to suburban America in the second half of the twentieth century affect the economics of department stores and grocery stores? Explain with examples. (pages 92–93, 96–97)

5. Why is it that General Motors can make millions of automobiles, without making a single tire to go on them, while Soviet enterprises not only tended to make all their own components, but sometimes even made the bricks for the buildings in which they operated? (pages 130, 134)

6. How did diseconomies of scale in agriculture affect the way tractor drivers plowed fields in the Soviet Union? What if agricultural enterprises had been privately owned and the tractor drivers were plowing their own fields? Would the work have been done differently and would the farm be likely to be as large? Explain why or why not. (pages 123–124)

7. When an economic project such as building a railroad or creating an airline requires far more money than any given individual can or will invest, what are some of the things that can facilitate or impede the pooling of the money of millions of people to finance the project? (pages 140–142)

8. Advertising, even when it is successful, is often considered to be a benefit only to those who advertise, but of no benefit to consumers, who have to pay the cost of the advertisements in the higher price of the products they buy. Evaluate this view from an economic perspective. (pages 120–121, 574–577)

9. "Inertia is common to people under both capitalism and socialism, but the market exacts a price for inertia." Explain how and why inertia among mail order houses, which were the leading retailers in the United States in the early twentieth century, was affected by the rise of department store chains. (pages 96–98, 182)

10. Why are retired people able to get much lower priced travel rates— on cruise ships, for example— than most other people? Explain the economic reasons. (pages 125–126)

11. Why is the perennial desire to "eliminate the middleman" perennially frustrated? (pages 130–133)

12. After the A & P grocery chain cut its profit margins on the goods it sold, back in the early twentieth century, its rate of profit on its investment rose well above the national average. Why? (page 118)

13. Why would luxury hotels be charging lower rates than economy hotels in the same city? (pages 126–127)

14. What is the difference between the government's protecting competition and protecting competitors? How does that affect the consumers' standard of living through its effect on the allocation of scarce resources which have alternative uses? (pages 161–165)

15. Stores in low–income neighborhoods tend to charge higher prices, in order to try to compensate for higher costs and for slower rates of turnover in their inventory. What limits the ability of these stores to completely compensate for these higher costs, so as to make the same rates of profits as stores in higher–income neighborhoods? (pages 118–119)

PART III: WORK AND PAY

1. What have been some of the economic and social consequences of the substitution of machine power for human strength, as a result of industrialization, and the growing importance of knowledge, skills, and experience in a high-tech economy? (pages 208–209)

2. Would you expect the average hammer in a factory to drive more nails per year in a richer country or a poorer country? Would you expect the average worker to produce more output per hour in a richer country or a poorer country? Explain the reasons in each case. (pages 216–217)

3. Some studies have attempted to determine how employment has changed in the wake of a minimum wage increase by surveying individual firms before and after the increase to find out how their employment has changed, and then adding up the results. What is the problem with this procedure? (page 225)

4. What has been the effect of multinational corporations in China on wages and working conditions there? (pages 245–247)

5. In the first half of 2010, the proportion of American adults with jobs had the largest decline in more than half a century. Yet the unemployment rate did not rise. How could this be? (pages 235–237)

6. Is it possible for per capita income to rise by 50 percent over a period of years while household income remains unchanged over those same years? (pages 202–203)

7. Although maximum wage laws existed long before minimum wage laws, only the latter are common today. However, in those special cases where there have been maximum wage laws— as under wage and price controls during World War II, for example— what effects would such laws have on discrimination against minorities and women? How would maximum wage laws and minimum wage laws differ in their effects on discrimination? (pages 214, 231–233)

8. Does inequality of income tend to be greater or less in the long run than in the short run? Why do many statistics about "the rich" and "the poor" include people who are neither rich nor poor in reality? (pages 199–200)

9. When drivers of municipal transit buses are unionized and paid more than they would be paid in a free, competitive market, what effect does that tend to have on the size of the buses and the waiting time between buses? (page 215)

10. How can differences in the quality of transportation systems or in the level of corruption in different countries affect the value of labor? (page 197)

11. Why would a South African manufacturer expand production by opening a plant in Poland, when there were large numbers of workers available in South Africa, where the unemployment rate was 26 percent, and where the average output per hour of South African workers was higher than the average output per hour of Polish workers? (pages 195–196, 227–228)

12. Why is the productivity of an individual not the same as the efficiency or merit of that individual? Give examples comparing workers in Third World countries with workers in more prosperous countries, and comparing different baseball players in different kinds of situations. (pages 196–197)

13. It has often been said that, over time, a higher percentage of the nation's total income goes to high income people. In what sense is this true and in what sense is it not true? (pages 203–207)

14. Why are wages lower, and working conditions worse, in Third World countries? What are the likely consequences of various possible ways of trying to improve either or both? (pages 244–247)

15. What are the implications of the fact that most people today reach their peak earnings years at later ages than in generations past— and that these peak earnings are now usually a larger number of times greater than the earnings of beginners than in times past? What further implications does this have for the changing differences in male and female earnings? (pages 208–209)

PART IV: TIME AND RISK

1. Does it make economic sense for a ninety-year-old man, with no heirs, to plant trees that will take 20 years to grow to maturity and bear fruit? (page 292)

2. Businesses raise money by issuing both stocks and bonds but individuals usually raise money by borrowing— the equivalent of issuing bonds. In some circumstances, however, individuals acquire resources by the equivalent of issuing stocks. What are those circumstances? Give specific examples and reasons. (pages 313–315)

3. Why may the statistics on the known reserves of a natural resource provide a misleading picture of how much of that resource there is in the ground? (pages 294–301)

4. Why is it common for "payday loans" to have annual interest rates of more than 100 percent, when other loans usually have interest rates that are a small fraction of that? (pages 281–283)

5. How does commodity speculation differ from gambling? What is the effect of commodity speculation on output? On the allocation of scarce resources which have alternative uses? (pages 283–289)

6. Why does it pay an insurance company or a commodity speculator to offer a deal in which they guarantee to pay a given sum of money to someone under given circumstances? And why does it pay for that person to accept the offer? (pages 288, 289, 316–317)

7. Why would a bus company owned or controlled by the government charge fares too low to replace existing buses as they wear out? What if the executives of a privately owned and privately controlled bus company decided to divert part of the money they received from bus fares toward paying themselves higher salaries, instead of setting aside enough money to replace buses as they wear out? What would happen to the value of the stock in their company and how would the stockholders be likely to react? (pages 337–338)

8. Many poor countries have confiscated businesses or land owned by wealthy foreign companies. Why has this seldom made the poor country more prosperous? (pages 340–341)

9. Can complex international commodity markets have much impact on small farmers in a Third World country? Can those Third World farmers, who are often poor and poorly educated, participate in international commodity markets? (pages 286–287)

10. Why does it make sense for an individual driver to get insurance on his automobile? Why then doesn't Hertz buy insurance for its automobiles? (pages 316–317)

11. How can government regulation of insurance companies improve the efficiency of the industry? How can it make the industry less efficient? Explain with examples of both. (pages 320–323)

12. Why do manufacturers in some countries keep an inventory of many months' supply of the materials needed in production, while manufacturers in some other countries do not keep an inventory of such materials sufficient to last all day? What are the implications for the allocation of scarce resources which have alternative uses? (pages 135–137, 289–291)

13. What kinds of income are called "unearned income" and why? (pages 278–280)

14. How does the interest rate allocate resources among contemporaries and between different present and future uses? (pages 273–276, 280–281)

15. Why would a state's bonds be downgraded by a bond-rating agency like Standard & Poor's, when that state was paying its bondholders regularly and had a surplus in its treasury? (page 292)

PART V: THE NATIONAL ECONOMY

1. How does the consumer price index tend to exaggerate the rate of inflation and how does that affect our attempts to measure real income? (pages 353–355)

2. Does the presence or absence of property rights make any difference to people who own no property? For example, are tenants affected economically by whether the community in which they rent apartments or houses allows unbridled property rights or reduces those property rights through zoning laws, open space laws, height restrictions on buildings, or rent control laws? (pages 400–404)

3. How does the level of honesty or corruption in a country affect the effectiveness of its economy? How do economic policies affect the level of honesty and corruption? (pages 394–396)

4. During the Great Depression of the 1930s, both Republican President Herbert Hoover and his successor, Democratic President Franklin D. Roosevelt, tried to keep up the prices of goods and labor. What was the rationale for these policies and what are the economic and social problems with such policies? (pages 375–376)

5. During a period of inflation, does money circulate faster or slower— and why? What are the consequences? What do you suppose happens during a period of deflation— and what are the consequences then? (pages 370–374)

6. During an all–out war, how can a country's military consumption plus civilian consumption add up to more than its output, without borrowing from other countries? (page 351)

7. Why is it difficult to make meaningful comparisons between the standard of living in a country whose population is, on average, many years younger than the population of another country with which it is being compared? (page 356)

8. In medieval times, the British economy lagged behind that of some economies in continental Europe but, in later centuries, Britain had the leading economy in Europe and led the world into the industrial age. How and why did foreigners play a major role in developing the British economy? (page 398)

9. Those who favor increases in tax rates are often disappointed that the additional revenue turns out to be less than they expected. Conversely, those who fear that cuts in tax rates will substantially reduce the government's revenues have often been surprised to find the government's revenues rising. Explain both phenomena. (pages 426–428)

10. Even if detailed statistics are available, why is it difficult to compare the national output at the beginning of the twentieth century with the national output at the beginning of the twenty-first century, and say by what percentage it has increased? Why is it hard even to say how much prices for particular goods have increased from one century to another? (pages 352–354)

11. Why would an Albanian bank, with 83 percent of the country's bank deposits, refuse to make any loans? And what were the consequences for the Albanian economy? (page 387)

12. Explain "the fallacy of composition" and give economic examples. (pages 346–347)

13. Since "money talks" in the marketplace, why would rich people want to shift some decisions out of the marketplace and have these decisions made politically or by the courts? (Hint: housing is a classic example.) (pages 402–403)

14. Under what conditions is the burden of the national debt passed on to future generations? Under what conditions is it not? (pages 437–438)

15. From time to time there are conflicting estimates of how much of the total taxes are paid for by various individuals and organizations. Why is it not easy to tell who is really bearing the burden of taxation? Explain with specific examples. (pages 428–432)

PART VI: THE INTERNATIONAL ECONOMY

1. If laws restrict the importation of a particular foreign product, in order to protect the jobs of domestic workers who produce that product, how is it possible that this can end up reducing domestic employment? (page 491)

2. Although Africa is more than twice the size of Europe, the European coastline is longer than the African coastline. How can that be, and— more important— what are the economic implications? (page 533)

3. If country *A* can produce a given product more cheaply than country *B*, what economic reason would cause it to buy that product from country *B*, instead of producing it itself? (pages 479–483)

4. Australia manufactures automobiles, but these are cars developed by Japanese or American car companies. Why would an advanced and prosperous country like Australia not design and produce its own cars? (pages 483–484)

5. What is meant by a "favorable balance of trade"? Why was it considered favorable? Is it also favorable to producing prosperity in the economy? (pages 476–478)

6. What economic effects do mountains have on (a) the people living in those mountains and (b) the people living below on the lands near those mountains? Explain why these economic effects are what they are. (pages 536–539)

7. What are some of the reasons for restrictions on international trade that economists usually recognize as valid? (pages 492–493)

8. In the absence of restrictions on international trade, would low-wage countries tend to take jobs away from high-wage countries through lower production costs that would allow them to sell at lower prices? Explain. (pages 486–489)

9. The United States has often been a "debtor nation" owing more to people in other countries than people in other countries owe to Americans, while Switzerland has often been a "creditor nation," to whom others owe more to the Swiss than the Swiss owe to others. What tends to lead to this difference and is it economically beneficial or harmful to Americans or Swiss? (pages 506–507)

10. How did the cultural universe and the disease universe of Europeans differ from that of the indigenous peoples of the Western Hemisphere, as of the time when they first came in contact with each other? Explain why— and the economic implications of those differences. (pages 539–541, 565–566)

11. If, instead of having international trade restrictions that save perhaps 200,000 jobs, the European Union allowed free trade and paid $100,000 to each individual who lost a job as a result, would the European Union come out ahead financially? (pages 498–499)

12. "Theoretically, investments might be expected to flow from where capital is abundant to where it is in short supply, much like water seeking its own level." What are some of the reasons why countries with abundant capital seldom invest much of it in countries where capital is much more scarce? (pages 503–505)

13. Name five reasons why one group of people might be more culturally isolated than another, and explain the economic implications of that isolation. (pages 536, 537–541, 549–551)

14. What are some of the problems in applying laws against "dumping"? (pages 493–495)

15. Why is free trade likely to be more valuable to producers in a small economy than to producers in a large economy? (pages 483–485)

PART VII: SPECIAL ECONOMIC ISSUES

1. Costly safety devices or policies have often been defended on grounds that "if it saves just one life, it is worth it." What is the problem with that reasoning? (pages 586–588)

2. What are some of the reasons why different prices are charged for things that are physically identical? (pages 572–573)

3. How did the mercantilist economists differ from classical economists such as Adam Smith? (pages 598–601)

4. What is the point of having different brands of the same product if in fact all the brands are of pretty much the same quality and sell for about the same price? What would happen in this situation if laws did away with brands, so that each consumer could only identify what the product was, but not who made it? (pages 574–578)

5. For about a century— from the 1770s to the 1870s— most of the leading economists believed that the relative prices of goods reflected their relative costs of production, especially the amount of labor they required. What are some of the problems with that theory? (pages 607–611)

6.   Explain how the presence or absence of the profit motive affects an organization's likelihood of achieving the purpose for which it was created, to the maximum extent possible with the resources at its disposal. (pages 578–580)

7.   During the era before there were laws against racial discrimination in employment, were black chemists more likely to be hired in profit-making businesses or in non-profit organizations such as colleges and universities— and why? (pages 581–582)

8.   Critics have claimed that profits exceed the value of the services performed by those who receive those profits. What empirical evidence could be used to test this belief? (pages 582–583)

9.   When fighting a war leads to a diversion of a substantial amount of resources from civilian to military purposes, most people would be more concerned to see that the poor could still get bread than that the rich could still get caviar. Then why not put price controls on bread but not on caviar? (pages 628–629)

10.   Some people regard economics as just the opinions of economists, reflecting their various ideological biases. Examine that belief in the light of the history of economics. (pages 621–622)

11.   Can government–imposed prices for medical care reduce the costs of that care? (page 573)

12.   It is common for politicians to set out to create a law or policy to solve a particular economic problem, and many in the media and among the public urge them to do that. In the light of economic theory in general, and general equilibrium theory in particular, what is wrong with that approach? (pages 612–613)

13. Where do natural disasters like earthquakes or hurricanes do the most damage in terms of financial costs and in terms of loss of human lives? (page 587)

14. A government official in India said: "I don't want multinational companies getting rich selling face creams to poor Indians." What does that statement imply? (pages 589–590)

15. Nobel Prizewinning economist F.A. Hayek said: "We shall not grow wiser before we learn that much that we have done was very foolish." What do you consider to be the three most foolish policies discussed in this book? Would you have considered those policies foolish before reading *Basic Economics*?

INDEX

A & P Grocery Chain, 90, 92–94, 118, 121, 151–152, 162, 163, 166, 172–173, 181, 641

Aaron, Henry, 196

Absolute Advantage (see also Comparative Advantage), 478–479

Adams, John, 475

Advanced Micro Devices, 112–113

Advertising, 120–121, 319, 574, 640

"Affordability," 39, 43, 44, 72, 83, 448, 449, 573

Africa, 24, 57, 73, 131–133, 137, 217–218, 226–227, 257, 273, 277, 296, 364, 394, 399, 409, 410, 483, 510, 512, 514, 515, 516, 521, 528, 529, 532–533, 534, 535–536, 539, 540–541, 547, 553, 557, 560, 561, 562, 563, 565n, 649

Age, 198–199, 212–213, 223, 231, 232–233, 236–237, 274–275, 321n, 333–334, 356, 593

Agents, 246, 315

Aggregate Demand, 345, 349, 350, 368, 375, 376, 385, 439, 605

Agriculture, 12, 16, 25, 53–58, 60, 73, 76, 80–81, 123–124, 131–132, 216, 250–251, 262–263, 285–289, 328, 335–336, 340, 373, 374, 376, 377–378, 400–401, 416, 444, 456, 457, 483, 490, 529–530, 539, 542, 545, 552, 564n, 640, 645

Airlines, 94, 160, 167–168

Albania, 387, 527, 537, 648

Alcoa, 146, 166

Alcohol, 78, 169, 418

Alexander the Great, 1, 366, 502

Allen, William R., ix

Allocation of Resources (see also Scarcity), 4, 6–7, 11, 16–17, 19–20, 24–25, 26, 27, 31, 44, 56, 57–63, 64, 72–73, 74, 89, 95, 101, 131, 142–143, 148, 149, 150–160, 188–189, 193, 248–250, 258, 275, 280–283, 288, 336, 388, 401, 425, 433, 434–435, 440–444, 447–448, 449, 571, 585, 587–588, 592, 599, 614, 624, 633, 638

efficiency: 4, 7, 27, 33, 44, 49, 84–85, 95, 97, 114, 130–131, 143–144, 148, 149, 155, 159, 162, 180, 182, 215–219, 250, 262, 277, 489

idle resources: 217, 229, 614